D1739879

Directors' Duties
A New Millennium, A New Approach?

STUDIES IN COMPARATIVE CORPORATE AND FINANCIAL LAW

Volume 7

Series Editor

Barry Rider
Institute of Advanced Legal Studies
University of London
Charles Clore House
17 Russell Square
London WC1B 5DR

The titles published in this series are listed at the end of this volume.

Directors' Duties
A New Millennium, A New Approach?

Bruce S. Butcher

B Juris (UWA), LLB (UWA), LLM (Lond), PhD (Cantab)
Solicitor of the Supreme Court of England and Wales,
Barrister and Solicitor of the Supreme Courts of New South Wales,
Victoria and Western Australia

KLUWER LAW INTERNATIONAL
THE HAGUE / LONDON / BOSTON

Library of Congress Cataloging-in-Publication Data

Butcher, Bruce S.
    Directors' duties : a new millenium, a new approach? / Bruce S. Butcher.
      p. cm. -- (Studies in comparative corporate and financial law ; v. 7)
    Includes index.
    ISBN 9041197885 (alk. paper)
    1. Directors of corporations--Legal status, laws, etc.--Australia. 2. Directors of corpo-
rations--Legal status, laws, etc.--Great Britain. I. Title. II. Series.

K1328.B88 2000
346'.06642--dc21
                                                      00-024919

ISBN 90-411-9788-5

Published by Kluwer Law International,
P.O. Box 85889, 2508 CN The Hague, The Netherlands

Sold and distributed in North, Central and South America
by Kluwer Law International,
675 Massachusetts Avenue, Cambridge, MA 02139, USA

In all other countries, sold and distributed
by Kluwer Law International, Distribution Centre
P.O. Box 322, 3300 AH Dordrecht, The Netherlands

Printed on acid-free paper

Printed and bound in Great Britain by Antony Rowe Limited.

Table of Contents

Preface

This book is written from a practising company lawyer's perspective and is principally concerned with two broad directors' duties: to act honestly, in good faith and for proper purposes, and to exercise care and diligence. Within this remit, this book examines the duties owed by directors of British and Australian companies and inquires into the role of parliament and the judiciary as the law responds to changes in public attitudes to corporate governance. Since the mid-1980s, public sentiment has altered towards directors and the business community's expectations in this respect have risen considerably. Parliament and the judiciary have come to recognise this and are adopting a new approach to directors' duties. This has led to case-law and statutory enactment which has widened the scope and applicability of duties imposed upon directors, focused upon areas previously regarded as being not properly the subject of attention and intervention, and adopted and encouraged a more robust approach to corporate governance. This new approach is to be welcomed.

There are strong historical links between English and Australian company law: legal, equitable and statutory. These links lend themselves to a comparative study across two jurisdictions with common roots, but at times different approaches and outlooks. This book draws from the rich experience of the English judiciary and the British Parliament, and from the significant contribution which Australian company law has recently made to the jurisprudence in this area. Over the past decade or so, the Australian judiciary has come to favour commercial certainty, tempered with a degree of commercial pragmatism in the light of the business community's expectations, in order to resolve the complex commercial disputes which today's companies face. This approach to directors' duties is gaining acceptance in English company law and is reflected in recent decisions by the English courts.

The cases mentioned throughout this book have been chosen very deliberately. Many have been analysed in detail. Moreover, there are many examples of Canadian and New Zealand company law cases which are cited and referred to throughout this book. Some of these are also analysed in detail as English and Australian company law are very much the richer for their influence: so too the jurisprudence of other Commonwealth countries. These cases serve to emphasise not only theoretical aspects of English and Australian company law, but very important practical aspects as well. This is important to the application of company law in every day practice and should prove useful to directors of British and Australian companies and those who advise them, and also to practitioners and students of this demanding and fascinating subject.

The law as it relates to the duties upon directors of British and Australian companies has proven to be unusually dynamic during the twilight years of the 20th century. It has been difficult keeping up with the many changes which have been made and those that are mooted to be made. On 4 March 1998, for instance, the President of the Board of Trade announced the launch of a fundamental review of the framework of core English company law. In February 1999, the Department of Trade and Industry released its consultation document entitled *Modern Company Law: The Strategic Framework*. This document identifies as an issue of general importance to the review those interests which English company law in the 21st century should serve and the means by which it should do so. It is intended that the review be completed in time for a detailed White Paper to be published in or about March 2001. Moreover, in September 1999, the Law Commission published its eagerly awaited report entitled *Company Directors: Regulating Conflicts of Interests and Formulating a Statement of Duties*. This report *inter alia* revives the push for the partial codification of the duty upon directors of British companies to exercise care, skill and diligence.

In addition, there have been a number of fresh legislative initiatives on the part of the Australian Parliament which complement and supplement the recent developments in this area of the law by the Australian judiciary. The recent Corporate Law Economic Reform Program, which has been partially implemented by the Australian Parliament, is an example of the determination which the Australian Government has for progressing a modernised and revitalised Australian company law into the 21st century. This approach to company law is being watched in England with considerable interest.

Whilst the topic of directors' duties might be described by some as a discrete aspect of company law, that would be to oversimplify its overall pervasive nature and the way in which it infects every aspect of modern company law. It is a topic of considerable theoretical and practical importance, and an area of increasing complexity as equitable doctrine more frequently impacts upon such diverse subjects as company law and insolvency law. Hence it invites analysis of the intricate relationship between statutory regulation and fiduciary law. This book suggests that a fundamental reassessment of traditional rules is required in order to refashion principles capable of resolving conflicts spawned by the complexities of modern corporate life. It inquires into the fundamental concepts, principles, policies and trends applicable to such complexities. It then explores the dynamics involved as the English and the Australian courts attempt to wade through the myriad of competing interests found within the morass of legal rules, equitable principles and statutory enactment which comprise modern company law.

Although the footnotes to this book are comprehensive and very detailed, no attempt has been made to refer to every major decision pronounced by the English and the Australian courts which touches upon directors' duties. Equally, not every article and journal which relate to the duties upon directors of British and Australian companies has been referred to. This selective treatment of the authorities was necessitated by the confines of space and the nature of this work. I have deliberately not undertaken a discussion, let alone an analysis, of the broader issues of company law. Even so, an attempt has been made to set the relevant legislation into the context of English and Australian company law, and to address some of the more interesting and sometimes controversial issues which relate to those cardinal duties under discussion. The many references not included can be readily found within any of the leading textbooks or casebooks on English and Australian company law. The views expressed in this book are mine. The law is stated as at 30 September 1999.

Bruce Butcher
London, 3 October 1999

Acknowledgments

It was with some trepidation that I embarked upon this project. As a practitioner in this field, I was only too well aware of the seemingly boundless nature of company law and the recent interest in the topic of directors' duties which has contributed exponentially to the growth of case-law and statutory enactment in this area. I was also very aware of my ongoing work commitments and the neglect that that has inflicted upon my family and friends over the past few years, without adding to my workload. Nonetheless, I pressed onwards as I wanted to write a book upon directors' duties and contribute in some small way to legal scholarship and the study of this intricate and exacting subject. The journey has been long, arduous and at times frustrating. But it has proven to be very rewarding. Even so, I am glad that the journey is now complete. That is largely through the efforts of others.

This book has benefited greatly from the very capable assistance provided by Heather Wilson who has proven to be a wonderful friend, supporter and assistant over the many years that it has been in the writing. My sincere appreciation to her is recorded here. I should also like to thank Professor Barry Rider who has provided me, as he has provided so many others, with his friendship, the opportunity of higher education and now publication of this book. His generosity often goes largely unnoticed, but is always appreciated. In addition, I am indebted to my family and friends for their considerable support. In particular, my parents, Patricia and Roy Heal, my brother Neil, my sisters Nita, Joy and Linda, and also Mark Balfour, who between them have held the fort at home during my many absences. Thank you.

Lastly, I should also express my gratitude to my publisher Kluwer Law International and to the way in which Lukas Claerhout and Nicki Judkins so quickly and so efficiently progressed my manuscript through the various stages and into print. My appreciation and gratitude is theirs. All errors and omissions are mine.

Bruce Butcher
London, 3 October 1999

Table of Abbreviations

ABLR	Australian Business Law Review
ABR	Australian Bar Review
AC	Appeal Cases
ACLC	Australian Company Law Cases
ACLR	Australian Company Law Reports
ACS	Australian Company Secretary
ACSR	Australian Corporations and Securities Reports
ACT	Australian Capital Territory
Adel LR	Adelaide Law Review
AGPS	Australian Government Publishing Service
AJCL	Australian Journal of Corporate Law
ALI	American Law Institute
ALJ	Australian Law Journal
ALJR	Australian Law Journal Reports
All ER	All England Law Reports
All ER Rep	All England Law Reports Reprint
ALR	Australian Law Reports
ALRC	Australian Law Reform Commission
App Cas	Appeal Cases
ASC	Australian Securities Commission
ASIC	Australian Securities and Investments Commission
ASLR	Australian Securities Law Reports
ASX	Australian Stock Exchange Ltd
Atk	Atkyns Reports
ATPR	Australian Trade Practices Reports
BCC	British Company Cases
BCLB	Butterworths Corporation Law Bulletin
BCLC	Butterworths Company Law Cases
Beav	Beavan Reports
BLR	Business Law Review
Bond LR	Bond University Law Review
Bus Law	Business Lawyer
Canta LR	Canterbury Law Review
CBLJ	Corporate and Business Law Journal
CCL	Current Commercial Law
CGPO	Commonwealth Government Printing Office
Ch	Chancery

Ch App	Chancery Appeals
Ch D	Chancery Division
Chan Rep	Chancery Reports
CLJ	Cambridge Law Journal
CLP	Current Legal Problems
CLR	Commonwealth Law Reports
Cmd/Cmnd	Command Paper
Co Dir	Company Director
Co Law	Company Lawyer
Colum LR	Columbia Law Review
Conv	Conveyancer and Property Lawyer
CP	Common Pleas
CPD	Common Pleas Division
CSLJ	Company and Securities Law Journal
Cth	Commonwealth
De G&J	De Gex and Jones Reports
De GJ&Sm	De Gex, Jones and Smith Reports
De GM&G	De Gex, Macnaghten and Gordon Reports
DLR	Dominion Law Reports
Dr&Sm	Drewry and Smale Reports
DTI	Department of Trade and Industry
EB&E	Ellis, Blackburn and Ellis Reports
E&B	Ellis and Blackburn Reports
Eden	Eden Reports
Eq	Equity
Eq Rep	Equity Reports
ER	English Reports Reprint
Ex D	Exchequer Division
F 2d	Federal Reporter 2nd series
FCT	Federal Commissioner of Taxation
Fed	Federal Reporter
FCR	Federal Court Reports
FLR	Federal Law Reports
H&M	Hemming and Miller Reports
Hare	Hare Reports
Harv LR	Harvard Law Review
HL	House of Lords
HLC	House of Lords Cases (Clark)
HMSO	Her/His Majesty's Stationery Office
ICLQ	International and Comparative Law Quarterly
ILJ	Insolvency Law Journal
IR	Irish Reports
JBFLP	Journal of Banking and Finance Law and Practice
JBL	Journal of Business Law
JCL	Journal of Contract Law
KB	King's Bench
LJ Ch	Law Journal Chancery
LJ PC	Law Journal Privy Council
Lloyd's Rep	Lloyd's List Law Reports

LQR	Law Quarterly Review
LR	Law Reports
LR (NSW)	Law Reports (New South Wales)
LR Eq	Equity Cases
LR HL	English and Irish Appeals
LSE	London Stock Exchange Ltd
LS Gaz	Law Society Gazette
LT	Law Times Reports
Mac&G	Macnaghten and Gordon Reports
Macq	Macqueen Reports
Melb ULR	Melbourne University Law Review
MLR	Modern Law Review
MULR	Monash University Law Review
My&Cr	Mylne and Craig Reports
NCSC	National Companies and Securities Commission
NE	North Eastern Reporter
NLJ	New Law Journal
NSW	New South Wales
NSWLR	New South Wales Law Reports
NSWR	New South Wales Reports
NT	Northern Territory
NZ	New Zealand
NZCLC	New Zealand Company Law Cases
NZLC	New Zealand Law Commission
NZLR	New Zealand Law Reports
NZULR	New Zealand Universities Law Review
OECD	Organisation of Economic Co-operation and Development
OHLJ	Osgoode Hall Law Journal
OJLS	Oxford Journal of Legal Studies
Ph	Phillips Reports
Plc	public limited company
PLR	Public Law Review
QB	Queen's Bench
QBD	Queen's Bench Division
Qd R	Queensland Reports
Qld	Queensland
RLV	Restitution Law Review
RSC	Rules of the Supreme Court
SA	South Australia
SASR	South Australian State Reports
Sc LR	Scottish Law Reporter
Sel Cas t King	Select Cases in Chancery
SI	Statutory Instrument
SLR	Stanford Law Review
SLT	Scots Law Times
Sm & Giff	Smale and Gifford Reports
Sol Jo	Solicitors' Journal and Reporter
SR(NSW)	State Reports (New South Wales)
St R (Qd)	State Reports (Queensland)

Str	Strange Reports
Syd LR	Sydney Law Review
Table A	Companies (Tables A to F) Regulations (SI 1985/805)
Tas	Tasmania
TLR	Times Law Reports
TSEC	Toronto Stock Exchange Committee
UCA	Uniform Companies Act
UCLR	University of Chicago Law Review
UK	United Kingdom
UNSWLJ	University of New South Wales Law Journal
US	United States Supreme Court Reports
USA	United States of America
UTLJ	University of Toronto Law Journal
UTLR	University of Tasmania Law Review
UWALR	University of Western Australia Law Review
V&B	Vesey and Beames Reports
V Conv R	Victorian Conveyancing Law and Practice
Ves Jun	Vesey Junior Reports
Ves Sen	Vesey Senior Reports
Vic	Victoria
VLR	Victorian Law Reports
VR	Victorian Reports
VUWLR	Victoria University of Wellington Law Review
WA	Western Australia
WAR	Western Australian Reports
WLR	Weekly Law Reports
WN	Weekly Notes
WN (NSW)	Weekly Notes (New South Wales)
Y&CCC	Younge and Collyer Reports
YLJ	Yale Law Journal

Table of Cases

Table of Statutes and Statutory Instruments

United Kingdom
"Bubble Act" 1719 (UK):   13
Companies (Consolidation) Act 1908 (UK):   171
Companies (Disqualification Orders) Regulations (SI 1986/2067) 1986 (UK):   263n
Companies (Tables A to F) Regulations (SI 1985/805) 1985 (UK):   98-99
Companies (Winding up) Act 1890 (UK):   188, 256
Companies Act 1862 (UK):   171n, 235
Companies Acts 1908 to 1917 (UK):   24, 231
Companies Act 1928 (UK):   197n, 234, 243
Companies Act 1929 (UK):   197n, 232, 234, 257, 258
Companies Act 1948 (UK):   171n, 179n, 198n, 232, 233, 234, 255, 257, 258, 266
Companies Act 1976 (UK):   263
Companies Act 1981 (UK):   227n
Companies Act 1985 (UK):   5n, 10n, 11n, 14n, 57, 98, 129n, 161n, 180n, 195n, 196n,
    230n, 232, 234, 235n, 236n, 237n, 242, 244n, 245n, 255, 257, 261, 263-264, 266,
    337
Companies Act 1989 (UK):   10n, 11n, 57, 337
Company Directors Disqualification Act 1986 (UK):   5n, 10n, 11n, 44, 53, 55, 58, 60,
    75, 90, 129n, 169n, 183, 188, 189n, 195n, 196, 206, 222n, 225, 227-228, 229, 230,
    231n, 232n, 234n, 235, 236, 237-238, 239-240, 242-255, 263, 264, 265n, 266, 267,
    271, 324, 331, 332, 333-334
Financial Services Act 1986 (UK):   5n, 10n, 11n, 61n, 129n, 228n, 234n, 235n, 236n
Insolvency Act 1976 (UK):   255, 263n
Insolvency Act 1985 (UK):   242, 255
Insolvency Act 1986 (UK):   5n, 10n, 11n, 44, 51n, 52n, 53, 58-60, 63, 74n, 90, 113,
    129n, 161n, 169n, 170n, 171n, 174n, 183, 185n, 188-189, 195n, 196, 197, 198, 206,
    215n, 220n, 222n, 225, 227, 228, 229, 230n, 231n, 232n, 234n, 236, 237, 240, 242,
    244n, 245, 255-262, 263, 264, 265n, 266, 271, 316n, 324, 326n, 331, 332, 333, 334
Joint Stock Companies Act 1844 (UK):   13
Joint Stock Companies Act 1856 (UK):   14
Joint Stock Companies Winding-up Act 1848 (UK):   255
Limitation Act 1980 (UK):   261n
Limited Liability Act 1855 (UK):   14
Supreme Court of Judicature Act 1873 (UK):   275n, 279n
Supreme Court of Judicature Act 1875 (UK):   275n, 279n

Australia

1

Directors' Duties:
Under The Corporate Spotlight

INTRODUCTION

The late 1980s and the early 1990s gave rise to many well-publicised corporate crashes. Those involving Robert Maxwell in England, Alan Bond in Australia and Allan Hawkins in New Zealand, for example, brought into sharp focus corporate governance in general;[1] and the topic of directors' duties in particular. This was recently acknowledged in the English courts by Hoffmann LJ[2] in *Bishopsgate Investment Management Ltd v Maxwell (No. 2)* where his Lordship recognised that the law, 'may be evolving in response to changes in public attitudes to corporate governance'.[3] It has also been acknowledged in the Australian courts. For instance, Perry J in *State of South Australia v Clark* posited that:

> Recent appellate decisions in Australia have gone a long way towards clarifying and re-expressing the duty of care owed by directors of a company vis à vis the company in terms more closely reflecting contemporary attitudes.[4]

The anodyne rubric 'corporate governance' is a popular catch-phrase which has assumed prominence in English company law since the committee chaired by Sir Adrian Cadbury ('Cadbury Committee') handed down its report ('Cadbury Report'),[5] together with a code of best practice ('Code') designed to achieve higher standards of corporate behaviour,[6] on 1 December 1992. The Cadbury Report described corporate governance as the system by which companies are directed and controlled.[7] It emphasised the importance of non-executive directors in publicly listed British

---

[1] Farrar J H, 'Corporate Governance, Business Judgement and the Professionalism of Directors' (1993) 6 CBLJ 1; and Stapledon G P, *Institutional Shareholders and Corporate Governance* Clarendon Press, Oxford, 1996; cf. The American Law Institute, *Principles of Corporate Governance: Analysis and Recommendations* St Paul, 1994.

[2] (Leggatt LJ agreed).

[3] [1994] 1 All ER 261 at 264.

[4] (1996) 19 ACSR 606 at 627.

[5] Committee on the Financial Aspects of Corporate Governance, *The Report of the Committee on the Financial Aspects of Corporate Governance* Gee and Co Ltd, London, 1992.

[6] Committee on the Financial Aspects of Corporate Governance, *The Code of Best Practice* Gee and Co Ltd, London, 1992.

[7] Committee on the Financial Aspects of Corporate Governance, *The Report of the Committee on the Financial Aspects of Corporate Governance* Gee and Co Ltd, London, 1992 at para 2.5.

companies as a means of setting and maintaining standards of corporate governance, the need for improved disclosure, and for better reporting and financial information.

The Cadbury Report recommended that the boards of all publicly listed British companies should comply with the Code, and further recommended that: (i) companies reporting in respect of years ending after 30 June 1993 should make a statement in their report and accounts about their compliance with the Code; and (ii) companies' statements of compliance should be reviewed by the auditors before publication.[8] This publication of a statement of compliance, reviewed by the auditors, was a critical aspect of the Cadbury Report and was to be made a continuing obligation of listing by the London Stock Exchange Ltd ('LSE').[9] On 24 May 1995, a sub-committee chaired by Cadbury published a further report entitled *The Report on Compliance with the Code of Best Practice*.[10] By way of preface, Cadbury proclaimed that in the intervening four year period since his original committee was established, 'Real progress in raising governance standards is being made and the task now is to maintain that momentum.'[11] Much of the 1990s was spent by various committees in England doing just that.

There have been a number of further reports on aspects of corporate governance in England since the Cadbury Report in 1992. The most notable of these are the reports which the committees chaired by Sir Richard Greenbury ('Greenbury Committee'),[12] and Sir Ronald Hampel ('Hampel Committee')[13] produced: the Greenbury Report and the Hampel Report respectively. The Greenbury Committee addressed the thorny issue of the remuneration of directors of publicly listed British companies. The Committee considered that the fundamental principles of accountability, transparency and performance, and the related arrangements and procedures for achieving that, ought to be encapsulated in a code of best practice on directors' remuneration which the LSE should encourage companies to observe and implement.[14] The Greenbury Report contained recommendations that directors' remuneration should be determined by a committee of non-executive directors, and that the remuneration committee should report annually to shareholders which should be included in the company's annual accounts.[15]

The Cadbury Report and the Greenbury Report have both been endorsed by the LSE and have proved very successful in raising the awareness of corporate governance issues generally.[16] The Cadbury Committee and the Greenbury Committee both recommended that a new committee should review the implementation of their findings. The Hampel Report is the culmination of that review committee's work. As the Hampel Committee observed:

---

[8] *Ibid* at paras 3.7-3.10.
[9] Committee on the Financial Aspects of Corporate Governance, *The Code of Best Practice* Gee and Co Ltd, London, 1992 at 3; note Belcher A, 'Compliance with the Cadbury Code and the reporting of corporate governance' (1996) 17 Co Law 11.
[10] Committee on the Financial Aspects of Corporate Governance, *The Report on Compliance with the Code of Best Practice* Gee Publishing Ltd, London, 1995.
[11] *Ibid* at 8.
[12] Study Group on Directors' Remuneration, *Directors' Remuneration* Gee Publishing Ltd, London, 1995.
[13] Committee on Corporate Governance, *Final Report* Gee Publishing Ltd, London, 1998.
[14] Study Group on Directors' Remuneration, *Directors' Remuneration* Gee Publishing Ltd, London, 1995 at paras 1.16, 2.4 and 3.3.
[15] *Ibid* at paras 1.18, 2.3 and 5.4.
[16] Dignam A, 'A principled approach to self-regulation? The report of the Hampel Committee on Corporate Governance' (1998) 19 Co Law 140 at 141.

Both the Cadbury and Greenbury reports were responses to things which were perceived to have gone wrong – corporate failures in the first case, unjustified compensation packages in the privatised utilities in the second. Understandably, both concentrated largely on the prevention of abuse. We are equally concerned with the positive contribution which good corporate governance can make.[17]

In addition to reviewing the findings of the Cadbury Committee and the Greenbury Committee, the Hampel Committee was asked to look afresh at the roles of directors, shareholders and auditors in corporate governance.[18] But, in this respect, the Hampel Report has been adversely criticised by some commentators. For instance, Barnard felt it to be less innovative than the Cadbury Report and the Greenbury Report given the Hampel Committee's failure: (i) to provide models for the behaviour it prescribed; (ii) to appreciate the annual general meeting for what it has become; and (iii) of nerve in declining to recommend that every publicly listed company adopt in-house compliance programs.[19] Riley too was critical of the Hampel Report. He considered most of its conclusions and recommendations to be, 'familiar, largely repeating and approving similar provisions in Cadbury and Greenbury.'[20] What refinements were suggested in the Hampel Report, Riley considered to be modest.[21] Dignam's criticisms were the most strident. Dignam concluded his review of the Hampel Report by stating that:

Its remit was wide which should have allowed for a considered response to all aspects of corporate governance. It chose to take a restrictive view of its remit and to avoid key corporate-governance issues. The Committee failed to exploit the potential for a wholesale review of corporate governance. The report largely confines itself to commenting on Cadbury and Greenbury and makes no attempt to expand or extend those recommendations. Indeed, at times it seems that the Committee is trying to do away with reforms instigated under those previous reports.[22]

In spite of the adverse comment directed towards aspects of the Hampel Report, the collective wisdom of the Cadbury, Greenbury and Hampel committees resulted in the publication by the Committee on Corporate Governance of *The Combined Code* in June 1998 under Hampel's chairmanship.[23] The Principles of Good Governance and the Code of Best Practice prepared by the Committee are now appended to, but do not form part of, the LSE's Listing Rules.[24] But their significance should not be underestimated as the LSE has adopted them.[25] When *The Combined Code* was published, the Institute of Chartered Accountants in England and Wales ('ICA') agreed with the LSE that it would establish a working party to provide guidance to assist publicly listed British companies

---

[17] Committee on Corporate Governance, *Final Report* Gee Publishing Ltd, London, 1998 at para 1.7.
[18] *Ibid* at para 1.6.
[19] Barnard J W, 'The Hampel Committee Report: a transatlantic critique' (1998) 19 Co Law 110 at 112 and 114.
[20] Riley C A, 'The Final Report of the Hampel Committee on corporate governance' (1998) 19 Co Law 179 at 179.
[21] *Ibid* at 180.
[22] Dignam A, 'A principled approach to self-regulation? The report of the Hampel Committee on Corporate Governance' (1998) 19 Co Law 140 at 152.
[23] Committee on Corporate Governance, *The Combined Code* Gee Publishing Ltd, London, 1998.
[24] Cf. London Stock Exchange Ltd's Listing Rules at chapter 12.43A.
[25] *The Times*, 28 September 1999.

to implement the new requirements relating to internal control.[26] In September 1999, the ICA published its final report entitled *Internal Control: Guidance for Directors on the Combined Code* ('guidance'),[27] being the product of the ICA's Internal Control Working Party under the chairmanship of Nigel Turnbull.[28] Within the foreword, the LSE's head of listing observed that the guidance, 'is consistent with both the requirements of the Combined Code and of the related Listing Rule disclosure requirements, and clarifies to boards of directors of listed companies what is expected of them.'[29] One of the stated objectives of the guidance contains the following statement:

> The guidance is based on the adoption by a company's board of a risk-based approach to establishing a sound system of internal control and reviewing its effectiveness. This should be incorporated by the company within its normal management and governance processes. It should not be treated as a separate exercise undertaken to meet regulatory requirements.[30]

The interest in corporate governance has not been confined to England. It has been widespread. As the Law Commission recently noted, the Organisation for Economic Co-operation and Development ('OECD') exercises an important role in setting global standards for corporate governance.[31] In May 1999, the OECD Council approved the publication of *OECD Principles of Corporate Governance.*[32] These principles cover the rights, the equitable treatment and the role of shareholders in corporate governance, the importance of disclosure and transparency, and the responsibilities of the board. Within the preamble, the OECD stated that:

> Good corporate governance should provide proper incentives for the board and management to pursue objectives that are in the interests of the company and shareholders and should facilitate effective monitoring, thereby encouraging firms to use resources more efficiently.[33]

It is evident that corporate governance is widely seen as a matter of great importance in modern company law. The plethora of reports, articles and books devoted to the subject is a testament to that. The 1990s, as Riley observes, 'seem in danger of becoming the decade of the corporate-governance committee.'[34] Whilst corporate governance is not only about directors and the boards of companies which they occupy, nonetheless, its omnipresence throughout the 1990s has put the corporate spotlight

---

[26] Institute of Chartered Accountants in England & Wales, *Internal Control* (a consultative document) Institute of Chartered Accountants in England & Wales, London, 1999 at foreword.

[27] Institute of Chartered Accountants in England & Wales, *Internal Control: Guidance for Directors on the Combined Code* Institute of Chartered Accountants in England & Wales, London, 1999.

[28] *Financial Times*, 27 September 1999.

[29] Institute of Chartered Accountants in England & Wales, *Internal Control: Guidance for Directors on the Combined Code* Institute of Chartered Accountants in England & Wales, London, 1999 at foreword.

[30] *Ibid* at para 9.

[31] Law Commission, *Company Directors: Regulating Conflicts of Interests and Formulating a Statement of Duties* HMSO, London, Cm 4436, 1999 at para 1.24.

[32] Organisation for Economic Co-operation and Development, *OECD Principles of Corporate Governance* OECD Publications, Paris, 1999.

[33] *Ibid* at 9.

[34] Riley C A, 'The Final Report of the Hampel Committee on corporate governance' (1998) 19 Co Law 179 at 179.

squarely upon directors of British and Australian companies.[35] This has brought the duties which they owe to their companies sharply into focus.

DIRECTORS: THEIR IMPACT AND REACH

In modern English and Australian company law, the topic of directors' duties is one which gives rise to substantial theoretical and practical difficulties.[36] It is a topic of considerable importance to directors and officers of British and Australian companies who fall within the expanded definition,[37] and those whom by their conduct are deemed to be performing relevant duties and therefore subject to corresponding responsibilities and obligations: whether as *de jure* directors, *de facto* directors or shadow directors.[38] As the Law Commission recently noted, directors' duties are essentially regulatory and prescriptive areas of the law. Their fundamental purpose is to regulate the conduct of directors; or, put another way, to promote high standards of behaviour.[39]

The publicity associated with those larger than life corporate personalities mentioned at the outset of this chapter,[40] whose infamy has made them household names, does unfortunately tend to distort, and detract from, the widely held view that the greater number of directors of British and Australian companies act with diligence and propriety befitting their positions of trust and responsibility. This is a view which has by and large persisted in England since 1926 when the committee chaired by Wilfrid Greene KC ('Greene Committee') noted that:

> The evidence satisfies us that the great majority of limited companies both public and private are honestly and conscientiously managed. Cases in which fraud or lesser forms of dishonesty or improper dealing occur are comparatively few, and the public interest which such cases naturally arouse tends to divert attention from the vast number of honestly conducted concerns and to create an exaggerated idea of the evils connected with limited companies and their activities.[41]

Nevertheless, such publicity does provide a timely reminder that within English and Australian company law there are, and probably have always been, those lesser lights

---

[35] *The Times*, 28 September 1999 and 29 April 1999; *The Sunday Times*, 25 April 1999; and *The Independent on Sunday*, 25 April 1999.

[36] Gibson P, 'Introduction' in McKendrick E (ed), *Commercial Aspects of Trusts and Fiduciary Obligations* Clarendon Press, Oxford, 1992 at 2.

[37] E.g., Companies Act 1985 (UK) ss309(3), 319-322, 322B and 330-346; and Corporations Law ss60 and 232(1); note Ford H A J, Austin R P and Ramsay I M, *Ford's Principles of Corporations Law* (9th ed) Reed International Books Australia Pty Ltd, Sydney, 1999 at para 8.020.

[38] Companies Act 1985 (UK) s741; Insolvency Act 1986 (UK) s251; Company Directors Disqualification Act 1986 (UK) s22; Financial Services Act 1986 (UK) s207; and Corporations Law s60; note *Re Lo-Line Electric Motors Ltd* (1988) 4 BCC 415 at 422 per Browne-Wilkinson VC; *Re Hydrodan (Corby) Ltd* [1994] BCC 161 at 162 per Millett J; and *Re Richborough Furniture Ltd* [1996] BCC 155 at 169 per Timothy Lloyd QC; cf. *Australian Securities Commission v AS Nominees Ltd* (1995) 133 ALR 1 at 51-53 per Finn J; *Mistmorn Pty Ltd v Yasseen* (1996) 21 ACSR 173 at 183 per Davies J; and *Deputy Commissioner of Taxation v Austin* (1998) 16 ACLC 1555 at 1559 per Madgwick J; see Carroll R, 'Third Party Liability for Corporate Activity: Recent Developments' (1996) 26 UWALR 332.

[39] Law Commission, *Company Directors: Regulating Conflicts of Interests and Formulating a Statement of Duties* HMSO, London, Cm 4436, 1999 at para 2.7.

[40] Robert Maxwell in England and Alan Bond in Australia.

[41] Company Law Amendment Committee, HMSO, London, Cmd 2657, 1926 at para 7.

who fail to meet levels of reasonable diligence and who flagrantly ignore the law's requirements of trust, confidence, good faith, honesty and integrity in favour of amorality, greed and selfishness; and, by doing so, bring English and Australian company law into disrepute.

In the mid-1990s the English courts played host to the most expensive trial in British legal history.[42] At that time we witnessed Robert Maxwell's sons, Ian and Kevin, embroiled in a complex fraud trial amidst allegations that they conspired with Maxwell to defraud companies, of which they were all directors, of corporate assets valued at tens of millions of pounds. Both sons were acquitted, but not before running up a multi-million pound legal aid bill in their defence.[43] Similarly, before the Australian courts, Alan Bond was charged with having conspired to, 'defraud Bell Resources Ltd, its subsidiaries and its shareholders' and, further, having failed to act honestly as a director of Freefold Pty Ltd relating to a $1bn transaction in the late 1980s.[44] On 5 February 1997, Bond was sentenced to four years imprisonment after pleading guilty to two charges of failing to act honestly as a director.[45] On appeal, this sentence was increased to seven years imprisonment by the Western Australian Court of Criminal Appeal on 22 August 1997.[46]

It is not surprising that the publicity generated by such high-profile corporate personalities has captured the public's imagination in England and in Australia.[47] The damage which some of these former directors have caused to corporate England and Australia, when coupled with the downturn in the property and commodity markets experienced across much of Europe and the Asia-Pacific region during the early 1990s,[48] consequent upon the collapse in October 1987 of the international share market, has, as Sealy laments:

> [Left] many investors and creditors with heavy losses: in the aftermath, critical public comment has often centered on the part played by directors, and on alleged weaknesses in the law.[49]

As we move into the next millennium, therefore, the corporate spotlight is very firmly upon directors and the enormous power and influence which they wield over corporate assets and also creditors, employees, shareholders and the like;[50] all of which can have serious ramifications for local, national and international communities. The modern corporate sector in England and in Australia has a profound effect on everyday life. It

---

[42] Sarker R, 'Maxwell: fraud trial of the century' (1996) 17 Co Law 116 at 116.
[43] *The Sunday Times*, 23 May 1999; and *Financial Times*, 29 July 1999.
[44] Following the takeover of Bell Resources Ltd by Bond's flagship, Bond Corporation Holdings Ltd.
[45] *The Age*, 23 August 1997.
[46] *The Australian Financial Review*, 25 August 1997.
[47] E.g., *Bishopsgate Investment Management Ltd v Maxwell (No. 2)* [1994] 1 All ER 261; *Commonwealth Bank of Australia v Friedrich* (1991) 5 ACSR 115; *Linter Group Ltd v Goldberg* (1992) 10 ACLC 739; *Equiticorp Finance Ltd v Bank of New Zealand* (1993) 11 ACLC 952; and *State of South Australia v Clark* (1996) 19 ACSR 606.
[48] *Financial Times*, 20 July 1999.
[49] Sealy L S, 'Reforming the Law on Directors' Duties' (1991) 12 Co Law 175 at 176.
[50] *The Sunday Times*, 25 April 1999; cf. *The Australian*, 23 April 1997; note Department of Trade and Industry, *Modern Company Law: For a Competitive Economy* (a consultative document) HMSO, London, 1998 at para 3.7; and Department of Trade and Industry, *Modern Company Law: The Strategic Framework* HMSO, London, 1999 at para 5.1.14.

is crucial to the creation of national wealth.[51] In Australia, for example, the corporate sector possesses most of Australia's assets and employs most of its workers. Similarly, according to the Cadbury Report, the British economy, 'depends upon the drive and efficiency of its companies.'[52] This was reinforced in July 1998 by the Chancellor of the Exchequer when he proclaimed that the related financial services industry, 'accounts for 7% of GDP and employs more than a million people in the City of London and around the country.'[53] Farther afield, the experience in the United States of America is an analogue of the Anglo-Australian as the following passage from Jackson J's judgment in *State Tax Commission of Utah v Aldrich* demonstrates:

> Of relatively recent growth, the corporation has become almost the unit of organization of our economic life. Whether for good or ill, the stubborn fact is that in our present system the corporation carries on the bulk of production and transportation, is the chief employer of both labor and capital, pays a large part of our taxes, and is an economic institution of such magnitude and importance that there is no present substitute for it except the state itself.[54]

From an economic standpoint, therefore, we look to companies for the innovation, enterprise and productivity needed to increase the wealth of our local, national and international communities. Company law, proclaimed the President of the Board of Trade in March 1998, lies at the heart of the British economy and, 'is fundamental to our national competitiveness.'[55] Directorial conduct and decision-making can positively influence economies in this regard. Conversely, directorial misconduct and decision-making can destroy economies; or, at the very least, weaken and suppress them.[56] Consequently, where a company is fraudulently, or even negligently operated, the potential for economic and social harm is tremendous. Bad and incompetent management places shareholders, creditors, employees, suppliers and consumers at risk.[57] Politically, it is expected that due regard will be given to community values and other matters such as, 'the company's workforce, its customers and clientele, its suppliers and creditors, more broadly, the local community, the national interest, exports, welfare, the environment.'[58] Thus, the ability, honesty, industry, ethical and moral outlook of directors affects many aspects of community life.[59]

The topic of directors' duties is, therefore, of vital concern to the community.[60] Writing in 1931, Dodd stated that public opinion ultimately makes the law. Dodd felt

---

[51] Senate Standing Committee on Legal and Constitutional Affairs, *Social and Fiduciary Duties and Obligations of Company Directors* AGPS, Canberra, 1989 at 7.

[52] Committee on the Financial Aspects of Corporate Governance, *The Report of the Committee on the Financial Aspects of Corporate Governance* Gee and Co Ltd, London, 1992 at para 1.1.

[53] HM Treasury, *Financial Services and Markets Bill: A Consultation Document, Part One* HMSO, London, 1998 at foreword.

[54] (1942) 316 US 174 at 192.

[55] Department of Trade and Industry, *Modern Company Law: For a Competitive Economy* (a consultative document) HMSO, London, 1998 at i.

[56] Senate Standing Committee on Legal and Constitutional Affairs, *Social and Fiduciary Duties and Obligations of Company Directors* AGPS, Canberra, 1989 at 7.

[57] Rider B A K, 'Amiable Lunatics and the Rule in Foss v Harbottle' [1978] CLJ 270 at 286-287.

[58] Sealy L S, 'Directors' "Wider" Responsibilities – Problems Conceptual, Practical and Procedural' (1987) 13 MULR 164 at 170; note Stapledon G P, *Institutional Shareholders and Corporate Governance* Clarendon Press, Oxford, 1996 at 8.

[59] *The Australian Financial Review*, 2 January 1996.

[60] Company Law Amendment Committee, HMSO, London, Cmd 2657, 1926 at paras 8-9.

that a, 'sense of social responsibility toward employees, consumers, and the general public may thus come to be regarded as the appropriate attitude to be adopted by those who are engaged in business'.[61] Others would argue that directors should be obliged to take a longer term view and act not only to protect the interests of their company's shareholders, but also to protect the interests of the future generation of shareholders' wealth, employees, customers, suppliers, the environment and the like.[62] In Canada, for instance, Berger J in *Teck Corporation Ltd v Millar*, when considering the issue of directors' duties, felt that:

> [The] law ought to take into account the fact that the corporation provides the legal framework for the development of resources and the generation of wealth in the private sector of the Canadian economy.[63]

A not dissimilar view was expressed by Kirby P in *Equiticorp Finance Ltd v Bank of New Zealand* where his Honour pronounced that company law, 'imposes on companies the beneficial discipline of the law for the protection of investors and creditors and, through them, of the community which is so dependent upon corporations for its economic well-being.'[64] But, in Dabner's view, 'it is naive to expect individual directors to operate corporations for the benefit of all. The welfare of the State is the realm of the government.'[65] And, in Heydon's view, such abstract matters as the national economic interest, the wishes of the government or the advancement of the environment ought only be considered by directors if such matters have a link with the interests of the company.[66] Heydon went on to explain that:

> A wide duty to consider anything which a good citizen might take into account will produce directors who cannot be brought to account. A narrow duty to consider particular material interests of particular classes will prevent directors having a proper degree of commercial freedom.[67]

These are weighty and complicated issues of vital import to the topic of directors' duties generally, but they are outside the remit of this book. Similarly, this book is not concerned with the more colourful and notorious of the corporate personalities themselves, or with the economic, environmental, political or social impact of their actions. The focus of this book is upon the judicial and legislative steps which have been recently taken by our courts and parliaments to combat the perception that company law is too lax and, thus, facilitative of the corporate abuses perpetrated by some directors during the 1980s and the early 1990s.[68] Abuses which resulted in vast

---

[61] Dodd E M Jr, 'For Whom are Corporate Managers Trustees?' (1931-1932) 45 Harv LR 1145 at 1160.
[62] *Financial Times*, 8 July 1999: 'The issue is between the supporters of the traditional view of the corporation as an agent for the shareholders and the fashionable alternative of a stakeholder corporation taking into account wider interests.'; and *Financial Times*, 21 July 1999.
[63] *Teck Corporation Ltd v Millar* (1972) 33 DLR (3d) 288 at 314.
[64] (1993) 11 ACLC 952 at 978-980.
[65] Dabner J, 'Directors' Duties – The Schizoid Company' (1988) 6 CSLJ 105 at 113.
[66] Heydon J D, 'Directors' Duties and the Company's Interests' in Finn P D (ed), *Equity and Commercial Relationships* The Law Book Company Ltd, Sydney, 1987 at 136.
[67] *Ibid.*
[68] Cf. *Re Swift 736 Ltd* [1993] BCC 312 at 315 per Nicholls VC (Farquharson and Steyn LJJ agreed); *Re Grayan Building Services Ltd* [1995] BCC 554 at 577 per Henry LJ; and *Re Living Images Ltd* [1996]

corporate losses for which these corporate high-flyers will long be remembered. Their legacy has led to a determined push on the part of our courts and parliaments, probably more so in Australia than in England, to raise levels of responsibility and accountability of directors of British and Australian companies more in keeping with public sentiment and the business community's expectations.[69]

DIRECTORS' DUTIES: REVIVED AND REFASHIONED

Throughout this book, it will be seen that raised levels of responsibility and accountability have been achieved by a more robust and interventionist approach by our courts and, within Australian company law in particular, the active support of parliamentary initiatives designed specifically to target errant directors and to meet new ideals of corporate governance.[70] This is a fresh initiative; a new approach, adopted and employed with specific ends in mind.[71] Ironically, the machinery for achieving these ends is not new. The legal rules and equitable principles employed by today's courts have governed directorial conduct and decision-making for several hundreds of years.[72] But it is only in the last decade or so that these traditional rules and principles have been refashioned by our courts, and applied in a more robust and interventionist manner in response to public calls for raised levels of directorial responsibility and accountability; specifically, to bring a measure of commercial pragmatism to bear upon the resolution of today's complex commercial and corporate disputes,[73] and to promote corporate integrity.

While the duties of directors are many, the leading textbooks on English and Australian company law treat directors of British and Australian companies as being

cont.
    BCC 112 at 115 per Laddie J; note Farrar J H, Furey N E, Hannigan B M and Wylie P, *Farrar's Company Law* (3rd ed) Butterworth & Co (Publishers) Ltd, London, 1991 at 397.

[69] See Prentice D D and Holland P R J, *Contemporary Issues in Corporate Governance* Oxford University Press, Oxford, 1993; Committee on the Financial Aspects of Corporate Governance, *The Report of the Committee on the Financial Aspects of Corporate Governance* Gee and Co Ltd, London, 1992; Farrar J H, 'Corporate Governance, Business Judgement and the Professionalism of Directors' (1993) 6 CBLJ 1; Whincop M J, 'An Economic Analysis of the Criminalisation and Content of Directors' Duties' (1996) 24 ABLR 273; and Stapledon G P, *Institutional Shareholders and Corporate Governance* Clarendon Press, Oxford, 1996.

[70] *Bishopsgate Investment Management Ltd v Maxwell (No. 2)* [1994] 1 All ER 261 at 264 per Hoffmann LJ (Leggatt LJ agreed) who recognised that the law, 'may be evolving in response to changes in public attitudes to corporate governance'; *Re Grayan Building Services Ltd* [1995] BCC 554 at 577 per Henry LJ, 'The statutory corporate climate is stricter than it has ever been, and those enforcing it should reflect the fact that Parliament has seen the need for higher standards.'; and *State of South Australia v Clark* (1996) 19 ACSR 606 at 627 per Perry J, 'Recent appellate decisions in Australia have gone a long way towards clarifying and re-expressing the duty of care owed by directors of a company vis á vis the company in terms more closely reflecting contemporary attitudes.'

[71] Committee on the Financial Aspects of Corporate Governance, *The Report on Compliance with the Code of Best Practice* Gee Publishing Ltd, London, 1995 at 8, 'Real progress in raising governance standards is being made and the task now is to maintain that momentum.'

[72] E.g., *The Earl of Oxford's Case* (1615) 1 Chan Rep 1; *The Charitable Corporation v Sutton* (1742) 2 Atk 400; and *The Overend & Gurney Company v Gibb* (1872) LR 5 HL 480.

[73] E.g., *Equiticorp Finance Ltd v Bank of New Zealand* (1993) 11 ACLC 952; *Bishopsgate Investment Management Ltd v Maxwell (No. 2)* [1994] 1 All ER 261; *Mallina Holdings Ltd v Biala Ltd* (1994) 15 ACSR 1; and *Daniels v Anderson* (1995) 13 ACLC 614; see Sealy L S, 'Directors' "Wider" Responsibilities – Problems Conceptual, Practical and Procedural' (1987) 13 MULR 164 at 169; and Sealy L S, '"Bona Fides" and "Proper Purposes" in Corporate Decisions' (1989) 15 MULR 265 at 265.

subject to two broad duties: (i) to act honestly, in good faith and for proper purposes; and (ii) to exercise care and diligence.[74] It is convenient to broadly categorise these duties in this way as cases involving allegations of breach of the former duty raise very different issues to those dealing with breach of the latter duty.[75] From an Australian company law perspective, companies legislation has always differentiated between the two duties.[76]

These duties emanated from cases now centuries old and have their roots in the fiduciary relationship which existed between directors, trustees and their companies. In Australian company law these duties are now reinforced, and partially codified, by statute.[77] In English company law they are more affected by statute. More will be said about this later.[78] But, in the analysis of the law relating to directors' duties which follows, it is important to be mindful that the image of company law as being all symmetry and design evinced by the leading textbooks is, more often than not, not the case in practice.[79] It is sometimes overlooked by commentators that the obligations and rights consequent upon directors' duties do not always have, 'the same abstract uniformity that a legal text book may give them, but translate into practical gains and losses for the parties in the real world of people and property'.[80] As this book will highlight, any attempt to categorise directors and to link duties to categories may over-simplify the reality that directors come in all shapes and sizes,[81] and that their duties range across a spectrum rather than fall into neatly defined categories.[82]

This book is written from a practising company lawyer's perspective and is concerned principally with these two broad duties: to act honestly, in good faith and for

[74] Davies P L, *Gower's Principles of Modern Company Law* (6th ed) Sweet & Maxwell Ltd, London, 1997 at 598-599; Ford H A J and Austin R P, *Ford's Principles of Corporations Law* (6th ed) Butterworths Pty Ltd, Sydney, 1992 at 430, 487 *et seq* and 524 *et seq*; Pennington R R, *Company Law* (6th ed) Butterworth & Co (Publishers) Ltd, London, 1990 at 583; Palmer F B, *Palmer's Company Law* (25th ed) Sweet & Maxwell Ltd, London, 1992 at 8.406 and 8.501 *et seq*; and Farrar J H, Furey N E, Hannigan B M and Wylie P, *Farrar's Company Law* (3rd ed) Butterworth & Co (Publishers) Ltd, London, 1991 at 380.

[75] Sievers A S, 'Farewell to the Sleeping Director – The Modern Judicial and Legislative Approach to Directors' Duties of Care, Skill and Diligence' (1993) 21 ABLR 111 at 111.

[76] Which relevantly began with Companies Act 1958 (Vic) s107(1).

[77] Corporations Law ss232(2) and 232(4).

[78] *The Times*, 25 January 1995 reported that the Institute of Directors, 'calculates that 750 different statutes directly affect the daily lives of company directors in the UK.'; see Davies P L, *Gower's Principles of Modern Company Law* (6th ed) Sweet & Maxwell Ltd, London, 1997 at 623-640; and, e.g., Companies Act 1985 (UK); Companies Act 1989 (UK); Insolvency Act 1986 (UK); Company Directors Disqualification Act 1986 (UK); and Financial Services Act 1986 (UK).

[79] Editorial comment (1994) 15 Co Law 34 at 34.

[80] Sealy L S, 'The Enforcement of Partnership Agreements, Articles of Association and Shareholder Agreements' in Finn P D (ed) *Equity and Commercial Relationships* The Law Book Company Ltd, Sydney, 1987 at 99.

[81] *In re City Equitable Fire Insurance Company Ltd* [1925] Ch 407 at 426-427 per Romer J; *Harris v S* (1976-1977) 2 ACLR 51 at 63-64 per Wells J; *Commonwealth Bank of Australia v Friedrich* (1991) 5 ACSR 115 at 125 per Tadgell J; *Standard Chartered Bank of Aust Ltd v Antico* (1995) 13 ACLC 1381 at 1436-1440 per Hodgson J; and *Australian Securities Commission v AS Nominees Ltd* (1995) 133 ALR 1 at 51-53 per Finn J; and *Deputy Commissioner of Taxation v Austin* (1998) 16 ACLC 1555 at 1558-1560 per Madgwick J; cf. *Dairy Containers Ltd v NZI Bank Ltd* [1995] 2 NZLR 30 at 90-91 per Thomas J; and *Re Richborough Furniture Ltd* [1996] 1 BCLC 507 at 524 per Timothy Lloyd QC; note Anderson C and Morrison D, 'Standard Chartered Bank of Australia Ltd v Antico: Towards a New Understanding of Insolvent Trading' (1996) 4 CCL 1 at 4-6; Baxt R, 'Shadow directors and Australian law' (1996) 70 ALJ 441 at 441-443; and Baxt R, commercial law note (1995) 69 ALJ 684 at 685-686.

[82] Shepherd J C, *The Law of Fiduciaries* The Carswell Company Ltd, Toronto, 1981 at 347-348.

proper purposes on the one hand, and to exercise care and diligence on the other hand. Relevantly, these duties stem from the fiduciary relationship between directors and their British and Australian companies, the general law, and the companies legislation which today regulates and shapes corporate England and Australia.[83] Because of the strong historical links between English and Australian company law, legal, equitable and statutory, this book draws from the rich experience of the English judiciary and the British Parliament, and also the dynamic approach to corporate regulation and company law reform taken by the Australian judiciary and the Australian Parliament over the past decade or so. Thus, Australian company law will be frequently resorted to, analogically and comparatively, in the many instances where it supplements and complements English company law; and, contrastingly, in those instances where it does not. Moreover, many examples of Canadian and New Zealand company law cases are cited and referred to. Some are analysed in detail as English and Australian company law are very much the richer for their influence: so too the jurisprudence of other Commonwealth countries.

Notwithstanding that Australian company law owes its heritage to, and is thus deeply indebted to, English company law, it is suggested that in recent years Australian company law has proven to be more adaptable, flexible and responsive to public demands and, thus, more attuned to, and in keeping with, public sentiment and the business community's expectations than has English company law.[84] It is considered that English company law has been somewhat reticent and impervious to change;[85] rooted in a bygone era,[86] seemingly hamstrung by conservative policies and steadfast in its refusal to respond to the times.[87] Although, it should be noted that on 4 March 1998, the President of the Board of Trade announced the launch of a fundamental review of the framework of core English company law. The consultation paper published at that time by the Department of Trade and Industry ('DTI') outlines the nature of the problems which the review is designed to address and its objectives, and relevantly provides that:

> The object of the review will be to bring forward proposals for a modern law for the modern world. The Government is determined that the nation should have an up-to-date framework which promotes the competitiveness of UK companies and so contributes to national competitiveness and increased prosperity.[88]

---

[83] E.g., Companies Act 1985 (UK); Companies Act 1989 (UK); Insolvency Act 1986 (UK); Company Directors Disqualification Act 1986 (UK); Financial Services Act 1986 (UK); and Corporations Act 1989 (Cth).

[84] Sealy L S, 'Reforming the Law on Directors' Duties' (1991) 12 Co Law 175 at 179.

[85] Finn P D, 'Fiduciary Law and the Modern Commercial World' in McKendrick E (ed), *Commercial Aspects of Trusts and Fiduciary Obligations* Clarendon Press, Oxford, 1992 at 40; and Sealy L S, 'Fiduciary Obligations, Forty Years On' (1995) 9 JCL 37 at 52-53.

[86] Department of Trade and Industry, *Modern Company Law: For a Competitive Economy* (a consultative document) HMSO, London, 1998 at para 1.1.

[87] Cf. *Bishopsgate Investment Management Ltd v Maxwell (No. 2)* [1994] 1 All ER 261 at 264 per Hoffmann LJ (Leggatt LJ agreed) who recognised that the law, 'may be evolving in response to changes in public attitudes to corporate governance'; and *Re Grayan Building Services Ltd* [1995] BCC 554 at 577 per Henry LJ, 'The statutory corporate climate is stricter than it has ever been, and those enforcing it should reflect the fact that Parliament has seen the need for higher standards.'

[88] Department of Trade and Industry, *Modern Company Law: For a Competitive Economy* (a consultative document) HMSO, London, 1998 at para 1.2.

In February 1999, the DTI released its consultation document entitled *Modern Company Law: The Strategic Framework* which identifies two particular issues of general importance to the review. First, the identification of the interests which English company law should serve and the means by which it should do so.[89] Secondly, the special needs of small and closely-held companies which were thought to be ill-served by the existing British companies legislation, and which constitute one of the key problem areas of English company law.[90] The aim of the Company Law Review Steering Group is to enable the DTI to publish a detailed White Paper in or about March 2001.[91] Given the breadth of core English company law, the DTI's review is being conducted against a tight timetable.[92]

AN HISTORICAL PERSPECTIVE

English company law has a long and distinguished pedigree. Its roots go back many centuries to a time when, undoubtedly, commerce in England was infected to some extent by continental influences.[93] Gradually, however, English company law developed its own distinctive personality; the historical origins of which are not only interesting in themselves, but additionally provide a necessary basis for the understanding of modern English company law.[94] The same is true for a proper appreciation of Australian company law.

It is instructive to recall that modern English company law evolved from the unincorporated association or joint stock company, an association akin to partnership, 'based on mutual agreement, rather than from the corporation, based on a grant from the state, and owes more to partnership principles than to rules based on corporate personality.'[95] Essentially, these unincorporated associations were formed under a deed of settlement not dissimilar to today's deed of partnership.[96] The deed of settlement constituted an agreement between trustees and the association's members as the original subscribers of capital. Inevitably, the deed provided for the appointment of directors to manage the enterprise. Thus, property would be held by trustees and managed by directors. It was a trust as Wedderburn explains:

---

[89] Department of Trade and Industry, *Modern Company Law: The Strategic Framework* HMSO, London, 1999 at chapter 5.1.

[90] *Ibid* at chapter 5.2; note Gower L C B, 'Some Contrasts Between British and American Corporation Law' (1955-1956) 69 Harv LR 1369 at 1373; Sealy L S, 'A Company Law for Tomorrow's World' (1981) 2 Co Law 195 at 200; and Rider B A K, 'Partnership Law and its Impact on "Domestic Companies"' [1979] CLJ 148 at 154; cf. *Mesenberg v Cord Industrial Recruiters Pty Ltd* (1996) 14 ACLC 519 at 528 per Young J; and *Glavanics v Brunninghausen* (1996) 19 ACSR 204 at 208 and 216-217 per Bryson J.

[91] Department of Trade and Industry, *Modern Company Law: For a Competitive Economy* (a consultative document) HMSO, London, 1998 at paras 1.5 and 8.2-8.3.

[92] Law Commission, *Company Directors: Regulating Conflicts of Interests and Formulating a Statement of Duties* HMSO, London, Cm 4436, 1999 at para 1.7.

[93] See Schmitthoff C M, 'The Origin of the Joint-Stock Company' (1939-1940) 3 UTLJ 74.

[94] Hein L W, 'The British Business Company: Its Origins and Its Control' (1963) 15 UTLJ 134 at 135.

[95] Gower L C B, 'Some Contrasts Between British and American Corporation Law' (1955-1956) 69 Harv LR 1369 at 1371-1372.

[96] Ford H A J, Austin R P and Ramsay I M, *Ford's Principles of Corporations Law* (9th ed) Reed International Books Australia Pty Ltd, Sydney, 1999 at para 2.160.

[To] which the proprietors would subscribe their money, being in the eye of the common law 'partners' (with full liability) in the enterprise, but with the crucial advantage of transferable 'shares'.[97]

These unincorporated associations functioned on a large scale with transferable shares, widespread membership, and capital raised by public subscription. It was even possible to achieve a measure of limited liability for shareholders by including appropriate provisions in contracts made with third parties. Incorporation, however, was only available through royal charter,[98] or act of parliament,[99] and was cumbersome and expensive. Companies incorporated pursuant to a special act of parliament were ordinarily granted the privilege of liability limited to the value of the paid-up shares.[100] Such a privilege, for example, was accorded to shareholders of the Bank of England.[101]

These were days of high adventure. Speculation was rife. Entrepreneurs would often pool their assets in order to, for example, jointly purchase and provision a ship for a trading venture; at the conclusion of which all would be sold and the proceeds divided. It is from this concept, says Hein, that the term joint stock derives;[102] although the more usual meaning of the term is that later enacted, namely:

> Every Partnership whereof the Capital is divided or agreed to be divided into Shares, and so as to be transferable without the express Consent of all the Copartners.[103]

As Gower observes, 'the wordy and obscure Bubble Act of 1719, was passed as a result of the speculative fever induced by the grandiose schemes of the ill-fated South Sea Company. The act was designed to curb the growth of unincorporated joint-stock companies, but its actual result was very different.'[104] Paradoxically, it seems that the so-called Bubble Act inhibited the granting of charters of incorporation which produced a rebirth of the unincorporated association which the Act had sought to destroy.[105] Hence, up until 1844 commerce in England continued to employ the unincorporated association and, thus, evaded the Bubble Act's prohibition against acting as a body corporate.[106]

Modern English company law has its genesis in three important statutory enactments from the 19th century. First, the Joint Stock Companies Act 1844 (UK) which enabled joint stock companies with transferable shares to become incorporated through the simple procedural device of registering a deed of settlement.[107] Thus, incorporation was made readily available in England. Upon incorporation the company assumed a corporate personality and was capable of suing, and being sued, in its own name. The

---

97 Wedderburn K W, 'Trust, Corporation and the Worker' (1985) 23 OHLJ 203 at 208.
98 The Muscovy Company chartered by King Edward VI in 1553 is considered to be the first joint stock company. The English East India Company was chartered in 1600.
99 E.g., statutory corporations were created to run such public utilities as railways, canals, docks and public water supplies.
100 Hein L W, 'The British Business Company: Its Origins and Its Control' (1963) 15 UTLJ 134 at 149.
101 The first joint stock company to give rise to the active trading of shares.
102 Hein L W, 'The British Business Company: Its Origins and Its Control' (1963) 15 UTLJ 134 at 143.
103 7&8 Vict c110 s2.
104 Gower L C B, 'Some Contrasts Between British and American Corporation Law' (1955-1956) 69 Harv LR 1369 at 1370-1371.
105 *Ibid* at 1371.
106 6 Geo I c18.
107 7&8 Vict c110 ss4 and 7.

quid pro quo, however, was the publicity given to the deed of settlement and the company register. Secondly, the Limited Liability Act 1855 (UK) which enabled limited liability to be enjoyed by those who so provided in their registered deed of settlement.[108] Thirdly, the Joint Stock Companies Act 1856 (UK) which abolished the deed of settlement and brought the memorandum of association and articles of association into existence.[109] Section 57 of this last Act repealed the 1844 and 1855 Acts and incorporated their essence into one Act. These Acts, therefore, 'introduced the great principle that any group of persons engaging in trade or commerce (other than insurance and banking) could be incorporated with a limited liability on satisfying certain specified requirements.'[110] It is from this point, says Keeton, that many of the most characteristic features of modern company practice, including the appointment of directors, the general and extraordinary meetings of shareholders, and the preparation and audit of an annual balance sheet derive.[111]

Incorporation and limited liability have been described as, 'the two greatest privileges available in the legal systems of the Western World'.[112] Yet, eminent jurists have failed to appreciate that, historically, limited liability and incorporation are divorced.[113] Equally, there are those who misconceive the seminal quality of the House of Lords' decision in *Salomon v A Salomon and Company Ltd*,[114] where the sanctity of the corporate entity was emphasised.[115] Additionally, the affinity between company law and partnership law is often overlooked. Nineteenth century British parliamentary intent, it would seem, was to restrict companies to large associations and partnerships to small associations given that partnership principles presuppose mutual trust and confidence among the members; which is impossible if their number is unduly large.[116]

The British Parliament did not contemplate the corporate form for use by the one-man firm or small family concern sanctified by the House of Lords in *Salomon*.[117] Consequently, as Sealy explains, this has resulted in 20th century English company law which is, 'too cumbersome to enable the small company to function freely, and too complex for the entrepreneur in the suburbs and the provinces to have ready access to proper advice.'[118] Although in many respects English and Australian company law is an analogue of partnership law, the concept of the close corporation or domestic

---

[108]   18&19 Vict c133 ss1 and 7.
[109]   19&20 Vict c47 ss3-13; cf. Companies Act 1985 (UK) s10.
[110]   Keeton G W, 'The Director as Trustee' (1952) 5 CLP 11 at 11-12.
[111]   *Ibid.*
[112]   Wedderburn K W, 'Trust, Corporation and the Worker' (1985) 23 OHLJ 203 at 204; note Whincup M, '"Inequitable Incorporation" – the Abuse of a Privilege' (1981) 2 Co Law 158 at 158.
[113]   *Dimbleby & Sons Ltd v National Union of Journalists* [1984] 1 WLR 427 at 435 per Lord Diplock; note Gower L C B, *Gower's Principles of Modern Company Law* (5th ed) Sweet & Maxwell Ltd, London, 1992 at 22-23 and 39 *et seq.*
[114]   [1897] AC 22; which Kahn-Freund O, 'Some Reflections on Company Law Reform' (1944) 7 MLR 54 at 54 described as that, 'calamitous decision'; cf. Wedderburn K W, 'Trust, Corporation and the Worker' (1985) 23 OHLJ 203 at 204; and Wedderburn K W, 'The Social Responsibility of Companies' (1985) 15 Melb ULR 4 at 8.
[115]   Baxt R, case note (1991) 65 ALJ 352 at 352.
[116]   Gower L C B, 'Some Contrasts Between British and American Corporation Law' (1955-1956) 69 Harv LR 1369 at 1372.
[117]   *Ibid* at 1373.
[118]   Sealy L S, 'A Company Law for Tomorrow's World' (1981) 2 Co Law 195 at 200.

company has been almost ignored.[119] However, as mentioned in an earlier part of this chapter, the Company Law Review Steering Group, which was appointed in 1998 under the auspices of the DTI to carry out a fundamental review of the framework of core English company law,[120] has recognised as an area of general importance to its review the special needs of small and closely-held companies which were thought to be ill-served by the existing British companies legislation. This is one of the key problem areas of English company law which the review is intent upon addressing.[121]

A MODERN PERSPECTIVE

Throughout this book, it should be borne in mind that the commercial and corporate disputes of the 20th century, particularly the latter part, were not those of the 18th century and the 19th century. Today, many of the commercial and corporate disputes which come before the English and Australian courts are so complex that the courts struggle to cope.[122] Offshore banking, tax havens, trusts, joint ventures, subsidiaries, corporate groups, satellites and the like have become *de rigueur* in today's commercial and corporate world.[123]

It is not surprising, therefore, that the application of traditional rules and principles to these modern day complex commercial and corporate problems is increasingly under attack. A fundamental reassessment of the way in which those traditional rules and principles are applied is required in order to refashion rules, principles and approaches considered applicable to resolving today's complex commercial and corporate disputes. The rules and principles are in need of a little dusting off and the courts, as Toohey J in *Jackson v Sterling Industries Ltd* observed, 'must respond to the situations of the time'.[124] That the Australian courts, in particular, have done this will be amply demonstrated throughout the succeeding chapters of this book.[125]

Directors' fiduciary duties have been criticised as being a creation of 19th century English law unable to cope with the complexities of the modern corporate world. The take-over bid, the shelf company, the multinational conglomerate and the offshore nominee did not, as Sealy explains, complicate the picture in Victorian days.[126] But the

---

[119] Rider B A K, 'Partnership Law and its Impact on "Domestic Companies"' [1979] CLJ 148 at 154; cf. *Mesenberg v Cord Industrial Recruiters Pty Ltd* (1996) 14 ACLC 519 at 528 per Young J; and *Glavanics v Brunninghausen* (1996) 19 ACSR 204 at 208 and 216-217 per Bryson J.

[120] Department of Trade and Industry, *Modern Company Law: The Strategic Framework* HMSO, London, 1999 at paras 1.1-1.2.

[121] *Ibid* at chapter 5.2.

[122] E.g., the acquittal of George Walker (the former chairman and chief executive of Brent Walker) during October 1994 of a £19.3m fraud charge involving evidence so complex as to tax even the most erudite of jurors; and the acquittal of several businessmen during March 1995 of fraud-related charges, part-way through a trial scheduled to last six months, when the judge ruled that the evidence was too difficult for the jury to understand: *The Times*, 23 March 1995; cf. *The Times*, 20 July 1999.

[123] House of Representatives Standing Committee on Legal and Constitutional Affairs, *Corporate Practices and the Rights of Shareholders* AGPS, Canberra, 1991 at 146.

[124] (1986-1987) 162 CLR 612 at 633.

[125] In a line of authority which relevantly began with *Darvall v North Sydney Brick & Tile Co Ltd (No. 2)* (1989) 7 ACLC 659 through to the recent decision in *Daniels v Anderson* (1995) 13 ACLC 614.

[126] Sealy L S, 'Directors' "Wider" Responsibilities – Problems Conceptual, Practical and Procedural' (1987) 13 MULR 164 at 169; see Sealy L S, '"Bona Fides" and "Proper Purposes" in Corporate Decisions' (1989) 15 MULR 265 at 265; and Gibson P, 'Introduction' in McKendrick E (ed), *Commercial Aspects of Trusts and Fiduciary Obligations* Clarendon Press, Oxford, 1992 at 2.

solution rests with the tradesman, not with his tools. Part of the reason for the inability of English and Australian company law to cope with the complexities of today's commercial and corporate world can be attributed to the failure on the part of many lawyers, judges and legislators to appreciate that the corporate structure in Robert Maxwell's day[127] is not the same as it was in the Marquis of Bute's day.[128] The modern day entrepreneur drives a very different corporate vehicle to that driven by Aron Salomon.[129]

The joint stock companies formed during the 19th century in order to raise capital for the construction of railways and canals in England stand in stark contrast to, for example, Allan Hawkins' Equiticorp group; a group of 140 or so companies intricately woven together as part of a multinational conglomerate. Its activities were principally investment in industrial and trading concerns and the lending of money. The Equiticorp group operated internationally through subsidiaries and related companies in Australia, Hong Kong, New Zealand, United Kingdom and other countries.[130] So too Alan Bond's corporate empire which, at its zenith, totalled 600 or so companies operating around the globe.[131] And, not to be outdone, Robert Maxwell's corporate empire which, at the time of his death on 5 November 1991, was of a size and intricacy that might never be fully understood nor totally unravelled.[132] One of the main groups of companies with which Maxwell was associated was that headed by Mirror Group Newspapers plc. In recent litigation involving it and the level of remuneration of certain receivers following their appointment in December 1991 over Maxwell's estate, Ferris J considered reports from the receivers where they found:

> [The] estate to be highly complex, giving rise to the need to make inquiries or take action in many countries other than the United Kingdom, including Liechtenstein, Switzerland, Luxembourg, France, the United States, Gibraltar, Israel, Portugal and Bulgaria.[133]

Today's English and Australian courts, therefore, must respond to these modern day challenges: not by adhering to traditional rules and principles out of step with today's complex commercial and corporate world; but by rising to the challenge of developing new rules and principles or, at the very least, refashioning those traditional rules and principles and applying them in a context more in keeping with today's requirements.[134] That this is possible is amply demonstrated by the recent opinion of the Privy Council in *Attorney General for Hong Kong v Reid*;[135] an opinion which will be analysed in detail in chapter nine of this book.

---

[127] *Mirror Group Newspapers plc v Maxwell (No. 2)* [1998] 1 BCLC 638 at 640 per Ferris J, 'the affairs of Mr Maxwell and of companies, trusts and organisations associated with him were of extreme intricacy ... [which] has led to a complex web of insolvencies, claims, cross-claims and other disputes.'

[128] *In re Cardiff Savings Bank* [1892] 2 Ch 100.

[129] Mannolini J J, 'Creditors' Interests in the Corporate Contract: A Case for the Reform of our Insolvent Trading Provisions' (1996) 6 AJCL 14 at 32-33.

[130] *Equiticorp Finance Ltd v Bank of New Zealand* (1993) 11 ACLC 952.

[131] Sykes T, *The Bold Riders* Allen & Unwin Pty Ltd, St Leonards, 1994 at 207.

[132] *The Sunday Times*, 8 August 1999.

[133] *Mirror Group Newspapers plc v Maxwell (No. 2)* [1998] 1 BCLC 638 at 641.

[134] Malcolm D, 'Directors' Duties: The Governing Principles' in Ramsay I M (ed), *Corporate Governance and the Duties of Company Directors* The Centre for Corporate Law and Securities Regulation, University of Melbourne, Parkville, 1997 at 60 and 80.

[135] [1994] 1 All ER 1 (on appeal from the New Zealand Court of Appeal).

DIRECTORS: PERSONAE AENIGMATICUS

In English and Australian company law, directors are creatures of statute who defy attempts at legal definition.[136] Although directors resemble agents, partners and trustees, a strict analysis of their theoretical status stands them apart and suggests that directors are more properly classified as *sui generis*.[137] Even so, within English and Australian company law it is considered that directors are agents of the company and that the acts of directors are the acts of the company,[138] and comparisons continue to be drawn between directors and trustees. Indeed, some of the older cases actually refer to directors as trustees.[139]

Similarly, there are parallels to be drawn between partnership law and the one-man or domestic companies. *A fortiori* in the context of the law relating to winding-up.[140] This, it has been seen, goes back to a time when companies were little more than unincorporated associations constituted by deeds of settlement prior to the passing of the 19th century Companies Acts;[141] a time when the English courts of chancery resorted to equitable principles, said to be derived from the fiduciary relationship between directors, trustees and their company, so as to resolve the commercial disputes of that time.[142]

The point is nicely illustrated by the judgment of James LJ in *Pearson's Case* where his Lordship spoke of the relevant director as a trustee who ought make restitution, 'to the company for whom he was trustee'.[143] At that time English courts of equity often regarded directors as trustees and their decisions, of course, reflect this.[144] The trustee analogy cannot be pressed too far, however, since the functions of directors and trustees are essentially quite different.[145] The director's role is to employ the company's assets

---

[136] *Regal (Hastings) Ltd v Gulliver* [1967] 2 AC 134 at 147 per Lord Russell; note *Standard Chartered Bank of Aust Ltd v Antico* (1995) 13 ACLC 1381 at 1436-1440 per Hodgson J; *Australian Securities Commission v AS Nominees Ltd* (1995) 133 ALR 1 at 51-53 per Finn J; *Mistmorn Pty Ltd v Yasseen* (1996) 21 ACSR 173 at 183 per Davies J; and *Deputy Commissioner of Taxation v Austin* (1998) 16 ACLC 1555 at 1559 per Madgwick J.

[137] Lindgren K E, 'The Fiduciary Nature of a Company Board's Power to Issue Shares' (1971-1972) 10 UWALR 364 at 366.

[138] Menzies D, 'Company Directors' (1959) 33 ALJ 156 at 157; see Heydon J D, 'Directors' Duties and the Company's Interests' in Finn P D (ed), *Equity and Commercial Relationships* The Law Book Company Ltd, Sydney, 1987 at 120; note *Aberdeen Railway Company v Blaikie Brothers* (1854) 1 Macq 461 at 471-472 per Lord Cranworth LC; *Richard Brady Franks Ltd v Price* (1937) 58 CLR 112 at 142-143 per Dixon J; and *Mills v Mills* (1938) 60 CLR 150 at 185 per Dixon J.

[139] *In re Forest of Dean Coal Mining Company* (1879) 10 Ch D 450 at 451 and 453 per Jessel MR; and *Hirsche v Sims* [1894] AC 654 at 667 per the Earl of Selborne; see Sealy L S, 'Fiduciary Relationships' [1962] CLJ 69; Finn P D, *Fiduciary Obligations* The Law Book Company Ltd, Sydney, 1977 at 89; Davies P L, *Gower's Principles of Modern Company Law* (6th ed) Sweet & Maxwell Ltd, London, 1997 at 598; and Ford H A J and Austin R P, *Ford's Principles of Corporations Law* (6th ed) Butterworths Pty Ltd, Sydney, 1992 at 487-488.

[140] Rider B A K, 'Partnership Law and its Impact on "Domestic Companies"' [1979] CLJ 148 at 156 *et seq*; note *Mesenberg v Cord Industrial Recruiters Pty Ltd* (1996) 14 ACLC 519 at 528 per Young J; and *Glavanics v Brunninghausen* (1996) 19 ACSR 204 at 208 and 216-217 per Bryson J.

[141] Keeton G W, 'The Director as Trustee' (1952) 5 CLP 11 at 16.

[142] Davies P L, *Gower's Principles of Modern Company Law* (6th ed) Sweet & Maxwell Ltd, London, 1997 at 598-599.

[143] *In re Caerphilly Colliery Company* (1877) 5 Ch D 336 at 342.

[144] *In re Wincham Shipbuilding, Boiler, and Salt Company* (1878) 9 Ch D 322 at 328-329 *per curiam*.

[145] *In re City Equitable Fire Insurance Company Ltd* [1925] 1 Ch 407 at 426 per Romer J.

in business. That involves risk-taking.[146] The trustee's role, on the other hand, is primarily to preserve the trust estate and safeguard it from risk.[147] However, whatever the correct analysis of the director's status may be, in equity it is indisputable that directors are fiduciaries.[148]

The word fiduciary comes from the Latin word *fudicia* meaning trust.[149] According to Finn, it is one of the most ill-defined if not altogether misleading terms in our law.[150] Its meaning may vary depending upon the particular context.[151] As a consequence, the inquiry as to whether or not a fiduciary relationship exists in any set of given facts is often plagued with uncertainty. Furthermore, even if it is determined that a fiduciary relationship does exist, ascertaining the precise scope and nature of the obligations that the fiduciary owes to the beneficiary is similarly beset with difficulty. Indeed, the relevant rules and principles have traditionally emerged from highly fact intensive case-law and are in a constant state of flux. The Law Commission, following its inquiry into conflicts of interest in the financial services industry, recently published its report entitled *Fiduciary Duties and Regulatory Rules* in which it formulated the view that:

> [A] fiduciary relationship is one in which a person undertakes to act on behalf of or for the benefit of another, often as an intermediary with a discretion or power which affects the interests of the other who depends on the fiduciary for information and advice.[152]

This broad statement is reminiscent of earlier attempts to identify whether a fiduciary relationship exists. For example, Finn has stated that a fiduciary is simply, 'someone who undertakes to act for or on behalf of another in some particular matter or matters'.[153] But whilst the exact definition of a fiduciary relationship is difficult to

---

[146] *Vrisakis v Australian Securities Commission* (1992-1993) 9 WAR 395 at 449-450 per Ipp J (Malcolm CJ agreed); see Sealy L S, 'Directors' "Wider" Responsibilities – Problems Conceptual, Practical and Procedural' (1987) 13 MULR 164 at 176; Sealy L S, 'The Director as Trustee' [1967] CLJ 83 at 89; The American Law Institute, *Principles of Corporate Governance: Analysis and Recommendations* St Paul, 1994, volume 1 at 174; and Commonwealth, House of Representatives, Parliamentary Debates, 3 November 1992 at 2402.

[147] Baker P V and Langan P St J, *Snell's Principles of Equity* (28th ed) Sweet & Maxwell Ltd, London, 1982 at 213; cf. Bishop W and Prentice D D, 'Some Legal and Economic Aspects of Fiduciary Remuneration' (1983) 46 MLR 289 at 291; see Sealy L S, 'The Director as Trustee' [1967] CLJ 83 at 89; note *Australian Securities Commission v AS Nominees Ltd* (1995) 133 ALR 1 at 12-15 per Finn J.

[148] Finn P D, *Fiduciary Obligations* The Law Book Company Ltd, Sydney, 1977 at 8; Ford H A J and Austin R P, *Ford's Principles of Corporations Law* (6th ed) Butterworths Pty Ltd, Sydney, 1992 at 487; and Davies P L, *Gower's Principles of Modern Company Law* (6th ed) Sweet & Maxwell Ltd, London, 1997 at 598-599; see *Castlereagh Motels Ltd v Davies-Roe* (1966) 67 SR (NSW) 279 at 285 per Jacobs and Asprey JJA; *Hospital Products Ltd v United States Surgical Corporation* (1984-1985) 156 CLR 41 at 68 per Gibbs CJ and at 96 per Mason J; and *Darvall v North Sydney Brick & Tile Co Ltd (No. 2)* (1989) 7 ACLC 659 at 662 per Kirby P.

[149] *Girardet v Crease & Company* (1987) 11 BCLR (2d) 361 at 362 per Southin J.

[150] Finn P D, *Fiduciary Obligations* The Law Book Company Ltd, Sydney, 1977 at 1; see Sealy L S, 'Fiduciary Relationships' [1962] CLJ 69 at 72-73; and Finn P D, 'The Fiduciary Principle' in Youdan T G (ed), *Equity, Fiduciaries and Trusts* The Law Book Company Ltd, Toronto, 1989 at 1, 'the peripatetic adjective.'

[151] *In re Coomber* [1911] 1 Ch 723 at 728-729 per Fletcher Moulton LJ; and *Kelly v CA & L Bell Commodities Corporation Pty Ltd* (1989) 18 NSWLR 248 at 256 per Mahoney JA.

[152] Law Commission, *Fiduciary Duties and Regulatory Rules* HMSO, London, Cm 3049, 1995 at para 1.3.

[153] Finn P D, *Fiduciary Obligations* The Law Book Company Ltd, Sydney, 1977 at 201; Shepherd J C, 'Towards a Unified Concept of Fiduciary Relationships' (1981) 97 LQR 51; Sealy L S, 'Fiduciary

formulate,[154] the relationship of director and company is nevertheless acknowledged to be fiduciary.[155] However, whether through ignorance or change in circumstance, the traditional application of the word fiduciary, as used by the judges in cases now centuries old, does not always accord with the way in which the word fiduciary is flung around now as if it applied to all breaches of duty by directors.[156] One needs to be careful, therefore, in recognising the director for what he or she really is, and the capacity in which he or she is then acting, when identifying the duties which flow from those actions *vis-à-vis* those duties which arise *ex officio*. All too often the word fiduciary has been, and perhaps unwittingly still is, used to describe true fiduciary duties when mere equitable, or even common law, duties are really in issue; albeit owed by a director in a fiduciary relationship. As Ipp J[157] observed in *Permanent Building Society v Wheeler*:

> It is essential to bear in mind that the existence of a fiduciary relationship does not mean that every duty owed by a fiduciary to the beneficiary is a fiduciary duty. In particular, a trustee's duty to exercise reasonable care, though equitable, is not specifically a fiduciary duty ... Similarly ... a director's duty to exercise reasonable care, though equitable (as well as legal) is not a fiduciary obligation.[158]

This distinction between legal, equitable and fiduciary duties is often overlooked and will be analysed in detail in chapter nine of this book. As chapter nine will demonstrate, the distinction is of critical import in the light of the doctrine of causation, the related issues of foreseeability and remoteness, and the securing of a remedy considered appropriate in the circumstances. From an orthodox perspective, the fiduciary relationship which directors enjoy with their company *ipso facto* imposes upon them fiduciary obligations of honesty and good faith.[159] In addition, the general law imposes

---

cont.

   Relationships' [1962] CLJ 69; and Sealy L S, 'Some Principles of Fiduciary Obligation' [1963] CLJ 119.

[154] *Hospital Products Ltd v United States Surgical Corporation* (1984-1985) 156 CLR 41 at 96-98 per Mason J; *In re Coomber* [1911] 1 Ch 723 at 728 per Fletcher Moulton LJ; *Chan v Zacharia* (1983-1984) 154 CLR 178 at 195 per Deane J; *Kelly v C A & L Bell Commodities Corporation Pty Ltd* (1989) 18 NSWLR 248 at 256 per Mahoney JA; and *Dowsett v Reid* (1912-1913) 15 CLR 695 at 703-704 per Griffith CJ.

[155] *Hospital Products Ltd v United States Surgical Corporation* (1984-1985) 156 CLR 41 at 68 per Gibbs CJ; *Australian Growth Resources Corporation Pty Ltd v van Reesema* (1988) 6 ACLC 529 at 535 per King CJ (Cox J agreed); Finn P D, *Fiduciary Obligations* The Law Book Company Ltd, Sydney, 1977 at 65; and Finn P D, 'The Fiduciary Principle' in Youdan T G (ed), *Equity, Fiduciaries and Trusts* The Law Book Company Ltd, Toronto, 1989 at 33.

[156] *Girardet v Crease & Company* (1987) 11 BCLR (2d) 361 at 362 per Southin J; note Sealy L S, 'Directors' "Wider" Responsibilities – Problems Conceptual, Practical and Procedural' (1987) 13 MULR 164 at 164, 'The language of nineteenth-centry [*sic*] chancery is imperfectly understood by most lawyers and is inconsistently applied.'

[157] (Malcolm CJ and Seaman J agreed).

[158] (1993-1994) 11 WAR 187 at 237-238; see *State of South Australia v Clark* (1996) 19 ACSR 606 at 631 per Perry J; note Finn P D, *Fiduciary Obligations* The Law Book Company Ltd, Sydney, 1977 at 78, 'The varying usage is unimportant provided one always recognises that a person is *not* a "fiduciary" ... until a duty applies to him. When one does, he then becomes a "fiduciary" ... but for the purposes of that duty only.'; also Sealy L S, 'Some Principles of Fiduciary Obligation' [1963] CLJ 119 at 137-140; cf. *Eromanga Hydrocarbons NL v Australis Mining NL* (1988) 6 ACLC 906 at 913 per Malcolm CJ.

[159] Heydon J D, 'Directors' Duties and the Company's Interests' in Finn P D (ed), *Equity and Commercial Relationships* The Law Book Company Ltd, Sydney, 1987 at 120; and Finn P D, 'The Fiduciary Principle'

duties upon directors of British and Australian companies to exercise care and diligence in the discharge of their obligations.[160]

These legal, equitable and fiduciary duties are owed by each director individually to the company.[161] Traditionally, this is understood to mean the shareholders collectively or the shareholders, present and future;[162] a principle regarded as firmly established by *Percival v Wright*.[163] But, as earlier alluded to in this chapter, the debate continues as to whether or not directors these days owe duties to, for example, the company's shareholders and its creditors direct, or, indeed, to an even wider constituency, or whether their interests must simply be taken into account.[164] There are some circumstances where a fiduciary relationship may exist, for example, between a director purchasing a shareholder's shares and that shareholder.[165] Conceptually, directors' duties in these circumstances raise quite different issues. But as Sealy stresses:

> [The] issue is not whether any of these 'wider' interests merits recognition and protection, but whether this can be satisfactorily achieved within the framework of

cont.

in Youdan T G (ed), *Equity, Fiduciaries and Trusts* The Law Book Company Ltd, Toronto, 1989; see *Aberdeen Railway Company v Blaikie Brothers* (1854) 1 Macq 461 at 471-472 per Lord Cranworth LC.

[160] *Australian Securities Commission v Gallagher* (1993) 11 ACLC 286 at 293-294 per Pidgeon J (Franklyn and Walsh JJ agreed); *Vrisakis v Australian Securities Commission* (1992-1993) 9 WAR 395 at 404 per Malcolm CJ; *Richard Brady Franks Ltd v Price* (1937) 58 CLR 112 at 142-143 per Dixon J; and *Elder's Trustee and Executor Company Ltd v Higgins* (1963-1964) 37 ALJR 132 at 141 per Dixon CJ, McTiernan and Windeyer JJ.

[161] Davies P L, *Gower's Principles of Modern Company Law* (6th ed) Sweet & Maxwell Ltd, London, 1997 at 599; Ford H A J and Austin R P, *Ford's Principles of Corporations Law* (6th ed) Butterworths Pty Ltd, Sydney, 1992 at 430; and Rider B A K, 'Partnership Law and its Impact on "Domestic Companies"' [1979] CLJ 148 at 148.

[162] Rider B A K, 'Partnership Law and its Impact on "Domestic Companies"' [1979] CLJ 148 at 157; and Finn P D, *Fiduciary Obligations* The Law Book Company Ltd, Sydney, 1977 at 66; see *The Australian Metropolitan Life Assurance Company Ltd v Ure* (1923-1924) 33 CLR 199; *Peters' American Delicacy Company Ltd v Heath* (1938-1939) 61 CLR 457; *Harlowe's Nominees Pty Ltd v Woodside (Lakes Entrance) Oil Company NL* (1969-1970) 121 CLR 483; *Greenhalgh v Arderne Cinemas Ld* [1951] Ch 286; and *Caparo Industries plc v Dickman* [1990] BCC 164 at 175 per Lord Bridge, 'The shareholders of a company have a collective interest in the company's proper management ... indistinguishable from the interest of the company itself'.

[163] [1902] 2 Ch 421; criticised by the Cohen committee (Report of the Committee on Company Law Amendment, HMSO, London, Cmd 6659, 1945 at paras 86-87); rejected by the Jenkins committee (Report of the Company Law Committee, HMSO, London, Cmnd 1749, 1962 at paras 89 and 99(b)); described by Loss L, 'The Fiduciary Concept as Applied to Trading by Corporate 'Insiders' in the United States' (1970) 33 MLR 34 at 40-41 as, 'a monument to the ability of lawyers to hypnotise themselves with their own creations'; but the decision, 'does not shock the conscience': *Coleman v Myers* [1977] 2 NZLR 225 at 329 per Cooke J; *Re Chez Nico (Restaurants) Ltd* [1991] BCC 736 at 750 per Browne-Wilkinson VC; note Rider B A K, 'Percival v Wright – Per Incuriam' (1977) 40 MLR 471; Rider B A K, 'Partnership Law and its Impact on "Domestic Companies"' [1979] CLJ 148 at 157; Keeton G W, 'The Director as Trustee' (1952) 5 CLP 11 at 16-18; Davies P L, *Gower's Principles of Modern Company Law* (6th ed) Sweet & Maxwell Ltd, London, 1997 at 599-600; and Lord Wilberforce, 'Law and Economics' [1966] JBL 301 at 307.

[164] Stapledon G P, *Institutional Shareholders and Corporate Governance* Clarendon Press, Oxford, 1996 at 8; cf. *The Australian Financial Review*, 2 January 1996.

[165] *Allen v Hyatt* (1914) 30 TLR 444 at 445 per Viscount Haldane LC; *Coleman v Myers* [1977] 2 NZLR 225 at 323 *et seq* per Woodhouse J, at 328 *et seq* per Cooke J and at 370 *et seq* per Casey J; *Glandon Pty Ltd v Strata Consolidated Pty Ltd* (1993) 11 ACSR 543 at 547 per Mahoney JA; and *Glavanics v Brunninghausen* (1996) 19 ACSR 204 at 215-219 and 222-224 per Bryson J; see Barrett R I, 'Directors' Duties to Creditors' (1977) 40 MLR 226 at 226-227.

company law as we know it, through the conceptual and remedial vehicle of directors' duties.[166]

It is ineluctable that remedies and *locus standi* are interdependent and throughout this book the question of standing will be contextually raised from time to time.[167] There can be little doubt that the complex issue of *locus standi* will increasingly tantalise the English and Australian courts as company law comes to recognise the influences of wider interests upon conventional company theory.[168] These are matters of great interest and of increasing importance to English and Australian company law. Regrettably, for reasons of space, this book will address in detail only one element of this wider constituency; namely, those interests of the company's creditors within the context of insolvency. This controversial issue has raised considerable interest in recent times,[169] given that the English and Australian courts have recognised an obligation at law on the part of directors of British and Australian companies to consider the interests of the company's creditors.[170]

It is significant for company law that the Australian Parliament has recently enacted Corporations Law Part 5.7B.[171] Within Part 5.7B, Corporations Law s588G statutorily obliges directors to prevent insolvent trading by their Australian companies. In chapters six and seven of this book, this novel statutory regime, and the directors' obligations in this regard, will be analysed in detail. Outside those chapters, however, this book's primary focus is upon the traditional repository of directors' duties; namely, the company as a whole.[172] Here the company is accorded its traditional constituency; namely, the shareholders collectively.[173]

---

[166] Sealy L S, 'Directors' "Wider" Responsibilities – Problems Conceptual, Practical and Procedural' (1987) 13 MULR 164 at 173.

[167] Cf. *Gray Eisdell Timms Pty Ltd v Combined Auctions Pty Ltd* (1995) 13 ACLC 965 at 971 per Young J, 'In seeking equitable relief, equity merely applies the maxim "Equity looks on that as done which ought to be done" and will not deprive a plaintiff of locus standi through a technicality brought about the [*sic*] by the defendant.'

[168] Wedderburn K W, 'Trust, Corporation and the Worker' (1985) 23 OHLJ 203 at 223-230; Sealy L S, 'Directors' "Wider" Responsibilities – Problems Conceptual, Practical and Procedural' (1987) 13 MULR 164; Sealy L S, 'The Enforcement of Partnership Agreements, Articles of Association and Shareholder Agreements' in Finn P D (ed) *Equity and Commercial Relationships* The Law Book Company Ltd, Sydney, 1987 at 109-110; Prentice D D, 'Directors, Creditors and Shareholders' in McKendrick E (ed), *Commercial Aspects of Trusts and Fiduciary Obligations* Clarendon Press, Oxford, 1992 at 73 *et seq*; note Panel on Take-overs and Mergers, *The City Code on Take-overs and Mergers* London, 1993 at General Principle 9; Companies Act 1985 (UK) ss309 and 719; and Insolvency Act 1986 (UK) s187.

[169] Renard I A, Commentary to Heydon, 'Directors' Duties and the Company's Interests' in Finn P D (ed), *Equity and Commercial Relationships* The Law Book Company Ltd, Sydney, 1987 at 137; note Prentice D D, 'Creditor's Interests and Director's Duties' (1990) 10 OJLS 265 at 277.

[170] In a line of authority which relevantly began with *Walker v Wimborne* (1976-1977) 137 CLR 1 through to the decision in *Equiticorp Finance Ltd v Bank of New Zealand* (1993) 11 ACLC 952 and beyond.

[171] Added by Act No. 210 of 1992 and effective 23 June 1993.

[172] Rixon F G, 'Competing Interests and Conflicting Principles: An Examination of the Power of Alteration of Articles of Association' (1986) 49 MLR 446 at 454 that, 'Delphic term employed by different judges in different circumstances to signify different things'; see Rajak H, *A Sourcebook of Company Law* Jordan & Sons Ltd, Bristol, 1989 at 518 *et seq*; cf. *Financial Times*, 21 July 1999.

[173] *The Australian Metropolitan Life Assurance Company Ltd v Ure* (1923-1924) 33 CLR 199 at 216-217 per Isaacs J; *Parke v Daily News Ltd* [1962] Ch 927 at 963 per Plowman J; and Wedderburn K W, 'Ultra Vires or Directors' Bona Fides?' (1967) 30 MLR 566 at 568.

PARTIAL CODIFICATION: THE DEBATE RESUMES

Ford, by way of preface, wrote in his first edition that, 'Company law is founded on enacted law but the legislation is not a self-sufficient code.'[174] This is as true today in Australian company law as when it was first written; notwithstanding the enactment of the Corporations Law,[175] a tome of legislative diktat, which has subjected Australian company law to considerable statutory intervention.[176] This was at the behest of an Australian Government determined to usher in to law a new era of corporate regulation and to, 'offer for the first time in the nation's history a single and truly national regulatory regime'.[177] However, few would disagree that the ever increasing volume of statutory rules and regulations, promulgated by the Australian Parliament in order to achieve this, has added to the difficulties and complexities associated with the day-to-day management of today's Australian companies.[178] This plethora of statutory material is somewhat difficult to reconcile with the traditional arguments in support of codification;[179] namely accessibility, certainty and clarity.[180] Rather, the sheer volume of statutory material is counter-supportive.[181]

Notwithstanding its daunting size, however, the Corporations Law has achieved a reasonable and workable balance in reconciling fundamental concepts, legal rules, equitable principles and policies within the clearly stated legislative intent behind its enactment.[182] This has been achieved largely through the adoption of broad general principles which leave the law flexible and permit the courts considerable latitude in which to manoeuvre,[183] rather than by resorting to a body of rigid rules.[184] Conceptually, this is important as many of these principles are based on current mores, philosophy, economic and social conditions; and, thus, subject to change.

Insofar as it deals with directors' duties, the Corporations Law is a partially codified reflection of current judicial trends; the culmination of English and Australian judicial development of legal rules and equitable principles considered appropriate to control and regulate directorial conduct and decision-making.[185] Much of this book will be devoted to these judicial trends. *A fortiori* in the light of the Law Commission's recently published report entitled *Company Directors: Regulating Conflicts of Interests*

---

[174] Ford H A J, *Principles of Company Law* (1st ed) Butterworths Pty Ltd, Sydney, 1974.

[175] Effective 1 January 1991.

[176] Ipp D A, 'The diligent director' (1997) 18 Co Law 162 at 162.

[177] Commonwealth, House of Representatives, Parliamentary Debates, 8 November 1990 at 3669.

[178] Mitchell V, 'Company law reviews in Australia and the United Kingdom' (1999) 20 Co Law 98 at 104.

[179] The Corporations Law does not, however, purport to be a code in the true sense, as no attempt is made to supersede the common law; *a fortiori* within the context of directors' duties, where the common law is expressly preserved: s232(11). On the distinction between a code and a statute see *The Governor and Company of The Bank of England v Vagliano Brothers* [1891] AC 107 at 144 per Lord Herschell; *Robinson v Canadian Pacific Railway Company* [1892] AC 481 at 487 per Lord Watson; and *In re English Bank of the River Plate; Ex Parte Bank of Brazil* [1893] 2 Ch 438 at 442 per Chitty J.

[180] Hahlo H R, 'Codifying the Common Law: Protracted Gestation' (1975) 38 MLR 23 at 23; cf. Rider B A K, 'Changes in Company Law – Directors' Duties' (1978) 128 NLJ 1116 at 1116.

[181] Report of the Company Law Committee, HMSO, London, Cmnd 1749, 1962 at paras 5-6.

[182] Commonwealth, House of Representatives, Parliamentary Debates, 26 February 1992 at 192, 'In developing the new Corporations and Securities Legislation the aim was to balance the conflicting interests of efficient business, shareholders and creditors, civil liberties and effective law enforcement, so as to achieve a workable result.'

[183] Cf. Lloyd D, 'Codifying English Law' (1949) 2 CLP 155 at 165.

[184] *Canson Enterprises Ltd v Boughton & Co* (1992) 85 DLR (4th) 129 at 136 per La Forest J.

[185] Cf. *State of South Australia v Clark* (1996) 19 ACSR 606 at 627 per Perry J.

and Formulating a Statement of Duties, which has as one of its central recommenda-tions that the duty upon directors of British companies to exercise care and diligence should be partially codified.[186] The Law Commission considers that the case for partial codification is a powerful one. The advantage of partial codification of directors' duties is that it achieves a balance between certainty and flexibility. This would make English company law more coherent and improve the international dimension.[187]

Throughout this book we will concern ourselves with Australian company law and the impact which Corporations Law ss232(2) and 232(4), and Corporations Law Parts 5.7B and 9.4B, have had upon that as a consequence of the partial codification of the duties upon directors of Australian companies. These aspects of the Corporations Law will be analysed in detail as they are demonstrative of the efficacy of partial codifica-tion in this challenging and complex area of the law.[188] The advantage of Australian company law in this respect, is that the Corporations Law expressly retains the general law within the setting of a legislative scheme.[189] As the Senate Standing Committee on Legal and Constitutional Affairs observed, following its inquiry into the duties and responsibilities of directors of Australian companies during the late 1980s:

> To some extent the rules of equity have been reproduced as statutory provisions, but they remain judge-made rules capable of judicial development to meet new situations and changing mores.[190]

Within that legislative scheme, therefore, the Australian courts remain free to do justice by the application of legal rules and equitable principles. Thus, the ability to lean in one direction rather than in the other, when considered desirable, is preserved. The judge, as Gibson observes, 'enjoys the flexibility thereby afforded, anxious to do what he sees as justice in the case before him.'[191] The corollary to this, however, is that such malleability can prove to be a recipe for uncertainty; although, as Rider notes, 'a degree of uncertainty and flexibility in the law may well be conducive to a greater degree of care and fair dealing.'[192] The Australian approach to partial codification of the duties upon directors of Australian companies should allay concerns which English lawyers, judges and academics might have at the prospect of English company law going the same way, in the event that the Law Commission's recent recommendations in this respect are accepted, and ultimately enacted, by the British Parliament. Moreover, as the Law Commission went to some lengths in its report to stress:

> It will, however, be clear from the Act that the intention of our *partial codification* is to state the principal duties and not to alter them in any respect. As with any Act of Parliament, the courts should give effect to the meaning of the words used by

---

[186] Law Commission, *Company Directors: Regulating Conflicts of Interests and Formulating a Statement of Duties* HMSO, London, Cm 4436, 1999 at paras 4.48, 5.19-5.20 and 5.38.

[187] *Ibid* at para 4.31.

[188] Cf. Reinhardt G, 'The Availability of Tracing to the Insolvency Administrator – Is the Remedy Adequate?' (1996) 4 ILJ 74 at 84.

[189] Corporations Law s232(11); note *The Governor and Company of the Bank of England v Vagliano Brothers* [1891] AC 107 at 144-145 per Lord Herschell.

[190] Senate Standing Committee on Legal and Constitutional Affairs, *Social and Fiduciary Duties and Obligations of Company Directors* AGPS, Canberra, 1989 at 37-38.

[191] Gibson P, 'Introduction' in McKendrick E (ed), *Commercial Aspects of Trusts and Fiduciary Obligations* Clarendon Press, Oxford, 1992 at 1.

[192] Rider B A K, 'Partnership Law and its Impact on "Domestic Companies"' [1979] CLJ 148 at 179.

Parliament. In the event of any ambiguity in the statutory statement, the courts could have regard to the general law that the statute was intended to codify.[193]

Whilst concern is expressed, from time to time, regarding the necessity for commerce to be able to operate within a legal system which is certain, and therefore predictable, and within which decisions may be made with confidence,[194] it is not possible nor, indeed, desirable to constrict equitable doctrine in such a way.[195] Because fiduciary law so dominates this area of English and Australian company law, there is a certain impossibility about codifying directors' duties.[196] There are so many matters to be taken into account that codification *per se* could not deal with them all. At the completion of its general review of the operation of the Companies Acts 1908 to 1917 (UK), the Greene Committee considered that any, 'attempt by statute to define the duties of directors would be a hopeless task'.[197] To attempt to do so would be to undermine the very concepts of flexibility, fairness and justice, which equitable doctrine has come to represent.[198] Similarly, the cumbersome machinery of amending legislation would constantly be invoked for almost as soon as, 'the ink on the code is dry the need for legislative amendments will become manifest.'[199] However, the Greene Committee did urge the British Parliament to immediately follow any amending Act by a consolidating Act given that:

> Constant reference has to be made to the Companies Acts by business men and the advantages of having the Statute Law embodied in a single code which can easily be referred to without the necessity for cross-reference are obvious.[200]

Within its terms of reference, the Law Commission was to consider the case for a statutory statement of the duties owed by directors of British companies to their company under the general law, including their fiduciary duties and their duty of care, and to make recommendations.[201] The Law Commission is of the view that full codification of the duties upon directors of British companies would be undesirable

---

[193] Law Commission, *Company Directors: Regulating Conflicts of Interests and Formulating a Statement of Duties* HMSO, London, Cm 4436, 1999 at para 4.36.

[194] *Maredelanto Compania Naviera SA v Bergbau-Handel GmbH (The Mihalis Angelos)* [1971] 1 QB 164 at 205 per Megaw LJ.

[195] Kennedy G A, 'Equity in a Commercial Context' in Finn P D (ed), *Equity and Commercial Relationships* The Law Book Company Ltd, Sydney, 1987 at 17.

[196] Beatson J, 'The Relationship Between Regulations Governing the Financial Services Industry and Fiduciary Duties under the General Law' in McKendrick E (ed), *Commercial Aspects of Trusts and Fiduciary Obligations* Clarendon Press, Oxford, 1992 at 56; and Law Commission, *Fiduciary Duties and Regulatory Rules* HMSO, London, Cm 3049, 1995 at paras 12.2 and 17.2; cf. *The Australian Financial Review*, 6 November 1995.

[197] Company Law Amendment Committee, HMSO, London, Cmd 2657, 1926 at para 46; note Report of the Company Law Committee, HMSO, London, Cmnd 1749, 1962 at paras 9 and 87.

[198] Meagher R P, Gummow W M C and Lehane J R F, *Equity Doctrines and Remedies* (3rd ed) Butterworths Pty Ltd, Sydney, 1992 at 3.

[199] Hahlo H R, 'Here Lies the Common Law: Rest in Peace' (1967) 30 MLR 241 at 250; note First Corporate Law Simplification Act 1995 (Cth): effective 9 December 1995.

[200] Company Law Amendment Committee, HMSO, London, Cmd 2657, 1926 at para 12.

[201] Law Commission, *Company Directors: Regulating Conflicts of Interests and Formulating a Statement of Duties* HMSO, London, Cm 4436, 1999 at para 1.4.

given that the law governing directors' duties is dynamic and continues to develop.[202] The Law Commission's reasons were amplified in this manner:

> We expect that the law will need to continue to evolve incrementally as circumstances require. The commercial context is constantly changing. It is important that the law retains the capacity to develop. For this reason we think that a *full codification* of directors' duties would not be desirable. To set out in statute duties that were still developing might restrict their ability to adapt to changing circumstances.[203]

The common law courts have always allowed for change and moulded with the times.[204] So too have the courts of equity, thereby honouring the maxim *aequitas sequitur legem*. Flexibility has always been amongst the common law's greatest virtues;[205] and, equally, is one of the hallmarks of equity.[206] Self-evidently, there is a need to preserve flexibility in order to deal with the increased complexity of commercial dealings and developments in the law relating to corporate relationships; for it is here that equity plays a significant and innovative role.[207] Its remedies, as chapter nine of this book will illustrate, are diverse and continuing.[208] As a consequence, the English and Australian courts need flexibility in order to meet the reality of the circumstances before them.[209] This is as true today as it was almost 400 years ago when Lord Ellesmere LC in *The Earl of Oxford's Case* explained that:

> The Cause why there is a Chancery is, for that Mens Actions are so divers and infinite, That it is impossible to make any general Law which may aptly meet with every particular Act, and not fail in some Circumstances.[210]

A little more recently in *Boulting v Association of Cinematograph, Television and Allied Technicians*, Upjohn LJ highlighted the utility of equity given that, 'it develops to meet the changing situations and conditions of the time'.[211] Moreover, as Lord Upjohn in *Boardman v Phipps* subsequently pointed out, 'Rules of equity have to be applied to such a great diversity of circumstances that they can be stated only in the most general terms and applied with particular attention to the exact circumstances of

---

[202] *Ibid* at para 4.27.
[203] *Ibid* at paras 4.27-4.28.
[204] Hahlo H R, 'Here Lies the Common Law: Rest in Peace' (1967) 30 MLR 241 at 245.
[205] Sealy L S, 'A Company Law for Tomorrow's World' (1981) 2 Co Law 195 at 200.
[206] Beatson J, 'The Relationship Between Regulations Governing the Financial Services Industry and Fiduciary Duties under the General Law' in McKendrick E (ed), *Commercial Aspects of Trusts and Fiduciary Obligations* Clarendon Press, Oxford, 1992 at 55.
[207] Austin R P, 'Fiduciary Accountability for Business Opportunities' in Finn P D (ed), *Equity and Commercial Relationships* The Law Book Company Ltd, Sydney, 1987 at 185; Austin R P, 'Commerce and Equity – Fiduciary Duty and Constructive Trust' (1986) 6 OJLS 444; and Kennedy G A, 'Equity in a Commercial Context' in Finn P D (ed), *Equity and Commercial Relationships* The Law Book Company Ltd, Sydney, 1987 at 17-18.
[208] *Gemstone Corporation of Australia Ltd v Grasso* (1994) 12 ACLC 653 at 658 per Prior J; see *Day v Mead* [1987] 2 NZLR 443 at 451 per Cooke P.
[209] Sealy L S, 'The Enforcement of Partnership Agreements, Articles of Association and Shareholder Agreements' in Finn P D (ed) *Equity and Commercial Relationships* The Law Book Company Ltd, Sydney, 1987 at 99.
[210] (1615) 1 Chan Rep 1 at 6.
[211] [1963] 2 QB 606 at 636.

each case.'[212] Thus, in a modern commercial and corporate setting, the pursuit of complete certainty will be unavailing.[213]

Partial codification permits an opportunity to develop a regulatory structure in the course of which legal and equitable duties can be either extended, limited or defined. The amendments to Corporations Law s232(4), and the introduction of Corporations Law Parts 5.7B and 9.4B,[214] within Australian company law, are illustrative of the way in which parliament can legislate so as to alter the focus of the general law by the statutory imposition of a fresh focus.[215] This will be borne out in chapters three, six, seven and eight of this book. However, in codifying basic principles of law and equity, it is generally recognised that parliament needs to ensure that no scope remains for any separation of legislative rules and equitable principles which might impede the achievement of a clearly understood body of law.[216]

One of the dangers of codification is that parliament may cease to frame its rules by reference to legal rules and equitable principles, thus denying the courts the freedom to respond to the needs of the individual circumstances of the case before it.[217] Too rigid an adherence to the letter of the law can lead to a disregard for the spirit of the law. Nowhere is this better exemplified than in fiduciary law which provides a standard set of mores for regulating the proper discharge by directors of their duties and sets a standard of commercial morality.[218] A court in the exercise of its equitable jurisdiction, as Lord Scarman explained, albeit there in a different context, in *National Westminster Bank Plc v Morgan*, 'is a court of conscience. Definition is a poor instrument when used to determine whether a transaction is or is not unconscionable: this is a question which depends upon the particular facts of the case.'[219] Accordingly, it is well within the courts' capacity, as Callaway observes, to adapt and develop the law relating to directors' duties on a case by case basis as legislation is not always the answer.[220] This was recognised almost a century ago in *Dovey v Cory* where Lord Macnaghten provided the following caveat:

> I do not think it desirable for any tribunal to do that which Parliament has abstained from doing – that is, to formulate precise rules for the guidance or embarrassment of business men in the conduct of business affairs. There never has been, and I think

[212] [1967] 2 AC 46 at 123.
[213] Kennedy G A, 'Equity in a Commercial Context' in Finn P D (ed), *Equity and Commercial Relationships* The Law Book Company Ltd, Sydney, 1987 at 18.
[214] Added by Act No. 210 of 1992 and effective 1 February 1993 and 23 June 1993.
[215] *The Governor and Company of the Bank of England v Vagliano Brothers* [1891] AC 107 at 145 per Lord Herschell.
[216] Beatson J, 'The Relationship Between Regulations Governing the Financial Services Industry and Fiduciary Duties under the General Law' in McKendrick E (ed), *Commercial Aspects of Trusts and Fiduciary Obligations* Clarendon Press, Oxford, 1992 at 58.
[217] Commonwealth, House of Representatives, Parliamentary Debates, 8 June 1994 at 1745, 'the current law governs the corporate sector and some reforms must continue to keep that law in tune with the rapidly changing commercial environment.'
[218] See Prentice D D, 'Directors, Creditors and Shareholders' in McKendrick E (ed), *Commercial Aspects of Trusts and Fiduciary Obligations* Clarendon Press, Oxford, 1992.
[219] [1985] AC 686 at 709.
[220] Callaway F H, Commentary to Sealy, 'The Enforcement of Partnership Agreements, Articles of Association and Shareholder Agreements' in Finn P D (ed), *Equity and Commercial Relationships* The Law Book Company Ltd, Sydney, 1987 at 119.

there never will be, much difficulty in dealing with any particular case on its own facts and circumstances ... I rather doubt the wisdom of attempting to do more.[221]

Given the diverse nature of commercial and corporate practices, and the disparity in corporate size, structure and operation,[222] the task of lawyers, judges and legislators in attempting to distil principles universally applicable to each and every director, and to formulate laws dealing with today's plethora of corporate practices is, undoubtedly, of *Sisyphean* proportion. Increasingly, directors of British and Australian companies find themselves involved in complex commercial dealings and affected by corporate relationships which, whether intentionally or unintentionally, involve dynamics not always present within other fiduciary relationships. It is, therefore, vitally important that company law remains fluid and, thus, capable of responding to the inevitable demands placed upon it by these complexities and the myriad of competing interests found within the morass of legal rules, equitable principles and statutory enactment which affect and determine directors' duties generally.[223] In this respect, it is useful to recall the Greene Committee's salutary remarks that:

> Many of the suggestions made to us show that the idea that fraud and lesser malpractices can be stopped by the simple expedient of a prohibition in an Act of Parliament, dies hard. Other witnesses with a view to making such malpractices impossible have advocated the imposition of statutory regulations and prohibitions calculated, not merely to put a stop to the activities of the wrongdoer, but to place quite intolerable fetters upon honest business. It is often forgotten that in dealing with a matter such as company law, which affects so closely the whole business life of the nation, a certain amount of elasticity is essential, if the system is to work in practice.[224]

It is considered virtually impossible for parliament to do other than provide guidance for the courts concerning the standards demanded of directors in the light of the business community's expectations.[225] The British and Australian Parliaments cannot legislate for, nor statutorily impose, corporate integrity.[226] The recent trend within

---

[221] [1901] AC 477 at 488; see *In re City Equitable Fire Insurance Company Ltd* [1925] 1 Ch 407 at 427 per Romer J; cf. Senate Standing Committee on Legal and Constitutional Affairs, *Social and Fiduciary Duties and Obligations of Company Directors* AGPS, Canberra, 1989 at 29, 'modern business practices seem to have developed to an extent unforeseen by Lord Macnaghten in 1901'.

[222] *In re City Equitable Fire Insurance Company Ltd* [1925] Ch 407 at 426-427 per Romer J; *Commonwealth Bank of Australia v Friedrich* (1991) 5 ACSR 115 at 125 per Tadgell J; and *Deputy Commissioner of Taxation v Austin* (1998) 16 ACLC 1555 at 1558-1560 per Madgwick J.

[223] Malcolm D, 'Directors' Duties: The Governing Principles' in Ramsay I M (ed), *Corporate Governance and the Duties of Company Directors* The Centre for Corporate Law and Securities Regulation, University of Melbourne, Parkville, 1997 at 60 and 80.

[224] Company Law Amendment Committee, HMSO, London, Cmd 2657, 1926 at para 8; note Report of the Company Law Committee, HMSO, London, Cmnd 1749, 1962 at para 11.

[225] During the second reading of the Corporations Legislation Amendment Bill 1991 (Cth), the Attorney-General proclaimed the need for the timely and effective enforcement of companies and securities laws to, 'clearly establish the standards of behaviour that the community is entitled to expect of its corporate directors': Commonwealth, House of Representatives, Parliamentary Debates, 29 May 1991 at 4213; cf. *The Australian Financial Review*, 6 November 1995.

[226] Cf. *Re Swift 736 Ltd* [1993] BCC 312 at 315 per Nicholls VC (Farquharson and Steyn LJJ agreed); *Re Grayan Building Services Ltd* [1995] BCC 554 at 577 per Henry LJ; and *Re Living Images Ltd* [1996] BCC 112 at 115 per Laddie J; note Farrar J H, Furey N E, Hannigan B M and Wylie P, *Farrar's Com-*

Australian company law to partial codification of directors' duties recognises this.[227] Irrespective of whether or not the recent views of the Law Commission advocating the partial codification of the duty upon directors of British companies to exercise care and diligence are ultimately embraced by the British Parliament,[228] legal rules and equitable principles will continue to prove a driving force in setting, enforcing and remedying the conduct and decision-making of directors of British companies well into the next millennium. The same will be true for directors of Australian companies.[229]

cont.

     pany Law (3rd ed) Butterworth & Co (Publishers) Ltd, London, 1991 at 397; and *The Australian Financial Review*, 2 January 1996.

[227] Corporations Law s232(11); note *The Governor and Company of the Bank of England v Vagliano Brothers* [1891] AC 107 at 144-145 per Lord Herschell; and Senate Standing Committee on Legal and Constitutional Affairs, *Social and Fiduciary Duties and Obligations of Company Directors* AGPS, Canberra, 1989 at 37-38.

[228] Law Commission, *Company Directors: Regulating Conflicts of Interests and Formulating a Statement of Duties* HMSO, London, Cm 4436, 1999 at paras 4.48, 5.19-5.20 and 5.38.

[229] Cf. *Australian Securities Commission v AS Nominees Ltd* (1995) 133 ALR 1 at 6 per Finn J, 'I would note in passing that here the emphasis in legal principle will be on the law of trusts and of fiduciary obligation more so than on company law.'

2

Directors' Legal and Equitable Duties to Exercise Care and Diligence

INTRODUCTION

The English courts of equity have long sought to promote high standards of business morality and ethical conduct. Throughout the cases, there is a long-standing tradition of intervention in the activities of directors of British companies in evidence.[1] As Sealy notes, 'the rules of chancery and the judges who administered them were well suited to enforcing standards of honesty and integrity'.[2] Consequently, there is an extensive body of case-law prescribing such standards of conduct for directors of British companies, and also for their Australian counterparts.

The duty to act honestly and in good faith can be traced back through decisions in the English courts of chancery spanning several hundreds of years and is part of fiduciary law. As we saw in the previous chapter of this book, this duty is closely linked with principles governing the obligations of trustees.[3] Not so, however, the requirement that directors exercise care and diligence: at least not by modern day standards. Its pedigree in English and Australian company law is far less distinguished. Compared with the fiduciary duty to act honestly and in good faith, the duty to exercise care and diligence has been described as remarkably low,[4] and light.[5]

The commentators have been almost universal in their deprecation of the duty to exercise care and diligence. Except for a few isolated examples,[6] one could be forgiven for believing that the English judiciary, in particular, was concerned only to intervene and regulate activity considered dishonest, or at least having the appearance of *mala fides*, on the part of the directors concerned. But this is only a mind-set, conditioned by today's standards and values,[7] as there has long been a duty to exercise care and diligence.

Jurisprudentially, *The Charitable Corporation v Sutton* is of interest for Lord Hardwicke LC there provided the earliest of the well-known formulations of directors' liability for negligence,[8] when he proclaimed that directors, 'may be guilty of acts of

---

[1]   Finn P D, *Fiduciary Obligations* The Law Book Company Ltd, Sydney, 1977 at 1.
[2]   Sealy L S, '"Bona Fides" and "Proper Purposes" in Corporate Decisions' (1989) 15 MULR 265 at 265.
[3]   See Sealy L S, 'The Director as Trustee' [1967] CLJ 83.
[4]   Corkery J F, *Directors' Powers and Duties* Longman Cheshire Pty Ltd, Melbourne, 1987 at 131.
[5]   Gower L C B, *Gower's Principles of Modern Company Law* (5th ed) Sweet & Maxwell Ltd, London, 1992 at 585; see *Lagunas Nitrate Company v Lagunas Syndicate* [1899] 2 Ch 392 at 418 per Romer J.
[6]   E.g., *The Charitable Corporation v Sutton* (1742) 2 Atk 400.
[7]   *Nestle v National Westminster Bank plc* [1994] 1 All ER 118 at 134 per Staughton LJ.
[8]   Trebilcock M J, 'The Liability of Company Directors for Negligence' (1969) 32 MLR 499 at 499.

commission or omission, of mal-feasance or non-feasance.'[9] Lord Hardwicke LC went on to affirm that by accepting a trust of this sort, 'a person is obliged to execute it with fidelity and reasonable diligence'.[10] The facts and the outcome in *Sutton* were briefly these. Fifty committee men of a chartered corporation were held liable for losses resulting from their failure to ensure that the activities of a warehouse-keeper, whose responsibility it was to make loans to poor people on the security of suitable pledges, were adequately supervised. As a consequence, some £350,000 was lost. And this in 1742. A corporate catastrophe to surely rival any of those one quarter of a millennium later! The way in which those moneys were lost; namely, 'the general and most destructive method was advancing money several times upon old pledges, which were not worth more than the first sum lent, or else giving credit upon imaginary pledges',[11] suggests that history does in fact repeat itself.[12]

Although the decision in *Sutton* stands in stark contrast to many that followed, where directors were excused from liability, given the language employed by Lord Hardwicke LC it is suggested that the finding of liability there was inevitable. Lord Hardwicke LC considered the directors to be within the realm of common trustees; obliged to execute their trust with fidelity and reasonable diligence. Notwithstanding that the language of reasonable diligence is employed, the outcome suggests that it was arrived at by treating the breach complained of as offending a true fiduciary duty.[13] Even so, this case has, as Trebilcock observes, 'been regarded as something of a high point in the duty of care the law has demanded of directors'.[14]

That duty of reasonable diligence identified by Lord Hardwicke LC in *Sutton* has essentially remained constant since 1742. Sometimes different words have been employed, for example, skill and negligence; and, the words care and diligence have not always been teamed together in the conjunctive manner suggested by this book. When describing the duty as the duty to exercise care and diligence, being the description preferred throughout this book, and also that enshrined in Australian companies legislation,[15] it is important to be aware that there is a distinction between skill on the one hand, and care on the other hand. This has not always been recognised. Skill involves the knowledge and experience that a director brings to his or her office.[16] Care involves the manner in which the skill is applied. Thus, each concept involves different elements.[17] Here we treat skill as a subset of care.

---

[9]   (1742) 2 Atk 400 at 404-406; note Trebilcock M J, 'The Liability of Company Directors for Negligence' (1969) 32 MLR 499 at 505 the only reported case in English law, 'where directors have been held liable for non-attendance'; Sealy L S, 'Fiduciary Relationships' [1962] CLJ 69 at 70; and Sealy L S, 'The Director as Trustee' [1967] CLJ 83 at 83-89.
[10] (1742) 2 Atk 400 at 404-406.
[11] *Ibid* at 402 per Lord Hardwicke LC.
[12] *Linter Group Ltd v Goldberg* (1992) 10 ACLC 739 at 749 per Southwell J.
[13] *Permanent Building Society v Wheeler* (1993-1994) 11 WAR 187 at 237-238 per Ipp J (Malcolm CJ and Seaman J agreed); and *State of South Australia v Clark* (1996) 19 ACSR 606 at 631 per Perry J; cf. Boyle A J, 'The Minority Shareholder in the Nineteenth Century: A Study in Anglo-American Legal History' (1965) 28 MLR 317 at 322.
[14] Trebilcock M J, 'The Liability of Company Directors for Negligence' (1969) 32 MLR 499 at 499-500.
[15] Corporations Law s232(4) provides that, 'In the exercise of his or her powers and the discharge of his or her duties, an officer of a corporation must exercise the degree of care and diligence that a reasonable person in a like position in a corporation would exercise in the corporation's circumstances.'
[16] *Daniels v Anderson* (1995) 13 ACLC 614 at 665 per Clarke and Sheller JJA.
[17] Ipp D A, 'The diligent director' (1997) 18 Co Law 162 at 163.

It helps to be mindful of this distinction, even though one need not be too pedantic as the requisite standard of care, skill or diligence is fixed by the court.[18] But terminology apart there was, and remains, a duty in existence seeking to prescribe standards of conduct for directors of British companies: irrespective of nomenclature. Cynics would say it was too often ignored though. And, by modern day standards, with some justification. What has changed over time, however, although not necessarily with the times, is the degree of care, skill or diligence required of directors; or, put in another form, the degree of negligence excused.[19] In this regard, the duty to exercise care and diligence is more protean than the duty to act honestly and in good faith; given that honesty is, and has always been, a *sine qua non* within commercial life.[20]

In analysing the standard of care and diligence required of directors of British and Australian companies,[21] therefore, there is a need to be mindful that the standard has gradually changed over time in keeping with felt needs of that time: as determined by the judiciary of the day.[22] It is with these changes to the standard of care and diligence, from the time of Sir Robert Sutton[23] to the present, that this chapter is principally concerned.

SOURCES OF THE DUTY

Chapter one of this book alluded to the difficulties one faces in practice when seeking to unravel the intricacies surrounding directors' duties which originated from the tangled web of ancient trust laws. The treatment by the textbooks of this difficult and demanding area of the law belies the skein which lies beneath the surface. Much of the confusion which permeates this area of English and Australian company law stems from judgments couched in language that no longer belongs to the present, and concepts and principles sometimes better consigned to the past. Thus, it is important to carefully distinguish between the several duties involved and their sources.

As Ford explains in his sixth edition, the duty to exercise care and diligence can arise by virtue of: (i) fiduciary obligations; (ii) contract;[24] (iii) *Donoghue v Stevenson* principles;[25] or (iv) statute.[26] The equitable duty to exercise care and diligence which

---

[18] *Re Landhurst Leasing plc* [1999] 1 BCLC 286 at 344 per Hart J.

[19] *Vrisakis v Australian Securities Commission* (1992-1993) 9 WAR 395 at 407-408 per Malcolm CJ.

[20] *Nocton v Lord Ashburton* [1914] AC 932 at 954 per Viscount Haldane LC (Lord Atkinson agreed); and *Darvall v North Sydney Brick & Tile Co Ltd (No. 2)* (1989) 7 ACLC 659 at 676 per Kirby P.

[21] E.g., Corporations Law s232(4).

[22] Inevitably there is some lead time, but lawyers, judges, and legislators ought not be condemned too harshly for failing to meet the standard of soothsayer by not predicting the public's moods and expectations in this regard.

[23] *The Charitable Corporation v Sutton* (1742) 2 Atk 400.

[24] *Hospital Products Ltd v United States Surgical Corporation* (1984-1985) 156 CLR 41 at 97 per Mason J; *Lister v Romford Ice and Cold Storage Co Ltd* [1957] AC 555; *Day v Mead* [1987] 2 NZLR 443 at 452 per Cooke P; note Birds J R, 'A code of directors' duties?' (1974) 124 NLJ 1163 at 1165; Shepherd J C, 'Towards a Unified Concept of Fiduciary Relationships' (1981) 97 LQR 51 at 66; Corkery J F, *Directors' Powers and Duties* Longman Cheshire Pty Ltd, Melbourne, 1987 at 139; and Black A, 'Recent Developments in Directors' Duties' (1991) 7 ABR 121 at 123.

[25] [1932] AC 562; see *Castlereagh Motels Ltd v Davies-Roe* (1966) 67 SR (NSW) 279 at 283 per Wallace P and at 285 per Jacobs and Asprey JJA; and *Daniels v Anderson* (1995) 13 ACLC 614 at 663 per Clarke and Sheller JJA.

[26] Ford H A J and Austin R P, *Ford's Principles of Corporations Law* (6th ed) Butterworths Pty Ltd, Sydney, 1992 at 524.

arises from the fiduciary relationship *per se* can, and often does, overlap with that at common law and, in doing so, can lead to confusion.[27] It is all too easy to blur the distinction that exists between the duty owed at law with that owed in equity. Equally, it is all too easy to place too much emphasis upon the fact that directors are fiduciaries and treat all duties as fiduciary duties when only some ought to be so attributed.

Equity should follow the law, not merge with it to a degree that allows for confusion and uncertainty as, 'equity and the law are set upon the same course'.[28] That confusion and uncertainty has happened in English and Australian company law, is apparent from a reading of some of the cases.[29] Why this confusion has been allowed to happen is a matter for conjecture. Perhaps the misconception which surrounds the fusion of law and equity is partly to blame;[30] or, perhaps the loose application of the word fiduciary by lawyers, judges and academics alike. But, for whatever reason, it is important to be aware that just because a fiduciary relationship exists, does not mean that every breach which arises from that relationship is one which automatically, 'carries the stench of dishonesty – if not of deceit, then of constructive fraud.'[31]

The Australian experience in this context is informative. One leading Australian decision which serves to clear the muddied waters is that of the Western Australian Full Court,[32] in *Permanent Building Society v Wheeler*.[33] The principal judgment was delivered by Ipp J,[34] and is impressive for its thorough review of the authorities and the manner in which his Honour distinguishes the several duties under discussion. Put shortly, the issue was whether one of the plaintiff building society's directors owed fiduciary duties to it to exercise a reasonable degree of care and diligence in the exercise of that director's powers and in the discharge of his duties. Counsel for the building society sought to characterise the claim as a breach of fiduciary duty; alternatively, a claim in negligence. In recognising that directors owe duties to exercise care and skill at law, and in equity, Ipp J considered that:

> [The] duties of directors are analogous to those of trustees, and, indeed, the duty of directors to exercise care and skill is essentially the same as that of trustees.[35]

However, in Ipp J's view, the duty to exercise care and skill does not stem from the requirements of trust and confidence imposed on a fiduciary and, 'has nothing to do with any position of disadvantage or vulnerability on the part of the company.'[36] The

---

[27] *Nocton v Lord Ashburton* [1914] AC 932 at 964 per Lord Dunedin; see Sealy L S, 'Some Principles of Fiduciary Obligation' [1963] CLJ 119 at 137 *et seq.*

[28] *Day v Mead* [1987] 2 NZLR 443 at 458 per Somers J; see *Canson Enterprises Ltd v Boughton & Co* (1992) 85 DLR (4th) 129 at 152 per La Forest J; note Mason A, 'The Place of Equity and Equitable Remedies in the Contemporary Common Law World' (1994) 110 LQR 238 at 244.

[29] *Wickstead v Browne* (1992-1993) 30 NSWLR 1 at 16 per Handley and Cripps JJA; and *Girardet v Crease & Company* (1987) 11 BCLR (2d) 361 at 362 per Southin J.

[30] Consequent upon the Supreme Court of Judicature Acts 1873 and 1875 (UK); note Muir G, 'Contract and Equity: Striking a Balance' (1985) 10 Adel LR 153 at 183.

[31] *Girardet v Crease & Company* (1987) 11 BCLR (2d) 361 at 362 per Southin J; and *LAC Minerals v International Corona Resources* (1989) 61 DLR (4th) 14 at 28 per La Forest J and at 61 per Sopinka J.

[32] (Malcolm CJ, Seaman and Ipp JJ).

[33] (1993-1994) 11 WAR 187.

[34] (Malcolm CJ and Seaman J agreed).

[35] (1993-1994) 11 WAR 187 at 235; see *The Overend & Gurney Company v Gibb* (1872) LR 5 HL 480 at 486-487 per Lord Hatherley LC; and *In re City Equitable Fire Insurance Company Ltd* [1925] Ch 407.

[36] (1993-1994) 11 WAR 187 at 239; see *Hospital Products Ltd v United States Surgical Corporation* (1984) 156 CLR 41 at 102 per Mason J.

Western Australian Full Court in *Wheeler* determined that the relevant director owed the building society a duty in law, and in equity, to exercise reasonable care and skill. However, 'the equitable duty is not to be equated or termed a "fiduciary" duty.'[37] Fiduciary obligations are imposed so as to preclude the fiduciary from being influenced by personal considerations, or from actually misusing his or her position for personal advantage;[38] considerations which have no application whatsoever to, for example, a breach of the directors' duty to exercise care and diligence. Millett LJ[39] in *Bristol and West Building Society v Mothew*, after referring to *Wheeler* and several passages from Ipp J's judgment, recently put the matter in this way:

> The nature of the obligation determines the nature of the breach. The various obligations of a fiduciary merely reflect different aspects of his core duties of loyalty and fidelity. Breach of fiduciary obligation, therefore, connotes disloyalty or infidelity. Mere incompetence is not enough. A servant who loyally does his incompetent best for his master is not unfaithful and is not guilty of a breach of fiduciary duty.[40]

With these few words of caution in place, and mindful of the legal vagaries which emerge from the cases from time to time concerning the duty to exercise care and diligence, it is opportune to now move on to consider the way in which the English and Australian courts have approached that vexed question: what is the standard of care and diligence required?

A TRADITIONAL PERSPECTIVE

Directors' legal and equitable duties to exercise care and diligence were traditionally stated in largely subjective terms so as to take into account the position and abilities of the individual director. As will be seen throughout this chapter, the law in this area resounds with echoes from the Victorian, and pre-Victorian, past when the English courts tended to take a gentle view,[41] and even appeared protective of directors of British companies.[42] Many commentators consider this to be an area where the law has not kept pace with public expectations.[43] An area where the authorities have not given any very clear answer to that vexed question posed by Romer J in *In re City Equitable Fire Insurance Company Ltd* concerning a director; *viz.*, what is the particular degree of skill and diligence required?[44] English company law, as Trebilcock notes, has consistently adopted the attitude that directors need have no special qualifications at all for office.[45] Consequently, as the learned authors of *Farrar's Company Law* bemoan:

---

[37] (1993-1994) 11 WAR 187 at 239 per Ipp J (Malcolm CJ and Seaman J agreed); see *State of South Australia v Clark* (1996) 19 ACSR 606 at 631 per Perry J.

[38] *Chan v Zacharia* (1983-1984) 154 CLR 178 at 198-199 per Deane J.

[39] (Otton LJ agreed).

[40] [1996] 4 All ER 698 at 712.

[41] Senate Standing Committee on Legal and Constitutional Affairs, *Social and Fiduciary Duties and Obligations of Company Directors* AGPS, Canberra, 1989 at 19.

[42] Rajak H, *A Sourcebook of Company Law* Jordan & Sons Ltd, Bristol, 1989 at 527.

[43] Nolan R C, 'Maxwell's improper purposes' (1994) 15 Co Law 85 at 87; and Farrar J H, Furey N E, Hannigan B M and Wylie P, *Farrar's Company Law* (3rd ed) Butterworth & Co (Publishers) Ltd, London, 1991 at 396.

[44] [1925] Ch 407 at 427.

[45] Trebilcock M J, 'The Liability of Company Directors for Negligence' (1969) 32 MLR 499 at 502.

This is an area where the common law has failed to keep pace with modern developments and instead presents a lamentably out of date view of directors' duties. In the past the courts have been reluctant to impose onerous standards of care and skill on directors and have been willing to impose liability only when a director's imprudence has been so great and so manifest as to amount to gross negligence.[46]

As mentioned in an earlier part of this chapter, and as will be seen from the discussion of the cases which follows, there was an early recognition by the English courts of a duty upon directors of British companies to exercise care and diligence.[47] That duty has, to all intents and purposes, survived virtually intact to the present day and strives to regulate directorial conduct in complex commercial and corporate situations for which the duty was not originally intended nor applied. Therein, it is suggested, lies the problem. Although the duty can be treated as having remained constant,[48] the principles developed by the courts, and the application of those principles, in order to measure the degree or the standard of care and diligence required in any given situation have not. It will be seen throughout the remainder of this chapter how the standard of care and diligence in English and Australian company law has evolved to the present day from a time:

> [When] directors were part-time officers, figureheads, adornments to the corporate Christmas tree, titled people with time on their hands. In keeping with this state of affairs, the courts regarded them as pleasant, if incompetent, amateurs who did not possess any particular executive skills and upon whom it would be unreasonable to impose onerous standards of care and skill.[49]

In order to illustrate these quintessential Victorian, and pre-Victorian, attitudes,[50] it is necessary only to mention three well-known cases where the court, in each, refused to accept that total inactivity could constitute an actionable claim in negligence.[51] The first of these cases is *Turquand v Marshall*,[52] where the liquidator of the Herefordshire Banking Company sought to render the directors liable for losses incurred by the company. One such loss concerned a loan to a director who died insolvent without repaying it. The court refused to hold the directors accountable. As there was no specific allegation of impropriety in lending the money, only default of judgment, it was Lord Hatherley LC's view that whatever may have been the amount which the

---

[46] Farrar J H, Furey N E, Hannigan B M and Wylie P, *Farrar's Company Law* (3rd ed) Butterworth & Co (Publishers) Ltd, London, 1991 at 396.

[47] *The Charitable Corporation v Sutton* (1742) 2 Atk 400.

[48] *Re Barings plc (No 5)* [1999] 1 BCLC 433 at 484 per Jonathan Parker J; cf. *Vrisakis v Australian Securities Commission* (1992-1993) 9 WAR 395 at 451 per Ipp J (Malcolm CJ agreed).

[49] Farrar J H, Furey N E, Hannigan B M and Wylie P, *Farrar's Company Law* (3rd ed) Butterworth & Co (Publishers) Ltd, London, 1991 at 396.

[50] Although, it must be said, carried well forward into the 20th century.

[51] Not something which the English or the Australian courts would condone today: *Bishopsgate Investment Management Ltd v Maxwell (No. 2)* [1994] 1 All ER 261 at 263-264 per Hoffmann LJ (Leggatt LJ agreed); *Permanent Building Society v Wheeler* (1993-1994) 11 WAR 187 at 241 per Ipp J (Malcolm CJ and Seaman J agreed); and *Daniels v Anderson* (1995) 13 ACLC 614 at 662 per Clarke and Sheller JJA.

[52] (1869) 4 Ch App 376.

directors lent and, 'however ridiculous and absurd their conduct might seem, it was the misfortune of the company that they chose such unwise directors'.[53]

Of equal interest is *In re Denham & Co*,[54] where a founding director of a quarrying and stone merchant's company was held not to be liable in negligence for recommending a payment of a dividend which was paid from capital; notwithstanding that the director concerned never attended a single board meeting during the four years in question. Chitty J's judgment is illuminative of those times. In his Lordship's view, whilst the director was guilty of considerable negligence in the discharge of the duties of his office, 'Mr *Crook* was not guilty of such gross and wilful negligence ... equivalent to fraud.'[55] Chitty J considered that Mr Crook was deceived by others and excused his failure to investigate the accounts on the grounds that, 'Mr *Crook* is a country gentleman, he is not a skilled accountant'.[56] The summons against the director was dismissed. But rather curiously, Chitty J ruled that, 'Justice will be done by not giving Mr *Crook* any costs'.[57] It would seem, therefore, that the court considered the director morally to blame, but not legally. Even so, this is a rather curious costs order; especially in the light of the practice of the House of Lords earlier restated in *Peek v Gurney*, where Lord Cairns gave the timely reminder that costs, 'should follow the result'.[58] As a rule of practice costs inevitably follow the event.[59]

This approach by the 19th century English courts is further exemplified in *In re Cardiff Savings Bank*,[60] where the Marquis of Bute had been appointed to the board of the Cardiff Savings Bank at the age of six months, having assumed the title of President upon his father's death. Only after he turned 21 years of age did he attend a board meeting; and, then, only one board meeting in almost 39 years. When the bank subsequently failed, the Marquis was held not to be liable in negligence for the mismanagement that had occurred. Stirling J determined that directors, 'are only bound to use fair and reasonable diligence in the management of their company's affairs'.[61] Stirling J considered that the Marquis was entitled to rely on the trustees and managers who attended the meetings and excused his total inactivity and failure to attend meetings.[62] The following extract from Stirling J's judgment is pertinent:

---

[53]   *Ibid* at 386; note Trebilcock M J, 'The Liability of Company Directors for Negligence' (1969) 32 MLR 499 at 500.

[54]   (1884) 25 Ch D 752.

[55]   *Ibid* at 766 per Chitty J; see *Dovey v Corey* [1901] AC 477 at 492 per Lord Davey.

[56]   (1884) 25 Ch D 752 at 767.

[57]   *Ibid* at 768.

[58]   (1873) LR 6 HL 377 at 413.

[59]   *Camiller v Commissioner of Police of the Metropolis: The Times*, 8 June 1999; *Edwards v Idaville Pty Ltd* (1996) 19 ACSR 556 at 565-566 per Nicholson J; and *Hughes v Western Australian Cricket Association (Inc)* (1986) 8 ATPR 48134 at 48236 per Toohey J; cf. *Turquand v Marshall* (1869) 4 Ch App 376 at 387 per Lord Hatherley LC, 'Each shareholder might have his remedy at law; but in order to mark the disapprobation of the Court, the bill must be dismissed without costs, and there would be no costs of the appeal.'

[60]   [1892] 2 Ch 100; see *In re New Mashonaland Exploration Company* [1892] 3 Ch 577 at 587 per Vaughan Williams J.

[61]   [1892] 2 Ch 100 at 108; see *In re Forest of Dean Coal Mining Company* (1879) 10 Ch D 450 at 452 per Jessel MR; and *In re Denham & Co* (1884) 25 Ch D 752.

[62]   Cf. *Re Kaytech International plc* [1999] BCC 390 at 403 per Robert Walker LJ (Stuart-Smith and Thorpe LJJ agreed); and *Re Brian D Pierson (Contractors) Ltd* [1999] BCC 26 at 55 per Hazel Williamson QC (sitting as a deputy High Court Judge).

Here the Marquis of *Bute* took no part in the conduct of the business of the bank. It may be that he neglected, as he certainly omitted, to attend the meetings to which he was summoned. But neglect or omission to attend meetings is not, in my opinion, the same thing as neglect or omission of a duty which ought to be performed at those meetings. If, indeed, he had had knowledge or notice either that no meetings of trustees or managers were being held, or that a duty which ought to be discharged at those meetings was not being performed, it might be right to hold that he was guilty of neglect or omission of the duty. That, however, is not this case.[63]

It is suggested that there are underlying reasons for this traditionally benign approach by the English judiciary to the duty upon directors of British companies to exercise care and diligence, which we have identified above. Two questions need to be asked in connection with the requisite standard of the day. The first is of relevance here and is this: why was the standard of care and diligence in these early cases so low by today's standards? The second question presumes an acceptance that over time the standard of care and diligence has increased and simply asks: why? But that question will be considered a little later in this chapter. For now, let us consider the first.

THE UNDERLYING REASONS

From a modern day perspective, looking back at these 19th century decisions by the English courts in *Turquand v Marshall*,[64] *In re Denham & Co*[65] and *In re Cardiff Savings Bank*,[66] for example, one could be forgiven for being a little cynical at not only the outcomes, but also the underlying reasons therefor. Was there a perception by the English judiciary rooted in Victorian, and pre-Victorian, attitudes, that a directorship was little more than a sinecure in which reasonable competence was a desirable but not a necessary qualification,[67] suitable for gentlemen as an appropriate diversion from their everyday lives?[68] Or, did the matter run deeper? A heretic might look at some of these, and other early cases, and liken the companies with which these cases are concerned – certainly the inner sanctum thereof – to gentlemen's clubs, whose members were sometimes not unlike Sir Arthur Aylmer, 'absolutely ignorant of business,' or perhaps akin to H W Tugwell, 'seventy five years of age and very deaf',[69] or even perhaps, 'Sir F Young, in the chair (an old gentleman upwards of 90 and since deceased)'.[70] And, preposterous though it might seem, that same heretic might suggest that the English courts respected, even protected,[71] that rather cosy existence.[72] Possibly for reasons

---

63   [1892] 2 Ch 100 at 109; cf. Stirling J, in earlier parallel proceedings involving a trustee and manager of the bank known as Davies, found Davies negligent given Davies' knowledge of certain irregularities which had occurred in the management of the bank: *In re Cardiff Savings Bank* [1892] 2 Ch 100.

64   (1869) 4 Ch App 376.

65   (1884) 25 Ch D 752.

66   [1892] 2 Ch 100.

67   Menzies D, 'Company Directors' (1959) 33 ALJ 156 at 163-164.

68   Macfarlan R B S, 'Directors' Duties after the National Safety Council Case Directors' Duty of Care' (1992) 9 ABR 269 at 270.

69   *In re Brazilian Rubber Plantations and Estates Ltd* [1911] 1 Ch 425 at 427; see Trebilcock M J, 'The Liability of Company Directors for Negligence' (1969) 32 MLR 499 at 503.

70   *Transvaal Lands Company v New Belgium (Transvaal) Land and Development Company* [1914] 2 Ch 488 at 500 per Swinfen Eady LJ.

71   Rajak H, *A Sourcebook of Company Law* Jordan & Sons Ltd, Bristol, 1989 at 527.

connected with peerage; or, at the very least, the retention of a socially acceptable level of class consciousness.[73] Such a concept does seem delightfully quaint by today's standards and values.

A more convincing argument,[74] as to why the standard of care and diligence in English company law was considered to be so low in earlier times, can be ascribed to the English judiciary's refusal to, 'interfere with the internal management of companies acting within their powers'.[75] Part of the English courts' reluctance to intervene in the activities of directors of British companies, absent dishonesty or *mala fides*, was on the one hand a belief that as the appointment of directors was a matter for the shareholders, so too was the level of a director's performance thereafter;[76] and, on the other hand, a sense of commercial inadequacy felt by the judiciary. Lord Hatherley LC in *The Overend & Gurney Company v Gibb* articulated the second of these two matters in this way:

> It would be extremely wrong to import into the consideration of the case of a person acting as a mercantile agent in the purchase of a business concern, those principles of extreme caution which might dictate the course of one who is not at all inclined to invest his property in any ventures of such a hazardous character.[77]

As to the concept of shareholder sovereignty, it is suggested that the pool of investors and shareholders subscribing to British companies in earlier times was very different in number and type to those on today's share registers with, 'fewer institutional shareholders and more of the human variety – interested, active and vocal'.[78] Directors were chosen out of trust.[79] Their appointment was a matter for the shareholders.[80] They were entitled to appoint directors of their choice.[81] Many were often known personally to investors and shareholders alike; and those investors and shareholders invariably held the whip hand inasmuch as it was they who could remove errant directors, overlook their shortcomings, forgive their misdeeds and ratify their excesses.

These earlier British companies were more the, 'instrument of investment and exploitation by people with substantial means, people who might be said to represent the monied class, or a class of professional investors'.[82] This community of professional

---

cont.

[72] Ipp D A, 'The diligent director' (1997) 18 Co Law 162 at 162.

[73] Keeton G W, 'The Director as Trustee' (1952) 5 CLP 11 at 19-20.

[74] And one which better preserves the judiciary's integrity.

[75] *Burland v Earle* [1902] AC 83 at 93 per Lord Davey; cf. Davies P L, *Gower's Principles of Modern Company Law* (6th ed) Sweet & Maxwell Ltd, London, 1997 at vi.

[76] Cf. Malcolm D, 'Directors' Duties: The Governing Principles' in Ramsay I M (ed), *Corporate Governance and the Duties of Company Directors* The Centre for Corporate Law and Securities Regulation, University of Melbourne, Parkville, 1997 at 60 and 80.

[77] (1872) LR 5 HL 480 at 495.

[78] Sealy L S, 'Directors' "Wider" Responsibilities – Problems Conceptual, Practical and Procedural' (1987) 13 MULR 164 at 165; note Stapledon G P, 'The Structure of Share Ownership and Control: The Potential for Institutional Investor Activism' (1995) 18 UNSWLJ 250 at 252; and Stapledon G P, 'Exercise of Voting Rights by Institutional Shareholders in the UK' (1995) 3 Corp Gov: Inter Rev 144 at 146; cf. *The Australian Financial Review*, 24 January 1997.

[79] *The Overend & Gurney Company v Gibb* (1872) LR 5 HL 480 at 495 per Lord Hatherley LC.

[80] Sealy L S, '"Bona Fides" and "Proper Purposes" in Corporate Decisions' (1989) 15 MULR 265 at 272.

[81] While today the usual form of articles provides that the directors themselves appoint directors with shareholder involvement being restricted to re-election at annual general meetings in accordance with retirement practices.

[82] Else-Mitchell J in Menzies D, 'Company Directors' (1959) 33 ALJ 156 at 171.

investors chose its directors for reasons known to advance their interests and for qualities pertaining to particular directors.[83] A community, the cases suggest, felt well able by the English judiciary to look after its own affairs and needs. Given that, it is not surprising that the courts should develop such a reluctance to interfere in areas in which clearly it was felt that the shareholders were seized of control and that such matters were really for them.

This sentiment is expressed rather nicely in *Shuttleworth v Cox Brothers and Company (Maidenhead) Ltd* by Scrutton LJ who noted, albeit in a slightly different context, but demonstrative nonetheless of the philosophy which underlies the courts' reluctance to supervise directors' activities, that it is not the business of the court, 'to manage the affairs of the company. That is for the shareholders and directors.'[84] Such was the attitude of the English judiciary which could boast a pedigree going back to Lord Eldon's famous statement in *Carlen v Drury* that:

> This Court is not to be required on every Occasion to take the Management of every Playhouse and Brewhouse in the Kingdom.[85]

Against that background, it is not surprising that the duty to exercise care and diligence in English company law was assessed subjectively by the courts in keeping with a measure of judicial deference for the businessman's judgment.[86] As foreshadowed by Lord Hatherley LC in *Overend*,[87] and as the next chapter of this book will suggest, it is arguable that the English judges of this time were simply not as alive to the commercial realities involved in the corporate world of their day as are today's judges concerning ours. Certainly they did not exhibit the same preparedness to enter the fray, and bring to account errant directors, in keeping with the more robust interventionist approach recently typified by, for example, the Australian judiciary.[88]

But the point is, in keeping with the public and judicial expression of their time, absent dishonesty and *mala fides*, the circumstances in which directors' conduct was thought to be properly the subject of judicial interference were very different to today, and the decisions of that time duly reflect that. However, having said that, what the English judges of the 19th century and the early 20th century did do, in formulating rules and principles which they considered appropriate to measure the requisite degree or standard of care and diligence for their time,[89] was to provide a rich legacy for later years.

Those traditional rules and principles have re-emerged today in English and Australian company law and provide the cornerstone upon which the modern day duty upon directors of British and Australian companies to exercise care and diligence is fashioned.[90] In the last few years we have witnessed the English and Australian courts

---

[83] Cf. *The Australian Financial Review*, 2 January 1996.

[84] [1927] 2 KB 9 at 23.

[85] (1812) 1 V&B 154 at 158.

[86] Tunc A, 'The Judge and the Businessman' (1986) 102 LQR 549 at 550.

[87] (1872) LR 5 HL 480 at 494-495.

[88] In a line of authority which relevantly began with *Darvall v North Sydney Brick & Tile Co Ltd (No. 2)* (1989) 7 ACLC 659 through to the recent decision in *Daniels v Anderson* (1995) 13 ACLC 614.

[89] But then, some might say, chose not to apply them.

[90] *Australian Securities Commission v Gallagher* (1993) 11 ACLC 286 at 294 per Pidgeon J (Franklyn and Walsh JJ agreed); *Vrisakis v Australian Securities Commission* (1992-1993) 9 WAR 395 at 449-451 per Ipp J (Malcolm CJ agreed); *National Companies and Securities Commission v Hurley* (1995) 13 ACLC

resorting to these traditional rules and principles. More and more we are hearing the corridors of justice echo to the strains of, 'the bold and robust principles of the early Chancery are alive and well'.[91]

THE STANDARD EVOLVES

It is instructive to briefly return to those earlier times in English company law and examine these traditional rules and principles so as to better understand and appreciate their shortcomings and failings, applicability or otherwise to today's complex commercial and corporate world in which we live and do business. Such an analysis is necessary, irrespective of whether or not directors' duties are codified. The Australian model presents as a good example in this respect, and will be considered in the next chapter of this book. From there, it will be seen that notwithstanding the partial codification in Australian company law of the duty upon directors to exercise care and diligence,[92] companies legislation in Australia has the general law as a background and the courts use that background in statutory interpretation. This is particularly relevant to English company law at present in the light of the Law Commission's recently published report entitled *Company Directors: Regulating Conflicts of Interests and Formulating a Statement of Duties*, which has as one of its central recommendations that the duty upon directors of British companies to exercise care and diligence should be partially codified.[93]

Technically, as Menzies observes, 'company law is statute law, but nobody could hope to become a company lawyer merely by reading and understanding the words of the statute.'[94] It is no accident that Australian companies legislation expressly preserves the general law duties.[95] Duties which, as we saw in the previous chapter of this book, evolved from the unincorporated association or joint stock company.[96] More recently, these duties find their watershed in the formulation by Romer J in *In re City Equitable Fire Insurance Company Ltd* of his celebrated three propositions.[97] It is significant that four well-known English company law cases proved decisive in Romer J's formulation of these propositions, and it will repay analysis to briefly mention each. The first is *The Overend & Gurney Company v Gibb*,[98] where Lord Hatherley LC[99] considered that the test to be applied in determining whether directors have exercised a reasonable degree of care and diligence, could be reduced to the following formula:

---

cont.

      1635 at 1641-1643 per Scott J (Malcolm CJ and Anderson J agreed); and *Daniels v Anderson* (1995) 13 ACLC 614 at 657-663 per Clarke and Sheller JJA.

[91]   Editorial comment (1994) 15 Co Law 34 at 34.

[92]   Corporations Law s232(4).

[93]   Law Commission, *Company Directors: Regulating Conflicts of Interests and Formulating a Statement of Duties* HMSO, London, Cm 4436, 1999 at paras 4.48, 5.19-5.20 and 5.38.

[94]   Menzies D, 'Company Directors' (1959) 33 ALJ 156 at 165.

[95]   Corporations Law s232(11); note *The Governor and Company of the Bank of England v Vagliano Brothers* [1891] AC 107 at 144-145 per Lord Herschell.

[96]   Gower L C B, 'Some Contrasts Between British and American Corporation Law' (1955-1956) 69 Harv LR 1369 at 1371-1372; note *Daniels v Anderson* (1995) 13 ACLC 614 at 656 per Clarke and Sheller JJA.

[97]   [1925] Ch 407 at 428-429.

[98]   (1872) LR 5 HL 480; see *Lagunas Nitrate Company v Lagunas Syndicate* [1899] 2 Ch 392 at 422-423 per Lindley MR.

[99]   (Lord Colonsay agreed).

[The] question is ... whether or not the directors exceeded the powers entrusted to them, or whether if they did not they were cognisant of circumstances of such a character, so plain, so manifest, and so simple of appreciation, that no men with any ordinary degree of prudence, acting on their own behalf, would have entered into such a transaction as they entered into?[100]

This classical *dictum* has survived the ravages of time, and continues to provide the foundation in Australian company law, for determining the relevant standard of care and diligence to which directors of Australian companies must conform at law, in equity and under statute.[101] Secondly, *Dovey v Cory*[102] merits attention. There, the facts were not dissimilar to those under discussion almost 100 years later in *Norman v Theodore Goddard*,[103] but rather surprisingly, it is suggested, not there relied upon. Cory, as the headnote recites, was a director who, in assenting to certain payments and advances, honestly relied on the judgment, information and advice of the chairman and general manager of the bank, by whose statements he was misled and whose integrity, skill and competence he had no reason for suspecting. In such circumstances, the House of Lords,[104] had little hesitation in finding that the director was not negligent of his duties. The Earl of Halsbury LC considered that in order to determine whether a director is in breach of duty, it is necessary to consider the nature of the company's business and the position of the director in relation to it.[105] In the Earl of Halsbury LC's opinion, it is unreasonable to expect a director to assume the role of auditor, managing director or chairman as the business of life could not go on, 'if people could not trust those who are put into a position of trust for the express purpose of attending to details of management.'[106]

Towards the latter part of Queen Victoria's reign, the degree of skill required was said to vary with the qualifications of the director and the nature of the company. In *Lagunas Nitrate Company v Lagunas Syndicate*, Lindley MR considered that if directors act within their powers and, 'if they act with such care as is reasonably to be expected from them, having regard to their knowledge and experience, and if they act honestly for the benefit of the company they represent, they discharge both their equitable as well as their legal duty to the company.'[107] Lastly, in *In re Brazilian Rubber Plantations and Estates Ltd*[108] Neville J explained that whilst directors were not responsible for errors of judgment, they should exercise reasonable care having regard to their knowledge and experience. Such reasonable care must, 'be measured by the

---

[100] (1872) LR 5 HL 480 at 486-487; see *In re City Equitable Fire Insurance Company Ltd* [1925] Ch 407 at 428 per Romer J.

[101] *Vrisakis v Australian Securities Commission* (1992-1993) 9 WAR 395 at 449-451 per Ipp J (Malcolm CJ agreed); and *National Companies and Securities Commission v Hurley* (1995) 13 ACLC 1635 at 1641-1643 per Scott J (Malcolm CJ and Anderson J agreed); cf. *Daniels v Anderson* (1995) 13 ACLC 614 at 663 per Clarke and Sheller JJA.

[102] [1901] AC 477.

[103] [1992] BCC 14.

[104] (Earl of Halsbury LC, Lords Macnaghten and Davey).

[105] [1901] AC 477 at 482-483.

[106] *Ibid* at 486; similarly at 492 per Lord Davey; see *In re City Equitable Fire Insurance Company Ltd* [1925] Ch 407 at 430 per Romer J; and *AWA Ltd v Daniels* (1992) 10 ACLC 933 at 1015 per Rogers CJ; cf. *Daniels v Anderson* (1995) 13 ACLC 614 at 663-666 per Clarke and Sheller JJA.

[107] [1899] 2 Ch 392 at 435; see *Australian Securities Commission v Gallagher* (1993) 11 ACLC 286 at 294 per Pidgeon J (Franklyn and Walsh JJ agreed); and *National Companies and Securities Commission v Hurley* (1995) 13 ACLC 1635 at 1641-1643 per Scott J (Malcolm CJ and Anderson J agreed).

[108] [1911] 1 Ch 425.

care an ordinary man might be expected to take in the same circumstances on his own behalf.'[109]

Each of these cases is a *cause célèbre* in its own right. Although the actual decision in each would not necessarily survive today, the principles that can be gleaned and refashioned from them, undoubtedly do. The *locus classicus* concerning the standard of care and diligence required by the general law is to be found in *City Equitable*.[110] There, Romer J[111] put forward the following three basic propositions: (i) in the performance of his duties, a director need not demonstrate a greater degree of skill than may reasonably be expected from a person of his knowledge and experience;[112] (ii) a director is not bound to give continuous attention to his company's affairs as his duties are of an intermittent nature to be performed at periodical board meetings;[113] and (iii) given the exigencies of business, and absent grounds for suspicion, a director is justified in relying upon and trusting others to properly perform all duties.[114] In the application of these propositions,[115] Romer J found the directors in *City Equitable* to be guilty of negligence. However, with the exception of Bevan, their wilfully negligent and fraudulent chairman, they escaped, 'scot-free because they were able to rely on a provision in the articles which exempted them from all liability apart from wilfully caused losses'.[116]

Over the next 50 years or so, little happened in the English courts by way of encouragement to those seeking raised levels of directorial responsibility and greater accountability in English company law. In *Pavlides v Jensen*,[117] for example, the sale of company assets at a considerable undervalue did not warrant intervention by the court. Danckwerts J indicated by his decision that a company must bear with, 'a set of amiable lunatics'.[118] To this point then, the standard of care and diligence required from directors of British companies in English company law could be described by today's expectations and requirements as being exceptionally lax.[119] The standard was considered to be too subjective with directors, 'only bound to use fair and reasonable

---

[109]   *Ibid* at 437 per Neville J.

[110]   [1925] Ch 407; see Corkery J F, *Directors' Powers and Duties* Longman Cheshire Pty Ltd, Melbourne, 1987 at 133-138.

[111]   In a judgment which, according to Pollock MR, on appeal, [1925] Ch 407 at 501, 'deserves more than a passing word of appreciation for its grasp of the details of a long and complicated case, and its co-ordination of the facts, as well as its application of the law to them'.

[112]   [1925] Ch 407 at 428; which prescribes a partly objective, partly subjective test.

[113]   *Ibid* at 429; which is directed solely to non-executive directors from whom little more than attendance at meetings was required. This is now a vestige of the past and no longer accords with modern expectations.

[114]   *Ibid*; a reflection of *Dovey v Cory* [1901] AC 477 at 492 per Lord Davey that the relevant director was entitled to rely upon, 'the judgment, information and advice, of the chairman and general manager, as to whose integrity, skill and competence he had no reason for suspicion.'

[115]   By which Farrar J H, Furey N E, Hannigan B M and Wylie P, *Farrar's Company Law* (3rd ed) Butterworth & Co (Publishers) Ltd, London, 1991 at 397 observes, 'The position at common law is dominated'.

[116]   Sealy L S, 'Company-Directors' "Duties" and Exempting Articles' [1987] CLJ 217; such a provision today would be void: Corporations Law s241.

[117]   [1956] Ch 565.

[118]   *Ibid* at 570; cf. Rider B A K, 'Amiable Lunatics and the Rule in Foss v Harbottle' [1978] CLJ 270 at 276-277.

[119]   Gower L C B, *Gower's Principles of Modern Company Law* (5th ed) Sweet & Maxwell Ltd, London, 1992 at 589.

diligence in the management of their company's affairs'.[120] In Menzies' view, if trouble brewed, 'the easiest and the safest course was to stay away from board meetings.'[121]

THE TIDE TURNS

In *Dorchester Finance Co Ltd v Stebbing*[122] a moneylending company had three directors, all of whom were experienced businessmen with considerable experience in accountancy. Only Stebbing worked for the company full time. The other two directors left all questions of management to him. They signed cheques in blank at Stebbing's request. With these he made illegal loans that were irrecoverable. No board meetings were ever held. In reliance upon *In re City Equitable Fire Insurance Company Ltd*,[123] Foster J held all three directors liable for the company's losses. In his Lordship's view, the non-executive directors, 'not only failed to exhibit the necessary skill and care in the performance of their duties as directors, but also failed to perform any duty at all as directors'.[124] It is suggested that Foster J's judgment was inevitable and appropriate for its time. Some commentators would view it as being not in keeping with the more *laissez-faire* approach hitherto displayed by the English courts. An aberration on the part of Foster J. But that is a little too cynical.

Some 15 years earlier, the Australian Capital Territory Supreme Court in *In Re Australasian Venezolana Pty Ltd*, when considering whether or not directors were negligent in *inter alia* signing cheques without inquiry as to the reason for the payments, felt the particular director concerned had erred in not having, 'taken reasonable steps to acquaint himself with the details of the company's business.'[125] It is suggested, therefore, that *Stebbing* was simply part of the gradual evolutionary path being trodden by the English judiciary towards higher levels of directorial responsibility and greater accountability.[126] The same path being trodden by their Australian counterparts in the overall, yet at that time underdeveloped, quest to implement more modern standards and principles commensurate with today's ideals of corporate governance.[127]

Not all commentators, however, would agree. Sievers, for example, was somewhat cynical and dismissive of *Stebbing* observing that, 'It now seems doubtful whether this case illustrates a general change in the attitude of English courts to enforcing the duty of care, skill and diligence'.[128] She treated the decision as being an exception to the same familiar pattern of directors escaping liability in the absence of dishonesty or good faith.[129] But, it is suggested that, it was not until recently that attitudes changed with

---

[120] *In re Cardiff Savings Bank* [1892] 2 Ch 100 at 108 per Stirling J.
[121] Menzies D, 'Company Directors' (1959) 33 ALJ 156 at 156; see Trebilcock M J, 'The Liability of Company Directors for Negligence' (1969) 32 MLR 499 at 504-506.
[122] [1989] BCLC 498.
[123] [1925] Ch 407.
[124] *Ibid* at 505.
[125] (1962) 4 FLR 60 at 66 per Eggleston J.
[126] Corkery J F, *Directors' Powers and Duties* Longman Cheshire Pty Ltd, Melbourne, 1987 at 135-136.
[127] See Farrar J H, 'Corporate Governance, Business Judgement and the Professionalism of Directors' (1993) 6 CBLJ 1; and Whincop M J, 'An Economic Analysis of the Criminalisation and Content of Directors' Duties' (1996) 24 ABLR 273 at 277 and 291.
[128] Sievers A S, 'Farewell to the Sleeping Director – The Modern Judicial and Legislative Approach to Directors' Duties of Care, Skill and Diligence' (1993) 21 ABLR 111 at 119.
[129] *Ibid*.

sufficient force and publicity to permeate judicial attitudes not previously attuned to change. *Stebbing* was decided at a time when expectations in English company law were not what they became towards the latter part of the 1980s.[130]

Even so, there have been critics of the lethargy displayed by the English and Australian courts in responding to calls for change. And, perhaps rightly so. But change is not always other than incremental;[131] something which is not necessarily a bad thing. Before change must come the necessary awareness to act as the catalyst. Gradual evolution accords with the law's heritage and its strict adherence to the doctrine of *stare decisis*.[132] Although occasionally there is a big bang,[133] more often than not change in company law tends to be sedate. Some would say pedestrian.[134]

A CHANGE IN CIRCUMSTANCES, ATTITUDE AND APPROACH

At this point it is expedient to recall the second of the two questions posed earlier in this chapter; namely, why has the standard of care and diligence required of British and Australian directors increased over time? The answer, in short, is because the public's expectations and requirements of directors in this regard have risen. In Australia especially, there has since the latter part of the 1980s been a rapid change in attitude by the Australian public to corporate governance.[135] The Australian courts have recognised and responded to this. For instance, Perry J in *State of South Australia v Clark* acknowledged that:

> Recent appellate decisions in Australia have gone a long way towards clarifying and re-expressing the duty of care owed by directors of a company vis á vis the company in terms more closely reflecting contemporary attitudes.[136]

The consequences of such changes in attitude are dealt with fully in the next chapter of this book. In England, on the other hand, we have not witnessed quite the same dynamics at work; although, undoubtedly, the levels of directorial responsibility and

---

[130] See Farrar J H, 'Corporate Governance, Business Judgement and the Professionalism of Directors' (1993) 6 CBLJ 1; and Whincop M J, 'An Economic Analysis of the Criminalisation and Content of Directors' Duties' (1996) 24 ABLR 273 at 277 and 291.

[131] Law Commission, *Company Directors: Regulating Conflicts of Interests and Formulating a Statement of Duties* HMSO, London, Cm 4436, 1999 at paras 4.27-4.28.

[132] See Kidd C J F, 'Stare Decisis in Intermediate Appellate Courts Practice in the English Court of Appeal, the Australian State Full Courts, and the New Zealand Court of Appeal' (1978) 52 ALJ 274; and Muir G, 'Contract and Equity: Striking a Balance' (1985) 10 Adel LR 153 at 183; note *Nguyen v Nguyen* (1989) 91 ALR 161 at 177-178 per Dawson, Toohey and McHugh JJ; and *Maguire v Makaronis* (1995) V Conv R 66314 at 66329-66330 per Nathan J.

[133] Although not cataclysmic, *Morley v Statewide Tobacco Services Ltd* (1992) 8 ACSR 305; *Group Four Industries Pty Ltd v Brosnan* (1992) 8 ACSR 463; and *Carrier Air-Conditioning Pty Ltd v Kurda* (1993) 11 ACSR 247 had somewhat of a cathartic effect upon corporate Australia.

[134] Cf. Department of Trade and Industry, *Modern Company Law: The Strategic Framework* HMSO, London, 1999 at para 8.5.

[135] See Farrar J H, 'Corporate Governance, Business Judgement and the Professionalism of Directors' (1993) 6 CBLJ 1; and Whincop M J, 'An Economic Analysis of the Criminalisation and Content of Directors' Duties' (1996) 24 ABLR 273 at 277 and 291.

[136] (1996) 19 ACSR 606 at 627.

accountability have risen.[137] This was recently acknowledged in the English courts by Hoffmann LJ[138] in *Bishopsgate Investment Management Ltd v Maxwell (No. 2)* where his Lordship recognised that:

> In the older cases the duty of a director to participate in the management of a company is stated in very undemanding terms. The law may be evolving in response to changes in public attitudes to corporate governance, as shown by the enactment of the provisions consolidated in the Company Directors Disqualification Act 1986.[139]

These changes have been more evident in the last few years than previously, and then noticeably within the context of insolvency where the British Parliament has seen fit to statutorily intervene in English company law in order to bring to account errant directors. With the enactment of the Company Directors Disqualification Act 1986 (UK) ('CDD Act') and the Insolvency Act 1986 (UK) ('IA 1986') this has not only permitted the disqualification of directors from holding office and also the payment of compensation to their companies for their directorial misconduct, but has generally raised the, 'standards of probity and competence to which the law requires company directors to conform.'[140] This statutory intervention represents, as Prentice observes, 'one of the most important developments in company law this century.'[141] It will be examined in detail in chapter eight of this book.

Today's commercial and corporate world is radically different to that identified in an earlier part of this chapter, and to that considered in the previous chapter of this book. There has been an explosion in the number of British and Australian companies doing business today in markets on a scale and magnitude unheard of in Victorian times. It is often the case that many directors of British and Australian companies these days are no longer known to investors and shareholders. Many of today's large public companies, 'consist of a greater number of shareholders than ever before and the holdings of individual shareholders are smaller than ever before.'[142] During its recent review of the findings of the committees chaired by Sir Adrian Cadbury[143] and Sir

---

[137] Stapledon G P, *Institutional Shareholders and Corporate Governance* Clarendon Press, Oxford, 1996 at 8; Whincop M J, 'An Economic Analysis of the Criminalisation and Content of Directors' Duties' (1996) 24 ABLR 273 at 277 and 291; Prentice D D and Holland P R J, *Contemporary Issues in Corporate Governance* Oxford University Press, Oxford, 1993; and Farrar J H, 'Corporate Governance, Business Judgement and the Professionalism of Directors' (1993) 6 CBLJ 1 at 2; note Committee on the Financial Aspects of Corporate Governance, *The Report of the Committee on the Financial Aspects of Corporate Governance* Gee and Co Ltd, London, 1992; and Committee on Corporate Governance, *Final Report* Gee Publishing Ltd, London, 1998; cf. The American Law Institute, *Principles of Corporate Governance: Analysis and Recommendations* St Paul, 1994.

[138] (Leggatt LJ agreed).

[139] [1994] 1 All ER 261 at 264; note *Re Landhurst Leasing plc* [1999] 1 BCLC 286 at 345 per Hart J.

[140] *Re Grayan Building Services Ltd* [1995] BCC 554 at 577 per Neill LJ.

[141] Prentice D D, 'Creditor's Interests and Director's Duties' (1990) 10 OJLS 265 at 277.

[142] Else-Mitchell J in Menzies D, 'Company Directors' (1959) 33 ALJ 156 at 171; prior to its collapse during 1991 (with group losses totalling $1.28bn) one of Australia's then industrial giants, Adelaide Steamship Company Ltd, had some 21,000 shareholders on its share register: Sykes T, *The Bold Riders* Allen & Unwin Pty Ltd, St Leonards, 1994 at 425 and 436.

[143] Committee on the Financial Aspects of Corporate Governance, *The Report of the Committee on the Financial Aspects of Corporate Governance* Gee and Co Ltd, London, 1992; and Committee on the Financial Aspects of Corporate Governance, *The Report on Compliance with the Code of Best Practice* Gee Publishing Ltd, London, 1995.

Richard Greenbury,[144] the Committee on Corporate Governance chaired by Sir Ronald Hampel ('Hampel Committee') found that:

> 60% of shares in listed UK companies are held by UK institutions – pension funds, insurance companies, unit and investment trusts. Of the remaining 40%, about half are owned by individuals and half by overseas owners, mainly institutions. ... Institutional investors are not an homogeneous group. They all have ... different investment objectives. The time period over which they seek to perform varies, as do their objectives for income and capital growth. Typically institutions used not to take much interest in corporate governance. They tried to achieve their target performance by buying and selling shares, relying on their judgement of the underlying strength of companies and their ability to exploit anomalies in share prices. Institutions tended not to vote their shares regularly, and to intervene directly with company managements only in circumstances of crisis.[145]

In the light of this it can be argued that there has been a dramatic erosion of the power and control previously wielded by shareholders in the day-to-day running of British companies.[146] This is true in the case of Australian companies as well. The sovereignty which shareholders earlier enjoyed has diminished.[147] It is sometimes the case that today's investors and shareholders are blissfully unaware of even the names of their directors, let alone the antecedents of those directors. More and more it is the case that directors are becoming professionals.[148] When investments are conducted through brokers it can even be the case that the investor himself or herself does not even know the proper name of the company to which he or she has subscribed, let alone who is running it. *A fortiori* where investors participate in pension schemes, take up units in trusts, or entrust their savings to investment managers whose portfolios include dozens, sometimes hundreds, of companies into which moneys are poured.[149] The options available to investors are limited solely by the imagination of their advisers.

The ways in which some of today's directors utilize proxies invariably results in their re-election and often leads to the self-perpetuation of virtually anonymous boards.[150] We are, thus, faced with management styles and techniques peculiar to today's complex commercial and corporate world. There are those who would argue that the annual general meeting as we knew it, has become an anachronism. Barnard suggests that the annual general meeting, 'provides an illusion of participatory democracy that really

---

144 Study Group on Directors' Remuneration, *Directors' Remuneration* Gee Publishing Ltd, London, 1995.

145 Committee on Corporate Governance, *Final Report* Gee Publishing Ltd, London, 1998 at paras 5.1-5.2.

146 Menzies D, 'Company Directors' (1959) 33 ALJ 156 at 174; Dawson J in Baxt R, 'Duties of directors with respect to creditors' (1989) 63 ALJ 846 at 846; and Wedderburn K W, 'Trust, Corporation and the Worker' (1985) 23 OHLJ 203 at 219-220; cf. Stapledon G P, 'Disincentives to Activism by Institutional Investors in Listed Australian Companies' (1996) 18 Syd LR 152; Stapledon G P, 'The Structure of Share Ownership and Control: The Potential for Institutional Investor Activism' (1995) 18 UNSWLJ 250; and Stapledon G P, 'Exercise of Voting Rights by Institutional Shareholders in the UK' (1995) 3 Corp Gov: Inter Rev 144.

147 *Biala Pty Ltd v Mallina Holdings Ltd* (1993) 11 ACSR 785 at 848 per Ipp J; cf. *The Australian Financial Review*, 2 January 1996.

148 Not in the sense of belonging to a profession such as law or medicine but rather full-time directors of, perhaps, several different companies, often with quite disparate interests; cf. *Daniels v Anderson* (1995) 13 ACLC 614 at 662 per Clarke and Sheller JJA.

149 Committee on Corporate Governance, *Final Report* Gee Publishing Ltd, London, 1998 at chapter 5.

150 Axworthy C S, 'Corporate Directors – Who Needs Them?' (1988) 51 MLR 273 at 288; and Hill J, 'Protecting Minority Shareholders and Reasonable Expectations' (1992) 10 CSLJ 86 at 87.

makes little sense in today's more complex world.'[151] In the result, there has been a shift in corporate power. Too often this has resulted in catastrophic consequences at the expense of thousands, if not tens of thousands, of investors and shareholders who have watched their savings dwindle, and more often than not disappear altogether, at the whim of powerful personalities over whom they have had little or no control.[152] As the learned authors of *Gower's Principles of Modern Company Law* observe:

> [In] relation to public listed companies, general meetings have proved a singularly ineffective way of making directors answerable to the general body of members who have no wish to play any role in the administration of the company and who, in most cases, will not attend general meetings unless their investment has proved so disappointing that they relish the opportunity of attending a meeting to tell the company's management what they think of it. Even then, most of them will decide instead to cut their losses by selling their shares if that is still possible. It is only institutional shareholders that the directors have to fear; if they get together the board can probably be ousted. Subject to that and to the risk of an unwelcome takeover bid, the boards of widely held public companies are self-perpetuating oligarchies which control the general meeting rather than it controlling them.[153]

These are some of the circumstances in which challenges are now being made to the English and the Australian judiciary's traditional approach of non-intervention with the internal management of companies.[154] As will be seen in subsequent chapters of this book, the Australian judges have become far more interventionist than their predecessors.[155] Consequently, in the last decade or so, corporate Australia has witnessed a dramatic tightening up of directorial responsibility and accountability, and the way in which directors of Australian companies are now required to go about their business.[156] The English judges would seem to have been more reticent in this respect. Although, in the cases which follow, we will discern a redefinition of traditional values in the context of a modern commercial and corporate setting which strongly suggests increased levels of responsibilities and greater accountability on the part of directors of British companies.[157]

---

[151] Barnard J W, 'The Hampel Committee Report: a transatlantic critique' (1998) 19 Co Law 110 at 114.

[152] E.g., the corporate collapses which gave rise to *Equiticorp Finance Ltd v Bank of New Zealand* (1993) 11 ACLC 952; and *Bishopsgate Investment Management Ltd v Maxwell (No. 2)* [1994] 1 All ER 261.

[153] Davies P L, *Gower's Principles of Modern Company Law* (6th ed) Sweet & Maxwell Ltd, London, 1997 at 597.

[154] *Burland v Earle* [1902] AC 83 at 93 per Lord Davey; see *Howard Smith Ltd v Ampol Petroleum Ltd* [1974] AC 821 at 832 per Lord Wilberforce; and *Harlowe's Nominees Pty Ltd v Woodside (Lakes Entrance) Oil Company NL* (1969-1970) 121 CLR 483 at 493 *per curiam*.

[155] *Kokotovich Constructions Pty Ltd v Wallington* (1995) 13 ACLC 1113 at 1125 per Kirby ACJ (Priestley and Handley JJA agreed), '[Whilst] Courts should hesitate before interfering with management decisions which have been reached bona fide ... this principle is of no application where, as in this case, the management decision was not *bona fide* arrived at. Indeed, it would be absurd to suggest that a court should forsake its responsibility to uphold the law in such a situation. If a director breaches his or her fiduciary duty in exercising a power for an improper purpose, not only is it desirable that the courts should intervene. They have a duty to do so.'

[156] In a line of authority which relevantly began with *Darvall v North Sydney Brick & Tile Co Ltd (No. 2)* (1989) 7 ACLC 659 through to the recent decision in *Daniels v Anderson* (1995) 13 ACLC 614.

[157] *Bishopsgate Investment Management Ltd v Maxwell (No. 2)* [1994] 1 All ER 261 at 264 per Hoffmann LJ (Leggatt LJ agreed) who recognised that the law, 'may be evolving in response to changes in public attitudes to corporate governance'; and *Re Grayan Building Services Ltd* [1995] BCC 554 at 577 per

A MODERN PERSPECTIVE

It is only in the last decade or so that English and Australian company law has expressed a willingness to recognise that a more modern approach is required in the light of the demands and the expectations of a more sophisticated and demanding business community. In recent years we have witnessed significant changes to the way in which companies have been structured, utilized and managed. There is less emphasis today upon the appointment of directors for reasons of status or as window-dressing than previously.[158] While it may have been perfectly acceptable for directors to absent themselves from board meetings for no particular reason during Mr Crook's time,[159] absence these days is only excused in, 'exceptional circumstances, such as illness or absence from the state'.[160]

From an academical and a practical perspective, it is not difficult to see that today's companies are dramatically different to those presided over by the likes of the Marquis of Bute.[161] For a time, however, lawyers, judges and legislators stood idly by, unable to appreciate that the traditional rules and principles which they sought to apply towards the latter part of the 20th century had grown out of laws developed during the 18th century and the 19th century to deal with 18th century and 19th century problems; and, as such, were not always relevant to latter-day problems. In the recent English and Australian company law cases, however, we are starting to witness new attitudes and approaches being embraced.[162]

Traditional rules and principles are being refashioned and applied in circumstances which evidence a somewhat revivified English and Australian judiciary. For example, in today's complex commercial and corporate world, delegation plays an increasingly important role in sound business practice and corporate governance. It has been seen that, absent reasonable grounds for suspicion, a director is justified in trusting his or her co-directors and the other officers of the company to perform honestly those duties which may properly be delegated or left to them.[163] However, duties must not be

---

cont.

Henry LJ, 'The statutory corporate climate is stricter than it has ever been, and those enforcing it should reflect the fact that Parliament has seen the need for higher standards.'

[158] Senate Standing Committee on Legal and Constitutional Affairs, *Social and Fiduciary Duties and Obligations of Company Directors* AGPS, Canberra, 1989 at 32; cf. Corkery J F, *Directors' Powers and Duties* Longman Cheshire Pty Ltd, Melbourne, 1987 at 137.

[159] *In re Denham & Co* (1884) 25 Ch D 752.

[160] *Vrisakis v Australian Securities Commission* (1992-1993) WAR 395 at 405 per Malcolm CJ; cf. *In re City Equitable Fire Insurance Company Ltd* [1925] Ch 407 at 444 per Romer J; note Harper J B and Browne A A, 'The Duties and Liabilities of a Director in 1973' (1973) 47 ALJ 447 at 451-452; and Malcolm D, 'Directors' Duties: The Governing Principles' in Ramsay I M (ed), *Corporate Governance and the Duties of Company Directors* The Centre for Corporate Law and Securities Regulation, University of Melbourne, Parkville, 1997 at 76.

[161] *In re Cardiff Savings Bank* [1892] 2 Ch 100.

[162] E.g., *Norman v Theodore Goddard* [1992] BCC 14 at 15 per Hoffmann J; *Re D'Jan of London Ltd* [1993] BCC 646 at 648-649 per Hoffmann LJ; *Vrisakis v Australian Securities Commission* (1992-1993) 9 WAR 395 at 451 per Ipp J (Malcolm CJ agreed); *Daniels v Anderson* (1995) 13 ACLC 614 at 662 per Clarke and Sheller JJA; *Androvin v Figliomeni* (1996) 14 ACLC 1461 at 1470 per Owen J (Kennedy and Franklyn JJ agreed); and *Re Barings plc* [1998] BCC 583 at 586 per Sir Richard Scott VC.

[163] *In re Brazilian Rubber Plantations and Estates Ltd* [1911] 1 Ch 425 at 438 per Neville J; note *Re Barings plc (No 5)* [1999] 1 BCLC 433 at 487 per Jonathan Parker J; and *Daniels v Anderson* (1995) 13 ACLC 614 at 663-666 per Clarke and Sheller JJA; see Davies P L, *Gower's Principles of Modern Company Law* (6th ed) Sweet & Maxwell Ltd, London, 1997 at 643-644.

entrusted to an obviously inappropriate or unqualified person.[164] This is an interesting area of the law which is still developing. The particular circumstances in each case, therefore, are clearly relevant.[165]

In the next chapter of this book we will analyse the Australian approach to delegation which is exemplified by Rogers CJ's decision in *AWA Ltd v Daniels*;[166] an approach recently amplified on appeal by the joint judgment of Clarke and Sheller JJA in the New South Wales Court of Appeal in *Daniels v Anderson*.[167] This approach is not dissimilar to that recently preferred in England. In *Norman v Theodore Goddard*,[168] for example, it was argued by way of third party proceedings that Quirk, the former director of a property company, was liable to replace moneys stolen from the company by Quirk's co-director Bingham, a partner in Theodore Goddard. The question was whether Quirk had taken reasonable care as a director. In finding in Quirk's favour, Hoffmann J mentioned two principles relevant to the extent of the duty of care owed by a director. His Lordship put the first of these in this way:

> [A] director performing active duties on behalf of the company need not exhibit a greater degree of skill than may reasonably be expected from a person undertaking those duties. ... It may be that in considering what a director ought reasonably to have known or inferred, one should also take into account the knowledge, skill and experience which he actually had in addition to that which a person carrying out his functions should be expected to have.[169]

In explaining the second of his two principles in *Theodore Goddard*, Hoffmann J reaffirmed Romer J's view in *In re City Equitable Fire Insurance Company Ltd*[170] that, absent reasonable grounds for suspicion, directors are entitled to rely upon others as business cannot be carried on upon principles of distrust.[171] In the light of the evidence which emerged, Hoffmann J considered that Quirk acted reasonably, 'in accepting that the information was true without asking more questions or making independent inquiry.'[172] Like *Dorchester Finance Co Ltd v Stebbing*,[173] the decision in *Theodore Goddard* has also received a measure of criticism.[174] But it is suggested that it is a decision, and an approach, which is incontestably correct. Directors cannot be expected to act as insurers. Business would simply not operate were directors obliged as a matter of course to check up on co-directors each and every step of the way irrespective of the

---

[164] It will be recalled that one of the grounds on which the directors in *In re City Equitable Fire Insurance Company Ltd* [1925] Ch 407 were held to have breached their duties, was that they had allowed the managing director to usurp functions not delegated to him and had permitted the company's stockbrokers to retain large sums without security in a manner more appropriate to bankers than to brokers.

[165] *Dovey v Cory* [1901] AC 477 at 488 per Lord Macnaghten; note Law Commission, *Company Directors: Regulating Conflicts of Interests and Formulating a Statement of Duties* HMSO, London, Cm 4436, 1999 at para 5.36.

[166] (1992) 10 ACLC 933 at 1015.

[167] (1995) 13 ACLC 614 at 663-666.

[168] [1992] BCC 14.

[169] *Ibid* at 15.

[170] [1925] Ch 407 at 429.

[171] [1992] BCC 14 at 16.

[172] *Ibid* at 19.

[173] [1989] BCLC 498.

[174] Sievers A S, 'Farewell to the Sleeping Director – The Modern Judicial and Legislative Approach to Directors' Duties of Care, Skill and Diligence' (1993) 21 ABLR 111 at 119-120; cf. Hicks A, 'Directors' Liability for Management Errors' (1994) 110 LQR 390 at 393.

particular circumstances involved; and, in default thereof, made personally liable.[175] The recent decision of the Court of Appeal[176] in *Re Westmid Packing Services Ltd*[177] is pertinent. Lord Woolf MR delivered the judgment of the Court of Appeal. His Lordship relevantly accepted as correct the following propositions:

> [The] collegiate or collective responsibility of the board of directors of a company is of fundamental importance to corporate governance under English company law. That collegiate or collective responsibility must however be based on individual responsibility. Each individual director owes duties to the company to inform himself about its affairs and to join with his co-directors in supervising and controlling them. A proper degree of delegation and division of responsibility is of course permissible, and often necessary, but not total abrogation of responsibility.[178]

Delegation is but one important function which directors of British and Australian companies regularly perform in the course of the day-to-day management of their companies.[179] It is inextricably interwoven with their duty to exercise care and diligence. This will be further borne out in our analysis of some of the cases which follow, and is dealt with in some detail in chapter eight of this book.

In today's corporate climate, many potential directors of British and Australian companies may understandably be dissuaded from accepting invitations to join boards believing that they face added responsibility and increased accountability;[180] even without the prospect of liability being automatically foisted upon them in the event of a co-director's breach of duty. Although Damocles' sword is heavy it is, and needs to remain, fairly suspended. It is only right that directors be responsible and accountable for their actions.[181] In some circumstances they should also be responsible for the actions of their co-directors; but not automatically, and not as a matter of course. Those circumstances in which directors ought be held accountable need to be carefully considered lest the scales tilt too far against the interests of commerce and snuff out the entrepreneurial flame.[182] Although Rugg CJ in *Goodwin v Agassiz* was relevantly dealing with the cases where directors incur fiduciary obligations to shareholders in purchases and sales of stock, nonetheless the following extract from his Honour's judgment is pertinent:

---

[175] *Dovey v Cory* [1901] AC 477 at 485-486 per the Earl of Halsbury LC.
[176] (Lord Woolf MR, Waller and Robert Walker LJJ).
[177] [1998] 2 All ER 124.
[178] *Ibid* at 130; note *Re Landhurst Leasing plc* [1999] 1 BCLC 286 at 346 per Hart J.
[179] Ford H A J, Austin R P and Ramsay I M, *Ford's Principles of Corporations Law* (9th ed) Reed International Books Australia Pty Ltd, Sydney, 1999 at para 8.330.
[180] Axworthy C S, 'Corporate Directors – Who Needs Them?' (1988) 51 MLR 273 at 275; note *In re Forest of Dean Coal Mining Company* (1879) 10 Ch D 450 at 451 per Jessel MR; cf. *The Australian Financial Review*, 2 January 1996.
[181] *Ibid.*
[182] Dwight F, 'Liability of Corporate Directors' (1907-1908) 17 YLJ 33 at 36, 'The canons of directorial responsibility are asserted bravely but almost invariably with a countervailing insistence upon preventing alarm to conscientious directors.'; note *Macquarie Bank Ltd v Fociri Pty Ltd* (1992) 10 ACLC 785 at 797 per Kirby P, 'There must be limits [to the imposition of greater liability] ... lest the brilliant idea which lay behind the separate legal personality of the corporation is undone to the disadvantage of the venturesome entrepreneurial spirit which is essential to driving a modern economy with its need for risk-taking.'

Fiduciary obligations of directors ought not to be made so onerous that men of experience and ability will be deterred from accepting such office. Law in its sanctions is not coextensive with morality. It cannot undertake to put all parties to every contract on an equality as to knowledge, experience, skill and shrewdness. It cannot undertake to relieve against hard bargains made between competent parties without fraud. On the other hand, directors cannot rightly be allowed to indulge with impunity in practices which do violence to prevailing standards of upright business men.[183]

As alluded to earlier in this chapter, one consequence of the growth in numbers of individual shareholders, each pursuing disparate interests in today's large public companies,[184] has been a more fragmented body of shareholders than in earlier times.[185] This has enabled some directors to enjoy the benefits of a divide and rule regime as so many of today's shareholders, including institutional shareholders, are passive investors who play no active role in the company's affairs.[186] They simply buy and sell their shares.[187] That in turn has enabled many of the corporate abuses which have been witnessed during the late 1980s and the early 1990s to be perpetrated in circumstances where little or no control was exercised over the directors by the company's shareholders;[188] often, with catastrophic consequences.[189]

In response to considerable public pressure, and in an attempt to exert a more meaningful influence and control over such practices, the courts have developed a more robust and interventionist approach to directorial misconduct and decision-making, and to the topic of directors' duties generally. The Australian courts probably more so than the English. In doing so, the courts have gradually abandoned their subjective approach in favour of a more objective assessment of standards of care and diligence considered more relevant to today's business community's requirements.[190] It is inevitable, however, that the court's first opportunity to intervene arrives too late. The company has collapsed in the face of a mountain of debts. The directors, should they ultimately be found liable to personally account, are often unable from their own personal resources to repair the company's losses.[191]

Highly relevant to this discussion, and among the more interesting cases recently before the English courts where the director concerned was held accountable, is

---

[183] (1933) 186 NER 659 at 661; see *Glavanics v Brunninghausen* (1996) 19 ACSR 204 at 219 per Bryson J.

[184] Committee on Corporate Governance, *Final Report* Gee Publishing Ltd, London, 1998 at para 5.2.

[185] Lord Wilberforce, 'Law and Economics' [1966] JBL 301 at 307; Farrar J H and Russell M, 'The Impact of Institutional Investment on Company Law' (1984) 5 Co Law 107 at 107-108; and Axworthy C S, 'Corporate Directors – Who Needs Them?' (1988) 51 MLR 273 at 277 and 285.

[186] With the advent of the institutional shareholder, and directors sitting on numerous boards, it is not hard to see how some of the difficulties which besieged corporate Australia, and to a certain extent England, during the 1980s came about.

[187] Kent W and Vary L, 'Compulsory Acquisition of Shares' (1991) 9 CSLJ 261 at 261; note Sealy L S, 'A Setback for the Minority Shareholder' [1982] CLJ 247 at 247.

[188] Cf. Davies P L, *Gower's Principles of Modern Company Law* (6th ed) Sweet & Maxwell Ltd, London, 1997 at 597.

[189] E.g., the corporate collapses which gave rise to *Equiticorp Finance Ltd v Bank of New Zealand* (1993) 11 ACLC 952; and *Bishopsgate Investment Management Ltd v Maxwell (No. 2)* [1994] 1 All ER 261.

[190] *State of South Australia v Clark* (1996) 19 ACSR 606 at 628-629 per Perry J.

[191] E.g., *Commonwealth Bank of Australia v Friedrich* (1991) 5 ACSR 115; *Linter Group Ltd v Goldberg* (1992) 10 ACLC 739; *Equiticorp Finance Ltd v Bank of New Zealand* (1993) 11 ACLC 952; and *State of South Australia v Clark* (1996) 19 ACSR 606.

Bishopsgate Investment Management Ltd v Maxwell (No. 2).[192] This case emerged by way of legacy following the death of Robert Maxwell on 5 November 1991. On an application for summary judgment against Ian Maxwell, one of the sons, it was alleged that acts or omissions by him in relation to doubtful transactions constituted a breach of his duties as a director of Bishopsgate. In essence, the claim against Maxwell was that he failed to take adequate steps to ensure that company assets were dealt with by the board in accordance with the articles. On the pleadings, this was put in various ways. Regrettably, the court felt constrained by the fact that matters before it were only at an interlocutory stage.[193] Chadwick J was not, therefore, prepared to rule whether or not Maxwell was negligent.[194] This serves to highlight the shortcomings, from an academical and a practical perspective, of decisions handed down on interlocutory applications as so many of the decisions in this area of English company law tend to be.[195]

That judgment in *Bishopsgate* went against Maxwell, on another footing, is now part of English company case-law and the subject of more detailed comment in chapters four and nine of this book. Before moving on, however, it should be noted that Maxwell's appeal to the Court of Appeal[196] was dismissed. The leading judgment was delivered by Hoffmann LJ[197] who was critical of Maxwell's lack of interest in the management of the company and his almost total inactivity.[198] In dismissing the appeal, Hoffmann LJ recognised that although in the older English company law cases the obligation upon directors to participate in company management was undemanding:

[The] existence of a duty to participate must depend upon how the particular company's business is organised and the part which the director could reasonably have been expected to play.[199]

Few would argue that today the objective test is to be preferred over the subjective test when subjecting the duty upon directors of British and Australian companies to exercise care and diligence to scrutiny; although, there will be a residual subjective element present as it applies to skill and the knowledge and experience that a particular director brings to bear.[200] As we have seen in the earlier parts of this chapter, the subjective test

---

[192] [1993] BCC 120; affirmed [1994] 1 All ER 261.

[193] Cf. *Facia Footwear Ltd v Hinchliffe* [1998] 1 BCLC 218 at 220, 228 and 233 per Sir Richard Scott VC; and *Balli Trading Ltd v Afalona Shipping Ltd* [1992] TLR 406 at 407 per Nourse LJ.

[194] Nolan R C, 'Maxwell's improper purposes' (1994) 15 Co Law 85 at 87, 'Nonetheless, hints of a possible shift in judicial attitudes to directors' duties of care and skill are given. Chadwick J entertained the possibility of a claim in tort by Bishopsgate against Ian Maxwell, based on Ian Maxwell's culpable inaction'.

[195] E.g., *Facia Footwear Ltd v Hinchliffe* [1998] 1 BCLC 218; and *Target Holdings Ltd v Redferns* [1995] 3 All ER 785.

[196] (Ralph Gibson, Leggatt and Hoffmann LJJ).

[197] (Leggatt LJ agreed).

[198] Cf. *Re Kaytech International plc* [1999] BCC 390 at 403 per Robert Walker LJ (Stuart-Smith and Thorpe LJJ agreed); and *Re Brian D Pierson (Contractors) Ltd* [1999] BCC 26 at 55 per Hazel Williamson QC (sitting as a deputy High Court Judge).

[199] [1994] 1 All ER 261 at 264; cf. *Joint Stock Discount Company v Brown* (1869) 8 LR Eq 381 at 404 per James VC.

[200] Ipp D A, 'The diligent director' (1997) 18 Co Law 162 at 163; note *State of South Australia v Clark* (1996) 19 ACSR 606 at 628 per Perry J; cf. Insolvency Act 1986 (UK) s214(4).

enjoyed pre-eminence during the 19th century,[201] and for much of the 20th century as well.[202] However, if the Australian experience can be relied upon, its demise is imminent.[203] The following passage from Tadgell J's judgment in *Commonwealth Bank of Australia v Friedrich*[204] explains why. There, his Honour noted that as the complexity of commerce has gradually intensified:

> [The] community has of necessity come to expect more than formerly from directors whose task it is to govern the affairs of companies ... In response, the parliaments and the courts have found it necessary in legislation and litigation to refer to the demands made on directors in more exacting terms than formerly; and the standard of capability required of them has correspondingly increased.[205]

Notwithstanding that the standard of care and diligence ought to be viewed objectively,[206] this area of the law continues to be pre-eminently an area where the legal result is highly sensitive to the particular facts,[207] and each case is to be determined upon its own merits.[208] As Finch explains, directors, 'do not form a homogeneous category and necessary skills vary according to differences in the sizes and purposes of companies, complexities of management structures, reliance on expert advisers and roles of the particular directors'.[209] Hence, it is not surprising that there is no catholicon available to the English and Australian courts, applicable to each and every case, to enable the courts to assess whether or not the director concerned has fallen below the standard expected of them. The presence of a residual subjective element ensures that. Given that directors need have no special qualifications at all for office,[210] this is an area where subjectivity is bound to encroach upon objectivity irrespective of the undesirability of its doing so.[211]

---

[201] E.g., *Turquand v Marshall* (1869) 4 Ch App 376 at 386 per Lord Hatherley LC; *In re Denham & Co* (1884) 25 Ch D 752 at 766 per Chitty J; and *In re Cardiff Savings Bank* [1892] 2 Ch 100 at 108-109 per Stirling J.

[202] E.g., *In re Brazilian Rubber Plantations and Estates Ltd* [1911] 1 Ch 425 at 427 per Neville J; *Transvaal Lands Company v New Belgium (Transvaal) Land and Development Company* [1914] 2 Ch 488 at 500 per Swinfen Eady LJ; and *Pavlides v Jensen* [1956] Ch 565 at 570 per Danckwerts J.

[203] Cf. *Bishopsgate Investment Management Ltd v Maxwell (No. 2)* [1994] 1 All ER 261 at 264 per Hoffmann LJ (Leggatt LJ agreed); note Senate Standing Committee on Legal and Constitutional Affairs, *Social and Fiduciary Duties and Obligations of Company Directors* AGPS, Canberra, 1989 at 29.

[204] (1991) 5 ACSR 115.

[205] *Ibid* at 126.

[206] E.g., *Norman v Theodore Goddard* [1992] BCC 14 at 15 per Hoffmann J; *Re D'Jan of London Ltd* [1993] BCC 646 at 648-649 per Hoffmann LJ; *Vrisakis v Australian Securities Commission* (1992-1993) 9 WAR 395 at 451 per Ipp J (Malcolm CJ agreed); *Daniels v Anderson* (1995) 13 ACLC 614 at 662 per Clarke and Sheller JJA; *Androvin v Figliomeni* (1996) 14 ACLC 1461 at 1470 per Owen J (Kennedy and Franklyn JJ agreed); and *Re Barings plc* [1998] BCC 583 at 586 per Sir Richard Scott VC.

[207] *Re Manlon Trading Ltd* [1995] 4 All ER 14 at 17 per Peter Gibson LJ.

[208] *Re Barings plc (No 5)* [1999] 1 BCLC 433 at 484 per Jonathan Parker J; note Malcolm D, 'Directors' Duties: The Governing Principles' in Ramsay I M (ed), *Corporate Governance and the Duties of Company Directors* The Centre for Corporate Law and Securities Regulation, University of Melbourne, Parkville, 1997 at 60 and 78.

[209] Finch V, 'Company Directors: Who Cares about Skill and Care?' (1992) 55 MLR 179 at 203; cf. *Deputy Commissioner of Taxation v Austin* (1998) 16 ACLC 1555 at 1558-1560 per Madgwick J.

[210] Trebilcock M J, 'The Liability of Company Directors for Negligence' (1969) 32 MLR 499 at 502.

[211] Cf. Insolvency Act 1986 (UK) s214(4); note Law Commission, *Company Directors: Regulating Conflicts of Interests and Formulating a Statement of Duties* HMSO, London, Cm 4436, 1999 at paras 5.19-5.20 and 5.38.

The lack of a yardstick, universal in its application to a director's obligations in all circumstances, and against which the standard of care and diligence required of the ubiquitous director can be measured, makes it very difficult to formulate meaningful guidelines to be followed by the English and Australian courts in order to delimit unacceptable behaviour.[212] Even though each case must be determined upon its own merits,[213] an approach entirely consistent with authority,[214] guidance can be found from the case-law. This is particularly so within the context of insolvency in English company law. There, the English courts have developed a substantial body of jurisprudence in respect to the appropriate standard of care and diligence expected of directors of British companies. This is of recent origin. It is a function of the increasing number of proceedings being instituted by the Secretary of State for Trade and Industry ('Secretary of State') and the liquidator, for relief considered appropriate under the CDD Act and the IA 1986 respectively.[215]

It is important to appreciate that the content of the duty owed by directors of British companies to exercise care and diligence remains constant.[216] This accords with the position in Australian company law.[217] Directors' obligations to their company are only fulfilled by the exercise of a reasonable degree of care and diligence. This was recently highlighted in *Re Barings plc*,[218] albeit there in the context of an application by the Secretary for State against Mr Maclean, a senior director within the Barings group, for a disqualification order under CDD Act s6. It was alleged that he was unfit to be a director. The facts in *Barings* are notorious. They were briefly these. Barings Bank was placed in administration on 26 February 1995. Nick Leeson, one of its employees, was responsible for massive losses in the region of £827m. The collapse of Barings raised the inevitable question: why was Leeson's unauthorised trading able to continue for so long, undetected and uncontrolled, as to bring down the oldest merchant bank in London?[219]

Following an in-depth investigation into Barings' management structure, its control system and the arrangements in place for funding the trading activities of its subsidiaries, disqualification proceedings were instituted in *Barings* against those directors considered responsible. In the result, Maclean was disqualified for a four year period. The interest in Sir Richard Scott VC's judgment for present purposes, however, is that it provides an interesting insight into the way in which the law is gradually evolving in response to changes in public attitudes to corporate governance and what today's directors of British companies must do in order to fulfil their obligations in that regard. The following extract from Sir Richard Scott VC's judgment is apposite:

[It] was the duty of Mr Maclean, once he became chairman of ALCO which had as part of its responsibilities the responsibility for monitoring risk that had previously

---

[212] Ipp D A, 'The diligent director' (1997) 18 Co Law 162 at 165.
[213] Malcolm D, 'Directors' Duties: The Governing Principles' in Ramsay I M (ed), *Corporate Governance and the Duties of Company Directors* The Centre for Corporate Law and Securities Regulation, University of Melbourne, Parkville, 1997 at 60 and 78.
[214] *Re Manlon Trading Ltd* [1995] 4 All ER 14 at 17 per Peter Gibson LJ.
[215] E.g., Comptroller and Auditor General, *The Insolvency Service Executive Agency: Company Director Disqualification – A Follow Up Report* The Stationery Office Ltd, London, 1999 at paras 1.6 and 1.15.
[216] *Re Barings plc (No 5)* [1999] 1 BCLC 433 at 484 per Jonathan Parker J.
[217] *Vrisakis v Australian Securities Commission* (1992-1993) 9 WAR 395 at 451 per Ipp J (Malcolm CJ agreed).
[218] [1998] BCC 583.
[219] Cf. *AWA Ltd v Daniels* (1992) 10 ACLC 933 at 937 per Rogers CJ.

been undertaken by the risk committee, to familiarise himself with that part of the committee's responsibility so as to exercise diligently and properly his office of chairman. ... [The] weight of responsibilities that the office carries with it, and those responsibilities require diligent attention from time to time to the question whether the system that has been put in place and over which the individual is presiding is operating efficiently, and whether individuals to whom duties ... have been delegated are discharging those duties efficiently. It plainly becomes individuals holding high office to be responsive to warning signs that indicate some failure in the system, or in the discharge by individuals within the system of their respective responsibilities.[220]

Irrespective of what a particular director's status might be, directors of British and Australian companies are duty bound to keep themselves regularly informed of their company's affairs.[221] It is incumbent upon directors to participate in the supervision and monitoring of their fellow directors and those to whom they delegate functions.[222] In this respect, Jonathan Parker J's recent judgment in *Re Barings plc (No 5)*,[223] greatly contributes to the development in English company law of the duty upon directors of British companies to exercise care and diligence. It also provides an impressive review of the authorities relevant to a determination of unfitness under CDD Act s6, as it was that which *Barings (No 5)* was concerned with. For present purposes, however, his Lordship's judgment is illuminating and most helpful. Jonathan Parker J was assisted by the following passage from the joint judgment of Clarke and Sheller JJA in *Daniels*, which his Lordship considered represented the law in England:[224]

A person who accepts the office of director of a particular company undertakes the responsibility of ensuring that he or she understands the nature of the duty a director is called upon to perform. That duty will vary according to the size and business of the particular company and the experience or skills that the director held himself or herself out to have in support of appointment to the office. None of this is novel. It turns upon the natural expectations and reliance placed by shareholders on the experience and skill of a particular director. ... The duty includes that of acting collectively to manage the company.[225]

Like its predecessor *Barings*,[226] *Barings (No 5)* was also concerned with an application by the Secretary of State for the disqualification under CDD Act s6 of certain directors within the Barings group. It was alleged that serious failures of management on the part of these directors were responsible for Nick Leeson's unauthorised trading activities in Singapore; which trading activities resulted in losses in the region of £827m, and brought down Barings Bank.[227] The only issue before the court in relation to the directors concerned was whether or not their conduct was such as to make them unfit

---

[220] [1998] BCC 583 at 586.
[221] *Re Westmid Packing Services Ltd* [1998] 2 All ER 124 at 130 per Lord Woolf MR (Waller and Robert Walker LJJ agreed).
[222] *Daniels v Anderson* (1995) 13 ACLC 614 at 663-666 per Clarke and Sheller JJA.
[223] [1999] 1 BCLC 433.
[224] *Ibid* at 488.
[225] (1995) 13 ACLC 614 at 665-666.
[226] [1998] BCC 583.
[227] Cf. *Re Barings plc* [1998] BCC 583 at 584 per Sir Richard Scott VC.

for the purposes of CDD Act s6. In short, it was the Secretary of State's general case that each of the directors was guilty of serious failures of management which demonstrated their incompetence to such a degree as to justify a disqualification order. In the result, Jonathan Parker J was satisfied that they should be disqualified and orders were made accordingly. In reaching this decision, his Lordship considered that the following general propositions could be derived from the authorities in respect to the duty upon directors of British companies to exercise care and diligence:

> (i) Directors have, both collectively and individually, a continuing duty to acquire and maintain a sufficient knowledge and understanding of the company's business to enable them properly to discharge their duties as directors. (ii) Whilst directors are entitled ... to delegate particular functions to those below them in the management chain, and to trust their competence and integrity to a reasonable extent, the exercise of the power of delegation does not absolve a director from the duty to supervise the discharge of the delegated functions. (iii) No rule of universal application can be formulated as to the duty referred to in (ii) above. The extent of the duty, and the question whether it has been discharged, must depend on the facts of each particular case, including the director's role in the management of the company.[228]

Within the present context of this chapter, *Barings (No 5)* is an important case. Jonathan Parker J's judgment provides impetus for the further expansion of the common law duty upon directors of British companies to exercise care and diligence by requiring them to take: (i) positive action to inform themselves about their company's affairs; and (ii) responsibility for the reasonable supervision and control of those to whom they delegate specific tasks and functions. As his Lordship explained, directors must appreciate that having delegated a particular function, they remain responsible and accountable for such delegated functions and will retain a residual duty of supervision and control.[229] This was the approach of the New South Wales Court of Appeal in *Daniels*;[230] an approach which is gradually coming to enjoy support in English company law.[231]

Even though the law surrounding directors' duties is today in a state of flux, in the light of such decisions as *Theodore Goddard*,[232] *Vrisakis v Australian Securities Commission*,[233] *Re D'Jan of London Ltd*,[234] *Daniels*,[235] and *Androvin v Figliomeni*,[236] where objective tests were applied, it is clear that subjectivity is rapidly losing ground to objectivity as the applicable test. Sir Richard Scott VC's judgment in *Barings* marks a further advance towards the development of an objective standard of care and diligence in English company law.[237] So too does Jonathan Parker J's judgment in *Barings (No 5)*.[238] This is to be welcomed. By way of comparison, in Australian

---

[228]   [1999] 1 BCLC 433 at 489.
[229]   *Ibid* at 487.
[230]   (1995) 13 ACLC 614 at 663-666 per Clarke and Sheller JJA.
[231]   Davies P L, *Gower's Principles of Modern Company Law* (6th ed) Sweet & Maxwell Ltd, London, 1997 at 643-644.
[232]   [1992] BCC 14.
[233]   (1992-1993) 9 WAR 395.
[234]   [1993] BCC 646.
[235]   (1995) 13 ACLC 614.
[236]   (1996) 14 ACLC 1461.
[237]   *Re Barings plc* [1998] BCC 583 at 586.
[238]   [1999] 1 BCLC 433.

company law the test of the reasonable person is now enshrined in statute law.[239] This will be examined in detail in the next chapter of this book. Within the context of insolvency, the duties upon directors of Australian companies operate, 'in the objective rather than the subjective sphere. The question is whether beliefs or expectations are "reasonable" in an objective sense.'[240] This will be examined in detail in chapters six and seven of this book.

As directors of British companies go bravely into the 21st century, it is considered that the English courts will more and more resort to the objective test as being the standard applicable to their determination of whether a particular director's conduct has met the requisite standard of care and diligence, or whether such conduct ought attract their disapprobation. It is evident from the brief discussion above that the traditional approach to the duty upon directors to exercise care and diligence is being gradually departed from. Until such time, however, as either the Court of Appeal or the House of Lords opines upon this fundamental duty and a definitive approach is thereby provided as to the modern standard expected of directors, English company law will remain of uncertain proportions in this important and challenging area. In the meantime, the development of the directors' duty to exercise care and diligence will continue to be *ad hoc* and incremental.[241]

The law regarding the duty upon directors of British and Australian companies to exercise care and diligence continues to evolve in response to changes in public attitudes to corporate governance.[242] This is a welcome change to, 'the low standards of skill and diligence required of directors by the nineteenth-century judges.'[243] It is to be encouraged. This change in approach will be amply demonstrated in the next chapter of this book where the more interventionist attitudes displayed by certain of the more robust judges within the Australian judiciary in recent years will be in evidence.[244] There, we will see the development in Australian company law of the statutory duty upon directors to exercise care and diligence.[245]

---

[239] Corporations Law s232(4).

[240] *Androvin v Figliomeni* (1996) 14 ACLC 1461 at 1470 per Owen J (Kennedy and Franklyn JJ agreed).

[241] Law Commission, *Company Directors: Regulating Conflicts of Interests and Formulating a Statement of Duties* HMSO, London, Cm 4436, 1999 at paras 4.27-4.28.

[242] Stapledon G P, *Institutional Shareholders and Corporate Governance* Clarendon Press, Oxford, 1996 at 8; Whincop M J, 'An Economic Analysis of the Criminalisation and Content of Directors' Duties' (1996) 24 ABLR 273 at 277 and 291; Prentice D D and Holland P R J, *Contemporary Issues in Corporate Governance* Oxford University Press, Oxford, 1993; and Farrar J H, 'Corporate Governance, Business Judgement and the Professionalism of Directors' (1993) 6 CBLJ 1 at 2; note Committee on the Financial Aspects of Corporate Governance, *The Report of the Committee on the Financial Aspects of Corporate Governance* Gee and Co Ltd, London, 1992; and Committee on Corporate Governance, *Final Report* Gee Publishing Ltd, London, 1998; cf. The American Law Institute, *Principles of Corporate Governance: Analysis and Recommendations* St Paul, 1994.

[243] Davies P L, *Gower's Principles of Modern Company Law* (6th ed) Sweet & Maxwell Ltd, London, 1997 at 656.

[244] In a line of authority which relevantly began with *Darvall v North Sydney Brick & Tile Co Ltd (No. 2)* (1989) 7 ACLC 659 through to the recent decision in *Daniels v Anderson* (1995) 13 ACLC 614.

[245] Which has its genesis in Companies Act 1958 (Vic) s107(1) and emerges as Corporations Law s232(4).

A STATUTORY DUTY UPON DIRECTORS OF BRITISH COMPANIES?

In contrast to the statutory duty upon directors of Australian companies to exercise care and diligence in Australian company law,[246] there is no corresponding statutory provision in English company law in either the Companies Act 1985 (UK) or the Companies Act 1989 (UK); notwithstanding an earlier attempt in the Companies Bill 1978 (UK) to codify directors' duties. Such attempt, as the learned authors of the fifth edition of *Gower's Principles of Modern Company Law* note:

> [Proved] abortive, to the regret of those of us who believe that a comprehensive statutory re-statement of those duties would make it more likely that they are observed; a belief strengthened by the fact that the main reason for giving up the attempt was the impossibility of obtaining agreement of the legal profession on precisely what the duties are.[247]

In the quest for codification, several White Papers have been presented to the British Parliament. That entitled *The Conduct of Company Directors*,[248] for example, recognised that directors were under fiduciary duties to act in the company's interests, and also under a duty to exercise care and skill in the discharge of their functions.[249] It was the British Government's then clearly stated intention to, 'introduce a provision requiring a director to observe the utmost good faith towards his company in all of his actions and to act honestly in the exercise of the powers and in the discharge of the duties of his office.'[250] As to the corresponding standard of skill and care expected of directors, it was intended by the British Government to codify the existing common law duty by requiring, 'a director to exercise that degree of care and diligence that a reasonably prudent person would exercise in comparable circumstances and the degree of skill which may reasonably be expected of a person of his knowledge and experience.'[251] But notwithstanding the tremendous amount of evidence which the Department of Trade and Industry ('DTI') received, the push for codification came to nought.[252]

The Law Commission in its recently published report entitled *Company Directors: Regulating Conflicts of Interests and Formulating a Statement of Duties*, has revived the push for codification. The report has as one of its central recommendations that the duty upon directors of British companies to exercise care and diligence should be partially codified.[253] The Law Commission considers that the case for partial codification is a powerful one. Not only would it achieve a balance between certainty and flexibility, but partial codification would make English company law more coherent and

---

[246] Corporations Law s232(4).

[247] Gower L C B, *Gower's Principles of Modern Company Law* (5th ed) Sweet & Maxwell Ltd, London, 1992 at 551; cf. Birds J R, 'Making Directors do their Duties' (1980) 1 Co Law 67 at 68.

[248] Department of Trade, *The Conduct of Company Directors* Cmnd 7037, 1977.

[249] *Ibid* at para 2.

[250] *Ibid* at para 3; cf. Corporations Law s232(2).

[251] Department of Trade, *The Conduct of Company Directors* Cmnd 7037, 1977 at para 4; standards which Rider B A K, 'The Conduct of Company Directors' (1978) 128 NLJ 27 at 28 felt were, 'a far too low level of responsibility.'; cf. Corporations Law s232(4).

[252] Rider B A K, 'The Conduct of Company Directors' (1978) 128 NLJ 27 at 27.

[253] Law Commission, *Company Directors: Regulating Conflicts of Interests and Formulating a Statement of Duties* HMSO, London, Cm 4436, 1999 at paras 4.48, 5.19-5.20 and 5.38.

improve the international dimension.[254] The Law Commission emphasises that in the important area of directors' duties, the law should aim to educate and inform directors, and not merely impose liabilities on them.[255] It is considered that a statutory statement of their duties would assist directors in this regard.

The Law Commission also believes that the topic of directors' duties ought to be viewed in a wider context; namely, the regulation of commercial activity so that it operates efficiently and promotes prosperity.[256] This particular standpoint is consistent with the philosophy and underlying rationale of the British Government, which is evident from the consultation paper published in March 1998 by the DTI foreshadowing the Company Law Review Steering Group's review of the framework of core English company law being presently undertaken. That consultation paper entitled *Modern Company Law: For a Competitive Economy* relevantly provides that:

> Simplification and rationalisation will be key themes at the heart of the review from the beginning. The Government is also determined to ensure that the new arrangements will support business activity and promote growth and competitiveness within a balanced framework rather than to act as a break or unnecessary constraint.[257]

The debate concerning the revivification and the refashioning of traditional directors' duties is becoming more vibrant and vocal. In chapter eight of this book we consider the effect which the CDD Act and the IA 1986 have had upon the development of the duty upon directors of British companies to exercise care and diligence, as the result of statutory intervention by the British Parliament within the context of insolvency. There, it will be seen that statutory guidance has been provided in circumstances constituting wrongful trading with the enactment of IA 1986 s214.[258] This section, 'measures a director's conduct against a minimum standard of commercial morality and competence.'[259] In such circumstances, more stringent standards of care and diligence have been imposed by the English courts. This augers well for the continued development of the duty to exercise care and diligence generally.[260]

Under IA 1986 s214(4), a director's conduct is assessed against that of a reasonably diligent person with the general knowledge, skill and experience reasonably expected of someone carrying out the same functions having the general knowledge, skill and experience that that director has.[261] Insofar as the standard of care and diligence required of directors of British companies generally is concerned, the Law Commission is in favour of a dual objective/subjective test based on that stipulated in IA 1986 s214(4). In expressing its preference for the codification of such an objective/subjective

---

[254] *Ibid* at para 4.31.

[255] *Ibid* at para 4.41.

[256] *Ibid* at para 2.8.

[257] Department of Trade and Industry, *Modern Company Law: For a Competitive Economy* (a consultative document) HMSO, London, 1998 at para 7.5.

[258] *Re Farmizer (Products) Ltd* [1997] BCC 655 at 662 per Peter Gibson LJ (Potter and Butler-Sloss LJJ agreed); note Davies P L, *Gower's Principles of Modern Company Law* (6th ed) Sweet & Maxwell Ltd, London, 1997 at 151.

[259] Schulte R, 'Enforcing wrongful trading as a standard of conduct for directors and a remedy for creditors: the special case of corporate insolvency' (1999) 20 Co Law 80 at 80.

[260] Prentice D D, 'Directors, Creditors and Shareholders' in McKendrick E (ed), *Commercial Aspects of Trusts and Fiduciary Obligations* Clarendon Press, Oxford, 1992 at 80-81; note Herzberg A, 'Insolvent Trading' (1991) 9 CSLJ 285 at 294.

[261] Insolvency Act 1986 (UK) s214(4); cf. Corporations Law s588G(2).

standard, the Law Commission considers it important that regard should be had to the functions of the particular directors and the circumstances of their particular company.[262] In this respect, the Law Commission recommends that:

> (1) a director's duty of care, skill and diligence to his company should be set out in statute; (2) the standard should be judged by a twofold objective/subjective test; and (3) regard should be had to the functions of the particular director and the circumstances [including size and type] of the company.[263]

The standard provided for in IA 1986 s214(4), as Hazel Williamson QC[264] in *Re Brian D Pierson (Contractors) Ltd* explained, 'is thus an objective minimum, although it may be raised by the particular attributes of the director in question.'[265] That is to say, the errant director's conduct must be looked at objectively; albeit given his or her general knowledge, skill and experience.[266] Thus, notes Finch, 'the honest incompetent and unjustified optimist now has something to fear.'[267] Indeed, that was the case in *Re DKG Contractors Ltd*.[268] There, John Weeks QC[269] found the directors' knowledge, skill and experience hopelessly inadequate for the task they undertook. Similarly, in *Re Produce Marketing Consortium Ltd*[270] the directors concerned were there found wanting. The judgment of Knox J in *Produce Marketing* merits attention as it was perhaps a harbinger of a more stringent attitude intended by the British Parliament to the requisite standard sought of directors of British companies in the context of insolvency. The following extract from his Lordship's judgment is pertinent:

> It is evident that Parliament intended to widen the scope of the legislation under which directors who trade on when the company is insolvent may ... be required to make a contribution to the assets of the company which, in practical terms, means its creditors. ... [The] test to be applied by the court has become one under which the director in question is to be judged by the standards of what can be expected of a person fulfilling his functions, and showing reasonable diligence in doing so.[271]

As the subjective test of the directors' duty to exercise care and diligence is more and more displaced by the English courts,[272] the lax behaviour hitherto tolerated of errant directors will gradually disappear.[273] As mentioned above, the law in this area is developing. Illustrative of this development is the decision by Hoffmann LJ[274] in *Re D'Jan of London Ltd*,[275] where his Lordship accepted that the duty of care owed by a

---

[262] Law Commission, *Company Directors: Regulating Conflicts of Interests and Formulating a Statement of Duties* HMSO, London, Cm 4436, 1999 at para 5.19.
[263] *Ibid* at para 5.20.
[264] Sitting as a deputy High Court Judge.
[265] [1999] BCC 26 at 49.
[266] Ipp D A, 'The diligent director' (1997) 18 Co Law 162 at 166.
[267] Finch V, 'Company Directors: Who Cares about Skill and Care?' (1992) 55 MLR 179 at 201.
[268] [1990] BCC 903.
[269] Sitting as a Chancery Judge.
[270] (1989) 5 BCC 569.
[271] *Ibid* at 594.
[272] Editorial comment, 'Other people's money' (1996) 17 Co Law 98 at 98.
[273] Gower L C B, *Gower's Principles of Modern Company Law* (5th ed) Sweet & Maxwell Ltd, London, 1992 at 589.
[274] Sitting as a Chancery Judge.
[275] [1993] BCC 646.

director at law is accurately stated in IA 1986 s214(4). In finding D'Jan negligent, Hoffmann LJ considered that both objectively and subjectively D'Jan did not show reasonable diligence and was, therefore, in breach of his duty to the company.[276]

These approaches by the English courts to the requisite standard required of directors of British companies, as prescribed by IA 1986 s214(4), are entirely consistent with that recently applied in respect to disqualification orders made by the courts pursuant to CDD Act s6. The recent judgments of Sir Richard Scott VC in *Barings*[277] and Jonathan Parker J in *Barings (No 5)*[278] are apposite. More and more applications are being brought under the CDD Act each year by the Secretary of State to have errant directors disqualified.[279] This, in conjunction with those applications brought by the liquidator pursuant to the IA 1986, ought lead to a raising of directorial standards over time.[280] As a matter of practice opines Farrar:

> [We] should see directors bringing greater care and skill to their positions as they attempt to avoid the personal liability and disqualification provided by those Acts for directors who fail to reach an appropriate standard of conduct. The existing case-law must now be read in the light of these legislative developments.[281]

In English company law there are parallels with Australian companies legislation[282] where situations of insolvency, near-insolvency or doubtful solvency,[283] have spawned considerable litigation regarding the duty upon directors of British and Australian companies to exercise care and diligence.[284] This will be examined at length in chapters six, seven and eight of this book. By looking to the experience of Australian company law in recent years, it is considered likely that English company law will follow suit. That, it is suggested, will result in continued moves towards strengthening the duty upon directors of British companies to exercise care and diligence. *A fortiori* in the event that the recent views of the Law Commission, advocating the partial codification of that duty,[285] are ultimately enacted by the British Parliament.

Irrespective of whether or not the duty upon directors of British companies to exercise care and diligence is partially codified, the case-law which has been briefly considered in this chapter will continue to evolve as the English courts respond to the

---

[276] *Ibid* at 648-649; see *Re Sherborne Associates Ltd* [1995] BCC 40; and *Re Landhurst Leasing plc* [1999] 1 BCLC 286 at 344 per Hart J.

[277] [1998] BCC 583 at 586.

[278] [1999] 1 BCLC 433.

[279] Comptroller and Auditor General, *The Insolvency Service Executive Agency: Company Director Disqualification – A Follow Up Report* The Stationery Office Ltd, London, 1999 at paras 1.6 and 1.15.

[280] Davies P L, *Gower's Principles of Modern Company Law* (6th ed) Sweet & Maxwell Ltd, London, 1997 at 642-643.

[281] Farrar J H, Furey N E, Hannigan B M and Wylie P, *Farrar's Company Law* (3rd ed) Butterworth & Co (Publishers) Ltd, London, 1991 at 397; see *Re Swift 736 Ltd* [1993] BCC 312 at 315 per Nicholls VC (Farquharson and Steyn LJJ agreed); *Re Grayan Building Services Ltd* [1995] BCC 554 at 577 per Henry LJ; *Re Living Images Ltd* [1996] BCC 112 at 115 per Laddie J; and *Re Richborough Furniture Ltd* [1996] 1 BCLC 507 at 520 per Timothy Lloyd QC.

[282] Companies Code s556; and Corporations Law ss592 and 588G.

[283] *Nicholson v Permakraft (NZ) Ltd* [1985] 1 NZLR 242 at 249 per Cooke J.

[284] In a line of authority which relevantly began with *Walker v Wimborne* (1976-1977) 137 CLR 1 through to the recent decision in *Hawcroft General Trading Co Ltd v Edgar* (1996) 20 ACSR 541.

[285] Law Commission, *Company Directors: Regulating Conflicts of Interests and Formulating a Statement of Duties* HMSO, London, Cm 4436, 1999 at paras 5.20 and 5.38.

call for raised levels of directorial responsibility and greater accountability.[286] A call perhaps more muted in England at present than that which has recently reverberated throughout corporate Australia.[287] However, within the current corporate regulatory climate over which the DTI,[288] and the Financial Services Authority to a lesser extent,[289] preside,[290] it is considered that those calls for raised levels of directorial responsibility and greater accountability will be clearly heard from Westminster to Canary Wharf. Furthermore, as the new millennium unfolds, those calls will be increasingly acted upon by the corporate regulators and the English courts. Directors of British companies must tread cautiously, therefore, as they take up the challenges of the 21st century.

[286] *Bishopsgate Investment Management Ltd v Maxwell (No. 2)* [1994] 1 All ER 261 at 264 per Hoffmann LJ (Leggatt LJ agreed) who recognised that the law, 'may be evolving in response to changes in public attitudes to corporate governance'; and *Re Grayan Building Services Ltd* [1995] BCC 554 at 577 per Henry LJ, 'The statutory corporate climate is stricter than it has ever been, and those enforcing it should reflect the fact that Parliament has seen the need for higher standards.'

[287] Ipp D A, 'The diligent director' (1997) 18 Co Law 162 at 166-167; Passmore C, 'Directors' Duties: Australian Style' (1997) 18 Co Law 158 at 159; and Nolan R, 'Care and skill in Australia – Daniels v Anderson' (1996) 17 Co Law 89 at 91.

[288] Davies P L, *Gower's Principles of Modern Company Law* (6th ed) Sweet & Maxwell Ltd, London, 1997 at 53 and 679.

[289] Financial Services Act 1986 (UK).

[290] See, e.g., *Financial Times*, 31 July 1999.

3

The Statutory Duty to Exercise Care and Diligence

INTRODUCTION

Legislation in English and Australian company law is omnipresent and imposes multifarious duties upon directors over a wide range of issues.[1] In Australia, for example, Federal legislation obliges directors to wrestle with *inter alia* income tax, company tax, sales tax, trade practices and industrial arbitration. Simultaneously, at state level, directors must deal with *inter alia* land tax, payroll tax, workers' compensation and stamp duty. The list of duties which the legislature has seen fit to impose on directors is a long one. So long in fact that the Senate Standing Committee on Legal and Constitutional Affairs, in its report on directors' duties ('Cooney Report'), described this anthology of duties as comprising a 'bewildering range of laws which govern directors'.[2]

In the previous chapter of this book, the development of the duty upon directors of British companies to exercise care and diligence was traced from the time of Sir Robert Sutton,[3] to the present day. A gradual evolution was noted in the standard required from a purely subjective test which, more often than not, permitted total inactivity on the part of directors disposed to a pastime befitting their status as gentlemen,[4] to an objective test giving vent to the public's more recent calls for stricter measures;[5] but tempered, nonetheless, by subjective considerations akin to those prescribed by Insolvency Act 1986 (UK) ('IA 1986') s214(4),[6] as applied by Hoffmann LJ in *Re D'Jan of London Ltd*.[7] Whilst such changes in attitude are welcome, the overall response time by the English judiciary to public demands remains pedestrian.[8] It should be noted, however,

---

[1] Harper J B and Browne A A, 'The Duties and Liabilities of a Director in 1973' (1973) 47 ALJ 447 at 454.

[2] Senate Standing Committee on Legal and Constitutional Affairs, *Social and Fiduciary Duties and Obligations of Company Directors* AGPS, Canberra, 1989 at 27.

[3] *The Charitable Corporation v Sutton* (1742) 2 Atk 400.

[4] *In re Denham & Co* (1884) 25 Ch D 752 at 766 per Chitty J.

[5] *Re Barings plc* [1998] BCC 583 at 586 per Sir Richard Scott VC; and *Bishopsgate Investment Management Ltd v Maxwell (No. 2)* [1994] 1 All ER 261 at 264 per Hoffmann LJ (Leggatt LJ agreed); cf. *Androvin v Figliomeni* (1996) 14 ACLC 1461 at 1470 per Owen J (Kennedy and Franklyn JJ agreed); and *State of South Australia v Clark* (1996) 19 ACSR 606 at 627 per Perry J.

[6] Law Commission, *Company Directors: Regulating Conflicts of Interests and Formulating a Statement of Duties* HMSO, London, Cm 4436, 1999 at paras 5.8-5.9, 5.19-5.20 and 5.38.

[7] [1993] BCC 646 at 648-649; see *Re Landhurst Leasing plc* [1999] 1 BCLC 286 at 344 per Hart J.

[8] Cf. Department of Trade and Industry, *Modern Company Law: The Strategic Framework* HMSO, London, 1999 at para 8.5.

that on 4 March 1998, the President of the Board of Trade announced the launch of a fundamental review of the framework of core English company law. The consultation paper published at that time by the Department of Trade and Industry ('DTI') outlines the nature of the problems which the review is designed to address and its objectives, and relevantly provides that:

> The object of the review will be to bring forward proposals for a modern law for the modern world. The Government is determined that the nation should have an up-to-date framework which promotes the competitiveness of UK companies and so contributes to national competitiveness and increased prosperity.[9]

In February 1999, the DTI released its consultation document entitled *Modern Company Law: The Strategic Framework* which identifies as an issue of general importance to the review those interests which English company law should serve and the means by which it should do so.[10] In addition, the Law Commission published in September 1999 its eagerly awaited report entitled *Company Directors: Regulating Conflicts of Interests and Formulating a Statement of Duties*. This revives the push for the partial codification of the duty upon directors of British companies to exercise care and diligence.[11] The Law Commission considers that the case for partial codification is a powerful one,[12] and advocates the enactment of a twofold objective/subjective test as the standard by which the duty upon directors of British companies to exercise care and diligence should be adjudged.[13]

Hence changes in English company law are mooted. Moves are afoot. But, quite properly, these things take time. The aim of the Company Law Review Steering Group, for instance, is to enable the DTI to publish a detailed White Paper in or about March 2001.[14] Given the breadth of the DTI's review, this looks to be a tight timetable.[15] Moreover, in the event that the recent views of the Law Commission advocating partial codification are embraced, and ultimately enacted, by the British Parliament, it will be some time before English company law benefits from that.

In contrast, since the latter part of the 1980s, Australian company law has witnessed a marked change in judicial attitudes and approaches,[16] coupled with a clearly stated Federal legislative intent,[17] designed to raise the level of directorial responsibility and to improve corporate governance generally.[18] Over the last decade or so, the Australian

---

9 Department of Trade and Industry, *Modern Company Law: For a Competitive Economy* (a consultative document) HMSO, London, 1998 at para 1.2.

10 Department of Trade and Industry, *Modern Company Law: The Strategic Framework* HMSO, London, 1999 at chapter 5.1.

11 Law Commission, *Company Directors: Regulating Conflicts of Interests and Formulating a Statement of Duties* HMSO, London, Cm 4436, 1999 at paras 4.48, 5.19-5.20 and 5.38.

12 *Ibid* at para 4.31.

13 *Ibid* at paras 5.19-5.20 and 5.38.

14 Department of Trade and Industry, *Modern Company Law: For a Competitive Economy* (a consultative document) HMSO, London, 1998 at paras 1.5 and 8.2-8.3.

15 Law Commission, *Company Directors: Regulating Conflicts of Interests and Formulating a Statement of Duties* HMSO, London, Cm 4436, 1999 at para 1.7.

16 In a line of authority which relevantly began with *Darvall v North Sydney Brick & Tile Co Ltd (No. 2)* (1989) 7 ACLC 659 through to the recent decision in *Daniels v Anderson* (1995) 13 ACLC 614.

17 Beginning with the Corporations Bill 1988 (Cth).

18 Stapledon G P, *Institutional Shareholders and Corporate Governance* Clarendon Press, Oxford, 1996 at 8; Whincop M J, 'An Economic Analysis of the Criminalisation and Content of Directors' Duties' (1996) 24 ABLR 273 at 277 and 291; Prentice D D and Holland P R J, *Contemporary Issues in Corpo-*

public's expectations and requirements of directors has risen sharply. The Australian courts have been quick to recognise this and to act upon it. So too has the Australian Parliament. That recognition, and the resultant action, has brought about a fresh legislative approach by the Australian Parliament and an enlightened judicial approach by the Australian courts to the whole question of company law in Australia; or as it is now more properly referred to, corporations law.[19]

In this chapter we will analyse the implications of partial codification in Australian company law which, as will be seen, is still in its infancy and, as a consequence, still suffering from growing pains.[20] It is suggested that such analysis is particularly timely in the light of the Law Commission's recent work in this area and its recommendations which favour partial codification of the duty upon directors of British companies to exercise care and diligence as the following extract from its report makes clear:

> (1) a director's duty of care, skill and diligence to his company should be set out in statute; (2) the standard should be judged by a twofold objective/subjective test; and (3) regard should be had to the functions of the particular director and the circumstances [including size and type] of the company.[21]

The law pertaining to directors' duties in English and Australian company law remains, therefore, in a state of flux: it continues to evolve. In the analysis which follows, it will become apparent that some formerly entrenched judicial attitudes, approaches, principles and standards, such as they were, affecting the directors' duties to exercise care and diligence, and which were distilled during a period in corporate history when a directorship was a sinecure in which reasonable competence was a desirable but not a necessary qualification,[22] are being gradually swept away. As Perry J in *State of South Australia v Clark* recently observed:

> Recent appellate decisions in Australia have gone a long way towards clarifying and re-expressing the duty of care owed by directors of a company vis á vis the company in terms more closely reflecting contemporary attitudes.[23]

At first, however, there was little enthusiasm for change and the Australian judiciary displayed a remarkable penchant for lethargy; seemingly content with that inherited

---

cont.

    rate Governance Oxford University Press, Oxford, 1993; and Farrar J H, 'Corporate Governance, Business Judgement and the Professionalism of Directors' (1993) 6 CBLJ 1 at 2; note Committee on the Financial Aspects of Corporate Governance, *The Report of the Committee on the Financial Aspects of Corporate Governance* Gee and Co Ltd, London, 1992; and Committee on Corporate Governance, *Final Report* Gee Publishing Ltd, London, 1998; cf. The American Law Institute, *Principles of Corporate Governance: Analysis and Recommendations* St Paul, 1994.

[19] Corporations Law s9.

[20] As evidenced by the ongoing amendments being made to the Corporations Law.

[21] Law Commission, *Company Directors: Regulating Conflicts of Interests and Formulating a Statement of Duties* HMSO, London, Cm 4436, 1999 at para 5.20.

[22] Menzies D, 'Company Directors' (1959) 33 ALJ 156 at 163-164.

[23] (1996) 19 ACSR 606 at 627; cf. *Bishopsgate Investment Management Ltd v Maxwell (No. 2)* [1994] 1 All ER 261 at 264 per Hoffmann LJ (Leggatt LJ agreed) who recognised that the law, 'may be evolving in response to changes in public attitudes to corporate governance'; and *Re Grayan Building Services Ltd* [1995] BCC 554 at 577 per Henry LJ, 'The statutory corporate climate is stricter than it has ever been, and those enforcing it should reflect the fact that Parliament has seen the need for higher standards.'

from English company law. Even after legislative intervention by State and Federal Parliaments, the pace of developments in this area remained undistinguished. Although, as we will see throughout the balance of this chapter, in the past decade or so, much has changed. Judges today are much more alive to the commercial realities involved,[24] and there has been an obvious commitment on the part of the Australian judiciary, probably more so than their English counterparts, which has led to a more dynamic approach to the directors' duties to exercise care and diligence.[25]

Initially, this development could be criticised on the grounds that progressive decisions seemed to emerge more by way of exception than by rule, and more out of *ad hoc* decision-making by the judges than by design. But Australian judges today are more interventionist than were their predecessors,[26] and the vigour and enthusiasm which has in recent times been displayed has meant a dramatic tightening up of directors' responsibilities and the way in which directors of Australian companies are now required to go about their business. Consequently, the specific statutory duty in Australian company law to exercise care and diligence,[27] which will now be considered in some detail, is probably more onerous than the common law and the equitable duties resorted to prior to its enactment.[28]

THE LATEST STATUTORY PROVISIONS

When the Corporations Bill 1988 (Cth) reached the Australian Senate on 14 October 1988, it heralded, 'a new direction in national companies and securities law and administration';[29] for the Bill sought to amalgamate into one law the areas at that time covered by the separate co-operative scheme codes referred to below. In doing so, the Australian Government sought to consolidate the existing law, remove much duplicated material, and rationalise the structure and arrangement of the legislation. Extensive changes to the existing law were not attempted. Nor was compliance with the Australian Constitution for, as history records, when the Corporations Act 1989 (Cth) was enacted by the Australian Parliament in 1989, aspects of it suffered the ignominy of being declared invalid by the High Court of Australia[30] in *New South Wales v Commonwealth of Australia*.[31] In short, prior to the Act being proclaimed to commence, New South Wales, South Australia and Western Australia brought these proceedings claiming that the Act was invalid to the extent that it provided for the incorporation of companies, or prevented companies being incorporated under the relevant State company law. By a majority of six to one,[32] the High Court held that the relevant

---

[24] With some members of the Australian judiciary having themselves served at some time or another as directors in either professional or personal capacities; note Sealy L S, 'Directors' "Wider" Responsibilities – Problems Conceptual, Practical and Procedural' (1987) 13 MULR 164 at 164.

[25] Ipp D A, 'The diligent director' (1997) 18 Co Law 162 at 167; and Passmore C, 'Directors' Duties: Australian Style' (1997) 18 Co Law 158 at 158-159.

[26] Being, it is suggested, more commercial and therefore having a better grasp of the commercial complexities and realities involved in matters before them than perhaps their predecessors; note Sealy L S, '"Bona Fides" and "Proper Purposes" in Corporate Decisions' (1989) 15 MULR 265 at 265.

[27] Corporations Law s232(4).

[28] *Daniels v Anderson* (1995) 13 ACLC 614 at 633 per Clarke and Sheller JJA.

[29] Commonwealth, Senate, Parliamentary Debates, 14 October 1988 at 1363.

[30] (Mason CJ, Brennan, Deane, Dawson, Toohey, Gaudron and McHugh JJ).

[31] (1989) 90 ALR 355.

[32] (Deane J dissented).

provisions were not supported by s51(xx) of the Constitution and were accordingly invalid.[33]

Notwithstanding this inauspicious start to modern corporate law reform, the Australian Parliament thereafter enacted the Corporations Legislation Amendment Act 1990 (Cth) in order to change the constitutional basis of the unproclaimed Corporations Act 1989 (Cth). As a consequence, each State and the Northern Territory then passed its own Corporations Act; s7 of which declared that the Corporations Law, as set out in Corporations Act 1989 (Cth) s82,[34] was to apply in their respective jurisdictions. There are, therefore, eight separate Corporations Laws: although each is uniform. For the purposes of this book, all subsequent references are to the Corporations Law as set out in Corporations Act 1989 (Cth) s82 which came into effect across Australia on 1 January 1991.[35]

During the second reading of the Corporations Legislation Amendment Bill 1990 (Cth), the Attorney-General reported in rather glowing terms that the proposed package of laws legislation will usher in a new era of corporate regulation as the national scheme embodied in that legislative package, 'will offer for the first time in the nation's history a single and truly national regulatory regime that can guarantee a sound and well regulated environment for corporate activity.'[36] Behind the rhetoric, no doubt, lay a desire on the part of the Australian Government to impress upon supporters and detractors alike the message that it was putting fresh initiatives into place which would end the reign of the Australian 'corporate cowboys'[37] who, it was considered by many, paid scant regard to laws hitherto in place and, in the process, had wreaked havoc upon a public ill-equipped to look after its own interests in the corporate sector.[38]

This new legislative package became the Corporations Law and was the Australian Government's show-piece at the time. It projected a strong image by adopting a tough new approach to the manner in which corporate activities were to be conducted. But in at least one significant respect, the Corporations Law fell short of the mark.[39] For when first enacted, Corporations Law s232(4) was simply a genderised restatement of its predecessor,[40] and provided that:

> An officer of a corporation shall at all times exercise a reasonable degree of care and diligence in the exercise of his or her powers and the discharge of his or her duties.

---

[33] Ford H A J, Austin R P and Ramsay I M, *Ford's Principles of Corporations Law* (9th ed) Reed International Books Australia Pty Ltd, Sydney, 1999 at paras 2.230-2.250.

[34] *Ibid* at para 1.020.

[35] Commonwealth, House of Representatives, Parliamentary Debates, 8 November 1990 at 3663.

[36] *Ibid* at 3669; cf. Ford H A J and Austin R P, *Ford's Principles of Corporations Law* (6th ed) Butterworths Pty Ltd, Sydney, 1992 at 19.

[37] Cf. Report of the Review Committee on Insolvency Law and Practice, HMSO, London, Cmnd 8558, 1982 at para 1742.

[38] See Sykes T, *The Bold Riders* Allen & Unwin Pty Ltd, St Leonards, 1994; Barry P, *The Rise and Fall of Alan Bond* Transworld Publishers (Australia) Pty Ltd, Sydney, 1990; and *The Australian Financial Review*, 6 November 1995.

[39] Since remedied by the Corporate Law Reform Act 1992 (Cth) which took heed of remarks in the report of the Senate Standing Committee on Legal and Constitutional Affairs, *Social and Fiduciary Duties and Obligations of Company Directors* AGPS, Canberra, 1989 at 29 that, 'the present state of law is not satisfactory' and the impassioned plea that, 'an objective duty of care for directors be provided in the companies legislation'.

[40] Companies Code s229(2).

Whilst a commendable exercise in politically correct genderisation by the inclusion of the words 'or her' as applicable, such cosmetic changes were hardly likely to guarantee a sound and well-regulated environment for corporate activity as originally proclaimed by the Attorney-General.[41] Furthermore, even though the enactment of the Corporations Law: (i) widened the statutory duties imposed upon directors of Australian companies by broadening the scope and applicability of those duties; (ii) focused upon areas not previously the subject of attention and intervention; and (iii) adopted a more robust approach to corporate governance, the Australian Parliament was not overly radical nor proactive in its implementation of this widened jurisdiction. It is suggested that the Australian Parliament was actually being less proactive than it sought credit for and was really more reactive by responding to judicial attitude, public opinion and various committee recommendations voiced during the preceding years.

In chapters six and seven of this book, examples of this judicial attitude and public opinion will be considered. Those chapters will also look at some of the committee recommendations concerned with bringing changes to those duties upon directors of Australian companies to exercise care and diligence. For the purposes of this chapter, however, and for the sake of brevity, our remarks will be confined to those recommendations in the Cooney Report which, significantly, resulted in amendments to, and a restatement of, Corporations Law s232(4). Chief amongst those recommendations was that, 'an objective duty of care for directors be provided in the companies legislation',[42] given the unsatisfactory state of the present law.[43]

On 3 November 1992, the Corporate Law Reform Bill 1992 (Cth) was introduced into the Australian Parliament. In the explanatory memorandum which accompanied the release of the Bill, the Australian Government paid tribute to the ability of the courts to develop principles in keeping with legislative intent. It then spelt out, for the judiciary's future guidance, that the Australian Government's decision to amend Corporations Law s232(4) was designed to reinforce that the duty to exercise care and diligence is an objective duty requiring directors to exercise the degree of care and diligence that a reasonable person in a like position would exercise in the corporation's circumstances.[44]

During the second reading of the Corporate Law Reform Bill 1992 (Cth), the Attorney-General reaffirmed that directors of Australian companies should show the degree of care and diligence that a reasonable person in their position would exercise and that, 'the courts should never apply hindsight to the decisions of directors, but should judge those decisions based on the information which was available to the director at the time the decision was made.'[45] But even before this proposed amendment to Corporations Law s232(4) was introduced, the debate as to the standard of care and

---

[41] Commonwealth, House of Representatives, Parliamentary Debates, 8 November 1990 at 3669; cf. Ford H A J and Austin R P, *Ford's Principles of Corporations Law* (6th ed) Butterworths Pty Ltd, Sydney, 1992 at 19.

[42] Senate Standing Committee on Legal and Constitutional Affairs, *Social and Fiduciary Duties and Obligations of Company Directors* AGPS, Canberra, 1989 at 29.

[43] *Ibid* at 32.

[44] Thereby adopting one of the Senate Standing Committee on Legal and Constitutional Affairs' more salutary recommendations; namely, that the required standard of care and diligence be determined objectively.

[45] Commonwealth, House of Representatives, Parliamentary Debates, 3 November 1992 at 2400; note Finch V, 'Company Directors: Who Cares about Skill and Care?' (1992) 55 MLR 179 at 189; and The American Law Institute, *Principles of Corporate Governance: Analysis and Recommendations* St Paul, 1994, volume 1 at 164.

diligence owed by a director at common law had been resolved in favour of an objective test by Australian courts in a series of decisions which will be considered shortly. In particular, the decisions in *Statewide Tobacco Services Ltd v Morley*,[46] *Commonwealth Bank of Australia v Friedrich*,[47] and *AWA Ltd v Daniels*,[48] were considered by the Australian Government to represent the position sought to be prescribed by the proposed amendment to s232(4).[49]

Thus, it is suggested that the legislative intent behind this aspect of the Corporations Law was simply to partially codify the directors' duty to exercise care and diligence as reflected by current judicial trends; being the culmination of the development of legal and equitable duties to that point. Hence Corporations Law s232(4) was intended to be confirmatory rather than innovatory.[50]

By virtue of the Corporate Law Reform Act 1992 (Cth), the Corporate Law Reform Bill 1992 (Cth) became law on 1 February 1993 and implemented some of the more salient recommendations made in the Cooney Report. Relevantly, for the purposes of this book, Corporations Law s232(4) was amended to expressly provide for an objective standard of care and diligence coupled with a very clear message from the Australian Parliament that in evaluating a director's compliance with the standard of care and diligence, the Australian courts are obliged to consider: (i) the special background, qualifications and management responsibilities of the particular director; and (ii) such matters as the state of the corporation's financial affairs, the size and nature of the corporation, the urgency and magnitude of any problem, the provisions of the corporation's constitution, and the composition of its board.[51]

At the same time, the Australian courts are to recognise that decisions must be made on the basis of the circumstances at the time and without the benefit of hindsight;[52] given that hindsight, as Cooke J in *Nicholson v Permakraft (NZ) Ltd* explained, 'can lead to a subconscious applying of too severe a standard.'[53] In addition, in the case of a business corporation, it is to be borne in mind that, 'corporate decisions involve risk taking'.[54] This philosophy is entirely consistent with that enjoyed in English company law.[55] As Tunc observes:

> Business life is made of reasoned acceptance of risks. To hold someone liable for the materialisation of a risk would paralyse initiative. The judge should be careful not

---

[46] (1990) 2 ACSR 405.

[47] (1991) 5 ACSR 115.

[48] (1992) 10 ACLC 933.

[49] Explanatory memorandum, *Corporate Law Reform Bill 1992* CCH Australia Ltd, Sydney, 1992 at 25.

[50] Cf. *State of South Australia v Clark* (1996) 19 ACSR 606 at 627-628 per Perry J.

[51] Cf. Law Commission, *Company Directors: Regulating Conflicts of Interests and Formulating a Statement of Duties* HMSO, London, Cm 4436, 1999 at paras 5.19-5.20 and 5.38; note *Deputy Commissioner of Taxation v Austin* (1998) 16 ACLC 1555 at 1558-1560 per Madgwick J.

[52] *Kong v Pilkington (Australia) Ltd* (1997) 15 ACLC 1561 at 1567 per Owen J (Franklyn and Murray JJ agreed); and *National Companies and Securities Commission v Hurley* (1995) 13 ACLC 1635 at 1642 per Scott J (Malcolm CJ and Anderson J agreed).

[53] [1985] 1 NZLR 242 at 253; see *In re Horsley & Weight Ltd* [1982] Ch 442 at 455 per Templeman LJ.

[54] Commonwealth, House of Representatives, Parliamentary Debates, 3 November 1992 at 2402; note Hopt K J, 'Directors' Duties to Shareholders, Employees, and Other Creditors: A View from the Continent' in McKendrick E (ed), *Commercial Aspects of Trusts and Fiduciary Obligations* Clarendon Press, Oxford, 1992 at 123.

[55] *Facia Footwear Ltd v Hinchliffe* [1998] 1 BCLC 218 at 228 per Sir Richard Scott VC; *Re Living Images Ltd* [1996] BCC 112 at 116-117 per Laddie J; and *Re Hitco 2000 Ltd* [1995] BCC 161 at 169 per Jules Sher QC.

to be 'wise after the event' and criticise as faulty a decision which turns out to be disappointing.[56]

As a consequence, when the courts come to take a more active role than has been traditional, as surely they must, it will be important to strike the right balance between meeting the standards required by contemporary business and retaining the essential spirit of enterprise.[57] In the light of this, in Australian company law an objective standard of care and diligence for directors is now prescribed by Corporations Law s232(4) which requires that:

> In the exercise of his or her powers and the discharge of his or her duties, an officer of a corporation must exercise the degree of care and diligence that a reasonable person in a like position in a corporation would exercise in the corporation's circumstances.[58]

Like its predecessors,[59] Corporations Law s232(4) preserves the common law position immediately prior to its enactment.[60] As s232(4) only came into effect on 1 January 1991, its statutory import, as such, is in its infancy and its effectiveness is too early to judge. *A fortiori* the changes brought about to that sub-section on 1 February 1993 by the importation of an objective test, consequent upon the Corporate Law Reform Act 1992 (Cth). Needless to say, there is little case-law specifically on s232(4); although more and more the cases are starting to appear in the reports.[61] A trilogy of these will be considered shortly.

Notwithstanding the dearth of case-law specifically on Corporations Law s232(4), given the Australian Government's widely flaunted and much publicised manifesto in regard to the implementation of the objective standard of care and diligence, and the reasons behind that, the way has been very clearly signposted for judicial interpretation. Such signposting will further strengthen the resolve of the Australian judiciary to lift standards of care and diligence required of directors of Australian companies, thus adding to the considerable gains already made.[62] Recent Australian cases which reflect these gains will be considered shortly. Many of these cases deal with the standard, as it was, under Companies Code s229(2) concerning breaches prior to 1 January 1991. Such decisions will apply with equal force to breaches occurring between 1 January 1991 and 1 February 1993, given that during this time Corporations Law s232(4) was, with the exception of the genderisation aspects introduced for reasons of political correctness, in terms identical with that of Companies Code s229(2).[63] Decisions on s229(2), therefore, remain relevant to any deliberations by the Australian courts upon

---

[56] Tunc A, 'The Judge and the Businessman' (1986) 102 LQR 549 at 554.

[57] Farrar J H, 'Corporate Governance, Business Judgement and the Professionalism of Directors' (1993) 6 CBLJ 1 at 3.

[58] Substituted by Act No. 210 of 1992 and effective 1 February 1993.

[59] Companies Act 1958 (Vic) s107(1); Companies Act 1961 (Vic) s124(1); and Companies Code s229(2).

[60] Corporations Law s232(11); note *The Governor and Company of the Bank of England v Vagliano Brothers* [1891] AC 107 at 144-145 per Lord Herschell.

[61] E.g., *Australian Securities Commission v Forem-Freeway Enterprises Pty Ltd* (1998-1999) 30 ACSR 339; *ASC v Donovan* (1998) 28 ACSR 583; *Gamble v Hoffman* (1997) 15 ACLC 1314; and *Re Property Force Consultancy Pty Ltd* [1997] 1 Qd R 300.

[62] Ipp D A, 'The diligent director' (1997) 18 Co Law 162 at 164-167; and Passmore C, 'Directors' Duties: Australian Style' (1997) 18 Co Law 158 at 158-159.

[63] *Re Property Force Consultancy Pty Ltd* [1997] 1 Qd R 300 at 305-306 per Derrington J.

Corporations Law s232(4).[64] However, case-law specifically upon s232(4) is starting to develop, and as we move into the next millennium that will continue to grow and soon be very much in evidence.

Before looking to the cases, however, it is instructive to return to those earlier attempts by State and Federal Parliaments to regulate the duties upon directors of Australian companies to exercise care and diligence, and to take a brief look at each. This is important for it provides an insight into some of the considerations which weighed heavily with the Australian judiciary during the formative years of the objective duty which is now enacted by Corporations Law s232(4).

THE FORMER STATUTORY PROVISIONS

The first Australian example of the statutory duty to exercise reasonable diligence appeared in the Companies Act 1958 (Vic) s107(1) which provided that, 'A director shall at all times act honestly and use reasonable diligence in the discharge of the duties of his office.' This enactment was the first of its kind in Australia to render a director failing to perform his or her duties of honesty and due diligence under the general law liable to be convicted of a criminal offence;[65] the penalty for which was a fine not to exceed £500.[66] Prior to 1958 it seems that there was no corresponding provision in the companies legislation of any other English speaking country.[67] But the Victorian Parliament saw to it that the common law duties were expressly preserved.[68] This statutory duty, as the learned authors of *Australian Company Law and Practice* note, was first introduced into the Victorian Parliament as Companies Bill 1958 (Vic) s107(1) on the basis that the section:

> [Is] declaratory of the existing law, but it is believed that a restatement of the princi-
> ples of honesty and good faith that should govern directors' conduct, clearly set out
> in the Act, will be an effective deterrent to misconduct and will free the courts from
> the technicalities of the existing law in dealing with all forms of dishonesty and
> impropriety by directors.[69]

Accordingly, when evaluating compliance with the section, the Australian courts continued to fall back upon Romer J's judgment in *In re City Equitable Fire Insurance Company Ltd*,[70] for guidance. The decision of the Victorian Full Court[71] in *Byrne v*

---

[64] *Daniels v Anderson* (1995) 13 ACLC 614 at 654 per Clarke and Sheller JJA.

[65] Wallace G and Young J McI, *Australian Company Law and Practice* The Law Book Company Ltd, Sydney, 1965 at 393; see *Vrisakis v Australian Securities Commission* (1992-1993) 9 WAR 395 at 404 per Malcolm CJ; and *Mesenberg v Cord Industrial Recruiters Pty Ltd* (1996) 14 ACLC 519 at 525 per Young J.

[66] Decimal currency was not introduced into Australia until 14 February 1966 when £AUP became $AUD.

[67] Brown S R and Grogan P R, *Company Directors* (3rd ed) The Law Book Company Ltd, Sydney, 1974 at 270.

[68] Companies Act 1958 (Vic) s107(4); note *The Governor and Company of the Bank of England v Vagliano Brothers* [1891] AC 107 at 144-145 per Lord Herschell.

[69] Wallace G and Young J McI, *Australian Company Law and Practice* The Law Book Company Ltd, Sydney, 1965 at 393.

[70] [1925] Ch 407.

[71] (Herring CJ, Smith and Adam JJ).

Baker[72] is apposite. In *Byrne* the Full Court examined Companies Act 1958 (Vic) s107(1) and, in a joint judgment, considered that in the discharge of his or her duties a director, 'must act honestly and must exercise such degree of both skill and diligence as would amount to the reasonable care which an ordinary man might be expected to take in the circumstances on his own behalf.'[73] The Full Court was of the view that Romer J's judgment in *City Equitable* had inspired the language of s107(1). What s107(1) demanded of honest directors was diligence only, and the degree of diligence demanded was that which was reasonable in the circumstances and no more.

Companies Act 1958 (Vic) was used as a template for a draft Companies Bill 1961. This was produced in an attempt to unify companies legislation throughout Australia. It was brought about largely by the inconvenience suffered by the business community given the varying legislative requirements as between the States and the Territories. This gave rise to each of the States and the Territories passing mainly uniform legislation across Australia which came to be known as the uniform Companies Acts.[74] At this point reference is made initially to the 1961 Victorian Act, since s124(1) of that Act was derived from Companies Act 1958 (Vic) s107,[75] and is illustrative of the position concerning directors' duties under the uniform Companies Acts across Australia at that time. Throughout the remainder of this book, reference will be made to the uniform Companies Acts as appropriate.

Companies Act 1961 (Vic) s124(1) referred to reasonable diligence in exactly the same terms as its predecessor.[76] The statutory duty so imposed reflected the general position at common law at that time;[77] and, like its earlier counterpart, expressly preserved that position.[78] Not surprisingly, therefore, when *Marchesi v Barnes*[79] came before the Victorian Supreme Court, as chapter five of this book will detail, Gowans J adopted the Victorian Full Court's view in *Byrne* that the source of the language used in s124(1) ought be attributed to Romer J in *City Equitable*. Thus, no great advances in the raising of standards were therefore made.[80] In taking this approach, Gowans J in *Marchesi* went on to affirm that effectively:

> [The] common law obligation in respect of acting honestly, as with the common law obligation to act with due diligence has been made a statutory duty, and failure to perform it, provided there is the proper mental element, has been made a criminal offence.[81]

---

[72] [1964] VR 443; see *Kimberley Mineral Holdings Ltd v Triguboff* [1978] 1 NSWLR 364 at 370 per Needham J; and *Vrisakis v Australian Securities Commission* (1992-1993) 9 WAR 395 at 409-411 per Malcolm CJ and at 442-443 per Ipp J (Malcolm CJ agreed).

[73] [1964] VR 443 at 450 *per curiam*; see Editorial comment (1964-1965) 38 ALJ 251 at 251; cf. Trebilcock M J, 'The Liability of Company Directors for Negligence' (1969) 32 MLR 499 at 502.

[74] Companies Act 1961 (NSW); Companies Act 1961 (Qld); Companies Act 1961 (Vic); Companies Act 1961 (WA); Companies Act 1962 (SA); Companies Act 1962 (Tas); Companies Ordinance 1962 (ACT); and Companies Ordinance 1963 (NT).

[75] Section 4(1) of the 1961 Act repealed the 1958 Act.

[76] Companies Act 1958 (Vic) s107(1).

[77] See Menzies D, 'Company Directors' (1959) 33 ALJ 156.

[78] Companies Act 1961 (Vic) s124(4).

[79] [1970] VR 434.

[80] Birds J R, 'A code of directors' duties?' (1974) 124 NLJ 1163 at 1165; note Corkery J F, *Directors' Powers and Duties* Longman Cheshire Pty Ltd, Melbourne, 1987 at 139-140.

[81] [1970] VR 434 at 438.

It is clear from these authorities that the relevant Australian companies legislation, prior to the enactment of Companies Code ss229(1) and 229(2), was simply a restatement of the common law obligation in respect of acting honestly coupled with the common law obligation to act with due diligence.[82] And little, if anything, was done in the way of raising standards. The *status quo* was preserved across another two decades of Australian company law.

By 1978 agreement had been reached on a State and Federal level to provide for a uniform system of law and administration in relation to Australian company law, and the regulation of the securities industry, by providing for a co-operative scheme involving the State and Federal Parliaments. Between 1981 and 1990 company law in Australia was regulated under this co-operative scheme. The Companies Act 1981 (Cth), which breathed life into this scheme, was assented to on 18 June 1981 and became effective as legislation of the Australian Capital Territory on 1 July 1982. To allow its provisions to apply in all participating jurisdictions, each State and the Northern Territory passed an enabling Act.[83] In each case the provisions of the Commonwealth Act applied as law of that particular jurisdiction.[84] The resultant legislation was simply referred to as the Companies ([name of State/Territory]) Code.[85] For the balance of this book, this will be generically referred to as the Companies Code in keeping with its homogeneity.[86]

Companies Code s229(2) is derived from the uniform Companies Acts (illustrative of which is Companies Act 1961 (Vic) s124(1)) which required a director at all times to act honestly and use reasonable diligence in the discharge of the duties of his or her office.[87] Relevantly, s229(2) provides that:

> An officer of a corporation shall at all times exercise a reasonable degree of care and diligence in the exercise of his powers and the discharge of his duties.

Like its predecessors,[88] Companies Code s229(2) preserves the common law position immediately prior to its enactment.[89] Decisions concerning breaches of the relevant duty under s229(2) have recently been handed down by the Australian courts.[90] Consequently, this case-law must be analysed in order to determine the relevant standard; for these decisions, and those before them, have been instrumental in shaping the applicable principles. From the previous chapter of this book, it will be recalled that the standard of care and diligence was said to be that which an ordinary or reasonable person might be expected to take, in the same circumstances, on his or her own behalf.[91]

---

[82] But converted into a criminal offence provided the proper mental element was present.

[83] The Companies (Application of Laws) Act: operative 1 July 1982 (cf. Northern Territory 1 July 1986).

[84] Subject to local modifications.

[85] Companies (New South Wales) Code; Companies (Queensland) Code; Companies (Victoria) Code; Companies (Western Australia) Code; Companies (South Australia) Code; Companies (Tasmania) Code; Companies (Australian Capital Territory) Code; and Companies (Northern Territory) Code.

[86] *Fitzsimmons v R* (1997) 23 ACSR 355 at 360 per Parker J.

[87] The duty to act honestly was made the subject of a separate provision in Companies Code s229(1).

[88] Companies Act 1958 (Vic) s107(1); and Companies Act 1961 (Vic) s124(1).

[89] Companies Code s229(10); note *The Governor and Company of the Bank of England v Vagliano Brothers* [1891] AC 107 at 144-145 per Lord Herschell.

[90] E.g., *The Duke Group Limited v Pilmer* (1998) 16 ACLC 567.

[91] *The Overend & Gurney Company v Gibb* (1872) LR 5 HL 480 at 486-487 per Lord Hatherley LC; and *In re Brazilian Rubber Plantations and Estates Ltd* [1911] 1 Ch 425 at 437 per Neville J.

Today, the statutory duty is to be objectively determined.[92] However, as there is no uniform standard applicable, the ambit of the duty and the standard of care required in Australian company law, 'depend on the particular circumstances.'[93] Thus the standard of care required of a director might vary from case to case; given that the proper performance of a director's duties is dependent upon: (i) his or her actual knowledge and experience; (ii) the nature and extent of the company's business; and (iii) the distribution of responsibilities within that company.[94]

The significant decisions concerning Companies Code s229(2) were handed down in 1992 and 1993: some ten years after the section came into effect. It is suggested that what prompted these actions, and many more like them, and which has resulted in a constant parade of directors before the Australian courts since, was the state of the Australian economy *post* 20 October 1987; a date which not only had serious global ramifications,[95] but locally marked the beginning of the end of the decade of greed,[96] and added fresh impetus to the push for stricter measures concerning corporate governance. Black Tuesday, as 20 October 1987 came to be known in financial markets and the media across Australia, also heralded a spate of insolvencies the likes of which in corporate Australia had not been previously known. The litigation spawned from record levels of insolvency was principally responsible for radical changes to traditional judicial attitudes and approaches by the Australian judiciary to corporate governance generally; and to demands concerning the directors' duty to exercise care and diligence specifically. *A fortiori* in the context of insolvency, near-insolvency or doubtful solvency.[97]

It is not surprising, therefore, that many of the significant advances in the strengthening of the duty upon directors of Australian companies to exercise care and diligence, arose out of litigation concerned with breaches by directors of insolvent trading provisions of the applicable companies legislation.[98] This has been the experience in English company law as well. In chapters six, seven and eight of this book, a number of these recent English and Australian decisions, in which more stringent standards of care and diligence have been imposed, will be analysed.[99] Although many of these cases are primarily concerned with insolvent trading claims, brought under the relevant companies legislation, they also raise wider issues as to the standards of care and

---

[92] Cf. Insolvency Act 1986 (UK) s214(4); note *Re D'Jan of London Ltd* [1993] BCC 646 at 648-649 per Hoffmann LJ; and *Re Barings plc* [1998] BCC 583 at 586 per Sir Richard Scott VC.

[93] *Vrisakis v Australian Securities Commission* (1992-1993) 9 WAR 395 at 451 per Ipp J (Malcolm CJ agreed); see *Gamble v Hoffman* (1997) 15 ACLC 1314 at 1318 per Carr J.

[94] *AWA Ltd v Daniels* (1992) 10 ACLC 933 at 1012 per Rogers CJ; see *Biala Pty Ltd v Mallina Holdings Ltd* (1993) 11 ACSR 785 at 856 per Ipp J; and *Vrisakis v Australian Securities Commission* (1992-1993) 9 WAR 395 at 451 per Ipp J (Malcolm CJ agreed).

[95] Cf. *Financial Times*, 20 July 1999.

[96] Commonwealth, House of Representatives, Parliamentary Debates, 29 May 1991 at 4213; cf. *The Australian*, 21 April 1997: 'Directors are more accountable to shareholders and they are more accountable to the community through beefed-up corporate laws … Yet the public is entitled to remain a little sceptical that company directors have learned the lesson that greed is not necessarily good.'

[97] *Nicholson v Permakraft (NZ) Ltd* [1985] 1 NZLR 242 at 249 per Cooke J.

[98] Companies Code s556; and Corporations Law s592.

[99] E.g., *Norman v Theodore Goddard* [1992] BCC 14; *Re D'Jan of London Ltd* [1993] BCC 646; *Australian Securities Commission v Gallagher* (1993) 11 ACLC 286; *Vrisakis v Australian Securities Commission* (1992-1993) 9 WAR 395; *Daniels v Anderson* (1995) 13 ACLC 614; *Re Barings plc* [1998] BCC 583; and *Re Barings plc (No 5)* [1999] 1 BCLC 433.

diligence now required of directors within English and Australian company law in general.[100]

In English company law for instance, Sir Richard Scott VC's recent judgment in *Re Barings plc* marks a further advance towards the development of an objective standard of care and diligence upon directors of British companies,[101] and is to be welcomed. So too does Jonathan Parker J's more recent judgment in *Re Barings plc (No 5).*[102] Even though *Barings* and *Barings (No 5)* were both concerned with Company Directors Disqualification Act 1986 (UK) ('CDD Act') s6, *dicta* from their Lordships' judgments are of broader application and relevantly apply to the directors' duty to exercise care and diligence generally.

Insofar as Australian company law is concerned, four Australian cases call for brief consideration here. These cases are of considerable import for they enlivened the debate on corporate governance in Australia and served as catalysts for the adoption of a more robust approach by the Australian judiciary in raising levels of directorial responsibility and greater accountability.[103]

THE LATE 1980s AND THE EARLY 1990s: A NEW APPROACH?

As we will see in more detail in chapter seven of this book, the New South Wales Court of Appeal[104] in *Metal Manufacturers Ltd v Lewis,*[105] dismissed an appeal by Metal Manufacturers Ltd in respect to its claim under Companies Code s556 against a wife who was one of two directors of a family company. In a strong dissent, Kirby P endorsed the raising of levels of responsibility for directors in the light of the overall legislative scheme signified by s556. In Kirby P's view, the relevant companies legislation must be read contextually against its predecessor section and other relevant sections designed to instil a high sense of responsibility in directors in the discharge of their duties.[106] Kirby P went on to relevantly state that:

> The time has passed when directors and other officers can simply surrender their duties to the public and those with whom the corporation deals by washing their hands, with impunity, leaving it to one director or a cadre of directors or to a general manager to discharge their responsibilities for them.[107]

On the facts in *Metal Manufacturers*, however, the majority[108] found in the defendant's favour. It was not long, however, before Kirby P's views on this subject were again ventilated. This time, in the Victorian Supreme Court where they were given more credence; curiously in a remarkably similar fact situation. In *Statewide Tobacco Services Ltd v Morley,*[109] the defendant was not so lucky. Ormiston J, at first instance,

---

[100] Sievers A S, 'Farewell to the Sleeping Director – The Modern Judicial and Legislative Approach to Directors' Duties of Care, Skill and Diligence' (1993) 21 ABLR 111 at 112 *et seq.*
[101] [1998] BCC 583 at 586.
[102] [1999] 1 BCLC 433.
[103] Ipp D A, 'The diligent director' (1997) 18 Co Law 162 at 164.
[104] (Kirby P, Mahoney and McHugh JJA).
[105] (1987-1988) 13 ACLR 357.
[106] *Ibid* at 360.
[107] *Ibid.*
[108] (Mahoney and McHugh JJA).
[109] (1990) 2 ACSR 405.

distinguished the majority judgments of the New South Wales Court of Appeal in *Metal Manufacturers* and advocated a stricter approach to directorial responsibility. Ormiston J denounced ignorance as an excuse for accountability, although he acknowledged that directors need not have omniscience.[110] However, his Honour considered that whilst directors are entitled to delegate to others the preparation of accounts and the carrying on of the day-to-day affairs of the company, they must exercise a reasonable degree of diligence and honesty and, 'try to understand or discover sufficient of the company's financial affairs'.[111] On appeal,[112] the Victorian Full Court[113] endorsed Ormiston J's approach and dismissed the appeal.

The South Australian Full Court[114] in *Group Four Industries Pty Ltd v Brosnan*,[115] favoured Ormiston J's approach in *Statewide*. There, the Full Court distinguished the majority judgments of the New South Wales Court of Appeal in *Metal Manufacturers*, and adopted Kirby P's reasons in his dissenting judgment. The question whether a director has discharged his or her duties is, in Debelle J's view, to be determined objectively in each case against the background of the duties which the statute imposes, and what, in all the circumstances, the director should have been reasonably required to have known. Thus the steps which a director should take, 'to discharge this duty will vary from company to company.'[116]

Lastly, *Commonwealth Bank of Australia v Friedrich*[117] completes this brief discussion concerning the development of the duty upon directors of Australian companies to exercise care and diligence, as a by-product of actions brought against directors under the insolvent trading provisions of relevant Australian companies legislation.[118] Integral in this development, *Friedrich* is a significant Australian case responsible for raising the standard of care and diligence expected of directors of Australian companies. The circumstances which gave rise to this development of the law relating to directors' duties were calamitous. *Friedrich* was typical of many of the financial disasters which befell corporate Australia during the second half of the 1980s and the early 1990s, and which fuelled the Australian Government's push for widened legislative powers in order to combat errant directors; and, thus, played an important role in the amplification of Corporations Law s232(4).

Although judgment in *Friedrich* was not handed down until July 1991, its shock-waves, and those caused by similar collapses, had been felt much earlier. By the start of 1990, politicians across Australia were reeling from the effects of an agitated media and an angry public.[119] The Cain Government in Victoria, in particular, was savagely mauled by adverse public opinion.[120] Corporate disaster after corporate disaster

---

[110] *Ibid* at 431.

[111] *Ibid* at 432.

[112] (1992) 8 ACSR 305.

[113] (Crockett, Southwell and Hedigan JJ).

[114] (Matheson, Olsson and Debelle JJ).

[115] (1992) 8 ACSR 463.

[116] *Ibid* at 513 per Debelle J; see *State Government Insurance Corporation v Pollock* (1993) 11 ACSR 333 at 343 per Seaman J.

[117] (1991) 5 ACSR 115.

[118] Companies Code s556; and Corporations Law s592.

[119] E.g., in Western Australia, Laurie Connell's merchant bank Rothwells Ltd collapsed into provisional liquidation during November 1988 with losses estimated at $600m. But not before the Western Australian Government had poured $150m of taxpayers' money into several abortive rescue attempts.

[120] But not just as a result of *Commonwealth Bank of Australia v Friedrich* (1991) 5 ACSR 115, for the State of Victoria was home to, not only John Friedrich, but also such corporate luminaries as George Herscu, Christopher Skase, Abe Goldberg and Bill Farrow.

unfolded on a scale and magnitude not previously known in that State's history.[121] The deleterious effect was considerable, not only upon the Victorian economy, but the Australian economy overall. It took a long time to recover. This angst and the public outcry it generated was to ignite and activate political forces across Australia.

Those political forces in Canberra were determined to bring about a new era of corporate regulation in Australia without which, 'business in this country cannot prosper as it should, and investors, both at home and abroad, will lack the security and confidence that is essential to our future economic growth and well-being.'[122] None of this, of course, would have been lost on the Australian judiciary. It is considered that those days of financial ruination for so many provided the necessary catalyst for change in judges' chambers and courts across Australia; change which has since had a profound effect upon the raising of standards of directorial conduct throughout Australian boardrooms, 'in terms more closely reflecting contemporary attitudes.'[123]

It is suggested that against this background it was, therefore, inevitable that when Mr Eise in *Friedrich* reached his day of reckoning in the Victorian Supreme Court, that Tadgell J should find him accountable.[124] His Honour considered that the relevant standard must be understood and applied against the background of the whole of the statute, and the legal rules and equitable principles which govern directors' duties and their discharge.[125] In Tadgell J's view:

> What constitutes the proper performance of the duties of a director of a particular company will be dictated by a host of circumstances, including no doubt the type of company, the size and nature of its enterprise, the provisions of its articles ... the composition of its board and the distribution of work between the board and other officers.[126]

Tadgell J's remarks in *Friedrich*, while generally consistent with those of Ormiston J in *Statewide*, subtly extended the duty of directors by reducing the scope for subjective criteria and limiting possible avenues of escape by errant directors from personal liability. Thus, directors of Australian companies are expected to understand and keep abreast of their company's affairs.[127] In the light of what has been seen, it might be considered that Tadgell J displayed remarkable restraint.

It is instructive to now move forward to more recent Australian cases concerned with the duty upon directors of Australian companies to exercise care and diligence under

---

[121] Many of which were politically disastrous for Victorian premier John Cain. Not least of which was the case of Pyramid Building Society, where assurances given in February 1990 by his Government's Treasurer, Rob Jolly, and the Attorney-General, Andrew McCutcheon, as to the financial security of Pyramid proved hopelessly wrong when only 10 months later the Pyramid group collapsed into liquidation with group losses estimated at approximately $1bn.

[122] Commonwealth, House of Representatives, Parliamentary Debates, 8 November 1990 at 3669.

[123] *State of South Australia v Clark* (1996) 19 ACSR 606 at 627 per Perry J.

[124] Cf. *In re City Equitable Fire Insurance Company Ltd* [1925] 1 Ch 407 at 457 per Romer J, 'It is impossible not to feel some sympathy for the respondent directors, hoodwinked as they were by a fraudulent chairman and not receiving proper protection from the officials in whom they placed their trust.'

[125] (1991) 5 ACSR 115 at 125.

[126] *Ibid*; cf. Law Commission, *Company Directors: Regulating Conflicts of Interests and Formulating a Statement of Duties* HMSO, London, Cm 4436, 1999 at paras 5.19-5.20 and 5.38; note *Deputy Commissioner of Taxation v Austin* (1998) 16 ACLC 1555 at 1558-1560 per Madgwick J.

[127] (1991) 5 ACSR 115 at 126 per Tadgell J; note Sievers A S, 'The National Safety Council Case' (1991) 9 CSLJ 338 at 338.

Companies Code s229(2). As earlier alluded to in this chapter, insofar as Corporations Law s232(4) is concerned, it is still early days. The courts are busier than at any earlier time with Corporations Law cases. Given the lead time involved with complex commercial and corporate litigation in the Australian courts,[128] however, decisions directly on s232(4) will take a little time to achieve prolificacy;[129] although cases directly in point are starting to appear in the reports.[130] That being the case, this book is restricted in the main to an analysis of the more recent Companies Code s229(2) cases in this context, but relevant Corporations Law s232(4) cases are considered where possible.

In spite of this dearth of case-law specifically upon Corporations Law s232(4), comfort can be drawn from the fact that this line of cases continues to focus upon the raising of levels of directorial responsibility and accountability in keeping with previously stated Australian judicial, Government and Parliamentary intent. Furthermore, in keeping with the doctrine of *stare decisis*,[131] the few relevant s232(4) cases that are now reaching the reports are consistent with authority, and the Australian courts are using those earlier decisions under Companies Code s229(2) as the foundation for their deliberations upon the requisite standard of care and diligence applicable to the circumstances before them. Absent statutory intervention, it is not expected that any dramatic changes to the standard of care and diligence which presently prevails in Australian company law will emerge;[132] even though the Australian judiciary has a recent history of pre-empting Federal Parliament in this respect.[133]

RECENT CASES: A NEW ERA FOR DIRECTORS?

The next major step in the development of the law in this area was provided by Rogers CJ in *AWA Ltd v Daniels*,[134] whose decision swept away the adage ignorance is bliss,[135] which had served the 18th century, the 19th century and the early 20th century English, and relevantly Australian, directors so well. In the course of what can only be described as an impressive judgment, Rogers CJ, probably more so than any other Australian

---

[128] An affliction suffered by the English courts as well.

[129] Notwithstanding the introduction into some Australian jurisdictions of special commercial lists designed to facilitate the fast-tracking of significant commercial and corporate disputes towards an expedited hearing; cf. the Practice Direction (Civil Litigation: Case management) handed down by the Lord Chief Justice in the English High Court on 24 January 1995.

[130] E.g., *Australian Securities Commission v Forem-Freeway Enterprises Pty Ltd* (1998-1999) 30 ACSR 339; *ASC v Donovan* (1998) 28 ACSR 583; *Gamble v Hoffman* (1997) 15 ACLC 1314; and *Re Property Force Consultancy Pty Ltd* [1997] 1 Qd R 300.

[131] See Kidd C J F, 'Stare Decisis in Intermediate Appellate Courts Practice in the English Court of Appeal, the Australian State Full Courts, and the New Zealand Court of Appeal' (1978) 52 ALJ 274; and Muir G, 'Contract and Equity: Striking a Balance' (1985) 10 Adel LR 153 at 183; note *Nguyen v Nguyen* (1989) 91 ALR 161 at 177-178 per Dawson, Toohey and McHugh JJ; and *Maguire v Makaronis* (1995) V Conv R 66314 at 66329-66330 per Nathan J.

[132] In a line of authority which relevantly began with *Darvall v North Sydney Brick & Tile Co Ltd (No. 2)* (1989) 7 ACLC 659 through to the recent decision in *Daniels v Anderson* (1995) 13 ACLC 614.

[133] *Morley v Statewide Tobacco Services Ltd* (1992) 8 ACSR 305; *Commonwealth Bank of Australia v Friedrich* (1991) 5 ACSR 115; and *AWA Ltd v Daniels* (1992) 10 ACLC 933; note Explanatory memorandum, *Corporate Law Reform Bill 1992* CCH Australia Ltd, Sydney, 1992 at 25.

[134] (1992) 10 ACLC 933.

[135] Gray T, *Ode on a Distant Prospect of Eton College* (1747) The Concise Oxford Dictionary of Quotations (3rd ed), Oxford University Press, Oxford, 1993; note Editorial comment, 'Directors – true or false?' (1997) 18 Co Law 129 at 129.

judge in recent times, crystallized the general duties which directors owe to their Australian companies in accordance with modern day expectations; and in a form to meet complex commercial and corporate requirements. Rogers CJ enunciated the view that not only must directors obtain at least a general understanding of the company's business, and the effect that a changing economy may have on that business, but additionally they should, 'bring an informed and independent judgment to bear on the various matters that come to the Board for decision'.[136] In doing so, Rogers CJ applied the judicial seal to what commentators had been advocating for years.[137]

The facts in *Daniels* appear in the headnote and it will repay analysis to briefly set them out.[138] AWA Ltd ('AWA') was a long established Australian company involved *inter alia* in the manufacture, import and export of electronic and electrical products. With a view to hedging against fluctuations in foreign exchange rates, AWA appointed a foreign exchange manager. Before long that appointment, to all outward appearances, displayed a veneer of handsome dividends; but in truth, and in reality, led to a loss of $49.8m from foreign exchange transactions. AWA's auditors carried out two audits. On neither occasion was the full extent of the foreign currency manager's operations, the deficiencies in the controls over the foreign currency operations, or the existence of loans covering the foreign currency losses, brought to management's attention. AWA sued its auditors for negligence. By way of cross-claim, the auditors alleged that AWA's directors were guilty of contributory negligence.[139] The non-executive directors argued that directors could not be tortfeasors because they could not be sued for liquidated damages at law in negligence.[140] This, it was said, was because directors' negligence is not negligence at law, but simply refers to their fiduciary or statutory liability.[141] It was held that the auditors were liable to AWA.[142]

However, for the purposes of this book, the more interesting aspect of the case centres upon the finding that AWA's management was negligent by failing to: (i) establish a proper structure of internal controls;[143] (ii) maintain a proper system of records; (iii) adequately supervise the activities of the foreign exchange manager;[144] and (iv) act on the auditor's warning that internal controls were inadequate.[145] Interestingly, however, the non-executive directors were found not to be negligent.[146] They had relied, and were entitled to so rely, on AWA's management and the auditors. There was a division of function between the non-executive directors and the chief executive, and other senior management, which entitled them to have confidence in AWA's senior

---

[136] (1992) 10 ACLC 933 at 1012-1013; see *Vrisakis v Australian Securities Commission* (1992-1993) 9 WAR 395 at 451 per Ipp J (Malcolm CJ agreed); and *Australian Securities Commission v Gallagher* (1993) 11 ACLC 286 at 294-295 per Pidgeon J (Franklyn and Walsh JJ agreed).

[137] Sealy L S, 'The Director as Trustee' [1967] CLJ 83 at 100-102.

[138] See also Nolan R, 'Care and skill in Australia – Daniels v Anderson' (1996) 17 Co Law 89.

[139] Hence obliged to contribute as tortfeasors under Law Reform (Miscellaneous Provisions) Act 1946 (NSW) s5.

[140] Cf. *Gamble v Hoffman* (1997) 15 ACLC 1314 at 1325 per Carr J.

[141] Ford H A J and Austin R P, *Ford's Principles of Corporations Law* (6th ed) Butterworths Pty Ltd, Sydney, 1992 at 524; note *Kimberley Mineral Holdings Ltd v Triguboff* [1978] 1 NSWLR 364; and *In re Claridge House Ltd* (1981) 28 SASR 481.

[142] On appeal that finding was affirmed but damages were reduced: *Daniels v Anderson* (1995) 13 ACLC 614.

[143] Cf. Institute of Chartered Accountants in England & Wales, *Internal Control: Guidance for Directors on the Combined Code* Institute of Chartered Accountants in England & Wales, London, 1999; note *Financial Times*, 27 September 1999.

[144] Cf. Bradley C, 'Corporate Control: Markets and Rules' (1990) 53 MLR 170 at 178.

[145] In the result, damages were reduced by reason of AWA's contributory negligence.

[146] Affirmed *Daniels v Anderson* (1995) 13 ACLC 614 at 672 per Clarke and Sheller JJA.

management. Absent information from senior management to the contrary, the non-executive directors were entitled to believe that the auditors had detected nothing untoward. This issue of reliance upon others was a critical aspect of the case. The general rule is that directors are guilty of negligence only where the actions by an officer or committee result in losses which could have been detected and prevented by proper supervision.[147] In this regard, Rogers CJ reaffirmed the approach taken by Lord Hatherley LC in *The Overend & Gurney Company v Gibb*,[148] and by Romer J in *In re City Equitable Fire Insurance Company Ltd*,[149] and determined that:

> Reliance would only be unreasonable where the director was aware of circumstances of such a character, so plain, so manifest and so simple of appreciation that no person, with any degree of prudence, acting on his behalf, would have relied on the particular judgment information and advice of the officers.[150]

Given the commercial exigencies of business,[151] which demand an intelligent devolution of labour,[152] such an approach is not surprising. However, on 15 May 1995, the New South Wales Court of Appeal[153] in *Daniels v Anderson*[154] delivered judgment in the long-awaited appeal from Rogers CJ's judgment at first instance. The majority's joint judgment,[155] relevantly affirmed Rogers CJ's findings as to directorial negligence and generally reaffirmed the legal, equitable and statutory bases in support thereof. Significantly, however, the majority considered that Rogers CJ's approach to the extent which directors are justified in trusting and relying upon others, 'does not accurately state the extent of the duty of directors whether non-executive or not in modern company law.'[156] In this regard, Clarke and Sheller JJA resorted to United States' authority and concluded that directorial conduct is to be, 'ordinarily measured by reference to what the reasonable man of ordinary prudence would do in the circumstances.'[157] It was considered that a director has a responsibility to ensure that the nature of the duty, that he or she is called upon to perform, is clearly understood. At law, Clarke and Sheller JJA considered directors of Australian companies to be under a duty which, 'includes that of acting collectively to manage the company.'[158]

Hence, positive action is contemplated.[159] If we cast our minds back to the earlier cases concerning directors' qualifications, or rather lack thereof,[160] and the requirements

---

[147]   Cf. *Re Barings plc* [1998] BCC 583 at 586 per Sir Richard Scott VC.
[148]   (1872) LR 5 HL 480 at 486-487.
[149]   [1925] Ch 407 at 428.
[150]   (1992) 10 ACLC 933 at 1015; see *Norman v Theodore Goddard* [1992] BCC 14 at 16 per Hoffmann J; and *Biala Pty Ltd v Mallina Holdings Ltd* (1993) 11 ACSR 785 at 856-857 per Ipp J.
[151]   *In re City Equitable Fire Insurance Company Ltd* [1925] Ch 407 at 429 per Romer J.
[152]   *Dovey v Cory* [1901] AC 477 at 485-486 per the Earl of Halsbury LC.
[153]   (Clarke, Sheller and Powell JJA).
[154]   (1995) 13 ACLC 614.
[155]   (Clarke and Sheller JJA).
[156]   (1995) 13 ACLC 614 at 663.
[157]   *Ibid* at 665.
[158]   *Ibid* at 666; see *Re Barings plc (No 5)* [1999] 1 BCLC 433 at 488 per Jonathan Parker J; note *Re Westmid Packing Services Ltd* [1998] 2 All ER 124 at 130 per Lord Woolf MR (Waller and Robert Walker LJJ agreed).
[159]   Cf. *Fitzsimmons v R* (1997) 23 ACSR 355 at 358 per Owen J; and *Permanent Building Society v Wheeler* (1993-1994) 11 WAR 187 at 241 per Ipp J (Malcolm CJ and Seaman J agreed).

as to their attendance at board meetings and the like,[161] it is hardly surprising that the law has been so accommodating of the delegation by directors of their duties to others.[162] However, the implications of Clarke and Sheller JJA's judgment in *Daniels* are such that more will need to be done by directors to ensure that not only do they have an understanding of the company's business, but that they are kept regularly informed by those in whom they invest trust, and upon whom they rely.

The protean quality of the directors' duties to exercise care and diligence, therefore, continues to expand into areas not hitherto contemplated. This is as true in English company law as it is in Australian company law.[163] Clearly this is of considerable import to directors of British and Australian companies, as the degree of specialisation required in today's complex commercial and corporate world makes it impossible for even the best qualified people to satisfactorily perform tasks outside what is often the narrow parameter of their field of expertise. Thus Rogers CJ's judgment, as amplified by Clarke and Sheller JJA, in *Daniels* has introduced into the Australian commercial and corporate sector a new era of responsibility for those who manage and control Australian companies. The same can now be said for those who manage and control British companies.[164] The significance of Rogers CJ's decision, and the manner in which the higher courts have embraced it, cannot be put too highly.[165]

Whilst the implications of the New South Wales Court of Appeal's decision in *Daniels* will take some time to settle, it appears that there are no earth-shattering revelations to be found within it. Put in its simplest form, the Court of Appeal has done little more than apply a traditional mix of principles which have long simmered in chancery's cauldrons, but have been too infrequently ladled out in either English or Australian company law. It is the mere application of tenets for so long ignored, by judges more interventionist than their predecessors, that has captured the imagination and created all the attention. And, why not? The ease with which directors of British and Australian companies had, in recent times, flouted what many saw as their responsibilities was being increasingly questioned. We all knew it was wrong, but until Rogers CJ took up the cudgels and adopted the stand he did, too many members of the

---

cont.

160 Trebilcock M J, 'The Liability of Company Directors for Negligence' (1969) 32 MLR 499 at 502; and Gower L C B, *Gower's Principles of Modern Company Law* (5th ed) Sweet & Maxwell Ltd, London, 1992 at 146.

161 *Vrisakis v Australian Securities Commission* (1992-1993) WAR 395 at 405 per Malcolm CJ; cf. *In re City Equitable Fire Insurance Company Ltd* [1925] Ch 407 at 444 per Romer J; note Menzies D, 'Company Directors' (1959) 33 ALJ 156 at 156; Harper J B and Browne A A, 'The Duties and Liabilities of a Director in 1973' (1973) 47 ALJ 447 at 451-452; and Malcolm D, 'Directors' Duties: The Governing Principles' in Ramsay I M (ed), *Corporate Governance and the Duties of Company Directors* The Centre for Corporate Law and Securities Regulation, University of Melbourne, Parkville, 1997 at 76.

162 Trebilcock M J, 'The Liability of Company Directors for Negligence' (1969) 32 MLR 499 at 506-508; see *In re Denham & Co* (1884) 25 Ch D 752; and *In re New Mashonaland Exploration Company* [1892] 3 Ch 577.

163 E.g., *Norman v Theodore Goddard* [1992] BCC 14 at 15 per Hoffmann J; *Re D'Jan of London Ltd* [1993] BCC 646 at 648-649 per Hoffmann LJ; *Vrisakis v Australian Securities Commission* (1992-1993) 9 WAR 395 at 451 per Ipp J (Malcolm CJ agreed); *Daniels v Anderson* (1995) 13 ACLC 614 at 662 per Clarke and Sheller JJA; *Androvin v Figliomeni* (1996) 14 ACLC 1461 at 1470 per Owen J (Kennedy and Franklyn JJ agreed); and *Re Barings plc* [1998] BCC 583 at 586 per Sir Richard Scott VC.

164 *Re Barings plc (No 5)* [1999] 1 BCLC 433 at 488 per Jonathan Parker J.

165 In the process, Rogers CJ foreclosed on Ford's assertion the previous year that, 'There is no judicial acceptance yet that the common law tortious duty of care involved in the tort of negligence applies to non-executive directors': Ford H A J and Austin R P, *Ford's Principles of Corporations Law* (6th ed) Butterworths Pty Ltd, Sydney, 1992 at 524.

Australian judiciary, and probably the English as well, blindly reached for shibboleths no longer in step with modern expectations. By entering the fray in this way, Rogers CJ has encouraged other judges to do likewise. *A fortiori* the approach taken by Clarke and Sheller JJA in the Court of Appeal in raising further the requirements of directorial responsibility and greater accountability in Australian company law; an approach which is now receiving recognition in English company law as well.[166]

Ultimately, the reticence traditionally displayed by the Australian judiciary, inherited no doubt from the English judiciary,[167] will evaporate in favour of judges who are more interventionist in outlook and who are willing to adopt more of a no-nonsense approach to their work.[168] A good illustration of the Australian courts' more robust and pragmatic approach to the interpretation of directors' duties was supplied by the Full Federal Court of Australia[169] in *Cummings v Claremont Petroleum NL*,[170] a case which reveals an all too familiar fact situation and is representative of the low points favoured by some directors within corporate Australia during the boom and bust days of the late 1980s where scant regard was had to ethics and, 'greed was good'.[171] The facts in *Claremont* appear in the headnote and were briefly these. Fuller and Cummings were strong personalities. As directors of Claremont Petroleum NL ('Claremont') their decisions invariably held sway.[172] They decided that Claremont should appoint their private consulting firms as consultants to Claremont as well as provide them personally with luxury motor vehicles.[173] Agreements reflecting those matters were duly executed.[174] Subsequently, further appointments were made to the board as a result of which the consultancy agreements were terminated, the motor vehicles offered for sale to Fuller and Cummings, and termination payments made in lieu thereof.[175]

In the proceedings which followed, Claremont sought to recover the termination payments on the basis that *inter alia* the transactions which gave rise to those payments, including the execution of the initial agreements, were the result of breaches by Fuller and Cummings of their statutory obligations to act with reasonable care and dili-

---

[166] Davies P L, *Gower's Principles of Modern Company Law* (6th ed) Sweet & Maxwell Ltd, London, 1997 at 643-644; note *Re Barings plc (No 5)* [1999] 1 BCLC 433 at 488 per Jonathan Parker J.

[167] Sealy L S, 'The Director as Trustee' [1967] CLJ 83 at 100.

[168] Finch V, 'Company Directors: Who Cares about Skill and Care?' (1992) 55 MLR 179 at 189 *et seq.*

[169] (Burchett, French and Lee JJ).

[170] (1993) 11 ACLC 125; note Baxt R, case note (1993) 67 ALJ 694 at 696.

[171] Commonwealth, House of Representatives, Parliamentary Debates, 29 May 1991 at 4213; cf. *The Australian*, 21 April 1997: 'Directors are more accountable to shareholders and they are more accountable to the community through beefed-up corporate laws ... Yet the public is entitled to remain a little sceptical that company directors have learned the lesson that greed is not necessarily good.'

[172] Cf. *Glavanics v Brunninghausen* (1996) 19 ACSR 204 at 208 per Bryson J, 'These were one man companies and they were not carried on in ways which respected or conformed to the organisational structure which the law requires companies to have.'

[173] Cf. *Gluckstein v Barnes* [1900] AC 240 at 258 per Lord Robertson, 'the company was paralyzed so far as vigilance and criticism were concerned; for the board-room was occupied by the enemy.'

[174] Breathing life into prophetic remarks made nearly a decade earlier by Bishop W and Prentice D D, 'Some Legal and Economic Aspects of Fiduciary Remuneration' (1983) 46 MLR 289 at 305, 'there will be the danger that trustees will have an incentive to write overly self-serving remuneration clauses in the trust deed.'

[175] Cf. *Neptune (Vehicle Washing Equipment) Ltd v Fitzgerald (No. 2)* [1995] BCC 1000 at 1017 per A G Steinfeld QC (sitting as a deputy Chancery Judge), 'It is difficult to conceive of a matter where there is a greater conflict between the personal interest of a director and his duties to the company than the question of whether the director's own service contract should be terminated and, if so, upon what terms as to compensation.'

gence.[176] At first instance, Wilcox J acceded to Claremont's application. On appeal, the Full Federal Court of Australia agreed. In the course of delivering their joint judgment, Burchett, French and Lee JJ denounced the, 'extraordinary conduct by Fuller and Cummings as executive directors' in failing to include provisions under which Claremont could terminate their contracts upon reasonable notice. In their Honours' view:

> Such conduct demonstrated a lack of exercise of a reasonable degree of care and diligence in the exercise of powers and discharge of duties as directors and could be taken into account with other evidence in deciding whether as directors Fuller and Cummings had at all times acted honestly in the exercise of those powers or had made improper use of their position as directors to gain an advantage for themselves or each other.[177]

In so ruling, the Full Federal Court of Australia in *Claremont* reiterated that the foundation of the statutory provision is the fiduciary relationship between directors and their company. The Full Court considered that the object of Companies Code s229, 'is to provide a statutory restatement of that duty with attached criminal responsibility and a statutory right for a company to recover compensation for loss or damage suffered as a result of a breach of that duty.'[178] In concluding its judgment, the Full Court sounded a strong message to corporate Australia and, in doing so, erected further signposts to foster in the judiciary a more robust and pragmatic approach to the interpretation of the duty upon directors of Australian companies to exercise care and diligence. The Full Court considered that given:

> [The] breadth of the right developed by the doctrines of equity to recover losses caused by and gains received by errant fiduciaries there is no reason to expect that the scope of s229 was intended to be in any way narrow or limited.[179]

This approach was fortified by the Western Australian Full Court[180] in *Australian Securities Commission v Gallagher*,[181] where a non-executive director was alleged to have breached Companies Code s229(2) by failing to exercise a reasonable degree of care and diligence in the exercise of his powers and the discharge of his duties. Gallagher was a casualty of the failed merchant bank Rothwells Ltd. In the Court of Petty Sessions the complaint was dismissed. On appeal, the Full Court affirmed the magistrate's decision. In doing so, Pidgeon J,[182] after reviewing the authorities and examining the decisions of Rogers CJ in *Daniels* and Romer J in *City Equitable* in particular, noted that in such cases the court is called upon to exercise a value judgment

---

[176] Companies Code s229(2).
[177] (1993) 11 ACLC 125 at 134; interestingly, the Full Federal Court of Australia (at 133) felt, 'The receipt of an unreasonable level of benefit may help to show that directors have failed to act honestly or failed to exercise a reasonable degree of care and diligence'. *Quaere* whether the rationale behind such *dictum* might have had a subliminal effect upon their Lordships' decision in *Guinness Plc v Saunders* [1990] 2 AC 663 to order repayment by Ward of £5.2m for services rendered.
[178] (1993) 11 ACLC 125 at 135 *per curiam*.
[179] *Ibid.*
[180] (Pidgeon, Franklyn and Walsh JJ).
[181] (1993) 11 ACLC 286; see *Biala Pty Ltd v Mallina Holdings Ltd* (1993) 11 ACSR 785 at 856 per Ipp J.
[182] (Franklyn and Walsh JJ agreed).

in order to determine whether directors have met the requisite standard of care and diligence. In Pidgeon J's judgment:

> [The] test is basically an objective one in the sense that the question is what an ordinary person, with the knowledge and experience of the defendant, might be expected to have done in the circumstances if he was acting on his own behalf.[183]

When dealing with the statutory duty prescribed by Companies Code s229(2), Pidgeon J in *Gallagher* considered that a non-executive director should take reasonable steps to place himself in a position so as, 'to be sufficiently informed of the company's affairs to make an independent judgment and to take appropriate action if matters did not proceed as matters should proceed' in such a company.[184]

Less than six months later, a differently constituted Western Australian Full Court,[185] in *Vrisakis v Australian Securities Commission*,[186] exonerated Vrisakis, another casualty of the failed merchant bank Rothwells Ltd,[187] from any wrongdoing under Companies Code s229(2). In the course of quashing the conviction, Ipp J[188] adopted Lord Hatherley LC's classical *dictum* in *Overend*,[189] and endorsed Pidgeon J's test in *Gallagher*;[190] as being apposite to the determination of whether or not directors of Australian companies have exercised a reasonable degree of care and diligence in accordance with the requisite standard. Additionally, Ipp J expressed the view that s229(2) requires a reasonable degree of care and diligence, objectively determined, as the following extract from his Honour's judgment attests:

> [The] duty imposed by the section is to be objectively determined. However, the ambit of the duty and the standard of care required (ie the specific functions with which particular directors are charged, and what is required to be done so that those functions are properly carried out) depend on the particular circumstances. There is no uniform standard applicable. ... It has often been pointed out that the duties of a director differ from case to case and are dependent entirely on the circumstances. The term 'duties' in this sense refers to the tasks undertaken by directors, in dis-

---

[183]   (1993) 11 ACLC 286 at 294; see *In re City Equitable Fire Insurance Company Ltd* [1925] Ch 407 at 427-428 per Romer J; *Lagunas Nitrate Company v Lagunas Syndicate* [1899] 2 Ch 392 at 435 per Lindley MR; and *National Companies and Securities Commission v Hurley* (1995) 13 ACLC 1635 at 1641-1643 per Scott J (Malcolm CJ and Anderson J agreed).

[184]   (1993) 11 ACLC 286 at 295-296; cf. *Daniels v Anderson* (1995) 13 ACLC 614 at 663-666 per Clarke and Sheller JJA.

[185]   (Malcolm CJ, Rowland and Ipp JJ).

[186]   (1992-1993) 9 WAR 395; see *Biala Pty Ltd v Mallina Holdings Ltd* (1993) 11 ACSR 785 at 856 per Ipp J.

[187]   *National Companies and Securities Commission v Hurley* (1995) 13 ACLC 1635 provides yet another example.

[188]   (Malcolm CJ agreed).

[189]   (1872) LR 5 HL 480 at 486-487.

[190]   (1993) 11 ACLC 286 at 294; see *In re City Equitable Fire Insurance Company Ltd* [1925] Ch 407 at 427-428 per Romer J; *Lagunas Nitrate Company v Lagunas Syndicate* [1899] 2 Ch 392 at 435 per Lindley MR; and *National Companies and Securities Commission v Hurley* (1995) 13 ACLC 1635 at 1641-1643 per Scott J (Malcolm CJ and Anderson J agreed).

charge of their office as such, and does not connote the duty to exercise a reasonable degree of care and diligence, the content of which remains constant.[191]

It is instructive to now turn briefly to three recent cases which specifically invoke Corporations Law s232(4). These will suffice to demonstrate its application by the Australian courts in practice. The first is *Gamble v Hoffman*.[192] There, the Federal Court of Australia was concerned with winding-up proceedings brought against the directors of an insolvent company by its liquidator. The facts are taken from the headnote and were briefly these. Mr and Mrs Hoffman were the directors of Tallimba Pty Ltd ('Tallimba'), the only shareholders in Sunhaven Nominees Pty Ltd ('Sunhaven') and two of five guarantors of Sunhaven's liabilities under a ten year lease that it held. Sunhaven ceased trading 18 months into that lease. Sixteen months later, it negotiated a surrender of the lease in return for a payment to the lessor of $80,000. Sunhaven was then hopelessly insolvent. Accordingly, the Hoffmans caused Tallimba to draw its cheque in the sum of $80,000 which was then used to pay out the lessor. Six months later Tallimba went into liquidation.

The liquidator in *Gamble* brought proceedings against the Hoffmans under Corporations Law s598 seeking repayment of the $80,000. Pursuant to s598, the court can order a person who is guilty of fraud, negligence, default, breach of trust or breach of duty in relation to a company, to *inter alia* pay money to that company. The proceedings alleged that the Hoffmans had been guilty of all but fraud. Although the case only involved a small sum of money, it is nonetheless interesting for several legal principles which were discussed. The matter was heard before Carr J who ultimately found in the liquidator's favour and against the Hoffmans. Carr J relied upon *dicta* from *Daniels*[193] and *Vrisakis*[194] in finding that the Hoffmans' conduct in causing Tallimba to make the payment fell short of their duty to take reasonable care in the performance of their office as directors. His Honour could find no benefit which Tallimba would derive from making that payment, particularly given Sunhaven's inability to repay those moneys.

Carr J found the Hoffmans guilty of negligence. He also considered them to be in breach of duty. Carr J found the Hoffmans' decision-making process, 'both objectively and in the light of their knowledge of the financial circumstances of Sunhaven',[195] to be wanting. In his Honour's judgment:

> They were in breach of their common law duty to exercise reasonable care. If there is a difference between that duty and the statutory duty imposed by s232(4) then I consider, for the same reasons as set out above, that they breached that statutory duty too.[196]

---

[191] (1992-1993) 9 WAR 395 at 451; see *Permanent Building Society v Wheeler* (1993-1994) 11 WAR 187 at 239-240 per Ipp J (Malcolm CJ and Seaman J agreed); and *National Companies and Securities Commission v Hurley* (1995) 13 ACLC 1635 at 1641-1643 per Scott J (Malcolm CJ and Anderson J agreed).

[192] (1997) 15 ACLC 1314.

[193] (1995) 13 ACLC 614 at 665-666 per Clarke and Sheller JJA.

[194] (1992-1993) 9 WAR 395 at 451 per Ipp J.

[195] (1997) 15 ACLC 1314 at 1323.

[196] *Ibid* at 1325.

In *ASC v Donovan*[197] the Federal Court of Australia held the directors of a company which sold growerships and quota for a fermented milk product to have breached Corporations Law s232(4). In short, the company was selling growerships and quota for substantial sums in order that the growers would produce a product for which there was then no market. The only purchaser for the product was the company. It could only finance the purchase of the product by selling more growerships and quota. Absent the establishment of an immediate real market for the product, Cooper J considered that the company was embarked upon a course which would lead to its insolvency. It was taking on financial obligations to purchase a product which it ultimately would not be able to discharge.[198] In Cooper J's judgment:

> Objectively, no person in the position of the respondents, with the knowledge the first respondent had and which the second respondent should have had, acting reasonably and exercising care and diligence, would have continued … selling growerships and quota to potential growers … In my view there is nothing in the material which makes the conduct of the directors, in allowing the company to continue to sell growerships and quota contrary to the expert advice which the company received, either reasonable or rational or conduct which satisfied the duty of care provided for in s232(4) … Absent a commercial market, to continue to sell growerships and quota was conduct in breach of the duty of care required by s232(4) … to be discharged by the respondents.[199]

Re Property Force Consultancy Pty Ltd[200] provides our third and final illustration of the application and efficacy of Corporations Law s232(4) in practice. There, the Queensland Supreme Court was faced with an application by the liquidator of a company seeking the recovery from one of two former directors of the proceeds of a cheque which was converted by the other former director, rather than being deposited into the company's bank account. Even though the cheque was converted by the other former director, it was deposited into their joint private bank account. As to s232(4), Derrington J had this to say:

> It follows the former s.229 … the object of the provision was to provide a statutory restatement of the fiduciary relationship between a company and its directors, attaching criminal responsibility for breach of that duty and providing a statutory right for the company to recover compensation for loss or damage suffered as a result of that duty[201] … This does not shed much light upon the present problem except to make it plain that all of the relevant circumstances of both the director and the company are to be taken into consideration in determining the standard of a reasonable person in that position.[202] More importantly, the section requires only the subjective elements of care and diligence but not the objective element of skill,

---

[197] (1998) 28 ACSR 583.
[198] *Ibid* at 600.
[199] *Ibid* at 601.
[200] [1997] 1 Qd R 300.
[201] *Cummings v Claremont Petroleum NL* (1993) 11 ACLC 125 at 135 *per curiam*.
[202] Cf. Law Commission, Company Directors: *Regulating Conflicts of Interests and Formulating a Statement of Duties* HMSO, London, Cm 4436, 1999 at paras 5.19-5.20 and 5.38.

though common law negligence,[203] including an element relating to skill,[204] would also seem to be available.[205]

In dismissing the liquidator's application, Derrington J considered that the respondent did not have notice of facts reasonably warning him of the true state of affairs, which facts would oblige him as a director to enquire and to prevent what happened. The respondent was not negligent in failing to ascertain that the cheque was the company's property in circumstances in which he had no reason to know anything about the obtaining of the company's cheque by his co-director nor to suspect, absent any indication to the contrary, that payment into their joint account had been improperly obtained. As such, and in the result, the respondent was not at fault.

The appeal in Derrington J's judgment in *Property Force*, however, lies in his Honour's treatment of the obligations upon a non-executive director outside his specific areas of expertise. Derrington J considered the respondent's value to the company to be in his management of its town planning and subdivision affairs for which he was an executive director only in respect of such matters. Even so, as Derrington J explained, this would not absolve the respondent of the ordinary duty of a non-executive director to have general supervision of the affairs of his company.[206] The following extract from Derrington J's judgment is of particular interest:

> His competence in his field was probably more useful in the directorate than any financial expertise, but he still had a general duty to pay attention to the company's affairs which might reasonably attract enquiry within his capacity, even outside the area of his expertise. He could not avoid responsibility simply by ignoring everything except the area of his speciality. In particular, if he had reason to suspect irregularity in the company's financial affairs, he was not entitled to ignore it, leaving it to the financial expert on the board, especially if the question involved some possible misconduct by that expert.[207]

These decisions upon Companies Code s229(2) and Corporations Law s232(4) are demonstrative of the way in which recent Australian judicial thinking is applied to the interpretation of the statutory duty upon directors of Australian companies to exercise care and diligence. There is a certain irony in the fact that two of Australia's top commercial and corporate judges, namely Malcolm CJ and Ipp J, who are perceived by the legal profession as being progressive, robust and interventionist, and whose judgments in this area of the law have been pre-eminent,[208] should revert to a 19th century standard first enunciated by Lord Hatherley LC in *Overend* over one century ago in order to refashion principles now considered applicable to resolving today's complex commercial and corporate disputes.[209] However, as we have seen from the

---

[203] Cf. *Vrisakis v Australian Securities Commission* (1992-1993) 9 WAR 395 at 407-408 per Malcolm CJ.
[204] Cf. Ipp D A, 'The diligent director' (1997) 18 Co Law 162 at 163.
[205] [1997] 1 Qd R 300 at 305-306.
[206] *Ibid* at 312.
[207] *Ibid.*
[208] E.g., *Vrisakis v Australian Securities Commission* (1992-1993) 9 WAR 395; *Permanent Building Society v Wheeler* (1993-1994) 11 WAR 187; and *National Companies and Securities Commission v Hurley* (1995) 13 ACLC 1635.
[209] (1872) LR 5 HL 480 at 486-487.

recent joint judgment of Clarke and Sheller JJA in *Daniels*, the application of these refashioned principles is very much with modern company law in mind.[210]

CIRCUMSTANCES OF THE SPECIFIC CASE

When one considers that directors, 'do not form a homogeneous category and necessary skills vary according to differences in the sizes and purposes of companies, complexities of management structures, reliance on expert advisers and roles of the particular directors',[211] it is not surprising that the Full Federal Court of Australia[212] in *Cummings v Claremont Petroleum NL*[213] determined to retain a flavour of subjectivity in its application of the statutory duty. Such an approach is consistent with the approach laid down by the High Court of Australia[214] in *Gould v The Mount Oxide Mines Ltd*,[215] over 80 years ago. It serves as a timely reminder that the diversity of companies and the variety of business endeavours do not allow of a uniform standard of care. And this, for the company lawyer, is the crux of the matter. *A fortiori* for the director himself or herself. The lack of a yardstick, universal in its application, and against which the standard of care and diligence required of the ubiquitous director can be measured, makes it very difficult to formulate meaningful guidelines to be followed in order to delimit unacceptable behaviour. This was recognised in 1916 by Isaacs and Rich JJ as the following extract from their joint judgment in *Gould* testifies:

> No rule of universal application can be formulated as to a director's obligation in all circumstances. The extent of his duty must depend on the particular function he is performing, the circumstances of the specific case, and the terms on which he has undertaken to act as a director.[216]

This philosophy and approach is as relevant to modern English company law as it is to modern Australian company law.[217] On this aspect of company law, it seems, there is no panacea. No quick fix. That which Isaacs and Rich JJ identified in *Gould* was encapsulated by the Senate Standing Committee on Legal and Constitutional Affairs when we were reminded that unlike recognised professions, there is no objective common law standard of the reasonably competent director given that the, 'activities of companies are diverse and consequently a range of skills and experience is useful on

---

[210] (1995) 13 ACLC 614 at 663.
[211] Finch V, 'Company Directors: Who Cares about Skill and Care?' (1992) 55 MLR 179 at 203; cf. *Deputy Commissioner of Taxation v Austin* (1998) 16 ACLC 1555 at 1558-1560 per Madgwick J.
[212] (Burchett, French and Lee JJ).
[213] (1993) 11 ACLC 125.
[214] (Griffith CJ, Isaacs and Rich JJ).
[215] (1916-1917) 22 CLR 490.
[216] *Ibid* at 531; similarly *Dovey v Cory* [1901] AC 477 at 488 per Lord Macnaghten; also *Commonwealth Bank of Australia v Friedrich* (1991) 5 ACSR 115 at 125 per Tadgell J, 'What constitutes the proper performance of the duties of a director of a particular company will be dictated by a host of circumstances'; cf. *Vrisakis v Australian Securities Commission* (1992-1993) 9 WAR 395 at 451 per Ipp J, 'The term "duties" in this sense refers to the tasks undertaken by directors, in discharge of their office as such, and does not connote the duties to exercise a reasonable degree of care and diligence, the content of which remains constant.'
[217] *Re Barings plc (No 5)* [1999] 1 BCLC 433 at 487 per Jonathan Parker J.

boards'.[218] Corporations Law s232(4) provides somewhat of a foil by introducing the concept of a reasonable person in a like position, in the corporation's circumstances.[219] The effect of this will be to engender more of an obligation on the part of directors to, 'take reasonable steps to place themselves in a position to guide and monitor the management of the company'[220] than hitherto has been the case; but implicit in the wording of the sub-section is a requirement upon the courts to continue this case by case approach.[221]

THE NEXT GENERATION

Notwithstanding the statutory obligation upon directors of Australian companies in contemporary Australian company law to exercise care and diligence, it should be remembered that Corporations Law s232(4) is just one part of the package of laws legislation which offers, 'for the first time in the nation's history a single and truly national regulatory regime'.[222] The whole, therefore, can be considered to be greater than the sum of its parts.[223] Consequently, an individual section, such as that presently under discussion, needs to be considered as part of an overall scheme which, so far as it impinges upon the duties of directors of Australian companies, has underlying policy implications.[224]

These policy implications are designed to restore public confidence in the corporate sector and, as such, extend beyond the black letter of the law. As we saw in chapter one of this book, directors of British and Australian companies wield enormous power and influence over corporate assets and also creditors, employees, shareholders and the like.[225] This can have serious ramifications for local, national and international communities. Thus, the modern corporate sector has a profound effect upon everyday life. The corporate sector possesses most of Australia's assets and employs most of its

---

[218] Senate Standing Committee on Legal and Constitutional Affairs, *Social and Fiduciary Duties and Obligations of Company Directors* AGPS, Canberra, 1989 at 28.

[219] The reference to 'in the corporation's circumstances' ought provide a timely reminder to directors that should their company be of questionable solvency then more might be expected of them so as not to jeopardise their company's creditors' interests: chapters six and seven.

[220] *AWA Ltd v Daniels* (1992) 10 ACLC 933 at 1012-1013 per Rogers CJ; affirmed *Daniels v Anderson* (1995) 13 ACLC 614 at 662 per Clarke and Sheller JJA.

[221] *Australian Securities Commission v Gallagher* (1993) 11 ACLC 286 at 294 per Pidgeon J (Franklyn and Walsh JJ agreed); note Callaway F H, Commentary to Sealy, 'The Enforcement of Partnership Agreements, Articles of Association and Shareholder Agreements' in Finn P D (ed), *Equity and Commercial Relationships* The Law Book Company Ltd, Sydney, 1987 at 119; and Malcolm D, 'Directors' Duties: The Governing Principles' in Ramsay I M (ed), *Corporate Governance and the Duties of Company Directors* The Centre for Corporate Law and Securities Regulation, University of Melbourne, Parkville, 1997 at 60.

[222] Commonwealth, House of Representatives, Parliamentary Debates, 8 November 1990 at 3669.

[223] *Cooper Brookes (Wollongong) Pty Ltd v The Commissioner of Taxation of the Commonwealth of Australia* (1980-1981) 147 CLR 297 at 304 per Gibbs CJ, 'Of course, no part of a statute can be considered in isolation from its context – the whole must be considered. If, when the section in question is read as part of the whole instrument, its meaning is clear and unambiguous, generally speaking "nothing remains but to give effect to the unqualified, words"'.

[224] Cf. *Capricorn Society Ltd v Linke* (1996) 14 ACLC 431 at 438-439 *per curiam*.

[225] *The Sunday Times*, 25 April 1999; cf. *The Australian*, 23 April 1997; note Department of Trade and Industry, *Modern Company Law: For a Competitive Economy* (a consultative document) HMSO, London, 1998 at para 3.7; and Department of Trade and Industry, *Modern Company Law: The Strategic Framework* HMSO, London, 1999 at para 5.1.14.

workers. Corporate England is to like effect.[226] Hence it is vital for economic, environmental, political and social reasons that the corporate sector, which is so crucial to the creation of national wealth,[227] has the confidence and support of the English and the Australian people.[228] The Australian judiciary, for example, has a critical role to play in maintaining this public confidence by interpreting the Australian Parliament's requirements, formulating sound principles in respect thereof, and then applying those principles in a direct and forthright way.

It is suggested that were the British Parliament to ultimately enact some of the Law Commission's recommendations in its recent report entitled *Company Directors: Regulating Conflicts of Interests and Formulating a Statement of Duties,*[229] then English company law, and the role of the English judiciary in that, would undoubtedly benefit from a close analysis of the Australian model which much of this chapter has been devoted to. *A fortiori* as the British Parliament statutorily intervenes more and more into English company law. Such statutory intervention on the part of the British Parliament is already on the increase with the enactment of the CDD Act and the IA 1986, as chapter eight of this book will demonstrate.

There is a perception in England and in Australia that the courts and the judges there could have done more to relieve against the harsh consequences occasioned by the events of the late 1980s and the early 1990s, which gave rise to many of the corporate crashes since consigned to company folklore. It was felt that some directors of British and Australian companies were lacking in responsibility and that not enough was being done by the English and the Australian judiciary to hold these directors accountable for their actions or inaction.[230] Some of the recent Australian decisions which have been considered in this chapter ameliorate this perspective and have, to a degree, raised levels of responsibility and accountability. In doing so, the Australian judiciary is restoring some sheen to its once tarnished image as it responds to the changes in public attitudes on corporate governance.[231] It is considered likely that with the passage of time, the gradual evolution of the standard pertaining to care and diligence, identified in the previous chapter of this book, will gain momentum: not only in corporate Australia, but in corporate England as well.[232] The implementation of Corporations Law

---

[226] Committee on the Financial Aspects of Corporate Governance, *The Report of the Committee on the Financial Aspects of Corporate Governance* Gee and Co Ltd, London, 1992 at 11; and HM Treasury, *Financial Services and Markets Bill: A Consultation Document, Part One* HMSO, London, 1998 at foreword.

[227] Senate Standing Committee on Legal and Constitutional Affairs, *Social and Fiduciary Duties and Obligations of Company Directors* AGPS, Canberra, 1989 at 7.

[228] Cf. *State Tax Commission of Utah v Aldrich* (1942) 316 US 174 at 192 per Jackson J.

[229] Law Commission, Company Directors: *Regulating Conflicts of Interests and Formulating a Statement of Duties* HMSO, London, Cm 4436, 1999 at paras 4.48, 5.19-5.20 and 5.38.

[230] Cf. *Re Kaytech International plc* [1999] BCC 390 at 403 per Robert Walker LJ (Stuart-Smith and Thorpe LJJ agreed); and *Re Brian D Pierson (Contractors) Ltd* [1999] BCC 26 at 55 per Hazel Williamson QC (sitting as a deputy High Court Judge).

[231] Farrar J H, 'Corporate Governance, Business Judgement and the Professionalism of Directors' (1993) 6 CBLJ 1 at 2; and Whincop M J, 'An Economic Analysis of the Criminalisation and Content of Directors' Duties' (1996) 24 ABLR 273 at 277 and 291.

[232] E.g., *Norman v Theodore Goddard* [1992] BCC 14 at 15 per Hoffmann J; *Re D'Jan of London Ltd* [1993] BCC 646 at 648-649 per Hoffmann LJ; V*risakis v Australian Securities Commission* (1992-1993) 9 WAR 395 at 451 per Ipp J (Malcolm CJ agreed); *Daniels v Anderson* (1995) 13 ACLC 614 at 662 per Clarke and Sheller JJA; *Androvin v Figliomeni* (1996) 14 ACLC 1461 at 1470 per Owen J (Kennedy and Franklyn JJ agreed); and *Re Barings plc* [1998] BCC 583 at 586 per Sir Richard Scott VC.

s232(4) within Australian company law has laid the foundation for that further development.

It is worth noting that Corporations Law s232(11) preserves the position at common law.[233] That sub-section expressly permits the continued development of independent, yet parallel, legal and equitable duties which oblige directors of Australian companies to exercise care and diligence. Unquestionably, these duties survive to the present; and actions continue to be maintained in respect to both, independently of statute.[234] Irrespective of whether the claim is legal or equitable, the test is the same.[235] That test, as stated earlier in *Australian Securities Commission v Gallagher*[236] and *Vrisakis v Australian Securities Commission*,[237] is derived from *The Overend & Gurney Company v Gibb*[238] and *In re City Equitable Fire Insurance Company Ltd*;[239] and, to all intents and purposes, accords with the statutory position. But the remedies, which will be considered in chapter nine of this book, do differ.[240] Significantly, the nature of the remedies sought is inevitably the determinative factor in whether legal, equitable or statutory relief is sought.[241] But, within that context, there exists the uniform aim in English and Australian company law of raising standards of directorial responsibility and accountability in keeping with equity's long-standing tradition of intervention in the activities of directors, in the cause of exacting high standards of business morality and ethical conduct.[242] The philosophy underlying, and the rationale behind, Corporations Law s232(4) is complementary to, and accords with, this tradition.

Menzies oft quoted prophecy that, 'what is in general expected of directors will tend to become the measure of what is required of them',[243] has become self-fulfilling. In reference to this observation, Tadgell J in *Commonwealth Bank of Australia v Friedrich*, noted that this has been borne out over the years and that as the complexity of commerce has gradually intensified:

> [The] community has of necessity come to expect more than formerly from directors whose task it is to govern the affairs of companies ... In response, the parliaments and the courts have found it necessary in legislation and litigation to refer to the

---

[233] Cf. *The Governor and Company of the Bank of England v Vagliano Brothers* [1891] AC 107 at 144-145 per Lord Herschell.

[234] *Permanent Building Society v Wheeler* (1993-1994) 11 WAR 187; note *Daniels v Anderson* (1995) 13 ACLC 614 at 665 per Clarke and Sheller JJA; and *Gamble v Hoffman* (1997) 15 ACLC 1314 at 1325 per Carr J.

[235] *Permanent Building Society v Wheeler* (1993-1994) 11 WAR 187 at 240 per Ipp J (Malcolm CJ and Seaman J agreed); note *Gamble v Hoffman* (1997) 15 ACLC 1314 at 1325 per Carr J.

[236] (1993) 11 ACLC 286.

[237] (1992-1993) 9 WAR 395.

[238] (1872) LR 5 HL 480 at 486-487 per Lord Hatherley LC.

[239] [1925] Ch 407 at 428 per Romer J.

[240] Doyle J J, Commentary to Kearney, 'Accounting for a Fiduciary's Gains in Commercial Contexts' in Finn P D (ed), *Equity and Commercial Relationships* The Law Book Company Ltd, Sydney, 1987 at 212-214; and Davidson I E, 'The Equitable Remedy of Compensation' (1982) 13 Melb ULR 349 at 352 *et seq*; note *McKenzie v McDonald* [1927] VLR 134.

[241] *Castlereagh Motels Ltd v Davies-Roe* (1966) 67 SR (NSW) 279 at 285-286 per Jacobs and Asprey JJA; note Finn P D, 'The Fiduciary Principle' in Youdan T G (ed), *Equity, Fiduciaries and Trusts* The Law Book Company Ltd, Toronto, 1989 at 56.

[242] Finn P D, *Fiduciary Obligations* The Law Book Company Ltd, Sydney, 1977 at 1.

[243] Menzies D, 'Company Directors' (1959) 33 ALJ 156 at 164.

demands made on directors in more exacting terms than formerly; and the standard of capability required of them has correspondingly increased.[244]

The aim and effect of partial codification under Corporations Law s232(4) has been to take these matters into account and to restructure the duty upon directors of Australian companies to exercise care and diligence as part of a determined push by the Australian Government for increased levels of responsibility, accountability and corporate governance overall.[245] In the process, a more robust and interventionist approach, which has been recently witnessed from certain members of the Australian judiciary,[246] has been endorsed at the expense of more traditional approaches. These approaches are gradually being imported into English company law as well,[247] as the English judiciary resorts more and more to the objective test, at the expense of the subjective test, by moving away from, 'the low standards of skill and diligence required of directors by the nineteenth-century judges.'[248] The recent judgments of Sir Richard Scott VC in *Re Barings plc*[249] and Jonathan Parker J in *Re Barings plc (No 5)*,[250] for example, are a testament to that.

In the continued quest for higher standards this approach will become the norm, rather than the exception, as English and Australian judges take a more commercial and pragmatic approach to the duties owed by directors of British and Australian companies,[251] in keeping with the business community's expectations.[252] This trend will be as evident, if not more so, in chapters four and five of this book when we come to consider, for example, the way in which the English and the Australian judiciary are reassessing the proper purposes doctrine. In doing so, the English and the Australian judiciary are tending to favour the promotion of commercial certainty, tempered with a degree of commercial pragmatism,[253] in the light of the business community's expectations,[254] in order to resolve today's complex commercial and corporate

---

[244] (1991) 5 ACSR 115 at 126.

[245] See Prentice D D and Holland P R J, *Contemporary Issues in Corporate Governance* Oxford University Press, Oxford, 1993; Committee on the Financial Aspects of Corporate Governance, *The Report of the Committee on the Financial Aspects of Corporate Governance* Gee and Co Ltd, London, 1992; Farrar J H, 'Corporate Governance, Business Judgement and the Professionalism of Directors' (1993) 6 CBLJ 1; Whincop M J, 'An Economic Analysis of the Criminalisation and Content of Directors' Duties' (1996) 24 ABLR 273; and Stapledon G P, *Institutional Shareholders and Corporate Governance* Clarendon Press, Oxford, 1996.

[246] In a line of authority which relevantly began with *Darvall v North Sydney Brick & Tile Co Ltd (No. 2)* (1989) 7 ACLC 659 through to the recent decision in *Daniels v Anderson* (1995) 13 ACLC 614.

[247] Davies P L, *Gower's Principles of Modern Company Law* (6th ed) Sweet & Maxwell Ltd, London, 1997 at 643; note *Re Barings plc (No 5)* [1999] 1 BCLC 433 at 488 per Jonathan Parker J.

[248] Davies P L, *Gower's Principles of Modern Company Law* (6th ed) Sweet & Maxwell Ltd, London, 1997 at 656.

[249] [1998] BCC 583 at 586.

[250] [1999] 1 BCLC 433.

[251] Malcolm D, 'Directors' Duties: The Governing Principles' in Ramsay I M (ed), *Corporate Governance and the Duties of Company Directors* The Centre for Corporate Law and Securities Regulation, University of Melbourne, Parkville, 1997 at 60, 78 and 80.

[252] Baxt R, 'The Role and Responsibilities of Nominee Directors in a Contested Takeover' a paper presented at the Corporate Law Workshop, conducted by the Business Law Section of the Law Council of Australia, Melbourne, October 1993 at 66.

[253] *Gray Eisdell Timms Pty Ltd v Combined Auctions Pty Ltd* (1995) 13 ACLC 965 at 974 per Young J; cf. Muir G, 'Contract and Equity: Striking a Balance' (1985) 10 Adel LR 153 at 183, 'But pragmatism must not always triumph over principle'.

[254] *Equiticorp Finance Ltd v Bank of New Zealand* (1993) 11 ACLC 952 at 1019 per Clarke and Cripps JJA.

disputes.[255] It can be argued, therefore, that the old values and traditions are no longer enough, and that a fresh approach is required to the complex and challenging topic of directors' duties in modern company law. This will have profound implications for directors of British and Australian companies of the 21st century.

---

[255] E.g., *Equiticorp Finance Ltd v Bank of New Zealand* (1993) 11 ACLC 952; *Bishopsgate Investment Management Ltd v Maxwell (No. 2)* [1994] 1 All ER 261; *Mallina Holdings Ltd v Biala Ltd* (1994) 15 ACSR 1; and *Daniels v Anderson* (1995) 13 ACLC 614; see Sealy L S, 'Directors' "Wider" Responsibilities – Problems Conceptual, Practical and Procedural' (1987) 13 MULR 164 at 169; and Sealy L S, '"Bona Fides" and "Proper Purposes" in Corporate Decisions' (1989) 15 MULR 265 at 265.

4

Directors' Fiduciary Duties to Act in Good Faith and for Proper Purposes

INTRODUCTION

It will be recalled from chapter one of this book that the leading textbooks on English and Australian company law treat directors as being subject to two broad duties; namely, to act honestly and in good faith on the one hand, and to exercise care and diligence on the other hand.[1] The broader of the two duties is the duty to act honestly and in good faith; itself a broad category encompassing a myriad of sub-categories each stemming from the principal duty to act in good faith.[2] To act honestly and in good faith might be described as tautologous or, at the very least, synonymous.[3] According to the view favoured by Ford in his fourth edition, the duty to act in good faith, 'can also be stated as a duty to act "honestly" using that word in a wide sense.'[4]

For the purposes of this book, to act honestly, in good faith and *bona fide* are considered to be different ways of expressing the one duty: each can be treated as being synonymous and interchangeable with the other. This is a view which accords with various dictionary meanings,[5] and one which prevails throughout the authorities.[6] The intricacies and complexities associated with this duty will soon unfold when we

---

[1] Ford H A J, Austin R P and Ramsay I M, *Ford's Principles of Corporations Law* (9th ed) Reed International Books Australia Pty Ltd, Sydney, 1999 at paras 8.070 and 8.200-8.355; Davies P L, *Gower's Principles of Modern Company Law* (6th ed) Sweet & Maxwell Ltd, London, 1997 at 598-599; Ford H A J and Austin R P, *Ford's Principles of Corporations Law* (6th ed) Butterworths Pty Ltd, Sydney, 1992 at 430, 487 *et seq* and 524 *et seq*; Palmer F B, *Palmer's Company Law* (25th ed) Sweet & Maxwell Ltd, London, 1992 at paras 8.406 and 8.501 *et seq*; Farrar J H, Furey N E, Hannigan B M and Wylie P, *Farrar's Company Law* (3rd ed) Butterworth & Co (Publishers) Ltd, London, 1991 at 380; and Pennington R R, *Company Law* (6th ed) Butterworth & Co (Publishers) Ltd, London, 1990 at 583.

[2] Finn P D, *Fiduciary Obligations* The Law Book Company Ltd, Sydney, 1977 at 78 *et seq*.

[3] Sealy L S, '"Bona Fides" and "Proper Purposes" in Corporate Decisions' (1989) 15 MULR 265 at 269; and Gower L C B, *Gower's Principles of Modern Company Law* (5th ed) Sweet & Maxwell Ltd, London, 1992 at 553-556.

[4] Ford H A J, *Principles of Company Law* (4th ed) Butterworths Pty Ltd, Sydney, 1986 at 381.

[5] Burke J, *Osborn's Concise Law Dictionary* (6th ed) Sweet & Maxwell Ltd, London, 1976 at 55; Ehrlich E, *Nil Desperandum: A Dictionary of Latin Tags and Useful Phrases* (1992 ed) BCA, London, 1992 at 62; and Allen R E, *The Concise Oxford Dictionary of Current English* (8th ed) BCA, London, 1990 at 125.

[6] *The Australian Metropolitan Life Assurance Company Ltd v Ure* (1923) 33 CLR 199 at 206 per Knox CJ.

introduce the proper purposes doctrine; long regarded as either synonymous with, or at least a manifestation of, lack of *bona fides*.[7]

It was argued in chapter one of this book that the English and the Australian judiciary must respond to modern day challenges brought about by the complexities of today's commercial and corporate world. It was there suggested that our courts need to rise to the challenge and develop new rules and principles or, at the very least, refashion traditional rules and principles, and apply them in a context more in keeping with today's requirements. This was recently recognised by the South Australian Supreme Court in *State of South Australia v Clark*, albeit there in the context of the directors' duty to exercise care and diligence, where Perry J observed that:

> Recent appellate decisions in Australia have gone a long way towards clarifying and re-expressing the duty of care owed by directors of a company vis á vis the company in terms more closely reflecting contemporary attitudes.[8]

The same argument has application to this chapter and the next, and will manifest itself when we come to consider the re-emergence of the proper purposes doctrine in particular. From chapters two and three of this book we have seen, and from chapters six, seven and eight of this book we will see, a change in circumstances, attitude and approach to the obligation upon directors of British and Australian companies to exercise care and diligence generally; and specifically, in the context of insolvency. In this chapter and the next a similar change in attitude and approach, especially by the Australian judiciary, will be in evidence when we consider the manner in which the English and Australian courts control the exercise by directors of corporate powers largely entrusted to them by their company's constitution and the relevant companies legislation.[9]

With the abolition in Australian company law of the *ultra vires* doctrine,[10] it has become commonplace to use corporate powers and directors' powers interchangeably in the context of misuse by directors of their powers.[11] While the scope for confusion has been removed, the proper distinction between the two was explained by the Queensland Full Court in *ANZ Executors & Trustee Co Ltd v Qintex Australia Ltd*.[12] For the purposes of this book, however, that distinction need not overly concern us for we are clearly dealing with directors' powers as, 'part and parcel of an established fiduciary relationship which is of a continuing nature.'[13] In this chapter and the next we are more concerned with the propriety of directors' decision-making which, traditionally, has been a matter solely for the *bona fide* subjective determination of the

---

[7] Lindgren K E, 'The Fiduciary Nature of a Company Board's Power to Issue Shares' (1971-1972) 10 UWALR 364 at 370.

[8] (1996) 19 ACSR 606 at 627.

[9] *Re Saul D Harrison & Sons plc* [1995] 1 BCLC 14 at 17-18 per Hoffmann LJ (Waite LJ agreed).

[10] Corporations Law ss124-125 (formerly Corporations Law ss160-162); cf. Companies Act 1985 (UK) ss35-35B.

[11] Ford H A J, Austin R P and Ramsay I M, *Ford's Principles of Corporations Law* (9th ed) Reed International Books Australia Pty Ltd, Sydney, 1999 at paras 12.060 and 12.100.

[12] (1990) 8 ACLC 980 at 988-989 per McPherson J (Lee and Mackenzie JJ agreed); see *Rolled Steel Products (Holdings) Ltd v British Steel Corporation* [1986] Ch 246 at 302-304 per Browne-Wilkinson LJ; and Sealy L S, '"Bona Fides" and "Proper Purposes" in Corporate Decisions' (1989) 15 MULR 265 at 271-274.

[13] Farrar J H, 'Abuse of Power by Directors' [1974] CLJ 221 at 222.

company's board. The English and Australian courts have been obstinate in their reluctance to intervene to overrule any such decision or to substitute their own view.[14]

However, as we have already seen from chapters two and three of this book, in Australian company law in particular, probably more so than in English company law, the whole topic of directors' duties in general has been seized of a new awareness over the last decade or so. With the pre-eminence of the proper purposes doctrine and its current resurgence in popularity with the English and Australian courts,[15] it is considered likely that the judiciary will become more and more involved in reviewing directors' decision-making.[16] *A fortiori* in the light of the abolition of the *ultra vires* doctrine in Australian company law, and its virtual abolition in English company law.[17] Given that, it is instructive to move on to explore the developments concerning the directors' duty to act in good faith and for proper purposes generally; and, specifically, the duty to act honestly in the light of partial codification in Australian company law.[18]

SOURCE OF DIRECTORS' POWERS

In English company law, a company derives its constitutional powers from its memorandum, its articles and the relevant companies legislation. So too in Australian company law. Although the enactment of the Company Law Review Act 1998 (Cth)[19] now means that in Australian company law the memorandum and articles of a company immediately before the commencement of the Act are taken together to make up the company's constitution after the Act's commencement.[20] Since 1 July 1998, therefore, in Australian company law a company's internal management may be governed by provisions of the Corporations Law that apply to the company as replaceable rules, by a constitution, or by a combination of both.[21] Insofar as this book is concerned, the company's articles remain significant. In English company law, and now to a lesser

---

[14] *Carlen v Drury* (1812) 1 V & B 154 at 158 per Lord Eldon; *Burland v Earle* [1902] AC 83 at 93 per Lord Davey; and *Shuttleworth v Cox Brothers and Company (Maidenhead) Ltd* [1927] 2 KB 9 at 23 per Scrutton LJ; note Sealy L S, 'The Director as Trustee' [1967] CLJ 83 at 100-101; and Editorial comment, 'Directors – true or false?' (1997) 18 Co Law 129 at 129.

[15] *Gambotto v WCP Ltd* (1995) 13 ACLC 342; *Kokotovich Constructions Pty Ltd v Wallington* (1995) 13 ACLC 1113; *Bishopsgate Investment Management Ltd v Maxwell (No. 2)* [1994] 1 All ER 261; and *Re BSB Holdings Ltd (No. 2)* [1996] 1 BCLC 155.

[16] A proposition consistent with Sealy's thesis that with the resurgence of the proper purposes test the more interventionist judges will lay bare the hitherto sanctity of the directors' subjective opinion when regard was more likely to be had to the *bona fides* test: Sealy L S, '"Bona Fides" and "Proper Purposes" in Corporate Decisions' (1989) 15 MULR 265.

[17] Birds J R, 'The demise of ultra vires?' (1986) 7 Co Law 203; Sealy L S, 'The bell tolls for ultra vires' (1986) 7 Co Law 90 at 90; Hannigan B M, 'The Reform of the Ultra Vires Rule' [1987] JBL 173 at 177-178; Editorial comment, 'Is Company Law Still in a Muddle?' (1991) 12 Co Law 42 at 42; Poole J, 'Abolition of the Ultra Vires Doctrine and Agency Problems' (1991) 12 Co Law 43; Ferran E, 'The Reform of the Law on Corporate Capacity and Directors' and Officers' Authority' (1992) 13 Co Law 124 and 177; and Davies P L, *Gower's Principles of Modern Company Law* (6th ed) Sweet & Maxwell Ltd, London, 1997 at 211-213.

[18] Companies Act 1958 (Vic) s107(1); Companies Act 1961 (Vic) s124(1); Companies Code s229(1); and Corporations Law s232(2).

[19] Added by Act No. 61 of 1998 and effective 1 July 1998.

[20] Corporations Law s1415; note Ford H A J, Austin R P and Ramsay I M, *Ford's Principles of Corporations Law* (9th ed) Reed International Books Australia Pty Ltd, Sydney, 1999 at paras 6.011, 6.020 and 6.090.

[21] Corporations Law s134.

extent in Australian company law, it remains that a company's articles largely regulate the company's internal government,[22] for it is they that largely empower directors.[23] In this regard, a company's articles are a *sine qua non* to the directors' empowerment as the following extract from Hoffmann LJ's judgment in *Re Saul D Harrison & Sons plc* amply testifies:

> The articles of association are just what their name implies: the contractual terms which govern the relationships of the shareholders with the company and each other. They determine the powers of the board and the company in general meeting and everyone who becomes a member of a company is taken to have agreed to them.[24]

In English company law, the Companies (Tables A to F) Regulations 1985 (SI 1985/805) made pursuant to Companies Act 1985 (UK) s8(5) set out in the time-honoured way a set of model regulations universally known as Table A. By virtue of Companies Act 1985 (UK) s8(2) these regulations have automatic application to companies limited by shares, yet permit exclusion or modification as required. Prior to 1 July 1998, similar considerations applied in Australian company law under the then Corporations Law s175 and Corporations Law Schedule 1 made pursuant to that. Since 1 July 1998, newly registered Australian companies will no longer be concerned with articles, but rather a table of replaceable rules.[25] Although existing companies may choose to retain them.[26] As matters presently stand, however, articles retain their significance for a great many Australian companies.

In this book we shall align ourselves with the English version of Table A which, in standard form, contemplates that the directors, rather than the general meeting, are empowered to manage the company and in doing so, 'may exercise all the powers of the company.'[27] It is with the exercise of these powers that this chapter and the next are largely concerned, absent any interference from the London Stock Exchange Ltd's Listing Rules in the case of listed public companies.[28] One can legitimately concentrate upon such powers when analysing the rules and principles applicable to directors' powers generally as most companies, according to Ford in his sixth edition, have an

---

[22] Ford H A J and Austin R P, *Ford's Principles of Corporations Law* (6th ed) Butterworths Pty Ltd, Sydney, 1992 at 56.

[23] *Guinness Plc v Saunders* [1990] 2 AC 663 at 689 per Lord Templeman (Lords Keith, Brandon and Griffiths agreed); see Hopkins J, case note [1990] CLJ 220; and *Bishopsgate Investment Management Ltd v Maxwell* [1993] BCC 120 at 136 per Chadwick J.

[24] [1995] 1 BCLC 14 at 17-18.

[25] Corporations Law s141; note Mitchell V, 'Company law reviews in Australia and the United Kingdom' (1999) 20 Co Law 98 at 99-100.

[26] Corporations Law s1415; note Ford H A J, Austin R P and Ramsay I M, *Ford's Principles of Corporations Law* (9th ed) Reed International Books Australia Pty Ltd, Sydney, 1999 at paras 6.011, 6.020 and 6.090.

[27] The Companies (Tables A to F) Regulations 1985 (SI 1985/805) Table A regulation 70; cf. Corporations Law Schedule 1 Table A regulation 66(1).

[28] This book ignores those Listing Rules, although clearly they are relevant: *Howard Smith Ltd v Ampol Petroleum Ltd* [1974] AC 821 at 835 per Lord Wilberforce; and *Flavel v Roget* (1990) 8 ACLC 237 at 243 per O'Loughlin; note Farrar J H, 'Abuse of Power by Directors' [1974] CLJ 221 at 223; and Davies P L, *Gower's Principles of Modern Company Law* (6th ed) Sweet & Maxwell Ltd, London, 1997 at vi, 'the Listing Rules of the Stock Exchange … have continued their move centre-stage as one of the leading sources of regulation of large companies.'

article like Table A regulation 66:[29] the Australian equivalent of Table A regulation 70. Relevantly, Table A regulation 70 provides that:

> Subject to the provisions of the Act, the memorandum and the articles and to any directions given by special resolution, the business of the company shall be managed by the directors who may exercise all the powers of the company. No alteration of the memorandum or articles and no such direction shall invalidate any prior act of the directors which would have been valid if that alteration had not been made or that direction had not been given. The powers given by this regulation shall not be limited by any special power given to the directors by the articles and a meeting of directors at which a quorum is present may exercise all powers exercisable by the directors.

The control of the company's business is usually the board's responsibility and it is well-settled that, under an article like regulation 70,[30] the shareholders in general meeting have no authority to interfere with the exercise of the directors' powers acting under such a provision.[31] Such powers typically include, 'borrowing money on behalf of the company, issuing debentures, issuing shares, making calls, receiving payments in advance of calls, causing shares to be forfeited, and filling casual vacancies on the board.'[32] But that is not to say that directors have *carte blanche* to do simply as they please, absent any consideration for propriety *per se* and directorial responsibility *vis-à-vis* their company's interests. The question which arises is: how does the law control the exercise by directors of British and Australian companies of these powers? In short, by treating directors as fiduciaries.[33]

DIRECTORS' FIDUCIARY DUTIES

Equity has a long-standing tradition of intervention in the activities of directors of British and Australian companies,[34] and has long sought to promote high standards of business morality and ethical conduct.[35] According to Wedderburn, 'the fiduciary duty is the main instrument which the Chancellor's courts bequeathed to today's judges by

---

[29] Ford H A J and Austin R P, *Ford's Principles of Corporations Law* (6th ed) Butterworths Pty Ltd, Sydney, 1992 at 432-434.

[30] Cf. Corporations Law s226A.

[31] *The Australian Metropolitan Life Assurance Company Ltd v Ure* (1923) 33 CLR 199 at 218 per Isaacs J; *ANZ Executors & Trustee Co Ltd v Qintex Australia Ltd* (1990) 8 ACLC 980 at 992 per McPherson J (Lee and Mackenzie JJ agreed); *Automatic Self-Cleansing Filter Syndicate Company Ltd v Cuninghame* [1906] 2 Ch 34; *Quin & Axtens Ltd v Salmon* [1909] AC 442; note Ferran E, 'The Reform of the Law on Corporate Capacity and Directors' and Officers' Authority' (1992) 13 Co Law 124 at 125 and 177; and Sealy L S, 'Company – Directors' Unconstitutional Acts' [1992] CLJ 229.

[32] Ford H A J, *Principles of Company Law* (4th ed) Butterworths Pty Ltd, Sydney, 1986 at 381; see Corporations Law s124.

[33] Bishop W and Prentice D D, 'Some Legal and Economic Aspects of Fiduciary Remuneration' (1983) 46 MLR 289 at 289.

[34] Finn P D, *Fiduciary Obligations* The Law Book Company Ltd, Sydney, 1977 at 1.

[35] *Aleyn v Belchier* (1758) 1 Eden 132 at 138 per Lord Northington, 'No point is better established than that, a person having a power, must execute it *bona fide* for the end designed, otherwise it is corrupt and void.'; see *Mills v Mills* (1938) 60 CLR 150 at 185 per Dixon J; and *Ngurli Ltd v McCann* (1953) 90 CLR 425 at 440 *per curiam*.

which to mark out certain basic social responsibilities of management.'[36] The English and Australian courts have always jealously guarded the fiduciary obligations owed by directors, and have sought to adapt those obligations to reflect changes over time. The rules of chancery, as Sealy notes, and the judges who administered them, were well-suited to enforcing standards of honesty and integrity.[37] Hence, in English and Australian company law there is an extensive body of case-law prescribing such standards and rules of conduct for directors.

These rules, according to Bishop, 'have been designed to operate prophylactically and place the maximum deterrent on a fiduciary benefiting from his position.'[38] Strict prophylactic rules designed to ensure certain minimum standards of behaviour from directors, backed up by onerous disclosure rules designed to prevent directors shrouding their transactions in secrecy.[39] For instance, the Earl of Halsbury LC in *Gluckstein v Barnes*, when faced with a scheme which generated a secret profit for the company's promoters, considered that the duty, 'is imposed by the plainest dictates of common honesty as well as by well-settled principles of common law.'[40] Thus by largely resorting to rules grounded in principles of honesty and integrity, the English and Australian courts were able to devise a means of controlling directors of British and Australian companies in the exercise of their powers.

By convention, four separate rules or equitable principles have emerged from the leading textbooks in an attempt to categorise directors' fiduciary duties;[41] notwithstanding Shepherd's caveat that company law is the most complex and difficult context in which fiduciary principles are applied, and that any attempt to build, 'tidy little theoretical cubbyholes in the corporate context is doomed to failure.'[42] These fiduciary duties prescribe that directors must: (i) act in good faith in what they believe to be the best interests of the company; (ii) not exercise the powers conferred upon them for purposes different from those for which they were conferred; (iii) not fetter their discretion as to how they shall act; and (iv) not, without the informed consent of the

---

[36] Wedderburn K W, 'The Social Responsibility of Companies' (1985) 15 Melb ULR 4 at 24.

[37] Sealy L S, '"Bona Fides" and "Proper Purposes" in Corporate Decisions' (1989) 15 MULR 265 at 265.

[38] Bishop W and Prentice D D, 'Some Legal and Economic Aspects of Fiduciary Remuneration' (1983) 46 MLR 289 at 309; see Jones G, 'Unjust Enrichment and the Fiduciary's Duty of Loyalty' (1968) 84 LQR 472 at 474 and 496; note *Midcon Oil & Gas Ltd v New British Dominion Oil Co Ltd* (1958) 12 DLR (2d) 705 at 716 per Rand J; and *Maguire v Makaronis* (1996-1997) 188 CLR 449 at 492 per Kirby J.

[39] Farrar J H, Furey N E, Hannigan B M and Wylie P, *Farrar's Company Law* (3rd ed) Butterworth & Co (Publishers) Ltd, London, 1991 at 379-380.

[40] [1900] AC 240 at 246.

[41] Ford H A J, Austin R P and Ramsay I M, *Ford's Principles of Corporations Law* (9th ed) Reed International Books Australia Pty Ltd, Sydney, 1999 at paras 8.070-8.160, 8.170-8.190, 8.200-8.280, 9.010-9.020 and 9.057-9.120; Davies P L, *Gower's Principles of Modern Company Law* (6th ed) Sweet & Maxwell Ltd, London, 1997 at 601; Ford H A J and Austin R P, *Ford's Principles of Corporations Law* (6th ed) Butterworths Pty Ltd, Sydney, 1992 at 430, 487 *et seq* and 524 *et seq*; Pennington R R, *Company Law* (6th ed) Butterworth & Co (Publishers) Ltd, London, 1990 at 583; Palmer F B, *Palmer's Company Law* (25th ed) Sweet & Maxwell Ltd, London, 1992 at 8.406 and 8.501 *et seq*; and Farrar J H, Furey N E, Hannigan B M and Wylie P, *Farrar's Company Law* (3rd ed) Butterworth & Co (Publishers) Ltd, London, 1991 at 380.

[42] Shepherd J C, *The Law of Fiduciaries* The Carswell Company Ltd, Toronto, 1981 at 347-348; Shepherd J C, 'Towards a Unified Concept of Fiduciary Relationships' (1981) 97 LQR 51 at 72; and Finn P D, *Fiduciary Obligations* The Law Book Company Ltd, Sydney, 1977 at 64 who regards directors as holding, 'the most complex fiduciary office'.

company, place themselves in a position in which their personal interests or duties to others are liable to conflict with their duties to the company.[43]

However, these categories should not be treated as exclusive, as in many respects they overlap with one another.[44] And, it is considered that there is no definite line of demarcation; such attempts at definition are often artificial and at times futile. Finn, for instance, would include each of the above four categories as sub-categories of the duty of good faith.[45] This chapter and the next will concentrate upon the first two categories; namely, the traditional company law doctrines of *bona fides* and proper purposes.[46] Both of these doctrines have application to the statutory duty in Australian company law to act honestly,[47] and are relevant in the context of the statutory remedy for oppression;[48] about which more will be said a little later in this chapter.

It is suggested that the treatment by the textbooks in this area of the law is both superficial and artificial. In categorising directors' fiduciary duties in this manner, the texts project a symmetry and design which to the practitioner may seem naive, or even academic.[49] For instance, as the learned editor of *The Company Lawyer* observes, directors are *inter alia* under a duty to:

> [Act] in good faith and to discharge their powers for a proper purpose. However, no matter how inspiring such grand principles may seem, they offer precious little guidance in resolving when a director should be held liable on the facts of specific cases.[50]

That observation cuts directly to the quick and reveals problems in this area of the law so often overlooked by the traditionalists. From the perspective of the practitioner, the academic and/or the businessman, this whole area of law to do with *bona fides* and proper purposes looks unpromising and is in a most unsatisfactory state. As a consequence, it is almost impossible to formulate guidelines of general application so as to delimit impropriety *vis-à-vis* directors' decision-making. Hence each case must, invariably, be considered on its own particular facts.[51]

This case by case approach is consistent with that laid down by the High Court of Australia in *Gould v The Mount Oxide Mines Ltd*,[52] over 80 years ago; yet is inconsis-

---

[43] Baxt R, 'Judges in their Own Cause: The Ratification of Directors' Breaches of Duty' (1978) 5 MULR 16 at 20-21; note *Bristol and West Building Society v Mothew* [1996] 4 All ER 698 at 712 per Millett LJ (Otton LJ agreed).

[44] Farrar J H, 'Abuse of Power by Directors' [1974] CLJ 221 at 221; and Lindgren K E, 'The Fiduciary Nature of a Company Board's Power to Issue Shares' (1971-1972) 10 UWALR 364 at 372; note *Chew v R* (1992) 10 ACLC 816 at 823 per Dawson J.

[45] Finn P D, *Fiduciary Obligations* The Law Book Company Ltd, Sydney, 1977 at 78 *et seq.*

[46] The other two categories are beyond the scope of this book.

[47] Corporations Law s232(2); note *Australian Growth Resources Corporation Pty Ltd v van Reesema* (1988) 6 ACLC 529 at 539 per King CJ (Cox J agreed); and *Residues Treatment & Trading Co Ltd v Southern Resources Ltd (No. 2)* (1989) 7 ACLC 1130 at 1152 per Perry J; affirmed *Southern Resources Ltd v Residues Treatment & Trading Co Ltd* (1990) 8 ACLC 1151 at 1167 *per curiam.*

[48] Corporations Law s246AA; note Corporations Law ss461(1)(e) and 461(1)(f).

[49] Editorial comment (1994) 15 Co Law 34 at 34.

[50] *Ibid.*

[51] *Re Barings plc (No 5)* [1999] 1 BCLC 433 at 484 per Jonathan Parker J; and *Fitzsimmons v R* (1997) 23 ACSR 355 at 358 per Owen J; note Malcolm D, 'Directors' Duties: The Governing Principles' in Ramsay I M (ed), *Corporate Governance and the Duties of Company Directors* The Centre for Corporate Law and Securities Regulation, University of Melbourne, Parkville, 1997 at 60 and 78.

[52] (1916-1917) 22 CLR 490 at 531 per Isaacs and Rich JJ.

tent with ideals of certainty, or even, predictability. Such an approach is of little comfort, therefore, for either the company lawyer or, more particularly, the director himself or herself who expects a degree of certainty in the law.[53] Similar problems were mentioned in the previous chapter of this book to those now raised, albeit there in the context of the duty upon directors of British and Australian companies to exercise care and diligence. Difficulties recognised also by Dixon J in *Peters' American Delicacy Company Ltd v Heath* where his Honour spoke of the, 'somewhat vague and unsatisfactory test to be applied when what is in question is the validity of an alteration of an article'.[54] But the level of unsatisfactoriness does not end there. It extends right across the directors' decision-making process and is of critical importance to all those affected, or likely to be affected, by corporate policy and those who frame and execute it.

It has been seen from previous chapters of this book that the relationship between directors and their company is acknowledged to be fiduciary.[55] As such, that fiduciary relationship *ipso facto* imposes upon directors fiduciary obligations which *inter alia* require directors to act in good faith and for proper purposes *vis-à-vis* their company;[56] and forms part of the, 'accepted mainstream of fiduciary obligation'.[57] Thus in our treatment of the directors' duties to act in good faith and for proper purposes, throughout this and the next chapter, we need not overly concern ourselves with the distinction observed in chapters one and two of this book between true fiduciary duties and mere equitable, or even common law, duties owed by a director in a fiduciary relationship.[58]

Directors' duties to act in good faith and for proper purposes strike at the very heart of trusts law and underpin the fiduciary obligations owed by directors to their British and Australian companies in English and Australian company law.[59] These fiduciary duties are premised upon honesty and integrity.[60] These are qualities which every director should have, are central to the discussion at hand and constitute a *sine qua non* to the fiduciary relationship between directors and their company.

---

[53] Baxt R, 'Judges in their Own Cause: The Ratification of Directors' Breaches of Duty' (1978) 5 MULR 16 at 18.

[54] (1938-1939) 61 CLR 457 at 515.

[55] Austin R P, 'Fiduciary Accountability for Business Opportunities' in Finn P D (ed), *Equity and Commercial Relationships* The Law Book Company Ltd, Sydney, 1987 at 150; and Rider B A K, 'Amiable Lunatics and the Rule in Foss v Harbottle' [1978] CLJ 270 at 270; see *Hospital Products Ltd v United States Surgical Corporation* (1984-1985) 156 CLR 41 at 68 per Gibbs CJ and at 96 per Mason J; and *Australian Growth Resources Corporation Pty Ltd v van Reesema* (1988) 6 ACLC 529 at 535-536 per King CJ (Cox J agreed).

[56] Heydon J D, 'Directors' Duties and the Company's Interests' in Finn P D (ed), *Equity and Commercial Relationships* The Law Book Company Ltd, Sydney, 1987 at 120; and Finn P D, 'The Fiduciary Principle' in Youdan T G (ed), *Equity, Fiduciaries and Trusts* The Law Book Company Ltd, Toronto, 1989; see *Aberdeen Railway Company v Blaikie Brothers* (1854) 1 Macq 461 at 471-472 per Lord Cranworth LC.

[57] Finn P D, *Fiduciary Obligations* The Law Book Company Ltd, Sydney, 1977 at 78.

[58] *Bristol and West Building Society v Mothew* [1996] 4 All ER 698 at 712 per Millett LJ (Otton LJ agreed); *Permanent Building Society v Wheeler* (1993-1994) 11 WAR 187 at 237-238 per Ipp J (Malcolm CJ and Seaman J agreed); *State of South Australia v Clark* (1996) 19 ACSR 606 at 631 per Perry J; and *Castlereagh Motels Ltd v Davies-Roe* (1966) 67 SR (NSW) 279 at 283 per Wallace P.

[59] There is a long line of authority from, recently, *Attorney General for Hong Kong v Reid* [1994] 1 All ER 1, which extends back, at least, to *Keech v Sandford* (1726) Sel Cas t King 61, with rules and principles applicable to fiduciary duties in uncompromising terms often, but not always, resulting in what might well be thought to be positive hardship to the fiduciary concerned.

[60] Qualities sadly lacking in some of today's boardrooms: *The Times*, 28 March 1995; note *Gluckstein v Barnes* [1900] AC 240 at 246 per the Earl of Halsbury LC.

CONTROL OVER DIRECTORS' DECISION-MAKING

This chapter and the next are concerned with the propriety of directors' decision-making within the confines of what English and Australian company law has come to recognise as the *bona fides* and the proper purposes doctrines. There is considerable debate as to whether the exercise by directors of their powers is governed by two separate duties in this regard,[61] or whether *bona fides* and proper purposes are more correctly described as being two halves of the one whole; with each supplementing and complementing the other, but at the same time being independently capable of striking down the exercise, or purported exercise, of a director's power where necessary. Although, as the general law has developed, it might be argued that each is independent of the other,[62] rather curiously both are found within the statutory obligation in Australian company law to act honestly.[63]

We shall focus upon the treatment by the English and Australian courts of the traditional doctrines of *bona fides* and proper purposes as specific requirements of English and Australian company law and analyse the way in which these requirements complement the relevant Australian companies legislation which obliges directors to act honestly. Especially in the light of the re-emergence of the proper purposes doctrine in recent English and Australian cases,[64] and the more commercial and pragmatic approach to directors' duties being currently displayed by the Australian courts[65] in an attempt to cope with the, 'treacherous currents of the 1980s',[66] those of the 1990s and the consequent, 'wreckage washed into the courts' from the ensuing corporate collapses.[67]

From the balance of this chapter, and throughout the next, it will be evident that for over a century now the English and Australian courts have grappled with the best approach to adopt when the exercise of directors' powers is challenged. From the cases it clearly emerges that two questions arise. First, were the directors acting in good faith and in what they considered to be the interests of the company as a whole?[68] Secondly, was the power exercised for the purpose for which it was conferred, or for some extraneous, improper or collateral purpose?[69]

However, the English and Australian courts remain unclear as to the circumstances which attract the application of one particular test in preference to the other. For

---

[61] Sealy L S, '"Bona Fides" and "Proper Purposes" in Corporate Decisions' (1989) 15 MULR 265 at 267; Sealy L S, 'Company Directors' Powers – Proper Motive but Improper Purpose' [1967] CLJ 33; and Sealy L S, 'Company – Directors' Unconstitutional Acts' [1992] CLJ 229.

[62] *Hogg v Cramphorn Ltd* [1967] Ch 254.

[63] Corporations Law s232(2); note *Australian Growth Resources Corporation Pty Ltd v van Reesema* (1988) 6 ACLC 529 at 539 per King CJ (Cox J agreed); and *Residues Treatment & Trading Co Ltd v Southern Resources Ltd (No. 2)* (1989) 7 ACLC 1130 at 1152 per Perry J; affirmed *Southern Resources Ltd v Residues Treatment & Trading Co Ltd* (1990) 8 ACLC 1151 at 1167 *per curiam*.

[64] *Gambotto v WCP Ltd* (1995) 13 ACLC 342; *Kokotovich Constructions Pty Ltd v Wallington* (1995) 13 ACLC 1113; *Bishopsgate Investment Management Ltd v Maxwell (No. 2)* [1994] 1 All ER 261; and *Re BSB Holdings Ltd (No. 2)* [1996] 1 BCLC 155.

[65] *Equiticorp Finance Ltd v Bank of New Zealand* (1993) 11 ACLC 952 at 1019 per Clarke and Cripps JJA; and *Glandon Pty Ltd v Strata Consolidated Pty Ltd* (1993) 11 ACSR 543 at 547-548 per Mahoney JA.

[66] Sykes T, *The Bold Riders* Allen & Unwin Pty Ltd, St Leonards, 1994 at 367.

[67] *Toycorp Ltd v Myer* (unreported, Supreme Court No. 2141/92, Victoria, Nathan J, 13 November 1992) at 8.

[68] *Clemens v Clemens Bros Ltd* [1976] 2 All ER 268 at 280 per Foster J.

[69] *Mills v Mills* (1938) 60 CLR 150 at 185 per Dixon J; see *Re BSB Holdings Ltd (No. 2)* [1996] 1 BCLC 155 at 243 per Arden J.

instance, the *bona fides* test has been almost universally applied by the courts to situations involving a challenge to shareholders' actions concerning alteration of a company's articles; relying upon, with almost religious fervour, Lindley MR's celebrated *dictum* in *Allen v Gold Reefs of West Africa Ltd*.[70] On 8 March 1995, however, the High Court of Australia[71] in *Gambotto v WCP Ltd*[72] rejected that test as being inapplicable. It had stood for almost a century. The High Court felt that the proper purposes doctrine was, in the circumstances, more appropriate. The High Court did, however, expressly preserve the *bona fides* test. The majority,[73] in a joint judgment, considered the expression for the benefit of the company as a whole to be, 'still in vogue in the context of the exercise by directors of their powers, particularly the power to issue or allot shares.'[74] It is instructive to now consider each of these doctrines in turn.

BONA FIDES DOCTRINE

Long considered the English and Australian courts' primary means of exercising control over directors' decision-making, the *bona fides* test developed amidst the type of *laissez-faire* philosophy witnessed in chapter two of this book; geared more or less to arrest dishonesty or *mala fides*, but well entrenched of a reluctance to interfere with the internal management of companies acting within their powers.[75] That the courts should develop such a reluctance to interfere in the exercise of directors' powers is not surprising for this was an area in which it was felt that the shareholders were seized of control, and that such matters were really for them.[76] And so, provided that directors of British and Australian companies acted *bona fide* in the interests of their company as a whole, it was felt shareholders had little cause for complaint. Thus, Foster J in *Clemens v Clemens Bros Ltd* considered that a director must, 'not only act within his powers but must also exercise them bona fide in what he believes to be the interests of the company.'[77] This approach accords with that recently taken by the South Australian Full Court[78] in *Grove v Flavel*; namely, that the duty of a director, 'is to act bona fide in the interests of the company as a whole.'[79]

---

70 [1900] 1 Ch 656 at 671.
71 (Mason CJ, Brennan, Deane, Dawson and McHugh JJ).
72 (1995) 13 ACLC 342; see Whitford K, 'The Year That Was: An Overview of Corporate Law 1995' (1996) 6 AJCL 1 at 7-8.
73 (Mason CJ, Brennan, Deane and Dawson JJ).
74 (1995) 13 ACLC 342 at 348; see *Richard Brady Franks Ltd v Price* (1937) 58 CLR 112 at 135 per Latham CJ; *Mills v Mills* (1938) 60 CLR 150 at 187-188 per Dixon J; *Ngurli Ltd v McCann* (1953) 90 CLR 425 at 440 *per curiam*; and *Harlowe's Nominees Pty Ltd v Woodside (Lakes Entrance) Oil Company NL* (1969-1970) 121 CLR 483 at 493 *per curiam*.
75 *Burland v Earle* [1902] AC 83 at 93 per Lord Davey; see Sealy L S, 'The Director as Trustee' [1967] CLJ 83 at 100-101.
76 *Shuttleworth v Cox Brothers and Company (Maidenhead) Ltd* [1927] 2 KB 9 at 23 per Scrutton LJ; note Editorial comment, 'Directors – true or false?' (1997) 18 Co Law 129 at 129.
77 [1976] 2 All ER 268 at 280; note Prentice D D, 'Restraints on the Exercise of Majority Shareholder Power' (1976) 92 LQR 502.
78 (Jacobs, Matheson and Olsson JJ).
79 (1986) 11 ACLR 161 at 166 *per curiam*; see Walsh J K, 'The Exercise of Powers in the Interests of a Company' (1967-1968) 8 UWALR 176 at 176.

However, such an approach begs two questions. First, what is meant by *bona fide*? Its meaning is not free from ambiguity.[80] As we have seen from an earlier part of this chapter, to act honestly, in good faith and *bona fide* have variously been described as synonymous. Throughout the authorities, these words are used interchangeably.[81] They have a certain fungibility about them.[82] Although *bona fide* might, according to Sealy, be better taken to mean genuine rather than honest.[83] Such an approach was favoured by Oliver J in *Re Halt Garage (1964) Ltd* where his Lordship struck down the payment of a substantial salary to a seriously ill and hospitalised director on the basis that it was not genuinely paid as the director's remuneration.[84] Malcolm CJ in *Chew v The Queen*, however, recently held that directors are required to act, 'in good faith in the interests of and for the benefit of the company as a whole'.[85] The turn of phrase and choice of words does, therefore, seem to fall to personal choice, and nothing turns upon it.

Secondly, what is meant by the company as a whole?[86] This is more controversial. Traditionally, the company has been understood to refer to the shareholders as a collective group,[87] usually qualified by a statement that the long term, as well as the short term, interests of the shareholders may be taken into account. Although the best interests of the company is an indefinite phrase, Dixon J in *Mills v Mills* felt, 'its meaning admits of little doubt.'[88] Whereas in Parsons' view, 'the concept remains miserably indeterminate.'[89] More recently, Kirby P in *Darvall v North Sydney Brick & Tile Co Ltd (No. 2)* was of the view that the best interests of the company as a whole, 'certainly included the interest of the shareholders as the corporators'.[90] Sealy, on the other hand, has argued for acceptance of the company as a commercial entity comprising, 'interests which collectively make up the enterprise'.[91] These are matters of great interest, and much could be written on this controversy as to the exact meaning of the

---

[80] Sealy L S, '"Bona Fides" and "Proper Purposes" in Corporate Decisions' (1989) 15 MULR 265 at 269.

[81] *The Australian Metropolitan Life Assurance Company Ltd v Ure* (1923) 33 CLR 199 at 206 per Knox CJ; cf. Walsh J K, 'The Exercise of Powers in the Interests of a Company' (1967-1968) 8 UWALR 176 at 181, 'The words "bona fide" add nothing to the test.'

[82] *Aleyn v Belchier* (1758) 1 Eden 132 at 138 per Lord Northington; *Hirsche v Sims* [1894] AC 654 at 665 per the Earl of Selborne; and *Lagunas Nitrate Company v Lagunas Syndicate* [1899] 2 Ch 392 at 435 per Lindley MR.

[83] Sealy L S, '"Bona Fides" and "Proper Purposes" in Corporate Decisions' (1989) 15 MULR 265 at 269.

[84] [1982] 3 All ER 1016 at 1040; note *Brady v Brady* [1989] 1 AC 755 at 777-778 per Lord Oliver that good faith required a, 'genuine belief that it is being done in the company's interest.'

[85] (1991) 4 WAR 21 at 49.

[86] *Richard Brady Franks Ltd v Price* (1937) 58 CLR 112 at 135-136 per Latham CJ; cf. *Ashburton Oil NL v Alpha Minerals NL* (1970-1971) 123 CLR 614 at 620 per Barwick CJ; see Barrett R I, 'Directors' Duties to Creditors' (1977) 40 MLR 226 at 226-227; Rixon F G, 'Competing Interests and Conflicting Principles: An Examination of the Power of Alteration of Articles of Association' (1986) 49 MLR 446 at 448, 'an ambiguous term.'; Sealy L S, '"Bona Fides" and "Proper Purposes" in Corporate Decisions' (1989) 15 MULR 265 at 269 a, 'phrase of notoriously elusive meaning.'; cf. Lindgren K E, 'The Fiduciary Nature of a Company Board's Power to Issue Shares' (1971-1972) 10 UWALR 364 at 368 words which, 'serve to emphasize that "the company" is not a mere majority of its shareholders.'

[87] *The Australian Metropolitan Life Assurance Company Ltd v Ure* (1923) 33 CLR 199 at 216-217 per Isaacs J.

[88] (1938) 60 CLR 150 at 188.

[89] Parsons R W, 'The Director's Duty of Good Faith' (1967) 5 MULR 395 at 396.

[90] (1989) 7 ACLC 659 at 676.

[91] Sealy L S, '"Bona Fides" and "Proper Purposes" in Corporate Decisions' (1989) 15 MULR 265 at 270; and Sealy L S, 'Directors' "Wider" Responsibilities – Problems Conceptual, Practical and Procedural' (1987) 13 MULR 164 at 174.

company as a whole.[92] Chapter six of this book will address this concept in some detail. But regrettably, for present purposes, our remit is limited. Thus, as mentioned in chapter one of this book, in this chapter and the next we accord the company its traditional constituency; namely, the shareholders collectively.[93]

DEVELOPMENT OF THE BONA FIDES DOCTRINE: AN ENGLISH PERSPECTIVE

From a traditional perspective, the way in which the *bona fides* doctrine has developed from humble origins into a primary means of controlling the exercise of directors' powers, is exemplified by the following brief discourse into the leading English and Australian authorities. From chapter two of this book, it will be recalled that in *Lagunas Nitrate Company v Lagunas Syndicate* Lindley MR considered that if directors act within their powers, do nothing *ultra vires*, and if fraud is not imputed, then any enquiry as to their decision-making, 'is reduced to want of care and bona fides'.[94] The words *bona fide* for the benefit of the company as a whole, which Lindgren designates a, 'linguistic formula',[95] were first used in a reported decision the following year in *Allen v Gold Reefs of West Africa Ltd*.[96] There, the Court of Appeal[97] reinforced the obligation of shareholders to act in the company's interests. In his oft quoted words, Lindley MR explained that:

> The power thus conferred on companies to alter the regulations contained in their articles is limited only by the provisions contained in the statute and the conditions contained in the company's memorandum of association. Wide, however, as the language of s.50 is, the power conferred by it must, like all other powers, be exercised subject to those general principles of law and equity which are applicable to all powers conferred on majorities and enabling them to bind minorities. It must be exercised, not only in the manner required by law, but also bonâ fide for the benefit of the company as a whole, and it must not be exceeded.[98]

Lindley MR's comments in *Gold Reefs* have not only been influential *vis-à-vis* an alteration of the articles by shareholders, but also in relation to the exercise of powers

---

[92] Ford H A J and Austin R P, *Ford's Principles of Corporations Law* (6th ed) Butterworths Pty Ltd, Sydney, 1992 at 466.

[93] *The Australian Metropolitan Life Assurance Company Ltd v Ure* (1923-1924) 33 CLR 199 at 216-217 per Isaacs J; *Parke v Daily News Ltd* [1962] Ch 927 at 963 per Plowman J; and Wedderburn K W, 'Ultra Vires or Directors' Bona Fides?' (1967) 30 MLR 566 at 568.

[94] [1899] 2 Ch 392 at 435; see *Australian Securities Commission v Gallagher* (1993) 11 ACLC 286 at 294 per Pidgeon J (Franklyn and Walsh JJ agreed); cf. *In re City Equitable Fire Insurance Company Ltd* [1925] Ch 407 at 429 per Romer J.

[95] Lindgren K E, 'The Fiduciary Nature of a Company Board's Power to Issue Shares' (1971-1972) 10 UWALR 364 at 367.

[96] [1900] 1 Ch 656.

[97] (Lindley MR, Vaughan Williams and Romer LJJ).

[98] [1900] 1 Ch 656 at 671; see *Punt v Symons & Co Ltd* [1903] 2 Ch 506 at 512 per Byrne J; *Shuttleworth v Cox Brothers and Company (Maidenhead) Ltd* [1927] 2 KB 9 at 17 per Bankes LJ; *Clemens v Clemens Bros Ltd* [1976] 2 All ER 268 at 281 per Foster J; *Re Halt Garage* (1964) Ltd [1982] 3 All ER 1016 at 1035 per Oliver J; and *Southern Resources Ltd v Residues Treatment & Trading Co Ltd* (1990) 8 ACLC 1151 at 1164 *per curiam*; cf. *Gambotto v WCP Ltd* (1995) 13 ACLC 342 at 345-348 per Mason CJ, Brennan, Deane and Dawson JJ.

by directors of British and Australian companies generally. The recent decision by the High Court of Australia in *Gambotto v WCP Ltd*,[99] however, has robbed Lindley MR of further influence in Australian company law, particularly concerning resolutions to alter articles. The decision in *Gambotto* will be examined a little later in this chapter.

It will repay analysis, however, to first consider the traditional approach. In *Shuttleworth v Cox Brothers and Company (Maidenhead) Ltd*,[100] the Court of Appeal[101] was concerned with a special resolution to alter the articles. Bankes LJ determined that any alteration must be for the company's benefit. In ascertaining that, his Lordship considered that the court is entitled to treat the conduct of shareholders as it does the verdict of a jury, and to say that the alteration shall not stand if it is such that no reasonable person could consider it for the company's benefit.[102] But, cautioned Scrutton LJ, 'I should be sorry to see the Court go beyond this and take upon itself the management of concerns which others may understand far better than the Court does.'[103] Although delivered in the context of shareholders' actions, Scrutton LJ's judgment sums up the reluctance of the English judiciary to review, or even consider, the directors' decision-making in the exercise of their powers.[104] A reluctance amply foreshadowed in chapter two of this book.

Of direct application to directors of British and Australian companies, and their professional advisers, is the well-known case of *In re Smith and Fawcett Ltd* where Lord Greene MR,[105] when considering the principles to be applied to directors transferring shares in accordance with a discretion conferred by the articles, was of the view that:

> [Directors] must exercise their discretion bona fide in what they consider – not what a court may consider – is in the interests of the company, and not for any collateral purpose.[106]

On the face of it, this is simply to display subjective good faith. But notwithstanding that it is for the directors, and not the court, to consider what is in the company's interests, directors may still breach that duty. For instance, where they have failed to direct their minds to the question whether a transaction was in fact in the company's interests.[107] Thus, the test is not entirely subjective and the courts do impose an objective threshold for reasons which emerged in *Hutton v West Cork Railway Company*, where Bowen LJ gave the timely reminder that:

---

[99] (1995) 13 ACLC 342 at 345-348 per Mason CJ, Brennan, Deane and Dawson JJ.
[100] [1927] 2 KB 9.
[101] (Bankes, Scrutton and Atkin LJJ).
[102] [1927] 2 KB 9 at 18-19; see *Allen v Gold Reefs of West Africa Ltd* [1900] 1 Ch 656 at 671 per Lindley MR.
[103] [1927] 2 KB 9 at 23-24; see *Teck Corporation Ltd v Millar* (1972) 33 DLR (3d) 288 at 316 per Berger J.
[104] *Carlen v Drury* (1812) 1 V & B 154 at 158 per Lord Eldon; *Burland v Earle* [1902] AC 83 at 93 per Lord Davey; and *Shuttleworth v Cox Brothers and Company (Maidenhead) Ltd* [1927] 2 KB 9 at 23 per Scrutton LJ; note Sealy L S, 'The Director as Trustee' [1967] CLJ 83 at 100-101; and Editorial comment, 'Directors – true or false?' (1997) 18 Co Law 129 at 129.
[105] (Luxmoore and Asquith LJJ agreed).
[106] [1942] Ch 304 at 306; see *Brady v Brady* (1987) 3 BCC 535 at 552 per Nourse LJ; and Farrar J H, Furey N E, Hannigan B M and Wylie P, *Farrar's Company Law* (3rd ed) Butterworth & Co (Publishers) Ltd, London, 1991 at 383.
[107] *Re BSB Holdings Ltd (No. 2)* [1996] 1 BCLC 155 at 243 per Arden J.

Bona fides cannot be the sole test, otherwise you might have a lunatic conducting the affairs of the company, and paying away its money with both hands in a manner perfectly *bonâ fide* yet perfectly irrational. The test must be what is reasonably incidental to, and within the reasonable scope of carrying on, the business of the company.[108]

Of similar notoriety is the decision in *Greenhalgh v Arderne Cinemas Ld*,[109] where the Court of Appeal[110] was asked to overturn the trial judge's decision that resolutions passed by the majority shareholders were valid. The litigation arose out of an agreement for the sale of a controlling interest in Arderne Cinemas Ld ('Arderne') which required a special resolution to be passed by Arderne's shareholders so as to alter the articles to give effect to the registration and transfer of the shares in question. Evershed MR,[111] who delivered the principal judgment, was of the view that the trial judge's decision should stand. In dismissing the appeal, Evershed MR said in an oft quoted passage:

[The phrase] 'bona fide for the benefit of the company as a whole' means ... that the shareholder must proceed upon what, in his honest opinion, is for the benefit of the company as a whole. ... [The] phrase, 'the company as a whole', does not (at any rate in such a case as the present) mean the company as a commercial entity, distinct from the corporators: it means the corporators as a general body. That is to say, the case may be taken of an individual hypothetical member and it may be asked whether what is proposed is, in the honest opinion of those who voted in its favour, for that person's benefit.[112]

One case where the directors' actions were successfully challenged was *In re W & M Roith Ltd*.[113] There, the controlling shareholder and director wished to make provision for his wife in the event of his death. Accordingly, he entered into a service agreement with the company whereby on his death she was to be entitled to a pension for life. On being satisfied that no thought had been given to the question whether the arrangement was for the benefit of the company and that, indeed, the sole object was to make provision for the widow, Plowman J held that the transaction was not binding on the company.[114]

A similar conclusion was reached in *Zemco Ltd v Jerrom-Pugh*,[115] where the Court of Appeal[116] was asked to determine the propriety of moneys withdrawn by a director from the bank account of Zemco Ltd following advice that the director's employment

---

[108] (1883) 23 Ch D 654 at 671; note Sealy L S, 'Company Directors' Powers – Proper Motive but Improper Purpose' [1967] CLJ 33 at 35.

[109] [1951] Ch 286; see *Australian Growth Resources Corporation Pty Ltd v van Reesema* (1988) 6 ACLC 529 at 535-536 per King CJ (Cox J agreed).

[110] (Evershed MR, Asquith and Jenkins LJJ).

[111] (Asquith and Jenkins LJJ agreed).

[112] [1951] Ch 286 at 291; see *Clemens v Clemens Bros Ltd* [1976] 2 All ER 268 at 281 per Foster J; *Ngurli Ltd v McCann* (1953) 90 CLR 425 at 438 *per curiam*; and *Gambotto v WCP Ltd* (1995) 13 ACLC 342 at 345-349 per Mason CJ, Brennan, Deane and Dawson JJ and at 354-355 per McHugh J; cf. Menzies D, 'Company Directors' (1959) 33 ALJ 156 at 168; Ford H A J and Austin R P, *Ford's Principles of Corporations Law* (6th ed) Butterworths Pty Ltd, Sydney, 1992 at 467; and Walsh J K, 'The Exercise of Powers in the Interests of a Company' (1967-1968) 8 UWALR 176 at 183.

[113] [1967] 1 WLR 432; see Wedderburn K W, 'Ultra Vires or Directors' Bona Fides?' (1967) 30 MLR 566.

[114] Cf. *In re Lee, Behrens and Co Ltd* [1932] 2 Ch 46 at 51 per Eve J.

[115] [1993] BCC 275.

[116] (Neill, Butler-Sloss and Hoffmann LJJ).

was to be terminated on three month's notice. The director argued an entitlement to those moneys by way of settlement. In finding against that argument, Hoffmann LJ[117] restated the trite proposition that directors are under an fiduciary obligation to their company to exercise powers of management *bona fide* in the company's interests. As the payment was made in breach of fiduciary duty, the director held the money as constructive trustee for the company.[118] A similar result was achieved in *Neptune (Vehicle Washing Equipment) Ltd v Fitzgerald (No. 2)*, where A G Steinfeld QC[119] reached the following decision:

> In my judgment the actions which he took were not taken bona fide in the interests of the company but were taken by the defendant solely in his own interests. On that basis, it seems to me, the plaintiff must, prima facie, be entitled to the repayment of the moneys which were paid to and received by the defendant in breach of his fiduciary duties.[120]

The last case for brief mention here is that decided by the Court of Appeal[121] in *Bishopsgate Investment Management Ltd v Maxwell (No. 2)*.[122] There, Hoffmann LJ[123] reminded us that should a director of a British company choose, 'to participate in the management of the company and exercise his powers on its behalf, he owes a duty to act bona fide in the interests of the company.'[124] From this brief excursion into the development of the *bona fides* doctrine, it can be seen from the cases mentioned above that there is a strong body of jurisprudence in evidence which supports this doctrine in English company law. It is instructive to now examine the corresponding position in Australian company law.

DEVELOPMENT OF THE BONA FIDES DOCTRINE: AN AUSTRALIAN PERSPECTIVE

The earlier Australian judges tended to be more ambivalent in their approach to the directors' duty to act in good faith than their English counterparts. In order to illustrate the somewhat confused approach within the Australian judiciary to the test to be applied to the exercise by directors of Australian companies of their powers,[125] it is necessary only to mention four well-known decisions of the High Court of Australia. The Australian judiciary's approach is considered to be confused because each of these

---

[117] (Neill and Butler-Sloss LJJ agreed).
[118] [1993] BCC 275 at 281; note *Maguire v Makaronis* (1996-1997) 188 CLR 449; *Westdeutsche Landesbank Girozentrale v Islington London Borough Council* [1996] AC 669; *Royal Brunei Airlines Sdn Bhd v Tan* [1995] 2 AC 378; *Attorney General for Hong Kong v Reid* [1994] 1 All ER 1; *United Dominions Corporation Ltd v Brian Pty Ltd* (1984-1985) 157 CLR 1; and *Chan v Zacharia* (1983-1984) 154 CLR 178.
[119] Sitting as a deputy Chancery Judge.
[120] [1995] BCC 1000 at 1021.
[121] (Ralph Gibson, Leggatt and Hoffmann LJJ).
[122] [1994] 1 All ER 261.
[123] (Leggatt LJ agreed).
[124] [1994] 1 All ER 261 at 265.
[125] E.g., in *The Australian Metropolitan Life Assurance Company Ltd v Ure* (1923) 33 CLR 199, although the conclusion was unanimous, the reasons differed dramatically. Knox CJ adopted the *bona fides* test, Isaacs J adopted the proper purposes test and Starke J applied a different test yet again.

four cases displays a measure of duality; with some judges advocating a test based upon *bona fides* whilst their brethren support, and rely upon, the independent existence of the proper purposes doctrine.

The first of these cases is *The Australian Metropolitan Life Assurance Company Ltd v Ure*,[126] where the High Court of Australia[127] rejected on the basis of a lack of evidence a challenge to the propriety of the directors' actions in refusing to register share transfers. The articles provided that the directors might refuse to register share transfers without giving any reason for doing so. The applicants failed to discharge the onus upon them of proving that, in exercising their power of refusal, the directors had not acted honestly or *bona fide* in the company's interests. The question for consideration, according to Knox CJ, was whether the evidence established that the directors, 'were not exercising their powers honestly or bona fide in what they believed to be the interests of the Company.'[128] Knox CJ dismissed the appeal as the respondents failed to show any want of *bona fides* or anything capricious or wanton even though the resolution would give the directors, 'power to allot 3,000 shares in their discretion; but this does not warrant the conclusion that the object of the proposal is to enable the directors to acquire an unfair advantage over other shareholders.'[129] On the other hand, Isaacs J was more attuned to proper purposes. In Isaacs J's judgment, the directors' power is gone if they are moved by some illegitimate consideration, or act upon some unworthy or extraneous reason.[130]

In *Richard Brady Franks Ltd v Price*,[131] the High Court of Australia[132] was asked to determine whether or not the directors, in issuing debentures to certain of the directors and other persons who, from time to time, lent money to the company on short call and had guaranteed the company's overdraft, had acted in the interests of the company and of the general body of shareholders; or whether they had acted in the interests of the proposed debenture holders. In finding that the plaintiff had not discharged the onus of establishing want of *bona fides* on the part of the directors *vis-à-vis* the issue of the debentures, Latham CJ explained that the court neither presumes impropriety nor determines the wisdom of the directors' actions. The question for the court, in Latham CJ's view, is whether it is shown that the directors, 'did not honestly act for what they regarded as the benefit of the company.'[133] However, Dixon J trod the proper purposes path. In doing so, his Honour reaffirmed that as directors are fiduciaries, their powers must be exercised honestly in furtherance of the purposes for which they are given.[134] Thus, the company's interests must not be sacrificed or disregarded.[135]

---

[126] (1923) 33 CLR 199; see *Australian Growth Resources Corporation Pty Ltd v van Reesema* (1988) 6 ACLC 529 at 535-536 per King CJ (Cox J agreed).
[127] (Knox CJ, Isaacs and Starke JJ).
[128] (1923) 33 CLR 199 at 206.
[129] *Ibid* at 210; see Finn P D, *Fiduciary Obligations* The Law Book Company Ltd, Sydney, 1977 at 75-76.
[130] (1923) 33 CLR 199 at 218; see *Allen v Hyatt* (1914) 30 TLR 444 at 445 per Viscount Haldane LC.
[131] (1937) 58 CLR 112; see *Australian Growth Resources Corporation Pty Ltd v van Reesema* (1988) 6 ACLC 529 at 535-536 per King CJ (Cox J agreed).
[132] (Latham CJ, Rich and Dixon JJ).
[133] (1937) 58 CLR 112 at 135-136; see *Allen v Gold Reefs of West Africa Ltd* (1900) 1 Ch 656 at 671 per Lindley MR; cf. *Gambotto v WCP Ltd* (1995) 13 ACLC 342 at 345-348 per Mason CJ, Brennan, Deane and Dawson JJ.
[134] (1937) 58 CLR 112 at 142-143.
[135] *Ibid* at 144-145 per Dixon J.

Similarly, in *Mills v Mills*[136] the High Court of Australia[137] was concerned with a challenge to the validity of a directors' resolution. The effect of the resolution was to increase the voting power of one of the directors. But the evidence established that when the resolution was passed, it was believed by the directors to be in the company's best interests. That evidence was unassailable and the High Court held that the mere fact that one of the directors derived some benefit from the passing of the resolution did not invalidate it. One of the grounds upon which the resolution was challenged was that it was not passed *bona fide* in the interests of the company; but, rather, in the interests of the managing director, with the intention of securing for him continued control of the company's operations.[138]

All members of the High Court of Australia in *Mills* embraced the primary judge's findings that except for the directors' desire to give ordinary shareholders a title to part of the reserve of profits, the resolution would not have been passed. Against that finding by the primary judge, the High Court was bound to find the resolution to have been validly passed. In so holding, Latham CJ emphasised that if directors act from an improper motive, arbitrarily or capriciously, and issue shares only for the purpose of conserving their own power, the resolution creating the shares will be set aside.[139] Dixon J, as he did in *Price*,[140] preferred the proper purposes approach. In a judgment which has been frequently referred to, Dixon J enunciated that:

> The application of the general equitable principle to the acts of directors ... must ... take the substantial object the accomplishment of which formed the real ground of the board's action. If this is within the scope of the power, then the power has been validly exercised. But if, except for some ulterior and illegitimate object, the power would not have been exercised, that which has been attempted as an ostensible exercise of the power will be void,[141] notwithstanding that the directors may incidentally bring about a result which is within the purpose of the power and which they consider desirable.[142]

The last of the four cases for consideration is *Peters' American Delicacy Company Ltd v Heath*.[143] There, the High Court of Australia[144] was faced with an attack upon a resolution concerning a bonus issue of shares as part of a scheme for the reorganisation of the company's affairs. Again, different approaches were taken by the members of the High Court in declaring the resolution valid. Latham CJ[145] opined that if the resolution was passed, 'fraudulently or oppressively or was so extravagant that no reasonable

---

[136] (1938) 60 CLR 150.
[137] (Latham CJ, Rich, Starke, Dixon and Evatt JJ).
[138] Which today would give rise to an action(s) under Corporations Law ss246AA and 461(1)(e).
[139] (1938) 60 CLR 150 at 162-163.
[140] (1937) 58 CLR 112 at 142-143.
[141] It is suggested that Dixon J inadvertently used *void* when in truth he meant *voidable* as this would accord with his earlier judgment in *Richard Brady Franks Ltd v Price* (1937) 58 CLR 112 at 142-143 and would also accord with subsequent authority.
[142] (1938) 60 CLR 150 at 185-186; see *Pine Vale Investments Ltd v McDonnell and East Ltd* (1983) 1 ACLC 1294 at 1303 per McPherson J; and *Darvall v North Sydney Brick & Tile Co Ltd (No. 2)* (1989) 7 ACLC 659 at 675-677 per Kirby P.
[143] (1938-1939) 61 CLR 457.
[144] (Latham CJ, Rich, Dixon and McTiernan JJ).
[145] (McTiernan J agreed).

person could believe that it was for the benefit of the company', it would be invalid.[146] In reaching the same decision, albeit by a different path, Rich J gave the timely reminder that:

> [The] power of alteration must be exercised bona fide with a view to the advancement of the company considered as a whole and not with a view to the advancement of the interests of a majority of voters or of a section of the company only.[147]

But, in the final analysis, it would seem that the High Court of Australia in *Peters'* fell back upon, 'general notions of fairness and propriety'.[148] In doing so, the High Court lost an opportunity to clarify the proper criteria to be followed in the event of a challenge to the exercise by directors of Australian companies of their powers. Although, it must be said that fairness, in view of the High Court of Australia's recent decision in *Gambotto v WCP Ltd*,[149] is now recognised as being integral to any deliberation upon oppression, and of increasing importance to any discussion in respect to proper purposes.[150] This is a discussion which will now be taken up.

PROPER PURPOSES DOCTRINE

In English and Australian company law, the duty upon directors of British and Australian companies to exercise powers for proper purposes has come to be regarded as separate from the duty to exercise powers *bona fide* in the interests of the company,[151] and is presently enjoying attention from courts of the highest authority.[152] The proper purposes test or, as it is also referred to, the collateral purposes test,[153] allows directors' acts to be reviewed by the courts upon a more objective basis than that which

---

[146] (1938-1939) 61 CLR 457 at 482; see *Gambotto v WCP Ltd* (1995) 13 ACLC 342 at 347 per Mason CJ, Brennan, Deane and Dawson JJ.

[147] (1938-1939) 61 CLR 457 at 495.

[148] *Ibid* at 507 per Dixon J; cf. *Mutual Life Insurance Co of New York v The Rank Organisation Ltd* [1985] BCLC 11 at 21 per Goulding J; and *Re BSB Holdings Ltd (No. 2)* [1996] 1 BCLC 155 at 247-249 per Arden J; see Walsh J K, 'The Exercise of Powers in the Interests of a Company' (1967-1968) 8 UWALR 176 at 183; and Finn P D, *Fiduciary Obligations* The Law Book Company Ltd, Sydney, 1977 at 41-42 and 64 *et seq*.

[149] (1995) 13 ACLC 342 at 349 per Mason CJ, Brennan, Deane and Dawson JJ and at 354-355 per McHugh J.

[150] Ford H A J, Austin R P and Ramsay I M, *Ford's Principles of Corporations Law* (9th ed) Reed International Books Australia Pty Ltd, Sydney, 1999 at para 24.190.

[151] Wedderburn K W, 'Shareholders' Control of Directors' Powers: A Judicial Innovation?' (1967) 30 MLR 77 at 79; Parsons R W, 'The Director's Duty of Good Faith' (1967) 5 MULR 395 at 419; and Birds J R, 'Proper Purposes as a Head of Directors' Duties' (1974) 37 MLR 580; cf. Slutsky B V, case note (1974) 37 MLR 457 at 460; Burridge S J, 'Wrongful Rights Issues' (1981) 44 MLR 40 at 50; and Sealy L S, 'Company – Directors' Unconstitutional Acts' [1992] CLJ 229.

[152] *Gambotto v WCP Ltd* (1995) 13 ACLC 342; and *Bishopsgate Investment Management Ltd v Maxwell (No. 2)* [1994] 1 All ER 261.

[153] *Darvall v North Sydney Brick & Tile Co Ltd (No. 2)* (1989) 7 ACLC 659 at 676 per Kirby P; *Equiticorp Finance Ltd v Bank of New Zealand* (1993) 11 ACLC 952 at 1018 per Clarke and Cripps JJA; *Permanent Building Society v Wheeler* (1993-1994) 11 WAR 187 at 193, 218, 226 and 234 per Ipp J (Malcolm CJ and Seaman J agreed); and *Re BSB Holdings Ltd (No. 2)* [1996] 1 BCLC 155 at 243 per Arden J.

has been traditionally applied in relation to *bona fides*.[154] Notwithstanding that directors may have acted honestly in what they believe to be in the company's interests, they may nevertheless be liable to the company if they have exercised their powers for a purpose different from that for which the powers were conferred upon them.[155] Strict adherence to the *bona fides* doctrine can permit of too much subjectivity in the directors' decision-making process. As we have seen from chapters two and three of this book, subjectivity *vis-à-vis* the directors' duty to exercise care and diligence was deprecated by the Australian business community and ultimately led to the statutory imposition of an objective test in Corporations Law s232(4).[156] The Law Commission, on the other hand, in its recent report entitled *Company Directors: Regulating Conflicts of Interests and Formulating a Statement of Duties*, is in favour of a dual objective/subjective test based on that enacted in Insolvency Act 1986 (UK) s214(4). In expressing its prefer-ence for the codification of such an objective/subjective standard, the Law Commission considers it important that regard should be had to the functions of the particular directors and the circumstances of their particular company.[157] In this respect, the Law Commission recommends that:

> (1) a director's duty of care, skill and diligence to his company should be set out in statute; (2) the standard should be judged by a twofold objective/subjective test; and (3) regard should be had to the functions of the particular director and the circum-stances [including size and type] of the company.[158]

The attractiveness of the proper purposes doctrine is that it introduces an objective element into the equation absent statutory interference. That satisfies some of the arguments which were considered in relation to the directors' duty to exercise care and diligence in chapters two and three of this book, and permits English and Australian courts with a more interventionist disposition to monitor more closely directors' decision-making.[159] In turn, that would seem to accord with the Australian judiciary's determined push for raised levels of responsibility and greater accountability in keeping with today's ideals of corporate governance;[160] and mesh rather nicely with the

---

[154] *Greenhalgh v Arderne Cinemas Ld* [1951] Ch 286 at 291 *per curiam*; and *Richard Brady Franks Ltd v Price* (1937) 58 CLR 112 at 135-136 per Latham CJ and at 216-217 per Isaacs J; note Birds J R, 'Mak-ing Directors do their Duties' (1980) 1 Co Law 67 at 70.

[155] *Fraser v Whalley* (1864) 2 H & M 10; *Punt v Symons & Co Ltd* [1903] 2 Ch 506; *Piercy v S Mills & Company Ltd* [1920] 1 Ch 77; *Ngurli Ltd v McCann* (1954) 90 CLR 425; *Hogg v Cramphorn Ltd* [1967] Ch 254; and *Howard Smith Ltd v Ampol Petroleum Ltd* [1974] AC 821.

[156] Senate Standing Committee on Legal and Constitutional Affairs, *Social and Fiduciary Duties and Obligations of Company Directors* AGPS, Canberra, 1989 at 29; note Explanatory memorandum, *Corporate Law Reform Bill 1992* CCH Australia Ltd, Sydney, 1992 at 25.

[157] Law Commission, *Company Directors: Regulating Conflicts of Interests and Formulating a Statement of Duties* HMSO, London, Cm 4436, 1999 at para 5.19.

[158] *Ibid* at para 5.20.

[159] Sealy L S, '"Bona Fides" and "Proper Purposes" in Corporate Decisions' (1989) 15 MULR 265 at 266; and Sealy L S, 'Company – Directors' Unconstitutional Acts' [1992] CLJ 229.

[160] See Prentice D D and Holland P R J, *Contemporary Issues in Corporate Governance* Oxford University Press, Oxford, 1993; Committee on the Financial Aspects of Corporate Governance, *The Report of the Committee on the Financial Aspects of Corporate Governance* Gee and Co Ltd, London, 1992; Farrar J H, 'Corporate Governance, Business Judgement and the Professionalism of Directors' (1993) 6 CBLJ 1; Whincop M J, 'An Economic Analysis of the Criminalisation and Content of Directors' Duties' (1996) 24 ABLR 273; and Stapledon G P, *Institutional Shareholders and Corporate Governance* Clarendon Press, Oxford, 1996.

Australian Government's self-proclaimed package of laws legislation in the pursuit of a uniform national regulatory regime.[161]

It is significant that the proper purposes doctrine has application where the directors' good faith is not challenged.[162] In *Winthrop v Winns*, for instance, Mahoney JA was of the view that the term collateral purpose is used, not to impute any personal dishonesty on the directors' part, but rather as indicative of whether or not the substantial object the accomplishment of which formed the real ground for their so acting was or was not a purpose of the company.[163] Since the proper purposes test may be applied independently of any question of motive, it becomes a question of law for the courts to determine in each case the proper limits upon the exercise of the power in question. This, as was seen earlier in this chapter in the context of the *bona fides* doctrine, must be ascertained largely by reference to the company's articles and, relevantly, any affecting legislation.[164]

There are those who would consider the utility of the proper purposes doctrine to exceed that of the *bona fides* doctrine. According to Walsh, for instance, 'the test of the interests of the company has proved difficult to apply and the courts have abandoned it when this became necessary'.[165] This is a view shared by Latham CJ in *Mills v Mills*.[166] If, as was suggested in *In re Smith and Fawcett Ltd*,[167] the duty to act in the company's interests is supplemented by the separate proviso that the directors must not act for any collateral purpose,[168] any exercise of the directors' powers for an improper purpose will be set aside, regardless of the fact that the directors may honestly have believed that they were acting in the company's interests.[169] For as Hodgson J in *Darvall v North Sydney Brick & Tile Co Ltd* observed:

> The existence of subjective good faith is insufficient to save the purported exercise of the power, if the power was exercised for a collateral purpose.[170]

It is, therefore, necessary to distinguish between an excess of authority and an act which *prima facie* is within the powers delegated to directors of British and Australian companies, but which they have abused by exercising for an improper purpose.[171]

---

[161] Commonwealth, House of Representatives, Parliamentary Debates, 8 November 1990 at 3669.

[162] *Hogg v Cramphorn Ltd* [1967] Ch 254; see Wedderburn K W, 'Shareholders' Control of Directors' Powers: A Judicial Innovation?' (1967) 30 MLR 77.

[163] (1975) ACLC 28401 at 28414; see Conway H M and Manuell R J, 'Duties of Company Directors and Ratification by General Meetings' (1977-1979) 8 Syd LR 493.

[164] Prentice D D, 'Expulsion of Members from a Company' (1970) 33 MLR 700 at 702-704; and Yeung K, 'Disentangling the Tangled Skein: The Ratification of Directors' Actions' (1992) 66 ALJ 343 at 345; note *Bishopsgate Investment Management Ltd v Maxwell* [1993] BCC 120 at 136 per Chadwick J.

[165] Walsh J K, 'The Exercise of Powers in the Interests of a Company' (1967-1968) 8 UWALR 176 at 182.

[166] (1938) 60 CLR 150 at 164; see *Hirsche v Sims* [1894] AC 654 at 660-661 per the Earl of Selborne; and *Howard Smith Ltd v Ampol Petroleum Ltd* [1974] AC 821 at 835 per Lord Wilberforce.

[167] [1942] Ch 304.

[168] Bradley C, 'Corporate Control: Markets and Rules' (1990) 53 MLR 170 at 178.

[169] *Australian Growth Resources Corporation Pty Ltd v van Reesema* (1988) 6 ACLC 529 at 538-539 per King CJ (Cox J agreed); and *Permanent Building Society v Wheeler* (1993-1994) 11 WAR 187 at 218 per Ipp J (Malcolm CJ and Seaman J agreed).

[170] (1988) 6 ACLC 154 at 174.

[171] Improper in the sense of, 'beyond the scope of or not justified by the instrument creating the power.': *Vatcher v Paull* [1915] AC 372 at 378 per Lord Parker; see Davies P L, *Gower's Principles of Modern Company Law* (6th ed) Sweet & Maxwell Ltd, London, 1997 at 606; and Rajak H, *A Sourcebook of Company Law* Jordan & Sons Ltd, Bristol, 1989 at 536.

Ascertainment of that purpose is a question of fact and the relevant question is whether the challenged power, 'would have been exercised *but for* the presence of the impermissible purpose'.[172] The authorities suggest that where a power is exercised for a purpose not within its proper scope, the transaction thereby effected is voidable rather than void.[173]

DEVELOPMENT OF THE PROPER PURPOSES DOCTRINE: AN ENGLISH PERSPECTIVE

The development by the English courts of the proper purposes doctrine has proved more than a useful adjunct to the *bona fides* doctrine. So much so that it must now be recognised as having evolved into a separate test to be applied in circumstances where *prima facie* the power complained of is within the scope of the directors' authority, but which they have abused by exercising for an improper purpose; often, so as to manipulate control.[174] The following cases highlight the way in which the proper purposes doctrine has evolved under the general law and it will repay analysis to briefly consider them. The first is *Fraser v Whalley*.[175] The essential facts appear within the following extract from Page Wood VC's judgment:

> The directors are informed that at the next general meeting they are likely to be removed; and therefore, on the very verge of a general meeting, they, without giving notice to anyone, with this indecent haste and scramble[176] which is shewn by the times at which the meetings were held, resolve that shares are, on the faith of this obsolete power entrusted to them for a different purpose, to be issued for the very purpose of controlling the ensuing general meeting.[177]

The Vice-Chancellor in *Whalley* felt that to be so gross a breach of trust as to merit the court's intervention. Page Wood VC expressed his dismay at the directors' attempts to clothe themselves with a trust to appropriate the shares by the use of such a power, 'for

---

[172] *Darvall v North Sydney Brick & Tile Co Ltd* (1988) 6 ACLC 154 at 174 per Hodgson J; see *Mills v Mills* (1938) 60 CLR 150 at 186 per Dixon J; *Whitehouse v Carlton Hotel Pty Ltd* (1987) 5 ACLC 421 at 427 per Mason CJ, Deane and Dawson JJ; also *Permanent Building Society v Wheeler* (1993-1994) 11 WAR 187 at 218 per Ipp J (Malcolm CJ and Seaman J agreed).

[173] *Bamford v Bamford* [1970] Ch 212 at 238 per Harman LJ and at 241-242 per Russell LJ (Karminski LJ agreed); *Ashburton Oil NL v Alpha Minerals NL* (1970-1971) 123 CLR 614 at 643 per Gibbs J; *Richard Brady Franks Ltd v Price* (1937) 58 CLR 112 at 142 per Dixon J; and *Winthrop v Winns* (1975) ACLC 28401 at 28415 per Mahoney JA.

[174] Wedderburn K W, 'Shareholders' Control of Directors' Powers: A Judicial Innovation?' (1967) 30 MLR 77 at 83; and Baxt R, *Afterman & Baxt's Cases and Materials on Corporations and Associations* (5th ed) Butterworths Pty Ltd, Sydney, 1988 at 554; note *Whitehouse v Carlton Hotel Pty Ltd* (1987) 5 ACLC 421 at 425 per Mason CJ, Deane and Dawson JJ.

[175] (1864) 2 H & M 10; note Lindgren K E, 'The Fiduciary Nature of a Company Board's Power to Issue Shares' (1971-1972) 10 UWALR 364 at 373; Birds J R, 'Proper Purposes as a Head of Directors' Duties' (1974) 37 MLR 580 at 581 and 586; and Sealy L S, 'Company – Directors' Unconstitutional Acts' [1992] CLJ 229.

[176] Cf. *Ashburton Oil NL v Alpha Minerals NL* (1970-1971) 123 CLR 614 at 642 per Gibbs J.

[177] (1864) 2 H & M 10 at 29.

a purpose not connected with the new constituency at all, but ... to keep themselves in office'.[178]

Such an approach was also adopted in *Punt v Symons & Company Ltd*,[179] where the directors had issued shares with the object of creating a sufficient majority to enable them to pass a special resolution depriving other shareholders of special rights conferred on them by the articles. In determining that the directors had acted improperly, Byrne J reaffirmed that directors must exercise their powers for the company's benefit. Although the power in question was primarily for the purpose of raising capital, his Lordship recognised that there might be occasions when the directors could fairly and properly issue shares for other reasons. However, a limited issue of shares to secure the necessary statutory majority in a particular interest is not, 'a fair and bonâ fide exercise of the power.'[180] Similarly, in *Piercy v S Mills & Company Ltd*, Peterson J held that directors are not entitled to use their powers of issuing shares merely for the purpose of maintaining control or defeating the wishes of the existing majority of shareholders.[181]

However, the case which probably more than any other gave recognition to a separate test over and above the traditional *bona fides* test, was *Hogg v Cramphorn Ltd*.[182] In *Hogg*, the directors had issued shares with special voting rights to the trustees of a scheme set up for the benefit of company employees in an attempt to forestall a takeover bid. While Buckley J accepted that the directors had acted in good faith, and that they honestly believed that what they had done would benefit the company, his Lordship observed nonetheless that, 'an essential element of the scheme, and indeed its primary purpose, was to ensure control of the company by the directors and those whom they could confidently regard as their supporters.'[183] Buckley J formed the view that the power to issue shares was fiduciary and if it was, 'exercised for an improper motive, the issue of these shares is liable to be set aside.'[184] The issue of shares was accordingly declared invalid. However, since the directors' breach of duty rendered their action

---

[178] *Ibid* at 29-30; see *Punt v Symons & Co Ltd* [1903] 2 Ch 506 at 516 per Byrne J; and *Piercy v S Mills & Company Ltd* [1920] 1 Ch 77 at 83; but the Vice-Chancellor's condemnation of the directors' behaviour in *Fraser v Whalley* (1864) 2 H & M 10 did little to assuage such corporate behaviour, for similar circumstances which persisted in 1864 were, regrettably, rife in boardrooms across England and Australia during the 1980s. Human frailties, it would seem, know no boundaries. Nor does time diminish reprehensible corporate practices.

[179] [1903] 2 Ch 506; see Sealy L S, 'Company Directors' Powers – Proper Motive but Improper Purpose' [1967] CLJ 33 at 34-35.

[180] [1903] 2 Ch 506 at 515-516 per Byrne J; see *Piercy v S Mills & Company Ltd* [1920] 1 Ch 77 at 84 per Peterson J; and *Hogg v Cramphorn Ltd* [1967] Ch 254 at 267 per Buckley J.

[181] [1920] 1 Ch 77 at 84; see *Hogg v Cramphorn Ltd* [1967] Ch 254 at 267 per Buckley J; *Lee Panavision Ltd v Lee Lighting Ltd* [1991] BCC 620 at 634 *per curiam*; and *Darvall v North Sydney Brick & Tile Co Ltd (No. 2)* (1989) 7 ACLC 659 at 676-677 per Kirby P; note Sealy L S, 'Company Directors' Powers – Proper Motive but Improper Purpose' [1967] CLJ 33 at 34-35.

[182] [1967] Ch 254; see *Punt v Symons & Co Ltd* [1903] 2 Ch 506; and *Piercy v S Mills & Company Ltd* [1920] 1 Ch 77; note Birds J R, 'Proper Purposes as a Head of Directors' Duties' (1974) 37 MLR 580 at 581 and 586; Chow K C K, 'Proper Purpose Doctrine and the Companies Bill' (1979) 129 NLJ 123 and 135; Davies P L, 'Directors' Fiduciary Duties and Individual Shareholders' in McKendrick E (ed), *Commercial Aspects of Trusts and Fiduciary Obligations* Clarendon Press, Oxford, 1992 at 102; cf. Sealy L S, 'Company Directors' Powers – Proper Motive but Improper Purpose' [1967] CLJ 33 at 34, 'these cases were not necessarily conclusive of the issue'; yet rejected in *Teck Corporation Ltd v Millar* (1972) 33 DLR (3d) 288 at 317 per Berger J (Slutsky B V, case note (1974) 37 MLR 457).

[183] [1967] Ch 254 at 266-267.

[184] *Ibid* at 269.

voidable rather than void,[185] it was capable of ratification by the shareholders in general meeting. The action was stood over and the allotment was later ratified. This decision in *Hogg* has excited a measure of controversy in English and Australian company law.[186] Whilst the topic of ratification is beyond the scope of this book, it is perhaps instructive to mention the interdiction on the use of ratification in Australian company law which the following passage from Santow J's judgment in *Miller v Miller* makes clear:

> Ratification is not available where it would constitute a fraud on the minority ... or misappropriation of company resources ... or was entered into by an insolvent company to the prejudice of creditors ... or defeated a member's personal right ... or was oppressive or where the majority in general meeting acted for the same improper purpose as directors ... It is also clear enough that ratification cannot cure a breach of statutory duty, more especially one imposing criminal liability. The most it can do is remove from the scope of technical dishonesty such actions as issuing shares for a purpose which is not a proper one, in the sense of not being for the benefit of the company as a whole.[187]

Buckley J's recognition in *Hogg* that subjective honesty of purpose was not always sufficient, launched proper purposes as a separate test; although its roots can be discerned in Bowen LJ's celebrated 'lunatic' *dictum* in *Hutton v West Cork Railway Company*.[188] The Court of Appeal[189] in *Bamford v Bamford*[190] soon afterwards endorsed, and itself relied upon, *Hogg* as an accurate statement of the law; although *Bamford* was principally concerned with the ratification of the directors' improper purpose behind the allotment of certain shares. Notwithstanding that, *Bamford* clearly recognises the separate nature of proper purposes.[191]

It is well established that the onus of showing that a director has not acted honestly in the exercise of his or her powers and the discharge of his or her office is upon the aggrieved party.[192] The point is well demonstrated in *Hindle v John Cotton Ltd*,[193] where the House of Lords[194] was asked to declare a resolution of the board void.

---

[185] *Bamford v Bamford* [1970] Ch 212 at 238 per Harman LJ and at 241-242 per Russell LJ (Karminski LJ agreed); *Ashburton Oil NL v Alpha Minerals NL* (1970-1971) 123 CLR 614 at 643 per Gibbs J; *Richard Brady Franks Ltd v Price* (1937) 58 CLR 112 at 142 per Dixon J; and *Winthrop v Winns* (1975) ACLC 28401 at 28415 per Mahoney JA.

[186] Baxt R, 'Judges in their Own Cause: The Ratification of Directors' Breaches of Duty' (1978) 5 MULR 16 at 29, 'Until the decision in *Hogg* ... it was the view that in such a case the acts of the directors were void and therefore not ratifiable.'; cf. Wedderburn K W, 'Shareholders' Control of Directors' Powers: A Judicial Innovation?' (1967) 30 MLR 77 at 81, 'The novelty of the judgment lies in the remarkable finding that a majority vote *could* ratify these improprieties.'

[187] (1995) 16 ACSR 73 at 89.

[188] (1883) 23 Ch D 654 at 671.

[189] (Harman, Russell and Karminski LJJ).

[190] [1970] Ch 212; see Baxt R, case note (1974) 48 ALJ 319 at 321.

[191] Cf. Farrar J H, 'Abuse of Power by Directors' [1974] CLJ 221 at 224.

[192] *The Australian Metropolitan Life Assurance Company Ltd v Ure* (1923) 33 CLR 199 at 219 per Isaacs J; and *Richard Brady Franks Ltd v Price* (1937) 58 CLR 112 at 135 per Latham CJ and at 138 per Rich J; cf. *Gambotto v WCP Ltd* (1995) 13 ACLC 342 at 349 per Mason CJ, Brennan, Deane and Dawson JJ, 'in the case of expropriation ... the onus lies on those supporting expropriation to show that the power is validly exercised.'

[193] (1919) 56 Sc LR 625.

[194] (Viscounts Finlay and Cave, Lords Dunedin, Shaw and Wrenbury).

Although the articles gave literal power to do what had been done, the House of Lords nonetheless granted the order sought. In doing so, Viscount Finlay[195] outlined the nature of the task that the court must undertake as the following passage from his celebrated speech to the House of Lords demonstrates:

> Where the question is one of abuse of powers, the state of mind of those who acted, and the motive on which they acted, are all important, and you may go into the question of what their intention was, collecting from the surrounding circumstances all the materials which genuinely throw light upon that question of the state of mind of the directors so as to show whether they were honestly acting in discharge of their powers in the interests of the company or were acting from some bye-motive, possibly of personal advantage, or for any other reason.[196]

On this point, Lord Shaw[197] in *Hindle* cautioned that the moving cause of the resolution must be the company's interests and not, 'the aggrandisement of the directors themselves.'[198]

For a more contemporary English perspective it is necessary to move forward to the mid-1970s. Although isolated cases can be found where the *bona fides* test has been applied, the latter day English courts have tended to promote, in preference, the proper purposes doctrine, which found very clear favour with the Privy Council[199] in *Howard Smith Ltd v Ampol Petroleum Ltd.*[200] There, the Privy Council was asked to consider whether or not the allotment and issue of certain shares to Howard Smith Ltd ('Howard Smith') was to satisfy the need for capital or whether the directors' primary purpose was to destroy the majority shareholding of Ampol Petroleum Ltd and another.

In delivering its opinion in *Howard Smith*, the Privy Council reaffirmed the judiciary's reluctance to interfere with, or even supervise, the merits of decisions within the powers of management honestly arrived at. But the Privy Council nonetheless considered that a court, 'is entitled to look at the situation objectively in order to estimate how critical or pressing, or substantial or, per contra, insubstantial an alleged requirement may have been.'[201] At first instance, Street J ruled that the power to issue and allot the shares was improperly exercised, notwithstanding that the directors were not motivated by any purpose of personal gain or advantage, or by any desire to retain

---

[195] (Viscount Cave and Lord Dunedin agreed).
[196] (1919) 56 Sc LR 625 at 630-631; see *The Australian Metropolitan Life Assurance Company Ltd v Ure* (1923) 33 CLR 199 at 220 per Isaacs J; *Howard Smith Ltd v Ampol Petroleum Ltd* [1974] AC 821 at 835 per Lord Wilberforce; *Equiticorp Finance Ltd v Bank of New Zealand* (1993) 11 ACLC 952 at 1017-1019 per Clarke and Cripps JJA; and *Southern Resources Ltd v Residues Treatment & Trading Co Ltd* (1990) 8 ACLC 1151 at 1164 *per curiam*.
[197] (Lord Wrenbury agreed).
[198] (1919) 56 Sc LR 625 at 631; see *The Australian Metropolitan Life Assurance Company Ltd v Ure* (1923) 33 CLR 199 at 219-220 per Isaacs J.
[199] (Lords Wilberforce, Diplock, Simon, Cross and Kilbrandon).
[200] [1974] AC 821; note Baxt R, case note (1974) 48 ALJ 319; Barrett R I, case note (1982) 56 ALJ 600; Sealy L S, 'Company – Directors' Unconstitutional Acts' [1992] CLJ 229; cf. Birds J R, 'Proper Purposes as a Head of Directors' Duties' (1974) 37 MLR 580 at 582 who was critical of the 'midway' approach adopted by their Lordships and found their Lordships' opinion, 'retrogressive'.
[201] [1974] AC 821 at 832 per Lord Wilberforce; see *Burland v Earle* [1902] AC 83 at 93 per Lord Davey; and *Imperial Mercantile Credit Association v Coleman* (1871) 6 Ch App 558 at 568 per Lord Hatherley LC; cf. Finn P D, *Equity and Commercial Relationships* The Law Book Company Ltd, Sydney, 1987 at 92; and Rider B A K, 'Amiable Lunatics and the Rule in Foss v Harbottle' [1978] CLJ 270 at 270-271.

their position on the board.[202] The Privy Council affirmed Street J's decision despite each director asserting that his primary purpose in voting for the allotment was to meet an urgent capital need.[203] The Privy Council considered that given the majority bloc in the share register, the directors' intention was to destroy its character as a majority,[204] so as to encourage Howard Smith to proceed with its takeover. The significance and the utility of the proper purposes test was highlighted by Lord Wilberforce, who delivered the advice of the Privy Council, when his Lordship explained that the use by directors of their fiduciary powers:

> [Solely] for the purpose of shifting the power to decide to whom and at what price shares are to be sold cannot be related to any purpose for which the power over the share capital was conferred upon them. That this is the position in law was in effect recognised by the majority directors themselves when they attempted to justify the issue as made primarily in order to obtain much needed capital for the company. And once this primary purpose was rejected, as it was by Street J, there is nothing legitimate left as a basis for their action, except honest behaviour. That is not, in itself, enough.[205]

The application of the proper purposes test in this manner, therefore, enables the directors' decision-making to be challenged without necessarily condemning their motives for so deciding. That in turn permits judges, of a more robust and interventionist disposition, to consider the decision itself rather than simply the decision-making process; thus giving rise to the review of business judgments of business men, long considered anathema to the English and the Australian judiciary.[206]

DEVELOPMENT OF THE PROPER PURPOSES DOCTRINE: AN AUSTRALIAN PERSPECTIVE

As mentioned earlier in this chapter, the High Court of Australia has been somewhat ambivalent in its treatment of the *bona fides* and the proper purposes doctrines. That ambivalence, which Birds describes as, 'a sort of midway view',[207] is carried forward in *Ngurli Ltd v McCann*.[208] There, the High Court of Australia[209] was faced with a challenge to an allotment of shares the effect of which was to favour a director over other minority shareholders. Those shareholders claimed that in allotting the shares the

---

[202] See Lindgren K E, case note (1973) 11 UWALR 68.

[203] The test is what the substantial or primary purpose was: *Hirsche v Sims* [1894] AC 654; *Hindle v John Cotton Ltd* (1919) 56 Sc LR 625; and *Mills v Mills* (1938) 60 CLR 150; cf. Birds J R, 'Proper Purposes as a Head of Directors' Duties' (1974) 37 MLR 580 at 585; and Burridge S J, 'Wrongful Rights Issues' (1981) 44 MLR 40 at 52.

[204] [1974] AC 821 at 833 per Lord Wilberforce.

[205] *Ibid* at 838; see *Darvall v North Sydney Brick & Tile Co Ltd (No. 2)* (1989) 7 ACLC 659 at 676 per Kirby P.

[206] Sealy L S, '"Bona Fides" and "Proper Purposes" in Corporate Decisions' (1989) 15 MULR 265 at 278; and Sealy L S, 'Company – Directors' Unconstitutional Acts' [1992] CLJ 229.

[207] Birds J R, 'Proper Purposes as a Head of Directors' Duties' (1974) 37 MLR 580 at 581.

[208] (1953) 90 CLR 425; see *Darvall v North Sydney Brick & Tile Co Ltd (No. 2)* (1989) 7 ACLC 659 at 676 per Kirby P.

[209] (Williams ACJ, Fullagar and Kitto JJ).

director concerned had neither acted in good faith nor in the company's interests, but rather for an ulterior purpose; namely, his own benefit. The High Court agreed.

In a joint judgment, the High Court of Australia in *Ngurli* reaffirmed that powers entrusted to directors by the articles are fiduciary powers and must be used *bona fide* for the purpose conferred;[210] in this case, to raise sufficient capital for the benefit of the company as a whole. As such, these powers must not be used to cloak the real purpose if that purpose is to benefit some shareholders at the expense of others or to 'wrest control of the company.'[211] But it was held that a director could take advantage of the power to benefit himself, if such a benefit was incidental to a *bona fide* exercise of the power. A director could not, however, either use the power for an ulterior purpose[212] or ostensibly to benefit the company, but really to benefit himself at the expense of other shareholders.[213]

Gradually, however, the Australian judiciary developed its reasoning beyond these earlier attempts at rationalisation and tended to embrace *bona fides* as a prime consideration in each instance, but proper purposes as determinative of the issue. *A fortiori* when considering the shareholders' interests *inter se*.[214] This development is exemplified in the cases which follow.

The decision of the High Court of Australia[215] in *Harlowe's Nominees Pty Ltd v Woodside (Lakes Entrance) Oil Company NL*[216] is apposite. There, the High Court was faced with an allegation by an existing shareholder that an allotment and issue of further shares was not made *bona fide* and in the interests of the company as a whole. The primary question was whether or not the directors of Woodside (Lakes Entrance) Oil Company NL were guilty of a misuse of power in allotting and issuing the shares. In concluding that the directors had not misused their powers, the High Court, in a joint judgment, recognised that there may be occasions when directors may fairly and properly issue shares for other reasons. Ultimately, the question must be whether in truth the issue was made honestly in the company's interests. The following extract from the joint judgment of Barwick CJ, McTiernan and Kitto JJ is pertinent:

> Directors in whom are vested the right and the duty of deciding where the company's interests lie and how they are to be served may be concerned with a wide range of practical considerations, and their judgment, if exercised in good faith and not for irrelevant purposes, is not open to review in the courts.[217]

---

[210] Cf. *Hogg v Cramphorn Ltd* [1967] Ch 254 at 269 per Buckley J.

[211] Sealy L S, 'The Director as Trustee' [1967] CLJ 83 at 94.

[212] (1953) 90 CLR 425 at 438 *per curiam*.

[213] *Ibid* at 439-440; see *Allen v Gold Reefs of West Africa Ltd* [1900] 1 Ch 656 at 671 per Lindley MR; cf. Walsh J K, 'The Exercise of Powers in the Interests of a Company' (1967-1968) 8 UWALR 176 at 185 that *Ngurli Ltd v McCann* injected, 'extraordinary confusion ... into the law'.

[214] *Mills v Mills* (1938) 60 CLR 150 at 164 per Latham CJ.

[215] (Barwick CJ, McTiernan and Kitto JJ).

[216] (1969-1970) 121 CLR 483.

[217] *Ibid* at 493; see *Howard Smith Ltd v Ampol Petroleum Ltd* [1974] AC 821 at 836 per Lord Wilberforce; *Whitehouse v Carlton Hotel Pty Ltd* (1987) 5 ACLC 421 at 424 per Mason CJ, Deane and Dawson JJ and at 431 per Wilson J; and *Darvall v North Sydney Brick & Tile Co Ltd (No. 2)* (1989) 7 ACLC 659 at 676 per Kirby P.

In *Pine Vale Investments Ltd v McDonnell and East Ltd*,[218] the Queensland Supreme Court was concerned with a proposed takeover. The issue which arose for determination was whether or not a proposed share issue was to be regarded as the product of a breach of duty by the directors of McDonnell and East Ltd. McPherson J concluded that the substantial object forming the board's action was to take advantage of a genuine commercially favourable opportunity rather than to frustrate the takeover. It did not, therefore, matter whether that opportunity was actively created by the company or dropped upon involuntarily. As McPherson J explained, once it is established that action is commercially justified in the corporate interest, 'it is difficult to understand why the directors should be reduced to inertia because of the pendency or possibility of a takeover offer.'[219]

Similarly, in *Winthrop Investments Ltd v Winns Ltd*[220] the New South Wales Supreme Court was concerned with allegations that the directors' decision to purchase a certain business was not a proper exercise of their powers of management; but, rather, was made in order to defeat a takeover offer. Waddell J adopted a commercial and pragmatic approach to the problem.[221] Whilst information that a takeover offer might be made had spurred the directors on, that was not, of itself, cause for complaint. In his Honour's view, such information should be regarded as having brought home to the directors rather forcibly the commercial necessity of acquiring new businesses. As a consequence, Waddell J considered that:

> The main or fundamental or basic object of the board in deciding to enter into the acquisition of the Mates stores was to improve the general financial position of the company and this clearly was a purpose for which each of the powers in question might validly have been exercised.[222]

As alluded to earlier in this chapter, the cases are concerned to establish as impermissible and invalid the exercise of directors' powers for the purpose of manipulating control.[223] The majority decision[224] in *Whitehouse v Carlton Hotel Pty Ltd*[225] bears testimony to that.[226] There, the High Court of Australia[227] was faced with an issue

---

[218] (1983) 1 ACLC 1294; see Ritson L, 'The "Proper Purposes" Duty of Directors and Defensive Measures against Company Takeovers' (1982-1985) 10 Syd LR 627.

[219] (1983) 1 ACLC 1294 at 1304; see *Mills v Mills* (1938) 60 CLR 150 at 185-186 per Dixon J; *Ashburton Oil NL v Alpha Minerals NL* (1970-1971) 123 CLR 614 at 620 per Barwick CJ; *Howard Smith Ltd v Ampol Petroleum Ltd* [1974] AC 821 at 831, 835 and 837 per Lord Wilberforce; and *Winthrop Investments Ltd v Winns Ltd* (1979) ACLC 32257 at 32265-32266 per Waddell J.

[220] (1979) ACLC 32257.

[221] Cf. *Gray Eisdell Timms Pty Ltd v Combined Auctions Pty Ltd* (1995) 13 ACLC 965 at 974 per Young J; note Muir G, 'Contract and Equity: Striking a Balance' (1985) 10 Adel LR 153 at 183, 'But pragmatism must not always triumph over principle'.

[222] (1979) ACLC 32257 at 32266 per Waddell J; see *Mills v Mills* (1938) 60 CLR 150 at 185-186 per Dixon J.

[223] Wedderburn K W, 'Shareholders' Control of Directors' Powers: A Judicial Innovation?' (1967) 30 MLR 77 at 83; and Baxt R, *Afterman & Baxt's Cases and Materials on Corporations and Associations* (5th ed) Butterworths Pty Ltd, Sydney, 1988 at 554; note *Whitehouse v Carlton Hotel Pty Ltd* (1987) 5 ACLC 421 at 425 per Mason CJ, Deane and Dawson JJ.

[224] (Mason CJ, Deane and Dawson JJ).

[225] (1987) 5 ACLC 421; see *Haselhurst v Wright* (1991) 9 ACLC 728 at 732 per Owen J; and *Chew v R* (1992) 10 ACLC 816 at 823 per Dawson J.

[226] (1987) 5 ACLC 421 at 425; see *Howard Smith Ltd v Ampol Petroleum Ltd* [1974] AC 821 at 835 and 837 per Lord Wilberforce; *Harlowe's Nominees Pty Ltd v Woodside (Lakes Entrance) Oil Company NL* (1969-1970) 121 CLR 483 at 493 *per curiam*; *Residues Treatment and Trading Co Ltd v Southern*

whether the purported allotment by Whitehouse to his sons, the appellants, of two 'B' class shares in the capital of Carlton Hotel Pty Ltd ('Carlton') was a valid exercise of the powers and discretion vested in him by Carlton's articles. In determining that it was not the majority explained that:

> In this as in other areas involving the exercise of fiduciary power, the exercise of a power for an ulterior or impermissible purpose is bad notwithstanding that the motives of the donee of the power in so exercising it are substantially altruistic.[228]

Although the majority of the High Court of Australia in *Whitehouse* found it unnecessary to expressly formulate the relevant test in cases where permissible purposes competed with impermissible purposes, their Honours did say that an, 'allotment will be invalidated if the impermissible purpose was causative in the sense that, but for its presence, "the power would not have been exercised"'.[229]

It is suggested that the Australian judiciary has, more recently, made a better job of analysing and applying the *bona fides* and the proper purposes doctrines than formerly. As previously mentioned in this chapter, there is much in the earlier decisions by the High Court of Australia which confuses and tends to blur the distinctions between the two doctrines; distinctions which today's judiciary seems better equipped to make. Take, for example, *Advance Bank Australia Ltd v FAI Insurances Ltd.*[230] There, the New South Wales Court of Appeal[231] was concerned with a challenge to the propriety of conduct by the directors of Advance Bank Australia Ltd ('Advance Bank') in electioneering prior to an annual general meeting at which four of a nine member board were due to retire and stand for re-election. The majority[232] dismissed the appeal and upheld Waddell CJ's view that the directors were in breach of their fiduciary duty to the company. While all parties generally accepted that the directors had acted *bona fide* and honestly, believing that the election of FAI Insurances Ltd nominees to the board would not be in Advance Bank's best interests, nonetheless, subjective honesty and good motives did not, in the majority's view, suffice to negate a breach of fiduciary duty.

The principal judgment in *Advance Bank* was delivered by Kirby P[233] who considered that merely because directors took advantage of conduct performed for a corporate purpose did not necessarily invalidate their actions, if those actions were otherwise lawful. However, the court should be vigilant for ulterior purposes of private advantage to be determined by reference to the real purposes which primarily motivate directors' actions. In Kirby P's judgment, statements by directors about their subjective intention, whilst relevant, are not conclusive of their *bona fides* or of the purposes for which they

---

cont.
   Resources Ltd (1988) 6 ACLC 1160 at 1164 *per curiam*; and *Darvall v North Sydney Brick & Tile Co Ltd (No. 2)* (1989) 7 ACLC 659 at 712-713 per Clarke JA.
[227] (Mason CJ, Deane, Dawson, Wilson and Brennan JJ).
[228] (1987) 5 ACLC 421 at 426 per Mason CJ, Deane and Dawson JJ; see *Advance Bank Australia Ltd v FAI Insurances Ltd* (1987) 5 ACLC 725 at 743 per Kirby P (Glass JA agreed); and *Darvall v North Sydney Brick & Tile Co Ltd (No. 2)* (1989) 7 ACLC 659 at 676 per Kirby P.
[229] (1987) 5 ACLC 421 at 427 per Mason CJ, Deane and Dawson JJ; see *Mills v Mills* (1938) 60 CLR 150 at 186 per Dixon J.
[230] (1987) 5 ACLC 725; see *Haselhurst v Wright* (1991) 9 ACLC 728 at 732 per Owen J.
[231] (Kirby P, Glass and Mahoney JJA).
[232] (Kirby P and Glass JA).
[233] (Glass JA agreed).

acted as they did. In this sense, Kirby P expressed an opinion which has much to commend it:

> [Although] the search is for the subjective intentions of the directors, it is a search which must be conducted objectively as the Court decides whether to accept or discount the assertions which the directors make about their motives and purposes.[234]

The last case for discussion here is *Darvall v North Sydney Brick & Tile Co Ltd (No. 2)*,[235] a case of considerable interest. In *Darvall* the New South Wales Court of Appeal[236] was concerned with Darvall's takeover offer of North Sydney Brick & Tile Co Ltd ('North Sydney Brick') of which he was a shareholder. The issue to be determined was whether North Sydney Brick's directors had an improper purpose, or alternatively abused their powers, in orchestrating a joint venture with independent financiers for the purpose of countering Darvall's offer by the making of offers independent to his. The primary judge found that relevant decisions were made for the substantial purpose of providing existing shareholders with alternatives which were more advantageous than the current bid, and to advance North Sydney Brick's commercial interests in relation to the development of certain land which was grossly undervalued on the company's books. The judge found that the transaction involving the joint venture would not have been entered into but for the making of the first bid;[237] but it was not a substantial purpose of the directors to prevent the first bid from succeeding, or to foreclose any amended takeover offer.

The majority of the New South Wales Court of Appeal[238] in *Darvall* affirmed the decision below. But Kirby P's dissenting judgment has merit, given his Honour's preparedness to superintend the performance of fiduciary obligations and intervene in the directors' decision-making when warranted.[239] Notwithstanding that Kirby P accepted the subjective honesty of the directors, he condemned the actions of the board, and the scheme in general, and classified the directors' conduct, 'as being on that side of the line which attracts the Court's intervention.'[240] In keeping with the determined push by the Australian judiciary to raise levels of directorial responsibility and accountability, Kirby P considered that to uphold the directors' decision in the light of all that had gone before, as being in the best interests of the company as a whole, would be to countenance an unacceptable standard of neglect of directors' obligations. And that in Kirby P's judgment:

---

[234] (1987) 5 ACLC 725 at 742; cf. *Cayne v Global Natural Resources plc* (unreported, Ch D, Megarry VC, 12 August 1982 (affirmed on another point [1984] 1 All ER 225)); see Barrett R I, case note (1982) 56 ALJ 600; and Ritson L, 'The "Proper Purposes" Duty of Directors and Defensive Measures against Company Takeovers' (1982-1985) 10 Syd LR 627 at 633 *et seq.*

[235] (1989) 7 ACLC 659; see Baxt R, 'Reforming the law relating to company directors' (1990) 64 ALJ 345 at 346 *et seq*; Baxt R, 'Second Guessing Directors' Decisions on Takeovers – A Mixed Message from the New South Wales Court of Appeal' (1990) 8 CSLJ 26; and Baxt R, 'The Role and Behaviour of Company Directors – Phase 2' (1990) 18 ABLR 53.

[236] (Kirby P, Mahoney and Clarke JJA).

[237] A 'well settled' principle: *Permanent Building Society v Wheeler* (1993-1994) 11 WAR 187 at 218 per Ipp J (Malcolm CJ and Seaman J agreed).

[238] (Mahoney and Clarke JJA).

[239] (1989) 7 ACLC 659 at 676; note *Permanent Building Society v Wheeler* (1993-1994) 11 WAR 187 at 218 per Ipp J (Malcolm CJ and Seaman J agreed), 'The issue is not whether a management decision was good or bad; it is whether the directors acted in breach of their fiduciary duties.'

[240] (1989) 7 ACLC 659 at 681.

[Would] be to sustain a passive conception of the duty of a fiduciary which has no place in company board rooms. Higher standards of vigilance and honesty are required there in dealing with other people's moneys.[241]

It is suggested that this approach to directorial responsibility and accountability of directors of Australian companies will enjoy continued support given Kirby J's elevation to the bench of the High Court of Australia. It is expected that his Honour's influence there will be profound. Kirby J's approach to directorial responsibility in Australian company law,[242] and his insistence upon the strict adherence by fiduciaries of their obligations in general, is well-known. His Honour's recent judgment in *Maguire v Makaronis* amply attests to that.[243] This approach on the part of Kirby J, and a recently re-constituted High Court of Australia, is considered in more detail in chapter nine of this book.

THE RE-EMERGENCE OF THE PROPER PURPOSES DOCTRINE

The proper purposes doctrine has recently enjoyed a measure of revivification in English company law at the hands of the Court of Appeal[244] in *Bishopsgate Investment Management Ltd v Maxwell (No. 2)*.[245] There, Ian Maxwell was found to be in breach of his fiduciary duty in signing various share transfers whereby shares were transferred for no consideration to another company controlling his father's private interests. The cause of action was constituted not by the failure to make enquiries, but by the improper transfer which had caused Bishopsgate Investment Management Ltd loss.[246] Chadwick J, at first instance, found Maxwell to be in breach of his fiduciary duty in signing the transfers and, as loss thereby resulted from the transfers, gave summary judgment against him. Given that the company was the trustee of various pension scheme assets, it was considered that the duties of the directors ought to be closely analogous to those of an individual trustee.[247] As such, it could not according to Chadwick J, 'be argued seriously that an individual trustee who signed a stock transfer form without considering whether the transfer was in the interests of his trust was not in breach of his fiduciary duty.'[248] In dismissing the appeal, Hoffmann LJ[249] reaffirmed that directors must exercise their powers solely for the purpose for which they are conferred. In Hoffmann LJ's judgment, the giving away of company assets for no consideration was

---

241 *Ibid.*
242 *Advance Bank Australia Ltd v FAI Insurances Ltd* (1987) 5 ACLC 725 at 742 per Kirby P (Glass JA agreed); *Darvall v North Sydney Brick & Tile Co Ltd (No. 2)* (1989) 7 ACLC 659 at 676 and 681 per Kirby P; and *Equiticorp Finance Ltd v Bank of New Zealand* (1993) 11 ACLC 952 at 979 per Kirby P.
243 (1996-1997) 188 CLR 449 at 492.
244 (Ralph Gibson, Leggatt and Hoffmann LJJ).
245 [1994] 1 All ER 261.
246 *Target Holdings Ltd v Redferns* [1994] 2 All ER 337 at 352-353 per Peter Gibson LJ (Hirst LJ agreed); on appeal *Target Holdings Ltd v Redferns* [1995] 3 All ER 785 at 793-794 per Lord Browne-Wilkinson (Lords Keith, Ackner, Jauncey and Lloyd agreed).
247 Cf. *In re Lands Allotment Company* [1894] 1 Ch 616 at 631 per Lindley LJ and at 638 per Kay LJ; note Ferran E, 'The Reform of the Law on Corporate Capacity and Directors' and Officers' Authority' (1992) 13 Co Law 124 and 177 at 179; and Ford H A J, Austin R P and Ramsay I M, *Ford's Principles of Corporations Law* (9th ed) Reed International Books Australia Pty Ltd, Sydney, 1999 at para 8.050.
248 [1993] BCC 120 at 137.
249 (Leggatt LJ agreed).

prima facie a use of directorial powers for an improper purpose and the burden was upon Maxwell to demonstrate its propriety.[250]

Of similar import in Australian company law is the more recent and controversial decision in *Gambotto v WCP Ltd*,[251] where the High Court of Australia[252] roundly endorsed the proper purposes doctrine in circumstances where a majority of shareholders, who held approximately 99.7 per cent of the company's shares, sought to amend the articles so as to permit compulsory acquisition of the remaining shares. It was conceded by the minority shareholders that the proposed acquisition price for their shares was fair and in excess of the current market price, however, they simply did not wish to sell. They sought to enjoin the company from resolving to alter the articles so as to effect the intended compulsory acquisition. The High Court determined that the proper purposes test was that applicable in the circumstances and firmly rejected the *bona fides* test applied by Lindley MR in *Allen v Gold Reefs of West Africa Ltd*.[253]

The principal judgment in *Gambotto* was jointly delivered by Mason CJ, Brennan, Deane and Dawson JJ who reaffirmed the illegitimacy of exercising powers simply for the purpose of aggrandizing the majority,[254] and proclaimed that, 'a power can be taken only if (i) it is exercisable for a proper purpose and (ii) its exercise will not operate oppressively in relation to minority shareholders.'[255] In their Honours' joint judgment, absent oppression to the minority shareholders, such an alteration would be valid where its substantial purpose is to secure the company from significant detriment or harm.[256] That will involve a value judgment on the part of the court and is yet another expression by the Australian judiciary of its preparedness to depart from the English and Australian courts' traditional reluctance to review or interfere with management decisions, expressed in a long line of authority extending back to *Carlen v Drury*.[257] As noted earlier in this chapter, an important aspect to the decision in *Gambotto* is the emphasis placed by all members of the High Court of Australia upon the requirement of fairness.[258] Any alteration to the company's articles will not be valid, 'simply because it was made for a proper purpose; it must also be fair in the circumstances.'[259] In this context, it should be noted that fairness has both procedural and substantive elements.[260]

---

[250] [1994] 1 All ER 261 at 265.

[251] (1995) 13 ACLC 342; see Whitford K, 'The Year That Was: An Overview of Corporate Law 1995' (1996) 6 AJCL 1 at 7-8; and Ramsay I M, *Gambotto v WCP Ltd: Its Implications for Corporate Regulation* The Centre for Corporate Law and Securities Regulation, University of Melbourne, Parkville, 1996 at 2.

[252] (Mason CJ, Brennan, Deane, Dawson and McHugh JJ).

[253] [1900] 1 Ch 656 at 671.

[254] Cf. *In re Bugle Press Ltd* [1961] Ch 270 at 286-288 per Lord Evershed MR (Donovan LJ agreed).

[255] (1995) 13 ACLC 342 at 348.

[256] Cf. *Brady v Brady* [1989] 1 AC 755 at 777-779 per Lord Oliver.

[257] (1812) 1 V & B 154 at 158 per Lord Eldon.

[258] Cf. Organisation for Economic Co-operation and Development, *OECD Principles of Corporate Governance* OECD Publications, Paris, 1999 at chapter II.

[259] (1995) 13 ACLC 342 at 349; see *Greenhalgh v Arderne Cinemas Ld* [1951] Ch 286 at 292 *per curiam*; note Walsh J K, 'The Exercise of Powers in the Interests of a Company' (1967-1968) 8 UWALR 176 at 183-184; and Ford H A J, Austin R P and Ramsay I M, *Ford's Principles of Corporations Law* (9th ed) Reed International Books Australia Pty Ltd, Sydney, 1999 at para 24.190.

[260] *Peters' American Delicacy Company Ltd v Heath* (1938-1939) 61 CLR 457 at 507 per Dixon J; cf. *Mutual Life Insurance Co of New York v The Rank Organisation Ltd* [1985] BCLC 11 at 21 per Goulding J; and *Re BSB Holdings Ltd (No. 2)* [1996] 1 BCLC 155 at 247-249 per Arden J; see Walsh J K, 'The Exercise of Powers in the Interests of a Company' (1967-1968) 8 UWALR 176 at 183; and Finn P D, *Fiduciary Obligations* The Law Book Company Ltd, Sydney, 1977 at 41-42 and 64 *et seq*.

Thus, if there was any doubt in English and Australian company law as to the existence of the proper purposes doctrine, as a separate means of exercising control over the way in which directors' wield their powers, then *Bishopsgate* and *Gambotto* most effectively dispel that. While *Gambotto* was limited to shareholders' powers, rather than directors' powers in the way in which *Gold Reefs* was, nonetheless, given the considerable influence which Lindley MR's judgment in that case had, and the way in which it was extended, adopted and applied, 'with remarkable consistency in cases concerned with alleged abuses of directorial powers',[261] it is suggested that the High Court of Australia's decision in *Gambotto* will have a profound influence upon Australian company law in general,[262] and will ultimately prove pre-eminent in this area of the law as well.

With this recent emphasis upon the proper purposes doctrine, the more robust and interventionist English and Australian judges will consider themselves empowered by revived and refashioned equitable rules and principles to play a much more active role in assessing the exercise of the powers by directors of British and Australian companies. In turn, this will inevitably lead to an evaluation of management decisions and the propriety of directors' decision-making;[263] notwithstanding that such an approach may be contrary to the advice of the Privy Council in *Howard Smith Ltd v Ampol Petroleum Ltd*,[264] and not in keeping with the judgment of the High Court of Australia in *Harlowe's Nominees Pty Ltd v Woodside (Lakes Entrance) Oil Company NL*.[265]

This fresh approach to intervention on the part of the Australian judiciary will be examined in detail in the next chapter of this book when we analyse the statutory duty in Australian company law to act honestly,[266] and the latest Australian cases in that regard. This is an area of company law deserving of comparative study. *A fortiori* as English company law resorts more and more to the Australian experience for guidance in this challenging and complex area of directors' duties.[267] For instance, in its consultation document entitled *Modern Company Law: The Strategic Framework*, which the Department of Trade and Industry ('DTI') published in February 1999, the DTI attaches, 'great importance to learning from the experience of other countries as we develop proposals for reform'.[268] The DTI specifically refers to Australian company law as being one of the models which its review will take cognisance of.[269] Hence

---

[261] Lindgren K E, 'The Fiduciary Nature of a Company Board's Power to Issue Shares' (1971-1972) 10 UWALR 364 at 367.

[262] Ramsay I M, *Gambotto v WCP Ltd: Its Implications for Corporate Regulation* The Centre for Corporate Law and Securities Regulation, University of Melbourne, Parkville, 1996 at 12; cf. Mitchell V, 'Company law reviews in Australia and the United Kingdom' (1999) 20 Co Law 98 at 103.

[263] *Kokotovich Constructions Pty Ltd v Wallington* (1995) 13 ACLC 1113 at 1125 per Kirby ACJ (Priestley and Handley JJA agreed), '[Whilst] Courts should hesitate before interfering with management decisions which have been reached bona fide ... this principle is of no application where, as in this case, the management decision was not *bona fide* arrived at. Indeed, it would be absurd to suggest that a court should forsake its responsibility to uphold the law in such a situation. If a director breaches his or her fiduciary duty in exercising a power for an improper purpose, not only is it desirable that the courts should intervene. They have a duty to do so.'

[264] [1974] AC 821 at 832 per Lord Wilberforce.

[265] (1969-1970) 121 CLR 483 at 493 *per curiam*.

[266] Companies Code s229(1); and Corporations Law s232(2).

[267] *Re Barings plc (No 5)* [1999] 1 BCLC 433 at 488 per Jonathan Parker J; note Davies P L, *Gower's Principles of Modern Company Law* (6th ed) Sweet & Maxwell Ltd, London, 1997 at 643.

[268] Department of Trade and Industry, *Modern Company Law: The Strategic Framework* HMSO, London, 1999 at para 4.1.

[269] *Ibid* at paras 4.8-4.11.

Mitchell's observation, in reference to the DTI's consultation paper released in March 1998 entitled *Modern Company Law: For a Competitive Economy*,[270] that a summary of the Australian experience and approach to date, 'could well be of assistance in any similar review in the United Kingdom',[271] is being borne out. The Law Commission's report entitled *Company Directors: Regulating Conflicts of Interests and Formulating a Statement of Duties*, published in September 1999, which recommends that not only should the duty upon directors of British companies to exercise care and diligence be partially codified,[272] but that there should also be 'a statutory statement of a director's main fiduciary duties',[273] is further testimony to that.

---

[270] Department of Trade and Industry, *Modern Company Law: For a Competitive Economy* (a consultative document) HMSO, London, 1998.

[271] Mitchell V, 'Company law reviews in Australia and the United Kingdom' (1999) 20 Co Law 98 at 98.

[272] Law Commission, *Company Directors: Regulating Conflicts of Interests and Formulating a Statement of Duties* HMSO, London, Cm 4436, 1999 at paras 5.19-5.20 and 5.38.

[273] *Ibid* at paras 4.48 and 4.68.

5

The Statutory Duty to Act Honestly

INTRODUCTION

Within Australian company law the statutory duty to act honestly has, to date, assumed a lower profile than the corresponding fiduciary duties upon directors of Australian companies to act in good faith and for proper purposes. These latter duties have been more in evidence in the day-to-day business of the Australian civil courts than the statutory duty. This is in spite of the fact that since 1958 there has been a statutory duty in Australian company law, the effect of which has been to oblige directors to act honestly in the discharge of their duties.[1] That duty has changed little so far as the black letter of the law is concerned and is now enacted in Corporations Law s232(2). It is of interest to note that the language employed in s232(2) is largely similar to that which first appeared in the statutes over 40 years ago.[2] We will consider its origins shortly.

It is significant that in Australian company law the statutory duty to act honestly is no longer restricted to directors,[3] but applies equally to any officers of the company who are authorised to act on its behalf.[4] Particularly to those acting in a managerial capacity.[5] In this book, however, we are concerned only with directors, and the duty upon them to act honestly remains dominated by equitable principles.[6] Equity here demands centre stage and affects vitally the directors' obligations to their Australian companies. For, independently of statute, 'the law has pitched the standard of honesty very high for directors, and this has been done simply enough by regarding a director as a person who occupies a fiduciary position.'[7] Equity, as Christie notes, 'retains a

---

[1]   Wallace G and Young J McI, *Australian Company Law and Practice* The Law Book Company Ltd, Sydney, 1965 at 393.

[2]   Companies Act 1958 (Vic) s107(1).

[3]   Corporations Law ss60, 232(1) and 232(2); cf. Company Directors Disqualification Act 1986 (UK) ss22(4) and 22(5); Financial Services Act 1986 (UK) s207(1); Insolvency Act 1986 (UK) ss214(7) and 251; and Companies Act 1985 (UK) ss309(3), 319-322, 322B, 330-346, 741(1) and 741(2).

[4]   Cf. *Secretary of State for Trade and Industry v Jones* [1999] BCC 336 at 349 per Jonathan Parker J; *Re Kaytech International plc* [1999] BCC 390 at 402-403 per Robert Walker LJ; *Secretary of State for Trade and Industry v Laing* [1996] 2 BCLC 324 at 337-339 per Evans-Lombe J; *Re Hydrodan (Corby) Ltd* [1994] BCC 161 at 162-163 per Millett J; and *Re Lo-Line Electric Motors Ltd* (1988) 4 BCC 415 at 421-422 per Browne-Wilkinson VC.

[5]   *Deputy Commissioner of Taxation v Austin* (1998) 16 ACLC 1555 at 1559 per Madgwick J; cf. *Canadian Aero Service Ltd v O'Malley* (1974) 40 DLR (3d) 371 at 381 per Laskin J.

[6]   Although, actionable fraud or deceit would give rise to a claim in damages at law: *Lagunas Nitrate Company v Lagunas Syndicate* [1899] 2 Ch 392 at 434-435 per Lindley MR; and *Castlereagh Motels Ltd v Davies-Roe* (1966) 67 SR (NSW) 279 at 283-284 per Wallace P and at 285 per Jacobs and Asprey JJA.

[7]   Menzies D, 'Company Directors' (1959) 33 ALJ 156 at 157.

primary role in ensuring that directors comply with the highest standards of conduct towards their companies.'[8] In the recent decision handed down by the Western Australian Full Court[9] in *Fitzsimmons v R*, Owen J echoed these remarks as the following extract from his Honour's judgment attests:

> It is a fundamental principle governing corporate governance that the relationship between a director and the company is a fiduciary one. The law imposes strict fiduciary and statutory obligations on a director so as to ensure high standards of loyalty in the performance of the duties of office.[10]

That much we have seen from the previous chapters of this book, and notwithstanding the recent trend within Australian company law to partial codification of directors' duties,[11] equitable, as well as legal, principles will continue to prove a driving force in setting, enforcing and remedying directors' conduct and decision-making well into the 21st century. *A fortiori* as the Australian judiciary strives to carry forward its revitalised approach to corporate governance,[12] and to implement the clearly stated intentions of the Australian Government to provide a sound and well-regulated environment for corporate activity.[13] Even so, the statutory duty in Australian company law to act honestly has not received the same parliamentary focus and attention that the statutory duty to exercise care and diligence has in recent years.[14]

From chapters two and three of this book, we have seen the effects of the Australian Government's deliberate push to strengthen extant legal and equitable duties upon directors of Australian companies to exercise care and diligence. This culminated in the introduction of a revivified Corporations Law s232(4) on 1 February 1993.[15] Deliberate steps taken in that regard by the Australian Government in response to a number of factors. For example, academic debate proved to be influential.[16] Moreover, the adverse publicity associated with the excesses and abuses perpetrated by some directors of Australian companies in the more widely publicised corporate crashes of the late 1980s and the early 1990s;[17] and the inevitable economic and social pressures consequent upon that. Furthermore, the Australian judiciary's attitudes to these excesses and abuses; such attitudes themselves being a reflection of, and in response to, earlier Australian parliamentary intent and changes in public opinion.[18]

It is interesting to note that no similar restructuring of either the directors' statutory duty to act honestly or the directors' fiduciary duties to act in good faith and for proper purposes has occurred in Australian company law *vis-à-vis* partial codification under

---

[8] Christie M, 'The Director's Fiduciary Duty not to Compete' (1992) 55 MLR 506 at 519.
[9] (Murray, Owen and Parker JJ).
[10] (1997) 23 ACSR 355 at 357.
[11] Cf. Law Commission, *Company Directors: Regulating Conflicts of Interests and Formulating a Statement of Duties* HMSO, London, Cm 4436, 1999 at paras 4.48, 5.19-5.20 and 5.38.
[12] Farrar J H, 'Corporate Governance, Business Judgement and the Professionalism of Directors' (1993) 6 CBLJ 1 at 2; and Whincop M J, 'An Economic Analysis of the Criminalisation and Content of Directors' Duties' (1996) 24 ABLR 273 at 277 and 291.
[13] Commonwealth, House of Representatives, Parliamentary Debates, 8 November 1990 at 3669; note Explanatory memorandum, *Corporate Law Economic Reform Program Bill 1998* CCH Australia Ltd, Sydney, 1999 at para 2.5.
[14] Cf. Corporate Law Economic Reform Program Bill 1998 (Cth) ss181 and 184.
[15] Added by Act No. 210 of 1992 and effective 1 February 1993.
[16] Cf. Editorial comment, 'Back to basics: company law reform' (1999) 20 Co Law 129 at 129.
[17] *The Australian Financial Review*, 21 April 1997; and *The Times*, 29 April 1999.
[18] Cf. *Glavanics v Brunninghausen* (1996) 19 ACSR 204 at 215 per Bryson J.

Corporations Law s232(2).[19] Indeed, very little in the way of amendment to the statutory duty to act honestly has taken place, and the duty has survived virtually intact since first introduced in Victoria via Companies Act 1958 (Vic) s107(1) which provided that:

> A director shall at all times act honestly and use reasonable diligence in the discharge of the duties of his office.

The reason for this static approach, it is suggested, is that the State and Federal Parliaments have considered the common law duties in this regard to be sufficiently well-developed so as not to warrant significant statutory intervention designed to dramatically alter the extant law; but, rather, merely statutory restatement designed to clarify the extant law and sharpen its focus.[20]

THE FORMER STATUTORY PROVISIONS

As we saw in chapter three of this book, Companies Act 1958 (Vic) s107(1) was the first of its kind in Australia to render a director, failing to perform his or her general law duty to act in good faith, liable to be convicted of a criminal offence.[21] Additionally, the director was, 'liable to the company for any profit made by him or for any damage suffered by the company as a result of the breach' of s107(1).[22] The directors' loyalties being very much in the company's favour. But, although the Victorian Parliament saw to it that the general law duty was expressly preserved,[23] the statutory duty to act honestly had very much a penal flavour with dishonest, that is to say fraudulent or criminal, overtones; rather than that actually intended by the Victorian Parliament.[24]

It is not surprising that Companies Act 1958 (Vic) s107(1) was under-utilised in the civil courts, tending to be more the vehicle for criminal prosecutions.[25] The imposition of penalties restricting its scope, 'to a greater extent than perhaps was originally intended.'[26] This is a phenomenon which has persisted to the present. But, notwithstanding this attempt at partial codification, when evaluating compliance with the

---

[19] Cf. Birds J R, 'A code of directors' duties?' (1974) 124 NLJ 1163 at 1166, 'it is more important to lay down by statute a modern standard of care and skill for the company director than to codify fiduciary duties which are already well established and clear.'

[20] Ford H A J, Austin R P and Ramsay I M, *Ford's Principles of Corporations Law* (9th ed) Reed International Books Australia Pty Ltd, Sydney, 1999 at paras 8.290-8.300.

[21] Wallace G and Young J McI, *Australian Company Law and Practice* The Law Book Company Ltd, Sydney, 1965 at 393; see *Vrisakis v Australian Securities Commission* (1992-1993) 9 WAR 395 at 404 per Malcolm CJ; and *Mesenberg v Cord Industrial Recruiters Pty Ltd* (1996) 14 ACLC 519 at 525 per Young J.

[22] Companies Act 1958 (Vic) s107(3).

[23] *Ibid* at s107(4); note *The Governor and Company of the Bank of England v Vagliano Brothers* [1891] AC 107 at 144-145 per Lord Herschell.

[24] *Corporate Affairs Commission v Papoulias* (1990) 8 ACLC 849 at 850-851 per Allen J.

[25] *Byrne v Baker* [1964] VR 443; the first reported prosecution of the statutory duty: Editorial comment (1964-1965) 38 ALJ 251 at 251.

[26] Editorial comment (1964-1965) 38 ALJ 251 at 251; note Parsons R W, 'The Director's Duty of Good Faith' (1967) 5 MULR 395 at 396.

section, the Australian courts continued to resort to equitable principles for guidance:[27] a practice which persists under current legislation.[28]

It will be recalled from chapter three of this book that Companies Act 1958 (Vic) was used as the model for a draft Companies Bill 1961, produced in an attempt to unify companies legislation throughout Australia. The resultant legislation came to be known as the uniform Companies Acts. Illustrative of the position concerning the duty upon directors of Australian companies to act honestly under the uniform Companies Acts across Australia at that time was Companies Act 1961 (Vic) s124(1), which referred to that duty in exactly the same terms as its predecessor.[29] The statutory duty so imposed reflected the general law position at that time and, like its earlier counterpart, expressly preserved that position.[30] This statutory duty, as the learned authors of *Australian Company Law and Practice* note, was first introduced into the Victorian Parliament as Companies Bill 1958 (Vic) s107(1) on the basis that the section:

> [Is] declaratory of the existing law, but it is believed that a restatement of the principles of honesty and good faith that should govern directors' conduct, clearly set out in the Act, will be an effective deterrent to misconduct and will free the courts from the technicalities of the existing law in dealing with all forms of dishonesty and impropriety by directors.[31]

It will also be recalled from chapter three of this book that when *Marchesi v Barnes*[32] came before the Victorian Supreme Court, Gowans J adopted the Victorian Full Court's view in *Byrne v Baker*[33] that the source of the language used in Companies Act 1961 (Vic) s124(1) should be attributed to Romer J in *In re City Equitable Fire Insurance Company Ltd*,[34] in order to conceptualise the statutory requirement necessary to discharge the duties of office by acting honestly. Gowans J in *Marchesi* also drew upon the judgments of Lindley MR in *Lagunas Nitrate Company v Lagunas Syndicate*,[35] and Lord Greene MR in *In re Smith and Fawcett Ltd*,[36] in order to provide background to s124(1).

The facts in *Marchesi* are stated in the headnote and were briefly these. Two directors were charged that they did not act honestly in the discharge of their duties contrary to Companies Act 1961 (Vic) s124(1). The charge in each case arose out of an allotment of shares; allegedly not made in the company's interests, but rather for the purpose of removing control from the existing shareholders. The proceedings came before the Victorian Supreme Court by way of order *nisi* to review and order *nisi* for

---

27 Menzies D, 'Company Directors' (1959) 33 ALJ 156 at 165; and *Byrne v Baker* [1964] VR 443.
28 *Vrisakis v Australian Securities Commission* (1992-1993) 9 WAR 395 at 404-411 per Malcolm CJ and at 442-443 per Ipp J (Malcolm CJ agreed); and *R v Yuill* (1994-1995) 15 ACSR 95 at 106-113 *per curiam.*
29 Companies Act 1958 (Vic) s107(1).
30 Companies Act 1961 (Vic) s124(4); note *The Governor and Company of the Bank of England v Vagliano Brothers* [1891] AC 107 at 144-145 per Lord Herschell.
31 Wallace G and Young J McI, *Australian Company Law and Practice* The Law Book Company Ltd, Sydney, 1965 at 393.
32 [1970] VR 434.
33 [1964] VR 443.
34 [1925] Ch 407.
35 [1899] 2 Ch 392.
36 [1942] Ch 304; note *The Duke Group Limited v Pilmer* (1998) 16 ACLC 567 at 663-664 per Mullighan J.

prohibition. Thus it was that the meaning of the statutory duty to act honestly first arrived for judicial interpretation in Australian company law. In Gowans J's view, the background to s124(1) permitted three conclusions: (i) the section is not concerned with directorial conduct in relation to creditors or others, only the company itself;[37] (ii) it is concerned with the directors' fiduciary duties to the company; and (iii) to act honestly refers to acting *bona fide* in the company's interests.[38]

Thus, prior to Companies Code s229(1), the relevant Australian companies legislation was simply a restatement of the general law obligation to act in good faith coupled with, 'the common law obligation to act with due diligence.'[39] It might be argued, however, that Gowans J's insistence in *Marchesi* that a breach of the duty involved, 'a consciousness that what is being done is not in the interests of the company',[40] suggests that absent consciousness the statutory duty would not be contravened even though the directors' decision was otherwise improper and voidable, and in contravention of the proper purposes doctrine.[41] Indeed, at first sight, the statutory duty appears narrower than the general law requirement encompassing *bona fides* and proper purposes. So much so that when the British Parliament was considering the introduction into English company law of a statutory duty to act honestly,[42] Birds felt that a statutory requirement to act honestly would be, 'incomplete and capable of being misleading on the ground that it ignores the aspect of directors' duties that has become known as the "proper purposes doctrine".'[43]

But this has not been the Australian experience. Quite the contrary. Gowans J in *Marchesi* clearly contemplated the proper purposes doctrine as falling within the statutory prescription to act honestly. The complaints before Gowans J charged the directors concerned with the improper purpose of removing control. The authorities which his Honour considered specifically related to the proper purposes doctrine, commencing with *Punt v Symons & Co Ltd*[44] and finishing with *Harlowe's Nominees Pty Ltd v Woodside (Lakes Entrance) Oil Company NL.*[45] This viewpoint is coincident with that of Allen J in *Corporate Affairs Commission v Papoulias.*[46] It is arguable, therefore, that the statutory duty to act honestly was from inception considered to collectively embrace the *bona fides* and the proper purposes doctrines. Malcolm CJ's judgment in *Eromanga Hydrocarbons NL v Australis Mining NL* supports this thesis.[47] Perry J has argued that this would have been made clearer had parliament at that time chosen simply to include the words, 'in the interests of the company as a whole' as

---

[37] No longer a credible proposition: *Flavel v Roget* (1990) 8 ACLC 237 at 247 per O'Loughlin J; *Morgan v Flavel* (1983) 1 ACLC 831 at 838 per White J; and *Southern Resources Ltd v Residues Treatment & Trading Co Ltd* (1990) 8 ACLC 1151 at 1168 *per curiam*.

[38] [1970] VR 434 at 438; see *Morgan v Flavel* (1983) 1 ACLC 831 at 837-838 per White J; and *Southern Resources Ltd v Residues Treatment & Trading Co Ltd* (1990) 8 ACLC 1151 at 1167 *per curiam*.

[39] *Marchesi v Barnes* [1970] VR 434 at 438 per Gowans J.

[40] *Ibid*.

[41] Ford H A J and Austin R P, *Ford's Principles of Corporations Law* (6th ed) Butterworths Pty Ltd, Sydney, 1992 at 489.

[42] Companies Bill 1973 (UK) cl 52; and Companies Bill 1978 (UK) cl 44.

[43] Birds J R, 'A code of directors' duties?' (1974) 124 NLJ 1163 at 1163.

[44] [1903] 2 Ch 506.

[45] (1969-1970) 121 CLR 483.

[46] (1990) 8 ACLC 849 at 851; cf. *Castlereagh Motels Ltd v Davies-Roe* (1966) 67 SR (NSW) 279 at 283 per Wallace P and at 285 per Jacobs and Asprey JJA; note *The Duke Group Limited v Pilmer* (1998) 16 ACLC 567 at 664 per Mullighan J.

[47] (1988) 6 ACLC 906 at 913.

being more readily demonstrative of its intention, 'to equate the statutory duty with that imposed in equity.'[48]

Within the relevant section, therefore, what is meant by the words: the duties of his office? The Victorian Full Court[49] in *Byrne*, in a joint judgment, considered that within the statutory context under discussion:

> [The] word 'duties' is used in a different sense from that in which the word 'duty' is used, when one is considering the duty owed by a director to his company and what he is bound to do or not to do in a set of circumstances.[50]

The Victorian Full Court in *Byrne* accepted the interpretation put upon those words by Romer J in *City Equitable* where his Lordship there explained the impossibility of describing the duty of directors in general terms and considered that to ascertain the directors' duties it is necessary to consider not only the nature of the company's business, but also the manner in which the company's work is distributed between the directors and the company's other officials.[51]

A similar approach was taken in *Commonwealth Bank of Australia v Friedrich* where Tadgell J considered that the proper performance of directors' duties will be dictated by a host of circumstances, including the type of company, the size and nature of its enterprise,[52] the provisions of its articles, the composition of its board and the distribution of work between the board and other officers.[53] Such an approach is consistent with that adopted by Rogers CJ in *AWA Ltd v Daniels*,[54] and Ipp J in *Vrisakis v Australian Securities Commission*.[55] Although the court in each of these cases was principally concerned with the directors' duty to exercise care and diligence, it is suggested that given the considerable overlap which infects that duty and the statutory duty to act honestly, similar considerations would apply.[56]

A SEPARATE STATUTORY PROVISION

We have seen from the treatment of Companies Code s229(2) in chapter three of this book, the way in which the Companies Code was brought into existence. It is not, therefore, proposed to re-canvass such matters in this chapter. The point to be made here is that Companies Code s229(1) is derived from the uniform Companies Acts of which Companies Act 1961 (Vic) s124(1) is illustrative. Section s229(1) relevantly provides that:

---

[48] *Residues Treatment and Trading Company Ltd v Southern Resources Ltd (No. 2)* (1989) 7 ACLC 1130 at 1152.
[49] (Herring CJ, Smith and Adam JJ).
[50] [1964] VR 443 at 450 *per curiam*; see *Gould v The Mount Oxide Mines Ltd* (1916-1917) 22 CLR 490 at 531 per Isaacs and Rich JJ; and *Vrisakis v Australian Securities Commission* (1992-1993) 9 WAR 395 at 451 per Ipp J (Malcolm CJ agreed).
[51] [1925] Ch 407 at 426-427; and Baxt R, *Afterman & Baxt's Cases and Materials on Corporations and Associations* (5th ed) Butterworths Pty Ltd, Sydney, 1988 at 554.
[52] Cf. *Deputy Commissioner of Taxation v Austin* (1998) 16 ACLC 1555 at 1558-1560 per Madgwick J.
[53] (1991) 5 ACSR 115 at 125.
[54] (1992) 10 ACLC 933 at 1012-1013.
[55] (1992-1993) 9 WAR 395 at 451.
[56] Birds J R, 'Making Directors do their Duties' (1980) 1 Co Law 67 at 70.

An officer of a corporation shall at all times act honestly in the exercise of his powers and the discharge of the duties of his office.

Like its predecessors,[57] Companies Code s229(1) preserves the general law position immediately prior to its enactment.[58] Unlike its predecessors, s229(1) deals solely with the duty to act honestly. The composite duty which required directors to act honestly and use reasonable diligence fell away. Thus, two separate and stand alone duties were enacted.[59] It is suggested that in practice the duties were always considered thus, but were, as we have seen, run together in composite form. In addition, s229(1) was extended to include the words, 'the exercise of his powers'.[60] This extension adds little to the section other than to make explicit what was already implicit. But, in doing so, these additional words sharpen the focus upon the proper purposes doctrine; a doctrine which is an integral part of the statutory duty to act honestly.[61]

Companies Code s229(1) came under consideration in *Flavel v Roget*,[62] where the South Australian Supreme Court dismissed an appeal from a magistrate concerning a charge against Roget that he did not act honestly in the discharge of his office by failing to comply with Stock Exchange of Adelaide Ltd listing requirements. The appeal was heard by O'Loughlin J who looked to *Marchesi v Barnes*[63] in order to consider the best interests of the company, an issue which his Honour considered to be imported into the subject charge.[64] O'Loughlin J accepted as a correct statement of law the following passage from Gowans J's judgment in *Marchesi*:

[The] language of the section [Companies Act 1961(Vic) s124(1)] appears to justify the conclusions, first, that the section is not concerned with the conduct of a director in relation to creditors or other persons dealing with or concerned with the company or anybody else but the company itself; secondly, that it is concerned with the performance of his fiduciary duty to the company; and, thirdly, that to 'act honestly' refers to acting bona fide in the interests of the company in the performance of the functions attaching to the office of director. A breach of the obligation to act bona fide in the interests of the company involves a consciousness that what is being done is not in the interests of the company, and deliberate conduct in disregard of that knowledge. This constitutes the element of *mens rea* in the criminal offence created by the statute. If the term 'fraud' is applicable in this section, it is only so in the sense of a 'fraud on the power'.[65] In effect, the common law obligation in respect of

---

57 Companies Act 1958 (Vic) s107(1); and Companies Act 1961 (Vic) s124(1).
58 Companies Code s229(10); note *The Governor and Company of the Bank of England v Vagliano Brothers* [1891] AC 107 at 144-145 per Lord Herschell.
59 Companies Code ss229(1) and 229(2); note Comerford A and Law L, 'Directors' Duty of Care and the Extent of "Reasonable" Reliance and Delegation' (1998) 16 CSLJ 103 at 106; and Ford H A J, Austin R P and Ramsay I M, *Ford's Principles of Corporations Law* (7th ed) Reed International Books Australia Pty Ltd, Sydney, 1995 at para 8142.
60 Cf. that recommended by the Jenkins' committee (Report of the Company Law Committee, HMSO, London, Cmnd 1749, 1962 at para 99(a)(i)) and which Companies Bill 1973 (UK) cl 52 was intended to enact, but which lapsed in February 1974.
61 *Australian Growth Resources Corporation Pty Ltd v van Reesema* (1988) 6 ACLC 529 at 539 per King CJ (Cox J agreed); and *Eromanga Hydrocarbons NL v Australis Mining NL* (1988) 6 ACLC 906 at 913 per Malcolm CJ.
62 (1990) 8 ACLC 237.
63 [1970] VR 434.
64 (1990) 8 ACLC 237 at 246-247.
65 Cf. *Eromanga Hydrocarbons NL v Australis Mining NL* (1988) 6 ACLC 906 at 913 per Malcolm CJ.

acting honestly, as with the common law obligation to act with due diligence has been made a statutory duty, and failure to perform it, provided there is the proper mental element, has been made a criminal offence.[66]

O'Loughlin J did, however, express reservations in *Flavel* as to whether or not in the light of *Walker v Wimborne*,[67] the proposition by Gowan J in *Marchesi* that the section is not concerned with creditors and others, remained valid.[68] This is a matter which will be considered further in chapters six and seven of this book.

THE LATEST STATUTORY PROVISION

Thirty years after the introduction into Australian company law of a statutory duty to act honestly, the Corporations Bill 1988 (Cth) was introduced into the Australian Parliament. After a false and ignominious start,[69] this ultimately led to the re-enactment of the statutory duty to act honestly.[70] Chapter three of this book details the history surrounding the Corporations Bill 1988 (Cth), the Corporations Act 1989 (Cth) and the way in which the Corporations Law was brought into effect across Australia on 1 January 1991.[71] It is not proposed to reflect upon those matters in this chapter. Suffice it to say that matters mentioned there apply *mutatis mutandis* here. Corporations Law s232(2) is simply a politically correct genderised restatement of its predecessor,[72] and relevantly provides that:

> An officer of a corporation shall at all times act honestly in the exercise of his or her powers and the discharge of the duties of his or her office.

Like its predecessors,[73] Corporations Law s232(2) preserves the general law position immediately prior to its enactment.[74] Unlike its predecessors, s232(2) attempts to do away with the penal flavour which pervaded earlier sections.[75] In a novel approach, the Australian Parliament initiated a fresh focus towards the statutory duties upon directors *inter alia* to act honestly on the one hand, and to exercise care and diligence on the other hand, by its enactment of the Corporate Law Reform Act 1992 (Cth),[76] various aspects of which came into effect on 1 February 1993 and on 23 June 1993.[77]

---

[66] [1970] VR 434 at 438.

[67] (1976-1977) 137 CLR 1.

[68] (1990) 8 ACLC 237 at 247; reservations earlier aired in *Morgan v Flavel* (1983) 1 ACLC 831 at 838 per White J; and subsequently aired in *Southern Resources Ltd v Residues Treatment & Trading Co Ltd* (1990) 8 ACLC 1151 at 1168 *per curiam*.

[69] *New South Wales v Commonwealth of Australia* (1989) 90 ALR 355.

[70] Corporations Law s232(2).

[71] Ford H A J, Austin R P and Ramsay I M, *Ford's Principles of Corporations Law* (9th ed) Reed International Books Australia Pty Ltd, Sydney, 1999 at paras 1.020 and 2.230-2.250.

[72] Companies Code s229(1).

[73] Companies Act 1958 (Vic) s107(1); Companies Act 1961 (Vic) s124(1); and Companies Code s229(1).

[74] Corporations Law s232(11); note *The Governor and Company of the Bank of England v Vagliano Brothers* [1891] AC 107 at 144-145 per Lord Herschell.

[75] *Corporate Affairs Commission v Papoulias* (1990) 8 ACLC 849 at 850-851 per Allen J.

[76] Introduced into the Australian Parliament on 3 November 1992.

[77] Act No. 210 of 1992 and effective 1 February 1993 and 23 June 1993.

This novel approach concerned the introduction of civil penalty provisions into Australian company law under a new regime found within Corporations Law Part 9.4B.[78] Civil penalty provisions will be considered in more detail in chapter eight of this book when we consider the topic of the disqualification of directors from holding office, and the payment of compensation. For present purposes, however, it should be noted that civil penalty provisions have application across the whole gamut of directors' statutory duties,[79] including those to act honestly on the one hand, and to exercise care and diligence on the other hand.[80] However, as Whincop has recently concluded, to the extent that civil penalty provisions create civil remedies, the statutory duties upon directors of Australian companies change little.[81]

This Australian parliamentary initiative which led to the introduction of civil penalty provisions was partly in response to a recommendation by the Senate Standing Committee on Legal and Constitutional Affairs in its report on directors' duties ('Cooney Report') that Australian company law be, wherever possible, decriminalised.[82] Prior to its repeal,[83] Corporations Law s232(3) provided that the penalty applicable to a contravention of Corporations Law s232(2) was:

(a) if the contravention was committed with intent to deceive or defraud the body corporate, members or creditors of the body corporate or creditors of any other person or for any other fraudulent purpose – $20,000 or imprisonment for 5 years, or both; or

(b) otherwise – $5,000.

Corporations Law Part 9.4B now implements the Senate Standing Committee's recommendations to the effect that: (i) criminal liability under the Corporations Law ought not apply in the absence of crimination; (ii) Corporations Law s232 be amended so that criminal liability only applies where conduct is genuinely criminal in nature;[84] and (iii) civil penalties be provided in the Corporations Law for breaches where no criminality is involved and that those suffering loss as a result of a breach be enabled

---

78   Added by Act No. 210 of 1992 and effective 1 February 1993.
79   E.g., Corporations Law s588G; see *Metropolitan Fire Systems Pty Ltd v Miller* (1997) 23 ACSR 699 at 701-703 per Einfeld J; and *Australian Securities Commission v Forem-Freeway Enterprises Pty Ltd* (1998-1999) 30 ACSR 339 at 340-341 per Madgwick J.
80   Corporations Law ss232(2) and 232(4); see Ford H A J, Austin R P and Ramsay I M, *Ford's Principles of Corporations Law* (9th ed) Reed International Books Australia Pty Ltd, Sydney, 1999 at paras 3.390, 8.360 and 9.288.
81   Whincop M J, 'An Economic Analysis of the Criminalisation and Content of Directors' Duties' (1996) 24 ABLR 273 at 280.
82   Senate Standing Committee on Legal and Constitutional Affairs, *Social and Fiduciary Duties and Obligations of Company Directors* AGPS, Canberra, 1989 at 58; note House of Representatives Standing Committee on Legal and Constitutional Affairs, *Corporate Practices and the Rights of Shareholders* AGPS, Canberra, 1991 at 211-213; Baxt R, 'Can the Law Relating to Directors' Duties be Reformed?' (1990) 8 CSLJ 110 at 114-115; and Sealy L S, 'Reforming the Law on Directors' Duties' (1991) 12 Co Law 175 at 178.
83   Omitted by Act No. 210 of 1992 and effective 1 February 1993.
84   Cf. *Proprietary Articles Trade Association v Attorney-General for Canada* [1931] AC 310 at 324 per Lord Atkin (Lords Blanesburgh, Merrivale, Russell and MacMillan agreed), 'Criminal Law connotes only the quality of such acts or omissions as are prohibited under appropriate penal provisions by authority of the State. The criminal quality of an act cannot be discerned by intuition; nor can it be discovered by reference to any standard but one: Is the act prohibited with penal consequences? Morality and criminality are far from co-extensive'.

to bring a claim for compensation.[85] By designating particular sections within the Corporations Law as civil penalty provisions, Part 9.4B draws those sections under its umbrella and provides civil and criminal consequences in the event of contravention, as appropriate.[86] These consequences are to be determined by separate proceedings, as the civil and criminal penalty regimes operate as alternatives.[87]

For present purposes, it should be noted that Corporations Law ss232(6B) and 1317DA expressly provide that Corporations Law s232(2) is a civil penalty provision and, thus, is subject to the new regime.[88] Significantly, criminality associated with the breach of duty prescribed by s232(2) now only attaches where a director has contravened a civil penalty provision knowingly, intentionally or recklessly,[89] and either: (i) dishonestly and intending to gain, whether directly or indirectly, an advantage for that or any other person; or (ii) intending to deceive or defraud someone.[90] This carries into effect the Cooney Report's recommendation that criminal liability should only apply, 'where conduct is genuinely criminal in nature.'[91] Sanctions hitherto attracted by contraventions of the duty upon directors of Australian companies to act honestly have now been reformed.[92]

If the wisdom of the Senate Standing Committee is to be accepted,[93] the removal of the criminal flavour from the statutory obligations upon directors of Australian companies, by the introduction of the new civil penalty provisions regime under Corporations Law Part 9.4B, should add a fresh impetus to civil litigants seeking to avail themselves of statutory rights and remedies stemming from Corporations Law

---

[85] Senate Standing Committee on Legal and Constitutional Affairs, *Social and Fiduciary Duties and Obligations of Company Directors* AGPS, Canberra, 1989 at 189-191; note House of Representatives Standing Committee on Legal and Constitutional Affairs, *Corporate Practices and the Rights of Shareholders* AGPS, Canberra, 1991 at 211-213.

[86] Commonwealth, House of Representatives, Parliamentary Debates, 3 November 1992 at 2403; and Commonwealth, Senate, Parliamentary Debates, 12 November 1992 at 2853.

[87] Bird H, 'The Problematic Nature of Civil Penalties in the Corporations Law' (1996) 14 CSLJ 405 at 407; note Corporate Law Economic Reform Program Bill 1998 (Cth) ss181 and 184.

[88] *Metropolitan Fire Systems Pty Ltd v Miller* (1997) 23 ACSR 699 at 713 per Einfeld J.

[89] Presumably in the *Derry v Peek* (1889) 14 App Cas 337 at 374 per Lord Herschell (Lords Halsbury LC and Watson agreed) sense; cf. *Regina v Mackinnon* [1959] 1 QB 150 at 153 per Salmon J; *The Queen v Phillips* [1971] 45 ALJR 467 at 478 per Windeyer J; *Manning v Cory* [1974] WAR 60 at 63 per Burt J; *Hyam v Director of Public Prosecutions* [1975] AC 55 at 74 per Lord Hailsham; *McL v Flavel* (1986) 4 ACLC 45 at 52-54 per Bollen J; *Brick and Pipe Industries Ltd v Occidental Life Nominees Pty Ltd* (1991-1992) 6 ACSR 464 at 478 *per curiam*; *Hatty v Pilkinton* (1992) 108 ALR 149 at 156-157 *per curiam*; and *Pollard v Commonwealth Director of Public Prosecutions* (1992) 8 ACSR 813 at 822-827 per Abadee J.

[90] Corporations Law s1317FA(1); Corporations Law Schedule 3 provides a penalty for the breach of s1317FA(1) in the form of a fine not exceeding $200,000 and/or imprisonment for a term not exceeding five years; note *R v Martyn* [1954] SASR 161 at 165 per Napier CJ; *Hardie v Hanson* (1960-1961) 105 CLR 451 at 456-460 per Dixon CJ; *Welham v Director of Public Prosecutions* [1961] AC 103 at 124-129 per Lord Radcliffe (Lords Tucker, Keith and Morris agreed); *Marchesi v Barnes* [1970] VR 434 at 437-438 per Gowans J; *Scott v Metropolitan Police Commissioner* [1975] AC 819 at 839 per Viscount Dilhorne (Lords Reid, Diplock, Simon and Kilbrandon agreed); *R v Ghosh* [1982] 2 All ER 689 at 695-696 per Lord Lane CJ (Lloyd and Eastham JJ agreed); *Corporate Affairs Commission v Papoulias* (1990-1991) 20 NSWLR 503 at 506 per Allen J; *Feil v Commissioner of Corporate Affairs* (1991) 9 ACLC 811 at 816-818 per O'Bryan J; and *Chew v The Queen* (1991-1992) 173 CLR 626 at 633-634 per Mason CJ, Brennan, Gaudron and McHugh JJ, at 637 per Deane J and at 640 per Dawson J.

[91] Senate Standing Committee on Legal and Constitutional Affairs, *Social and Fiduciary Duties and Obligations of Company Directors* AGPS, Canberra, 1989 at 190.

[92] Bird H, 'The Problematic Nature of Civil Penalties in the Corporations Law' (1996) 14 CSLJ 405 at 409.

[93] Senate Standing Committee on Legal and Constitutional Affairs, *Social and Fiduciary Duties and Obligations of Company Directors* AGPS, Canberra, 1989 at 58.

s232,[94] where applicable. The inhibitory effect of this criminal flavour which has in the past infected s232(2) ought disappear. The Australian civil courts should now be more inclined to find against errant directors than hitherto has been the case.[95] As a consequence, it is considered that the under-utilisation of ss232(2) and 232(4), identified a little earlier in this chapter, will be gradually reversed.[96] By virtue of Corporations Law s1317EB(1), however, it will be the Australian Securities and Investments Commission ('ASIC'),[97] Australia's corporate regulator, which mainly brings these actions.[98] As such, the challenge is now with ASIC, as Gething observes:

> [To] use the regime it has at its disposal fully, effectively and creatively to ensure that directors comply with the civil penalty provisions in a way that maintains, facilitates and improves the performance of companies and the efficiency and development of the economy.[99]

Research conducted during 1998 by the Centre for Corporate Law and Securities Regulation, under the auspices of the University of Melbourne, however, suggests that ASIC has not fully taken up this challenge. The Centre found that ASIC had commenced only 14 civil penalty applications relating to ten case situations from the inception of civil penalty provisions on 1 February 1993.[100] Even so, it should be remembered that the sixth anniversary of the introduction into Australian company law of civil penalty provisions has only been reached, and the statutory import of Corporations Law Part 9.4B, and Corporations Law ss232 and 588G as a whole for that matter, remains in its infancy. Thus, its effectiveness is perhaps a little too early to judge. Needless to say, there is little case-law specifically on these new sections within Part 9.4B, although it is starting to emerge.[101] However, it is acknowledged that Part 9.4B

---

[94] Whincop M J, 'An Economic Analysis of the Criminalisation and Content of Directors' Duties' (1996) 24 ABLR 273 at 274; cf. *Mesenberg v Cord Industrial Recruiters Pty Ltd* (1996) 14 ACLC 519 at 526-527 per Young J; note Baxt R, 'Doubt on statutory derivative action' (1996) 12 Co Dir 4 at 5-6.

[95] *Group Four Industries Pty Ltd v Brosnan* (1991) 9 ACLC 1181 at 1190 per Duggan J.

[96] *Airpeak Pty Ltd v Jetstream Aircraft Ltd* (1997) 15 ACLC 715 at 720-721 per Einfeld J; *Australian Securities Commission v Forem-Freeway Enterprises Pty Ltd* (1998-1999) 30 ACSR 339; and *ASC v Donovan* (1998) 28 ACSR 583; cf. *Mesenberg v Cord Industrial Recruiters Pty Ltd* (1996) 14 ACLC 519 at 526-527 per Young J; note Baxt R, 'Doubt on statutory derivative action' (1996) 12 Co Dir 4 at 5-6.

[97] Australian Securities and Investments Commission Act 1989 (Cth).

[98] *Metropolitan Fire Systems Pty Ltd v Miller* (1997) 23 ACSR 699 at 713 per Einfeld J; *Airpeak Pty Ltd v Jetstream Aircraft Ltd* (1997) 15 ACLC 715 at 720 per Einfeld J; cf. *Titlow v Intercapital Group (Australia) Pty Ltd* (1996) 20 ACSR 201 at 204 per Lehane J; note Corporations Law s1317HD(1); and Whincop M J, 'An Economic Analysis of the Criminalisation and Content of Directors' Duties' (1996) 24 ABLR 273 at 280.

[99] Gething M, 'Do We Really Need Criminal and Civil Penalties for Contraventions of Directors' Duties?' (1996) 24 ABLR 375 at 390.

[100] Bird H L, Gilligan G and Ramsay I M, *Regulating Directors' Duties – How Effective are the Civil Penalty Sanctions in the Australian Corporations Law?* The Centre for Corporate Law and Securities Regulation, The University of Melbourne, Parkville, 1999 at vii and 23.

[101] *Australian Securities Commission v Major* (unreported, Federal Court of Australia, Queensland District Registry No. QG3011/96, Drummond J, 16 August 1996) and *Stargard Security Systems Pty Ltd v Goldie* (1994) 13 ACSR 805 were concerned with Corporations Law s588G and appear to be amongst the first decisions involving Corporations Law Part 9.4B; see also *ASC v Donovan* (1998) 28 ACSR 583; *Simar Transit Mixers Pty Ltd v Baryczka* (1998) 28 ACSR 238; *Australian Securities Commission v Spencer* (1997) 25 ACSR 143; *Metropolitan Fire Systems Pty Ltd v Miller* (1997) 23 ACSR 699; and *Airpeak Pty Ltd v Jetstream Aircraft Ltd* (1997) 15 ACLC 715; cf. *Mesenberg v Cord Industrial Recruiters Pty Ltd* (1996) 14 ACLC 519.

has its genesis in, and is an analogue of, Trade Practices Act 1974 (Cth) Part VI. It is therefore considered likely that the Australian courts will look to, and draw upon, decisions which are affected by that legislation,[102] in the event that civil penalty provisions are availed of by ASIC more than presently seems to be the case.[103] Chapter eight of this book addresses these matters in some detail.

Notwithstanding the dearth of case-law directly upon Corporations Law s232(2), however, given the Australian Government's widely flaunted and much publicised manifesto in regard to the implementation of the objective standard of care and diligence under Corporations Law s232(4), and the reasons behind that, the way has been very clearly signposted for judicial interpretation *vis-à-vis* s232 generally; especially given the context within which s232(2) is to be found in the Corporations Law.[104] Such signposting will further strengthen the resolve of the Australian judiciary in promoting and preserving the integrity of Australian company law and the great many Australians affected by companies in their everyday lives; economically, politically, socially and environmentally.[105]

Within Australian company law there is an increasing insistence on the part of the Australian judiciary of the requirement of objectivity against which directors' conduct and decision-making is to be measured.[106] As a consequence, directors' subjectivity for so long associated with the application of the *bona fides* doctrine is gradually being departed from. This should assist those seeking to bring to account errant directors as raised levels of responsibility and greater accountability become the norm.[107] The

---

[102] E.g., *Trade Practices Commission v Prestige Motors Pty Ltd* (1994) 16 ATPR 42693; and *Trade Practices Commission v TNT Australia Pty Ltd* (1995) 17 ATPR 40161.

[103] Bird H L, Gilligan G and Ramsay I M, *Regulating Directors' Duties – How Effective are the Civil Penalty Sanctions in the Australian Corporations Law?* The Centre for Corporate Law and Securities Regulation, The University of Melbourne, Parkville, 1999 at vii and 23.

[104] *R v Yuill* (1994-1995) 15 ACSR 95 at 106-107 per Hunt CJ, Abadee and Simpson JJ.

[105] Cf. HM Treasury, *Financial Services and Markets Bill: A Consultation Document, Part One* HMSO, London, 1998 at foreword; Department of Trade and Industry, *Modern Company Law: For a Competitive Economy* (a consultative document) HMSO, London, 1998 at I; Stapledon G P, *Institutional Shareholders and Corporate Governance* Clarendon Press, Oxford, 1996 at 8; *The Australian Financial Review*, 2 January 1996; Committee on the Financial Aspects of Corporate Governance, *The Report of the Committee on the Financial Aspects of Corporate Governance* Gee and Co Ltd, London, 1992 at para 1.1; Senate Standing Committee on Legal and Constitutional Affairs, *Social and Fiduciary Duties and Obligations of Company Directors* AGPS, Canberra, 1989 at 7; and Sealy L S, 'Directors' "Wider" Responsibilities – Problems Conceptual, Practical and Procedural' (1987) 13 MULR 164 at 170; cf. Dwight F, 'Liability of Corporate Directors' (1907-1908) 17 YLJ 33 at 34; note *State Tax Commission of Utah v Aldrich* (1942) 316 US 174 at 192 per Jackson J.

[106] *Carter v Drake* (1992-1993) 9 WAR 82 at 94 per Malcolm CJ; see *Lyford v Commonwealth Bank of Australia* (1995) 13 ACLC 900 at 914 per R D Nicholson J; *Permanent Building Society v Wheeler* (1993-1994) 11 WAR 187 at 218 per Ipp J (Malcolm CJ and Seaman J agreed); *Southern Resources Ltd v Residues Treatment & Trading Co Ltd* (1990) 8 ACLC 1151 at 1164 *per curiam*; *Darvall v North Sydney Brick & Tile Co Ltd (No. 2)* (1989) 7 ACLC 659 at 676 per Kirby P; *Australian Growth Resources Corporation Pty Ltd v van Reesema* (1988) 6 ACLC 529 at 535-536 per King CJ (Cox J agreed); and *Richard Brady Franks Ltd v Price* (1937) 58 CLR 112 at 135 per Latham CJ; cf. *Howard Smith Ltd v Ampol Petroleum Ltd* [1974] AC 821 at 835 per Lord Wilberforce; *Hindle v John Cotton Ltd* (1919) 56 ScLR 625 at 630-631 per Viscount Finlay; and *Allen v Gold Reefs of West Africa Ltd* [1900] 1 Ch 656 at 671 per Lindley MR.

[107] *Daniels v Anderson* (1995) 13 ACLC 614 at 662-666 per Clarke and Sheller JJA; and *Kokotovich Constructions Pty Ltd v Wallington* (1995) 13 ACLC 1113 at 1125 per Kirby ACJ (Priestley and Handley JJA agreed); cf. *Re Grayan Building Services Ltd* [1995] BCC 554 at 577 per Henry LJ, 'The statutory corporate climate is stricter than it has ever been, and those enforcing it should reflect the fact that Parliament has seen the need for higher standards.'

application of objective standards in this way should encourage directors of Australian companies to pursue corporate goals in their company's interests, thus permitting of less subjectivity as to directors' intentions or beliefs than hitherto has been the case.[108] Thus, no longer will honest or altruistic behaviour by directors deny a finding of improper conduct if that conduct, objectively determined, was carried out for an improper purpose.[109]

In *Australian Growth Resources Corporation Pty Ltd v van Reesema* King CJ[110] observed that a director, 'may be in breach of his fiduciary duties notwithstanding the subjective honesty of his motives.'[111] Thus, a director must act for the benefit of the company as a whole; and, as King CJ went on to explain, it is not to the point that a director genuinely considers his purposes to be honest, if those purposes are not in the company's interests.[112] However, as Mullighan J in *The Duke Group Limited v Pilmer* recently noted, albeit in passing only, King CJ's observations in *van Reesema* which are extracted above in respect to honesty were not, 'necessarily equating fiduciary duty with the obligation under [Companies Code] s229(1) although the same conduct may constitute a breach of both.'[113] It is suggested that with the implementation of Corporations Law Part 9.4B and the introduction of the civil penalty regime,[114] King CJ's approach to the intractable concept of honesty is likely to be increasingly favoured by the Australian judiciary. As the learned authors of *Ford's Principles of Corporations Law* observe in this respect:

> The result is probably that [Corporations Law] s232(2) now applies to any breach of the duty to act in good faith in the interests of the company and the duty to act for proper purposes, whether or not the director subjectively and honestly believed that he or she was acting in the company's interests, but unless conscious dishonesty or an intention to deceive is present, there is no criminal offence.[115]

It should be briefly mentioned here that in 1995 the Corporations Law Simplification Task Force proposed that the statutory duty in Australian company law to act honestly be rewritten, without changing its meaning, to reflect the fiduciary concept of honesty, and to avoid any inconsistent use of the word honestly throughout the Corporations Law.[116] It was proposed at that time that Corporations Law s232(2) be redrafted so that directors of Australian companies were required to, 'act in good faith in the best

---

[108] *Permanent Building Society v Wheeler* (1993-1994) 11 WAR 187 at 218 per Ipp J (Malcolm CJ and Seaman J agreed); and *Bishopsgate Investment Management Ltd v Maxwell (No. 2)* [1994] 1 All ER 261 at 268-269 per Ralph Gibson LJ.

[109] *Whitehouse v Carlton Hotel Pty Ltd* (1987) 5 ACLC 421 at 426 per Mason CJ, Deane and Dawson JJ; *Advance Bank Australia Ltd v FAI Insurances Ltd* (1987) 5 ACLC 725 at 743 per Kirby P (Glass JA agreed); and *Darvall v North Sydney Brick & Tile Co Ltd (No. 2)* (1989) 7 ACLC 659 at 676 per Kirby P; note Birds J R, 'Making Directors do their Duties' (1980) 1 Co Law 67 at 70.

[110] (Cox J agreed).

[111] (1988) 6 ACLC 529 at 538; see *Nocton v Lord Ashburton* [1914] AC 932 at 954 per Viscount Haldane LC (Lord Atkinson agreed).

[112] (1988) 6 ACLC 529 at 538.

[113] (1998) 16 ACLC 567 at 665.

[114] Added by Act No. 210 of 1992 and effective 1 February 1993.

[115] Ford H A J, Austin R P and Ramsay I M, *Ford's Principles of Corporations Law* (9th ed) Reed International Books Australia Pty Ltd, Sydney, 1999 at para 8.300.

[116] *Ibid*; and Ford H A J, Austin R P and Ramsay I M, *Ford's Principles of Corporations Law* (7th ed) Reed International Books Australia Pty Ltd, Sydney, 1995 at para 8144.

interests of the company and for a proper purpose'.[117] With the change in government, the Task Force found disfavour and in March 1997 the newly elected Australian Government established the Corporate Law Economic Reform Program in its stead. The aim of this program is to reform key areas of Australian companies law, to make it easier for new businesses to be established, and to reduce the cost of business regulation.[118]

This Australian Government initiative has relevantly spawned the Corporate Law Economic Reform Program Bill 1998 (Cth) which proposes that the extant statutory duty upon directors of Australian companies to act honestly be replaced by an obligation that they exercise their powers and discharge their duties: (i) in good faith in what they believe to be in the best interests of the corporation; and (ii) for a proper purpose.[119] It is proposed, therefore, that the word honestly be written out of the legislation so as to avoid any inconsistent use of it and to emphasise the fiduciary principles which underpin the statutory obligation.[120] If enacted, this is unlikely to significantly impact upon the way in which the Australian courts have recently interpreted, and will continue to interpret, the requisite duty.[121]

A PERSPECTIVE FROM THE LATE 1980s AND THE EARLY 1990s

It is expedient to now move on to consider several Australian cases which reflect the perspective of the Australian judiciary to the duty upon directors of Australian companies to act honestly during the late 1980s and the early 1990s. These cases deal with the prevailing attitudes under Companies Code s229(1) concerning breaches prior to 1 January 1991 and before the introduction into Australian company law of Corporations Law s232(2). Given the interchangeability between Companies Code s229(1) and Corporations Law s232(2), however, these decisions clearly will have application to s232(2). If anything, such decisions upon the duty to act honestly will understate the latest attitudes fuelled by the ongoing quest for raised levels of directorial responsibility and greater accountability in Australian company law.[122]

---

[117] Corporations Law Simplification Task Force, *Officers and related party transactions: Proposal for simplification* Canberra, 1995 at 10-11. Such an approach is consistent with that taken in *Marchesi v Barnes* [1970] VR 434 at 438 per Gowans J; *Australian Growth Resources Corporation Pty Ltd v van Reesema* (1988) 6 ACLC 529 at 539 per King CJ (Cox J agreed); *Residues Treatment and Trading Company Ltd v Southern Resources Ltd (No. 2)* (1989) 7 ACLC 1130 at 1152 per Perry J; *Corporate Affairs Commission v Papoulias* (1990) 8 ACLC 849 at 851 per Allen J; and *Feil v Commissioner of Corporate Affairs* (1991) 9 ACLC 811 at 817 per O'Bryan J.

[118] Parliamentary Joint Committee on Corporations and Securities, *Report on the Corporate Law Economic Reform Program Bill 1998* AGPS, Canberra, 1999 at para 1.1.

[119] Corporate Law Economic Reform Program Bill 1998 (Cth) s181(1).

[120] Explanatory memorandum, *Corporate Law Economic Reform Program Bill 1998* CCH Australia Ltd, Sydney, 1999 at para 4.2.

[121] *Permanent Building Society v Wheeler* (1993-1994) 11 WAR 187 at 218 per Ipp J (Malcolm CJ and Seaman J agreed); *Carter v Drake* (1992-1993) 9 WAR 82 at 94 per Malcolm CJ; *Southern Resources Ltd v Residues Treatment & Trading Co Ltd* (1990) 8 ACLC 1151 at 1164 *per curiam*; *Darvall v North Sydney Brick & Tile Co Ltd (No. 2)* (1989) 7 ACLC 659 at 676 per Kirby P; *Eromanga Hydrocarbons NL v Australis Mining NL* (1988) 6 ACLC 906 at 913 per Malcolm CJ; *Australian Growth Resources Corporation Pty Ltd v van Reesema* (1988) 6 ACLC 529 at 535-536 and 539 per King CJ (Cox J agreed); and *Richard Brady Franks Ltd v Price* (1937) 58 CLR 112 at 135 per Latham CJ.

[122] Cf. *Re Grayan Building Services Ltd* [1995] BCC 554 at 577 per Henry LJ, 'The statutory corporate climate is stricter than it has ever been, and those enforcing it should reflect the fact that Parliament has seen the need for higher standards.'

Absent criminal law considerations, the impact upon Australian company law of the statutory duty to act honestly has, to date, been minimal. Little has happened to affect the day-to-day business of the courts. Because of the penal flavour to the section, and the uncertainty and utility surrounding statutory remedies consequent upon a proven breach, civil litigants have largely shied away from invoking the relevant section; preferring to resort to better understood, and more familiar, equitable bases for relief. These are examined in detail in chapter nine of this book. Arguments also persist that given the penal flavour which has in the past infected the statutory duties to act honestly and also to exercise care and diligence, the judiciary has at times been shy to fix errant directors with liability; especially where their conduct was, 'honest but careless.'[123]

In the main, therefore, the Australian civil courts continue to treat directors as fiduciaries,[124] resort to time-honoured equitable principles, and assess the propriety of directors' decision-making accordingly;[125] as they have done for well over a century. Even so, the manner in which today's courts apply the traditional equitable principles, associated with the statutory duty to act honestly, to the complex commercial and corporate disputes which so dominate today's litigious arena, has changed. In Australian company law especially, there is a new breed of commercial judge, more robust and interventionist than his or her predecessor. Judges prepared to revive and refashion traditional rules, principles and approaches considered applicable to resolving today's complex commercial and corporate disputes.[126] Thus, it is to equity and the case-law that we must continue to look in order to discern the relevant principles when analysing the directors' statutory duty to act honestly.

One of the principal decisions to emerge during this period is *Australian Growth Resources Corporation Pty Ltd v van Reesema*,[127] where the South Australian Full Court[128] found the directors concerned to be in breach of Companies Code s229(1) and, in doing so, recognised that a director may fail to act honestly within the meaning of the section without fraud. Furthermore, a director who exercises his or her powers for a purpose which the law deems to be improper, infringes the section notwithstanding that they believe themselves to be acting honestly.[129] In the course of so finding, King CJ[130] reaffirmed the fiduciary character of the director/company relationship and the primary consequence that a director is bound to exercise his or her powers *bona fide* in the company's interests. Thus, the exercise of a fiduciary power for a purpose beyond

---

[123] *Permanent Building Society v Wheeler* (1993-1994) 11 WAR 187 at 247 per Ipp J (Malcolm CJ and Seaman J agreed).

[124] Ford H A J, Austin R P and Ramsay I M, *Ford's Principles of Corporations Law* (9th ed) Reed International Books Australia Pty Ltd, Sydney, 1999 at para 8.010.

[125] E.g., *Daniels v Anderson* (1995) 13 ACLC 614; *Kokotovich Constructions Pty Ltd v Wallington* (1995) 13 ACLC 1113; and *State of South Australia v Clark* (1996) 19 ACSR 606.

[126] E.g., *Equiticorp Finance Ltd v Bank of New Zealand* (1993) 11 ACLC 952; *Bishopsgate Investment Management Ltd v Maxwell (No. 2)* [1994] 1 All ER 261; *Mallina Holdings Ltd v Biala Ltd* (1994) 15 ACSR 1; and *Daniels v Anderson* (1995) 13 ACLC 614; see Sealy L S, 'Directors' "Wider" Responsibilities – Problems Conceptual, Practical and Procedural' (1987) 13 MULR 164 at 169; and Sealy L S, '"Bona Fides" and "Proper Purposes" in Corporate Decisions' (1989) 15 MULR 265 at 265.

[127] (1988) 6 ACLC 529.

[128] (King CJ, Cox and Johnston JJ).

[129] Cf. *Marchesi v Barnes* [1970] VR 434 at 438 per Gowans J; Ford H A J and Austin R P, *Ford's Principles of Corporations Law* (6th ed) Butterworths Pty Ltd, Sydney, 1992 at 488-490; and *Permanent Building Society v Wheeler* (1993-1994) 11 WAR 187 at 218 per Ipp J (Malcolm CJ and Seaman J agreed).

[130] (Cox J agreed).

its legitimate scope is invalid.[131] On the statutory duty to act honestly, King CJ considered the section to embody a concept analogous to constructive fraud, 'a species of dishonesty which does not involve moral turpitude.'[132] As a consequence, a director who exercises his or her powers for an improper purpose, infringes the statutory duty notwithstanding that according to their own lights they may be acting honestly.[133]

With the introduction of Corporations Law Part 9.4B into Australian company law on 1 February 1993,[134] and the emphasis now upon civil penalty provisions, King CJ's judgment in *van Reesema* has been very clearly borne out.[135] A similar approach was taken in *Eromanga Hydrocarbons NL v Australis Mining NL*,[136] where the Western Australian Supreme Court was asked to determine whether the directors concerned acted otherwise than in good faith and in the interests of Australis Mining NL in making a placement of shares to the third defendant. In considering whether or not the allotment was for an improper purpose, Malcolm CJ explained that the duty to act honestly involves a duty to act in good faith.[137] The two duties are coincident and, 'it is of no moment that the duty of directors has been elevated to a statutory duty of honesty'.[138]

The statutory duty to act honestly often falls for consideration within the context of takeovers. *Southern Resources Ltd v Residues Treatment & Trading Co Ltd*[139] is apposite. There, the South Australian Full Court[140] was concerned with the propriety of directors resolving to make a takeover offer in the face of objections by minority shareholders. Perry J, the trial judge, held that certain of the directors were motivated by improper purposes in propounding the takeover offer and that *inter alia* they were in breach of their fiduciary duty to act *bona fide* in the interests of the company as a whole and, further, in breach of their corresponding statutory duty under Companies Code s229(1). The Full Court, in a joint judgment, agreed. Although the Full Court considered that conceptually honesty may differ according to the circumstances,[141] it felt bound to follow the South Australian Full Court's decision in *van Reesema*,[142] that the fiduciary duty to act honestly is to be equated with the statutory duty.[143]

Another South Australian case which reinforces the relationship between the fiduciary duty and the statutory duty is *Gemstone Corporation of Australia Ltd v*

---

[131] (1988) 6 ACLC 529 at 535-536; see *Richard Brady Franks Ltd v Price* (1937) 58 CLR 112 at 135 per Latham CJ; *The Australian Metropolitan Life Assurance Company Ltd v Ure* (1923) 33 CLR 199 at 217 per Isaacs J; *Greenhalgh v Arderne Cinemas Ld* [1951] Ch 286 at 291 per Evershed MR; *Walker v Wimborne* (1976-1977) 137 CLR 1 at 7 per Mason J; and *Southern Resources Ltd v Residues Treatment & Trading Co Ltd* (1990) 8 ACLC 1151 at 1164 *per curiam*.

[132] (1988) 6 ACLC 529 at 539; cf. *Marchesi v Barnes* [1970] VR 434 at 438 per Gowans J; and *Re Living Images Ltd* [1996] BCC 112 at 116 per Laddie J; see Ford H A J and Austin R P, *Ford's Principles of Corporations Law* (6th ed) Butterworths Pty Ltd, Sydney, 1992 at 488-490.

[133] (1988) 6 ACLC 529 at 539 per King CJ (Cox J agreed).

[134] Added by Act No. 210 of 1992 and effective 1 February 1993.

[135] Cf. Ford H A J, Austin R P and Ramsay I M, *Ford's Principles of Corporations Law* (9th ed) Reed International Books Australia Pty Ltd, Sydney, 1999 at para 8.300.

[136] (1988) 6 ACLC 906.

[137] *Ibid* at 913; cf. *State of South Australia v Clark* (1996) 19 ACSR 606; note *Mid Density Developments Pty Ltd v Rockdale Municipal Council* (1993) 116 ALR 460.

[138] (1988) 6 ACLC 906 at 913 per Malcolm CJ.

[139] (1990) 8 ACLC 1151; see Black A, 'Recent Developments in Directors' Duties: A Postscript' (1991) 8 ABR 10.

[140] (Jacobs ACJ, Prior and Mullighan JJ).

[141] (1990) 8 ACLC 1151 at 1166-1167 *per curiam*.

[142] (1988) 6 ACLC 529 at 539 per King CJ (Cox J agreed).

[143] Black A, 'Recent Developments in Directors' Duties: A Postscript' (1991) 8 ABR 10 at 10.

Grasso.[144] The South Australian Full Court[145] found Grasso, a director of Gemstone Corporation of Australia Ltd ('Gemstone'), to be in breach of his fiduciary duties to Gemstone by causing another company of which he was a director and shareholder to take up partly-paid shares in Gemstone when that other company never had any assets and, for that reason, could never answer any call on the Gemstone shares from its own resources. The case was argued before Perry J on the basis that Grasso was in breach of general law duties as well as statutory duties under Companies Code ss229(1) and 229(2). As to the relationship between those duties, Perry J was of the view that the scope of the statutory duty was no different from that which is imposed on a fiduciary in equity.[146] On appeal, however, the Full Court reached its decision by resorting to Grasso's fiduciary obligations to the company only, and ignored any statutory considerations.

Although *Jenkins v Enterprise Gold Mines NL*[147] was concerned with an attack upon certain decisions being taken by directors common to a group of companies, which resulted in discrimination against certain minority shareholders, what fell from the Western Australian Full Court[148] in the course of giving judgment is apposite to the discussion at hand. Consequent upon certain directorial decisions, large sums of money left Enterprise Gold Mines NL ('Enterprise') to the advantage of other companies within the group; the effect of which was to, in many cases, discriminate against the minority shareholders in Enterprise. In many cases this occurred without any adequate explanation of the conflict of interest of some directors involved, or of the commercial advantages to Enterprise, where not only was the transaction one which apparently involved unnecessary risk, but where large sums of money were subsequently lost to Enterprise without any explanation as to the reasons for the transaction in the first place, or any explanation how the directors or those involved in the transactions fulfilled their fiduciary duty. In a joint judgment, Malcolm CJ, Rowland and Franklyn JJ expressed the view that:

> The principles relating to conflict of interests are an extension of the requirement that the directors act in good faith in the interests and for the benefit of the company and its shareholders as a whole.[149]

Consistent with the English approach exemplified in *Charterbridge Corporation Ltd v Lloyds Bank Ltd*,[150] the Western Australian Full Court in *Jenkins* considered that it was not open to consider the benefit of the group as a whole without giving separate consideration to that of the company alone. In doing so, the Full Court favoured Pennycuick J's view that the proper test, 'must be whether an intelligent and honest man in the position of a director of the company concerned, could, in the whole of the existing circumstances, have reasonably believed that the transactions were for the

---

[144]   (1994) 12 ACLC 653.
[145]   (Matheson, Prior and Olsson JJ).
[146]   (1993) 11 ACLC 1161 at 1176.
[147]   (1992) 10 ACLC 136.
[148]   (Malcolm CJ, Rowland and Franklyn JJ).
[149]   (1992) 10 ACLC 136 at 146; see *Richard Brady Franks Ltd v Price* (1937) 58 CLR 112 at 137 per Latham CJ.
[150]   [1970] Ch 62; note Schmitthoff C M, 'The Wholly Owned and the Controlled Subsidiary' [1978] JBL 218 at 219 *et seq*.

benefit of the company.'[151] The Full Court explained that the directors' failure to act in the company's interest in relation to a transaction with another company in the group would involve a breach of fiduciary duty in terms of both the general law and the statutory duty to act honestly.[152] In doing so, the Full Court reaffirmed the Australian judiciary's approach; namely, that the statutory duty to act honestly encapsulates the *bona fides* and the proper purposes doctrines.[153]

As such, and in the light of the re-emergence of the proper purposes doctrine,[154] there is considerable scope for judges of a robust and interventionist disposition to further raise levels of directorial responsibility and accountability in keeping with that witnessed in chapters two and three of this book *vis-à-vis* the directors' non-statutory, and statutory, duties to exercise care and diligence.[155]

RECENT CASES: A NEW ERA FOR DIRECTORS?

Against this background, and in the light of the very clear Australian judicial and parliamentary intent to give effect to raised levels of responsibility and accountability, insofar as directors of Australian companies are concerned, one can be fairly confident as to the direction in which the Australian judiciary will continue to move as the new millennium unfolds.[156] The recent decision of the Western Australian Full Court[157] in *Australian Securities Commission v Gallagher*,[158] although strictly on Companies Code s229(2), showed amply that any attempt to categorise directors and to link duties to categories may oversimplify the reality that directors come in all shapes and sizes and that their duties range across a spectrum rather than fall into neatly defined categories.[159] As a consequence, many of the more recent Australian cases, which deal with matters presently under discussion, involve considerations which fall to be discussed under both Corporations Law ss232(2) and 232(4). Often, circumstances which give

---

[151] [1970] Ch 62 at 74; see *Reid Murray Holdings Ltd v David Murray Holdings Pty Ltd* (1972-1973) 5 SASR 386 at 402 per Mitchell J; and *Japan Abrasive Materials Pty Ltd v Australian Fused Materials Pty Ltd* (1998) 16 ACLC 1172 at 1180 per Templeman J; cf. *Equiticorp Finance Ltd v Bank of New Zealand* (1993) 11 ACLC 952 at 1018 per Clarke and Cripps JJA.

[152] (1992) 10 ACLC 136 at 147 *per curiam*; see *Walker v Wimborne* (1976-1977) 137 CLR 1 at 6 per Mason J (Barwick CJ agreed).

[153] *Eromanga Hydrocarbons NL v Australis Mining NL* (1988) 6 ACLC 906 at 913 per Malcolm CJ.

[154] *Gambotto v WCP Ltd* (1995) 13 ACLC 342; *Kokotovich Constructions Pty Ltd v Wallington* (1995) 13 ACLC 1113; *Bishopsgate Investment Management Ltd v Maxwell (No. 2)* [1994] 1 All ER 261; and *Re BSB Holdings Ltd (No. 2)* [1996] 1 BCLC 155.

[155] E.g., *Norman v Theodore Goddard* [1992] BCC 14 at 15 per Hoffmann J; *Re D'Jan of London Ltd* [1993] BCC 646 at 648-649 per Hoffmann LJ; *V risakis v Australian Securities Commission* (1992-1993) 9 WAR 395 at 451 per Ipp J (Malcolm CJ agreed); *Daniels v Anderson* (1995) 13 ACLC 614 at 662 per Clarke and Sheller JJA; *Androvin v Figliomeni* (1996) 14 ACLC 1461 at 1470 per Owen J (Kennedy and Franklyn JJ agreed); and *Re Barings plc* [1998] BCC 583 at 586 per Sir Richard Scott VC.

[156] Cf. *Re Grayan Building Services Ltd* [1995] BCC 554 at 577 per Henry LJ, 'The statutory corporate climate is stricter than it has ever been, and those enforcing it should reflect the fact that Parliament has seen the need for higher standards.'

[157] (Pidgeon, Franklyn and Walsh JJ).

[158] (1993) 11 ACLC 286.

[159] Shepherd J C, *The Law of Fiduciaries* The Carswell Company Ltd, Toronto, 1981 at 347-348; and Shepherd J C, 'Towards a Unified Concept of Fiduciary Relationships' (1981) 97 LQR 51 at 77; note *In re City Equitable Fire Insurance Company Ltd* [1925] Ch 407 at 426-427 per Romer J; *Commonwealth Bank of Australia v Friedrich* (1991) 5 ACSR 115 at 125 per Tadgell J; and *Deputy Commissioner of Taxation v Austin* (1998) 16 ACLC 1555 at 1558-1560 per Madgwick J.

rise to the breach of one duty will also ground the breach of the other duty. It is inevitable that these duties overlap, intertwine and form a continuum. As such, they are often not easily separable.

A good example of this is *Cummings v Claremont Petroleum NL*,[160] which was considered in chapter three of this book. From there, it will be recalled that the Full Federal Court of Australia[161] was concerned with a publicly listed company controlled by a powerful personality whose decisions invariably held sway.[162] The Full Court determined that the receipt by directors of unreasonable benefits at the company's expense may show that directors have failed to act honestly or failed to exercise care and diligence in the discharge of their duties.[163] The Full Court deplored the directors' conduct in preparing consultancy agreements more favourable to their own interests than those of the company whose interests they were bound to protect.[164] Such conduct, the Full Court felt, demonstrated a lack of care and diligence and could be taken into account with other evidence in deciding whether or not the directors concerned had acted honestly in the exercise of their powers.[165] In the result, the Full Court endorsed the trial judge's finding that the directors had breached Companies Code s229(1); and, in doing so, reaffirmed that directors' duties are stringent given that the foundation of the statutory duty is the fiduciary relationship between directors and their company.[166]

Another example is *Hannes v MJH Pty Ltd*.[167] There, the New South Wales Court of Appeal[168] was concerned with a small family company dominated by one man within a corporate setting considered virtually his own. Hannes utilised the company's memorandum and articles to justify the company entering into a service agreement with him to include a payment of $500,000 upon termination of his employment. In addition, resolutions were passed to allot shares to Hannes. Subsequently, the other shareholders challenged the validity of the allotment and the service agreement upon the basis that *inter alia* the directors were in breach of their fiduciary and statutory duties to the company. The Court of Appeal condemned the directors' use of powers in this manner and held Hannes to be in breach of his fiduciary duty and also in breach of Companies Code s229(1). The principal judgment was delivered by Sheller JA[169] who denounced the promotion of Hannes' self-interest at the expense of those purposes for which the company was incorporated.[170]

---

[160] (1993) 11 ACLC 125; note Baxt R, case note (1993) 67 ALJ 694 at 696.

[161] (Burchett, French and Lee JJ).

[162] Cf. *Glavanics v Brunninghausen* (1996) 19 ACSR 204 at 208 per Bryson J, 'These were one man companies and they were not carried on in ways which respected or conformed to the organisational structure which the law requires companies to have.'

[163] (1993) 11 ACLC 125 at 133 *per curiam*.

[164] Cf. *Gluckstein v Barnes* [1900] AC 240 at 258 per Lord Robertson, 'the company was paralyzed so far as vigilance and criticism were concerned; for the board-room was occupied by the enemy.'

[165] (1993) 11 ACLC 125 at 134 *per curiam*; see *Australian Growth Resources Corporation Pty Ltd v van Reesema* (1988) 6 ACLC 529 at 539 per King CJ (Cox J agreed).

[166] (1993) 11 ACLC 125 at 135 *per curiam*; cf. *Neptune (Vehicle Washing Equipment) Ltd v Fitzgerald (No. 2)* [1995] BCC 1000 at 1017 per A G Steinfeld QC (sitting as a deputy Chancery Judge), 'It is difficult to conceive of a matter where there is a greater conflict between the personal interest of a director and his duties to the company than the question of whether the director's own service contract should be terminated and, if so, upon what terms as to compensation.'

[167] (1992) 10 ACLC 400.

[168] (Samuels, Clarke and Sheller JJA).

[169] (Samuels and Clarke JJA agreed).

[170] (1992) 10 ACLC 400 at 409; cf. *Neptune (Vehicle Washing Equipment) Ltd v Fitzgerald (No. 2)* [1995] BCC 1000 at 1017 per A G Steinfeld QC (sitting as a deputy Chancery Judge), 'the court's concern is

The New South Wales Court of Appeal in *Hannes* considered that a director's state of mind and the motive for which he or she acted are all important in determining whether that director was acting honestly in the company's interests or acting to achieve some ulterior purpose, for personal advantage or other illegitimate reason.[171] To decide that, the court may go into the question of what the intention was, 'collecting from the surrounding circumstances all the materials which genuinely throw light on that question.'[172] In confirming the trial judge's finding, Sheller JA was of the view that self-interest formed the real ground of Hannes' action and that once that is acknowledged, 'there is no legitimate basis left for his actions even if they were intra vires.'[173]

At the other end of the spectrum is *Linter Group Ltd v Goldberg*.[174] This case epitomises many of the major corporate crashes across England and Australia during the late 1980s and the early 1990s,[175] and the complex litigation thereby spawned. We have earlier considered some of the flotsam[176] from this inauspicious period in English and Australian corporate history and will consider more later in this chapter.[177] The facts in *Goldberg* were briefly these. During an attempted takeover of the British textile company Tootal Ltd, funds originally advanced to Linter Group Ltd ('Linter') by Citibank Ltd ('Citibank') were channelled off to various corporate entities controlled by Goldberg; the effect of which was to leave Linter exposed to Citibank and others in circumstances constituting breaches by Goldberg of his fiduciary duty to Linter to act honestly and in good faith. In the Victorian Supreme Court, Southwell J found that the use of Linter's funds in this manner constituted breaches of the fiduciary duty which Goldberg owed to Linter given that:

[The] impugned directors masterminded a transaction which involved the expenditure of $205 million, some 77% of Linter's funds, by way of a grossly inadequately secured loan to a $2 company, which was not even a subsidiary of Linter, in circumstances ... which were designed to preclude and did preclude the lender from obtaining security in the acquired asset, and which were designed to ensure that the benefits of ownership of that asset would flow not to the lender but to the private family interests of the directors.[178]

The above extract from Southwell J's judgment typifies some of the deplorable practices throughout corporate Australia during the 1980s and the early 1990s; practices

cont.
> bound to be even greater – and hence its scrutiny of the transaction even closer – where the transaction is determined by that director alone acting as sole director.'; note *Glavanics v Brunninghausen* (1996) 19 ACSR 204 at 208 per Bryson J.
[171] Cf. *Carter v Drake* (1992-1993) 9 WAR 82 at 94 per Malcolm CJ; and *Permanent Building Society v Wheeler* (1993-1994) 11 WAR 187 at 218 per Ipp J (Malcolm CJ and Seaman J agreed).
[172] (1992) 10 ACLC 400 at 409 per Sheller JA (Samuels and Clarke JJA agreed); see *Hindle v John Cotton Ltd* (1919) 56 Sc LR 625 at 630-631 per Viscount Finlay (Viscount Cave and Lord Dunedin agreed); and *Mills v Mills* (1938) 60 CLR 150 at 186 per Dixon J.
[173] (1992) 10 ACLC 400 at 409; see *Howard Smith Ltd v Ampol Petroleum Ltd* [1974] AC 821 at 834 per Lord Wilberforce.
[174] (1992) 10 ACLC 739.
[175] *The Australian Financial Review*, 21 April 1997; and *The Times*, 29 April 1999.
[176] *Commonwealth Bank of Australia v Friedrich* (1991) 5 ACSR 115; cf. *Bishopsgate Investment Management Ltd v Maxwell (No. 2)* [1994] 1 All ER 261.
[177] E.g., *Equiticorp Finance Ltd v Bank of New Zealand* (1993) 11 ACLC 952.
[178] (1992) 10 ACLC 739 at 749; cf. *Gemstone Corporation of Australia Ltd v Grasso* (1990) 8 ACLC 1151, albeit on a much smaller scale.

which infected corporate England as well during this unedifying period of our corporate history.[179]

A MORE INTERVENTIONIST APPROACH

From chapters two and three of this book, it will be recalled that the English and Australian courts have placed significance upon Lord Hatherley LC's judgment in *The Overend & Gurney Company v Gibb*,[180] concerning the test to be applied in determining whether or not directors of British and Australian companies have exercised a reasonable degree of care and diligence.[181] The relevant question, it will be recalled, was reduced to:

> [Whether] or not the directors exceeded the powers entrusted to them, or whether if they did not they were cognisant of circumstances of such a character, so plain, so manifest, and so simple of appreciation, that no men with any ordinary degree of prudence, acting on their own behalf, would have entered into such a transaction as they entered into?[182]

Thus, argues Sealy, the courts have retained a residual power to interfere based on a minimum objective standard.[183] This is an argument echoed by the High Court of Australia[184] in *Wayde v New South Wales Rugby League Ltd*.[185] Although the court may not intervene and hold a decision invalid if it thinks the decision unreasonable, in Brennan J's view it may do so if it considers that, 'no reasonable board of directors could think the decision to be substantially for a purpose for which the power was conferred ... for the court will not substitute its discretion for the discretion exercised in good faith by the directors.'[186]

One of the principal authorities cited in support of a non-interventionist policy is that of the High Court of Australia[187] in *Harlowe's Nominees Pty Ltd v Woodside (Lakes Entrance) Oil Company NL*.[188] There, Barwick CJ, McTiernan and Kitto JJ in a joint judgment said that:

> Directors in whom are vested the right and the duty of deciding where the company's interests lie and how they are to be served may be concerned with a wide range of

---

[179]   *The Australian*, 20 September 1996; and *The Independent on Sunday*, 25 April 1999.
[180]   (1872) LR 5 HL 480.
[181]   *Lagunas Nitrate Company v Lagunas Syndicate* [1899] 2 Ch 392 at 422-423 per Lindley MR; *In re City Equitable Fire Insurance Company Ltd* [1925] Ch 407 at 428 per Romer J; and *Vrisakis v Australian Securities Commission* (1992-1993) 9 WAR 395 at 450 per Ipp J (Malcolm CJ agreed).
[182]   *The Overend & Gurney Company v Gibb* (1872) LR 5 HL 480 at 486-487 per Lord Hatherley LC.
[183]   Sealy L S, 'The Director as Trustee' [1967] CLJ 83 at 95.
[184]   (Mason ACJ, Wilson, Brennan, Deane and Dawson JJ).
[185]   (1985) 3 ACLC 799; see *Gaiman v National Association for Mental Health* [1971] Ch 317; and Prentice D D, 'Expulsion of Members from a Company' (1970) 33 MLR 700.
[186]   (1985) 3 ACLC 799 at 805; see *Howard Smith Ltd v Ampol Petroleum Ltd* [1974] AC 821 at 832 per Lord Wilberforce; *Shuttleworth v Cox Brothers and Company (Maidenhead) Ltd* [1927] 2 KB 9 at 23-24 per Scrutton LJ; *Peters' American Delicacy Company Ltd v Heath* (1938-1939) 61 CLR 457 at 481 per Latham CJ; and *Harlowe's Nominees Pty Ltd v Woodside (Lakes Entrance) Oil Company NL* (1969-1970) 121 CLR 483 at 493 *per curiam*.
[187]   (Barwick CJ, McTiernan and Kitto JJ).
[188]   (1969-1970) 121 CLR 483.

practical considerations, and their judgment, if exercised in good faith and not for irrelevant purposes, is not open to review in the courts.[189]

Equally, the leading authority *Howard Smith Ltd v Ampol Petroleum Ltd*[190] is often considered to stand firmly against courts reviewing the merits of management decisions honestly arrived at.[191] But within the advice of the Privy Council, which was delivered by Lord Wilberforce, there is sufficient latitude for those of an interventionist disposition to review directors' decision-making as the following passage suggests:

> But accepting all of this, when a dispute arises where the directors ... made a particular decision for one purpose or for another, or whether, there being more than one purpose, one or another purpose was the substantial or primary purpose, the court ... is entitled to look at the situation objectively in order to estimate how critical or pressing, or substantial or, per contra, insubstantial an alleged requirement may have been.[192]

It is the allegation of impropriety that opens the door. It is then up to the judge as to how far he or she steps inside. Although the cases are replete with caveats reminding judges not to second guess business decisions,[193] when faced with allegations that those business decisions are improper, more and more are today's judges obliged to test those decisions against objective criteria.[194] It is inevitable that that will require the directors whose decisions are under attack to give evidence of their subjective intentions in that regard. That in turn obliges judges to step upon dangerous ground for proper purposes focuses upon the decision itself and, 'calls for a more interventionist line, reviewing the business judgments of business men.'[195] The decision in *Kokotovich Constructions Pty Ltd v Wallington* is apposite as the following extract from the judgment of Kirby ACJ[196] attests:

> [Whilst] Courts should hesitate before interfering with management decisions which have been reached bona fide ... this principle is of no application where, as in this case, the management decision was not *bona fide* arrived at. Indeed, it would be absurd to suggest that a court should forsake its responsibility to uphold the law in such a situation. If a director breaches his or her fiduciary duty in exercising a power

---

[189] *Ibid* at 493.
[190] [1974] AC 821.
[191] The issue was put rather nicely in *Equiticorp Finance Ltd v Bank of New Zealand* (1993) 11 ACLC 952 at 977 per Kirby P, 'I am not concerned with the merits of what Mr Hawkins did. My sole concern is with its lawfulness.'
[192] [1974] AC 821 at 832.
[193] *Equiticorp Finance Ltd v Bank of New Zealand* (1993) 11 ACLC 952 at 977 per Kirby P; note *The Times*, 21 July 1999.
[194] *Androvin v Figliomeni* (1996) 14 ACLC 1461 at 1470 per Owen J (Kennedy and Franklyn JJ agreed); *Daniels v Anderson* (1995) 13 ACLC 614 at 662 per Clarke and Sheller JJA; *Lyford v Commonwealth Bank of Australia* (1995) 13 ACLC 900 at 914 per R D Nicholson J; *Carter v Drake* (1992-1993) 9 WAR 82 at 94 per Malcolm CJ; and *Vrisakis v Australian Securities Commission* (1992-1993) 9 WAR 395 at 451 per Ipp J (Malcolm CJ agreed).
[195] Sealy L S, 'Company – Directors' Unconstitutional Acts' [1992] CLJ 229 at 229.
[196] (Priestley and Handley JJA agreed).

for an improper purpose, not only is it desirable that the courts should intervene. They have a duty to do so.[197]

But as Ipp J[198] in *Permanent Building Society v Wheeler* reminded us, the issue is, 'not whether a management decision was good or bad; it is whether the directors acted in breach of their fiduciary duties.'[199] That involves a determination of whether but for the improper purpose the directors would have performed the act impugned.[200]

With the enactment of Corporations Law s232(2), coupled with the very clear expression by the Australian Government that the Australian judiciary is to become more interventionist, the duty to act honestly is to be interpreted as an invitation, or perhaps an instruction, to the courts to intervene in directors' decision-making when considered appropriate.[201] Thus, it can be argued that the analytical distinction between the *bona fides* and the proper purposes doctrines is becoming increasingly academic. In more practical terms, whether or not *bona fides* and proper purposes are separate doctrines or simply different ways of saying, or at least achieving, the same thing is no longer to the point, or greatly relevant, in Australian company law. Proper purposes requires an objective approach, and it is now generally accepted that the question whether directors have acted *bona fide* in their company's interest is also to be objectively determined, 'although the evidence of the directors as to their respective subjective intentions will be relevant for that purpose.'[202]

This united and somewhat refashioned approach will go some way towards ameliorating the lack of certainty and the confusion which has surrounded the application of the *bona fides* and the proper purposes doctrines identified in the previous chapter of this book. Times have changed since the classical expositions of Lord Eldon in *Carlen v Drury*,[203] Lord Davey in *Burland v Earle*,[204] Lord Wilberforce in *Howard Smith*,[205] and the joint judgment of Barwick CJ, McTiernan and Kitto JJ in *Harlowe's*.[206] Gone are the days when Australian courts sit idly back and ignore

---

[197] (1995) 13 ACLC 1113 at 1125.
[198] (Malcolm CJ and Seaman J agreed).
[199] (1993-1994) 11 WAR 187 at 218; see *Japan Abrasive Materials Pty Ltd v Australian Fused Materials Pty Ltd* (1998) 16 ACLC 1172 at 1180 per Templeman J; cf. *Carter v Drake* (1992-1993) 9 WAR 82 at 94-95 per Malcolm CJ; *Mills v Mills* (1938) 60 CLR 150 at 185 per Dixon J; and *Howard Smith Ltd v Ampol Petroleum Ltd* [1974] AC 821 at 838 per Lord Wilberforce.
[200] *Darvall v North Sydney Brick & Tile Co Ltd (No. 2)* (1989) 7 ACLC 659 at 676 per Kirby P; and *Kokotovich Constructions Pty Ltd v Wallington* (1995) 13 ACLC 1113 at 1124 per Kirby ACJ (Priestley and Handley JJA agreed).
[201] *Kokotovich Constructions Pty Ltd v Wallington* (1995) 13 ACLC 1113 at 1125 per Kirby ACJ (Priestley and Handley JJA agreed).
[202] *Carter v Drake* (1992-1993) 9 WAR 82 at 94 per Malcolm CJ; see *Lyford v Commonwealth Bank of Australia* (1995) 13 ACLC 900 at 914 per R D Nicholson J; *Permanent Building Society v Wheeler* (1993-1994) 11 WAR 187 at 218 per Ipp J (Malcolm CJ and Seaman J agreed); *Southern Resources Ltd v Residues Treatment & Trading Co Ltd* (1990) 8 ACLC 1151 at 1164 *per curiam*; *Darvall v North Sydney Brick & Tile Co Ltd (No. 2)* (1989) 7 ACLC 659 at 676 per Kirby P; *Australian Growth Resources Corporation Pty Ltd v van Reesema* (1988) 6 ACLC 529 at 535-536 per King CJ (Cox J agreed); and *Richard Brady Franks Ltd v Price* (1937) 58 CLR 112 at 135 per Latham CJ; cf. *Howard Smith Ltd v Ampol Petroleum Ltd* [1974] AC 821 at 835 per Lord Wilberforce; *Hindle v John Cotton Ltd* (1919) 56 ScLR 625 at 630-631 per Viscount Finlay; and *Allen v Gold Reefs of West Africa Ltd* [1900] 1 Ch 656 at 671 per Lindley MR.
[203] (1812) 1 V&B 154 at 158.
[204] [1902] AC 83 at 93.
[205] [1974] AC 821 at 832.
[206] (1969-1970) 121 CLR 483 at 493.

decisions made by businessmen and businesswomen which fly in the face of public expectations and, more recently, parliamentary decree; such idleness brought about largely by a sense of commercial inadequacy historically felt by the English and the Australian judiciary.[207]

In today's commercial environment, even though a director of an Australian company may act honestly, nonetheless, if an Australian court considers that that director has acted improperly, then the court will intervene.[208] Kirby P in *Darvall v North Sydney Brick & Tile Co Ltd (No. 2)* explained that the rationale and the purpose of the court's jurisdiction in such circumstances was not to substitute an *ex post* decision for that of the directors, but rather, 'to assure the integrity of their decision at the time in the exercise of their fiduciary powers.'[209]

COMMERCIAL PRAGMATISM

It is suggested that as many of today's Australian judges, probably much more so than their English counterparts, have actually sat in boardrooms and/or run their own businesses and legal practices, they are better equipped than at any time earlier to, metaphorically speaking, roll up their shirt-sleeves, enter the fray and attack complex commercial and corporate disputes at the grass roots level. It is considered that by tackling the fundamentals in this manner, with the object of achieving a more pragmatic and commercially acceptable solution to the problem, the community's business interests will better be served than by the application of esoteric principles, no longer considered relevant, to very much changed situations to those in which they were developed.[210]

Commercial pragmatism, or the 'commercial reality principle' as Malcolm labels it,[211] is more and more proving a decisive factor in the resolution of complex commercial and corporate disputes which so dominate today's Australian corporate sector.[212] The approach favoured by the New South Wales Court of Appeal[213] in *Equiticorp Finance Ltd v Bank of New Zealand*[214] is apposite.[215] There, the Court of Appeal was faced with one of the consequences of the many corporate collapses of the late 1980s. The case is interesting, not least for the fact that it brings home just how complex and intricate modern commercial and corporate life can be. As noted in chapter one of this

---

[207] *Carlen v Drury* (1812) 1 V & B 154 at 158 per Lord Eldon; *Burland v Earle* [1902] AC 83 at 93 per Lord Davey; and *Shuttleworth v Cox Brothers and Company (Maidenhead) Ltd* [1927] 2 KB 9 at 23 per Scrutton LJ; note Sealy L S, 'The Director as Trustee' [1967] CLJ 83 at 100-101; and Editorial comment, 'Directors – true or false?' (1997) 18 Co Law 129 at 129.

[208] *Kokotovich Constructions Pty Ltd v Wallington* (1995) 13 ACLC 1113 at 1125 per Kirby ACJ (Priestley and Handley JJA agreed).

[209] (1989) 7 ACLC 659 at 678.

[210] *Biala Pty Ltd v Mallina Holdings Ltd* (1993) 11 ACSR 785 at 848 per Ipp J.

[211] Malcolm D, 'Directors' Duties: The Governing Principles' in Ramsay I M (ed), *Corporate Governance and the Duties of Company Directors* The Centre for Corporate Law and Securities Regulation, University of Melbourne, Parkville, 1997 at 60.

[212] *Gray Eisdell Timms Pty Ltd v Combined Auctions Pty Ltd* (1995) 13 ACLC 965 at 974 per Young J; cf. Muir G, 'Contract and Equity: Striking a Balance' (1985) 10 Adel LR 153 at 183, 'But pragmatism must not always triumph over principle'.

[213] (Kirby P, Clarke and Cripps JJA).

[214] (1993) 11 ACLC 952; see Baxt R, 'Duties to a Corporate Group – One Step Forward or Two Steps Backwards?' (1994) 22 ABLR 138.

[215] (1993) 11 ACLC 952 at 1019 per Clarke and Cripps JJA.

book, *Equiticorp* highlights a modern corporate phenomenon; namely, the intricate web of interrelated companies which, more often than not, operates in today's international conglomerate world. And, as is sometimes the case, under the direction of one man.[216]

In short, the facts in *Equiticorp* were these. Bank of New Zealand ('BNZ'), the Equiticorp group's bankers, lent Equiticorp Tasman Ltd, or a wholly owned subsidiary thereof, a $200m loan facility to finance the takeover by the Equiticorp group of an Australian publicly listed group of companies. In so doing a complicated series of transactions was set in train. The appellants ('EFSA' and 'EFL') had between them approximately $50m on deposit with BNZ; which moneys were ultimately applied in the reduction of another Equiticorp group company's indebtedness *vis-à-vis* the $200m facility originally advanced by BNZ. Both appellants went into liquidation. The liquidators claimed that the application of the $50m on deposit in this way was procured *inter alia* in breach of the directors' fiduciary duties to the companies and in breach of Companies Code s229. Giles J, at first instance, found for BNZ on all matters.[217]

On appeal, the liquidators in *Equiticorp* unsuccessfully argued that in the application of the liquidity reserve towards the discharge of the other company's debt, no consideration was given to the interests of EFL or EFSA, but rather those companies were deprived of their liquidity reserve for what was perceived to be the interests of the Equiticorp group as a whole. That, ran the liquidators' argument, necessarily meant that there had been a breach of the fiduciary duty owed by the directors of EFL and EFSA. In addressing that argument, the majority,[218] in a joint judgment, referred to the decisions in *Charterbridge Corporation Ltd v Lloyds Bank Ltd*,[219] *Walker v Wimborne*[220] and *Kinsela v Russell Kinsela Pty Ltd*,[221] before reaffirming the trite proposition that directors must, 'exercise their powers, bona fide, in what they consider is in the interests of the company and not for any collateral purpose.'[222] Clarke and Cripps JJA then, however, took a more commercial and pragmatic approach in deciding that it was proper, in all the circumstances, to deploy the liquidity reserve in that manner. In their Honours' view the alternative was, 'possible disaster for the whole group including the two companies.'[223]

But *Equiticorp* has particular appeal for the dissenting judgment of Kirby P and his unwavering adherence to the application of traditional company law principles in a modern-day setting, in the face of complex and entangled corporate practices. From a policy perspective, Kirby P's approach has merit and its underlying message ought not be lost sight of. For, whilst there are benefits which flow from a pragmatic approach, one needs to ensure that there is no debasement to the integrity of English and

---

[216] Thus, the checks and balances which boardroom decision-making is designed to provide is open to abuse when the *presidium* is at the beck and call of just one powerful personality; as evidenced by this, and the litany of recent cases, to like effect; note *The Times*, 29 April 1999; and Committee on the Financial Aspects of Corporate Governance, *The Report of the Committee on the Financial Aspects of Corporate Governance* Gee and Co Ltd, London, 1992 at para 4.2.

[217] *Bank of New Zealand v Equiticorp Finance Ltd* (1993) 11 ACLC 84.

[218] (Clarke and Cripps JJA).

[219] [1970] Ch 62.

[220] (1976-1977) 137 CLR 1.

[221] [1986] 4 NSWLR 722.

[222] (1993) 11 ACLC 952 at 1017-1018 per Clarke and Cripps JJA.

[223] *Ibid* at 1019.

Australian company law, and that companies operate according to the law.[224] Kirby P sought to preserve that ideal and was quick to point out that:

> The law has not yet come to the point of ignoring the requirements of due formality. Such requirements are protective of shareholders, creditors, employees and the community. The suggested imperative of 'realism' and the *Realpolitik* of corporate control does not authorize courts to ride roughshod over the due observance of company law.[225]

Thus, Kirby P in *Equiticorp* took a more traditional line. In Kirby P's view, the intelligent and honest director test formulated by Pennycuick J in *Charterbridge*,[226] led inexorably to the conclusion that no intelligent and honest person, 'in the position of a director of EFL or EFSA could, in the circumstances described, have considered that it was in the best interests of those companies to authorise the deployment of their liquidity reserves for the purpose for which they were used'.[227] However, notwithstanding Kirby P's caveat extracted above, the Australian judiciary will continue to favour corporate certainty tempered with a degree of commercial pragmatism in the light of community expectations in order to resolve the complex commercial disputes which today's companies face.

The recent cases reflect a more pragmatic approach which the judges are being forced to adopt,[228] and demonstrate a willingness on the part of the Australian judiciary to be more flexible in its application of strict general law duties.[229] There is a willingness to take on board a changed approach to meet changed circumstances, albeit by the application of tried and proven traditional principles.[230] In this regard, *Glandon Pty Ltd v Strata Consolidated Pty Ltd*[231] is of interest. There, the New South Wales Court of Appeal[232] was presented with an argument by the plaintiffs that a fiduciary relationship existed between them and those defendants who were directors of companies in which shares were held by the plaintiffs' interests, which relationship required that the defendants inform the plaintiffs of the offers which had been made to relevant companies for land held by them. Failure to reveal such offers *inter alia* was a basis, claimed the plaintiffs, for the relief sought.

The New South Wales Court of Appeal in *Glandon* unanimously rejected the argument that a fiduciary relationship existed in the commercial context before it. That

---

[224] *Gray Eisdell Timms Pty Ltd v Combined Auctions Pty Ltd* (1995) 13 ACLC 965 at 974 per Young J; cf. Muir G, 'Contract and Equity: Striking a Balance' (1985) 10 Adel LR 153 at 183, 'But pragmatism must not always triumph over principle'.

[225] (1993) 11 ACLC 952 at 979; cf. *Brady v Brady* (1987) 3 BCC 535 at 552-553 per Nourse LJ, 'But there is a higher principle at stake, which is that the formalities of company law must be rigorously upheld.'

[226] [1970] Ch 62 at 74; see *Japan Abrasive Materials Pty Ltd v Australian Fused Materials Pty Ltd* (1998) 16 ACLC 1172 at 1180 per Templeman J.

[227] (1993) 11 ACLC 952 at 985.

[228] Baxt R, 'The Role and Responsibilities of Nominee Directors in a Contested Takeover' a paper presented at the Corporate Law Workshop, conducted by the Business Law Section of the Law Council of Australia, Melbourne, October 1993 at 66.

[229] Teele R, 'The Necessary Reformulation of the Classic Fiduciary Duty to Avoid a Conflict of Interest or Duties' (1994) 22 ABLR 99 at 100.

[230] *Coleman v Myers* [1977] 2 NZLR 225 at 324-325 per Woodhouse J.

[231] (1993) 11 ACSR 543.

[232] (Mahoney, Clarke and Cripps JJA).

relationship was of vendor and purchaser.[233] Nothing which the plaintiffs did was with reference to or in reliance upon any purported fiduciary relationship. The leading judgment was delivered by Mahoney JA who reaffirmed conventional English and Australian company theory that, without more, the relationship of director and shareholder, as such, does not give rise to a fiduciary relationship. Mahoney JA recognised that the absence of the relationship of confidence is relevant in deciding whether fiduciary duties exist;[234] although, having regard to the position of the directors *vis-à-vis* shareholders, that is not conclusive.[235] Such considerations suggest, in Mahoney JA's judgment, that:

> [A] director purchasing the shares of a shareholder is in a position of advantage and that that advantage is of a special kind which, in appropriate circumstances, may give rise to fiduciary obligations.[236]

Mahoney JA's judgment in *Glandon* is also of interest for his treatment of *Percival v Wright*; long considered by many to have been wrongly decided, but at no point overruled.[237] Mahoney JA's judgment is supportive of the pragmatic approach being adopted in contemporary Australian company law which recognises that the judiciary's, and the business community's, attitudes are changing and that while a legal principle may remain, the application of that principle may require reconsideration where the factual context has changed.[238]

---

[233] Cf. *Glavanics v Brunninghausen* (1996) 19 ACSR 204 at 228 per Bryson J, 'In my opinion no policy considerations could support the advance of negligence law into the new province of relationships between vendor and purchaser, where the law is in a mature state and a consideration of dominating importance is the law's requirement that parties to sales should be vigilant in their own interests. The transformation of the relationship of vendor and purchaser and the introduction of fresh complexities would be most impolitic.'

[234] *Dowsett v Reid* (1913) 15 CLR 695 at 704-705 per Griffith CJ; *Hospital Products Ltd v United States Surgical Corporation* (1984-1985) 156 CLR 41 at 69-72 per Gibbs CJ; and *Coleman v Myers* [1977] 2 NZLR 225 at 325 per Woodhouse J.

[235] *Coleman v Myers* [1977] 2 NZLR 225 at 277-278 per Mahon J; and Rider B A K, 'A Special Relationship on the Special Facts' (1978) 41 MLR 585.

[236] (1993) 11 ACSR 543 at 547 per Mahoney JA.

[237] [1902] 2 Ch 421; criticised by the Cohen committee (Report of the Committee on Company Law Amendment, HMSO, London, Cmd 6659, 1945 at paras 86-87); rejected by the Jenkins committee (Report of the Company Law Committee, HMSO, London, Cmnd 1749, 1962 at paras 89 and 99(b)); described by Loss L, 'The Fiduciary Concept as Applied to Trading by Corporate 'Insiders' in the United States' (1970) 33 MLR 34 at 40-41 as, 'a monument to the ability of lawyers to hypnotise themselves with their own creations'; but the decision, 'does not shock the conscience': *Coleman v Myers* [1977] 2 NZLR 225 at 329 per Cooke J; *Re Chez Nico (Restaurants) Ltd* [1991] BCC 736 at 750 per Browne-Wilkinson VC; note Rider B A K, 'Percival v Wright – Per Incuriam' (1977) 40 MLR 471; Rider B A K, 'Partnership Law and its Impact on "Domestic Companies"' [1979] CLJ 148 at 157; Keeton G W, 'The Director as Trustee' (1952) 5 CLP 11 at 16-18; Davies P L, *Gower's Principles of Modern Company Law* (6th ed) Sweet & Maxwell Ltd, London, 1997 at 599-600; and Lord Wilberforce, 'Law and Economics' [1966] JBL 301 at 307.

[238] (1993) 11 ACSR 543 at 547-548; cf. *Mesenberg v Cord Industrial Recruiters Pty Ltd* (1996) 14 ACLC 519 at 526-528 per Young J; note *Glavanics v Brunninghausen* (1996) 19 ACSR 204 at 216-217 and 224 per Bryson J.

THE WAY FORWARD

It is suggested that the days when directors of British and Australian companies could, 'immure themselves from a scrutiny of their purposes by asserting that they acted honestly and with good intention' are gone.[239] Today's Australian courts, probably more so than their English counterparts, are inclined to subject these purposes to scrutiny to see whether or not they should be accepted.[240] Kirby P in *Darvall v North Sydney Brick & Tile Co Ltd (No. 2)* put the proposition in this way:

> Directors of corporations cannot immure themselves from a scrutiny of their purposes by asserting that they acted honestly and with good intention for this or that legitimate purpose. The purpose may be scrutinised by a court to see if this assertion should be accepted. The directors cannot, by donning blinkers, ignore the plain facts disclosed to them and then assert that they acted bona fide in the best interests of the company. A more rigorous standard of conduct is required by the law.[241]

This revitalised approach to contemporary Australian company law was recently exemplified in *Biala Pty Ltd v Mallina Holdings Ltd*;[242] a case which typifies today's complex commercial and corporate litigation. In essence, the dispute centred upon a joint venture development of what was intended to become a major petrochemical project in Western Australia, the participants in which included two of Australia's corporate high-flyers throughout the 1980s and the early 1990s.[243] The circumstances which gave rise to this, and related, litigation resulted in catastrophic losses totalling hundreds of millions of dollars which fell, ultimately, to the Western Australian taxpayers. The trial brought into disrepute the evidence of one of those corporate personalities, Dallas Dempster, and also, in part, evidence given by the Western Australian Premier, at the relevant time, Brian Burke.

The essential facts in *Biala* were briefly these. Biala Pty Ltd ('Biala'), as a minority shareholder in Mallina Holdings Ltd ('Mallina'), brought an action against Mallina, Dempster (a former director of Mallina), a Dempster controlled company, and others. Dempster was the instigator of, and the prime mover behind, a feasibility study into the development of a petrochemical project. Mallina was a principal participant. Subsequently, Dempster disassociated himself with Mallina and went on to form a joint venture with another party. Dempster then arranged for Mallina's interests in the project to be bought out by third parties for $150,000. Those third parties, in which Dempster retained an interest, ultimately on-sold their interests in the project for $400m. Interests related to Dempster received $50m. In these circumstances, it was alleged *inter alia* that Dempster was in breach of a fiduciary duty owed to Mallina in relation to the joint venture. The matter came on before Ipp J in whose judgment Dempster and Dempster's controlled company were found to be in breach of fiduciary duties owed to Mallina. Judgment was entered accordingly.

---

[239] *Darvall v North Sydney Brick & Tile Co Ltd (No. 2)* (1989) 7 ACLC 659 at 679 per Kirby P.

[240] *Advance Bank Australia Ltd v FAI Insurances Ltd* (1987) 5 ACLC 725 at 742-743 per Kirby P (Glass JA agreed); and *Kokotovich Constructions Pty Ltd v Wallington* (1995) 13 ACLC 1113 at 1123-1125 per Kirby ACJ (Priestley and Handley JJA agreed).

[241] (1989) 7 ACLC 659 at 679.

[242] (1993) 11 ACSR 785.

[243] Laurie Connell (formerly chief executive of the failed merchant bank Rothwells Ltd); and Dallas Dempster.

On appeal, the Western Australian Full Court[244] in *Mallina Holdings Ltd v Biala Ltd*[245] unanimously affirmed Ipp J's judgment below in *Biala*. Ipp J's judgment provides a useful analysis of the applicable remedies. There is also a detailed treatment of these remedies provided on appeal by Rowland J.[246] These are explored in chapter nine of this book. For present purposes, however, Ipp J's judgment at first instance importantly advances the so-called fifth exception to the rule in *Foss v Harbottle*;[247] thereby broadening the scope and entitlement of a shareholder to bring a derivative action on the general ground that considerations of justice require such an action to be brought.[248] In Ipp J's view, 'the courts should not shrink from determining whether the justice of the case should allow a shareholder to proceed with a derivative action.'[249] Such an approach is in keeping with the more robust and interventionist approach which has recently found favour with the Australian judiciary,[250] and is one well-suited to resolving today's complex commercial and corporate disputes.

This approach is consistent with that taken in *Residues Treatment & Trading Company Ltd v Southern Resources Ltd*,[251] where the South Australian Full Court[252] reinstated the statement of claim of Residues Treatment & Trading Company Ltd on appeal. The effect of so doing was to permit a shareholder *locus standi* to prosecute an action to challenge an allotment of shares made by the directors for an improper purpose. The principal judgment was delivered by King CJ,[253] in whose opinion:

> [There] is a clear trend in cases of the highest authority tending to indicate the existence of a personal right in a shareholder, grounded upon equitable principles, to have the voting power of his shares undiminished by improper actions on the part

---

[244] (Pidgeon, Rowland and Seaman JJ).

[245] (1994) 15 ACSR 1.

[246] *Mallina Holdings Ltd v Biala Ltd* (1994) 15 ACSR 1 at 48 *et seq.*

[247] (1843) 2 Hare 461.

[248] (1993) 11 ACSR 785 at 844; cf. *Cape Breton Company v Fenn* (1881) 17 Ch D 198 at 208 per Cotton LJ; *Ferguson v Wallbridge* [1935] 3 DLR 66 at 83-84 per Lord Blanesburgh (Lords Thankerton, Russell and Alness, and Sir Sidney Rowlatt agreed); *Hawkesbury Development Co Ltd v Landmark Finance Pty Ltd* (1969) 92 WN (NSW) 199 at 208 per Street J; *Fargro Ltd v Godfroy* [1986] 1 WLR 1134 at 1138 per Walton J; *Scarel Pty Ltd v City Loan & Credit Corporation Pty Ltd* (1988) 17 FCR 344 at 347-352 per Gummow J; and *Zempilas v JN Taylor Holdings Ltd* (1990-1991) 5 ACSR 28 at 30 per Debelle J; cf. *Christianos v Aloridge Pty Ltd* (1995) 18 ACSR 272 at 281 per Beaumont, Whitlam and Tamberlin JJ, 'Although a member who is dissatisfied with a liquidator's reluctance to sue cannot rely on the exceptions to the rule in *Foss v Harbottle*, it is clear that other remedies may be available, for instance, the member may use the statutory procedure to ask the court to order the liquidator to bring the proceedings'.

[249] (1993) 11 ACSR 785 at 846; cf. *Russell v Wakefield Waterworks Company* (1875) 20 LR Eq 474 at 482 per Sir George Jessel MR, 'As I have said before, the rule is a general one, but it does not apply to a case where the interests of justice require the rule to be dispensed with.'

[250] Ford H A J, Austin R P and Ramsay I M, *Ford's Principles of Corporations Law* (7th ed) Reed International Books Australia Pty Ltd, Sydney, 1995 at paras 11148-11149; cf. *Mesenberg v Cord Industrial Recruiters Pty Ltd* (1996) 14 ACLC 519 at 523 per Young J, 'Although there is doubt as to whether this exception is part of the law, there are weighty judgments which, despite indication of doubt, would conceive that it might exist'.

[251] (1988) 6 ACLC 1160.

[252] (King CJ, Matheson and Bollen JJ).

[253] (Matheson and Bollen JJ agreed).

of the directors and of his *locus standi* to institute and prosecute proceedings to protect that right.[254]

The South Australian Full Court, by its judgment in *Residues*, considered that the time had arrived for the Australian courts to give unequivocal recognition to such a right.[255] Thus, complex questions of *locus standi* are gradually being simplified; and more and more are those aggrieved by directors' decision-making being permitted to prosecute their complaints in the interests of justice.[256] This is in keeping with today's business community's expectations and will assist in the advancement of modern ideals of corporate governance,[257] and will lead further to raised levels of responsibility and greater accountability on the part of directors of Australian companies in general.

With the pre-eminence of the proper purposes doctrine, and its current resurgence in popularity with the English and Australian courts,[258] it is considered likely that the judiciary will become more and more involved in reviewing directors' decision-making in order to determine whether in fact decisions which directors assert on oath, as having been made *bona fide* in the interests of the company as a whole, accord with a strict application of the proper purposes doctrine.[259] Mere assertion of subjective honesty will no longer be considered enough to hold the day.[260]

The implementation of Corporations Law s232(2) into Australian company law requires a new vigilance on the part of the Australian judiciary and encourages judges of a robust and interventionist disposition to exact even higher standards from directors of Australian companies. It is considered that more and more the Australian courts will grant disgruntled shareholders *locus standi* in order to bring to account errant directors and to attack decisions either improperly made or lacking in good faith.[261]

This revivified and refashioned approach by the Australian judiciary invites, not unnaturally, an equally revivified and refashioned approach to the issue of remedies as well. Indeed, some commentators suggest that the whole question of *bona fides* and

---

[254] (1988) 6 ACLC 1160 at 1165; see *Re Sherborne Park Residents Co Ltd* (1986) 2 BCC 99528; and *Eromanga Hydrocarbons NL v Australis Mining NL* (1988) 6 ACLC 906 at 912 per Malcolm CJ.

[255] (1988) 6 ACLC 1160 at 1165 per King CJ (Matheson and Bollen JJ agreed).

[256] *Biala Pty Ltd v Mallina Holdings Ltd* (1993) 11 ACSR 785 at 846 per Ipp J; note *Russell v Wakefield Waterworks Company* (1875) 20 LR Eq 474 at 482 per Sir George Jessel MR, 'As I have said before, the rule is a general one, but it does not apply to a case where the interests of justice require the rule to be dispensed with.'

[257] See Prentice D D and Holland P R J, *Contemporary Issues in Corporate Governance* Oxford University Press, Oxford, 1993; Committee on the Financial Aspects of Corporate Governance, *The Report of the Committee on the Financial Aspects of Corporate Governance* Gee and Co Ltd, London, 1992; Farrar J H, 'Corporate Governance, Business Judgement and the Professionalism of Directors' (1993) 6 CBLJ 1 at 2; Whincop M J, 'An Economic Analysis of the Criminalisation and Content of Directors' Duties' (1996) 24 ABLR 273 at 277 and 291; and Stapledon G P, *Institutional Shareholders and Corporate Governance* Clarendon Press, Oxford, 1996 at 8.

[258] *Gambotto v WCP Ltd* (1995) 13 ACLC 342; *Kokotovich Constructions Pty Ltd v Wallington* (1995) 13 ACLC 1113; *Bishopsgate Investment Management Ltd v Maxwell (No. 2)* [1994] 1 All ER 261; and *Re BSB Holdings Ltd (No. 2)* [1996] 1 BCLC 155.

[259] *Kokotovich Constructions Pty Ltd v Wallington* (1995) 13 ACLC 1113 at 1125 per Kirby ACJ (Priestley and Handley JJA agreed).

[260] *Permanent Building Society v Wheeler* (1993-1994) 11 WAR 187 at 218 per Ipp J (Malcolm CJ and Seaman J agreed); and *Bishopsgate Investment Management Ltd v Maxwell (No. 2)* [1994] 1 All ER 261 at 268-269 per Ralph Gibson LJ.

[261] *Residues Treatment and Trading Co Ltd v Southern Resources Ltd* (1988) 6 ACLC 1160 at 1162 per King CJ (Matheson and Bollen JJ agreed); and *Biala Pty Ltd v Mallina Holdings Ltd* (1993) 11 ACSR 785 at 848 per Ipp J; note Birds J R, 'Making Directors do their Duties' (1980) 1 Co Law 67 at 70.

proper purposes ought focus more on the end product; that is to say, rather than get too caught up in the detail of categorisation, one ought treat these doctrines as being merely facilitative of a challenge to a corporate decision on the basis that that decision is irregular.[262] Such an approach has merit, especially in the light of the vast array of remedies, statutory and non-statutory, which are now available to those aggrieved by the improper exercise of directors' powers. The traditional remedies have been given a new lease of life. In chapters eight and nine of this book, this new lease of life will be considered in detail.

Why have the English and Australian courts become more interventionist in their consideration of the exercise of the powers of directors of British and Australian companies?[263] In short, because the public's expectations and requirements of directors in this regard have risen. In England and in Australia there has, since the latter 1980s, been a rapid change in attitude by the English and Australian public to corporate governance.[264] In today's judicial climate of raised levels of responsibility and greater accountability, in keeping with today's ideals of corporate governance,[265] the exercise by directors of British and Australian companies of their powers is likely to be monitored and scrutinised more closely than at anytime previously.[266] One area in which the English and Australian courts particularly have displayed a measure of alacrity, in adopting a more robust and interventionist role *vis-à-vis* directors' decision-making, is in the context of insolvency. This important and challenging area of the law is considered in detail in chapters six, seven and eight of this book.

---

[262] Sealy L S, '"Bona Fides" and "Proper Purposes" in Corporate Decisions' (1989) 15 MULR 265 at 268 *et seq.*

[263] Cf. *Carlen v Drury* (1812) 1 V & B 154 at 158 per Lord Eldon; *Burland v Earle* [1902] AC 83 at 93 per Lord Davey; and *Shuttleworth v Cox Brothers and Company (Maidenhead) Ltd* [1927] 2 KB 9 at 23 per Scrutton LJ; note Sealy L S, 'The Director as Trustee' [1967] CLJ 83 at 100-101; and Editorial comment, 'Directors – true or false?' (1997) 18 Co Law 129 at 129.

[264] See Prentice D D and Holland P R J, *Contemporary Issues in Corporate Governance* Oxford University Press, Oxford, 1993; Committee on the Financial Aspects of Corporate Governance, *The Report of the Committee on the Financial Aspects of Corporate Governance* Gee and Co Ltd, London, 1992; Farrar J H, 'Corporate Governance, Business Judgement and the Professionalism of Directors' (1993) 6 CBLJ 1 at 2; Whincop M J, 'An Economic Analysis of the Criminalisation and Content of Directors' Duties' (1996) 24 ABLR 273 at 277 and 291; and Stapledon G P, *Institutional Shareholders and Corporate Governance* Clarendon Press, Oxford, 1996 at 8.

[265] *The Australian Financial Review*, 2 January 1996; *The Australian*, 21 April 1997; *The Independent on Sunday*, 25 April 1999; *The Times*, 29 April 1999; *Financial Times*, 8 June 1999; and *The Times*, 21 July 1999.

[266] *Darvall v North Sydney Brick & Tile Co Ltd (No. 2)* (1989) 7 ACLC 659 at 679 per Kirby P.

6

A Duty to Creditors
in the Context of Insolvency?

INTRODUCTION

As we saw in chapter one of this book, the traditional acceptance that the duties upon directors of British and Australian companies are confined to their companies has come under pressure as more and more interest groups, long considered unqualified for admission to 'corporate membership',[1] compete for recognition in modern English and Australian company law.[2] The list of those considered to be on the periphery includes *inter alia* employees, customers, suppliers, consumers, contractors, competitors, creditors, local and national interests, exports, welfare and the environment.[3] Interests long considered extraneous to company law.[4] In earlier chapters of this book, we examined the duties upon directors of British and Australian companies to act honestly, in good faith and for proper purposes on the one hand, and also to exercise care and diligence on the other hand. There, the company was seen to be the repository of these non-statutory, and statutory, duties.[5] In each case the company was accorded its traditional constituency; namely, the shareholders collectively.[6]

---

[1] Sealy L S, 'Directors' "Wider" Responsibilities – Problems Conceptual, Practical and Procedural' (1987) 13 MULR 164 at 173.

[2] Heydon J D, 'Directors' Duties and the Company's Interests' in Finn P D (ed), *Equity and Commercial Relationships* The Law Book Company Ltd, Sydney, 1987 at 134; and Renard I A, Commentary to Heydon, 'Directors' Duties and the Company's Interests' in Finn P D (ed), *Equity and Commercial Relationships* The Law Book Company Ltd, Sydney, 1987 at 137; note *Financial Times*, 8 July 1999; and *The Times*, 21 July 1999.

[3] Ford H A J and Austin R P, *Ford's Principles of Corporations Law* (6th ed) Butterworths Pty Ltd, Sydney, 1992 at 466-470; Senate Standing Committee on Legal and Constitutional Affairs, *Social and Fiduciary Duties and Obligations of Company Directors* AGPS, Canberra, 1989 at 11; Sealy L S, 'Directors' "Wider" Responsibilities – Problems Conceptual, Practical and Procedural' (1987) 13 MULR 164 at 170; and Sealy L S, 'Reforming the Law on Directors' Duties' (1991) 12 Co Law 175 at 178.

[4] Wedderburn K W, 'Trust, Corporation and the Worker' (1985) 23 OHLJ 203 at 223-230; Sealy L S, 'Directors' "Wider" Responsibilities – Problems Conceptual, Practical and Procedural' (1987) 13 MULR 164; Sealy L S, 'The Enforcement of Partnership Agreements, Articles of Association and Shareholder Agreements' in Finn P D (ed) *Equity and Commercial Relationships* The Law Book Company Ltd, Sydney, 1987 at 109-110; Prentice D D, 'Directors, Creditors and Shareholders' in McKendrick E (ed), *Commercial Aspects of Trusts and Fiduciary Obligations* Clarendon Press, Oxford, 1992 at 73 *et seq*; note Panel on Take-overs and Mergers, *The City Code on Take-overs and Mergers* London, 1993 at General Principle 9; Companies Act 1985 (UK) ss309 and 719; Insolvency Act 1986 (UK) s187; *Financial Times*, 8 July 1999; and *The Times*, 21 July 1999.

[5] Davies P L, *Gower's Principles of Modern Company Law* (6th ed) Sweet & Maxwell Ltd, London, 1997 at 599; Ford H A J and Austin R P, *Ford's Principles of Corporations Law* (6th ed) Butterworths Pty

In this chapter we will consider the developing argument that the conventional treatment of English and Australian company law as such, should be departed from so as to impart upon directors of British and Australian companies an obligation to recognise, and to take into account, the company's creditors' interests as part of the day-to-day management requirements of directors.[7] In that event, should such an obligation on the part of directors run in parallel with their traditional obligation to consider the interests of the company's shareholders? Or is co-existence mutually exclusive? Barrett recognises the potential for conflict. In Barrett's view, inconvenience and uncertainty will follow:

> [If] directors of a company are always under an abstract duty to 'take account of the interests of its shareholders and its creditors,' since there will often be insoluble problems of reconciling the conflicting interests of these two groups.[8]

Do we require new rules and principles to accommodate such a departure from the traditional perspective of English and Australian company law? Certainly, the Senate Standing Committee on Legal and Constitutional Affairs, following its inquiry into the duties and responsibilities of directors of Australian companies during the late 1980s, felt that, 'a re-think of some of the fundamentals of company law would be required.'[9] Once more we find ourselves faced with the prospect of embarking upon a fundamental reassessment of the way in which traditional rules and principles are applied in order to refashion rules, principles and approaches considered applicable to resolving today's complex commercial and corporate problems. For, as will be seen shortly in this chapter, support is mounting for the definition of a duty upon directors of British and Australian companies, 'to act bona fide in the interests of the company as encompassing creditor interests in some circumstances.'[10]

In the next chapter of this book, we will analyse the development of the statutory duty in Australian company law which obliges directors of Australian companies to take positive steps to ensure that the company's creditors' interests are not put at risk where there are reasonable grounds for suspecting insolvency. With the enactment of Corporations Law s588G,[11] the debate as to whether or not creditors have an individual right, independent of that statutorily decreed liquidators in the overall interests of all creditors, to lay direct claim upon the directors for the recovery of losses, has been revivified. For, as the next chapter will evince, creditors of Australian companies, relying upon the Corporations Law, may only bring a personal action directly against the directors with the liquidator's written consent or, after having given the liquidator

---

cont.

  Ltd, Sydney, 1992 at 430; and Rider B A K, 'Partnership Law and its Impact on "Domestic Companies"' [1979] CLJ 148 at 148.

[6] *The Australian Metropolitan Life Assurance Company Ltd v Ure* (1923-1924) 33 CLR 199 at 216-217 per Isaacs J; *Parke v Daily News Ltd* [1962] Ch 927 at 963 per Plowman J; and Wedderburn K W, 'Ultra Vires or Directors' Bona Fides?' (1967) 30 MLR 566 at 568.

[7] Cf. *Financial Times*, 8 July 1999; and *The Times*, 21 July 1999.

[8] Barrett R I, 'Directors' Duties to Creditors' (1977) 40 MLR 226 at 230-231; note Riley C A, 'Directors' duties and the interests of creditors' (1989) 10 Co Law 87 at 90.

[9] Senate Standing Committee on Legal and Constitutional Affairs, *Social and Fiduciary Duties and Obligations of Company Directors* AGPS, Canberra, 1989 at 12.

[10] Farrar J H, Furey N E, Hannigan B M and Wylie P, *Farrar's Company Law* (3rd ed) Butterworth & Co (Publishers) Ltd, London, 1991 at 386.

[11] Added by Act No. 210 of 1992 and effective 23 June 1993.

a notice of intention to bring such an action and the liquidator refuses his or her consent, with the leave of the court.[12]

CREDITORS: A PROBLEM STATED

Whether or not creditors can look to the directors of British and Australian companies for payment of the company's debts will depend upon legal rules, equitable principles and any statutory obligations upon those directors to safeguard the interests of the creditors concerned. As a general rule, creditors are bound to look to the company for payment. This is a function of contract law,[13] and the doctrine of separate legal entity which establishes that a company is a legal person distinct from its directors and shareholders.[14] It is also a function of agency law.[15] No liability is assumed by directors for transactions which they conduct as their company's agents. In the White Paper entitled *A Revised Framework for Insolvency Law* presented to the British Parliament in 1984 by the Secretary of State for Trade and Industry ('1984 White Paper'),[16] as a result of recommendations within the Cork Report,[17] the Department of Trade and Industry ('DTI') advocated the introduction as soon as possible of measures to curb and to penalise the activities of irresponsible directors of British companies.[18] In doing so, the DTI relevantly observed that:

> Directors of companies, unlike bankrupts who are personally liable for all their debts, are, in the absence of fraudulent trading, misfeasance or breach of trust, generally under no personal liability, even though the financial loss suffered as a result of the irresponsibility of a director is often much greater than the damage caused by a bankrupt.[19]

As a consequence of British and Australian companies being discrete legal entities, those minded to commence trading with and give credit to a company, as Cooke J pointed out in *Nicholson v Permakraft (NZ) Ltd*, 'must normally take the company as

---

[12]   Corporations Law ss588M and 588R-588U; note *Stoland Pty Ltd v Thurn* (1998) 29 ACSR 280 at 289 per Lehane J; and *Quick v Stoland Pty Ltd* (1998) 29 ACSR 130 at 146 per Finkelstein J (Branson and Emmett JJ agreed); cf. *Ferguson v Wallbridge* [1935] 3 DLR 66 at 83 per Lord Blanesburgh (Lords Thankerton, Russell and Alness and Sir Sidney Rowlatt agreed), 'it is open to the Court, on cause shown, either to direct the liquidator to proceed in the company's name or on proper terms as to indemnity, and otherwise to give to the applicant leave to use the company's name as plaintiff in any action necessary to be brought for the vindication of the company's rights.'

[13]   *Wilson v Lord Bury* (1880) 5 QBD 518 at 525-526 per Brett LJ; and *Ferguson v Wilson* (1866) 2 Ch App 77 at 85 and 88-89 per Turner LJ; note Menzies D, 'Company Directors' (1959) 33 ALJ 156 at 157.

[14]   *Salomon v A Salomon and Company Ltd* [1897] AC 22; see Corporations Law s124 (formerly Corporations Law s161); cf. Companies Act 1985 (UK) ss35-35B.

[15]   *Ferguson v Wilson* (1866) 2 Ch App 77 at 89-90 per Cairns LJ; cf. *New Zealand Guardian Trust Co Ltd v Brooks* [1995] BCC 407 at 409-410 per Lord Keith.

[16]   Department of Trade and Industry, *A Revised Framework for Insolvency Law* HMSO, London, Cmnd 9175, 1984.

[17]   Report of the Review Committee on Insolvency Law and Practice, HMSO, London, Cmnd 8558, 1982.

[18]   Cf. Report of the Committee on Company Law Amendment, HMSO, London, Cmd 6659, 1945 at para 150; and Report of the Company Law Committee, HMSO, London, Cmnd 1749, 1962 at paras 80, 85(b), 497-499 and 503(a)-(d).

[19]   Department of Trade and Industry, *A Revised Framework for Insolvency Law* HMSO, London, Cmnd 9175, 1984 at para 14.

it is when they elect to do business with it. Short of fraud they must be the guardians of their own interests.'[20] The House of Lords[21] in *J H Rayner (Mincing Lane) Ltd v Department of Trade and Industry*[22] reiterated that a company is a legal person and that no one can sue on a contract save the parties to the contract. In Lord Templeman's speech to the House of Lords,[23] we were given the salutary reminder that:

> Since *Salomon's* case, traders and creditors have known that they do business with a corporation at their peril if they do not require guarantees from members of the corporation or adequate security.[24]

As such, creditors ought take the necessary steps to ensure that in the event of corporate failure their position is secure.[25] Indeed, as Lord Macnaghten pointed out in *Salomon v A Salomon and Company Ltd*, 'Every creditor is entitled to get and to hold the best security the law allows him to take.'[26] The use of directors' guarantees is one common way in which security might be achieved.[27] The ideal is easy to state.[28] But in practice it is not always that easy to achieve. In many cases, companies will only conduct business on a take it or leave it basis. In other cases, the commercial exigencies of getting the business done often do not allow for the requisite attention to detail. And so all too often such matters, although commercially critical, are simply overlooked. The ease with which credit is extended, and the folly of sometimes doing so, has long been recognised. The Greene Committee, for instance, was appointed at the beginning of 1925 under the chairmanship of Wilfrid Greene KC,[29] and presented its report on 8 May 1926. Whilst the Committee felt that no alteration of the law was desirable to meet the special case of private companies,[30] nonetheless, in the area of undischarged bankrupts as directors of British companies, the Greene Committee relevantly observed that:

> In many cases, traders have been far too ready to give credit to private companies of which they know nothing, without making any or sufficient inquiries as to the financial standing of the company or the persons who control it, and to this extent it may fairly be said that the trouble lies at their own door. This is particularly the case where manufacturers in periods of trade depression have been eager at any risk to find a sale for their goods.[31]

---

[20]   [1985] 1 NZLR 242 at 250.
[21]   (Lords Keith, Brandon, Templeman, Griffiths and Oliver).
[22]   [1989] 3 WLR 969; note Greenwood C, 'The Tin Council Litigation in the House of Lords' [1990] CLJ 8.
[23]   (Lords Keith, Brandon and Griffiths agreed).
[24]   [1989] 3 WLR 969 at 986.
[25]   Ford H A J, Austin R P and Ramsay I M, *Ford's Principles of Corporations Law* (9th ed) Reed International Books Australia Pty Ltd, Sydney, 1999 at paras 20.020 and 20.280.
[26]   [1897] AC 22 at 52.
[27]   *McLean v Burns Philp Trustee Company Pty Ltd* (1984-1985) 9 ACLR 926 at 940 per Young J.
[28]   The New Zealand Law Commission when declining to recommend the imposition of any new fiduciary duties on directors in respect of creditors observed, 'It is, of course, always open to a creditor to contract for higher protection.': New Zealand Law Commission, Report No. 9, *Company Law Reform and Restatement* Wellington, 1989 at paras 216-218.
[29]   By minutes dated 6 January 1925 and 19 February 1925.
[30]   Company Law Amendment Committee, HMSO, London, Cmd 2657, 1926 at para 86.
[31]   *Ibid* at para 56; see Report of the Review Committee on Insolvency Law and Practice, HMSO, London, Cmnd 8558, 1982 at para 90.

Almost 75 years later it seems that the lessons from the past have still not been learned. But it should be noted that creditors cannot guard against every eventuality. Business involves taking risks. The extension of credit is no different. Almost by definition businesses, new and old, will fail. This was recognised in the DTI's 1984 White Paper, for example, where the DTI reported that:

> The extension of credit has always involved a degree of risk and will continue to do so and it is inevitable that not every new commercial venture will be successful or that all established concerns will be able to adapt successfully to changing patterns of competition.[32]

It is fortunate that in most cases the company will meet the creditors' requirements and there is no reason to look further. But when the company cannot pay creditors may need to look to the directors personally. Secured creditors, however, if their advisers have done their job properly, should always be in a position to recover from the company the moneys which they are owed. In general it is unsecured creditors, who have no legal or equitable interest in the company's assets, who are most at risk.[33] *A fortiori* when those company assets are either lost or put beyond their reach. In these circumstances, one avenue for redress is perceived to be the directors themselves. This is especially so when the company is insolvent, but the directors are not. This chapter and the next will focus upon the unsecured creditor and the insolvent, or near-insolvent, company.

DO THE COMPANY'S INTERESTS INCLUDE CREDITORS?

The orthodox view in English and Australian company law is that the duties of directors of British and Australian companies are owed to the company. This principle is firmly established by *Percival v Wright*.[34] Traditionally, it is said that there is no separate legal or equitable duty owed by directors to their company's creditors.[35] Fiduciary obligations do not, however, exclude outside interests being taken into account, as long as in

---

[32] Department of Trade and Industry, *A Revised Framework for Insolvency Law* HMSO, London, Cmnd 9175, 1984 at para 12.

[33] *Macaura v Northern Assurance Company Ltd* [1925] AC 619 at 633 per Lord Wrenbury.

[34] [1902] 2 Ch 421; criticised by the Cohen committee (Report of the Committee on Company Law Amendment, HMSO, London, Cmd 6659, 1945 at paras 86-87); rejected by the Jenkins committee (Report of the Company Law Committee, HMSO, London, Cmnd 1749, 1962 at paras 89 and 99(b)); described by Loss L, 'The Fiduciary Concept as Applied to Trading by Corporate 'Insiders' in the United States' (1970) 33 MLR 34 at 40-41 as, 'a monument to the ability of lawyers to hypnotise themselves with their own creations'; but the decision, 'does not shock the conscience': *Coleman v Myers* [1977] 2 NZLR 225 at 329 per Cooke J; *Re Chez Nico (Restaurants) Ltd* [1991] BCC 736 at 750 per Browne-Wilkinson VC; note Rider B A K, 'Percival v Wright – Per Incuriam' (1977) 40 MLR 471; Rider B A K, 'Partnership Law and its Impact on "Domestic Companies"' [1979] CLJ 148 at 157; Keeton G W, 'The Director as Trustee' (1952) 5 CLP 11 at 16-18; Davies P L, *Gower's Principles of Modern Company Law* (6th ed) Sweet & Maxwell Ltd, London, 1997 at 599-600; and Lord Wilberforce, 'Law and Economics' [1966] JBL 301 at 307.

[35] *Bath v Standard Land Company Ltd* [1911] 1 Ch 618 at 627 per Cozens-Hardy MR; *In re Horsley & Weight Ltd* [1982] Ch 442 at 453-454 per Buckley LJ (Cumming-Bruce LJ agreed); and *Multinational Gas and Petrochemical Co v Multinational Gas and Petrochemical Services Ltd* [1983] Ch 258 at 288 per Dillon LJ; note Sealy L S, *Disqualification and Personal Liability of Directors* (4th ed) CCH Editions Ltd, Bicester, 1993 at 47; and Rajak H, *A Sourcebook of Company Law* Jordan & Sons Ltd, Bristol, 1989 at 518.

doing so the interests of the company are also served.[36] From earlier chapters of this book, it has been seen that the fiduciary relationship enjoyed between directors and their company imposes duties upon those directors *inter alia* to act honestly and in good faith, and also to exercise care and diligence towards their company. The juridical basis for this derives from trusts law and is centuries old. The English courts of chancery were not concerned to focus upon matters then considered to be outside the trust relationship. As a consequence, directors do not by reason only of their position as directors owe any duty to the company's creditors.[37] According to Lord Greene MR[38] in *In re Smith and Fawcett Ltd*:

> [Directors] must exercise their discretion bona fide in what they consider – not what a court may consider – is in the interests of the company, and not for any collateral purpose.[39]

Lord Greene MR's formula in *Fawcett* seems deceptively straightforward. But it is a formula which has been glossed in a succession of cases. Particularly, as Sealy notes, 'in regard to the meaning of the term "the company", in whose interests the directors must act.'[40] Although conventional wisdom dictates that directors of British and Australian companies must act in the company's interests, can that obligation extend to the company's creditors?[41] Are creditors' interests consonant with those of the company? Should directors be obliged to take into account the company's creditors' interests when considering the interests of the company?[42] The debate in English and Australian company law these days depends very much upon whether or not the company is faced with a situation of insolvency, near-insolvency or doubtful solvency.[43]

THE INTERESTS OF THE COMPANY AS A WHOLE

As we saw in chapter four of this book, it is trite law that the pre-eminent duty of a director of a British and Australian company is to act *bona fide* in the interests of the company as a whole.[44] However, as Ford in his sixth edition notes, there is controversy as to the exact meaning of this phrase, 'when it refers to "company as a whole". Does it mean the existing members, does it extend to the future members, the creditors and

---

36 Heydon J D, 'Directors' Duties and the Company's Interests' in Finn P D (ed), *Equity and Commercial Relationships* The Law Book Company Ltd, Sydney, 1987 at 134-135; and *Hurley v BGH Nominees Pty Ltd* (1982) 6 ACLR 791.

37 *Kuwait Asia Bank EC v National Mutual Life Nominees Ltd* [1990] 3 WLR 297 at 315 per Lord Lowry; see Farrar J H, Furey N E, Hannigan B M and Wylie P, *Farrar's Company Law* (3rd ed) Butterworth & Co (Publishers) Ltd, London, 1991 at 385.

38 (Luxmoore LJ and Asquith J agreed).

39 [1942] Ch 304 at 306; see *Brady v Brady* (1987) 3 BCC 535 at 552 per Nourse LJ.

40 Sealy L S, 'Directors' "Wider" Responsibilities – Problems Conceptual, Practical and Procedural' (1987) 13 MULR 164 at 166.

41 Cf. *Financial Times*, 8 July 1999; and *The Times*, 21 July 1999.

42 See Barrett R I, 'Directors' Fiduciary Duties' (1985) 59 ALJ 46.

43 *Nicholson v Permakraft (NZ) Ltd* [1985] 1 NZLR 242 at 249 per Cooke J.

44 *Grove v Flavel* (1986) 11 ACLR 161 at 166 *per curiam*; note *Clemens v Clemens Bros Ltd* [1976] 2 All ER 268 at 280 per Foster J.

others who have relations with the company?'[45] Historically, as we have seen, the company was understood to mean the shareholders collectively or the shareholders, present and future.[46]

In *The Australian Metropolitan Life Assurance Company Ltd v Ure* Isaacs J was of the view that the company comprised, 'the shareholders as a whole'.[47] In *Peters' American Delicacy Company Ltd v Heath* Dixon J determined that the company as a whole was to be considered, 'a corporate entity consisting of all the shareholders.'[48] In *Harlowe's Nominees Pty Ltd v Woodside (Lakes Entrance) Oil Company NL* the High Court of Australia,[49] in a joint judgment, declared that the company comprised, 'the general body of shareholders'.[50] And in *Greenhalgh v Arderne Cinemas Ld*, Evershed MR[51] considered that the company as a whole meant, 'the corporators as a general body'.[52]

Notwithstanding this rather impressive array of judicial pronouncement, the sermon is the same throughout. The underlying premise is clear. Conventional English and Australian company theory simply does not permit of consideration of the creditors' interests. It is the shareholders' interests with which directors have traditionally been concerned. In *In re Wincham Shipbuilding, Boiler, and Salt Company*, for instance, Jessel MR[53] put the matter in this way:

> It has always been held that the directors are trustees for the shareholders, that is, for the company. ... But directors are not trustees for the creditors of the company. The creditors have certain rights against a company and its members, but they have no greater rights against the directors than against any other members of the company. They have only those statutory rights against the members which are given them in the winding-up.[54]

Over 100 years later this classical position was reaffirmed by Dillon LJ in *Multinational Gas and Petrochemical Co v Multinational Gas and Petrochemical Services Ltd*, where his Lordship explained rather eloquently and succinctly that:

> [The] directors indeed stand in a fiduciary relationship to the company, as they are appointed to manage the affairs of the company and they owe fiduciary duties to the company though not to the creditors, present or future, or to individual shareholders.[55]

---

[45]   Ford H A J and Austin R P, *Ford's Principles of Corporations Law* (6th ed) Butterworths Pty Ltd, Sydney, 1992 at 466.

[46]   Finn P D, *Fiduciary Obligations* The Law Book Company Ltd, Sydney, 1977 at 66.

[47]   (1923) 33 CLR 199 at 216-217.

[48]   (1938-1939) 61 CLR 457 at 512.

[49]   (Barwick CJ, McTiernan and Kitto JJ).

[50]   (1969-1970) 121 CLR 483 at 493 *per curiam*.

[51]   (Asquith and Jenkins LJJ agreed).

[52]   [1951] Ch 286 at 291; see *Ngurli Ltd v McCann* (1953-1954) 90 CLR 425 at 438 *per curiam*; cf. Virgo G, 'Stealing from the Small Family Business' [1991] CLJ 464 at 484.

[53]   (James and Bramwell LJJ agreed).

[54]   (1878) 9 Ch D 322 at 328-329; see *Kuwait Asia Bank E C v National Mutual Life Nominees Ltd* [1990] 3 WLR 297 at 316 per Lord Lowry.

[55]   [1983] Ch 258 at 288; cf. *Liquidator of West Mercia Safetywear Ltd v Dodd* (1988) 4 BCC 30 at 33 per Dillon LJ (Croom-Johnson LJ and Caulfield J agreed); note Sealy L S, 'The Enforcement of Partnership

As Gower in his fifth edition points out, the English courts have been reluctant to recognise that, 'directors have any right, let alone duty, to have regard to the interests of creditors.'[56] Other commentators view the notion of a duty owed to creditors as contrary to principle and to long-established authority, and inherently at odds with the essential nature of a director's duty.[57] But there can be little doubt that since the mid-1970s, and more especially the mid-1980s, more and more attention has been given to this subject.[58] The upshot of this has been to challenge the traditional compass of the British and the Australian company, and the duties of directors said to be owed to them.

Thus, the whole concept of what comprises the interests of the company is being reappraised by the English and the Australian judiciary. One recent meaning of this provocative phrase was delivered by the Western Australian Full Court[59] in *Vrisakis v Australian Securities Commission*, where Ipp J[60] amplified the traditional approach, and dealt with the matter in this way:

> In determining what is in the 'interests of a company', the company means the corporate entity itself, the shareholders, and, where the financial position of the company is precarious, the creditors of the company.[61]

Ipp J's formulation in *Vrisakis* was not, however, too radical. It was based upon what fell earlier from Malcolm CJ's judgment in *Chew v The Queen*; namely, that if a company's financial position is precarious, 'the interests of the creditors may become the dominant factor in what constitutes the "benefit of the company as a whole"'.[62] Moreover, in the House of Lords a decade earlier, Lord Diplock had said in *Lonrho Ltd v Shell Petroleum Co Ltd* that the best interests of the company, 'are not exclusively those of its shareholders but may include those of its creditors.'[63] And notwithstanding his earlier comments in *Multinational*,[64] Dillon LJ[65] considered that the director in *Liquidator of West Mercia Safetywear Ltd v Dodd*[66] did owe a duty to have regard to the interests of the company's creditors. Dillon LJ distinguished his earlier comments in *Multinational* on the grounds that the relevant transaction there was made at a time when the company was solvent. In his Lordship's view, the director concerned in *Dodd*

---

cont.

Agreements, Articles of Association and Shareholder Agreements' in Finn P D (ed) *Equity and Commercial Relationships* The Law Book Company Ltd, Sydney, 1987 at 109.

[56] Gower L C B, *Gower's Principles of Modern Company Law* (5th ed) Sweet & Maxwell Ltd, London, 1992 at 555.

[57] Renard I A, Commentary to Heydon, 'Directors' Duties and the Company's Interests' in Finn P D (ed), *Equity and Commercial Relationships* The Law Book Company Ltd, Sydney, 1987 at 140.

[58] Cf. *Financial Times*, 8 July 1999; and *The Times*, 21 July 1999.

[59] (Malcolm CJ, Rowland and Ipp JJ).

[60] (Malcolm CJ agreed).

[61] (1992-1993) 9 WAR 395 at 450.

[62] (1991) 4 WAR 21 at 49.

[63] [1980] 1 WLR 627 at 634; see Barrett R I, 'Directors' Duties to Creditors' (1977) 40 MLR 226; and Wedderburn K W, 'The Social Responsibility of Companies' (1985) 15 Melb ULR 4 at 10, where Lord Diplock's views were described as, 'a rather daring innovation'.

[64] [1983] Ch 258 at 288; cf. *Liquidator of West Mercia Safetywear Ltd v Dodd* (1988) 4 BCC 30 at 33 per Dillon LJ (Croom-Johnson LJ and Caulfield J agreed); note Sealy L S, 'The Enforcement of Partnership Agreements, Articles of Association and Shareholder Agreements' in Finn P D (ed) *Equity and Commercial Relationships* The Law Book Company Ltd, Sydney, 1987 at 109.

[65] (Croom-Johnson LJ and Caulfield J agreed).

[66] (1988) 4 BCC 30.

was guilty of misfeasance and in breach of a fiduciary duty to the company, 'in making that transfer by way of fraudulent preference'.[67]

A CHANGE IN CIRCUMSTANCES, ATTITUDE AND APPROACH

The last decade or so, has seen courts at the very highest level in England and in Australia give recognition to interests traditionally considered extraneous to British and Australian companies. But what is the reason for this recognition? In short, the run on insolvency, and the public reaction to that. Economic recession has motivated the English and Australian courts to adopt a harder attitude towards directors of failing companies and, in Farrar's view, the modern trend, 'is to incorporate regard for the creditor interest in the directors' fiduciary duty to the company as a whole.'[68]

As we have seen from previous chapters of this book, times and attitudes change to meet felt needs of the day.[69] It is suggested that a new awareness *vis-à-vis* directors' duties has permeated the English and the Australian judiciary. We saw this in chapters two and three of this book where the Australian courts since the mid-1980s, probably more so than their English counterparts, have developed a far more robust and interventionist approach to the degree of care and diligence expected of directors in their management of today's companies.[70] Likewise, this was evident throughout chapters four and five of this book. There, we witnessed a far more commercial and pragmatic approach being taken by the Australian judiciary,[71] again probably more so than the English judiciary, in the light of the business community's expectations,[72] in order to resolve today's complex commercial and corporate disputes;[73] and the re-emergence of the proper purposes doctrine in keeping with that.[74]

Many of the Australian cases which gave rise to this new approach were concerned with insolvent trading provisions of the relevant Australian companies legislation.[75] These matters were considered in chapter three of this book and will receive further

---

[67] *Ibid* at 32; cf. Sealy L S, 'Directors' Duties – An Unnecessary Gloss' [1988] CLJ 175.

[68] Farrar J H, 'The Responsibility of Directors and Shareholders for a Company's Debts' (1989) 4 Canta LR 12 at 31.

[69] Cf. Company Law Amendment Committee, HMSO, London, Cmd 2657, 1926 at para 6.

[70] E.g., *Norman v Theodore Goddard* [1992] BCC 14 at 15 per Hoffmann J; *Vrisakis v Australian Securities Commission* (1992-1993) 9 WAR 395 at 451 per Ipp J (Malcolm CJ agreed); *Daniels v Anderson* (1995) 13 ACLC 614 at 662 per Clarke and Sheller JJA; *Androvin v Figliomeni* (1996) 14 ACLC 1461 at 1470 per Owen J (Kennedy and Franklyn JJ agreed); and *Re Barings plc* [1998] BCC 583 at 586 per Sir Richard Scott VC.

[71] *Gray Eisdell Timms Pty Ltd v Combined Auctions Pty Ltd* (1995) 13 ACLC 965 at 974 per Young J; cf. Muir G, 'Contract and Equity: Striking a Balance' (1985) 10 Adel LR 153 at 183, 'But pragmatism must not always triumph over principle'.

[72] *Equiticorp Finance Ltd v Bank of New Zealand* (1993) 11 ACLC 952 at 1019 per Clarke and Cripps JJA; and *Glandon Pty Ltd v Strata Consolidated Pty Ltd* (1993) 11 ACSR 543 at 547-548 per Mahoney JA.

[73] E.g., *Equiticorp Finance Ltd v Bank of New Zealand* (1993) 11 ACLC 952; *Bishopsgate Investment Management Ltd v Maxwell (No. 2)* [1994] 1 All ER 261; *Mallina Holdings Ltd v Biala Ltd* (1994) 15 ACSR 1; and *Daniels v Anderson* (1995) 13 ACLC 614; see Sealy L S, 'Directors' "Wider" Responsibilities – Problems Conceptual, Practical and Procedural' (1987) 13 MULR 164 at 169; and Sealy L S, '"Bona Fides" and "Proper Purposes" in Corporate Decisions' (1989) 15 MULR 265 at 265.

[74] *Gambotto v WCP Ltd* (1995) 13 ACLC 342; *Kokotovich Constructions Pty Ltd v Wallington* (1995) 13 ACLC 1113; *Bishopsgate Investment Management Ltd v Maxwell (No. 2)* [1994] 1 All ER 261; and *Re BSB Holdings Ltd (No. 2)* [1996] 1 BCLC 155.

[75] Companies Code s556; and Corporations Law s592; cf. Insolvency Act 1986 (UK) ss212-214; and Company Directors Disqualification Act 1986 (UK) ss2, 4, 6, 8 and 10.

scrutiny in the next chapter. What we are concerned with here is the development, independently of statute, of an obligation on the part of directors of British and Australian companies to consider, at least in the context of insolvency, the company's creditors' interests. Part of the debate which has emerged, consequent upon the recognition by the English and the Australian judiciary that such an obligation exists, centres upon the repository of that duty; that is to say, whether the duty is directly owed to the creditors, or whether along more traditional lines to the company itself. If the latter, then the question arises as to whether or not there is really a need for such a novel development; given the traditional rules and principles relating to, 'misfeasance, the expropriation of corporate assets or fraudulent preference'.[76]

THE MISFEASANCE CASES REVISITED

We have briefly considered some of the cases which ground the so-called duty upon directors of British and Australian companies to consider the company's creditors' interests in the context of insolvency.[77] When we come to consider further cases, it will become apparent that the English and Australian courts do seem intent upon framing such an obligation upon directors in terms of an independent duty. As such, certain issues emerge which we will consider a little later in this chapter.

At this point, however, the question arises whether this development is not simply a refashioning of traditional rules and principles by the English and the Australian judiciary in an attempt to bring a fresh approach to the whole topic of directors' duties generally. An instance of re-labelling of the type identified by Rogers CJ in *AWA Ltd v Daniels*.[78] It is suggested that the so-called duty upon directors of British and Australian companies to consider the company's creditors' interests stems from the misfeasance summons: a procedural device empowering liquidators in given circumstances to recover from directors who have done wrongly by misapplying or retaining the company's moneys, 'or by which the company's property has been wasted, or the company's credit improperly pledged.'[79]

As such, the concept is not new as the law has a long history of imposing liability in such circumstances.[80] But what is misfeasance? To constitute misfeasance, according to Mason J in *Walker v Wimborne*, 'it must appear that there has been something more than mere negligence; it must be shown that what occurred amounted to a breach of duty.'[81] Jacobs J later amplified this in his judgment in *Wimborne*, when his Honour explained that the court must be satisfied that the director impugned:

[76] Sealy L S, 'Directors' Duties – An Unnecessary Gloss' [1988] CLJ 175 at 175; note Insolvency Act 1986 (UK) ss212-214; cf. Corporations Law s598.
[77] *Lonrho Ltd v Shell Petroleum Co Ltd* [1980] 1 WLR 627 at 634 per Lord Diplock; and *Liquidator of West Mercia Safetywear Ltd v Dodd* (1988) 4 BCC 30 at 32 per Dillon LJ (Croom-Johnson LJ and Caulfield J agreed); cf. *Chew v The Queen* (1991) 4 WAR 21 at 49 per Malcolm CJ; and *Vrisakis v Australian Securities Commission* (1992-1993) 9 WAR 395 at 450 per Ipp J (Malcolm CJ agreed).
[78] (1992) 10 ACLC 933 at 1019.
[79] *In re Canadian Land Reclaiming and Colonizing Company* (1880) 14 Ch D 660 at 670 per James LJ.
[80] *In re Forest of Dean Coal Mining Company* (1879) 10 Ch D 450; *In re City Equitable Fire Insurance Company Ltd* [1925] Ch 407; *In re Etic Limited* [1928] Ch 861 at 875 per Maugham J; *Couve v J Pierre Couve Ltd* (1933) 49 CLR 486 at 495 *per curiam*; and *Walker v Wimborne* (1976-1977) 137 CLR 1 at 14 per Jacobs J.
[81] (1976-1977) 137 CLR 1 at 8; note *Kimberley Mineral Holdings Ltd v Triguboff* [1978] 1 NSWLR 364 at 368-369 per Needham J.

[Was] in breach of a fiduciary duty or 'something in the nature' thereof for which he is accountable in a court applying principles of Equity. That is what is meant by 'breach of duty' in [that] context.[82]

In expressing this view, it is clear that Jacobs J in *Wimborne* was simply adopting that which fell earlier from Maugham J's judgment in *In re Etic Limited*;[83] and, which in turn, was approved by the High Court of Australia[84] in *Couve v J Pierre Couve Ltd.*[85] The authorities upon the scope of misfeasance proceedings were collected and examined by Maugham J in *Etic*, where his Lordship concluded that Companies (Consolidation) Act 1908 (UK) s215:[86]

> [Is] not applicable to all cases in which the company has a right of action against an officer of the company. It is limited to cases where there has been something in the nature of a breach of duty by an officer of the company as such which has caused pecuniary loss to the company. Breach of duty of course would include a misfea-sance or a breach of trust in the stricter sense, and the section will apply to a true case of misapplication of money or property of the company, or a case where there has been retention of money or property which the officer was bound to have paid or returned to the company.[87]

In many of the cases which follow, the proceedings are brought by either liquidators alleging misfeasance in reliance upon statutory assistance granted them or corporate regulators as part of the administration or winding-up procedures of British and Australian companies in liquidation. Such legislation has long been enacted in English and Australian company law.[88] It has inevitably referred to misfeasance, breach of duty or breach of trust on the part of errant directors, and has enabled recovery action against them accordingly. Hence, it can be argued that today's judges are simply re-visiting old procedures and dressing them up as a new independent duty.[89] But in the process of doing that, it is suggested that the whole concept of the traditional model of English and Australian company law has not been sufficiently thought through; for reasons that will emerge a little later in this chapter.

THE CONCEPT OF A SEPARATE DUTY

The South Australian Full Court[90] in *Grove v Flavel*[91] rejected the argument that there was a general duty owed by directors of Australian companies to protect the interests

---

[82] (1976-1977) 137 CLR 1 at 14-15.
[83] [1928] Ch 861.
[84] (Dixon, Evatt and McTiernan JJ).
[85] (1933) 49 CLR 486 at 495 *per curiam*.
[86] Cf. Companies Act 1899 (NSW) s162.
[87] [1928] Ch 861 at 875; see *Couve v J Pierre Couve Ltd* (1933) 49 CLR 486 at 495 *per curiam*; and *Walker v Wimborne* (1976-1977) 137 CLR 1 at 14 per Jacobs J.
[88] E.g., Companies Act 1899 (NSW) s162; Companies Act 1936 (NSW) s308; Companies Act 1961 (NSW) s367B; Companies Code s542; and Corporations Law s598; cf. Companies Act 1862 (UK) s165; Companies (Consolidation) Act 1908 (UK) s215; Companies Act 1948 (UK) s333; and Insolvency Act 1986 (UK) s212.
[89] Menzies D, 'Company Directors' (1959) 33 ALJ 156 at 166.
[90] (Jacobs, Matheson and Olsson JJ).

of creditors, irrespective of the company's financial position. The Full Court held, however, that directors who act to the detriment of creditors knowing that the company faces a real risk of liquidation are acting improperly.[92] However, in *Jeffree v National Companies & Securities Commission*[93] the Western Australian Full Court[94] went much further, when it held that directors owed fiduciary duties to present and future creditors of the company.[95] In doing so, the Full Court cited with approval comments which Lord Templeman made during his speech to the House of Lords in *Winkworth v Edward Baron Development Co Ltd*.[96] Comments which we will consider shortly. The philosophy and underlying rationale for this departure from the traditional view of English and Australian company law was identified by the House of Representatives Standing Committee on Legal and Constitutional Affairs in its report entitled *Corporate Practices and the Rights of Shareholders* ('Lavarch Report'), where the Committee recognised that:

> Increasingly companies have resorted to debt rather than equity for meeting their capital requirements.[97] This has affected the traditional relationships between directors and shareholders by introducing new factors into the equation. It needs to be noted that the interests of shareholders can be effected [*sic*] as creditors have priority to shareholders in the winding up of a company.[98]

The argument runs, therefore, that in the context of insolvency, with the consequent loss of the company's capital, the shareholders have no financial interest in the company. In those circumstances, directors must have regard to the company's creditors' interests. Dabner, for instance, argues that it is only in the context of insolvency that the rights of shareholders give way to those of creditors, because it is the creditors' investment that is then at stake.[99] This approach has much to commend it. The English and Australian courts have embraced this argument and the concept of a separate duty. There is now clear authority in England and in Australia that directors must have regard to the company's creditors' interests where the company is insolvent. For directors to do otherwise, constitutes an actionable misfeasance.

In Australia, the High Court of Australia[100] in *Walker v Wimborne*[101] was instrumental in extending directors' duties to embrace the company's creditors' interests within

---

cont.

91 (1986) 11 ACLR 161; cf. Farrar J H, 'The Responsibility of Directors and Shareholders for a Company's Debts' (1989) 4 Canta LR 12 at 19; note *McNamara v Flavel* (1987-1988) 13 ACLR 619.
92 (1986) 11 ACLR 161 at 170 *per curiam*.
93 (1989) 15 ACLR 217; note Baxt R, 'Duties of directors with respect to creditors' (1989) 63 ALJ 846 at 847-849; and Baxt R, 'Reforming the law relating to company directors' (1990) 64 ALJ 345 at 345-346; see *Re Avon Chambers Ltd* [1978] 2 NZLR 638.
94 (Wallace, Brinsden and Pidgeon JJ).
95 (1989) 15 ACLR 217 at 221-222 per Wallace J and at 227-228 per Brinsden J (Pidgeon J agreed with both).
96 [1987] 1 All ER 114 at 118.
97 Figures for the relevant decade indicate that credit to the business sector by financial intermediaries rose from $43bn in 1981 to $213bn in June 1990: Reserve Bank of Australia Bulletin, December 1991, Table D.4 at 555.
98 House of Representatives Standing Committee on Legal and Constitutional Affairs, *Corporate Practices and the Rights of Shareholders* AGPS, Canberra, 1991 at para 5.3.17; see Grantham R, 'The Judicial Extension of Directors' Duties to Creditors' [1991] JBL 1.
99 Dabner J, 'Directors' Duties – The Schizoid Company' (1988) 6 CSLJ 105 at 114.
100 (Barwick CJ, Mason and Jacobs JJ).

the context of insolvency.[102] The Senate Standing Committee on Legal and Constitutional Affairs in its report entitled *Social and Fiduciary Duties and Obligations of Company Directors* explained the rationale for such an extension as being that, 'at times of insolvency, or near-insolvency, it is the funds of the creditors, rather than those of the shareholders, with which the directors are dealing.'[103] For, it is said that where the company is solvent, albeit in liquidation, the real interest in how the liquidation is effected lies with the shareholders, as the creditors will be paid in any event. The focus must be upon those whose real interests are affected by the state of insolvency, or otherwise, of the company.[104] To some, *Wimborne* is considered to be the genesis of what is now widely accepted as the extended common law obligation of directors to consider their company's creditors' interests in the context of insolvency.[105] It is a case deserving of study.

WALKER v WIMBORNE: A LANDMARK DECISION

In *Walker v Wimborne*[106] the company was one of a group controlled by common directors.[107] Shortly before the company went into liquidation, its directors paid certain moneys to related companies in circumstances where there was no obvious benefit to the company in making any of the payments. Subsequently, the liquidator sought to recover those moneys as having been paid in circumstances constituting either a breach of duty or a breach of trust within the applicable companies legislation.[108] The High Court of Australia[109] found that by moving moneys between their related companies, the directors had disregarded the interests of the company and its creditors in circumstances constituting misfeasance. In reaching this conclusion, Mason J,[110] who delivered the leading judgment, emphasised that:

> [The] directors of a company in discharging their duty to the company must take account of the interest of its shareholders and its creditors. Any failure by the directors to take into account the interests of creditors will have adverse consequences for the company as well as for them. The creditor of a company, whether it be a member of a 'group' of companies in the accepted sense of that term or not, must look to that

---

cont.

[101] (1976-1977) 137 CLR 1.

[102] Cf. Barrett R I, 'Directors' Duties to Creditors' (1977) 40 MLR 226 at 229, 'Mason J seems to infer that creditors' interests must be taken into account even before insolvency'.

[103] Senate Standing Committee on Legal and Constitutional Affairs, *Social and Fiduciary Duties and Obligations of Company Directors* AGPS, Canberra, 1989 at 66.

[104] Finn P D, *Fiduciary Obligations* The Law Book Company Ltd, Sydney, 197 at 61.

[105] Goldberg A H, 'Who'd be a Company Director' a paper presented at the Second Business Lawyers' Conference, conducted by the Business Law Section of the Law Council of Australia, Melbourne, 10 April 1989 at 6.

[106] (1976-1977) 137 CLR 1.

[107] See Baxt R, 'The Duties of Directors of Public Companies – The Realities of Commercial Life, The Contradictions of the Law, And the Need for Reform' (1976) BLR 289.

[108] Companies Act 1961 (NSW) s367B(1)(b).

[109] (Barwick CJ, Mason and Jacobs JJ).

[110] (Barwick CJ agreed).

company for payment. His interests may be prejudiced by the movement of funds between companies in the event that the companies become insolvent.[111]

Whether or not Mason J was seeking to establish an independent duty upon directors of Australian companies as such, subsequent cases have, nevertheless, treated the decision by the High Court of Australia in *Wimborne* as a landmark decision. Mason J's celebrated *dictum* is considered as authority for extending directors' duties to include an obligation to take into account the creditors' interests of an insolvent company. Heydon, however, felt that *Wimborne* had been misread.[112] He thought it extremely doubtful that Mason J's comments were intended to suggest that directors owe an independent duty directly to creditors. Heydon's opinion has received a measure of judicial support and, it is suggested, is correct.[113]

To interpret Mason J's comments in *Wimborne* otherwise, would be to fly in the face of established insolvency law.[114] But that is very different to extending the parameter of directors' duties to include an obligation to have regard to the company's creditors' interests in the context of insolvency. The duty in such circumstances being owed to the company, not to its creditors. However, Mason J's recognition in *Wimborne* that creditors' interests are vital is to be welcomed. In Baxt's view, this merely emphasises that:

> [In] commerce the directors of companies do not see their obligation as resting entirely with their shareholders. Surely these interests are paramount in their thinking but it must be recalled that a company does not exist by shareholders alone![115]

Notwithstanding that subsequent decisions at the highest level have enshrined Mason J's comments as part of Australian legal gospel,[116] it remains important to balance such developments in English and Australian company law with conventional insolvency theory so that hitherto well established principles do not collide.

---

[111] (1976-1977) 137 CLR 1 at 7; see *Equiticorp Finance Ltd v Bank of New Zealand* (1993) 11 ACLC 952 at 1015 per Clarke and Cripps JJA.

[112] Heydon J D, 'Directors' Duties and the Company's Interests' in Finn P D (ed), *Equity and Commercial Relationships* The Law Book Company Ltd, Sydney, 1987 at 126 and 134.

[113] *Sycotex Pty Ltd v Baseler* (1994) 122 ALR 531 at 549-550 per Gummow J; cf. Chernov A, 'The Role of Corporate Governance Practices in the Development of Legal Principles Relating to Directors' in Ramsay I M (ed), *Corporate Governance and the Duties of Company Directors* The Centre for Corporate Law and Securities Regulation, University of Melbourne, Parkville, 1997 at 46, 'since *Walker v Wimborne*, legal principles have evolved, albeit on a dubious jurisprudential basis'.

[114] *Re Oasis Merchandising Services Ltd* [1997] BCC 282 at 291 *per curiam*; cf. Insolvency Act 1986 (UK) s107; note Villiers C, 'Employees as creditors: a challenge for justice in insolvency law' (1999) 20 Co Law 222 at 228; Schulte R, 'Corporate groups and the equitable subordination of claims on insolvency' (1997) 18 Co Law 2 at 2 and 11; Bean G M D, 'Debt subordination validated' (1994) 15 Co Law 52 at 52; and Sealy L S, 'Directors' Duties – An Unnecessary Gloss' [1988] CLJ 175 at 177; see Report of the Review Committee on Insolvency Law and Practice, HMSO, London, Cmnd 8558, 1982 at para 1396.

[115] Baxt R, 'The Duties of Directors of Public Companies – The Realities of Commercial Life, The Contradictions of the Law, And the Need for Reform' (1976) BLR 289 at 298-299.

[116] *Australian Growth Resources Corporation Pty Ltd v van Reesema* (1988) 6 ACLC 529 at 535-536 per King CJ (Cox J agreed); *Chew v The Queen* (1991) 4 WAR 21 at 49 per Malcolm CJ; and *Glandon Pty Ltd v Strata Consolidated Pty Ltd* (1993) 11 ACSR 543 at 557 per Cripps JA.

DEVELOPMENT OF A SEPARATE DUTY: AN AUSTRALIAN AND NEW ZEALAND PERSPECTIVE

Since *Walker v Wimborne*, there have been a number of Australian and New Zealand cases which have taken Mason J's comments[117] as their basis for accepting that directors, in some circumstances, do owe an independent fiduciary duty to take into account the company's creditors' interests. In order to demonstrate this acceptance by the judiciary, that directors are so obliged, it is only necessary to mention the following four well-known cases. In each case, action was taken by the liquidator to recover moneys on behalf of the company's creditors.

The first of these cases is *Re Avon Chambers Ltd*.[118] Briefly, the facts were these. Several days before the appointment of an arbitrator to fix the rental over the company's premises, the effect of which would inevitably result in an obligation upon the company to meet substantial arrears of rental, the company declared and paid a dividend to its principal shareholder and director. During the winding-up of the company, under the relevant companies legislation, the liquidator applied for repayment of the dividend; alleging that its procurement, at the instance of the director concerned, constituted misfeasance on the director's part. The court agreed.

Casey J, before whom *Avon* was argued, adopted the meaning of misfeasance as that earlier prescribed by Mason J in *Wimborne*.[119] Misfeasance, in Casey J's judgment, includes actions within the directors' powers which cause the company loss and which are not done for its benefit. Casey J considered that the situation before him constituted misfeasance and was not, 'mere negligence or error of judgment; it was a deliberate attempt to put funds beyond the reach of creditors and to benefit the shareholders.'[120] Although not clear from the report, it would seem that Casey J considered that the company's virtual insolvency at the relevant time, was such as to oblige the director concerned to have regard to the company's contingent creditors. If that be the case, then Casey J was pre-empting the approach subsequently taken by the Western Australian Full Court in *Jeffree v National Companies & Securities Commission*;[121] a case it will be recalled from a little earlier in this chapter, involving strikingly similar facts.

In *Ring v Sutton*[122] the New South Wales Court of Appeal[123] was asked to consider the rights of creditors in proceedings brought by the company's liquidator against a director claiming damages for misfeasance. The misfeasance, it was said, concerned personal loans from the company the terms of which were commercially questionable. Rather curiously, the Court of Appeal found that the loans amounted to a breach of duty on the director's part and ordered that the moneys borrowed be repaid at commercial rates of interest. The Court of Appeal cited *Wimborne* with approval and recognised a right in the liquidator to challenge the loans in the company's creditors' interests. But, in doing so, the Court of Appeal failed to actually go on and state why it was that the

---

[117] (1976-1977) 137 CLR 1 at 7.
[118] [1978] 2 NZLR 638.
[119] (1976-1977) 137 CLR 1 at 14-15.
[120] [1978] 2 NZLR 638 at 641.
[121] (1989) 15 ACLR 217; note Baxt R, 'Duties of directors with respect to creditors' (1989) 63 ALJ 846 at 847-849; and Baxt R, 'Reforming the law relating to company directors' (1990) 64 ALJ 345 at 345-346; see *Re Avon Chambers Ltd* [1978] 2 NZLR 638.
[122] (1980) 5 ACLR 546.
[123] (Moffitt P, Hope and Glass JJA).

principle enunciated by Mason J in *Wimborne* was applicable. On the facts, the decision in *Sutton* looks suspect: a view which is shared by several commentators.[124]

Of more interest to the present discussion is *Nicholson v Permakraft (NZ) Ltd.*[125] There, the liquidator unsuccessfully sought to recover moneys distributed to shareholders as a result of a restructuring of the company's assets. The New Zealand Court of Appeal[126] took the opportunity to discuss the position concerning creditors' rights. The leading judgment was given by Cooke J who undertook a detailed examination in this regard. In Cooke J's judgment, whilst directors' duties are owed to the company, particular cases may require the directors to consider *inter alia* creditors' interests. For instance, 'if the company is insolvent, or near-insolvent, or of doubtful solvency, or if a contemplated payment or other course of action would jeopardise its solvency.'[127]

Conceptually, Cooke J in *Permakraft* considered such an obligation to be an analogue of the neighbour principle and the linking of power with obligation, and opined that in a situation of marginal commercial solvency, 'creditors may fairly be seen as beneficially interested in the company or contingently so.'[128] Cooke J was concerned to link this obligation upon directors to consider creditors' interests to *Salomon's* charter of limited liability on the basis that whilst limited liability is a privilege, it is open to abuse through irresponsible structural engineering to the prejudice of creditors: 'a mischief to which the Courts should be alive.'[129] In expressing this view, Cooke J was concerned at the time it took for information concerning the company's financial position, which if not actually in the directors' hands ought to have been, to reach its creditors.[130] It was during that interval that he felt creditors ought be protected.

It could be argued, however, that such is commercial life. Implicit in business is the element of risk.[131] Creditors must be taken to know that their intelligence may not always meet that of their debtors. That is one of the reasons why the law of securities has played such a prominent part in commerce over the centuries. Creditors have available to them a level of protection commensurate with the risks they take.[132] Why should additional avenues be made available to creditors, if they choose not to avail

124 Sealy L S, 'Directors' "Wider" Responsibilities – Problems Conceptual, Practical and Procedural' (1987) 13 MULR 164 at 172, 175 and 180; Sealy L S, 'Directors' Duties – An Unnecessary Gloss' [1988] CLJ 175 at 176; and Barrett R I, case note (1982) 56 ALJ 189.
125 [1985] 1 NZLR 242.
126 (Cooke, Richardson and Somers JJ).
127 [1985] 1 NZLR 242 at 249 per Cooke J.
128 *Ibid*; which Farrar J H, 'The Responsibility of Directors and Shareholders for a Company's Debts' (1989) 4 Canta LR 12 at 15 described as, 'interesting philosophical remarks on the question of a duty to creditors'; note Farrar J H, 'The Obligation of a Company's Directors to its Creditors Before Liquidation' [1985] JBL 413 at 415, 'The test is *ought* the directors to have known that the particular thing was likely to cause loss to creditors'; cf. Sealy L S, 'Directors' Duties – An Unnecessary Gloss' [1988] CLJ 175 at 177.
129 [1985] 1 NZLR 242 at 250; note Baxt R, case note (1988) 62 ALJ 643 at 645.
130 Cf. Davies P L, *Gower's Principles of Modern Company Law* (6th ed) Sweet & Maxwell Ltd, London, 1997 at 537.
131 *Macquarie Bank Ltd v Fociri Pty Ltd* (1992) 10 ACLC 785 at 797 per Kirby P; and *Vrisakis v Australian Securities Commission* (1992-1993) 9 WAR 395 at 449-450 per Ipp J (Malcolm CJ agreed); note Sealy L S, 'Directors' "Wider" Responsibilities – Problems Conceptual, Practical and Procedural' (1987) 13 MULR 164 at 176; Sealy L S, 'The Director as Trustee' [1967] CLJ 83 at 89; The American Law Institute, *Principles of Corporate Governance: Analysis and Recommendations* St Paul, 1994, volume 1 at 174; and Commonwealth, House of Representatives, Parliamentary Debates, 3 November 1992 at 2402.
132 Posner R A, 'The Rights of Creditors of Affiliated Corporations' (1975-1976) 43 UCLR 499 at 507-509.

themselves of remedies already amply provided? The point was made rather nicely more than a century ago by Lord Watson in his speech to the House of Lords[133] in *Salomon v A Salomon and Company Ltd*, where his Lordship boldly asserted that:

> [A] creditor who will not take the trouble to use the means which the statute provides for enabling him to protect himself must bear the consequence of his own negligence.[134]

But, in any event, these progressive views articulated by Cooke J in *Permakraft* did not receive support from his brethren, both of whom expressly declined to comment. First, upon whether anything short of insolvency was sufficient to ground an action for breach of duty; and secondly, whether the duty could be said to be directly owed to the creditors concerned. On the facts of the present case, the company was, at the relevant time, solvent. It is suggested that Cooke J's views were, therefore, largely gratuitous. Richardson J, on the other hand, saw the issue in this way:

> If a company is solvent in the sense of its assets exceeding its liabilities there can ... be no question of a separate duty to creditors: they have their ordinary remedies if their accounts are not paid. If it is insolvent the creditors have an interest in the company and the directors might be said to have a duty to them for creditors' money is then at stake. It is in the intermediate situation of near insolvency or doubtful insolvency that greater difficulties of legal principle arise.[135]

However, Richardson J in *Permakraft* baulked at tackling the difficult issues thus identified. So too did Somers J, who would not be drawn on the debate; for in his view, the company was clearly solvent. Somers J did, however, reaffirm that where the company is insolvent, its directors must have regard to the creditors' interests; for the directors are trading with the creditors' money.[136]

Lastly, it is important to consider *Kinsela v Russell Kinsela Pty Ltd*,[137] where the New South Wales Court of Appeal[138] endorsed the approaches of Mason J in *Wimborne* and Cooke J in *Permakraft*. In doing so, the Court of Appeal upheld the liquidator's claim to avoid a private lease arrangement which was entered into by the directors in order to place the company's assets beyond the immediate reach of its creditors.[139] The Court of Appeal's reasons were given by Street CJ[140] who recognised that in a solvent company the shareholders' proprietary interests entitle them as a general body to be regarded as the company. But where a company is insolvent, the creditors' interests intrude. It is in these circumstances that Street CJ considered that:

> [The creditors] become prospectively entitled, through the mechanism of liquidation, to displace the power of the shareholders and directors to deal with the company's assets. It is in a practical sense their assets and not the shareholders' assets that,

---

[133]   (Lords Halsbury LC, Watson, Herschell, Macnaghten, Morris and Davey).
[134]   [1897] AC 22 at 40.
[135]   [1985] 1 NZLR 242 at 254.
[136]   *Ibid* at 255.
[137]   [1986] 4 NSWLR 722.
[138]   (Street CJ, Hope and McHugh JJA).
[139]   [1986] 4 NSWLR 722 at 727 per Street CJ.
[140]   (Hope and McHugh JJA agreed).

through the medium of the company, are under the management of the directors pending either liquidation, return to solvency, or the imposition of some alternative administration.[141]

After reviewing *Wimborne* and *Permakraft*, Street CJ accepted that, 'the directors' duty to a company as a whole extends in an insolvency context to not prejudicing the interests of creditors'.[142] Street CJ had little difficulty in finding in the liquidator's favour; for in his Honour's view, the company was plainly insolvent at the relevant time and its collapse was imminent. In these circumstances, the directors' actions were in breach of their duty to the company in that they directly prejudiced the company's creditors.[143]

DEVELOPMENT OF A SEPARATE DUTY: AN ENGLISH PERSPECTIVE

In English company law a similar trend to that witnessed in Australian and New Zealand company law has occurred. By way of comparative analysis, however, it is instructive to consider four cases decided by the English courts which have led to an obligation on the part of directors of British companies to have regard to the company's creditors' interests in the context of insolvency. The facts of each are well-known and so it is not necessary, therefore, to dwell too much upon their factual background.

The existence of an independent duty in English company law upon directors of British companies to consider the company's creditors' interests, has been ascribed to Lord Templeman in *Winkworth v Edward Baron Development Co Ltd*.[144] However, it was recognised as early as 1980 by Lord Diplock in *Lonrho Ltd v Shell Petroleum Co Ltd* that:

> [It] is the duty of the board to consider ... the best interests of the company. These are not exclusively those of its shareholders but may include those of its creditors.[145]

Whilst the House of Lords[146] in *Lonrho* was not concerned with the question of a duty being owed by the directors to the company's creditors in the context of insolvency, or otherwise, Lord Diplock's comments extracted above from his Lordship's speech to the

---

[141] [1986] 4 NSWLR 722 at 730; see *Australian Growth Resources Corporation Pty Ltd v van Reesema* (1988) 6 ACLC 529 at 535-536 per King CJ (Cox J agreed); *McNamara v Flavel* (1987-1988) 13 ACLR 619 at 625 per Millhouse J; *Liquidator of West Mercia Safetywear Ltd v Dodd* (1988) 4 BCC 30 at 33 *per curiam*; *Lee Panavision Ltd v Lee Lighting Ltd* [1991] BCC 620 at 635 *per curiam*; and *Equiticorp Finance Ltd v Bank of New Zealand* (1993) 11 ACLC 952 at 1016-1017 per Clarke and Cripps JJA; cf. Callaway F H, Commentary to Sealy, 'The Enforcement of Partnership Agreements, Articles of Association and Shareholder Agreements' in Finn P D (ed), *Equity and Commercial Relationships* The Law Book Company Ltd, Sydney, 1987 at 119; note Prentice D D, 'Directors, Creditors and Shareholders' in McKendrick E (ed), *Commercial Aspects of Trusts and Fiduciary Obligations* Clarendon Press, Oxford, 1992 at 78-80.

[142] [1986] 4 NSWLR 722 at 732.

[143] *Ibid* at 733 per Street CJ.

[144] [1987] 1 All ER 114 at 118.

[145] [1980] 1 WLR 627 at 634.

[146] (Lords Diplock, Edmund-Davies, Fraser, Russell and Keith).

House of Lords do, nevertheless, provide judicial recognition of the highest order that directors ought be alive to their company's creditors' interests.[147]

In re Horsley & Weight Ltd[148] has generated much judicial comment, both in England and in Australia. There, the liquidator sought a declaration that the purchase of a pension policy by the company was *ultra vires* its articles. The liquidator claimed that the particular director involved, by procuring the company to take out the policy for his benefit, was guilty of misfeasance and breach of trust. As such, the liquidator claimed the pension scheme as an asset in the winding-up.[149] The Court of Appeal[150] rejected the liquidator's claim. In doing so, Buckley LJ,[151] who delivered the principal judgment, was of the view that directors owe a duty to the company not to permit any unlawful reduction of capital to occur and that, 'if the company is put into liquidation when paid-up capital has been improperly repaid, the liquidator owes a duty to the creditors to enforce any right to repayment which is available to the company.'[152]

The other members of the Court of Appeal in *Horsley* were of the view that because there was no proof that the directors should have appreciated that the payment was likely to cause loss to the creditors, the directors could not be guilty of misfeasance. Had there been such proof, then the Court of Appeal would have found the directors liable, notwithstanding that the purchase by them of the pension policy was clearly *intra vires*. Templeman LJ noted that if the company had been doubtfully solvent at the date of the grant to the directors' knowledge, 'the grant would have been both a misfeasance and a fraud, on the creditors for which the directors would remain liable.'[153] Templeman LJ went on to explain that absent fraud the directors might still have been guilty of negligence where the company had cash flow and profitability problems. In such circumstances it would have been, 'negligent of the directors to pay out £10,000 for the benefit of the respondent at that juncture. There could have been gross negligence, amounting to misfeasance.'[154]

The next development in English company law appeared five years later. Again, Lord Templeman was involved. This time in *Winkworth*,[155] where the facts were briefly these. A husband and wife were the shareholders and directors of a company which purchased a freehold property, which they then occupied as their home. Upon the sale of the former matrimonial home, the husband and wife paid the proceeds into the company's bank account in reduction of its overdraft facility. Some months later, without the wife's knowledge or consent, the company mortgaged the property to Winkworth. In the process, the wife's signature was forged by the husband. Subsequently, the company became insolvent and went into liquidation. Winkworth, as mortgagee, brought an action for possession. Although neither the company nor the husband resisted the action, the wife did. She claimed that the proceeds from the sale of the former matrimonial home which were paid into the company's bank account, prior to the legal charge executed in favour of Winkworth, gave her an equitable

---

[147] (All members of the House agreed).
[148] [1982] Ch 442; see *Brady v Brady* (1987) 3 BCC 535 at 546 per Croom-Johnson LJ.
[149] Companies Act 1948 (UK) s333(1).
[150] (Buckley, Cumming-Bruce and Templeman LJJ).
[151] (Cumming-Bruce LJ agreed).
[152] [1982] Ch 442 at 453-454.
[153] *Ibid* at 455.
[154] *Ibid*.
[155] [1987] 1 All ER 114.

interest in the property which overrode Winkworth's interest. The House of Lords[156] rejected the wife's claim. In doing so, Lord Templeman[157] determined that:

> [A] company owes a duty to its creditors, present and future. ... [The] company owes a duty to its creditors to keep its property inviolate and available for the repayment of its debts. ... A duty is owed by the directors to the company and to the creditors of the company to ensure that the affairs of the company are properly administered and that its property is not dissipated or exploited for the benefit of the directors themselves to the prejudice of the creditors.[158]

What Lord Templeman meant by these remarks, which are taken from his Lordship's speech to the House of Lords in *Winkworth*, is a matter of conjecture and some doubt. Farrar has suggested that Lord Templeman's comments are too widely stated. In Farrar's view, they are either a restatement of the capital maintenance doctrine or, 'an equitable extension of that doctrine from the core of stated capital to a penumbra of guaranteed solvency'.[159] Support for Farrar's view can be found in an earlier article in which Barrett notes that:

> [The] rules as to the maintenance of capital exist for the benefit of creditors and that after liquidation has commenced creditors have a statutory right to seek the assistance of the court in compelling directors to make good to the company such loss as it has sustained through breach of their duties to it.[160]

Although *Horsley* was not referred to in argument in *Winkworth*, there are parallels to be drawn between that passage from Lord Templeman's speech to the House of Lords extracted above, and the approach taken by Buckley LJ in *Horsley*, whose comments were referred to a little earlier in this chapter.[161] Lord Templeman, it will be recalled, sat with Buckley LJ as a member of the Court of Appeal which heard the appeal in *Horsley*.

The last of the four cases to be considered here is *Brady v Brady*.[162] There, the Court of Appeal[163] was asked to determine whether or not the disposition of one half of the company's assets for the benefit of one of its two major shareholders was valid. In deciding that it was not, the Court of Appeal displayed a remarkable lack of unanimity. O'Connor LJ felt that the scheme fell short of the statutory requirement contained in Companies Act 1985 (UK) s153(2)(b) that, 'assistance is given in good faith in the interests of the company' and could constitute misfeasance on the part of the directors. Nourse LJ agreed, but felt the scheme was simply *ultra vires* and void. Croom-Johnson

---

[156] (Lords Keith, Templeman, Griffiths, Mackay and Ackner).

[157] (All members of the House agreed).

[158] [1987] 1 All ER 114 at 118; cf. Sealy L S, 'Directors' Duties – An Unnecessary Gloss' [1988] CLJ 175 at 176; note Baxt R, 'Duties of directors with respect to creditors' (1989) 63 ALJ 846 at 847 who described Lord Templeman's remarks as, 'rather extravagant'.

[159] Farrar J H, 'The Obligation of a Company's Directors to its Creditors Before Liquidation' [1985] JBL 413; and Farrar J H, 'The Responsibility of Directors and Shareholders for a Company's Debts' (1989) 4 Canta LR 12 at 14.

[160] Barrett R I, 'Directors' Duties to Creditors' (1977) 40 MLR 226 at 230.

[161] [1982] Ch 442 at 453-454.

[162] (1987) 3 BCC 535; note Polack K, 'Companies Act 1985 – "The Interests of the Company"' [1988] CLJ 24.

[163] (O'Connor, Croom-Johnson and Nourse LJJ).

LJ on the other hand dissented. His Lordship determined that the transaction complained of was *intra vires* the company's powers as described in its memorandum. As it would benefit and promote prosperity, it was therefore in the company's interests. Croom-Johnson LJ felt that no issue of creditors' interests arose as the company was solvent at all times. Nourse LJ in disposing of the *ultra vires* argument stated that:

> [The] corollary of limited liability, [is] that the integrity of a company's assets, except to the extent allowed by its constitution, must be preserved for the benefit of all those who are interested in them, most pertinently its creditors.[164]

As to whether or not the dispositions in *Brady* were made in the interests of the company, Nourse LJ considered this expression to be sometimes misunderstood and capable of slightly different meanings in different contexts. In Nourse LJ's judgment:

> The interests of a company ... cannot be distinguished from the interests of the persons who are interested in it. Who are those persons? Where a company is both going and solvent, first and foremost come the shareholders, present and no doubt future as well. ... Conversely, where the company is insolvent, or even doubtfully solvent, the interests of the company are in reality the interests of existing creditors alone.[165]

On appeal,[166] the House of Lords[167] in *Brady* overturned the Court of Appeal's findings and reinstated the decision of the primary judge. The principal speech to the House of Lords was delivered by Lord Oliver.[168] His Lordship felt that the transaction complained of was *intra vires* and that as both companies were solvent at the relevant time, there could be no question of misfeasance on the part of the directors. And given that the transaction was carried out, 'not only with the knowledge and assent of all the shareholders but with their active co-operation and at their instigation',[169] there was no avenue left, in that regard, for complaint. *A fortiori* when to do otherwise would be to invite the, 'total termination and extinction of its business'.[170] In such circumstances, the creditors' interests would be sacrificed and totally defeated. Hence the reorganisation could only improve the creditors' position.[171] Lord Oliver's approach is refreshing for it lends weight to the more commercial and pragmatic approach which, it is considered, is required of today's judiciary in order to resolve the complexities of today's commercial and corporate disputes.[172]

---

[164] (1987) 3 BCC 535 at 550.

[165] *Ibid* at 552; note Grantham R, 'Directors' Duties and Insolvent Companies' (1991) 54 MLR 576 at 578.

[166] [1989] AC 755; note Polack K, 'Companies Act 1985 – Scope of Section 153' [1988] CLJ 359.

[167] (Lords Keith, Havers, Templeman, Griffiths and Oliver).

[168] (All members of the House agreed).

[169] [1989] AC 755 at 776 per Lord Oliver.

[170] *Ibid.*

[171] *Ibid* at 778.

[172] *Equiticorp Finance Ltd v Bank of New Zealand* (1993) 11 ACLC 952 at 1019 per Clarke and Cripps JJA; *Glandon Pty Ltd v Strata Consolidated Pty Ltd* (1993) 11 ACSR 543 at 547-548 per Mahoney JA; and *Gray Eisdell Timms Pty Ltd v Combined Auctions Pty Ltd* (1995) 13 ACLC 965 at 974 per Young J; cf. Muir G, 'Contract and Equity: Striking a Balance' (1985) 10 Adel LR 153 at 183, 'But pragmatism must not always triumph over principle'.

SOME UNRESOLVED ISSUES

The effect of the decisions in *Walker v Wimborne*,[173] *Nicholson v Permakraft (NZ) Ltd*[174] and *Kinsela v Russell Kinsela Pty Ltd*[175] was sufficient for Corkery to conclude that these cases firmly established the principle that, 'directors of insolvent companies must act in the interests of creditors.'[176] That much is clear. The English cases, which have just been considered, bear this out too. But some issues remain unresolved in English and Australian company law. The authorities have, for example, shied away from formulating the extent of the duty, and when it becomes operative, in circumstances where the company's financial position is neither plainly solvent nor insolvent. A situation described in *Permakraft* as, 'the intermediate situation of near-insolvency or doubtful insolvency'.[177]

Another unresolved issue for discussion concerns the actual repository of the duty. To whom is the duty owed? Who has the correlative right to enforce it? Do creditors, for instance, have a right of action against the directors independently of the rights statutorily granted the liquidator upon a winding-up?[178] In addition, there is the question of financial stability versus risk.[179] As was evident throughout the earlier chapters of this book, directors of British and Australian companies are constantly being asked to juggle these competing interests. It is difficult, some would say impossible, to achieve the correct balance. The list goes on. This is why it was mentioned a little earlier in this chapter that before departing from the traditional model of English and Australian company law, the whole process needs to be very clearly thought through.

Whereas it might be permissible for British and Australian Parliaments to tinker at the edges, the English and the Australian judiciary ought be dissuaded from doing so unnecessarily, and on an *ad hoc* basis, lest more issues be raised than are resolved. By way of illustration, it is instructive to move on to consider three such unresolved issues. The first of these is recognised by Farrar. The learned author acknowledges that:

> [There is] difficulty in gauging the point at which shareholders cease to be the dominant concern, as they are when the company is solvent, and creditors become the focus for directors, as they do when the company is insolvent or possibly of doubtful solvency. Identifying the point in time when that shift in emphasis occurs may be difficult.[180]

At what point then does the duty crystallise? This is the moot point as the whole concept of insolvency is fraught with imprecision.[181] Insolvency has always been, and

---

[173] (1976-1977) 137 CLR 1.

[174] [1985] 1 NZLR 242.

[175] [1986] 4 NSWLR 722.

[176] Corkery J F, *Directors' Powers and Duties* Longman Cheshire Pty Ltd, Melbourne, 1987 at 69.

[177] [1985] 1 NZLR 242 at 254 per Richardson J.

[178] *Allen v Atalay* (1994) 12 ACLC 7 at 10 per Hayne J; note Baxt R, commercial law note (1994) 68 ALJ 758 at 758-759; and Baxt R, commercial law note (1995) 69 ALJ 940 at 943-944.

[179] *Kinsela v Russell Kinsela Pty Ltd* [1986] 4 NSWLR 722 at 733 per Street CJ.

[180] Farrar J H, Furey N E, Hannigan B M and Wylie P, *Farrar's Company Law* (3rd ed) Butterworth & Co (Publishers) Ltd, London, 1991 at 389; note *Nicholson v Permakraft (NZ) Ltd* [1985] 1 NZLR 242 at 254 per Richardson J.

[181] *Rees v Bank of New South Wales* (1963-1964) 111 CLR 210 at 218 per Barwick CJ; *Bank of Australasia v Hall* (1907) 4 CLR 1514 at 1528 per Griffith CJ; and *Sandell v Porter* (1965-1966) 115 CLR 666 at 670-671 *per curiam*.

remains, a notoriously difficult state to pin down. A company's financial position may fluctuate so that technically it moves in and out of insolvency.[182] To make matters more difficult to conceptualize, we find that common usage, case-law and legislation have each permitted several variations of the same theme: in English and in Australian company law.

In Australian company law, for instance, Corporations Law s95A(1) defines an insolvent company as one which is unable to pay all its debts as and when they become due and payable.[183] In *Statewide Tobacco Services Ltd v Morley* Ormiston J said that insolvency, 'is intended to refer to the commercial insolvency of a company, that is, the inability of a company to pay all its debts as and when they fall due.'[184] Ormiston J was distinguishing commercial insolvency from balance sheet insolvency.[185]

Whilst that seems reasonably straightforward, but in practice seldom is, note the confusion, or perhaps the lack of clarity, which prevails in English company law. Sealy in his third edition, for instance, condemns the different meanings ascribed to insolvency which appear in various sections of the Insolvency Act 1986 (UK) ('IA 1986'), the Insolvency Rules 1986 (UK) and the Company Directors Disqualification Act 1986 (UK) ('CDD Act').[186] The learned author decries the lack of any statutory definition of the word insolvent and the confusion thereby occasioned.

For the English and Australian courts to entertain a duty in circumstances of near-insolvent, or of doubtful solvency presents, therefore, an even more daunting task.[187] Sealy, however, is more positive. In his view:

> Company law can, however, adjust to accept the notion of a duty to take account of creditors' interests in a situation of doubtful solvency. But this is only likely to be achieved if the courts are prepared to accept a more interventionist role than has been traditional and to review directors' commercial and policy decisions.[188]

Such a change in approach by the English and Australian courts to that traditionally adopted, is something which was witnessed in earlier chapters of this book. There, it was evident that the Australian courts, probably more so than their English counterparts, are adjusting to, and pursuing, a more commercial and pragmatic approach.[189] This approach was also evident in *Brady v Brady*.[190] Gradually, therefore, the judges

---

[182] Sealy L S, 'Directors' "Wider" Responsibilities – Problems Conceptual, Practical and Procedural' (1987) 13 MULR 164 at 179.

[183] *Stargard Security Systems Pty Ltd v Goldie* (1994) 13 ACSR 805 at 811-813 per Master Bredmeyer.

[184] (1990) 2 ACSR 405 at 433.

[185] *Nicholson v Permakraft (NZ) Ltd* [1985] 1 NZLR 242 at 249 per Cooke J; cf. *Lee Panavision Ltd v Lee Lighting Ltd* [1991] BCC 620 at 622 per Harman J and at 635 per Dillon LJ; note Farrar J H, 'The Responsibility of Directors and Shareholders for a Company's Debts' (1989) 4 Canta LR 12 at 19.

[186] Sealy L S and Milman D, *Annotated Guide to the 1986 Insolvency Legislation* (3rd ed) CCH Editions Ltd, Bicester, 1991 at 260; cf. Riley C A, 'Directors' duties and the interests of creditors' (1989) 10 Co Law 87 at 88.

[187] *Nicholson v Permakraft (NZ) Ltd* [1985] 1 NZLR 242 at 249 per Cooke J.

[188] Sealy L S, 'Directors' "Wider" Responsibilities – Problems Conceptual, Practical and Procedural' (1987) 13 MULR 164 at 188; cf. Barrett R I, 'Directors' Duties to Creditors' (1977) 40 MLR 226 at 230-231.

[189] *Equiticorp Finance Ltd v Bank of New Zealand* (1993) 11 ACLC 952 at 1019 per Clarke and Cripps JJA; *Glandon Pty Ltd v Strata Consolidated Pty Ltd* (1993) 11 ACSR 543 at 547-548 per Mahoney JA; and *Gray Eisdell Timms Pty Ltd v Combined Auctions Pty Ltd* (1995) 13 ACLC 965 at 974 per Young J; cf. Muir G, 'Contract and Equity: Striking a Balance' (1985) 10 Adel LR 153 at 183, 'But pragmatism must not always triumph over principle'.

[190] [1989] AC 755 at 776-778 per Lord Oliver.

are abandoning their well-documented reluctance to review directors' judgmental and policy decision-making in favour of adopting a fresh approach that will permit of interference in the internal management of companies.[191] It is suggested that such an approach will, if the English and Australian courts are so minded, permit of further development in this area of the law and clarify many of the unresolved issues with which we are at present left to ponder.

The second unresolved issue which emerges from the English and Australian cases in this intriguing area of the law is whether or not the duty upon directors of British and Australian companies ought be confined to a consideration of the interests of existing creditors only, or whether the duty might include future creditors as well. In *Jeffree v National Companies & Securities Commission*,[192] it will be recalled that the Western Australian Full Court[193] held that a director had a duty to protect the interests of a person who, by virtue of a pending arbitration, was likely to become a creditor of the company in the near future. The Full Court adopted Lord Templeman's comments in *Winkworth v Edward Baron Development Co Ltd* that the duty extended to creditors present and future.[194] In doing so, the Full Court seems to have been even more liberal in its application of the duty than, say, Cooke J in *Permakraft* who felt that while it is appropriate for directors to consider whether what they do will prejudice their company's ability to promptly discharge debts owed to current and likely continuing trade creditors, 'to make out a duty to future *new* creditors would be much more difficult.'[195]

However, quite apart from the extent of the duty, and somewhat more fundamental, is the fact that neither the English nor the Australian judiciary has determined unequivocally to whom the duty is owed. Is it owed to the company? Or is it owed to the creditors themselves? The difference is crucial. A duty owed directly to creditors will permit them to bring actions in their own right, and for their own benefit. Whilst that would obviate any awkward question of *locus standi* of creditors,[196] it would nevertheless cut across fundamental principles of English and Australian insolvency law. Hence it is important to ask: does the existence of such a duty permit a creditor to bring an action in his, her or its own right against the directors, independently of statute, for its breach? The commentators differ on this vexed question.[197] The answer will lie

---

[191] *Carlen v Drury* (1812) 1 V & B 154 at 158 per Lord Eldon; *Burland v Earle* [1902] AC 83 at 93 per Lord Davey; and *Shuttleworth v Cox Brothers and Company (Maidenhead) Ltd* [1927] 2 KB 9 at 23 per Scrutton LJ; cf. *Howard Smith Ltd v Ampol Petroleum Ltd* [1974] AC 821 at 832 per Lord Wilberforce; and *Harlowe's Nominees Pty Ltd v Woodside (Lakes Entrance) Oil Company NL* (1969-1970) 121 CLR 483 at 493 *per curiam*; note Sealy L S, 'The Director as Trustee' [1967] CLJ 83 at 100-101; and Editorial comment, 'Directors – true or false?' (1997) 18 Co Law 129 at 129.

[192] (1989) 15 ACLR 217; note Baxt R, 'Duties of directors with respect to creditors' (1989) 63 ALJ 846 at 847-849; and Baxt R, 'Reforming the law relating to company directors' (1990) 64 ALJ 345 at 345-346; see *Re Avon Chambers Ltd* [1978] 2 NZLR 638.

[193] (Wallace, Brinsden and Pidgeon JJ).

[194] [1987] 1 All ER 114 at 118; cf. Sealy L S, 'Directors' Duties – An Unnecessary Gloss' [1988] CLJ 175 at 176; note Baxt R, 'Duties of directors with respect to creditors' (1989) 63 ALJ 846 at 847 who described Lord Templeman's remarks as, 'rather extravagant'.

[195] [1985] 1 NZLR 242 at 250.

[196] Farrar J H, 'The Responsibility of Directors and Shareholders for a Company's Debts' (1989) 4 Canta LR 12 at 20.

[197] Corkery J F, *Directors' Powers and Duties* Longman Cheshire Pty Ltd, Melbourne, 1987 at 67; Heydon J D, 'Directors' Duties and the Company's Interests' in Finn P D (ed), *Equity and Commercial Relationships* The Law Book Company Ltd, Sydney, 1987 at 131-133; and Sealy L S, 'Directors' "Wider" Responsibilities – Problems Conceptual, Practical and Procedural' (1987) 13 MULR 164 at 177 and 184.

first, by looking to whom the duty is owed; and secondly, by looking at the nature of the duty itself. That is to say, is it really a duty as such? Let us return to this in a moment.

Of the cases referred to earlier in this chapter, only Cooke J in *Permakraft*,[198] Wallace and Brinsden JJ in *Jeffree*,[199] and Lord Templeman in *Winkworth*,[200] have expressed a willingness to contemplate a duty owed directly to creditors.[201] The preponderance of authority suggests that it is the company that is the repository of the duty.[202] This accords with conventional English and Australian company theory. But in the day-to-day business of the English and Australian courts, the issue barely surfaces. The cases which have reached the Australian courts, for example, have mainly involved actions brought by liquidators on behalf of the creditors as a whole, pursuant to Australian companies legislation which has developed as an offshoot to insolvency law.[203] Such legislation initially sought to discourage directors from abusing their office by the imposition of penal sanctions. Out of that has grown an independent statutory duty upon directors of Australian companies to prevent insolvent trading by their companies.[204] This statutory duty will be examined in the next chapter of this book.

The third unresolved issue, therefore, is whether or not creditors have a right of action. As we have seen, it is a general rule that unsecured creditors have no proprietary interest in the company's assets. As such, creditors have no standing to interfere in the company's affairs, short of obtaining a mareva injunction when appropriate,[205] or subjecting the company to official management or liquidation.[206] The usual situation, therefore, is where the liquidator brings the action in the name of the company, thus ensuring that any proceeds will be shared by all unsecured creditors; rather than that creditor with sufficient resources to bring an individual action direct. This concept of all unsecured creditors sharing in any proceeds recovered, is consistent with the philosophy underlying English and Australian insolvency law.[207]

---

[198] [1985] 1 NZLR 242 at 249-250.

[199] (1989) 15 ACLR 217 at 221-222 per Wallace J and at 227-228 per Brinsden J (Pidgeon J agreed with both).

[200] [1987] 1 All ER 114 at 118; cf. Sealy L S, 'Directors' Duties – An Unnecessary Gloss' [1988] CLJ 175 at 176; note Baxt R, 'Duties of directors with respect to creditors' (1989) 63 ALJ 846 at 847 who described Lord Templeman's remarks as, 'rather extravagant'.

[201] Cf. *Hilton International Ltd v Hilton* (1988) 4 NZCLC 96-265 at 64750-64751 per Tipping J who held that directors owed a duty when declaring a dividend, 'not only to the company but also to its creditors'.

[202] Sealy L S, 'Directors' Duties – An Unnecessary Gloss' [1988] CLJ 175 at 175.

[203] *Grove v Flavel* (1986) 11 ACLR 161 and *Jeffree v National Companies & Securities Commission* (1989) 15 ACLR 217 provide exceptions.

[204] Corporations Law s588G; see *Metropolitan Fire Systems Pty Ltd v Miller* (1997) 23 ACSR 699 at 701-703 per Einfeld J; and *Australian Securities Commission v Forem-Freeway Enterprises Pty Ltd* (1998-1999) 30 ACSR 339 at 340-341 per Madgwick J.

[205] *Jackson v Sterling Industries Ltd* (1986-1987) 162 CLR 612.

[206] *Mills v Northern Railway of Buenos Ayres Company* (1870) 5 Ch App 621 at 628 per Lord Hatherley LC; and *Siskina v Distos Compania Naviera SA* [1979] AC 210 at 260-261 per Lord Hailsham; cf. Heydon J D, 'Directors' Duties and the Company's Interests' in Finn P D (ed), *Equity and Commercial Relationships* The Law Book Company Ltd, Sydney, 1987 at 133.

[207] *Re Oasis Merchandising Services Ltd* [1997] BCC 282 at 291 *per curiam*; cf. Insolvency Act 1986 (UK) s107; note Villiers C, 'Employees as creditors: a challenge for justice in insolvency law' (1999) 20 Co Law 222 at 228; Schulte R, 'Corporate groups and the equitable subordination of claims on insolvency' (1997) 18 Co Law 2 at 2 and 11; Bean G M D, 'Debt subordination validated' (1994) 15 Co Law 52 at 52; and Sealy L S, 'Directors' Duties – An Unnecessary Gloss' [1988] CLJ 175 at 177; see Report of the Review Committee on Insolvency Law and Practice, HMSO, London, Cmnd 8558, 1982 at para 1396.

Notwithstanding this, the issue remains live. By virtue of Corporations Law s588P, the ability of creditors to bring direct actions against the directors of Australian companies for the breach of a legal or equitable duty is arguably preserved. The way is therefore open to creditors, provided that they are of sufficient means and determination, to pursue errant directors outside the statutory scheme; if they can convince a court that they have a right to be heard. If creditors can establish such a right, then their rewards may well be greater than were they to rely upon a liquidator. It is that establishment of the correlative right that gives meaning to the existence of the duty. Equally, the range of remedies available upon a breach, or threatened breach, of the duty speaks volumes for whether or not the duty rings hollow.[208] But this, like the issue surrounding insolvency, is by no means trouble free and remains unresolved.

Whether or not directors of British and Australian companies are liable as such to creditors of the company, it should be noted that a director may, by agreement or representation, assume a special duty to a creditor of the company. A director may accept or assume a duty of care in supplying information to a creditor analogous to the duty described by the House of Lords in *Hedley Byrne & Co Ltd v Heller & Partners Ltd*.[209] Equally, although statutorily, in Australian company law the Trade Practices Act 1974 (Cth) also affords creditors remedies against the directors of an insolvent company where, for example, the directors have made representations about the financial viability of the company when in fact it is insolvent and those creditors rely upon those representations to their cost. In such circumstances creditors can bring actions against the directors of Australian companies personally under s52 and, if successful, recover damages pursuant to s82 of the Act.

Until recently, the emphasis in Australian company law has been to permit creditors relief pursuant to the applicable Australian companies legislation.[210] Creditors have brought personal actions directly against the directors of Australian companies under Companies Code s556[211] and Corporations Law s592.[212] Under these statutory provisions, it is the liquidator who lacks standing. The liquidator does not become the creditors' agent so as to be able to bring an action on their behalf.[213] However, with the enactment of the Corporate Law Reform Act 1992 (Cth), and the consequent introduction of Corporations Law s588G,[214] the Australian Parliament has discouraged the bringing of such individual actions by making creditors stand behind the liquidator, unless the liquidator fails to take action, and the court otherwise orders.[215]

---

[208] Renard I A, Commentary to Heydon, 'Directors' Duties and the Company's Interests' in Finn P D (ed), *Equity and Commercial Relationships* The Law Book Company Ltd, Sydney, 1987 at 140.

[209] [1964] AC 465; see *Esso Petroleum Co Ltd v Mardon* [1976] QB 801; *Yianni v Edwin Evans & Sons* [1982] QB 438; *Smith v Eric S Bush* [1990] 1 AC 831; *Morgan Crucible Co Plc v Hill Samuel & Co Ltd* [1991] Ch 295; and *Williams v Natural Life Health Foods Plc* [1998] 1 BCLC 689; cf. *Caparo Industries Plc v Dickman* [1990] 2 AC 605.

[210] Corporations Law s588G has shifted the focus.

[211] Baxt R, 'Reforming the law relating to company directors' (1990) 64 ALJ 345 at 346.

[212] *3M Australia Pty Ltd v Watt* (1984) 2 ACLC 621; on appeal *Watt v 3M Australia Pty Ltd* (1985) 3 ACLC 324; note *EL Bell Packaging Pty Ltd v Allied Seafoods Ltd* (1990) 8 ACLC 1135.

[213] *Ross McConnel Kitchen & Co Pty Ltd v Ross (No. 2)* [1985] 1 NSWLR 238.

[214] Added by Act No. 210 of 1992 and effective 23 June 1993.

[215] Corporations Law ss588M and 588R-588U; note *Stoland Pty Ltd v Thurn* (1998) 29 ACSR 280 at 289 per Lehane J; and *Quick v Stoland Pty Ltd* (1998) 29 ACSR 130 at 146 per Finkelstein J (Branson and Emmett JJ agreed); cf. *Ferguson v Wallbridge* [1935] 3 DLR 66 at 83 per Lord Blanesburgh (Lords Thankerton, Russell and Alness and Sir Sidney Rowlatt agreed), 'it is open to the Court, on cause shown, either to direct the liquidator to proceed in the company's name or on proper terms as to indemnity, and

This new approach was introduced into Australian company law following recommendations made by the Australian Law Reform Commission in its report entitled *General Insolvency Inquiry* ('Harmer Report'),[216] and also by the House of Representatives Standing Committee on Legal and Constitutional Affairs in the Lavarch Report.[217] These recommendations were to the effect that the liquidator ought have the primary responsibility to determine if an action should be brought. The liquidator, it was felt, should be given standing to bring an action against errant directors of Australian companies for the benefit of all unsecured creditors, rather than just the first creditor who takes action. The underlying philosophy and rationale for this finds its roots in English and Australian insolvency law which subscribes to equality as a fundamental principle.[218] This principle was earlier acknowledged in English company law by the review committee appointed on 27 January 1977 under the chairmanship of Sir Kenneth Cork ('Cork Committee'). The Cork Committee was appointed to carry out a fundamental and exhaustive reappraisal of all aspects of the insolvency laws in England and Wales at a time when no comprehensive statement of insolvency law was then in existence: merely, 'a patchwork of materials dealing with the subject.'[219] The Committee undertook its task at a time when the technical state of the law and its objectives were both in disarray.[220] The Committee reaffirmed in its 1982 report that:

> It is a fundamental objective of the law of insolvency to achieve a rateable, that is to say *pari passu*, distribution of the uncharged assets of the insolvent among the unsecured creditors.[221]

Conceptually, there are advantages to individual creditors in recognising a creditor's right of action against directors at law and, more especially, in equity. But whether the Australian Parliament will permit that to continue, when to do so is to cut across recommendations contained within the Harmer Report and the Lavarch Report, and is *per contra* insolvency law, remains to be seen. At present, only a window of opportunity remains. Arguably, that window is opened by invoking Corporations Law s588P. That section was brought into force by the Corporate Law Reform Act 1992 (Cth), two and one half years after the principal Act became effective.[222]

---

cont.
   otherwise to give to the applicant leave to use the company's name as plaintiff in any action necessary to be brought for the vindication of the company's rights.'
[216]   Australian Law Reform Commission, Report No. 45 (vol 1), *General Insolvency Inquiry* AGPS, Canberra, 1988 at paras 313-316.
[217]   House of Representatives Standing Committee on Legal and Constitutional Affairs, *Corporate Practices and the Rights of Shareholders* AGPS, Canberra, 1991 at paras 5.4.13-5.4.17.
[218]   *Re Oasis Merchandising Services Ltd* [1997] BCC 282 at 291 *per curiam*; cf. Insolvency Act 1986 (UK) s107; note Villiers C, 'Employees as creditors: a challenge for justice in insolvency law' (1999) 20 Co Law 222 at 228; Schulte R, 'Corporate groups and the equitable subordination of claims on insolvency' (1997) 18 Co Law 2 at 2 and 11; Bean G M D, 'Debt subordination validated' (1994) 15 Co Law 52 at 52; and Sealy L S, 'Directors' Duties – An Unnecessary Gloss' [1988] CLJ 175 at 177; see Report of the Review Committee on Insolvency Law and Practice, HMSO, London, Cmnd 8558, 1982 at para 1396.
[219]   Report of the Review Committee on Insolvency Law and Practice, HMSO, London, Cmnd 8558, 1982 at para 26.
[220]   Finch V, 'The Measures of Insolvency Law' (1997) 17 OJLS 227 at 228.
[221]   Report of the Review Committee on Insolvency Law and Practice, HMSO, London, Cmnd 8558, 1982 at para 1396.
[222]   Corporations Act 1989 (Cth) s82; see Corporations Law s592.

Thus, it would seem that whilst the preferred path from a policy perspective is that trodden by the liquidator on behalf of all creditors generally,[223] it is nevertheless considered expedient to allow an occasional deviation from that path, should the circumstances of the case permit. It is suggested that expressly and by implication, therefore, the Australian Parliament does seem intent upon preserving creditors' legal and equitable rights against errant directors outside the legislative scheme; although, this does seem somewhat inconsistent with the overall intent of that legislative scheme.[224]

The statutory position in English company law, as was evident from chapter two of this book, and which is examined in detail in chapter eight of this book, is governed principally by the IA 1986 and bolstered by the CDD Act; and, as such, it is not proposed to re-canvass here matters which are mentioned there. The IA 1986, as Farrar notes:

> [Does] not impose duties on directors vis-à-vis creditors but it does assess directors' conduct on a company going into insolvency in the light of, inter alia, the effect of that conduct on the company's creditors.[225]

What is of interest, from the perspective of English company law, is the enactment of IA 1986 s212. However, s212 does not, of itself, create any new rights.[226] IA 1986 s212 provides the statutory machinery which enables liquidators and creditors *inter alios* to apply for relief in the course of a winding-up along the traditional lines of the misfeasance summons referred to earlier in this chapter.[227] IA 1986 s212 permits the English courts to examine the conduct of a person concerned where it appears to the official receiver, the liquidator, or any creditor or contributory, that that person has misapplied or retained, or become accountable for, any money or other property of the company, or been guilty of any misfeasance or breach of any fiduciary or other duty in relation to the company.[228] Its pedigree extends back to Companies (Winding up) Act 1890 s10.[229] Section 212, in essence, as Hoffmann LJ explained in his judgment in *Re D'Jan of London Ltd*, 'is a summary procedure which used to be called a misfeasance

---

[223] Cf. *Cape Breton Company v Fenn* (1881) 17 Ch D 198 at 208 per Cotton LJ; *Ferguson v Wallbridge* [1935] 3 DLR 66 at 83-84 per Lord Blanesburgh (Lords Thankerton, Russell and Alness and Sir Sidney Rowlatt agreed); *Fargro Ltd v Godfroy* [1986] 1 WLR 1134 at 1138 per Walton J; *Scarel Pty Ltd v City Loan & Credit Corporation Pty Ltd* (1988) 17 FCR 344 at 347-352 per Gummow J; *Zempilas v JN Taylor Holdings Ltd* (1990-1991) 5 ACSR 28 at 30 per Debelle J; and *Christianos v Aloridge Pty Ltd* (1995) 18 ACSR 272 at 280-281 per Beaumont, Whitlam and Tamberlin JJ.

[224] Cf. *Scarel Pty Ltd v City Loan & Credit Corporation Pty Ltd* (1988) 17 FCR 344 at 350 per Gummow J, 'The scheme of the statute is that it is the liquidator who is the appropriate party to decide whether to continue for the company litigation such as this, subject to the control of the Companies Court over the liquidator.'

[225] Farrar J H, Furey N E, Hannigan B M and Wylie P, *Farrar's Company Law* (3rd ed) Butterworth & Co (Publishers) Ltd, London, 1991 at 388; note *Re Sherborne Associates Ltd* [1995] BCC 40 at 45 per Jack J.

[226] *In re Forest of Dean Coal Mining Company* (1879) 10 Ch D 450; *In re City Equitable Fire Insurance Company Ltd* [1925] Ch 407; *In re Etic Limited* [1928] Ch 861 at 875 per Maugham J; *Couve v J Pierre Couve Ltd* (1933) 49 CLR 486 at 495 *per curiam*; and *Walker v Wimborne* (1976-1977) 137 CLR 1 at 14 per Jacobs J.

[227] Cf. Corporations Law s598.

[228] E.g., *Re Barton Manufacturing Co Ltd* [1999] 1 BCLC 740; cf. Corporations Law s598; note *Gamble v Hoffman* (1997) 15 ACLC 1314 at 1316 per Carr J; and *Re Property Force Consultancy Pty Ltd* [1997] 1 Qd R 300 at 304-316 per Derrington J.

[229] Cf. *In re Lands Allotment Company* [1894] 1 Ch 616.

summons but has been extended to include breaches of any duty including the duty of care.'[230] Its application by the English courts today, however, is considered to be largely uncontroversial.[231] But it should be noted that s212 is not available to an individual creditor to assert a personal right against a director,[232] nor does it enable the company to recover from a director a mere monetary claim owed to the company.[233] The ability of creditors to seek summary relief in limited circumstances is preserved;[234] although moneys recovered, consistent with English and Australian insolvency law, are for the benefit of all creditors generally.[235]

DOES IT MATTER WHETHER CREDITORS HAVE A RIGHT OF ACTION?

In the light of extant British and Australian companies legislation,[236] which provides the statutory machinery for bringing to account errant directors in the context of insolvency, it may seem merely academic as to whether or not creditors do enjoy a personal right of action directly against directors of British and Australian companies. But it is not. Whilst Goldberg observes that the controversy surrounding the issue, 'whether directors have a duty outside the Companies Code to creditors will remain substantially academic because of the specific standing of provisions found in sections 556 and 557',[237] his comments do not take into account the recent enactment of Corporations Law s588G and the sections which follow that.[238] Equally, Goldberg's comments overlook the greater flexibility that a creditor has in being able to choose whether to proceed statutorily or non-statutorily against an errant director. But this, of course, begs the question: do creditors have such a right in any event?

There is no definitive answer to this question, and the issues surrounding that remain largely unresolved in English and Australian company law. But, importantly, the possibility in Australian company law has been statutorily preserved.[239] This is important because a creditor's interests may not be best served by invoking the applicable companies legislation so as to secure a statutory remedy at the expense of

---

[230] [1993] BCC 646 at 647.

[231] Schulte R, 'Corporate groups and the equitable subordination of claims on insolvency' (1997) 18 Co Law 2 at 9.

[232] *Yukong Line Ltd of Korea v Rendsburg Investments Corp of Liberia (No. 2)* [1998] 4 All ER 82 at 99 per Toulson J.

[233] *In re Etic Limited* [1928] Ch 861 at 873-876 per Maugham J.

[234] Cf. *In re Hill's Waterfall Estate and Gold Mining Company* [1896] 1 Ch 947.

[235] *Re Oasis Merchandising Services Ltd* [1997] BCC 282 at 291 *per curiam*; cf. Insolvency Act 1986 (UK) s107; note Villiers C, 'Employees as creditors: a challenge for justice in insolvency law' (1999) 20 Co Law 222 at 228; Schulte R, 'Corporate groups and the equitable subordination of claims on insolvency' (1997) 18 Co Law 2 at 2 and 11; Bean G M D, 'Debt subordination validated' (1994) 15 Co Law 52 at 52; and Sealy L S, 'Directors' Duties – An Unnecessary Gloss' [1988] CLJ 175 at 177; see Report of the Review Committee on Insolvency Law and Practice, HMSO, London, Cmnd 8558, 1982 at para 1396.

[236] E.g., Insolvency Act 1986 (UK) ss212-214; and Company Directors Disqualification Act 1986 (UK) ss2, 4, 6, 8 and 10; cf. Corporations Law s588G.

[237] Goldberg A H, 'Who'd be a Company Director' a paper presented at the Second Business Lawyers' Conference, conducted by the Business Law Section of the Law Council of Australia, Melbourne, 10 April 1989 at 16.

[238] Added by Act No. 210 of 1992 and effective 23 June 1993.

[239] Corporations Law s588P.

other options.[240] It is suggested that there are three important issues which creditors must deal with when deciding which course of action to take against the directors of an insolvent company. First, the question of standing. Secondly, the nature of the remedy being sought. Thirdly, the conduct of the litigation itself.[241]

If creditors can overcome the *locus standi* hurdle, then careful consideration needs to be given as to whether a statutory remedy or an equitable remedy will best achieve the objects of the litigation.[242] For, as Austin notes, equitable remedies can reach an asset in the hands of a third party and allow for the tracing of assets; whereas an action brought by a creditor pursuant to companies legislation, will lead only to, at best, a claim upon the errant director's personal assets.[243] That may, or may not, satisfy a judgment awarded in the creditor's favour. Equitable remedies are the subject of chapter nine of this book.

Dabner, however, argues that as the liquidator brings actions for breach of duty for the collective good of the creditors, the lack of an independent cause of action presents no conceptual difficulties.[244] Strictly speaking this is true. From an individual creditor's standpoint, however, and with the greatest respect, Dabner misses the point. So too does Farrar when he opines that:

> Nevertheless, at the end of the day it is unlikely that a creditor will pursue either remedy in normal circumstances. First, it will not make economic sense for him to do so. He will want to be repaid, not to intermeddle in the affairs of his debtor or expose himself to the hazards of tricky litigation.[245]

It is respectfully suggested that whilst such viewpoints are proper, they are not always commercially acceptable. When it comes to litigation, irate creditors all too often become unreasonable plaintiffs; their reasons for litigating being as varied as human nature itself. A creditor may not wish to share his or her spoils with the general body of creditors. A creditor may not wish to have to rely upon the liquidator to prosecute an action against the directors. He or she may wish to set their own timetable. They may wish to recover on an action *in rem* rather than *in personam*.[246] They may wish simply to embarrass or cause financial, mental and/or social anguish to the director or directors concerned.[247] Such reasons may not sit comfortably with academical ideals, but at the coalface there are many who actually subscribe to them.[248]

---

[240] But what of, for example, others' best interests? Therein lies one of the major difficulties – the competition between so many diverse interest groups.

[241] Whilst the liquidator's costs of conducting the litigation will be shared amongst all creditors, creditors may be faced with the frustrations of having a third party take decisions on their behalf.

[242] *Castlereagh Motels Ltd v Davies-Roe* (1966) 67 SR (NSW) 279 at 285-286 per Jacobs and Asprey JJA.

[243] Austin R P, 'Constructive Trusts' in Finn P D (ed), *Essays in Equity* The Law Book Company Ltd, Sydney, 1985 at 196; cf. Goff R and Jones G, *The Law of Restitution* (3rd ed) Sweet & Maxwell Ltd, London, 1986 at 78; note *Maguire v Makaronis* (1996-1997) 188 CLR 449; *Westdeutsche Landesbank Girozentrale v Islington London Borough Council* [1996] AC 669; *Royal Brunei Airlines Sdn Bhd v Tan* [1995] 2 AC 378; *Attorney General for Hong Kong v Reid* [1994] 1 All ER 1; *United Dominions Corporation Ltd v Brian Pty Ltd* (1984-1985) 157 CLR 1; and *Chan v Zacharia* (1983-1984) 154 CLR 178.

[244] Dabner J, 'Directors' Duties – The Schizoid Company' (1988) 6 CSLJ 105 at 114.

[245] Farrar J H, 'The Responsibility of Directors and Shareholders for a Company's Debts' (1989) 4 Canta LR 12 at 31.

[246] *Shepherd v Australia and New Zealand Banking Group Ltd* (1996) 20 ACSR 81 at 96 per Bryson J.

[247] *Financial Times*, 25 June 1999; note e.g., the plight of Jonathan Aitken, the former Conservative cabinet minister, who has been paraded through the press since 10 May 1994 when *The Guardian* exposed his

To give effect to his or her wishes, however, the creditor must be able to rely upon the breach of a duty owed to them. And, as we have seen throughout this chapter, independently of statute, the authorities in English and Australian company law are not clear as to the existence of such a duty giving rise to a justiciable issue on the part of creditors. Cooke J's comments in *Nicholson v Permakraft (NZ) Ltd* do not go far enough,[249] and little comfort can be drawn from *Jeffree v National Companies & Securities Commission.*[250] *Winkworth v Edward Baron Development Co Ltd*[251] has been much criticised and *Hilton International Ltd v Hilton*[252] is a decision at first instance only, and then not strictly in point.

One possibility for clarification in Australian company law was *Allen v Atalay.*[253] In the course of considering, at an interlocutory stage, an application by a creditor under Corporations Law s1324 for damages, resulting from alleged breaches of the directors' duties under Corporations Law s232, Hayne J ruled that the creditor had an arguable case and that there was a serious question to be tried. This ruling attracted a degree of interest and excitement amongst Australian academics given that, at that interlocutory stage, counsel for the creditor foreshadowed an amendment to the pleadings to include an allegation that the directors concerned were in breach of their duty to the creditors.

But, on the pleadings as they then stood, *Atalay* was substantively concerned with the question of *locus standi* of creditors seeking an injunction and/or damages against directors pursuant to Corporations Law s1324. It was considered that such an avenue might prove useful for creditors in their efforts to circumvent the thrust of the statutory scheme which, as earlier identified, is largely supportive of traditional insolvency law principles.[254] Regrettably, from an academical perspective, however, the action has been settled. In the course of finalising the appropriate orders as to costs, Hayne J somewhat commiseratively remarked:

> I have had every academic in Australia trying to find out what was happening in this case ... They will be sorely disappointed.[255]

cont.
    stay at the Paris Ritz, which put in train a catastrophic series of events and led to Aitken declaring himself bankrupt on 10 May 1999, and ultimately being convicted then sentenced to 18 months imprisonment on 8 June 1999 for perjury and conspiracy to pervert the course of justice: *The Times*, 9 June 1999; and see *The Times*, 19 August 1999.

[248] Cf. *Barrett v Duckett* [1995] BCC 362.

[249] [1985] 1 NZLR 242 at 249-250.

[250] (1989) 15 ACLR 217 at 221-222 per Wallace J and at 227-228 per Brinsden J (Pidgeon J agreed with both); cf. Baxt R, 'Duties of directors with respect to creditors' (1989) 63 ALJ 846 at 849.

[251] [1987] 1 All ER 114 at 118 per Lord Templeman.

[252] (1988) 4 NZCLC 96-265.

[253] (1994) 12 ACLC 7; note Baxt R, commercial law note (1994) 68 ALJ 758 at 758-759; and Baxt R, commercial law note (1995) 69 ALJ 940 at 943-944.

[254] *Re Oasis Merchandising Services Ltd* [1997] BCC 282 at 291 *per curiam*; cf. Insolvency Act 1986 (UK) s107; note Villiers C, 'Employees as creditors: a challenge for justice in insolvency law' (1999) 20 Co Law 222 at 228; Schulte R, 'Corporate groups and the equitable subordination of claims on insolvency' (1997) 18 Co Law 2 at 2 and 11; Bean G M D, 'Debt subordination validated' (1994) 15 Co Law 52 at 52; and Sealy L S, 'Directors' Duties – An Unnecessary Gloss' [1988] CLJ 175 at 177; see Report of the Review Committee on Insolvency Law and Practice, HMSO, London, Cmnd 8558, 1982 at para 1396.

[255] *Allen v Atalay* (1994) (unreported, Victorian Supreme Court No. 2126/93, Hayne J , 16 August 1994) at 5.

Notwithstanding these possibilities, and even given the provisions of Corporations Law s588P, it remains difficult to comprehend of an Australian court flying in the face of traditional insolvency law by permitting some creditors a remedy which favoured them at the expense of others. To do so, would be to run counter to principle.[256]

Throughout this chapter, it has been evident that the English and the Australian judiciary seem intent upon, at least in the context of insolvency, obliging directors of British and Australian companies to consider the company's creditors' interests in circumstances which invite a reassessment of conventional English and Australian company theory. It will be recalled from *Kinsela v Russell Kinsela Pty Ltd*, that Street CJ found it difficult to formulate any general test as to the degree of financial instability necessary to trigger this so-called duty upon directors.[257] In the course of grappling with that, Street CJ reminded us that courts have traditionally and properly been cautious about pronouncing upon the commercial justification of particular executive decisions given the wholly differing considerations applicable from one corporate situation to the next.[258]

However, in the intervening years since judgment was handed down in *Kinsela*, significant changes in attitude by the Australian judiciary to this issue have been in evidence. Most recently by the New South Wales Court of Appeal[259] in *Daniels v Anderson*, where Clarke and Sheller JJA emphasised a positive approach to corporate management in modern company law where directors of Australian companies must make it their business to understand, and be kept regularly informed of, their company's business.[260] This approach is now receiving recognition in English company law as well.[261] The focus upon raised levels of directorial responsibility and greater accountability, therefore, becomes ever sharper as we move into the next millennium.

It should be borne in mind, however, that making directors of British and Australian companies more responsible and accountable, in keeping with today's ideals of corporate governance,[262] enlarges the scope of insolvency law on the one hand, and tends to erode the corporate immunity enjoyed since Aron Salomon's days,[263] on the other hand.[264] This, it might be argued, is to undermine the very premise upon which the modern theory of English and Australian company law is based and invites caution. To promote, therefore, the further development of the so-called duty upon directors of British and Australian companies to consider the company's creditors' interests, is to radically depart from traditional company law tenets. That, according to some, is a job for the British and Australian Parliaments and not the English and the Australian

---

[256] Sealy L S, 'Directors' "Wider" Responsibilities – Problems Conceptual, Practical and Procedural' (1987) 13 MULR 164 at 186.

[257] [1986] 4 NSWLR 722 at 733.

[258] *Ibid.*

[259] (Clarke, Sheller and Powell JJA).

[260] (1995) 13 ACLC 614 at 663-666.

[261] Davies P L, *Gower's Principles of Modern Company Law* (6th ed) Sweet & Maxwell Ltd, London, 1997 at 643-644; cf. *Re Barings plc (No 5)* [1999] 1 BCLC 433 at 488 per Jonathan Parker J.

[262] See Prentice D D and Holland P R J, *Contemporary Issues in Corporate Governance* Oxford University Press, Oxford, 1993; Committee on the Financial Aspects of Corporate Governance, *The Report of the Committee on the Financial Aspects of Corporate Governance* Gee and Co Ltd, London, 1992; Farrar J H, 'Corporate Governance, Business Judgement and the Professionalism of Directors' (1993) 6 CBLJ 1; Whincop M J, 'An Economic Analysis of the Criminalisation and Content of Directors' Duties' (1996) 24 ABLR 273; and Stapledon G P, *Institutional Shareholders and Corporate Governance* Clarendon Press, Oxford, 1996.

[263] *Salomon v A Salomon and Company Ltd* [1897] AC 22.

[264] Prentice D D, 'Creditor's Interests and Director's Duties' (1990) 10 OJLS 265 at 277.

judiciary.[265] Chapters seven and eight of this book will consider how the British and Australian Parliaments have responded to these challenges to conventional company theory which affect the duties upon directors of British and Australian companies in the context of insolvency.

---

[265] Senate Standing Committee on Legal and Constitutional Affairs, *Social and Fiduciary Duties and Obligations of Company Directors* AGPS, Canberra, 1989 at 18; Sealy L S, 'Directors' Duties – An Unnecessary Gloss' [1988] CLJ 175 at 177; and Riley C A, 'Directors' duties and the interests of creditors' (1989) 10 Co Law 87 at 92.

7

The Statutory Duty to Prevent Insolvent Trading

INTRODUCTION

It is trite law that British and Australian companies conduct their affairs through their directors who, as a general rule, assume no personal liability for the transactions which they conduct as their companies' agents.[1] However, where the actions of the directors contribute significantly to a company's insolvency, the English and the Australian judiciary, and also the British and Australian Parliaments, have recognised that creditors who face the prospect of receiving no payment, or part-payment only, of their debts do have a legitimate grievance.[2] A *fortiori* when the insolvency was occasioned by unreasonable risks undertaken by the directors in reliance upon credit given by those creditors.[3]

In this chapter we will briefly consider the earlier statutory attempts by the Australian Parliament to regulate the conduct of directors in this regard, and then move on to analyse the development of the statutory duty in Australian company law which today obliges directors of Australian companies to take positive steps to ensure that their company's creditors' interests are not put at risk where there are reasonable grounds for suspecting insolvency.[4] Unlike earlier statutory provisions,[5] creditors of Australian companies, relying upon the Corporations Law today,[6] may only bring a personal action directly against the errant directors with the liquidator's written consent or, after having given the liquidator a notice of intention to bring such an action and the liquidator refuses his or her consent, with the leave of the court.[7]

---

[1]   *Ferguson v Wilson* (1866) 2 Ch App 77 at 89-90 per Cairns LJ; cf. *New Zealand Guardian Trust Co Ltd v Brooks* [1995] BCC 407 at 409-410 per Lord Keith; see Corporations Law s124 (formerly Corporations Law s161); cf. Companies Act 1985 (UK) ss35-35B.

[2]   Insolvency Act 1986 (UK) ss212-214; Company Directors Disqualification Act 1986 (UK) ss2, 4, 6, 8 and 10; cf. Corporations Law s588G.

[3]   Cf. Sealy L S, 'Directors' "Wider" Responsibilities – Problems Conceptual, Practical and Procedural' (1987) 13 MULR 164 at 181.

[4]   Corporations Law s588G; see *Metropolitan Fire Systems Pty Ltd v Miller* (1997) 23 ACSR 699 at 701-703 per Einfeld J; and *Australian Securities Commission v Forem-Freeway Enterprises Pty Ltd* (1998-1999) 30 ACSR 339 at 340-341 per Madgwick J.

[5]   Companies Code s556; and Corporations Law s592; note Herzberg A, 'Insolvent Trading' (1991) 9 CSLJ 285 at 287-289.

[6]   Added by Act No. 210 of 1992 and effective 1 February 1993 and 23 June 1993.

[7]   Corporations Law ss588M and 588R-588U; note *Stoland Pty Ltd v Thurn* (1998) 29 ACSR 280 at 289 per Lehane J; and *Quick v Stoland Pty Ltd* (1998) 29 ACSR 130 at 146 per Finkelstein J (Branson and Emmett JJ agreed); cf. *Ferguson v Wallbridge* [1935] 3 DLR 66 at 83 per Lord Blanesburgh (Lords Thankerton, Russell and Alness and Sir Sidney Rowlatt agreed), 'it is open to the Court, on cause shown, either to direct the liquidator to proceed in the company's name or on proper terms as to indemnity, and

This chapter will also introduce, and the next chapter of this book will analyse in detail, the development of the statutory machinery in English company law within the Company Directors Disqualification Act 1986 (UK) ('CDD Act') for disqualifying errant directors from acting as directors, or being in any way concerned in the management, of British companies by reason of their unfitness to do so: either generally,[8] or given that they have engaged in either fraudulent trading[9] or wrongful trading[10] within the context of insolvency. The British Parliament has also seen fit to provide a legislative framework within Insolvency Act 1986 (UK) ('IA 1986') ss212-214,[11] which permits the liquidator to apply to the court for an order that the errant directors concerned are to restore the company's assets or make whatever contribution to the company's assets by way of compensation which the court thinks appropriate.[12] This too is analysed in detail in the next chapter of this book.

In this way, therefore, the English and Australian courts are able to redress instances of egregious behaviour on the part of directors for their misconduct and decision-making and, by doing so, generally raise the, 'standards of probity and competence to which the law requires company directors to conform.'[13] Although the Australian judiciary has recognised a non-statutory duty upon directors of Australian companies to have regard for their company's creditors' interests within the context of insolvency,[14] there remain a number of unresolved issues. In practical terms, the effect of Corporations Law s588G is not necessarily to resolve these issues, but rather to put them to one side in the day-to-day business of the courts. Significantly, the introduction of s588G has meant a return to insolvency law principles of equality amongst unsecured creditors.[15] This means that most relevant actions before the courts today are those brought by liquidators in the interests of unsecured creditors as a whole. As such, the legal niceties which were identified and explored in part in the previous chapter of this book, seldom arise for either consideration or determination by the Australian courts. As a consequence, at law those unresolved issues may remain just that.

---

cont.

    otherwise to give to the applicant leave to use the company's name as plaintiff in any action necessary to be brought for the vindication of the company's rights.'

8 Company Directors Disqualification Act 1986 (UK) ss6 and 8.

9 *Ibid* at ss4, 6, 8 and 10; and Companies Act 1985 (UK) s458; see Insolvency Act 1986 (UK) s213.

10 Company Directors Disqualification Act 1986 (UK) ss6, 8 and 10; see Insolvency Act 1986 (UK) s214.

11 Cf. Company Directors Disqualification Act 1986 (UK) ss4, 6, 8 and 10.

12 *Re Farmizer (Products) Ltd* [1997] BCC 655 at 657 per Peter Gibson LJ (Potter and Butler-Sloss LJJ agreed).

13 *Re Grayan Building Services Ltd* [1995] BCC 554 at 577 per Neill LJ.

14 *Walker v Wimborne* (1976-1977) 137 CLR 1 at 7 per Mason J; *Grove v Flavel* (1986) 11 ACLR 161 at 170 *per curiam*; *Kinsela v Russell Kinsela Pty Ltd* [1986] 4 NSWLR 722 at 730 and at 732-733 per Street CJ; and *Jeffree v National Companies & Securities Commission* (1989) 15 ACLR 217 at 221-222 per Wallace J and at 227-228 per Brinsden J (Pidgeon J agreed with both).

15 *Re Oasis Merchandising Services Ltd* [1997] BCC 282 at 291 *per curiam*; cf. Insolvency Act 1986 (UK) s107; note Villiers C, 'Employees as creditors: a challenge for justice in insolvency law' (1999) 20 Co Law 222 at 228; Schulte R, 'Corporate groups and the equitable subordination of claims on insolvency' (1997) 18 Co Law 2 at 2 and 11; Bean G M D, 'Debt subordination validated' (1994) 15 Co Law 52 at 52; and Sealy L S, 'Directors' Duties – An Unnecessary Gloss' [1988] CLJ 175 at 177; see Report of the Review Committee on Insolvency Law and Practice, HMSO, London, Cmnd 8558, 1982 at para 1396.

THE FORMER STATUTORY PROVISIONS

The quest by the British and Australian Parliaments, and also the English and the Australian judiciary, to make directors more responsible and accountable in keeping with today's ideals of corporate governance,[16] has enlarged the scope of insolvency law on the one hand, and has eroded the corporate immunity enjoyed since Aron Salomon's days on the other hand. [17] As Ford in his sixth edition notes:

> The high water mark of immunity for managers of companies seems to have been the period from *Salomon's* case[18] in 1897 to 1928. Since 1928 the legislation has been progressively amended towards something like the *commenda* principle.[19]

It is instructive to briefly look back over the last 70 years or so at some of the key points in time which have proved instrumental in leading to the enactment of Corporations Law s588G.[20] A convenient starting point is the English Company Law Amendment Committee's report ('Greene Report') produced under the chairmanship of Wilfrid Greene KC on 8 May 1926. The Greene Report recommended that where in the winding-up of a British company it appeared that the directors had carried on the company's business with intent to defraud, those directors should *inter alia* be liable without limitation for the company's debts.[21] This recommendation was subsequently enacted in England and in Wales,[22] and was the forerunner to the fraudulent trading provision in English company law which exists today as IA 1986 s213.[23]

In Australian company law, a fraudulent trading provision appeared first in Queensland's statutes in 1931. Other States soon followed suit. In 1961 the uniform companies legislation[24] adopted a new criminal offence where it appeared, in the course of a winding-up, that an officer of an Australian company was a party to the incurring of a debt by the company without a reasonable expectation that the debt could be paid.[25] In 1962 the English Company Law Committee's report ('Jenkins Report'), produced under the chairmanship of Lord Jenkins on 30 May 1962, recommended that a statutory provision be introduced into English company law so as to make directors of a British

---

[16] See Prentice D D and Holland P R J, *Contemporary Issues in Corporate Governance* Oxford University Press, Oxford, 1993; Committee on the Financial Aspects of Corporate Governance, *The Report of the Committee on the Financial Aspects of Corporate Governance* Gee and Co Ltd, London, 1992; Farrar J H, 'Corporate Governance, Business Judgement and the Professionalism of Directors' (1993) 6 CBLJ 1; Whincop M J, 'An Economic Analysis of the Criminalisation and Content of Directors' Duties' (1996) 24 ABLR 273; and Stapledon G P, *Institutional Shareholders and Corporate Governance* Clarendon Press, Oxford, 1996.

[17] Prentice D D, 'Creditor's Interests and Director's Duties' (1990) 10 OJLS 265 at 277.

[18] *Salomon v A Salomon and Company Ltd* [1897] AC 22.

[19] Ford H A J and Austin R P, *Ford's Principles of Corporations Law* (6th ed) Butterworths Pty Ltd, Sydney, 1992 at 87; note Schmitthoff C M, 'The Origin of the Joint-Stock Company' (1939-1940) 3 UTLJ 74 at 86; and *Macquarie Bank Ltd v Fociri Pty Ltd* (1992) 10 ACLC 785 at 797 per Kirby P.

[20] Added by Act No. 210 of 1992 and effective 23 June 1993.

[21] Company Law Amendment Committee, HMSO, London, Cmd 2657, 1926 at para 62.

[22] Companies Act 1928 (UK) s75; and Companies Act 1929 (UK) s275.

[23] *Re Farmizer (Products) Ltd* [1997] BCC 655 at 660 per Peter Gibson LJ (Potter and Butler-Sloss LJJ agreed); and *Re Oasis Merchandising Services Ltd* [1997] BCC 282 at 291 *per curiam*.

[24] Companies Act 1961 (NSW); Companies Act 1961 (Qld); Companies Act 1961 (Vic); Companies Act 1961 (WA); Companies Act 1962 (SA); Companies Act 1962 (Tas); Companies Ordinance 1962 (ACT); and Companies Ordinance 1963 (NT).

[25] E.g., Companies Act 1961 (NSW) s303(3).

company, who had carried on the company's business in a reckless manner, personally responsible in a winding-up without limitation for the company's debts.[26]

On 27 January 1977, the Review Committee on Insolvency Law and Practice under the chairmanship of Sir Kenneth Cork ('Cork Committee') was appointed to carry out a fundamental and exhaustive reappraisal of all aspects of the insolvency laws in England and Wales. The Cork Committee's final report was presented in June 1982 ('Cork Report').[27] The Committee expressed the view that the law as it then stood was sufficiently flexible to enable a liquidator to recover compensation from errant directors of an insolvent British company in respect of a broad range of breaches of fiduciary duties. However, in certain situations, the Committee considered that the law was powerless to intervene. For example, where the directors' misfeasance or breach of trust was instigated or ratified by the shareholders, and also where the company was insolvent, but its directors permitted it to continue to trade and to obtain further credit.[28] The Cork Report recommended that the new concept of wrongful trading be introduced to supplement and complement the fraudulent trading provisions in English company law.[29]

As chapters two, three, six and eight of this book explain, this recommendation within the Cork Report was subsequently enacted in England and in Wales, and became known as the wrongful trading provision in English company law which appears today as IA 1986 s214.[30] In Australia, a statutory civil liability for incurring a debt without reasonable expectation of payment was first introduced in New South Wales in 1964. Civil liability was, however, only consequent upon a conviction for the associated criminal offence.[31] The relevant provision enabled the court to declare a director liable to pay all or part of the company's debt to the creditor concerned.

In 1971 the question of the civil liability of directors of Australian companies was again addressed by the legislature in Australia.[32] It was made clear that any amount recovered from a director, for incurring a debt without reasonable expectation of payment, would be paid to the company and be for the benefit of all creditors. In 1981 the nature of the civil liability changed. It will be recalled from chapter three of this book that, in an attempt to unify companies legislation throughout Australia, each Australian State and Territory enacted largely uniform legislation as part of a co-operative scheme which regulated Australian company law between 1981 and 1990.[33] The resultant legislation was simply referred to as the Companies ([name of

---

[26] Report of the Company Law Committee, HMSO, London, Cmnd 1749, 1962 at para 503.
[27] Report of the Review Committee on Insolvency Law and Practice, HMSO, London, Cmnd 8558, 1982.
[28] *Ibid* at paras 1754-1757.
[29] *Ibid* at para 1774 and chapter 44.
[30] E.g., *Re Brian D Pierson (Contractors) Ltd* [1999] BCC 26; *Re Oasis Merchandising Services Ltd* [1997] BCC 282; *Re Hydrodan (Corby) Ltd* [1994] BCC 161; *Re D'Jan of London Ltd* [1993] BCC 646; *Re Produce Marketing Consortium Ltd* (1989) 5 BCC 569; and *Re Bath Glass Ltd* (1988) 4 BCC 130.
[31] Companies Act 1961 (NSW) s304 (1A); cf. Companies Act 1948 (UK) s332.
[32] Companies Act 1961 (NSW) s304 (1A) was repealed and replaced by Companies Act 1961 (NSW) s374D.
[33] See Rumble G A, 'The Commonwealth/State Co-Operative Basis for the Australian Wheat Board and the National Companies and Securities Commission: Some Constitutional Issues' (1980) 7 Adel LR 348; note Ford H A J, Austin R P and Ramsay I M, *Ford's Principles of Corporations Law* (9th ed) Reed International Books Australia Pty Ltd, Sydney, 1999 at paras 2.210-2.220.

State/Territory]) Code.[34] Throughout this book, this uniform legislation is generically referred to as the Companies Code in keeping with its homogeneity.[35]

Companies Code s556 was an attempt on the part of the Australian Parliament, and those of its States and Territories, to make directors of Australian companies liable for their company's debts where the company's business was conducted fraudulently or without due regard to the company's ability to pay its debts. It could be directly enforced by a creditor for the personal benefit of that creditor. There was no necessity for a prior conviction. To the chagrin of many insolvency law practitioners, liquidators were precluded from being able to take action against errant directors for civil recovery. Thus s556 was novel in Australian company law.[36] Gleeson CJ recognised this novelty in *Hawkins v Bank of China*, as the following passage from his Honour's judgment makes clear:

> The nature of the liability, both civil and criminal, created by s556 is unusual, and it depends upon a combination of facts and circumstances some of which may require retrospective consideration of events. For example, the section may be invoked in relation to a company that was not a company to which it applied when the relevant debt was incurred, but which became such a company at a later time.[37]

This novelty was earlier recognised in *Metal Manufacturers Ltd v Lewis* where Kirby P acknowledged the exceptional and reformatory nature of the section in the context of the history of Australian company law.[38] The enactment of Companies Code s556 sought to attach civil and criminal liability to directors of a company which incurred a debt during a time at which, broadly speaking, the company was insolvent. However, rather than specifically address the duties upon directors of Australian companies as such,[39] s556 imposed liability on the directors of companies that incurred debts when there were no reasonable grounds to expect solvency. Its application was dependent upon the company being wound up, or in the course of being wound up, having ceased to carry on business or being unable to pay its debts.[40]

The broad purpose of Companies Code s556, according to Starke, was to pierce the corporate veil.[41] As such, the enactment of s556 represented a significant break from traditional concepts of English and Australian company law.[42] In Kennett's view, the purpose of s556 was twofold. First, to lift the corporate veil to allow action by creditors. Secondly, to urge directors to take particular care in the incurring of debts by the company during times of financial difficulty.[43] Whilst s556 remains in force and operative upon debts incurred up to and including 31 December 1990, it was superseded

---

[34] Companies (New South Wales) Code; Companies (Queensland) Code; Companies (Victoria) Code; Companies (Western Australia) Code; Companies (South Australia) Code; Companies (Tasmania) Code; Companies (Australian Capital Territory) Code; and Companies (Northern Territory) Code.

[35] *Fitzsimmons v R* (1997) 23 ACSR 355 at 360 per Parker J.

[36] *Capricorn Society Ltd v Linke* (1996) 14 ACLC 431 at 434 *per curiam*; note *Hawkins v Bank of China* (1992) 26 NSWLR 562 at 567 per Gleeson CJ.

[37] (1992) 26 NSWLR 562 at 567.

[38] (1987-1988) 13 ACLR 357 at 358.

[39] Cf. *3M Australia Pty Ltd v Watt* (1984) 2 ACLC 621 at 624 per Rogers J, 'The action contemplated by the section was for breach of fiduciary duty owed to the debtor company.'

[40] Companies Code s553(1).

[41] Starke J G, 'Liability of Individuals Connected with Company' (1991) 65 ALJ 300 at 300.

[42] Kennett G R, case note (1989) 63 ALJ 502 at 502.

[43] *Ibid* at 503.

by Corporations Law s592 on 1 January 1991.[44] With the passage of time, however, the cases expressly upon s556 have all but dried up. Section 556 was part of an overall integrated legislative framework designed to provide uniform companies legislation across Australia and was instrumental in the development of a national approach to Australian company law. Kirby P recognised this in *Hawkins*, where his Honour put the matter in this way:

> It is obviously highly desirable that the Code, and the equivalent provisions of the *Corporations Law*, should have a uniform interpretation throughout Australia. The principal purpose of the development of a national approach to company law in Australia has been to recognise the vital importance of corporations to the economic well-being of the whole country; the typical organisation of many corporations today on a national basis; and the inefficiency and uncertainty caused by differing constructions of the same law in different parts of Australia.[45]

It will be recalled from chapter three of this book that notwithstanding the Australian Attorney-General's rhetoric on 8 November 1990 that the proposed package of laws legislation, 'will together usher in a new era of corporate regulation in this country',[46] Corporations Law s232(4) was little more than an re-enactment of Companies Code s229(2), albeit in more politically correct language. Similarly, the insolvent trading provisions under Companies Code s556 were simply re-enacted to become Corporations Law s592.[47] This is hardly credible testimony, therefore, to the Attorney-General's proclamation that the Corporations Law will, 'guarantee a sound and well regulated environment for corporate activity.'[48]

It is suggested that this re-labelling process was somewhat surprising given the considerable debate across Australia at that time, fuelled by the corporate excesses and abuses of the 1980s,[49] which resulted in major blue chip companies, banks and building societies *inter alios* collapsing across Australia under mountains of debt.[50] Some of these major corporate collapses were earlier identified in chapters two and three of this book. As such, considerable economic and social pressures were brought to bear upon the Australian Government in an environment which stimulated and enlivened academic debate.[51] There was, therefore, no shortage of publicity crying out for change and for the raising of levels of directorial responsibility and greater accountability. In addition, the Australian Law Reform Commission had by then published its report entitled *General Insolvency Inquiry* following on from its far-reaching inquiry into the law and

---

[44] Noble T, 'When Does a Company Incur a Debt Under the Insolvent Trading Provisions of the Corporations Law?' (1994) 12 CSLJ 297 at 297-298.

[45] (1992) 26 NSWLR 562 at 573-574.

[46] Commonwealth, House of Representatives, Parliamentary Debates, 8 November 1990 at 3669; note Explanatory memorandum, *Corporate Law Economic Reform Program Bill 1998* CCH Australia Ltd, Sydney, 1999 at para 2.5.

[47] *Hawkins v Bank of China* (1992) 26 NSWLR 562 at 565 per Gleeson CJ and at 573 per Kirby P; and *Sycotex Pty Ltd v Baseler* (1994) 122 ALR 531 at 539 per Gummow J.

[48] Commonwealth, House of Representatives, Parliamentary Debates, 8 November 1990 at 3669; note Explanatory memorandum, *Corporate Law Economic Reform Program Bill 1998* CCH Australia Ltd, Sydney, 1999 at para 2.5.

[49] *The Australian Financial Review*, 6 November 1995 and 2 January 1996; *The Australian*, 20 September 1996; *The Independent on Sunday*, 25 April 1999; and *The Times*, 29 April 1999.

[50] *The Australian Financial Review*, 6 November 1995 and 21 April 1997.

[51] Cf. Editorial comment, 'Back to basics: company law reform' (1999) 20 Co Law 129 at 129.

practice relating to the insolvency of both individuals and bodies corporate ('Harmer Report').[52]

Against this background, it is suggested that it is somewhat disappointing that the Australian Parliament chose not to do more with Corporations Law s592. The Harmer Report recommended that Companies Code s556 be overhauled in favour of a positive duty upon directors of Australian companies to prevent insolvent trading.[53] Although these recommendations were well-received, the Australian Parliament chose to simply re-label Companies Code s556 as Corporations Law s592. The Harmer Report's recommendation of a positive duty was shelved and the *status quo* was preserved. Corporations Law s592, therefore, simply carries forward the provisions of Companies Code s556 and makes it an offence for directors of Australian companies to allow their company to incur a debt when at the time there are reasonable grounds to expect that the company will not be able to pay all its debts as and when they fall due. In those circumstances, the directors are jointly and severally liable for payment of the debt.[54] Gummow J in *Stanley Street v Retravision (NSW) Pty Ltd* explained the operation of s592 in the following manner:

> Like its immediate predecessor, s. 556 of the Code, s. 592 has a dual aspect or operation. This is that a person may be convicted of an offence under sub-s. 592(1) and that proceedings may be brought under the same sub-section against the same person for the recovery of the debt in respect of the incurring of which there has been the conviction. Sub-section 592(3) so provides. Furthermore, sub-s. 592(4) makes it clear that in a proceeding for the recovery of a debt liability may be established on the balance of probabilities.[55]

Given the almost identical wording of Companies Code s556 and Corporations Law s592, it is possible to treat one section as being interchangeable with the other when examining the cases below.[56] In the analysis of the cases which follows, we will trace the recent development within the Australian judiciary of a more robust and interventionist approach to directors' duties in general. This revitalised judicial approach was principally responsible for the positive duty which is now statutorily imposed upon directors of Australian companies to ensure that their company's creditors' interests are not put at risk where there are reasonable grounds for suspecting insolvency.[57]

THE LATE 1980s AND THE EARLY 1990s

As we saw in chapter three of this book, in *Metal Manufacturers Ltd v Lewis*[58] a family company was operated by a husband and wife team as sole directors. Typically, the

---

52 Australian Law Reform Commission, Report No. 45, *General Insolvency Inquiry* AGPS, Canberra, 1988.

53 *Ibid* at vol 1 at paras 283, 286, 313 and 325.

54 *Macquarie Bank Ltd v Fociri Pty Ltd* (1992) 10 ACLC 785 at 798 per Kirby P, 'Again, stated generally, the object [of Companies Code s556] is to inculcate a heightened sense of responsibility in directors and other officers in charge of insolvent companies.'

55 (1995) 13 ACLC 757 at 761.

56 *Rema Industries and Services Pty Ltd v Coad* (1992) 7 ACSR 251 at 252 per Lockhart J.

57 Corporations Law s588G; see *Metropolitan Fire Systems Pty Ltd v Miller* (1997) 23 ACSR 699 at 701-703 per Einfeld J; and *Australian Securities Commission v Forem-Freeway Enterprises Pty Ltd* (1998-1999) 30 ACSR 339 at 340-341 per Madgwick J.

58 (1987-1988) 13 ACLR 357.

wife took no part in the running of the company's business. That was managed by the husband. The wife was a director for signing purposes only. Upon the winding-up of the relevant company, Metal Manufacturers Ltd brought an action against the wife under Companies Code s556 to recover the cost of goods supplied to the company prior to the winding-up. The issue for determination was whether or not the wife, by allowing her husband to act as managing director and run the company's business, gave her express or implied authority or consent to the contracting of a debt in the ordinary course of the company's business.[59]

Consistent with the mood of the judiciary at that time, the New South Wales Court of Appeal[60] in *Metal Manufacturers* ruled that the wife was not liable to her company's creditor. The wife's acquiescence in her husband being the company's managing director did not *ipso facto* mean that she had impliedly authorised or consented to him incurring debts on behalf of the company.[61] Whilst the wife's non-participation is consistent with Romer J's third proposition in *In re City Equitable Fire Insurance Company Ltd*,[62] nonetheless, in Baxt's view:

> [The] failure of directors to give continuous attention to the affairs of the company or the expedient of delegating to others can be taken too far.[63]

For the purposes of this book, however, *Metal Manufacturers* is significant for the dissenting views expressed by Kirby P. His Honour asserted that the overall legislative scheme signified by Companies Code s556 raised levels of directorial responsibility and was intended to instil in directors, during times of insolvency or economic difficulty, a proper concern to take particular care in the incurring of debts by the company with third parties.[64] After exploring the development of the section from one which simply provided for an offence, to one which provided for the recovery of the debt from a director, Kirby P went on to explain that s556 was to be understood as part of an integrated legislative scheme which requires of directors higher levels of attention to the company's affairs and its dealings with the outside world than was hitherto the case.[65]

In finding against the defendant in *Metal Manufacturers*, Kirby P strongly condemned those willing to accept the privileges of directorships, but without the responsibilities. The following caveat is found within Kirby P's judgment:

> People should not become ... directors ... if they wish to avoid exposing themselves and their assets to the liabilities now imposed by s556. If they are directors, they should exercise the reasonable care and diligence which the Code now requires of them. They cannot surround themselves with a shield of immunity from the operation of s556, by the simple expedient of washing their hands of the company's affairs

---

[59] Companies Code s556(2)(a).

[60] (Kirby P, Mahoney and McHugh JJA).

[61] Cf. *Androvin v Figliomeni* (1996) 14 ACLC 1461 at 1468-1469 per Owen J (Kennedy and Franklyn JJ agreed); and *Standard Chartered Bank of Aust Ltd v Antico* (1995) 13 ACLC 1381 at 1473 per Hodgson J.

[62] [1925] Ch 407 at 429.

[63] Baxt R, case note (1988) 62 ALJ 643 at 645.

[64] (1987-1988) 13 ACLR 357 at 360; see *EL Bell Packaging Pty Ltd v Allied Seafords Ltd* (1990) 8 ACLC 1135 at 1144 per Vincent J.

[65] *Ibid*; see *Group Four Industries Pty Ltd v Brosnan* (1992) 8 ACSR 463 at 471 per Matheson J and at 489 per Olsson J.

and leaving it to a co-director to attend to those affairs and to incur the debts with third parties which it is the very purpose of s556 to control.[66]

Kirby P was robust in his opposition to any attempt by directors of Australian companies to thwart the legislative intent of Companies Code s556 by the simple expedient of, 'donning the blinkers of indifference to, and assuming the bridle of neglect of, the interest in the company's affairs', and surrendering their powers to a co-director or managing director.[67] However, the other members of the Court of Appeal[68] in *Metal Manufacturers*, rather fortuitously for the defendant, did not share Kirby P's strict interpretation of s556.

With the passage of time, however, and given the recent dramatic shift in judicial attitudes to such matters, it is difficult to comprehend of an Australian court these days reaching a decision at odds with that of Kirby P in *Metal Manufacturers*. But at that time the mood of the Australian public was such that it took the judiciary another two years before it was to pick up on the message which underpinned Kirby P's strong dissent. That happened in *Statewide Tobacco Services Ltd v Morley*,[69] where Ormiston J was called upon to interpret both defences available under Companies Code s556(2) in a fact situation with 'striking similarities'[70] to that in *Metal Manufacturers*, but where the defendant's understanding of the company's affairs was even more negligible than that of Mrs Lewis.

The facts in *Statewide* were briefly these. Mrs Morley was an inactive female director who had never taken any part in the day-to-day running of the business. She was told 'remarkably little about its activities'[71] and allowed the business to be run first by her husband and then by her son. The question for determination was the extent to which a director, who takes no effective part in the company's management, may be liable for the company's debts in circumstances where it continues to trade while insolvent. While arriving at a conclusion consonant with Kirby P's dissent in *Metal Manufacturers*, Ormiston J expressly stated that he preferred his own line of reasoning.

Ormiston J distinguished the majority judgments of the New South Wales Court of Appeal[72] in *Metal Manufacturers*, and found against the defendant in *Statewide*. In formulating his reasons for doing so, Ormiston J examined the legislative position in Australian company law prior to Companies Code s556 and explored the reasons behind the parliamentary changes which led to its enactment.[73] Not surprisingly, therefore, Ormiston J's reasons are peppered with references to the parliamentary intent behind s556 and his desire to meet that intent, by interpreting s556 accordingly, is evident throughout. Thus, in Ormiston J's judgment:

---

[66] (1987-1988) 13 ACLR 357 at 362; thus, notes Sievers A S, 'The National Safety Council Case' (1991) 9 CSLJ 338 at 338, 'it is no longer acceptable for non-executive directors to leave the affairs of a company in the hands of the full-time executives. Passivity is not good enough.'

[67] (1987-1988) 13 ACLR 357 at 363; see *Group Four Industries Pty Ltd v Brosnan* (1992) 8 ACSR 463 at 490-491 per Olsson J; Kirby P's approach, according to Baxt R, case note (1988) 62 ALJ 643 at 645, 'clearly implies that society expects that limited liability would not be taken advantage of in a way which would result in abuse of this privilege.'

[68] (Mahoney and McHugh JJA).

[69] (1990) 2 ACSR 405; note Baxt R, 'Directors Cannot Escape Liability by Doing Nothing' (1990) ABLR 405 at 405.

[70] (1990) 2 ACSR 405 at 423 per Ormiston J.

[71] *Ibid* at 408.

[72] (Mahoney and McHugh JJA).

[73] (1990) 2 ACSR 405 at 410-411.

[A] more rigorous approach should now be taken by the courts in the light of the scope of remedies thereunder and of other legislative changes.[74]

In *Statewide*, Ormiston J considered that directors of Australian companies should be obliged to take all steps practicable to prevent insolvent trading. If a director is unable to persuade his or her fellow directors accordingly, they should seek to have the company wound up or resign.[75] Thus, in Ormiston J's judgment, directors should apply their minds to the company's overall financial position. Whilst a director may be able to show that he or she acted reasonably, for example, by appointing suitable and appropriate accountants and other executives, they should, even in a small company, ask for and receive figures, albeit of a basic kind, on a more or less regular basis.[76] However, Ormiston J considered that:

> Directors cannot be required to make their own further investigations or to 'audit' the accounts provided, unless they have particular responsibilities or expertise, and they can only be required to seek more information if the company's accounts, together with any other information from the company's executives, put them on inquiry.[77]

On appeal,[78] the Victorian Full Court[79] in *Statewide* unanimously approved Ormiston J's endeavours at placing more stringent obligations upon directors of Australian companies in the light of, 'the realities of the day-to-day management of companies.'[80] After quoting at length from Ormiston J's reasons, and referring favourably to Hodgson J's reasons at first instance in *Metal Manufacturers*,[81] and also those of Tadgell J in *Commonwealth Bank of Australia v Friedrich*,[82] the Full Court, in a joint judgment, reaffirmed that today's directors should not be allowed to escape liability by pleading their own ignorance of the relevant facts.[83]

Rather curiously, however, in *Group Four Industries Pty Ltd v Brosnan*,[84] Duggan J expressly declined to follow Ormiston J's judgment in *Statewide*. Duggan J held that a director whose husband had, 'assumed complete de facto control',[85] could rely on the

---

[74] *Ibid* at 412.

[75] *Ibid* at 422; note *Group Four Industries Pty Ltd v Brosnan* (1992) 8 ACSR 463 at 509 per Debelle J; see *Re Bike World (Wholesale) Pty Ltd* (1991-1992) 6 ACSR 681; cf. *Fitzsimmons v R* (1997) 23 ACSR 355 at 358 per Owen J; and *Secretary of State for Trade and Industry v Gash* [1997] 1 BCLC 341 at 349 per Chadwick J; note Corporations Law ss588G(5) and 588G(6); and Trethowan I, 'Directors' Personal Liability for Insolvent Trading: At Last, a Degree of Consensus' (1993) 11 CSLJ 102 at 113.

[76] Cf. *Re Barings plc (No 5)* [1999] 1 BCLC 433 at 486-488 per Jonathan Parker J; *Re Kaytech International plc* [1999] BCC 390 at 403 per Robert Walker LJ (Stuart-Smith and Thorpe LJJ agreed); *Re Brian D Pierson (Contractors) Ltd* [1999] BCC 26 at 55 per Hazel Williamson QC (sitting as a deputy High Court Judge); *Re Westmid Packing Services Ltd* [1998] 2 All ER 124 at 130 per Lord Woolf MR (Waller and Robert Walker LJJ agreed); and *Re Barings plc* [1998] BCC 583 at 585-586 per Sir Richard Scott VC.

[77] (1990) 2 ACSR 405 at 431.

[78] *Morley v Statewide Tobacco Services Ltd* (1992) 8 ACSR 305.

[79] (Crockett, Southwell and Hedigan JJ).

[80] (1990) 2 ACSR 405 at 419 per Ormiston J.

[81] (1986) 11 ACLR 122.

[82] (1991) 5 ACSR 115.

[83] (1992) 8 ACSR 305 at 320 *per curiam*; see *Group Four Industries Pty Ltd v Brosnan* (1992) 8 ACSR 463 at 482 per Matheson J.

[84] (1991) 9 ACLC 1181.

[85] *Ibid* at 1189.

defences available to her under Companies Code s556. In doing so, it is suggested that Duggan J was influenced by the penal flavour of the section which led to a narrower interpretation.[86] Moreover, Duggan J did not have the advantage of either the Victorian Full Court's reasons in *Statewide*, or Lockhart J's reasons in *Rema Industries and Services Pty Ltd v Coad*.[87] Thus, Duggan J must have felt constrained to follow the majority judgments in *Metal Manufacturers*;[88] rather than the more enlightened views there delivered by Kirby P.

On appeal to the South Australian Full Court,[89] Duggan J's decision in *Brosnan* was overruled.[90] By this time, the Victorian Full Court had affirmed Ormiston J's decision in *Statewide* and the Federal Court of Australia, through Lockhart J, had handed down its decision in *Rema*. In overruling Duggan J's decision, the Full Court quoted extensively from Kirby P's dissenting judgment in *Metal Manufacturers*, and also from Ormiston J's judgment in *Statewide*. Reliance was also placed upon Lockhart J's decision in *Rema*. By doing so, the Full Court considered that it was giving effect to parliamentary legislative intent. Hence considerable weight was thereby added to the push for change within corporate Australia to make directors more responsible for their actions, and more accountable for their failings, of office. In finding against the defendant in *Brosnan*, Olsson J considered that the very facts known to Mrs Brosnan:

> [Must] have led any reasonable, intelligent person of average competence to suspect that all was not well and to seek information. She was not entitled merely to sit back in self-imposed ignorance and then seek to rely on that ignorance.[91]

Debelle J, like the other members of the South Australian Full Court in *Brosnan*, was clearly influenced by parliament's desire to see an increase in directors' responsibilities in relation to their company's financial affairs. Debelle J considered that Companies Code s556 was enacted to impose greater responsibility on directors of Australian companies. His Honour invoked Companies Code ss229(2) and 269(9)(a)(iii)[92] as supporting an overall shift in attitude towards the duties upon directors in general.[93] In Debelle J's view:

> [Directors] who stand by and, by their inactivity, allow the managing director to incur debts give their implied authority or consent to the incurring of those debts.[94]

If fellow directors engage in insolvent trading, Debelle J considered that the other director should seek to have the company wound up or resign.[95] Debelle J gave careful

---

[86] *Ibid* at 1190.
[87] (1992) 7 ACSR 251.
[88] (Mahoney and McHugh JJA).
[89] (Matheson, Olsson and Debelle JJ).
[90] (1992) 8 ACSR 463.
[91] *Ibid* at 499; cf. *Re Kaytech International plc* [1999] BCC 390 at 403 per Robert Walker LJ (Stuart-Smith and Thorpe LJJ agreed); and *Re Brian D Pierson (Contractors) Ltd* [1999] BCC 26 at 55 per Hazel Williamson QC (sitting as a deputy High Court Judge).
[92] Cf. Corporations Law s301(5) (repealed by Act No. 61 of 1998 and effective 1 July 1998).
[93] (1992) 8 ACSR 463 at 502-503.
[94] *Ibid* at 509; cf. *Standard Chartered Bank of Aust Ltd v Antico* (1995) 13 ACLC 1381 at 1473-1474 per Hodgson J; note *Capricorn Society Ltd v Linke* (1996) 14 ACLC 431 at 442 per Lander J (Cox and Perry JJ agreed), 'It cannot be said that in all circumstances inactivity will mean that implied authority or consent can be inferred.'

consideration to the interpretation of the defence in Companies Code s556 and the fact that the provision imposes criminal as well as civil liability.[96] As to the level of acceptable conduct on the part of directors,[97] Debelle J agreed with Ormiston J's view in *Statewide*[98] that rather than catalogue directorial reasonableness, each case should be individually considered.[99] Thus, although directors have a duty to monitor the level of the company's debt and its capacity to pay, as the circumstances of individual companies will vary, 'so the steps which directors will need to take will also vary.'[100] As a consequence, a directorship in today's corporate climate involves duties and obligations which require an active interest to be displayed in the company's affairs.[101]

This approach on the part of Olsson and Debelle JJ in *Brosnan* is very much at odds with that adopted by the English courts a century earlier when considering the methods of corporate governance practised by such corporate luminaries as the Marquis of Bute,[102] and Mr Crook.[103] However, since the enactment of the CDD Act and the IA 1986, and the more vigorous approach to the interpretation and application of these Acts by the English courts, there has been a move away from, 'the low standards of skill and diligence required of directors by the nineteenth-century judges.'[104] This is happening more and more in English and Australian company law as we confront the challenges of the 21st century. Today's directors of British and Australian companies must, therefore, be more vigilant of their obligations and responsibilities than were their predecessors. The experience of the past decade or so testifies to that.[105]

A further development in this revitalised approach to directorial responsibility in Australian company law within the context of insolvency was provided by the Victorian Supreme Court in *Friedrich*,[106] where Tadgell J was faced with one of Australia's major corporate financial disasters when the National Safety Council of Australia Victorian Division ('NSC') collapsed in 1989 with a deficiency of assets in the order of $258m.[107]

---

cont.

[95] (1992) 8 ACSR 463 at 509; note *Statewide Tobacco Services Ltd v Morley* (1990) 2 ACSR 405 at 422 per Ormiston J; cf. *Fitzsimmons v R* (1997) 23 ACSR 355 at 358 per Owen J; and *Secretary of State for Trade and Industry v Gash* [1997] 1 BCLC 341 at 349 per Chadwick J.

[96] Cf. Corporations Law s588G; and Corporations Law Part 9.4B.

[97] Companies Code s556(2)(b).

[98] (1990) 2 ACSR 405 at 431-432.

[99] Cf. *Commonwealth Bank of Australia v Friedrich* (1991) 5 ACSR 115 at 125 and 197 per Tadgell J; note *Androvin v Figliomeni* (1996) 14 ACLC 1461 at 1470 per Owen J (Kennedy and Franklyn JJ agreed).

[100] (1992) 8 ACSR 463 at 513 per Debelle J; see *State Government Insurance Corporation v Pollock* (1993) 11 ACSR 333 at 343 per Seaman J.

[101] *Group Four Industries Pty Ltd v Brosnan* (1992) 8 ACSR 463 at 513-514 per Debelle J; and *Daniels v Anderson* (1995) 13 ACLC 614 at 663-666 per Clarke and Sheller JJA; cf. *Re Barings plc* [1998] BCC 583 at 586 per Sir Richard Scott VC; and *Re Barings plc (No 5)* [1999] 1 BCLC 433 at 488 per Jonathan Parker J.

[102] *In re Cardiff Savings Bank* [1892] 2 Ch 100.

[103] *In re Denham & Co* (1883) 25 Ch D 752.

[104] Davies P L, *Gower's Principles of Modern Company Law* (6th ed) Sweet & Maxwell Ltd, London, 1997 at 656.

[105] E.g., *Norman v Theodore Goddard* [1992] BCC 14 at 15 per Hoffmann J; *Vrisakis v Australian Securities Commission* (1992-1993) 9 WAR 395 at 451 per Ipp J (Malcolm CJ agreed); *Daniels v Anderson* (1995) 13 ACLC 614 at 662 per Clarke and Sheller JJA; *Androvin v Figliomeni* (1996) 14 ACLC 1461 at 1470 per Owen J (Kennedy and Franklyn JJ agreed); and *Re Barings plc* [1998] BCC 583 at 586 per Sir Richard Scott VC.

[106] (1991) 5 ACSR 115; see *Australian Securities Commission v Gallagher* (1993) 11 ACLC 286.

[107] The State of Victoria is still suffering from the effects of its collapse.

The collapse was brought about by the elaborate fraud of its chief executive John Friedrich.[108]

The facts in *Friedrich* are well-documented in the reports and elsewhere,[109] but were briefly these. Nine of the company's eleven directors were non-executive. Of those, none had demonstrated financial expertise, although one was better versed than the others. All gave their time on a voluntary basis. Other than for out-of-pocket expenses, no payments were received by the non-executive directors. The board's control over loan approval was strikingly lax and was recorded in the vaguest terms, even though multi-million dollar sums were involved. Statutory requirements in relation to the accounts were not met and bundles of documents were signed without consideration.[110] Following liquidation, the State Bank of Victoria, a major creditor of the NSC, sought to recover approximately $97m from the directors, one of whom was Mr Eise. Eise's attempt to rely on the defence under Companies Code s556(2)(b) failed.[111]

While conceding that Eise was an active director, deceived by a fraudster who had also taken in creditors and accountants, Tadgell J underlined the persistent breaches of the Companies Code and the failure to take reasonable steps that were available to obtain proper financial information.[112] Lacking such information, Eise nevertheless signed reports and statements. Tadgell J determined that Eise was not entitled to rely on the fact that he had not read those reports.[113] It was noted that accountants were engaged in late 1988, but that they did not suspect insolvency for a further three months. Tadgell J accepted that the accountants' initial brief was not an insolvency investigation and that their short acquaintance with the company's affairs could be contrasted with Eise's long-standing connection. In Tadgell J's judgment:

> [A director] properly doing his job, and using no more than common sense, [would] have called for and considered both the accounts and the report in a relatively short time … He would have done so in order to keep himself abreast of the company's affairs for the purpose of carrying out his director's duties. … It is of the essence of the responsibilities of the directors … that they should take reasonable steps to place

---

[108] (1991) 5 ACSR 115 at 118 per Tadgell J, 'The detail and magnitude of Friedrich's deceit are not readily grasped'; a modern day equivalent of the rogue Bevan in *In re City Equitable Fire Insurance Company Ltd* [1925] Ch 407 described at 474 per Romer J as, 'a daring and unprincipled scoundrel'.

[109] Sievers A S, 'Farewell to the Sleeping Director – The Modern Judicial and Legislative Approach to Directors' Duties of Care, Skill and Diligence' (1993) 21 ABLR 111 at 131-134.

[110] Regrettably, a scenario all too common to corporate Australia during the 1980s: Sykes T, *The Bold Riders* Allen & Unwin Pty Ltd, St Leonards, 1994; and Barry P, *The Rise and Fall of Alan Bond* Transworld Publishers (Australia) Pty Ltd, Sydney, 1990; cf. *Bishopsgate Investment Management Ltd v Maxwell (No. 2)* [1994] 1 All ER 261.

[111] *Quaere* whether Eise would have been made liable had this action come before Jessel MR in the light of Jessel MR's remarks in *In re Forest of Dean Coal Mining Company* (1879) 10 Ch D 450 at 454.

[112] Cf. *Re Hitco 2000 Ltd* [1995] BCC 161 at 167 per Jules Sher QC (sitting as a deputy High Court Judge), 'In my judgment the respondent's greatest failing is that he did not ensure that he was provided with regular financial management information so as to enable him to answer that most difficult question which every director who trades with the privilege of limited liability is obliged to confront, especially in straitened financial circumstances, "should I cease trading?".'

[113] (1991) 5 ACSR 115 at 183-184, cf. *Re D'Jan of London Ltd* [1993] BCC 646 at 648-649 per Hoffmann LJ.

themselves in a position to guide and monitor the management of the company by reference to information appropriate for the purpose.[114]

Tadgell J condemned Eise's actions, or rather inaction, in *Friedrich* by allowing Friedrich a free rein and for not having the intestinal fortitude to stand up to Friedrich when Eise's suspicions were aroused that all at the company was not well. Such behaviour on Eise's part facilitated the perpetration of Friedrich's massive fraud on the company and its creditors. As we have witnessed in chapter three of this book, and as we shall see in the next chapter of this book, Tadgell J's remarks, while generally consistent with those of Ormiston J in *Statewide*,[115] subtly extended the duty upon directors of Australian companies to exercise care and diligence by reducing the scope for subjective criteria and limiting possible avenues of escape from personal liability.[116]

At least one commentator[117] has argued that Tadgell J in *Friedrich* set out to define a duty of financial competence.[118] Whether or not that was so, clearly Tadgell J was intent upon a more rigorous approach,[119] and was looking to impose upgraded levels of vigilance and financial standards upon directors in an era of increasing insolvency. That approach, it is suggested, reflected contemporary community expectations at that time and fuelled the desire for legislative reform in Australian company law.

Before turning to the matter of reform, however, it is instructive to briefly consider several more recent decisions which serve to emphasise the revitalised approach on the part of the Australian judiciary to directorial responsibility and greater accountability in this context. First, *Rema Industries and Services Pty Ltd v Coad*.[120] There, the Federal Court of Australia was asked to consider an application under Corporations Law s592 that one working director of an insolvent company, who had the management of its day-to-day business, and two non-working directors were jointly and severally liable for the company's debts. Lockhart J found against all defendants on the grounds that neither Coad, the working director, nor one of the non-working directors established their defences under s592(2)(b)(i) as they ought to have informed themselves far more fully than they did about the company's financial affairs and its trading relationship with Rema Industries and Services Pty Ltd.[121] In reviewing the legislative intent behind s592, Lockhart J considered that the recent legislation reflects:

[The] tendency of parliament in recent times to place greater responsibility on persons who are directors and managers of companies at times when debts are

---

[114] (1991) 5 ACSR 115 at 184; note Sievers A S, 'The National Safety Council Case' (1991) 9 CSLJ 338 at 342, 'Tadgell J is speaking here in the context of s556 (now s592) but his remarks are equally valid in the wider context of directors' duties generally.'

[115] (1990) 2 ACSR 405 at 422 and at 431.

[116] Ipp D A, 'The diligent director' (1997) 18 Co Law 162 at 164-165.

[117] Dodds J, 'New Developments in Directors' Duties – The Victorian Stance on Financial Competence' (1991) 17 MULR 132 at 147.

[118] Such a requirement would represent a departure from a traditional tenet of company law with wide-reaching implications for the commercial community.

[119] Cf. *Statewide Tobacco Services Ltd v Morley* (1990) 2 ACSR 405 at 412 per Ormiston J.

[120] (1992) 7 ACSR 251; see *Taylor v Darke* (1992) 10 ACLC 1516; note Noble T, 'When Does a Company Incur a Debt Under the Insolvent Trading Provisions of the Corporations Law?' (1994) 12 CSLJ 297 at 306.

[121] The second non-working director failed to attend the hearing and judgment went against him by default.

incurred in circumstances where there is no reasonable prospect of the companies being able to pay their debts.[122]

In considering the standard which directors are expected to meet, Lockhart J in *Rema* adopted the test formulated by Foster J in *3M Australia Pty Ltd v Kemish*; namely, that the reasonableness of the grounds relied upon must be judged by the standard appropriate to a director of ordinary competence.[123] This is not to be measured by subjective considerations personal to the defendant.[124] In Lockhart J's view, as a defence under Corporations Law s592(2)(b), reasonable cause imports an objective standard. But this must be applied to the facts and circumstances known to the director, and the facts and circumstances which, by reason of his or her duties as a director, ought to have been known to them.[125]

These tests enunciated by Lockhart J in *Rema* have subsequently met with widespread judicial approval throughout Australia.[126] The decision in *State Government Insurance Corporation v Pollock*[127] is apposite. There, the Western Australian Supreme Court was concerned with the payment of an insurance premium. The issue before the court was whether or not that premium constituted a debt within the meaning of Companies Code s556. The matter came on for hearing before Seaman J who cited *Rema* with approval in holding, and reaffirming, that:

> The reasonable grounds referred to in ... [Companies Code s556(1)(b)] are grounds which are reasonable according to the standards of directors ... who are of reasonable ability. Reasonable ability is a relative concept designed to be applied with some flexibility. The test is objective and not measured by the subjective considerations personal to the defendant.[128]

When examining the second limb of the defence under Companies Code s556(2) in *Rema*, Seaman J felt that to be a matter to be judged by the standard appropriate to a director of ordinary competence, 'in the light of the facts and circumstances which were known or ought to have been known to such a director'.[129]

As this raft of decisions mentioned above demonstrates, the Australian judiciary was at that time very much on the move. Just three days later, another step was taken by the Australian judiciary to offset, 'the traditionally benign view that company directors,

---

[122] (1992) 7 ACSR 251 at 257-258.

[123] (1986) 4 ACLC 185 at 187; see *Taylor v Powell* (1993) 11 ACLC 311.

[124] (1992) 7 ACSR 251 at 259; see *State Government Insurance Corporation v Pollock* (1993) 11 ACSR 333 at 341 per Seaman J; note *Gamble v Hoffman* (1997) 15 ACLC 1314 at 1318 per Carr J.

[125] (1992) 7 ACSR 251 at 259 per Lockhart J; see *Taylor v Powell* (1993) 11 ACLC 311 at 316 per Davies J, 'the test of "reasonable cause" involves a "blending of subjective and objective considerations" as discussed by the High Court in *Shapowloff v Dunn*'.

[126] E.g., *Carrier Air Conditioning Pty Ltd v Kurda* (1993) 11 ACSR 247; *State Government Insurance Corporation v Pollock* (1993) 11 ACSR 333; *Travel Compensation Fund v Dunn* (unreported, Federal Court of Australia, New South Wales District Registry No. G777/91, Wilcox J, 2 December 1992); and *Taylor v Darke* (1992) 10 ACLC 1516.

[127] (1993) 11 ACSR 333.

[128] *Ibid* at 341.

[129] *Ibid* at 343; note *3M Australia Pty Ltd v Kemish* (1986) 4 ACLC 185 at 190-191 per Foster J; *Grimm v Roy Galvin & Co Pty Ltd* (1988) 6 ACLC 852; and *Rema Industries and Services Pty Ltd v Coad* (1992) 7 ACSR 251.

particularly if non-executive, were not required, as a matter of law, to be competent'.[130] In *Carrier Air Conditioning Pty Ltd v Kurda*,[131] the South Australian Full Court[132] found the directors of the insolvent company under consideration personally liable under Companies Code s556(1) for the cost of airconditioning equipment sold and supplied to their company. The principal decision in *Carrier* was delivered by Debelle J[133] who, in reliance upon the decisions in *Statewide*, *Brosnan*, *Friedrich* and *Rema* mentioned above, reaffirmed that the proper discharge of directorial duties in Australian company law obliges directors:

> [To] act in accordance with the duties of a director as prescribed by the Code, the common law and equity duties which include the obligation to keep himself informed of the financial affairs of the company.[134]

Debelle J's judgment in *Carrier* is consistent with those promoting a more rigorous and interventionist approach to the issue of directors' duties in general. This robust attitude is evident from an analysis of the cases earlier mentioned, and is demonstrative of the strong push by the Australian judiciary in recent years towards making directors of Australian companies more responsible and accountable for their actions, and inaction, of office.[135] Throughout this book we have witnessed a change in circumstances, attitude and approach to the whole topic of directors' duties generally: in English and Australian company law. So much so that in today's corporate climate it is widely accepted that:

> [If] people choose to use a corporate vehicle to carry on their business activities, then they must accept the consequential responsibilities imposed by law.[136]

This approach to corporate governance accords with that recently intended by the Australian Parliament, and is more in keeping with that recently called for by the Australian public, in order to meet the rising expectations of directors of Australian companies.[137] It is an approach which is at last gaining recognition and acceptance in English company law as well.[138] That will be borne out in the next chapter of this book when we examine the effect which statutory intervention on the part of the British Parliament has had upon the duties of directors of British companies.

---

[130] Dodds J, 'New Developments in Directors' Duties – The Victorian Stance on Financial Competence' (1991) 17 MULR 132 at 134.

[131] (1993) 11 ACSR 247.

[132] (Cox, Duggan and Debelle JJ).

[133] (Cox and Duggan JJ agreed).

[134] (1993) 11 ACSR 247 at 250.

[135] *Capricorn Society Ltd v Linke* (1996) 14 ACLC 431 at 444 per Perry J; *Standard Chartered Bank of Aust Ltd v Antico* (1995) 13 ACLC 1381 at 1443-1444 per Hodgson J; and *Southern Star Group Pty Ltd v Byron* (1995) 13 ACLC 1622 at 1628-1630 per Young J; cf. *Re Kaytech International plc* [1999] BCC 390 at 403 per Robert Walker LJ (Stuart-Smith and Thorpe LJJ agreed); and *Re Brian D Pierson (Contractors) Ltd* [1999] BCC 26 at 55 per Hazel Williamson QC (sitting as a deputy High Court Judge).

[136] *Statewide Tobacco Services Ltd v Morley* (1990) 2 ACSR 405 at 432 per Ormiston J.

[137] E.g., *The Australian Financial Review*, 6 November 1995, 2 January 1996 and 21 April 1997; and *The Australian*, 21 April 1997; cf. *The Times*, 29 April 1999; and *Financial Times*, 8 June 1999.

[138] *Re Barings plc (No 5)* [1999] 1 BCLC 433 at 488 per Jonathan Parker J; note Davies P L, *Gower's Principles of Modern Company Law* (6th ed) Sweet & Maxwell Ltd, London, 1997 at 643.

A DUTY TO ACTIVELY PARTICIPATE?

In order to avoid personal liability for debts incurred by their insolvent companies, directors of Australian companies must ensure that these days they make sufficient enquiries to regularly acquaint themselves with the company's financial situation.[139] The prevailing attitude is such that a non-participating director is now in a perilous position.[140] Directors who fail to participate *ipso facto* do so at their own peril. They can no longer remain in total ignorance of the company's affairs by conferring a general authority upon another to run the company.[141] This is not to be confused with reasonable and proper delegation of the type contemplated by Rogers CJ in *AWA Ltd v Daniels*,[142] and recognised by Hoffmann LJ as being appropriate in *Norman v Theodore Goddard*.[143] Within the context of active participation on the part of directors, what recently fell from the Western Australian Full Court[144] in *Androvin v Figliomeni* warrants mention. The judgment of the Full Court was delivered by Owen J[145] who addressed the matter in this way:

> The duties which a director has in relation to the affairs of the company cannot be circumvented by mere inaction. A director who, for whatever reason, decides to take no part in the affairs of the company does so at his or her own risk and cannot then rely on inaction to avoid liability. Passive acquiescence in the incurring of a debt on behalf of a company can be evidence of authority or consent and may, depending on the circumstances, be sufficient to justify a finding that such authority or consent existed.[146]

While it is true that an ordinary director does not have the ability to restrict the actions of a managing director whose powers are derived from the company's articles, or its replaceable rules as the articles are now referred to in Australian company law,[147] this does not mean that a director cannot actively indicate his or her disapproval of the managing director's conduct. Surely, says Trethowan, if it were recorded in board minutes, or other documentary evidence existed, to show that the director had objected to the continued incurring of debts whilst the company was insolvent, that would go far to enable the director to take advantage of the defence in Corporations Law

---

[139]   *Group Four Industries Pty Ltd v Brosnan* (1992) 8 ACSR 463 at 513-514 per Debelle J; and *Daniels v Anderson* (1995) 13 ACLC 614 at 663-666 per Clarke and Sheller JJA; note Australian Law Reform Commission, Report No. 45 (vol 1), *General Insolvency Inquiry* AGPS, Canberra, 1988 at paras 302-305. Such enquiries must be made, in any case, to properly comply with, e.g., Corporations Law s232; cf. *Re Hitco 2000 Ltd* [1995] BCC 161 at 167 per Jules Sher QC (sitting as a deputy High Court Judge).

[140]   Sievers A S, 'The National Safety Council Case' (1991) 9 CSLJ 338 at 338; cf. *Bishopsgate Investment Management Ltd v Maxwell (No. 2)* 1 All ER 261 at 264 per Hoffman LJ, 'the existence of a duty to participate must depend upon how the particular company's business is organised and the part which the director could reasonably have been expected to play.'

[141]   *Group Four Industries Pty Ltd v Brosnan* (1992) 8 ACSR 463 at 499 per Olsson J; and *Capricorn Society Ltd v Linke* (1996) 14 ACLC 431 at 443-444 *per curiam*; cf. *Re Westmid Packing Services Ltd* [1998] 2 All ER 124 at 130 per Lord Woolf MR (Waller and Robert Walker LJJ agreed).

[142]   (1992) 10 ACLC 933 at 1015.

[143]   [1992] BCC 14 at 15-16 and 19.

[144]   (Kennedy, Franklyn and Owen JJ).

[145]   (Kennedy and Franklyn JJ agreed).

[146]   (1996) 14 ACLC 1461 at 1468-1469.

[147]   Corporations Law ss134-135, 141 and 1415 (added by Act No. 61 of 1998 and effective 1 July 1998).

s592(2)(a).[148] Perhaps. Although as Young J's judgment in *Southern Star Group Pty Ltd v Byron* cautions, 'It may be that resignation is his only escape because he may not have the status, especially if he is a minority director who has no shareholding to approach the Court for winding up.'[149] Almost certainly, however, if the insolvent trading continued after the director had so objected, it would be necessary for the director to resign from the board to negate an inference of acquiescence in the continuing insolvent trading. This is treacherous ground for directors of Australian companies as Hodgson J's judgment in *Standard Chartered Bank of Aust Ltd v Antico* conveys succinctly:

> I do consider that there may be circumstances in which the failure of a single director to seek to persuade a managing director not to incur a debt, or to call a directors' meeting with a view to stopping the incurring of debts, or to resign, or to seek to have the company wound up, could amount to giving authority or consent to the incurring of a debt.[150]

It will be recalled from *Group Four Industries Pty Ltd v Brosnan*, that Debelle J was firmly of the view that a director was obliged to regularly and frequently monitor the company's solvency and could not escape responsibility upon the pretext of being unable to influence or control other board members.[151] In Debelle J's opinion, if the managing director refused to act as requested, 'the other director should seek to have the company wound up or resign.'[152] Few would contend that the dramatic change in attitude displayed by the Australian judiciary over the last decade or so, which has been briefly analysed and considered throughout this chapter, was other than a positive development in the overall raising of levels of directorial responsibility and account-ability, and in keeping with today's ideals of corporate governance.[153] But *quaere* whether or not the particular defendants involved could be seen as victims of an abrupt judicial change in direction.[154] However, be that as it may, clearly the Australian judiciary felt that the time was ripe for a shake-out of the old values and the ushering in of a new era in corporate responsibility.[155]

---

[148] Trethowan I, 'Directors' Personal Liability for Insolvent Trading: At Last, a Degree of Consensus' (1993) 11 CSLJ 102 at 112.

[149] (1995) 13 ACLC 1622 at 1629.

[150] (1995) 13 ACLC 1381 at 1473; note *Southern Star Group Pty Ltd v Byron* (1995) 13 ACLC 1622 at 1627-1628 per Young J.

[151] (1992) 8 ACSR 463 at 509; cf. *Secretary of State for Trade and Industry v Gash* [1997] 1 BCLC 341 at 349 per Chadwick J.

[152] (1992) 8 ACSR 463 at 509; note *Statewide Tobacco Services Ltd v Morley* (1990) 2 ACSR 405 at 422 per Ormiston J; cf. *Fitzsimmons v R* (1997) 23 ACSR 355 at 358 per Owen J; and *Secretary of State for Trade and Industry v Gash* [1997] 1 BCLC 341 at 349 per Chadwick J.

[153] See Prentice D D and Holland P R J, *Contemporary Issues in Corporate Governance* Oxford University Press, Oxford, 1993; Committee on the Financial Aspects of Corporate Governance, *The Report of the Committee on the Financial Aspects of Corporate Governance* Gee and Co Ltd, London, 1992; Farrar J H, 'Corporate Governance, Business Judgement and the Professionalism of Directors' (1993) 6 CBLJ 1; Whincop M J, 'An Economic Analysis of the Criminalisation and Content of Directors' Duties' (1996) 24 ABLR 273; and Stapledon G P, *Institutional Shareholders and Corporate Governance* Clarendon Press, Oxford, 1996.

[154] Dodds J, 'New Developments in Directors' Duties – The Victorian Stance on Financial Competence' (1991) 17 MULR 132 at 132.

[155] A view strongly embraced by Rogers CJ in *AWA Ltd v Daniels* (1992) 10 ACLC 933; affirmed *Daniels v Anderson* (1995) 13 ACLC 614.

THE CALL FOR CHANGE AND PARLIAMENT'S RESPONSE

It is indisputable that in recent years there has been a strong push by the Australian Parliament to place more responsibility and greater accountability upon the shoulders of directors of Australian companies.[156] As we have seen throughout this and the previous chapters of this book, this trend was identified and advanced by the Australian courts in such cases as *Morley v Statewide Tobacco Services Ltd*,[157] *Group Four Industries Pty Ltd v Brosnan*,[158] *Commonwealth Bank of Australia v Friedrich*[159] and *Rema Industries and Services Pty Ltd v Coad*.[160] The combined judicial weight behind the decisions in these cases is quite considerable. Baxt foreshadowed the significance of these decisions when he wrote that:

> The decision of the superior courts on these questions will be important in the light of the pressures on the [Australian] Government to amend legislation to impose harsher responsibilities and more wide-ranging duties on directors.[161]

Baxt's prophecy has been fulfilled as that forecast on his part has now come to pass. Given the perception that Australian company law was too lax during the late 1980s, public discontent became evident within the Australian business and legal communities. Pressures mounted upon the Australian Government for change. Committees had been established with briefs that included, at least in part, an examination of the obligations and responsibilities of directors of Australian companies. *A fortiori* in the context of insolvency.[162] Recommendations for change were made repeatedly. The Australian academics and commentators weighed in with their support.[163] To their credit, the Australian Government and the Australian Parliament responded in a positive and timely fashion.

The evolution of directors' duties and responsibilities, which we identified in chapter two of this book concerning the duty to exercise care and diligence, for example, moved forwards. Along the way, judicial attitudes and approaches changed. For instance, traditional recovery procedures directed at directors of insolvent Australian companies, via the mechanism of the misfeasance summons,[164] were refashioned and gave rise to what many considered to be an independent fiduciary duty upon directors of Australian companies to have regard for the interests of their company's creditors.[165] Whilst the end result was preserved, the approach was considered in a different light. Statutorily,

---

[156] *Rema Industries and Services Pty Ltd v Coad* (1992) 7 ACSR 251 at 257-258 per Lockhart J.

[157] (1992) 8 ACSR 305.

[158] (1992) 8 ACSR 463.

[159] (1991) 5 ACSR 115.

[160] (1992) 7 ACSR 251.

[161] Baxt R, 'Sleeping Directors Get a Second Chance' (1992) 20 ABLR 78 at 81.

[162] E.g., Australian Law Reform Commission, Report No. 45, *General Insolvency Inquiry* AGPS, Canberra, 1988; Senate Standing Committee on Legal and Constitutional Affairs, *Social and Fiduciary Duties and Obligations of Company Directors* AGPS, Canberra, 1989; and The Companies and Securities Advisory Committee, *Report on Reform of the Law Governing Corporate Financial Transactions* AGPS, Canberra, 1991.

[163] Cf. Editorial comment, 'Back to basics: company law reform' (1999) 20 Co Law 129 at 129.

[164] Cf. Corporations Law s598; see *Gamble v Hoffman* (1997) 15 ACLC 1314 at 1316 per Carr J.

[165] In a line of authority which relevantly began with *Walker v Wimborne* (1976-1977) 137 CLR 1 through to the recent decision in *Equiticorp Finance Ltd v Bank of New Zealand* (1993) 11 ACLC 952; cf. *3M Australia Pty Ltd v Watt* (1984) 2 ACLC 621 at 624 per Rogers J, 'The action contemplated by the section was for breach of fiduciary duty owed to the debtor company.'

creditors were given a personal right of action directly against errant directors, thus overcoming any perceived shortcomings in the common law duty said to arise upon Mason J's celebrated *dictum* in *Walker v Wimborne*.[166] But, even so, the metamorphosis was not yet complete.

Less than two years after Corporations Law s592 came into effect,[167] the Corporate Law Reform Bill 1992 (Cth) ('Bill') was introduced into the Australian Parliament on 3 November 1992. In its explanatory memorandum which accompanied the release of the Bill,[168] the Australian Government paid tribute to the ability of the Australian courts to develop principles in keeping with legislative intent. The Government then spelt out, for the future guidance of the judiciary, that in the context of insolvency what constituted the proper performance of directors' duties ought, in its view, be influenced by matters such as the state of the company's financial affairs, the size and nature of the company, the urgency and magnitude of any problem, the provisions of the company's constitution and the composition of its board.[169] Matters which we have seen throughout this book that have application to the duties upon directors of British and Australian companies in general.[170]

The Bill addressed *inter alia* the following three major Australian law reform reports: (i) the Cooney Report;[171] (ii) the Harmer Report;[172] and (iii) the Advisory Committee Report.[173] Relevantly, the Cooney Report made recommendations concerning the duty upon directors to exercise care and diligence, the decriminalisation of directors' duties in appropriate circumstances and the introduction of civil penalties for breaches of the legislation. It did not, however, focus upon the issue of whether or not directors could be said to owe a duty to creditors and to future creditors in certain circumstances.[174] Baxt was critical of that oversight.[175]

Of these reports, the Harmer Report was, within the context of this chapter, the most significant. It was five years in the making. The Australian Law Reform Commission had been given its terms of reference on 20 November 1983. Although major reviews of insolvency law had been undertaken in England, Canada and the United States, corporate insolvency had never been reviewed in Australia. It was, thus, a heavy brief. The Harmer Report was critical of parliament's earlier legislative shortcomings in failing to give creditors, as a class, a suitable remedy against directors of Australian companies for incurring debts without a reasonable prospect of payment.[176]

---

[166] (1976-1977) 137 CLR 1 at 7.

[167] Added by Act No. 110 of 1990 and effective 1 January 1991.

[168] Explanatory memorandum, *Corporate Law Reform Bill 1992* CCH Australia Ltd, Sydney, 1992.

[169] A view earlier espoused in *Commonwealth Bank of Australia v Friedrich* (1991) 5 ACSR 115 at 125 per Tadgell J; cf. *Deputy Commissioner of Taxation v Austin* (1998) 16 ACLC 1555 at 1558-1560 per Madgwick J.

[170] Sievers A S, 'The National Safety Council Case' (1991) 9 CSLJ 338 at 342.

[171] Senate Standing Committee on Legal and Constitutional Affairs, *Social and Fiduciary Duties and Obligations of Company Directors* AGPS, Canberra, 1989.

[172] Australian Law Reform Commission, Report No. 45 (vol 1), *General Insolvency Inquiry* AGPS, Canberra, 1988.

[173] The Companies and Securities Advisory Committee, *Report on Reform of the Law Governing Corporate Financial Transactions* AGPS, Canberra, 1991.

[174] Cf. *Jeffree v National Companies & Securities Commission* (1989) 15 ACLR 217.

[175] Baxt R, 'Reforming the law relating to company directors' (1990) 64 ALJ 345 at 346.

[176] Australian Law Reform Commission, Report No. 45 (vol 1), *General Insolvency Inquiry* AGPS, Canberra, 1988 at para 279.

The Harmer Report noted that Companies Code s556 contained a curious mixture of civil and criminal sanctions and criticised its operation.[177] Relevantly, recommendations were made to the effect that: (i) directors have a duty to prevent a company trading when it is unable to pay its debts; and (ii) liquidators be able to sue directors who breach this duty, with the proceeds to be applied for the benefit of all unsecured creditors, rather than just the first creditor who takes action.[178] By virtue of the Corporate Law Reform Act 1992 (Cth),[179] the Bill became law and implemented these, and many other, recommendations made in these reports.[180]

The metamorphosis was now complete. The Australian Parliament had introduced into Australian company law a positive statutory duty upon directors of Australian companies to prevent insolvent trading by their companies.[181] It is opportune to now move on to consider this duty in some detail and to see what effect the new legislation has had on those issues which were left unresolved in the previous chapter of this book.

THE LATEST STATUTORY PROVISIONS

In Australian company law, Corporations Law Part 5.7B[182] establishes a regime whereby the company's liquidator may seek compensation from a director of an Australian company who has been in breach of Corporations Law s588G by permitting the company to trade while insolvent.[183] The effect of Part 5.7B is to reinstate traditional principles of insolvency law by discouraging independent actions brought directly against errant directors by the insolvent company's creditors. However, it will be recalled from the previous chapter of this book that, by virtue of Corporations Law s588P, the creditors' ability to bring such personal actions for the breach of either legal or equitable duties, is arguably preserved.[184] For reasons there explained, this issue, regrettably, remains unresolved. Irrespective of that, however, Corporations Law s588R(1) expressly provides that:

> A creditor of a company that is being wound up may, with the written consent of the company's liquidator, begin proceedings under section 588M in relation to the incurring by the company of a debt that is owed to the creditor.

Absent the liquidator's consent under Corporations Law s588R(1), a creditor may nonetheless bring an action against an errant director under Corporations Law s588M(3) should the liquidator fail to initiate proceedings within three months of a request by the

---

[177] Which criticism applies with equal force to Corporations Law s592.

[178] Australian Law Reform Commission, Report No. 45 (vol 1), *General Insolvency Inquiry* AGPS, Canberra, 1988 at paras 313-314, 316 and 327.

[179] Added by Act No. 210 of 1992 and effective 23 June 1993.

[180] Noble T, 'When Does a Company Incur a Debt Under the Insolvent Trading Provisions of the Corporations Law?' (1994) 12 CSLJ 297 at 297.

[181] Corporations Law s588G; see *Metropolitan Fire Systems Pty Ltd v Miller* (1997) 23 ACSR 699 at 701-703 per Einfeld J; and *Australian Securities Commission v Forem-Freeway Enterprises Pty Ltd* (1998-1999) 30 ACSR 339 at 340-341 per Madgwick J.

[182] Added by Act No. 210 of 1992 and effective 23 June 1993.

[183] Corporations Law s588M(2); cf. Insolvency Act 1986 (UK) ss213-214.

[184] Sealy L S, 'Directors' "Wider" Responsibilities – Problems Conceptual, Practical and Procedural' (1987) 13 MULR 164 at 186.

creditor to do so by virtue of Corporations Law s588T(2).[185] Hence, where an errant director is liable to pay the debts of his or her company that were incurred by that company in consequence of the application of Corporations Law s588G, those debts are either recoverable by the liquidator pursuant to Corporations Law s588M(2) or by the creditor pursuant to s588M(3). As Finkelstein J[186] observed in *Quick v Stoland Pty Ltd*:

> If the debts are recovered by the liquidator they will form part of the estate of the company that is available for distribution among its creditors and contributories. If recovered by the creditor they will be retained by him or her. However, a director cannot be subjected to competing claims. It is for the liquidator to decide whether he or she will bring the claim or allow the creditor to bring it. To ensure that the decision remains with the liquidator s588R(1) provides that the creditor is not able to bring proceedings under s588M without the consent of the liquidator.[187]

Where the liquidator takes action under Corporations Law Part 5.7B, any amounts paid are paid as compensation to the company for the unsecured creditors' benefit.[188] Secured creditors will only receive money in this manner if they prove as outstanding unsecured creditors, or where there are no unsecured debts. The duty is owed to the insolvent company;[189] and, thus, one unresolved issue from the previous chapter of this book is laid to rest under the statutory scheme.

Whereas Corporations Law s592 applies to all those who took part in the company's management, Corporations Law s588G applies only to directors of Australian companies. This more limited focus is an analogue of that which prevails in English company law under the wrongful trading provision imposed by IA 1986 s214. The application of s588G to directors only makes sense in Herzberg's view, as managers do not generally have the power to initiate insolvency administration should the company's financial position require that.[190] Furthermore, the former Corporations Law s301(5) obliged directors, not managers, to certify that for the relevant accounting period there were reasonable grounds to believe that the company would be able to pay its debts as and when they fell due.[191] The Australian Law Reform Commission in its report entitled *General Insolvency Inquiry* took the view that it is the directors who have a duty to

---

[185] Mescher B, 'Personal Liability of Company Directors for Company Debts' (1996) 70 ALJ 837 at 850.
[186] (Branson and Emmett JJ agreed).
[187] (1998) 29 ACSR 130 at 146.
[188] *Re Oasis Merchandising Services Ltd* [1997] BCC 282 at 291 *per curiam*; cf. Insolvency Act 1986 (UK) s107; note Villiers C, 'Employees as creditors: a challenge for justice in insolvency law' (1999) 20 Co Law 222 at 228; Schulte R, 'Corporate groups and the equitable subordination of claims on insolvency' (1997) 18 Co Law 2 at 2 and 11; Bean G M D, 'Debt subordination validated' (1994) 15 Co Law 52 at 52; and Sealy L S, 'Directors' Duties – An Unnecessary Gloss' [1988] CLJ 175 at 177; see Report of the Review Committee on Insolvency Law and Practice, HMSO, London, Cmnd 8558, 1982 at para 1396.
[189] *Cape Breton Company v Fenn* (1881) 17 Ch D 198 at 208 per Cotton LJ; *Ferguson v Wallbridge* [1935] 3 DLR 66 at 83-84 per Lord Blanesburgh (Lords Thankerton, Russell and Alness and Sir Sidney Rowlatt agreed); *Fargro Ltd v Godfroy* [1986] 1 WLR 1134 at 1138 per Walton J; *Scarel Pty Ltd v City Loan & Credit Corporation Pty Ltd* (1988) 17 FCR 344 at 347-352 per Gummow J; *Zempilas v JN Taylor Holdings Ltd* (1990-1991) 5 ACSR 28 at 30 per Debelle J; and *Christianos v Aloridge Pty Ltd* (1995) 18 ACSR 272 at 280-281 per Beaumont, Whitlam and Tamberlin JJ.
[190] Herzberg A, 'Insolvent Trading' (1991) 9 CSLJ 285 at 291; note *Deputy Commissioner of Taxation v Austin* (1998) 16 ACLC 1555 at 1559 per Madgwick J; cf. *Canadian Aero Service Ltd v O'Malley* (1974) 40 DLR (3d) 371 at 381 per Laskin J.
[191] Repealed by Act No. 61 of 1998 and effective 1 July 1998.

oversee the company's management and that only they should owe the duty to prevent insolvent trading.[192] This change is unlikely to have any significant ramifications given that most of the relevant cases before the Australian courts have, to date, involved only directors of Australian companies in any event.[193] Section 588G relevantly provides that:

(1) This section applies if:
   (a) a person is a director of a company at the time when the company incurs a debt; and
   (b) the company is insolvent at that time, or becomes insolvent by incurring that debt, or by incurring at that time debts including that debt; and
   (c) at that time, there are reasonable grounds for suspecting that the company is insolvent, or would so become insolvent, as the case may be; and
   (d) that time is at or after the commencement of this Part.
(2) By failing to prevent the company from incurring the debt, the person contravenes this section if:
   (a) the person is aware at that time that there are such grounds for so suspecting; or
   (b) a reasonable person in a like position in a company in the company's circumstances would be so aware.

On the face of the legislative material itself, it can be seen that there are a number of differences between Companies Code s556, Corporations Law s592 and Corporations Law s588G.[194] Some of the more interesting differences are these. First, it will be recalled that under Companies Code s556 and Corporations Law s592, liability is imposed where there are reasonable grounds to expect that the company would not be able to pay its debts.[195] Under Corporations Law s588G, it will be sufficient if there are reasonable grounds for suspecting insolvency.[196] The common denominator throughout is the objective standard imported by the use of the words reasonable grounds.[197] The reasonableness of the grounds relied upon must be judged by the standard appropriate to a director of ordinary competence.[198] As Mescher observes:

> The relationship between ss232(4) and 588G(1) was explained when s588G was introduced. The standard attributable to a director who is the subject of an insolvent

---

[192] Australian Law Reform Commission, Report No. 45 (vol 1), *General Insolvency Inquiry* AGPS, Canberra, 1988 at para 325; note Herzberg A, 'Insolvent Trading' (1991) 9 CSLJ 285 at 286.

[193] Cf. *Taylor v Darke* (1992) 10 ACLC 1516; *Holpitt Pty Ltd v Swaab* (1992) 6 ACSR 488; and *Shepherd v Australia and New Zealand Banking Group Ltd* (1996) 20 ACSR 81.

[194] *Stargard Security Systems Pty Ltd v Goldie* (1994) 13 ACSR 805 at 806 per Master Bredmeyer; and *Stanley Street v Retravision (NSW) Pty Ltd* (1995) 13 ACLC 757 at 758 per Gummow J.

[195] *Kong v Pilkington (Australia) Ltd* (1997) 15 ACLC 1561 at 1574-1575 per Owen J (Franklyn and Murray JJ agreed); and *Hawcroft General Trading Co Ltd v Edgar* (1996) 20 ACSR 541 at 548 per Tamberlin J.

[196] Australian Law Reform Commission, Report No. 45 (vol 1), *General Insolvency Inquiry* AGPS, Canberra, 1988 at paras 302-305.

[197] *Rema Industries and Services Pty Ltd v Coad* (1992) 7 ACSR 251 at 258-259 per Lockhart J; see *Group Four Industries Pty Ltd v Brosnan* (1992) 8 ACSR 463 at 512-514 per Debelle J.

[198] *State Government Insurance Corporation v Pollock* (1993) 11 ACSR 333 at 343 per Seaman J; note *3M Australia Pty Ltd v Kemish* (1986) 4 ACLC 185 at 190-191 per Foster J; *Grimm v Roy Galvin & Co Pty Ltd* (1988) 6 ACLC 852; and *Rema Industries and Services Pty Ltd v Coad* (1992) 7 ACSR 251.

trading offence is to be consistent with the general test of care and diligence in s232(4).[199]

Secondly, Corporations Law s588G(3) provides that s588G is a civil penalty provision as defined by Corporations Law s1317DA,[200] so that Corporations Law Part 9.4B provides for civil and criminal consequences of contravening it, or of being involved in a contravention of it.[201] Corporations Law s79 makes it clear that this is to include those who aid and abet any such contravention.[202]

In spite of Lehane J's remarks in *Stoland Pty Ltd v Thurn* that Corporations Law s588H provides for statutory defences in terms which are similar to those found within Corporations Law s592(2),[203] there are important differences.[204] For instance, in order for a director of an Australian company to establish a defence under s588H(2), the onus of which lies on the person seeking to invoke it,[205] it will be necessary to establish that there were reasonable grounds to expect solvency.[206] It is suggested that the ramifications of this change will be significant. It has been held that expecting is synonymous with predicting and is quite different from suspecting.[207] An expectation goes beyond a mere hope or possibility.[208] It implies a measure of confidence in the outcome of what is expected. A prediction that something will happen or turn out. An expectation connotes or implies some form of confidence about the outcome of a situation. In *Carrier Air Conditioning Pty Ltd v Kurda*, Debelle J considered that the meaning of the word expect should not lead to difficulty as it is to be understood, 'according to its usage in ordinary parlance, namely, "to regard as likely to happen" or "to expect to find" or "to expect that it will turn out that".'[209]

To assist with the meaning of suspecting it is helpful to call upon the way in which that word has been interpreted by the Australian courts within the context of Bankruptcy Act 1966 (Cth) s122(4)(c).[210] Decisions upon s122(4)(c) will be authoritative.[211] In *Queensland Bacon Pty Ltd v Rees*, for instance, Kitto J explained the meaning of suspect in the following manner:

---

[199] Mescher B, 'Personal Liability of Company Directors for Company Debts' (1996) 70 ALJ 837 at 839.

[200] *Australian Securities Commission v Forem-Freeway Enterprises Pty Ltd* (1998-1999) 30 ACSR 339 at 341 per Madgwick J.

[201] Ford H A J, Austin R P and Ramsay I M, *Ford's Principles of Corporations Law* (9th ed) Reed International Books Australia Pty Ltd, Sydney, 1999 at para 20.110.

[202] Mescher B, 'Personal Liability of Company Directors for Company Debts' (1996) 70 ALJ 837 at 842.

[203] (1998) 29 ACSR 280 at 282.

[204] *Metropolitan Fire Systems Pty Ltd v Miller* (1997) 23 ACSR 699 at 702 per Einfeld J.

[205] *Androvin v Figliomeni* (1996) 14 ACLC 1461 at 1469 per Owen J (Kennedy and Franklyn JJ agreed); and *Metropolitan Fire Systems Pty Ltd v Miller* (1997) 23 ACSR 699 at 711 per Einfeld J.

[206] Similarly with Corporations Law s588H(3).

[207] *3M Australia Pty Ltd v Kemish* (1986) 4 ACLC 185 at 192 per Foster J; *Commonwealth Bank of Australia v Friedrich* (1991) 9 ACLC 946 at 956-957 per Tadgell J; and *TCN Channel Nine Pty Ltd v Scotney* (1995) 17 ACSR 116 at 118 per Tamberlin J.

[208] *Dunn v Shapowloff* [1978] 2 NSWLR 235 at 249 per Mahoney JA; and *TCN Channel Nine Pty Ltd v Scotney* (1995) 17 ACSR 116 at 118 per Tamberlin J.

[209] (1993) 11 ACSR 247 at 250; note *Amatek Ltd v Botman* (1995) 13 ACLC 1729 at 1742 per Steytler J.

[210] Bankruptcy Act 1966 (Cth) s122(4)(c) qualifies the defence available to a creditor under s122(2) against a claim under s122 that a transaction between the company and the creditor is void as a preference.

[211] Ford H A J, Austin R P and Ramsay I M, *Ford's Principles of Corporations Law* (9th ed) Reed International Books Australia Pty Ltd, Sydney, 1999 at para 20.160.

[The] precise force of the word 'suspect' needs to be noticed. A suspicion that something exists is more than a mere idle wondering whether it exists or not; it is a positive feeling of actual apprehension or mistrust, amounting to 'a slight opinion, but without sufficient evidence' ... Consequently, a reason to suspect that a fact exists is more than a reason to consider or to look into the possibility of its existence.[212]

To suspect something means that the person has a positive feeling of apprehension or mistrust that a situation exists such as the fact that the company is insolvent. The positive feeling may amount to an opinion on the issue, but without sufficient evidence of the matter. Conventional wisdom suggests that to suspect something requires a lower threshold of knowledge or awareness than to expect a state of affairs to exist.[213] This wisdom was recently affirmed by the Federal Court of Australia in *TCN Channel Nine Pty Ltd v Scotney*, where Tamberlin J expressed the following view:

The 'expectation' must be more than a hope, possibility or suspicion. The term is used in the sense of 'to regard as about to happen; to anticipate the occurrence or the coming of' ... By contrast the test used in [Corporations Law] s588G is whether there are reasonable grounds for 'suspecting'. This is a lower threshold than reasonable grounds to 'expect'.[214]

Thus, by enacting Corporations Law Part 5.7B,[215] the Australian Parliament has determined that directors of Australian companies are to focus their minds upon the day-to-day management of their companies,[216] and to familiarise themselves with company financial matters,[217] in a manner not hitherto contemplated in Australian company law. A suspicion of doubtful solvency, therefore, should be sufficient to set the alarm bells ringing. This may go some way towards making the unresolved controversy under discussion in the previous chapter of this book, concerning the point at which insolvency crystallizes, seem less relevant. Today's complex commercial and corporate world demands that its directors actively participate in management.[218] As Mescher notes, 'directors are expected to monitor their company's performance closely and recognise the warning signs of insolvency.'[219] For directors to ignore such counsel is to invite the court to order that they are to assume personal liability for the debts of their insolvent Australian company.[220]

---

[212] (1965-1966) 115 CLR 266 at 303.
[213] *Stoland Pty Ltd v Thurn* (1998) 29 ACSR 280 at 288 per Lehane J.
[214] (1995) 17 ACSR 116 at 118; see *Hawcroft General Trading Co Ltd v Edgar* (1996) 20 ACSR 541 at 548 per Tamberlin J.
[215] Added by Act No. 210 of 1992 and effective 23 June 1993.
[216] *Capricorn Society Ltd v Linke* (1996) 14 ACLC 431 at 438-439 *per curiam*.
[217] *Daniels v Anderson* (1995) 13 ACLC 614 at 662-666 per Clarke and Sheller JJA; cf. *Re Barings plc* [1998] BCC 583 at 586 per Sir Richard Scott VC; and *Re Barings plc (No 5)* [1999] 1 BCLC 433 at 488 per Jonathan Parker J.
[218] Sievers A S, 'The National Safety Council Case' (1991) 9 CSLJ 338 at 338; cf. *Bishopsgate Investment Management Ltd v Maxwell (No. 2)* 1 All ER 261 at 264 per Hoffman LJ, 'the existence of a duty to participate must depend upon how the particular company's business is organised and the part which the director could reasonably have been expected to play.'
[219] Mescher B, 'Personal Liability of Company Directors for Company Debts' (1996) 70 ALJ 837 at 850.
[220] *Australian Securities Commission v Forem-Freeway Enterprises Pty Ltd* (1998-1999) 30 ACSR 339 at 349 per Madgwick J.

It is suggested that Corporations Law s588G does more than former statutory provisions did to expose directors of Australian companies to personal consequences in circumstances where directors fail to meet raised levels of care and diligence required by today's business community. As we have seen, the question of culpability is now to be determined objectively.[221] But not, as we were recently reminded by Jack J in *Re Sherborne Associates Ltd*, with the benefit of hindsight.[222] Whilst this principle is easy to state in practice, its application is somewhat more difficult in English and Australian company law where the court must be alert to the dangers of hindsight, and not fall into the trap of being too wise after the event.[223] In *Re Hitco 2000 Ltd*, for instance, Jules Sher QC[224] addressed the issue of hindsight in this way:

> With hindsight, of course, it is plain that trading should have stopped then, if not before. Nobody is of course gifted with hindsight but I can see very little in the evidence that could, with foresight, have justified continued trading in January 1990.[225]

It is suggested that the defences available under Corporations Law ss588H(2) and 588H(3) are less broad and ambiguous than were the defences available under Companies Code s556 and Corporations Law s592.[226] This is a further distinction between Companies Code s556, Corporations Law s592 and Corporations Law s588G. As a consequence, these defences would seem to hold out little hope for non-participating directors of insolvent Australian companies.[227] The reason, it is suggested, is quite simple. The philosophy and rationale underpinning the introduction of the specific defences in s588H is that directors are to be encouraged to act with reasonable care and diligence and to actively participate in their company's management.[228] Directors are, thus, encouraged to face important issues and to make critical decisions. Those that do are to be given protection. Sections 588H(5) and 588H(6),[229] when read together, oblige a director who has been alerted to the danger that his or her company is insolvent, or near-insolvent, to take positive steps either to have an

---

[221] *Sycotex Pty Ltd v Baseler* (1994) 122 ALR 531 at 539 per Gummow J; *TCN Channel Nine Pty Ltd v Scotney* (1995) 17 ACSR 116 at 118 per Tamberlin J; and *Hawcroft General Trading Co Ltd v Edgar* (1996) 20 ACSR 541 at 548 per Tamberlin J.

[222] [1995] BCC 40 at 54; see *In re Horsley & Weight Ltd* [1982] Ch 442 at 455 per Templeman LJ; and *Re Hitco 2000 Ltd* [1995] BCC 161 at 169 per Jules Sher QC; cf. *Nicholson v Permakraft (NZ) Ltd* [1985] 1 NZLR 242 at 253 per Cooke J; and *Kong v Pilkington (Australia) Ltd* (1997) 15 ACLC 1561 at 1567 per Owen J (Franklyn and Murray JJ agreed); note Commonwealth, House of Representatives, Parliamentary Debates, 3 November 1992 at 2400; see Finch V, 'Company Directors: Who Cares about Skill and Care?' (1992) 55 MLR 179 at 189; and The American Law Institute, *Principles of Corporate Governance: Analysis and Recommendations* St Paul, 1994, volume 1 at 164.

[223] *Re Living Images Ltd* [1996] BCC 112 at 116-117 per Laddie J; and *Facia Footwear Ltd v Hinchliffe* [1998] 1 BCLC 218 at 228 per Sir Richard Scott VC.

[224] Sitting as a deputy High Court Judge.

[225] [1995] BCC 161 at 169.

[226] Trethowan I, 'Directors' Personal Liability for Insolvent Trading: At Last, a Degree of Consensus' (1993) 11 CSLJ 102 at 114-116.

[227] Ford H A J, Austin R P and Ramsay I M, *Ford's Principles of Corporations Law* (9th ed) Reed International Books Australia Pty Ltd, Sydney, 1999 at para 20.180.

[228] Cf. *Re Grayan Building Services Ltd* [1995] BCC 554 at 577 per Neill LJ, 'Those who trade under the regime of limited liability and who avail themselves of the privileges of that regime, must accept the standards of probity and competence to which the law requires company directors to conform.'

[229] Cf. Insolvency Act 1986 (UK) s214(3).

administrator appointed to the company,[230] or to petition for the winding-up of the company.[231]

This brings us to another important and interesting difference between the latest, and the former, statutory provisions; namely, the introduction of company administrators. The appointment of an administrator as part of a voluntary administration procedure is a novelty in Australian company law.[232] During the second reading of the Corporate Law Reform Bill 1992 (Cth) on 3 November 1992, the Attorney-General explained that when a basically sound company faces solvency difficulties what is really needed is a capacity for that company to obtain a breathing-space. Directors will be able to appoint an administrator, 'who will have the benefit of a moratorium on actions against the company while formulating a plan of action for consideration by the creditors.'[233]

This gave rise to Corporations Law s588H(6), the wording of which is deceptively simple. Nevertheless, it calls for drastic action on the part of directors of Australian companies. Although expressly not limited to matters set out in that sub-section, s588H(6) does appear to present the director within its province with a *fait accompli*. On the face of it, there would seem little else that a director could do other than apply for the appointment of an administrator to the company.[234]

Corporations Law s588H(6) would appear to exclude the ability of a director to avoid personal liability by simply speaking against a resolution at a board meeting, at which the transaction relating to the incurring of the debt is discussed, and then voting against the resolution.[235] The director must do more. Were the director to then go on and resign, he or she might escape liability. But it would seem that the section is again asking for more;[236] namely, positive action by the director designed to wrest control of the company away from the current board in favour of an administrator or other court appointed officer.[237] If that be correct then directors are being asked to shoulder novel and rather weighty obligations by virtue of their office.[238] Not too weighty, it is to be hoped, to dissuade others from taking up office as directors.[239] But it should be self-

---

[230] In an attempt to preserve the creditors' interests or possibly even to turn the company around: see *Foxcroft v The Ink Group Pty Ltd* (1994) 12 ACLC 1063.

[231] At which stage notes Trebilcock M J, 'The Liability of Company Directors for Negligence' (1969) 32 MLR 499 at 512, 'the company is usually so hopelessly insolvent that there is little or nothing that can be salvaged'.

[232] Ford H A J, Austin R P and Ramsay I M, *Ford's Principles of Corporations Law* (9th ed) Reed International Books Australia Pty Ltd, Sydney, 1999 at paras 20.198 and 26.020.

[233] Commonwealth, House of Representatives, Parliamentary Debates, 3 November 1992 at 2404.

[234] Cf. *Re Bike World (Wholesale) Pty Ltd* (1991-1992) 6 ACSR 681.

[235] Cf. Trethowan I, 'Directors' Personal Liability for Insolvent Trading: At Last, a Degree of Consensus' (1993) 11 CSLJ 102 at 112.

[236] *Statewide Tobacco Services Ltd v Morley* (1990) 2 ACSR 405 at 422 per Ormiston J; and *Group Four Industries Pty Ltd v Brosnan* (1992) 8 ACSR 463 at 509 per Debelle J.

[237] Cf. *Secretary of State for Trade and Industry v Gash* [1997] 1 BCLC 341 at 346 per Chadwick J.

[238] Note *Wagner v International Health Promotions* (1994) 12 ACLC 986 where Santow J ruled invalid the appointment of an administrator due to the board's failure to resolve that the company was insolvent.

[239] Axworthy C S, 'Corporate Directors – Who Needs Them?' (1988) 51 MLR 273 at 275; and Dwight F, 'Liability of Corporate Directors' (1907-1908) 17 YLJ 33 at 36, 'The canons of directorial responsibility are asserted bravely but almost invariably with a countervailing insistence upon preventing alarm to conscientious directors.'; note *The Australian Financial Review*, 2 January 1996; cf. *The Times*, 29 April 1999; see *In re Forest of Dean Coal Mining Company* (1879) 10 Ch D 450 at 451 per Jessel MR; and *Macquarie Bank Ltd v Fociri Pty Ltd* (1992) 10 ACLC 785 at 797 per Kirby P, 'There must be limits [to the imposition of greater liability] ... lest the brilliant idea which lay behind the separate legal personality of the corporation is undone to the disadvantage of the venturesome entrepreneurial spirit which is essential to driving a modern economy with its need for risk-taking'.

evident that these are very real concerns for today's directors of Australian companies as the implications for them are profound. So too for their English counterparts,[240] as the next chapter of this book will attest.

THE WAY FORWARD

English and Australian company law has evolved to the point where directors of British and Australian companies owe statutory, and non-statutory, duties to take into account their company's creditors' interests in the context of insolvency.[241] These duties have been briefly considered in this and the previous chapter, and will be considered further in the next chapter of this book. Insofar as Corporations Law s588G is concerned, it is suggested that the Australian courts will interpret the statutory duty in this regard by building upon earlier decisions; and, by doing so, give effect to the, 'Intention of the Legislature.'[242] For, as we argued in chapter three of this book in respect to Corporations Law s232(4), the legislative intent behind that section was to partially codify current judicial trends to that point.[243] This is equally true of s588G.

It is suggested that Corporations Law s588G is essentially a reflection of current judicial trends and was enacted *inter alia* in response to the strong and clear message sounded by the Australian judiciary in recent years.[244] Section 588G governs the liability imposed upon directors of Australian companies in the case of debts incurred by an insolvent company after 23 June 1993.[245] Given that the sixth anniversary of s588G has only recently arrived, there is an insubstantial body of jurisprudence directly upon it at this stage.[246] In spite of that, however, we can be confident that when more authoritative cases roll off the judicial press, espousing the views of the superior courts

---

[240] Insolvency Act 1986 (UK) s214(3); cf. Company Directors Disqualification Act 1986 (UK) ss6, 8 and 10.

[241] E.g., *Walker v Wimborne* (1976-1977) 137 CLR 1 at 7 per Mason J; *Lonrho Ltd v Shell Petroleum Co Ltd* [1980] 1 WLR 627 at 634 per Lord Diplock; *Kinsela v Russell Kinsela Pty Ltd* [1986] 4 NSWLR 722 at 727 and 730-733 per Street CJ; *Winkworth v Edward Baron Development Co Ltd* [1987] 1 All ER 114 at 118 per Lord Templeman; *Liquidator of West Mercia Safetywear Ltd v Dodd* (1988) 4 BCC 30 at 32 per Dillon LJ (Croom-Johnson LJ and Caulfield J agreed); *Australian Growth Resources Corporation Pty Ltd v van Reesema* (1988) 6 ACLC 529 at 535-536 per King CJ (Cox J agreed); *Jeffree v National Companies & Securities Commission* (1989) 15 ACLR 217 at 221-222 per Wallace J and at 227-228 per Brinsden J (Pidgeon J agreed with both); *Chew v The Queen* (1991) 4 WAR 21 at 49 per Malcolm CJ; *Vrisakis v Australian Securities Commission* (1992-1993) 9 WAR 395 at 450 per Ipp J (Malcolm CJ agreed); *Equiticorp Finance Ltd v Bank of New Zealand* (1993) 11 ACLC 952 at 1015 per Clarke and Cripps JJA; and *Glandon Pty Ltd v Strata Consolidated Pty Ltd* (1993) 11 ACSR 543 at 557 per Cripps JA; note Insolvency Act 1986 (UK) ss212-214; and Corporations Law s588G.

[242] *Salomon v A Salomon and Company Ltd* [1897] AC 22 at 38 per Lord Watson, 'a common but very slippery phrase'.

[243] Cf. Law Commission, *Company Directors: Regulating Conflicts of Interests and Formulating a Statement of Duties* HMSO, London, Cm 4436, 1999 at paras 4.48, 4.68, 5.19-5.20 and 5.38.

[244] *Morley v Statewide Tobacco Services Ltd* (1992) 8 ACSR 305; *Commonwealth Bank of Australia v Friedrich* (1991) 5 ACSR 115; and *AWA Ltd v Daniels* (1992) 10 ACLC 933; note Explanatory memorandum, *Corporate Law Reform Bill 1992* CCH Australia Ltd, Sydney, 1992 at 25.

[245] *Quick v Stoland Pty Ltd* (1998) 29 ACSR 130 at 142 per Finkelstein J (Branson and Emmett JJ agreed); and *Metropolitan Fire Systems Pty Ltd v Miller* (1997) 23 ACSR 699 at 701 per Einfeld J.

[246] E.g., *Stargard Security Systems Pty Ltd v Goldie* (1994) 13 ACSR 805; *TCN Channel Nine Pty Ltd v Scotney* (1995) 17 ACSR 116; *Metropolitan Fire Systems Pty Ltd v Miller* (1997) 23 ACSR 699; *Quick v Stoland Pty Ltd* (1998) 29 ACSR 130; *Stoland Pty Ltd v Thurn* (1998) 29 ACSR 280; and *Australian Securities Commission v Forem-Freeway Enterprises Pty Ltd* (1998-1999) 30 ACSR 339.

in Australia, the raised levels of directorial responsibility and greater accountability achieved to date in Australian company law will not only be reinforced, but also advanced.[247] Those cases are eagerly awaited.

In the meantime, without much in the way of specific judicial guidance as to the way in which the many facets of Corporations Law ss588G and 588H will be applied, the prudent director would be well advised to follow the path laid out by the Australian appellate courts in *Morley v Statewide Tobacco Services Ltd*,[248] *Group Four Industries Pty Ltd v Brosnan*[249] and *Carrier Air Conditioning Pty Ltd v Kurda*.[250] A path recently reaffirmed by the South Australian Full Court[251] in *Capricorn Society Ltd v Linke*,[252] and by the Western Australian Full Court[253] in *Androvin v Figliomeni*.[254] A prudent director, seeking to rely upon the statutory defence provided by ss588H(5) and 588H(6), should take the steps referred to in s588H(6) and have an administrator appointed to the company.[255] While this may seem a little draconian at first, it is often better to tread cautiously and allow others to test the water. The prudent director ought, therefore, be content to allow the courts to establish, at the imprudent director's expense, the guidelines to be followed in applying the sub-section; for, it is well known that: *vis consili expers mole ruit sua.*

In the explanatory memorandum which accompanied the release of the Corporate Law Reform Bill 1992 (Cth), the Australian Government recognised that corporate decisions involve risk-taking. The Government, it explained, was aware that courts had in the past: (i) recognised that directors are not liable for honest errors of judgment;[256] (ii) shown a reluctance to review business judgments taken in good faith;[257] and (iii) exercised their discretion to excuse directors who have acted honestly and who ought fairly to be excused.[258] As a consequence, therefore, and in keeping with parliamentary intent, in the interpretation of Corporations Law ss588G and 588H, the Australian courts will need to balance the activities of an entrepreneurial director against the imposition of responsibilities and obligations thought necessary to promote fairness between the competing interests which make up the company as a whole.

---

[247] Noble T, 'When Does a Company Incur a Debt Under the Insolvent Trading Provisions of the Corporations Law?' (1994) 12 CSLJ 297 at 298.

[248] (1992) 8 ACSR 305.

[249] (1992) 8 ACSR 463.

[250] (1993) 11 ACSR 247.

[251] (Lander, Cox and Perry JJ).

[252] (1996) 14 ACLC 431.

[253] (Kennedy, Franklyn and Owen JJ).

[254] (1996) 14 ACLC 1461 at 1468 per Owen J (Kennedy and Franklyn JJ agreed).

[255] Cf. *Velkovski v Ryan* (1996) 19 ACSR 514.

[256] Ford H A J and Austin R P, *Ford's Principles of Corporations Law* (6th ed) Butterworths Pty Ltd, Sydney, 1992 at 528-529.

[257] *Wayde v New South Wales Rugby League Ltd* (1985) 3 ACLC 799 at 805 per Brennan J; see *Howard Smith Ltd v Ampol Petroleum Ltd* [1974] AC 821 at 832 per Lord Wilberforce; *Shuttleworth v Cox Brothers and Company (Maidenhead) Ltd* [1927] 2 KB 9 at 23-24 per Scrutton LJ; *Peters' American Delicacy Company Ltd v Heath* (1938-1939) 61 CLR 457 at 481 per Latham CJ; and *Harlowe's Nominees Pty Ltd v Woodside (Lakes Entrance) Oil Company NL* (1969-1970) 121 CLR 483 at 493 *per curiam.*

[258] *Perrins v Bellamy* [1899] 1 Ch 797 at 801 per Lindley MR (Romer LJ agreed); *In re Claridge's Patent Asphalte Company Ltd* [1921] 1 Ch 543 at 548-549 per Astbury J; *In re Duomatic Ltd* [1969] 2 Ch 365 at 377 per Buckley J; *Re Welfab Engineers Ltd* [1990] BCC 600 at 604 per Hoffmann J; and *Neptune (Vehicle Washing Equipment) Ltd v Fitzgerald (No. 2)* [1995] BCC 1000 at 1021 per A G Steinfeld QC (sitting as a deputy Chancery Judge); note Corporations Law s1318 which contains such a provision; cf. Companies Act 1985 (UK) s727.

It is important to recognise that a successful business depends upon an entrepreneurial spirit which demands a certain amount of risk-taking.[259] Conceptually, few would baulk at that. The difficulty, however, creeps in when one tries to marry risk-taking with an obligation on the part of directors to consider their company's creditors' interests. Such a marriage is not made in heaven as competing interests are involved.[260] Sealy appreciated the argument that conventional English and Australian company theory is predicated on the concept of risk-taking when he expressed, contextually, the following view:

> What the law has to ensure is that the risks which that company elects to embrace fall within the range of legitimate business risks, consistently with the expectations of all those whose interests are at stake, creditors and members alike.[261]

By enacting Corporations Law Part 5.7B, the Australian Parliament is progressing the Australian Government towards its stated goal; namely, an integrated code of Australian company law detailing the overall duties owed by directors as a function of modern corporate life.[262] It is suggested that the implementation of Part 5.7B is merely one aspect of a much bigger whole.[263] Within chapter three of this book, a similar viewpoint was expressed in respect to Corporations Law s232(4). The same applies to Corporations Law s232(2). From this book's treatment of the relevant cases, and from its consideration of Hansard and the various reports, it clearly emerges that statutory duties upon directors of Australian companies are to be viewed as falling within, and comprising an integral part of, an overall legislative scheme designed to usher in a new era of corporate regulation under a national regulatory regime, 'that can guarantee a sound and well regulated environment for corporate activity.'[264]

By its enactment of Corporations Law s588G,[265] the Australian Parliament has undoubtedly introduced a novel concept within the traditional framework of directors' duties.[266] The implementation of a statutory duty upon directors to prevent insolvent trading by their Australian companies, in conjunction with those statutory, and non-statutory, duties explored in the previous chapters of this book, and to be explored in chapters eight and nine of this book, will provide the Australian judiciary with a flexible and powerful array of remedies in order to combat directorial misconduct and

---

[259] *Macquarie Bank Ltd v Fociri Pty Ltd* (1992) 10 ACLC 785 at 797 per Kirby P; and *Vrisakis v Australian Securities Commission* (1992-1993) 9 WAR 395 at 449-450 per Ipp J (Malcolm CJ agreed); note Sealy L S, 'Directors' "Wider" Responsibilities – Problems Conceptual, Practical and Procedural' (1987) 13 MULR 164 at 176; Sealy L S, 'The Director as Trustee' [1967] CLJ 83 at 89; The American Law Institute, *Principles of Corporate Governance: Analysis and Recommendations* St Paul, 1994, volume 1 at 174; and Commonwealth, House of Representatives, Parliamentary Debates, 3 November 1992 at 2402.

[260] *Facia Footwear Ltd v Hinchliffe* [1998] 1 BCLC 218 at 228 per Sir Richard Scott VC.

[261] Sealy L S, 'Directors' "Wider" Responsibilities – Problems Conceptual, Practical and Procedural' (1987) 13 MULR 164 at 181.

[262] Cf. *Metal Manufacturers Ltd v Lewis* (1987-1988) 13 ACLR 357 at 360 per Kirby P.

[263] *Capricorn Society Ltd v Linke* (1996) 14 ACLC 431 at 438-439 *per curiam*.

[264] Commonwealth, House of Representatives, Parliamentary Debates, 8 November 1990 at 3669; cf. Explanatory memorandum, *Corporate Law Economic Reform Program Bill 1998* CCH Australia Ltd, Sydney, 1999 at para 2.5; see *Metal Manufacturers Ltd v Lewis* (1987-1988) 13 ACLR 357 at 360 per Kirby P; and *Hawkins v Bank of China* (1992) 26 NSWLR 562 at 573-574 per Kirby P.

[265] Added by Act No. 210 of 1992 and effective 23 June 1993.

[266] Noble T, 'When Does a Company Incur a Debt Under the Insolvent Trading Provisions of the Corporations Law?' (1994) 12 CSLJ 297 at 297.

decision-making. In contrast, in English company law there is no corresponding duty upon directors of British companies to prevent insolvent trading. As Chadwick J in *Secretary of State for Trade and Industry v Gash* observed:

> The companies legislation does not impose on directors a statutory duty to ensure that their company does not trade while insolvent; nor does that legislation impose an obligation to ensure that the company does not trade at a loss.[267]

In spite of this, the introduction into English company law of the CDD Act and the IA 1986, and the frequency with which the English courts are today approached for declaratory relief in respect to these Acts,[268] has endowed the English judiciary with effective measures designed to, 'protect the public, and in particular potential creditors of companies, from losing money through companies becoming insolvent when the directors of those companies are people unfit to be concerned in the management of a company.'[269] Thus, notwithstanding the absence from the British statute books of a statutory duty upon directors to prevent insolvent trading by their British companies, revived and refashioned traditional legal rules and equitable principles,[270] which boast a long and distinguished pedigree in English company law, coupled with the limited but effective measures provided for under the CDD Act and the IA 1986,[271] do provide the English judiciary with an array of remedies comparable to those which their Australian counterparts have become accustomed to deploying. In chapters eight and nine of this book, some of the more controversial and effective of these remedies will be considered.

---

[267] [1997] 1 BCLC 341 at 348.

[268] Comptroller and Auditor General, *The Insolvency Service Executive Agency: Company Director Disqualification – A Follow Up Report* The Stationery Office Ltd, London, 1999 at paras 1.6 and 1.15.

[269] *Re Sevenoaks Stationers (Retail) Ltd* [1990] BCC 765 at 773 per Dillon LJ (Butler-Sloss and Staughton LJJ agreed); note *Re Grayan Building Services Ltd* [1995] BCC 554 at 577 per Henry LJ; *Re Richborough Furniture Ltd* [1996] BCC 155 at 166 per Timothy Lloyd QC; *Re Continental Assurance Co of London plc* [1997] 1 BCLC 48 at 59 per Chadwick J; and *Re Blackspur Group plc* [1998] 1 BCLC 676 at 680 and 688 per Lord Woolf MR (Millett and Mummery LJJ agreed).

[270] Cf. Malcolm D, 'Directors' Duties: The Governing Principles' in Ramsay I M (ed), *Corporate Governance and the Duties of Company Directors* The Centre for Corporate Law and Securities Regulation, University of Melbourne, Parkville, 1997 at 60 and 80.

[271] *Re Blackspur Group plc* [1998] 1 BCLC 676 at 681 per Lord Woolf MR (Millett and Mummery LJJ agreed).

8

Statutory Intervention: Disqualifying Directors and the Payment of Compensation

INTRODUCTION

Legislative reform in English company law in the area of directors' duties has remained relatively static over the past decade or so.[1] This has been in contrast to the active legislative reform programs regularly undertaken by the Australian Parliament in Australian company law throughout the corresponding period.[2] The preference in English company law, as the previous chapters of this book have demonstrated, has been to leave to the English courts the control of directorial misconduct by largely relying upon traditional remedies, 'determined by extensive and complex case law which does not find expression in the Act.'[3] *A fortiori* where directors have breached duties to act honestly, in good faith and for proper purposes on the one hand, and to exercise care and diligence on the other hand.

Where the British Parliament has seen fit to statutorily intervene in English company law in order to bring to account errant directors, has been in the context of insolvency. It is this significant statutory intervention, relevantly enacted in 1986,[4] which permits the disqualification of directors from holding office and also the payment of compensation to their companies for their directorial misconduct, that this chapter is largely concerned with. This statutory intervention represents, as Prentice observes, 'one of the most important developments in company law this century.'[5]

Directors of British companies who fall foul of such provisions, relevantly those contained within Insolvency Act 1986 (UK) ('IA 1986') Part IV Chapter X, may be disqualified from acting as directors or taking part in the management of a company[6] for up to 15 years[7] by virtue of the Company Directors Disqualification Act 1986 (UK)

---

[1] Davies P L, *Gower's Principles of Modern Company Law* (6th ed) Sweet & Maxwell Ltd, London, 1997 at v.

[2] E.g., Corporations Legislation Amendment Act 1991 (Cth); Corporate Law Reform Act 1992 (Cth); Corporate Law Reform Act 1994 (Cth); First Corporate Law Simplification Act 1995 (Cth); Company Law Review Act 1998 (Cth); Managed Investments Act 1998 (Cth); and Financial Sector Reform (Amendments and Transitional Provisions) Act 1998. Moreover, fresh initiatives are to be re-introduced into the Australian Parliament with the Corporate Law Economic Reform Program Bill 1998 (Cth) expected to be enacted in the first half of 2000.

[3] Report of the Company Law Committee, HMSO, London, Cmnd 1749, 1962 at para 86.

[4] Company Directors Disqualification Act 1986 (UK); and Insolvency Act 1986 (UK).

[5] Prentice D D, 'Creditor's Interests and Director's Duties' (1990) 10 OJLS 265 at 277.

[6] Cf. Corporations Law s91A.

[7] Companies Act 1981 (UK) s93 increased the maximum period of a disqualification order from five years to 15 years.

('CDD Act').[8] The CDD Act provides a number of grounds for the disqualification of errant directors. In some respects these overlap. For example, that which might ground an application under CDD Act ss2, 3 or 4 might also constitute 'unfitness' for the purposes of CDD Act s6. Unfitness in the context of s6, as Jonathan Parker J in *Re Barings plc (No 5)* recently explained, 'may be shown by conduct which is dishonest (including conduct showing a want of probity or integrity) or by conduct which is merely incompetent.'[9] This will be enlarged upon a little later in this chapter. Furthermore, where a court makes a declaration under either IA 1986 ss213 or 214 that the person concerned is to make such contribution to the company's assets considered appropriate in the circumstances, the court may also, by virtue of CDD Act s10(1), make a disqualification order against the person to whom the declaration relates.[10]

Generally, however, proceedings under the CDD Act and those under the IA 1986 are discrete. It will usually fall to the Secretary of State for Trade and Industry ('Secretary of State') to initiate disqualification proceedings under the CDD Act. Applications under IA 1986 ss212-214, on the other hand, are usually brought by the liquidator of the company concerned. In this way, therefore, the English courts are able to redress instances of egregious behaviour on the part of directors for their misconduct and decision-making and, by doing so, generally raise the, 'standards of probity and competence to which the law requires company directors to conform.'[11]

Whilst there are statutory provisions that have a similar effect in Australian company law,[12] detailed analysis of them is outside the remit of this book. However, at the end of this chapter we will look briefly at the recent experience of the radical civil penalty provisions introduced into Australian company law by Corporations Law Part 9.4B;[13] pursuant to which errant directors may be prohibited from managing a company, and the payment of compensation from errant directors can be ordered.[14]

One of the features of modern English and Australian company law has been the recognition by the British and Australian Parliaments that what is needed in corporate regulation is a watchdog empowered to take action on behalf of companies and their shareholders by investigations, inspections and the institution of civil and criminal proceedings.[15] In the English company law field that watchdog is the Department of Trade and Industry ('DTI'),[16] the government department responsible since 1970 for English company law, and now also for the administration of the IA 1986 and the CDD Act.[17] Thus, in many of the cases involving these Acts, it is the Secretary of State who initiates proceedings. In the related field of English financial services law that watchdog is the Financial Services Authority.[18] In Australian company law that responsibility falls

---

[8]   Company Directors Disqualification Act 1986 (UK) ss2, 4, 6 and 10.
[9]   [1999] 1 BCLC 433 at 483.
[10]   *Re Brian D Pierson (Contractors) Ltd* [1999] BCC 26 at 58 per Hazel Williamson QC (sitting as a deputy High Court Judge).
[11]   *Re Grayan Building Services Ltd* [1995] BCC 554 at 577 per Neill LJ.
[12]   E.g., Corporations Law ss229, 230, 588J, 588K, 588M, 592, 596, 598, 599, 600 and 1317EA(3).
[13]   Added by Act No. 210 of 1992 and effective 1 February 1993.
[14]   Corporations Law s1317EA(3); see *ASC v Donovan* (1998) 28 ACSR 583.
[15]   Cf. Company Law Amendment Committee, HMSO, London, Cmd 2657, 1926 at paras 58 and 60.
[16]   Formerly the Board of Trade; see Report of the Company Law Committee, HMSO, London, Cmnd 1749, 1962 at para 505.
[17]   Davies P L, *Gower's Principles of Modern Company Law* (6th ed) Sweet & Maxwell Ltd, London, 1997 at 53 and 679.
[18]   Financial Services Act 1986 (UK).

to the Australian Securities and Investments Commission ('ASIC'),[19] which has enjoyed a widened remit since 1 July 1998.[20]

Within Australian company law statutory intervention is playing an increasingly important role. That is evident from the earlier chapters in this book. In the context of insolvency, for example, Corporations Law Part 5.7B establishes a novel regime whereby the company's liquidator may seek compensation from an errant director who has been in breach of Corporations Law s588G by permitting the company to trade while insolvent.[21] The effect of Part 5.7B is to reinstate traditional principles of insolvency law by discouraging independent actions brought directly against directors of Australian companies by the insolvent company's creditors, although expressly permitting them in defined limited circumstances,[22] thus enabling a *pari passu* distribution of assets in keeping with such traditional principles and the statutory scheme of liquidation.[23]

British companies legislation on the other hand does not impose on directors of British companies a statutory duty to ensure that their company does not trade whilst insolvent. Where directors do permit their company to trade whilst insolvent, they run the risk of becoming personally liable for the amount, 'by which the company's assets can be discerned to have been depleted by the director's conduct',[24] and being prosecuted by the Secretary of State under the CDD Act for their disqualification.[25] By virtue of the provisions within the IA 1986,[26] the director concerned may well find himself or herself engaged in litigation with the company's liquidator who, like his or her Australian counterpart, will be seeking to recover the company's assets to permit a *pari passu* distribution of assets in order to satisfy time-honoured principles of equality within insolvency law.[27]

The distinction between English and Australian company law in this respect, therefore, is the absence in England of any duty upon directors to prevent their companies from trading whilst insolvent; a duty statutorily imposed upon directors of Australian companies.[28] Thus, in English company law directors may properly take the view that it is in the interests of the company and of its creditors that, although insolvent, the company should continue to trade out of its difficulties.[29] This point was

---

[19]   Ford H A J, Austin R P and Ramsay I M, *Ford's Principles of Corporations Law* (9th ed) Reed International Books Australia Pty Ltd, Sydney, 1999 at paras 3.060, 3.120 and 3.140.

[20]   Australian Securities and Investments Commission Act 1989 (Cth) s1, amended by Act No. 54 of 1998 and effective 1 July 1998.

[21]   Added by Act No. 210 of 1992 and effective 23 June 1993.

[22]   Corporations Law ss588M, 588P, 588R, 588S, 588T and 588U.

[23]   *Re Esal (Commodities) Ltd* [1997] 1 BCLC 705 at 715 per Peter Gibson LJ (Hirst and Ralph Gibson LJJ agreed); cf. Corporations Law ss588J, 588K, 588M, 588N and 588Y.

[24]   *Re Produce Marketing Consortium Ltd* (1989) 5 BCC 569 at 597 per Knox J; see *Re Purpoint Ltd* [1991] BCC 121 at 128 per Vinelott J.

[25]   Company Directors Disqualification Act 1986 (UK) ss2, 4, 6, 8 and 10.

[26]   Insolvency Act 1986 (UK) ss212-214.

[27]   *Re Oasis Merchandising Services Ltd* [1997] BCC 282 at 291 *per curiam*; cf. Insolvency Act 1986 (UK) s107; note Villiers C, 'Employees as creditors: a challenge for justice in insolvency law' (1999) 20 Co Law 222 at 228; and Schulte R, 'Corporate groups and the equitable subordination of claims on insolvency' (1997) 18 Co Law 2 at 2 and 11.

[28]   Corporations Law s588G; see *Metropolitan Fire Systems Pty Ltd v Miller* (1997) 23 ACSR 699 at 701-703 per Einfeld J; and *Australian Securities Commission v Forem-Freeway Enterprises Pty Ltd* (1998-1999) 30 ACSR 339 at 340-341 per Madgwick J.

[29]   Cf. Prentice D D, 'Creditor's Interests and Director's Duties' (1990) 10 OJLS 265 at 265.

made by Chadwick J in *Secretary of State for Trade and Industry v Gash* where his Lordship went on to say of directors in such circumstances that:

> They may properly take the view that it is in the interests of the company and its creditors that some loss-making trade should be accepted in anticipation of future profitability. They are not to be criticised if they give effect to such view. But the legislation imposes on directors the risk that trading while insolvent may lead to personal liability. Section 214 of the Insolvency Act imposes that liability where the director knew, or ought to have concluded, that there was no reasonable prospect that the company would avoid going into insolvent liquidation.[30]

However, liability may personally attach to an errant director in the context of insolvency in the event that the company's assets were depleted at the expense of its creditors in circumstances where the director concerned: (i) was guilty of any misfeasance or breach of duty to the company;[31] (ii) intended to defraud the company's creditors;[32] or (iii) permitted that through lack of reasonable diligence.[33] In such circumstances, the director concerned will not only be liable to make good the company's assets, or at least make a contribution to them, but may also be liable to disqualification.[34] Generally speaking, however, outside CDD Act s10(1),[35] such proceedings are discrete and the applicants are different.

The statutory machinery for achieving this within English company law is largely procedural in nature and capable, therefore, of somewhat less controversial application than remedies which other breaches of fiduciary, legal and equitable duties are currently attracting.[36] These remedies are the subject of the next chapter of this book. Nonetheless, given the increasing use to which disqualification orders are being put by the English judiciary today, and the effect that that is having upon errant directors by indirectly extending the duty to exercise care and diligence,[37] it is instructive to briefly consider four major reviews upon relevant aspects of English company law and insolvency law completed in England between 1926 and 1982,[38] and the resultant

---

[30] [1997] 1 BCLC 341 at 349; see *Simar Transit Mixers Pty Ltd v Baryczka* (1998) 28 ACSR 238 at 243-244 per Doyle CJ; cf. *Metropolitan Fire Systems Pty Ltd v Miller* (1997) 23 ACSR 699 at 710 per Einfeld J.

[31] Insolvency Act 1986 (UK) s212; cf. Companies Act 1985 (UK) s458.

[32] Insolvency Act 1986 (UK) s213.

[33] *Ibid* at s214.

[34] Company Directors Disqualification Act 1986 (UK) ss2, 4, 6 and 10; see, e.g., *Re Barings plc (No 5)* [1999] 1 BCLC 433.

[35] *Re Brian D Pierson (Contractors) Ltd* [1999] BCC 26 at 58 per Hazel Williamson QC (sitting as a deputy High Court Judge).

[36] E.g., *Kelly v Cooper* [1993] AC 205; *Clark Boyce v Mouat* [1994] 1 AC 428; *Attorney General for Hong Kong v Reid* [1994] 1 All ER 1; *Target Holdings Ltd v Redferns* [1995] 3 All ER 785; *Bristol and West Building Society v Mothew* [1996] 4 All ER 698; *Swindle v Harrison* [1997] 4 All ER 705; and *Westdeutsche Landesbank Girozentrale v Islington London Borough Council* [1996] AC 669.

[37] Gower L C B, *Gower's Principles of Modern Company Law* (5th ed) Sweet & Maxwell Ltd, London, 1992 at 589.

[38] Company Law Amendment Committee, HMSO, London, Cmd 2657, 1926; Report of the Committee on Company Law Amendment, HMSO, London, Cmd 6659, 1945; Report of the Company Law Committee, HMSO, London, Cmnd 1749, 1962; and Report of the Review Committee on Insolvency Law and Practice, HMSO, London, Cmnd 8558, 1982.

legislation which now impacts upon directors of British companies in the light of those reviews.[39]

MAJOR REVIEWS UPON COMPANY LAW AND INSOLVENCY LAW

The Greene Committee was appointed at the beginning of 1925,[40] under the chairmanship of Wilfrid Greene KC, to consider and report what amendments were then considered desirable insofar as the Companies Acts 1908 to 1917 (UK) were concerned. This was the first general review of the operation of the Companies Acts in 20 years.[41] The Committee presented its report on 8 May 1926 ('Greene Report'). In general terms, the Committee considered that the system of English company law and practice then in force had gradually evolved to meet the needs of the British community at large and the commercial community in particular. It was felt that English company law had stood the test of years, was well understood by those who were accustomed to dealing with it and should not, therefore, be altered unnecessarily.[42]

Within the context of private companies, the Greene Committee was satisfied that the great majority were honestly conducted. The Committee considered that much of the criticism to which private companies were then subjected was, 'directed to cases of fraudulent trading by undischarged bankrupts and others through the medium of a private company and cases of directors holding debentures which they enforce at a time convenient to themselves'.[43] Whilst the Committee felt that no alteration of the law was desirable to meet the special case of private companies,[44] nonetheless in the area of fraudulent trading the Greene Report relevantly recommended that:

> Where in the course of winding up a company it appears that any business of the company has been carried on with the intent to defraud creditors of the company or of any other company or person or for any fraudulent or illegal purpose the Court should be empowered upon the application of the official receiver or of the liquidator or of any creditor or contributory to declare that all or any of the responsible directors of the company present or past shall be subject to unlimited personal liability in respect of all or any of the debts or other liabilities of the company and to make any necessary consequential orders for the purpose of enforcing such liability.[45]

The Greene Report followed up this recommendation for amendment to the existing British companies legislation, by also recommending that:

> Where the Court makes a declaration under this section or where there has been a conviction the Court should be empowered to order that the person affected by the declaration or conviction shall not without the leave of the Court be a director of or

---

[39] Company Directors Disqualification Act 1986 (UK); and Insolvency Act 1986 (UK).
[40] By minutes dated 6 January 1925 and 19 February 1925.
[41] Company Law Amendment Committee, HMSO, London, Cmd 2657, 1926 at 3.
[42] *Ibid* at 4.
[43] *Ibid* at para 86.
[44] *Ibid.*
[45] *Ibid* at para 62, 1(a).

in any way directly or indirectly be concerned or take part in the management of a company for a period not exceeding five years.[46]

These recommendations were spawned out of the concern which the Greene Committee had in circumstances where the director controlling the company held a floating charge over the company's assets and then, in the knowledge that the company is on the verge of liquidation, 'fills up' his security by means of goods obtained on credit and then appoints a receiver.[47] That state of affairs was, in the Committee's view, unsatisfactorily dealt with by the law as it then stood. In such circumstances, therefore, it was considered necessary on the part of the Committee that that person should not only be found guilty of fraudulent trading, but that, 'trading of this character should be made a criminal offence in the directors in so far as it may not be one already, and should be a ground for disqualification to act as a director ... for a period of years.'[48] Insofar as disqualification is concerned, that has now come to pass.[49]

The second major review commenced on 26 June 1943 when the Cohen Committee was appointed. It was asked to consider and report what major amendments were then considered desirable in the Companies Act 1929 (UK) and, in particular, to review the requirements prescribed in regard to the formation and affairs of companies and the safeguards afforded for investors and for the public interest. The Committee was chaired by Mr Justice Lionel Cohen and presented its report on 11 June 1945 ('Cohen Report').[50] In respect to Companies Act 1929 (UK) s275, the Cohen Report vainly recommended that a new s275A be added in these terms:

> If in the course of a winding-up it appears that any director or other officer of the company, past or present, has committed any breach of duty in respect of the management of the affairs of the company, the Court, on the application of the official receiver or the liquidator or any creditor or contributory of the company, may, if it thinks proper so to do, declare that that person shall not, without the leave of the Court, be a director of or in any way, whether directly or indirectly, be concerned in or take part in the management of a company for such period, not exceeding five years.[51]

The third major review warranting mention began with the appointment of the Jenkins Committee on 10 December 1959. The Committee's mandate was to review and report upon the provisions and working of *inter alia* the Companies Act 1948 (UK) and to consider in the light of modern conditions and practices then prevailing what should be the duties of directors and the rights of shareholders, and generally to recommend what changes in the law were then considered desirable. The Committee was chaired by Lord Jenkins and presented its report on 30 May 1962 ('Jenkins Report').[52] In its review, the Committee acknowledged that:

---

[46]   *Ibid* at para 62, 1(e).
[47]   *Ibid* at para 61.
[48]   *Ibid*.
[49]   Insolvency Act 1986 (UK) s213; Companies Act 1985 (UK) s458; and Company Directors Disqualification Act 1986 (UK) ss2, 4, 6 and 10; cf. Corporations Law ss229, 230, 588J, 588K, 588M, 592, 596, 598, 599 and 600.
[50]   Report of the Committee on Company Law Amendment, HMSO, London, Cmd 6659, 1945.
[51]   *Ibid* at 97 para XI(1).
[52]   Report of the Company Law Committee, HMSO, London, Cmnd 1749, 1962.

There is widespread criticism that the Companies Act as a whole does not at present deal adequately with the situation arising from fraud and incompetence on the part of directors – particularly directors of insolvent companies.[53]

The Jenkins Committee was of the view that English company law would benefit were legislation enacted to permit disqualification of directors in circumstances where they had been: (i) persistently in default in complying with the provisions of the Companies Act; or (ii) shown to have acted recklessly or incompetently in relation to the affairs of any company of which they are or were directors.[54] By legislating in this respect, the Committee believed that, 'a major point of criticism in this field will be met.'[55] Whilst the Jenkins Report recommended an expansion of existing provisions to include directors who could be shown to have acted 'recklessly or incompetently' in relation to the affairs of their companies,[56] those proposals were never implemented by the British Parliament.

The last, and most significant, review for present purposes was that chaired by Sir Kenneth Cork. On 27 January 1977, the Cork Committee was appointed to carry out a fundamental and exhaustive reappraisal of all aspects of the insolvency laws in England and Wales at a time when no comprehensive statement of insolvency law was then in existence: merely, 'a patchwork of materials dealing with the subject.'[57] The Committee undertook its task at a time when the technical state of the law and its objectives were both in disarray.[58] Its final report was presented in June 1982 ('Cork Report'). Within its terms of reference, the Committee identified the two main means by which it considered financial compensation might be obtained by the company, or its creditors, for any damage or loss sustained in consequence of misconduct by the directors of an insolvent company. The Cork Report recognised that proceedings could be brought for: (i) misfeasance or breach of trust in relation to the company under Companies Act 1948 (UK) s333; and (ii) fraudulent trading under Companies Act 1948 (UK) s332.[59]

When Companies Act 1948 (UK) s333 was enacted, it was intended to provide a quick mechanism for bringing before the English courts civil claims against those who had been concerned with the affairs of a company and who had been guilty of a breach of a fiduciary duty owed to it. The Cork Committee expressed the view that the law as it then stood was sufficiently flexible to enable a liquidator to recover compensation from errant directors of an insolvent company in respect of a broad range of breaches of fiduciary duty. However, in certain situations, the Committee considered that the law was powerless to intervene. For example, where the director's misfeasance or breach of trust was instigated or ratified by the shareholders, and also where the company was insolvent, but its directors permitted it to continue to trade and to obtain further credit.[60]

---

[53] *Ibid* at para 497.
[54] *Ibid* at para 498.
[55] *Ibid* at para 499.
[56] *Ibid* at para 498.
[57] Report of the Review Committee on Insolvency Law and Practice, HMSO, London, Cmnd 8558, 1982 at para 26.
[58] Finch V, 'The Measures of Insolvency Law' (1997) 17 OJLS 227 at 228.
[59] Report of the Review Committee on Insolvency Law and Practice, HMSO, London, Cmnd 8558, 1982 at para 1753.
[60] *Ibid* at paras 1754-1757.

The concept of fraudulent trading within the context of insolvency was introduced by Companies Act 1928 (UK) s75, which became Companies Act 1929 (UK) s275.[61] In its original form this only permitted proceedings to be brought against directors,[62] but that was widened with the enactment of Companies Act 1948 (UK) s332 to include any persons who were knowingly parties to the fraudulent trading. This was a Cohen Committee initiative, although that enacted was not quite in the same format as that recommended.[63] These earlier sections imposed both a civil and a criminal responsibility on persons who knowingly had been parties to the carrying on of a company's business with intent to defraud creditors of the company, or creditors of any other person or for any fraudulent purpose.[64] Civil and criminal responsibility for fraudulent trading was, however, separated during the British companies legislative reforms of the mid-1980s. IA 1986 s213 now has application to only civil responsibility for fraudulent trading. That which survives today as Companies Act 1985 (UK) s458, preserves only criminal responsibility for fraudulent trading in these terms:

> If any business of a company is carried on with intent to defraud creditors of the company or creditors of any other person, or for any fraudulent purpose, every person who was knowingly a party to the carrying on of the business in that matter is liable to imprisonment or a fine, or both. This applies whether or not the company has been, or is in the course of being, wound up.[65]

The Cork Report recommended that the new concept of wrongful trading be introduced to supplement and complement the fraudulent trading provisions.[66] That too has come to pass,[67] and will be considered shortly. First, it is instructive to briefly observe just how elastic the meaning of a 'director' has become in this context, and to elucidate the approach taken by the British Parliament and the English judiciary in extending the definition of a director,[68] in order to ensure that the relevant legislation[69] has maximum effect.

---

[61] *Re Farmizer (Products) Ltd* [1997] BCC 655 at 660 per Peter Gibson LJ (Potter and Butler-Sloss LJJ agreed).

[62] *Re Esal (Commodities) Ltd* [1997] 1 BCLC 705 at 711 per Peter Gibson LJ (Hirst and Ralph Gibson LJJ agreed).

[63] Report of the Committee on Company Law Amendment, HMSO, London, Cmd 6659, 1945 at para 149 and at 97 para X.

[64] Companies Act 1929 (UK) s275(1).

[65] Cf. Corporations Law s592(6).

[66] Report of the Review Committee on Insolvency Law and Practice, HMSO, London, Cmnd 8558, 1982 at para 1774 and chapter 44.

[67] Insolvency Act 1986 (UK) s214.

[68] Companies Act 1985 (UK) s741; Insolvency Act 1986 (UK) s251; Company Directors Disqualification Act 1986 (UK) s22; Financial Services Act 1986 (UK) s207; and Corporations Law s60; note *Re Lo-Line Electric Motors Ltd* (1988) 4 BCC 415 at 422 per Browne-Wilkinson VC; *Re Hydrodan (Corby) Ltd* [1994] BCC 161 at 162 per Millett J; and *Re Richborough Furniture Ltd* [1996] BCC 155 at 169 per Timothy Lloyd QC (sitting as a deputy High Court Judge); cf. *Australian Securities Commission v AS Nominees Ltd* (1995) 133 ALR 1 at 51-53 per Finn J; *Mistmorn Pty Ltd v Yasseen* (1996) 21 ACSR 173 at 183 per Davies J; and *Deputy Commissioner of Taxation v Austin* (1998) 16 ACLC 1555 at 1559 per Madgwick J; see Carroll R, 'Third Party Liability for Corporate Activity: Recent Developments' (1996) 26 UWALR 332.

[69] Company Directors Disqualification Act 1986 (UK); and Insolvency Act 1986 (UK).

SHADOW DIRECTORS AND DE FACTO DIRECTORS

Before examining the CDD Act and the IA 1986 in detail, it is important to first mention 'shadow' directors and *de facto* directors in this context, for much of the case-law in this area is concerned with their influence over the management of the British companies concerned.[70] Moreover, it is a precondition under both CDD Act s6 and IA 1986 s214 that the person concerned is or has been a director of the relevant company.[71] Of those sections considered within this chapter, these two are the most commonly resorted to by the Secretary of State and the liquidator respectively. To assist in meeting this preliminary point, CDD Act s22(4) and IA 1986 s251 each provide in identical language that a director, 'includes any person occupying the position of director, by whatever name called'.[72] Insofar as CDD Act ss6-9 are concerned, it is expressly provided therein, and by virtue of CDD Act s22(4), that a director includes a shadow director. IA 1986 s214 is to like effect.[73] In spite of these statutory definitions, it remains necessary to consider the case-law in order to examine how the English courts assess whether or not someone is a director, and to witness the way in which these sections are applied in practice.

A *de facto* director is someone who assumes to act as a director and is held out as such by the company.[74] He or she claims and purports to be a director, although was never actually or validly appointed as such. Whilst a *de facto* director does not find expression in British companies legislation, it has enjoyed common usage for some time.[75] Jessel MR in *In re Canadian Land Reclaiming and Colonizing Company*, for instance, when considering whether or not the persons there concerned were liable for misfeasance within the meaning of Companies Act 1862 (UK) s165, had this to say about *de facto* directors:

> No doubt they were not properly elected, and were, therefore, not *de jure* directors of the company; but that they were *de facto* directors of the company is equally beyond all question. The point I have to consider is whether the person who acts as *de facto* director is a director within the meaning of this section, or whether he can afterwards be allowed to deny that he was a director within the meaning of this section. I think he cannot. We are familiar in the law with a great number of cases in which a man who assumes a position cannot be allowed to deny in a Court of Justice that he really was entitled to occupy that position. The most familiar instance

---

[70] Cf. Report of the Committee on Company Law Amendment, HMSO, London, Cmd 6659, 1945 at 97 para XI(2).

[71] *Re Kaytech International plc* [1999] BCC 390 at 398-399 per Robert Walker LJ (Stuart-Smith and Thorpe LJJ agreed); and *Secretary of State for Trade and Industry v Tjolle* [1998] BCC 282 at 288 per Jacob J.

[72] Cf. Companies Act 1985 (UK) s741(1); and Financial Services Act 1986 (UK) s207(1).

[73] Insolvency Act 1986 (UK) ss214(7) and 251; note Prentice D D, 'Creditor's Interests and Director's Duties' (1990) 10 OJLS 265 at 267-268.

[74] Davies P L, *Gower's Principles of Modern Company Law* (6th ed) Sweet & Maxwell Ltd, London, 1997 at 182.

[75] Cf. Corporations Law s60; see *Deputy Commissioner of Taxation v Austin* (1998) 16 ACLC 1555 at 1559 per Madgwick J; and *Mistmorn Pty Ltd v Yasseen* (1996) 21 ACSR 173 at 183 per Davies J; note Ford H A J, Austin R P and Ramsay I M, *Ford's Principles of Corporations Law* (9th ed) Reed International Books Australia Pty Ltd, Sydney, 1999 at para 8.020.

is that of executor *de son tort*. In like manner, it seems to me, in an application under this section, the *de facto* director is a director for the purposes of the section.[76]

In contrast, a shadow director claims not to be a director and is not held out by the company as a director.[77] A shadow director, as Millett J in *Re Hydrodan (Corby) Ltd* explained, 'lurks in the shadows, sheltering behind others who, he claims, are the only directors of the company to the exclusion of himself.'[78] A shadow director is a creature of statute.[79] CDD Act s22(5) and IA 1986 s251 each provide in identical language that in relation to a company, a shadow director means:

> [A] person in accordance with whose directions or instructions the directors of the company are accustomed to act (but so that a person is not deemed a shadow director by reason only that the directors act on advice given by him in a professional capacity).[80]

The English courts are therefore obliged to consider whether in the circumstances alleged it is appropriate to disqualify *de jure* directors, *de facto* directors and shadow directors from in any way, whether directly or indirectly, being concerned or taking part in the promotion, formation or management of a company for a specified period.[81] By virtue of IA 1986 ss212-214, the English courts are empowered to declare that errant *de jure* directors, *de facto* directors and shadow directors are to restore the company's assets or make whatever contribution to the company's assets by way of compensation which the court thinks appropriate.[82]

This is of considerable importance to directors and officers of British companies who fall within the expanded definition,[83] and those whom by their conduct are deemed to be performing relevant duties and therefore subject to corresponding responsibilities and obligations.[84] As Prentice observes, this extension of liability may well mean that in many situations a parent company will be liable for the debts of its subsidiary, and so also may others who have had a significant involvement in the management of a company's affairs; for example, a company's bank.[85] It is equally important to the corporate regulators as it is all too common for those who engage in misconduct of the

---

[76] (1880) 14 Ch D 660 at 664-665.

[77] Davies P L, *Gower's Principles of Modern Company Law* (6th ed) Sweet & Maxwell Ltd, London, 1997 at 183.

[78] [1994] BCC 161 at 163; see *Secretary of State for Trade and Industry v Laing* [1996] 2 BCLC 324 at 337-339 per Evans-Lombe J.

[79] Cf. Corporations Law s60; see *Australian Securities Commission v AS Nominees Ltd* (1995) 133 ALR 1 at 51-53 per Finn J; note Ford H A J, Austin R P and Ramsay I M, *Ford's Principles of Corporations Law* (9th ed) Reed International Books Australia Pty Ltd, Sydney, 1999 at para 8.020.

[80] Cf. Companies Act 1985 (UK) s741(2).

[81] Company Directors Disqualification Act 1986 (UK) s1(1).

[82] *Re Farmizer (Products) Ltd* [1997] BCC 655 at 657 per Peter Gibson LJ (Potter and Butler-Sloss LJJ agreed).

[83] E.g., Companies Act 1985 (UK) ss309(3), 319-322, 322B and 330-346; cf. Corporations Law s232(1).

[84] Companies Act 1985 (UK) s741; Insolvency Act 1986 (UK) s251; Company Directors Disqualification Act 1986 (UK) s22; Financial Services Act 1986 (UK) s207; cf. Corporations Law s60; note *Australian Securities Commission v AS Nominees Ltd* (1995) 133 ALR 1 at 51-53 per Finn J; *Mistmorn Pty Ltd v Yasseen* (1996) 21 ACSR 173 at 183 per Davies J; and *Deputy Commissioner of Taxation v Austin* (1998) 16 ACLC 1555 at 1559 per Madgwick J; see Carroll R, 'Third Party Liability for Corporate Activity: Recent Developments' (1996) 26 UWALR 332.

[85] Prentice D D, 'Creditor's Interests and Director's Duties' (1990) 10 OJLS 265 at 267-268.

type warranting disqualification, to either seek to deliberately conceal their managerial or directorial relationship with a company, or overlook, or simply not bother with, the legal niceties imposed by companies legislation designed specifically to guard against the misconduct complained of.[86] The distinctions between *de jure* directors, *de facto* directors and shadow directors, however, remain important as Browne-Wilkinson VC in *Re Lo-Line Electric Motors Ltd* explained:

> [It] is not possible to treat a de facto director as a 'director' for all the purposes in the 1985 Act[87] ... in some sections the word director must include a person who is not a de jure director. Thus sec. 285 validates acts of a director notwithstanding a defect in his appointment i.e. the acts of someone who is not a de jure director. It follows that the word director is capable of including de facto directors but may not do so. The meaning of director varies according to the context in which it is to be found.[88]

Hydrodan is a case in point. There, the court was concerned with IA 1986 s214 and whether or not liability for wrongful trading thereby imposed extended to *de facto* directors as well as to *de jure* directors and shadow directors.[89] The matter was argued before Millett J on appeal from the Northampton County Court. After noting that IA 1986 s214(7) provides that a 'director' includes a shadow director which, in turn, is defined in IA 1986 s251, Millett J went on to say that:

> It appears to me that that concession [that the liability imposed by s214 extends to de facto directors as well as to de jure and shadow directors] is plainly correct. Liability for wrongful trading is imposed by the Act on those persons who are responsible for it, that is to say, who were in a position to prevent damage to creditors by taking proper steps to protect their interests. Liability cannot sensibly depend upon the validity of the defendant's appointment. Those who assume to act as directors and who thereby exercise the powers and discharge the functions of a director, whether validly appointed or not, must accept the responsibilities which are attached to the office.[90]

Millett J's reasoning in *Hydrodan* for including shadow directors and *de facto* directors within the generic description of a 'director' under the wrongful trading provision proscribed by IA 1986 s214, was adopted by Timothy Lloyd QC[91] in *Re Richborough Furniture Ltd* and was there extended to the meaning of a 'director' found within CDD Act s6.[92] In doing so, Timothy Lloyd QC accepted the earlier reasoning of Browne-Wilkinson VC in *Lo-Line* to like effect.[93] On the facts before him, however, it was decided that the person concerned in *Richborough* was not a *de facto* director for the

---

[86] *Yukong Line Ltd of Korea v Rendsburg Investments Corp of Liberia (No. 2)* [1998] 4 All ER 82 at 98 per Toulson J.
[87] E.g., Companies Act 1985 (UK) ss282, 288, 291 and 293(2).
[88] (1988) 4 BCC 415 at 421-422.
[89] [1994] BCC 161.
[90] *Ibid* at 162.
[91] Sitting as a deputy High Court Judge.
[92] [1996] BCC 155 at 169.
[93] (1988) 4 BCC 415 at 422.

purposes of CDD Act s6.[94] Timothy Lloyd QC considered that for someone to be liable in such circumstances, there would need to be clear evidence that the person concerned:

> [Had] been either the sole person directing the affairs of the company ... or, if there were others who were true directors, that he was acting on an equal footing with the others in directing the affairs of the company.[95]

Regrettably, these remarks have introduced uncertainty into the proper test to be applied in order to determine whether or not someone is to be treated as a *de facto* director for the purposes of the legislation. This 'equal footing' test postulated by Timothy Lloyd QC was considered by Jacob J in *Secretary of State for Trade and Industry v Tjolle*.[96] The essential facts in *Tjolle* were these. Mrs Kenning joined the company concerned as a part-time administrative assistant. She worked her way up in the company, becoming principally concerned with sales, marketing and customer care. She assumed the title 'director', and variations of that. The Secretary of State contended that Kenning had held herself out as a director in circumstances which constituted her a *de facto* director and, given her alleged unfitness, was liable to disqualification under CDD Act s6. Jacob J did not agree. Whilst Kenning was obviously a very capable manager, 'she did not form part of the real corporate governance of the company.'[97] In reaching this decision, Jacob J examined those passages from the judgments of Millett J in *Hydrodan*, and Timothy Lloyd QC in *Richborough*, extracted above. His Lordship acknowledged the difficulty in postulating any one decisive test and opined that:

> I think what is involved is very much a question of degree. The court takes into account all the relevant factors. Those factors include at least whether or not there was a holding out by the company of the individual as a director, whether the individual used the title, whether the individual had proper information ... on which to base decisions, and whether the individual has to make major decisions and so on. Taking all these factors into account, one asks 'was this individual part of the corporate governing structure?' ... There would be no justification for the law making a person liable to misfeasance or disqualification proceedings unless they were truly in a position to exercise the powers and discharge the functions of a director. Otherwise they would be made liable for events over which they had no real control, either in fact or law.[98]

In the result, Jacob J considered that Kenning neither satisfied Millett J's test nor Timothy Lloyd QC's test. Rather, it is incumbent upon the court in each case to consider the overall picture in order to determine whether or not the alleged *de facto* director has assumed the position of a director. Another variation of this approach was recently employed by Jonathan Parker J in *Secretary of State for Trade and Industry v Jones*.[99] After reviewing the 'equal footing' test and determining that the alleged *de*

---

[94] *Re Sykes (Butchers) Ltd* [1998] BCC 484 provides an example of where the person concerned was a *de facto* director.
[95] [1996] BCC 155 at 170.
[96] [1998] BCC 282.
[97] *Ibid* at 300-301.
[98] *Ibid* at 290.
[99] [1999] BCC 336.

facto director there had in fact assumed the position of a director, his Lordship considered that:

> [The] correct approach in deciding whether or not a respondent is a de facto director is to look at his conduct as found by the court in the round and, so approaching it, to reach a conclusion as to whether or not the respondent in fact assumed the role of a director of the company, notwithstanding that he had not been formally appointed as such.[100]

Re Kaytech International plc[101] appears to be the first occasion upon which the Court of Appeal[102] has considered the proper test to be applied for determining whether or not someone is a *de facto* director for the purposes of CDD Act s6. There, the relevant *dicta* from *Lo-Line*, *Hydrodan*, *Richborough* and *Tjolle*, which we have considered above, was cited in argument and reviewed by the Court of Appeal. Robert Walker LJ delivered the only reasoned judgment.[103] It is evident that his Lordship saw much force in Jacob J declining to formulate a single test in *Tjolle*, as he placed emphasis upon that passage from Jacob J's judgment extracted above.[104] However, Robert Walker LJ explained that Jacob J was not enumerating tests in *Tjolle* which must all be satisfied in order to establish that someone is a *de facto* director, but rather was drawing attention to some only of the relevant factors.[105] In the course of finding that each of the three persons concerned was a director for the purposes of CDD Act s6, what Robert Walker LJ had to say concerning one of them in particular is worthy of note as it has broader application to the directors' duty to exercise care and diligence, and is a useful signpost to the way in which the English courts are gradually heading. His Lordship had this to say:

> The judge observed, correctly, that complete inactivity by a director can constitute unfitness. ... It was Mr Solly's duty to inform himself about the affairs of the company ... His honest but thoroughly unreasonable belief that he was not a director cannot in my judgment be a defence. The law should give no encouragement to the notion that if a man takes on so many directorships that he cannot remember them, he is thereby released from the heavy responsibility which he has undertaken.[106]

In spite of the uncertainty which surrounds the correct approach to be taken in determining whether someone is or is not a *de facto* director, the important point to note, according to the learned authors of *Disqualification of Directors: Law & Practice*, 'is that a judge who places greater emphasis on the protective aspect of the legislation might well take a broader view as to what constitutes *de facto* directorship.'[107] If that be correct, then the philosophy and rationale underlying the enactment by the British

---

[100]   *Ibid* at 349.
[101]   [1999] BCC 390.
[102]   (Stuart-Smith, Thorpe and Robert Walker LJJ).
[103]   (Stuart-Smith and Thorpe LJJ agreed).
[104]   [1998] BCC 282 at 290 per Jacob J.
[105]   [1999] BCC 390 at 402.
[106]   *Ibid* at 403.
[107]   Walters A and Davis-White M, *Directors' Disqualification: Law & Practice* Sweet & Maxwell Ltd, London, 1999 at chapter 3.011.

Parliament of the CDD Act will be met.[108] Moreover, that in turn ought lead to a gradual overall raising of the standards of directorial conduct and decision-making on the part of directors of British companies in keeping with the community's, and the commercial world's, changing expectations.[109] *A fortiori* as the common law relating to the directors' duty to exercise care and diligence continues to evolve, and the objective standard of care and diligence further develops at the expense of subjectivity.[110]

There are few reported decisions in English company law concerning shadow directors and their disqualification under the CDD Act. *Re Tasbian Ltd (No. 3)*[111] is one of them. There, David Nixon a chartered accountant and 'company doctor' was appointed as a consultant to Tasbian Ltd ('Tasbian') by a finance company which financed its business as a shareholder and debenture holder. One of the issues before the Court of Appeal[112] was the sufficiency of the evidence necessary to disclose an arguable case that Nixon was either a shadow director or a *de facto* director. Balcombe LJ delivered the only reasoned judgment.[113] After referring to the statutory definitions found within CDD Act ss22(4) and 22(5), his Lordship felt that allegations that Nixon: (i) monitored Tasbian's trading and controlled its bank account; (ii) was usurping the directors' functions (given complaints to that effect); and (iii) decided which cheques drawn by Tasbian could and which could not be submitted to the bank, all pointed towards Nixon being able to control Tasbian's affairs. As such, Balcombe LJ considered it to be at least arguable that Nixon was either a shadow director or a *de facto* director. That finding satisfied that aspect of the appeal, and is useful as it identifies some of the indicia which it might be said are hallmarks of a shadow director. But, in isolation, *Tasbian* is of limited utility.[114]

Within the context of IA 1986 s214, however, the courts have more frequently been called upon to determine whether someone is or is not a shadow director. As the statutory definition of shadow director in CDD Act s22(5) and IA 1986 s251 is the same, decisions on one are directly referable to decisions upon the other. The dearth of authority in this respect concerning the CDD Act does not, therefore, present as too much of a concern. In this context, both *Hydrodan* and *Re Unisoft Group Ltd (No. 2)*[115]

---

[108] Hoey A, 'Disqualifying delinquent directors' (1997) 18 Co Law 130 at 130; and Walters A and Davis-White M, *Directors' Disqualification: Law & Practice* Sweet & Maxwell Ltd, London, 1999 at chapter 2; note *Re Swift 736 Ltd* [1993] BCC 312 at 315 per Nicholls VC (Farquharson and Steyn LJJ agreed); *Re Grayan Building Services Ltd* [1995] BCC 554 at 577 per Henry LJ; *Re Westmid Packing Services Ltd* [1998] 2 All ER 124 at 131-132 per Lord Woolf MR (Waller and Robert Walker LJJ agreed); *Re Barings plc* [1998] BCC 583 at 590 per Sir Richard Scott VC; and *Re Barings plc (No 5)* [1999] 1 BCLC 433 at 482 per Jonathan Parker J.

[109] Cf. Malcolm D, 'Directors' Duties: The Governing Principles' in Ramsay I M (ed), *Corporate Governance and the Duties of Company Directors* The Centre for Corporate Law and Securities Regulation, University of Melbourne, Parkville, 1997 at 78.

[110] E.g., *Norman v Theodore Goddard* [1992] BCC 14 at 15 per Hoffmann J; *Vrisakis v Australian Securities Commission* (1992-1993) 9 WAR 395 at 451 per Ipp J (Malcolm CJ agreed); *Daniels v Anderson* (1995) 13 ACLC 614 at 662 per Clarke and Sheller JJA; *Androvin v Figliomeni* (1996) 14 ACLC 1461 at 1470 per Owen J (Kennedy and Franklyn JJ agreed); and *Re Barings plc* [1998] BCC 583 at 586 per Sir Richard Scott VC.

[111] [1992] BCC 358.

[112] (Lord Donaldson, Balcombe and Stuart-Smith LJJ).

[113] (Lord Donaldson and Stuart-Smith LJ agreed).

[114] Cf. *Re Kaytech International plc* [1999] BCC 390 at 402 per Robert Walker LJ (Stuart-Smith and Thorpe LJJ agreed); and *Secretary of State for Trade and Industry v Tjolle* [1998] BCC 282 at 290 per Jacob J.

[115] [1994] BCC 766.

are apposite. The following passage from Millett J's judgment in *Hydrodan* warrants particular attention:

> To establish that a defendant is a shadow director of a company it is necessary to allege and prove: (1) who are the directors of the company, whether de facto or de jure; (2) that the defendant directed those directors how to act in relation to the company or that he was one of the persons who did so; (3) that those directors acted in accordance with such directions; and (4) that they were accustomed so to act. What is needed is, first, a board of directors claiming and purporting to act as such; and, secondly, a pattern of behaviour in which the board did not exercise any discretion or judgment of its own, but acted in accordance with the directions of others.[116]

Harman J's judgment in *Unisoft* was complementary and sympathetic to that extracted above. In his Lordship's view, unless the governing majority of the board is accustomed to act on the directions of the person concerned, he or she cannot be a shadow director.[117] Furthermore, Harman J considered that there must be, 'more than one act and a course of conduct.'[118] However, these indicia of shadow directors are not conclusive. Each case must be examined on its own facts. It is perhaps worth noting that most of the reported decisions on shadow directors in English company law have been decided in favour of the so-called shadow director.[119]

From this brief excursion into the law pertaining to shadow directors and *de facto* directors, it can readily be seen that there are several intractable issues which must first be resolved in order to invoke the relevant legislation;[120] issues which can at times bedevil the English courts. Nevertheless, the approaches on the part of the English judiciary considered above enable liability to be properly imposed upon those responsible for the demise of their company's fortunes, and the diminution of their company's creditors' financial resources, rather than hinge upon the validity of a defendant's appointment.[121] The English courts are, therefore, empowered within the context of insolvency to disqualify those who, by their actions or inaction, bring English company law into disrepute: whether validly appointed directors or not.[122]

---

[116] [1994] BCC 161 at 163.

[117] [1994] BCC 766 at 775.

[118] *Ibid.*

[119] Walters A and Davis-White M, *Directors' Disqualification: Law & Practice* Sweet & Maxwell Ltd, London, 1999 at chapter 3.013.

[120] *Re Kaytech International plc* [1999] BCC 390 at 398-399 per Robert Walker LJ (Stuart-Smith and Thorpe LJJ agreed); and *Secretary of State for Trade and Industry v Tjolle* [1998] BCC 282 at 288 per Jacob J.

[121] Bhattacharyya G, 'Re Hydrodan (Corby) Ltd – shadow directors and wrongful trading' (1994) 15 Co Law 151 at 151.

[122] Cf. Corporations Law s60; note *Australian Securities Commission v AS Nominees Ltd* (1995) 133 ALR 1 at 51-53 per Finn J; *Mistmorn Pty Ltd v Yasseen* (1996) 21 ACSR 173 at 183 per Davies J; and *Deputy Commissioner of Taxation v Austin* (1998) 16 ACLC 1555 at 1559 per Madgwick J; see Carroll R, 'Third Party Liability for Corporate Activity: Recent Developments' (1996) 26 UWALR 332.

COMPANY DIRECTORS DISQUALIFICATION ACT 1986 (UK)

In the White Paper entitled *A Revised Framework for Insolvency Law* presented to the British Parliament in 1984 by the Secretary of State,[123] as a result of recommendations within the Cork Report,[124] the DTI advocated the introduction as soon as possible of measures to curb and to penalise the activities of irresponsible directors.[125] In particular, the DTI saw the principal role of legislation in this context and that of insolvency law as: (i) providing a statutory framework to encourage directors to pay careful attention to their company's financial circumstances so as to recognise difficulties at an early stage and before the interests of creditors are seriously prejudiced; and (ii) deterring and penalising irresponsible behaviour and malpractice on the part of those who manage a company's affairs.[126] Some of these measures have been addressed by the enactment of the CDD Act. Other recommendations, directed specifically towards insolvency legislation, will be considered shortly.

Prior to the enactment of the CDD Act, provisions empowering the English courts to disqualify those undeserving of being able to act as directors, or be concerned in the management,[127] of British companies and thereby enjoy the privileges of limited liability,[128] had previously been divided between the Insolvency Acts 1985 and 1986 (UK) and the Companies Act 1985 (UK).[129] In keeping with the somewhat pedestrian approach historically adopted by the British Parliament to English company law reform,[130] and the piecemeal approach to its development,[131] a number of reviews upon relevant aspects of company law and insolvency law were completed before their enactment: relevantly, the four major reviews which have been mentioned above.[132] As Lord Hoffmann recently observed, 'disqualification is a very serious matter.'[133] This was echoed even more recently by Jonathan Parker J in *Re Barings plc (No 5)*.[134]

---

[123] Department of Trade and Industry, *A Revised Framework for Insolvency Law* HMSO, London, Cmnd 9175, 1984.

[124] Report of the Review Committee on Insolvency Law and Practice, HMSO, London, Cmnd 8558, 1982.

[125] Cf. Report of the Committee on Company Law Amendment, HMSO, London, Cmd 6659, 1945 at para 150; and Report of the Company Law Committee, HMSO, London, Cmnd 1749, 1962 at paras 80, 85(b), 497-499 and 503(a)-(d).

[126] Department of Trade and Industry, *A Revised Framework for Insolvency Law* HMSO, London, Cmnd 9175, 1984 at 5.

[127] Cf. Corporations Law s91A.

[128] *Re Sevenoaks Stationers (Retail) Ltd* [1990] BCC 765 at 773 per Dillon LJ (Butler-Sloss and Staughton LJJ agreed); *Re Swift 736 Ltd* [1993] BCC 312 at 315 per Nicholls VC (Farquharson and Steyn LJJ agreed); *Re Grayan Building Services Ltd* [1995] BCC 554 at 574 per Hoffmann LJ (Henry and Neill LJJ agreed), at 577 per Henry LJ and at 577 per Neill LJ; *Re Richborough Furniture Ltd* [1996] BCC 155 at 166 per Timothy Lloyd QC (sitting as a deputy High Court Judge); *Re Continental Assurance Co of London plc* [1997] 1 BCLC 48 at 59 per Chadwick J; and *Re Blackspur Group plc* [1998] 1 BCLC 676 at 680 and 688 per Lord Woolf MR (Millett and Mummery LJJ agreed).

[129] Davies P L, *Gower's Principles of Modern Company Law* (6th ed) Sweet & Maxwell Ltd, London, 1997 at 51.

[130] Cf. Department of Trade and Industry, *Modern Company Law: The Strategic Framework* HMSO, London, 1999 at para 8.5.

[131] Finch V, 'The Measures of Insolvency Law' (1997) 17 OJLS 227 at 228.

[132] Company Law Amendment Committee, HMSO, London, Cmd 2657, 1926; Report of the Committee on Company Law Amendment, HMSO, London, Cmd 6659, 1945; Report of the Company Law Committee, HMSO, London, Cmnd 1749, 1962; and Report of the Review Committee on Insolvency Law and Practice, HMSO, London, Cmnd 8558, 1982.

[133] Hoffmann L H, 'The Fourth Annual Leonard Sainer Lecture' (1997) 18 Co Law 194 at 197.

[134] [1999] 1 BCLC 433 at 484.

Moreover, the seriousness with which conduct meriting disqualification is to be viewed is reflected in the provisions of the CDD Act itself.[135] Viewed in this light, it is understandable that some time would be taken by the British Parliament to implement that legislation considered most appropriate in the circumstances.

The desirability of a disqualification regime in English company law cannot be faulted. It seeks to deter errant directors from abusing their position of limited liability,[136] and creates an incentive for directors of British companies to behave honestly and efficiently in the discharge of their corporate responsibilities.[137] For those directors who are not deterred from so acting, the regime provides for their removal in order to protect the public.[138] This philosophy is borne out in the recent report by the Comptroller and Auditor General entitled *The Insolvency Service Executive Agency: Company Director Disqualification – A Follow Up Report* ('Comptroller's Follow Up Report') which relevantly provides that:

> The disqualification arrangements help to promote confidence and risk-taking in the market, by assuring those who do business with limited liability companies that directors who are unfit will be disqualified from being involved in the management of those companies. If unfit directors were able to continue in business without the sanction of disqualification, confidence in the market would be undermined.[139]

Insofar as deterrence is concerned, it is interesting to note that which the Senate Standing Committee on Legal and Constitutional Affairs discovered in respect to the efficacy of disqualification upon infelicitous directors, following its inquiry into the duties and responsibilities of directors of Australian companies during the late 1980s. The Committee had this to say of disqualification:

> Evidence was given to the Committee that disqualification from office was the greatest threat to directors, notwithstanding possible gaol sentences and financial penalties, and therefore was an effective sanction.[140]

The power to disqualify directors from office in English company law for engaging in fraudulent trading within the context of insolvency was first recognised in Companies Act 1928 (UK) s75(4). It has come a long way since, and the implications and effect which disqualification can today have upon directors, their companies, corporate regulation and English company law in general, can be profound.[141] Hence, this is an important area of the law where there is *multum in parvo*.

---

[135] *Re Swift 736 Ltd* [1993] BCC 312 at 315 per Nicholls VC (Farquharson and Steyn LJJ agreed).

[136] Hoey A, 'Disqualifying delinquent directors' (1997) 18 Co Law 130 at 130.

[137] See Walters A and Davis-White M, *Directors' Disqualification: Law & Practice* Sweet & Maxwell Ltd, London, 1999 at chapter 2.

[138] *Re Westmid Packing Services Ltd* [1998] 2 All ER 124 at 131-132 per Lord Woolf MR (Waller and Robert Walker LJJ agreed); *Re Barings plc* [1998] BCC 583 at 590 per Sir Richard Scott VC; and *Re Barings plc (No 5)* [1999] 1 BCLC 433 at 482 per Jonathan Parker J.

[139] Comptroller and Auditor General, *The Insolvency Service Executive Agency: Company Director Disqualification – A Follow Up Report* The Stationery Office Ltd, London, 1999 at para 3.2.

[140] Senate Standing Committee on Legal and Constitutional Affairs, *Social and Fiduciary Duties and Obligations of Company Directors* AGPS, Canberra, 1989 at 194.

[141] Cf. Hicks A, *Disqualification of Directors: No Hiding Place for the Unfit?* The Association of Chartered Certified Accountants, London, 1998 at 67-78 and 99.

The CDD Act classifies the circumstances in which the English courts may order that a person be disqualified from acting as a director of a British company for a specified period. A disqualification order may be made for misconduct in relation to a company where the person concerned has, for example: (i) been convicted of an indictable offence in connection with a company;[142] (ii) committed persistent breaches of companies legislation relating to the delivery of documents or returns to the registrar of companies as required;[143] (iii) participated in fraudulent trading;[144] or (iv) committed other fraud or a breach of duty which comes to light in the course of a winding-up.[145] It is worthy of mention that companies themselves may also be the subject of CDD Act proceedings.[146] *Official Receiver v Brady*[147] appears to be the first occasion upon which two Jersey companies falling within the CDD Act s22(4) definition of director were disqualified from so acting: in that case for the maximum period of 15 years.[148]

The applicant for a disqualification order in these circumstances may be the Secretary of State, the official receiver, the liquidator or any past or present member or creditor of any company in relation to which the person concerned is alleged to have offended.[149] The court has a discretion of whether or not to make an order, which may provide for disqualification for a maximum of either five or 15 years depending upon the section of the CDD Act under which the person concerned is prosecuted, and the seriousness of the allegations proven. A disqualification order may also be made for unfitness under either CDD Act ss6[150] or 8. Applications under the latter are less common than under the former,[151] but important nevertheless.

CDD Act s8 empowers the court to make a disqualification order if it is satisfied that the conduct of any person who is or has been a director or shadow director of any company makes him or her unfit to be concerned in the management of a company. The relevant information going to unfitness is that which comes to light following the exercise of one or more of those statutory powers of investigation stipulated in s8(1).[152] One of the advantages of proceeding under s8 is that it can be used even if the company has not become insolvent.[153] Even so, the majority of those disqualified under the CDD Act occur as a result of applications brought under CDD Act s6. During 1997-1998, for example, 87 per cent of director disqualifications were brought about through s6 proceedings.[154] It is, therefore, deserving of study. CDD Act s6(1) requires that:

> The court shall make a disqualification order against a person in any case where, on an application under this section, it is satisfied –

---

[142] Company Directors Disqualification Act 1986 (UK) s2.
[143] *Ibid* at ss3 and 5.
[144] *Ibid* at s4; and Companies Act 1985 (UK) s458; cf. Insolvency Act 1986 (UK) s213.
[145] Company Directors Disqualification Act 1986 (UK) s4.
[146] *Ibid* at s14.
[147] [1999] BCC 258.
[148] *Ibid* at 259 per Jacob J.
[149] Company Directors Disqualification Act 1986 (UK) s16(2).
[150] Formerly Companies Act 1985 (UK) s300.
[151] *Re Rex Williams Leisure plc* [1994] BCC 551 at 553 per Hoffmann LJ (Russell LJ agreed).
[152] See Walters A and Davis-White M, *Directors' Disqualification: Law & Practice* Sweet & Maxwell Ltd, London, 1999 at chapter 3.
[153] *Re Barings plc (No 5)* [1999] 1 BCLC 433 at 482 per Jonathan Parker J; and *Re Rex Williams Leisure plc* [1994] BCC 551 at 553 per Hoffmann LJ (Russell LJ agreed).
[154] Comptroller and Auditor General, *The Insolvency Service Executive Agency: Company Director Disqualification – A Follow Up Report* The Stationery Office Ltd, London, 1999 at para 1.6.

(a) that he is or has been a director of a company which has at any time become insolvent (whether while he was a director or subsequently), and

(b) that his conduct as a director of that company (either taken alone or taken together with his conduct as a director of any other company or companies) makes him unfit to be concerned in the management of a company.[155]

Application for an order under this section can be made only by the Secretary of State[156] or, if he so directs, by the official receiver.[157] Where the Secretary of State considers it expedient in the public interest that a disqualification order under s6 should be made against any person who is or who has been a director of a British company, he may apply to the court for the making of such an order.[158] The burden of proof to make good the allegations being made against the director concerned, 'rests firmly on the shoulders of the Secretary of State.'[159] Furthermore, participants in fraudulent trading[160] or wrongful trading[161] are similarly at risk of an application being made for their disqualification.[162] In this respect, CDD Act s10(1) relevantly provides that:

> Where the court makes a declaration under section 213 or 214 of the Insolvency Act that a person is liable to make a contribution to a company's assets, then, whether or not an application for such an order is made by any person, the court may, if it thinks fit, also make a disqualification order against the person to whom the declaration relates.

Whereas under CDD Act ss2, 3, 4, 5, 8 and 10 the court may make a disqualification order in the circumstances stipulated, under s6 the court must make a disqualification order for not less than two nor more than 15 years where the company has at any time become insolvent, and the director's conduct makes him or her unfit to be concerned in the management of *any* company.[163] If satisfied upon the two matters mentioned in s6(1), the court has no discretion: it must disqualify. But, the court has a discretion as to the period of disqualification.[164] One of the preconditions mentioned in s6(1) is that the court must be satisfied that the person concerned is or has been a director. This serves to highlight the significance of the debate which surrounds the classification of directors into either *de jure* directors, *de facto* directors or shadow directors,[165] and the test applicable in the circumstances. This was discussed in some detail in an earlier part of this chapter.

---

155 Under Company Directors Disqualification Act 1986 (UK) s9 the court is required to have regard in particular to the matters prescribed in Schedule 1 to the Act in determining unfitness: *Re Bath Glass Ltd* (1988) 4 BCC 130 at 132-133 per Peter Gibson J.

156 *Re Barings plc (No 2)* [1999] 1 All ER 311 at 334 per Chadwick LJ.

157 Company Directors Disqualification Act 1986 (UK) s7(1).

158 *Ibid.*

159 *Secretary of State for Trade and Industry v Laing* [1996] 2 BCLC 324 at 340 per Evans-Lombe J.

160 Insolvency Act 1986 (UK) s213; cf. Companies Act 1985 (UK) s458.

161 Insolvency Act 1986 (UK) s214.

162 *Re Brian D Pierson (Contractors) Ltd* [1999] BCC 26 at 58 per Hazel Williamson QC (sitting as a deputy High Court Judge).

163 *Re Barings plc (No 2)* [1999] 1 All ER 311 at 340 per Waller LJ; cf. *Re Barings plc (No 5)* [1999] 1 BCLC 433 at 482 per Jonathan Parker J.

164 *Re Swift 736 Ltd* [1993] BCC 312 at 313 per Nicholls VC (Farquharson and Steyn LJJ agreed).

165 *Secretary of State for Trade and Industry v Tjolle* [1998] BCC 282 at 288-291 per Jacob J.

Disqualification proceedings are civil and not criminal,[166] notwithstanding that under CDD Act s2 the disqualification order may be made following criminal proceedings by the court which convicted the person concerned. It is well established that the purpose of disqualification is directed at the protection of the public and not punishment.[167] Hence, the standard of proof is on the balance of probabilities[168] and not beyond reasonable doubt, 'but regard has to be had to the seriousness of the issues raised.'[169] *A fortiori* where the complaints against the errant director are, 'in the main of lack of probity and not of negligence or incompetence and are therefore very serious.'[170] But, as Chadwick J noted in *Re Continental Assurance Co of London plc*:

> The prohibition is not an absolute prohibition against being a director of any company or being concerned with the management of any company. It is a prohibition against being a director without the leave of the court.[171]

The first appeal against a disqualification order to have reached the Court of Appeal[172] concerning the CDD Act was *Re Sevenoaks Stationers (Retail) Ltd*.[173] There, the opportunity was taken to review decisions of courts of first instance, particularly in relation to mandatory disqualification under s6 for unfitness, and a three tier tariff was suggested.[174] The judgment of the Court of Appeal was delivered by Dillon LJ.[175] In his Lordship's view, a director's unfitness did not demand dishonesty as, 'incompetence or negligence in a very marked degree ... is enough to render him unfit ... to take part in the management of a company.'[176] In reaching this view, Dillon LJ distanced himself from that earlier pronounced by Browne-Wilkinson VC in *Re Lo-Line Electric Motors Ltd*, where the Vice-Chancellor had opined that:

> Ordinary commercial misjudgment is in itself not sufficient to justify disqualification. In the normal case, the conduct complained of must display a lack of commercial probity although I have no doubt that in an extreme case of gross negligence or total incompetence disqualification could be appropriate.[177]

---

[166] *R v Secretary of State for Trade and Industry, ex parte McCormick* [1998] BCC 379 at 392 per Morritt LJ (Waller LJ agreed); cf. Corporations Law s1317ED(1).

[167] *Re Lo-Line Electric Motors Ltd* (1988) 4 BCC 415 at 422 per Browne-Wilkinson VC; *Re Sevenoaks Stationers (Retail) Ltd* [1990] BCC 765 at 773 per Dillon LJ (Butler-Sloss and Staughton LJJ agreed); note *Re Grayan Building Services Ltd* [1995] BCC 554 at 577 per Henry LJ; *Re Richborough Furniture Ltd* [1996] BCC 155 at 166 per Timothy Lloyd QC (sitting as a deputy High Court Judge); *Re Continental Assurance Co of London plc* [1997] 1 BCLC 48 at 59 per Chadwick J; and *Re Blackspur Group plc* [1998] 1 BCLC 676 at 680 and 688 per Lord Woolf MR (Millett and Mummery LJJ agreed); cf. *Australian Securities Commission v Forem-Freeway Enterprises Pty Ltd* (1998-1999) 30 ACSR 339 at 349 per Madgwick J.

[168] Griffin S, 'Standard of proof applicable to s6 of the Company Directors Disqualification Act 1986' (1997) 18 Co Law 24 at 24.

[169] *Re Dominion International Group plc (No. 2)* [1996] 1 BCLC 572 at 576 per Knox J.

[170] *Ibid.*

[171] [1997] 1 BCLC 48 at 59; note Company Directors Disqualification Act 1986 (UK) ss1 and 17.

[172] (Dillon, Butler-Sloss and Staughton LJJ).

[173] [1990] BCC 765.

[174] *Ibid* at 771-772 per Dillon LJ.

[175] (Butler-Sloss and Staughton LJJ agreed).

[176] [1990] BCC 765 at 780.

[177] (1988) 4 BCC 415 at 419.

Whilst Dillon LJ in *Sevenoaks* considered such statements to be helpful in identifying particular circumstances in which a person would clearly be unfit, he did not think it necessary for incompetence to be 'total' as suggested by Browne-Wilkinson VC in *Lo-Line*.[178] But what the court must decide, in its application of the CDD Act, is whether or not the director's conduct, 'viewed cumulatively and taking account of any extenuating circumstances, has fallen below the standards of probity and competence appropriate for persons fit to be directors of companies.'[179] Within the context of insolvency, therefore, the court must pass judgment on the way in which the directors conducted the affairs of their company over a period of days, weeks or possibly months. In doing so, the court must be alert to the dangers of hindsight[180] and not fall into the trap of being too wise after the event.[181] When asked to disqualify a director under CDD Act s6 in *Re Bath Glass Ltd*, Peter Gibson J determined that:

> To reach a finding of unfitness the court must be satisfied that the director has been guilty of a serious failure or serious failures, whether deliberately or through incompetence, to perform those duties of directors which are attendant on the privilege of trading through companies with limited liability. Any misconduct of the respondent qua director may be relevant, even if it does not fall within a specific section of the Companies Acts or the Insolvency Act.[182]

According to the Comptroller's Follow Up Report, 1,267 of the 1,460 director disqualifications during 1997-1998 arose from civil proceedings brought under CDD Act s6 against the directors of failed companies.[183] This represents a three-fold increase over the 399 disqualifications secured during 1993-1994.[184] However, the impact of such statistics upon the business community at large is questionable.[185] During the corresponding period that 1,267 directors were disqualified, there were 1.32 million British companies registered with Companies House.[186] Given that there are some three million directors who run these companies,[187] one might empathise with the remarks of the learned editor of *The Company Lawyer* that, 'a large adult population capable of

---

[178] [1990] BCC 765 at 773 and 780; note *Re Barings plc* [1998] BCC 583 at 589 per Sir Richard Scott VC.

[179] *Re Living Images Ltd* [1996] BCC 112 at 115 per Laddie J; cf. *Secretary of State for Trade and Industry v Hickling* [1996] BCC 678 at 693 per Judge Weeks QC, 'In this case I have found no dishonesty, no breach of common standards of commercial morality, no cynical disregard for others' interests and no gross incompetence on the part of either [director] … At worst they were guilty of naivety, over-optimism and misplaced trust. In my judgment, their conduct as directors of Moonlight was not such as to make them unfit to be concerned in the management of a company.'

[180] *In re Horsley & Weight Ltd* [1982] Ch 442 at 455 per Templeman LJ; and *Re Hitco 2000 Ltd* [1995] BCC 161 at 169 per Jules Sher QC; cf. *Nicholson v Permakraft (NZ) Ltd* [1985] 1 NZLR 242 at 253 per Cooke J; and *Kong v Pilkington (Australia) Ltd* (1997) 15 ACLC 1561 at 1567 per Owen J (Franklyn and Murray JJ agreed).

[181] *Re Living Images Ltd* [1996] BCC 112 at 116-117 per Laddie J; and *Facia Footwear Ltd v Hinchliffe* [1998] 1 BCLC 218 at 228 per Sir Richard Scott VC.

[182] (1988) 4 BCC 130 at 133.

[183] Comptroller and Auditor General, *The Insolvency Service Executive Agency: Company Director Disqualification – A Follow Up Report* The Stationery Office Ltd, London, 1999 at para 1.6.

[184] *Ibid* at para 1.15.

[185] Hicks A, *Disqualification of Directors: No Hiding Place for the Unfit?* The Association of Chartered Certified Accountants, London, 1998 at 67-78 and 99.

[186] Department of Trade and Industry, *Modern Company Law: The Strategic Framework* HMSO, London, 1999 at Annex D.

[187] Comptroller and Auditor General, *The Insolvency Service Executive Agency: Company Director Disqualification – A Follow Up Report* The Stationery Office Ltd, London, 1999 at para 1.2.

buying a company off the shelf and running it wholly without any prior qualification or competence, something over 1,000 disqualification orders a year makes little impact on the potential legions of the unfit.'[188] Nonetheless, at least anecdotally the threat of disqualification presents as a deterrent.[189] Moreover, at present disqualification is, 'the only curtailment of the statutory privilege to form limited liability companies.'[190]

In order to determine whether or not a director's conduct renders him unfit to be concerned in the management of a British company,[191] statutory guidance has been provided by the British Parliament.[192] Under CDD Act s9(1), a court determining whether a person's conduct as a director makes him unfit to be concerned in the management of a company shall have regard in particular to the matters mentioned in CDD Act Schedule 1 Part I and, where the company has become insolvent, to the matters mentioned in CDD Act Schedule 1 Part II.[193] Part I, for instance, provides that the breach of any fiduciary or other duties by the director in relation to the company is a matter applicable in all cases for determining whether or not that director is unfit to be concerned in the management of a company.[194] However, there is an absence of statutory guidance as to the point at which a director's misconduct is said to breach the duty to exercise care and diligence owed by him or her to the British company concerned.

In *Re Barings plc (No 2)*[195] Chadwick LJ emphasised that it was the person's conduct as a director which was central to the disqualification proceedings. That will necessarily involve an investigation into what responsibility the person concerned had as a director for the insolvency of his or her company. In his Lordship's judgment:

> The relevant question will be whether ... [the director's] acts or omissions fell so far short of the competence required of a director of ... [the company] that the court ought to reach the conclusion that he is unfit to be concerned in the management of a company – that is to say, any company.[196]

In gauging the appropriate standard of care and diligence below which the director's conduct will attract the disapprobation of the English courts, and result in that director's disqualification, therefore, it falls to the common law to assist in determining whether or not the director concerned has met that standard.[197] This, as we have seen from earlier chapters in this book, is not always that easy to formulate. It is exacerbated by the uncertainty which surrounds the appropriate test to be applied by the English courts. Since the celebrated *dicta* of Lord Hatherley LC in *The Overend & Gurney Company*

---

[188] Editorial comment, 'Director disqualification: upping the ante?' (1999) 20 Co Law 97 at 97.
[189] Senate Standing Committee on Legal and Constitutional Affairs, *Social and Fiduciary Duties and Obligations of Company Directors* AGPS, Canberra, 1989 at 194.
[190] Ong K T W, 'Disqualification of directors: a faulty regime?' (1998) 19 Co Law 7 at 7.
[191] Company Directors Disqualification Act 1986 (UK) s6(1).
[192] *Re Barings plc* [1998] BCC 583 at 584 per Sir Richard Scott VC; and *Re Westmid Packing Services Ltd* [1998] 2 All ER 124 at 127 per Lord Woolf MR (Waller and Robert Walker LJJ agreed).
[193] Schulte R, 'Enforcing wrongful trading as a standard of conduct for directors and a remedy for creditors: the special case of corporate insolvency' (1999) 20 Co Law 80 at 82.
[194] *Re Barings plc (No 5)* [1999] 1 BCLC 433 at 483 per Jonathan Parker J; and *Re Bath Glass Ltd* (1988) 4 BCC 130 at 132-133 per Peter Gibson J.
[195] [1999] 1 All ER 311.
[196] *Ibid* at 338-339.
[197] Cf. Report of the Company Law Committee, HMSO, London, Cmnd 1749, 1962 at para 86.

v Gibb,[198] Lindley MR in *Lagunas Nitrate Company v Lagunas Syndicate*,[199] the Earl of Halsbury LC in *Dovey v Cory*,[200] Neville J in *In re Brazilian Rubber Plantations and Estates Ltd*,[201] and Romer J in *In re City Equitable Fire Insurance Company Ltd*,[202] the emergence of an objective test has enjoyed some recognition and a measure of judicial support in English company law, albeit limited.

Few would argue that today the objective test is to be preferred over the subjective test when subjecting the conduct of the director concerned to scrutiny. As we have seen, the subjective test enjoyed pre-eminence during the 19th century,[203] and for much of the 20th century as well.[204] However, if the Australian experience can be relied upon, its demise is imminent.[205] The following passage from Tadgell J's judgment in *Commonwealth Bank of Australia v Friedrich*[206] explains why. There, his Honour noted that as the complexity of commerce has gradually intensified:

> [The] community has of necessity come to expect more than formerly from directors whose task it is to govern the affairs of companies ... In response, the parliaments and the courts have found it necessary in legislation and litigation to refer to the demands made on directors in more exacting terms than formerly; and the standard of capability required of them has correspondingly increased.[207]

In spite of the fact that the conduct of the director concerned ought to be viewed objectively,[208] this area of the law continues to be pre-eminently an area where the legal result is highly sensitive to the particular facts,[209] and each case is to be determined upon its own merits.[210] As Finch explains, directors, 'do not form a homogeneous category and necessary skills vary according to differences in the sizes and purposes of companies, complexities of management structures, reliance on expert advisers and

---

[198] (1872) LR 5 HL 480 at 486-487.

[199] [1899] 2 Ch 392 at 435.

[200] [1901] AC 477 at 482-483.

[201] [1911] 1 Ch 425 at 437.

[202] [1925] Ch 407 at 428.

[203] E.g., *Turquand v Marshall* (1869) 4 Ch App 376 at 386 per Lord Hatherley LC; *In re Denham & Co* (1884) 25 Ch D 752 at 766 per Chitty J; and *In re Cardiff Savings Bank* [1892] 2 Ch 100 at 108-109 per Stirling J.

[204] E.g., *In re Brazilian Rubber Plantations and Estates Ltd* [1911] 1 Ch 425 at 427 per Neville J; *Transvaal Lands Company v New Belgium (Transvaal) Land and Development Company* [1914] 2 Ch 488 at 500 per Swinfen Eady LJ; and *Pavlides v Jensen* [1956] Ch 565 at 570 per Danckwerts J.

[205] Cf. *Bishopsgate Investment Management Ltd v Maxwell (No. 2)* [1994] 1 All ER 261 at 264 per Hoffmann LJ (Leggatt LJ agreed); note Senate Standing Committee on Legal and Constitutional Affairs, *Social and Fiduciary Duties and Obligations of Company Directors* AGPS, Canberra, 1989 at 29.

[206] (1991) 5 ACSR 115.

[207] *Ibid* at 126.

[208] E.g., *Norman v Theodore Goddard* [1992] BCC 14 at 15 per Hoffmann J; *Vrisakis v Australian Securities Commission* (1992-1993) 9 WAR 395 at 451 per Ipp J (Malcolm CJ agreed); *Daniels v Anderson* (1995) 13 ACLC 614 at 662 per Clarke and Sheller JJA; *Androvin v Figliomeni* (1996) 14 ACLC 1461 at 1470 per Owen J (Kennedy and Franklyn JJ agreed); and *Re Barings plc* [1998] BCC 583 at 586 per Sir Richard Scott VC.

[209] *Re Manlon Trading Ltd* [1995] 4 All ER 14 at 17 per Peter Gibson LJ.

[210] *Re Barings plc (No 5)* [1999] 1 BCLC 433 at 484 per Jonathan Parker J; note Malcolm D, 'Directors' Duties: The Governing Principles' in Ramsay I M (ed), *Corporate Governance and the Duties of Company Directors* The Centre for Corporate Law and Securities Regulation, University of Melbourne, Parkville, 1997 at 60 and 78.

roles of the particular directors'.[211] Hence, it is not surprising that there is no catholicon available to the English courts, applicable to each and every case, to enable the courts to assess whether or not the director concerned has fallen below the standard expected of them. As Lord Hoffmann pointed out when he gave the Leonard Sainer Lecture in London on 26 November 1996, 'where the law does not require any kind of qualification for becoming a director, it is not easy to fix an *ex post facto* standard of competence for disqualification.'[212]

The lack of a yardstick, universal in its application to a director's obligations in all circumstances, and against which the standard of care and diligence required of the ubiquitous director can be measured, makes it very difficult to formulate meaningful guidelines to be followed by the English courts in order to delimit unacceptable behaviour.[213] Notwithstanding that each case must be determined upon its own merits,[214] an approach entirely consistent with authority,[215] guidance can be found from the case-law. Within the context of CDD Act s6, a substantial body of jurisprudence has developed in respect to the appropriate standard of care and diligence expected of directors of British companies. It should be remembered, however, that the CDD Act is directed towards the abuse of limited liability, 'and the obligations of a businessman to his creditors rather than general questions of corporate government.'[216] As Lord Hoffmann recently pointed out:

> The Company Directors Disqualification Act is concerned with an altogether different problem. The directors against whom applications for disqualification are made are for the most part sole traders, beneficial owners of the whole issued share capital of a company using the corporate structure simply for the advantages of limited liability.[217]

Even so, the content of the duty owed by directors of British companies in such circumstances must remain constant.[218] Their obligations to the company are only fulfilled by the exercise of a reasonable degree of care and diligence. This was recently highlighted in *Re Barings plc*,[219] although it involved a company and its directors very much at the other end of the scale to that contemplated by Lord Hoffmann, as the remarks attributed to him above suggest.[220] The facts in *Barings* were briefly these. Barings Bank was placed in administration on 26 February 1995. Nick Leeson, one of its employees, was responsible for massive losses in the region of £827m. The collapse of Barings raised the inevitable question: why was Leeson's unauthorised trading able

---

[211] Finch V, 'Company Directors: Who Cares about Skill and Care?' (1992) 55 MLR 179 at 203; cf. *Deputy Commissioner of Taxation v Austin* (1998) 16 ACLC 1555 at 1558-1560 per Madgwick J.

[212] Hoffmann L H, 'The Fourth Annual Leonard Sainer Lecture' (1997) 18 Co Law 194 at 197.

[213] Ipp D A, 'The diligent director' (1997) 18 Co Law 162 at 165.

[214] Malcolm D, 'Directors' Duties: The Governing Principles' in Ramsay I M (ed), *Corporate Governance and the Duties of Company Directors* The Centre for Corporate Law and Securities Regulation, University of Melbourne, Parkville, 1997 at 60 and 78.

[215] *Re Manlon Trading Ltd* [1995] 4 All ER 14 at 17 per Peter Gibson LJ.

[216] Hoffmann L H, 'The Fourth Annual Leonard Sainer Lecture' (1997) 18 Co Law 194 at 197; cf. *Secretary of State for Trade and Industry v Tjolle* [1998] BCC 282 at 290 and 300-301 per Jacob J.

[217] Hoffmann L H, 'The Fourth Annual Leonard Sainer Lecture' (1997) 18 Co Law 194 at 196.

[218] *Re Barings plc (No 5)* [1999] 1 BCLC 433 at 484 per Jonathan Parker J; cf. *Vrisakis v Australian Securities Commission* (1992-1993) 9 WAR 395 at 451 per Ipp J (Malcolm CJ agreed).

[219] [1998] BCC 583.

[220] Hoffmann L H, 'The Fourth Annual Leonard Sainer Lecture' (1997) 18 Co Law 194 at 196.

to continue for so long, undetected and uncontrolled, as to bring down the oldest merchant bank in London?[221]

Following an in-depth investigation into Barings' management structure, its control system and the arrangements in place for funding the trading activities of its subsidiaries, proceedings were instituted by the Secretary for State against ten directors, one of whom was Mr Maclean a senior director within the Barings group. Maclean acknowledged that in the circumstances a disqualification order under CDD Act s6 was appropriate. Sir Richard Scott VC felt that a four year disqualification period was fitting. His Lordship's judgment provides an interesting insight into the way in which the law is gradually evolving in response to changes in public attitudes to corporate governance and what today's directors of British companies must do in order to fulfil their obligations in that regard, and also under the CDD Act. The following extract from Sir Richard Scott VC's judgment is apposite:

[It] was the duty of Mr Maclean, once he became chairman of ALCO which had as part of its responsibilities the responsibility for monitoring risk that had previously been undertaken by the risk committee, to familiarise himself with that part of the committee's responsibility so as to exercise diligently and properly his office of chairman. ... [The] weight of responsibilities that the office carries with it, and those responsibilities require diligent attention from time to time to the question whether the system that has been put in place and over which the individual is presiding is operating efficiently, and whether individuals to whom duties ... have been delegated are discharging those duties efficiently. It plainly becomes individuals holding high office to be responsive to warning signs that indicate some failure in the system, or in the discharge by individuals within the system of their respective responsibilities.[222]

Irrespective of what a particular director's status might be, directors of British and Australian companies are duty bound to keep themselves regularly informed of their company's affairs.[223] It is incumbent upon directors to participate in the supervision and monitoring of their fellow directors and those to whom they delegate functions.[224] As Walters observes:

Directors who abdicate their responsibilities, fail to keep themselves properly informed and/or seek to disassociate themselves completely from the supervision of the company's activities risk disqualification and possible liability for misfeasance should it become insolvent.[225]

The Australian experience, in this respect, is informative and particularly helpful. For instance, it will be recalled that the statutory duty under Corporations Law s232(4) requires a reasonable degree of care and diligence from a director of an Australian company. The decision by the Western Australian Full Court[226] in *Vrisakis v Australian*

---

[221] Cf. *AWA Ltd v Daniels* (1992) 10 ACLC 933 at 937 per Rogers CJ.
[222] [1998] BCC 583 at 586.
[223] *Re Westmid Packing Services Ltd* [1998] 2 All ER 124 at 130 per Lord Woolf MR (Waller and Robert Walker LJJ agreed).
[224] *Daniels v Anderson* (1995) 13 ACLC 614 at 663-666 per Clarke and Sheller JJA.
[225] Walters A, 'Directors' duties and shareholder remedies' (1999) 20 Co Law 138 at 142.
[226] (Malcolm CJ, Rowland and Ipp JJ).

Securities Commission[227] is useful for an appreciation for, and an understanding of, the way in which the appellate courts in Australia are approaching the appropriate standard of care and diligence required in this context. The judgment of Ipp J is most illuminating for present purposes. His Honour dealt with the matter in this way:

> [The] duty imposed by the section is to be objectively determined. However, the ambit of the duty and the standard of care required (ie the specific functions with which particular directors are charged, and what is required to be done so that those functions are properly carried out) depend on the particular circumstances. There is no uniform standard applicable. ... It has often been pointed out that the duties of a director differ from case to case and are dependent entirely on the circumstances. The term 'duties' in this sense refers to the tasks undertaken by directors, in discharge of their office as such, and does not connote the duty to exercise a reasonable degree of care and diligence, the content of which remains constant.[228]

This approach is gradually receiving recognition in English company law. Although *Vrisakis* was not cited in *Barings (No 5)*,[229] nonetheless, the approach taken by Jonathan Parker J in his recent judgment is consistent with that adopted by Ipp J. Jonathan Parker J's judgment in *Barings (No 5)* is impressive: not merely for its length, but rather for its review of the authorities relevant to a determination of unfitness under CDD Act s6, and also for his Lordship's contribution to the development in English company law of the directors' duty to exercise care and diligence generally. In this respect, Jonathan Parker J was assisted by the following passage from the joint judgment of Clarke and Sheller JJA in *Daniels v Anderson*,[230] which his Lordship considered represented the law in England,[231] insofar as the directors' duty to exercise care and diligence is concerned:

> A person who accepts the office of director of a particular company undertakes the responsibility of ensuring that he or she understands the nature of the duty a director is called upon to perform. That duty will vary according to the size and business of the particular company and the experience or skills that the director held himself or herself out to have in support of appointment to the office. None of this is novel. It turns upon the natural expectations and reliance placed by shareholders on the experience and skill of a particular director. ... The duty includes that of acting collectively to manage the company.[232]

Barings (No 5) was concerned with the Secretary of State's application for the disqualification under CDD Act s6 of the remaining three directors, of the initial ten directors, within the Barings group against whom it was alleged that serious failures of management on their part were responsible for Nick Leeson's unauthorised trading activities in Singapore; which trading activities resulted in losses in the region of

---

[227] (1992-1993) 9 WAR 395.
[228] *Ibid* at 451.
[229] [1999] 1 BCLC 433.
[230] Where *Vrisakis v Australian Securities Commission* was referred to: see (1995) 13 ACLC 614 at 662 per Clarke and Sheller JJA.
[231] [1999] 1 BCLC 433 at 488.
[232] (1995) 13 ACLC 614 at 665-666.

£827m and brought down Barings Bank.[233] The only issue before the court in relation to Andrew Tucker, Ronald Baker and Anthony Gamby was whether or not their conduct as directors was such as to make them unfit for the purposes of CDD Act s6. In short, it was the Secretary of State's general case that each was guilty of serious failures of management which demonstrated their incompetence to such a degree as to justify a disqualification order. In the result, Jonathan Parker J was satisfied that Tucker, Baker and Gamby should be disqualified and orders were made accordingly. In reaching this decision, his Lordship considered that the following general propositions could be derived from the authorities in respect to the directors' duty to exercise care and diligence:

> (i) Directors have, both collectively and individually, a continuing duty to acquire and maintain a sufficient knowledge and understanding of the company's business to enable them properly to discharge their duties as directors. (ii) Whilst directors are entitled ... to delegate particular functions to those below them in the management chain, and to trust their competence and integrity to a reasonable extent, the exercise of the power of delegation does not absolve a director from the duty to supervise the discharge of the delegated functions. (iii) No rule of universal application can be formulated as to the duty referred to in (ii) above. The extent of the duty, and the question whether it has been discharged, must depend on the facts of each particular case, including the director's role in the management of the company.[234]

Barings (No 5) is an important case as Jonathan Parker J's judgment is declaratory of important aspects of what constitutes unfitness for the purpose of CDD Act s6, and also provides impetus for the further expansion of the common law duty upon directors of British companies to exercise care and diligence by requiring them to take: (i) positive action to inform themselves about their company's affairs; and (ii) responsibility for the reasonable supervision and control of those to whom they delegate specific tasks and functions. As his Lordship explained, directors must appreciate that having delegated a particular function, they remain responsible and accountable for such delegated functions and will retain a residual duty of supervision and control.[235]

This was the approach of the New South Wales Court of Appeal in *Daniels*;[236] an approach which is gradually coming to enjoy support in English company law.[237] Thus, the envelope is being gradually pushed by the English courts. Until such time, however, as either the Court of Appeal or the House of Lords opines upon these important aspects of the duties which directors owe to their British companies, and a definitive approach is thereby provided as to the modern standard expected of them, English company law will remain of uncertain dimensions in this important and challenging area. In the interim, the development of the directors' duty to exercise care and diligence will continue to be *ad hoc* and incremental.[238]

---

[233] Cf. *Re Barings plc* [1998] BCC 583 at 584 per Sir Richard Scott VC.
[234] [1999] 1 BCLC 433 at 489.
[235] *Ibid* at 487.
[236] (1995) 13 ACLC 614 at 663-666 per Clarke and Sheller JJA.
[237] Davies P L, *Gower's Principles of Modern Company Law* (6th ed) Sweet & Maxwell Ltd, London, 1997 at 643-644.
[238] Law Commission, *Company Directors: Regulating Conflicts of Interests and Formulating a Statement of Duties* HMSO, London, Cm 4436, 1999 at paras 4.27-4.28.

Even though the law surrounding directors' duties is today in a state of flux, in the light of such decisions as *Norman v Theodore Goddard*,[239] *Vrisakis*,[240] *Re D'Jan of London Ltd*,[241] *Daniels*,[242] and *Androvin v Figliomeni*,[243] where objective tests were applied, it is clear that subjectivity is rapidly losing ground to objectivity as the applicable test. Sir Richard Scott VC's judgment in *Barings* marks a further advance towards the development of an objective standard of care and diligence in English company law, and is to be welcomed.[244] So too does Jonathan Parker J's judgment in *Barings (No 5)*.[245] By way of comparison, in Australian company law the test of the reasonable person is now enshrined in statute law.[246] Within the context of insolvency, the duties upon directors of Australian companies operate, 'in the objective rather than the subjective sphere. The question is whether beliefs or expectations are "reasonable" in an objective sense.'[247]

As we go bravely into the 21st century, it is considered that the English courts will more and more resort to the objective test as being the standard applicable to their determination of whether or not a particular director's conduct ought attract their disapprobation, and result in that director's disqualification on the basis that he or she is unfit to be concerned in the management of a British company.[248] This is entirely consistent with the British parliamentary intent behind the enactment of the CDD Act,[249] and was recognised as such by Nicholls VC[250] in *Re Swift 736 Ltd* in these terms:

> Limited liability is a valuable tool in the promotion of trade and business, but it must not be misused. Those who make use of limited liability must do so with a proper sense of responsibility. The director disqualification procedure is an important sanction introduced by Parliament to raise standards in this regard. Those who take advantage of limited liability must conduct their companies with due regard to the ordinary standards of commercial morality. They must also be punctilious in observing the safeguards laid down by Parliament for the benefit of others who have dealings with their companies.[251]

Given the increasing use now being made of disqualification orders,[252] this goes part of the way, as Gower in his fifth edition observes, 'to make up for the fact that no

---

[239]   [1992] BCC 14.
[240]   (1992-1993) 9 WAR 395.
[241]   [1993] BCC 646.
[242]   (1995) 13 ACLC 614.
[243]   (1996) 14 ACLC 1461.
[244]   *Re Barings plc* [1998] BCC 583 at 586.
[245]   [1999] 1 BCLC 433.
[246]   E.g., Corporations Law s232(4).
[247]   *Androvin v Figliomeni* (1996) 14 ACLC 1461 at 1470 per Owen J (Kennedy and Franklyn JJ agreed).
[248]   Company Directors Disqualification Act 1986 (UK) s6(1).
[249]   See, e.g., Walters A and Davis-White M, *Directors' Disqualification: Law & Practice* Sweet & Maxwell Ltd, London, 1999 at chapter 2; note *Re Grayan Building Services Ltd* [1995] BCC 554 at 577 per Henry LJ.
[250]   (Farquharson and Steyn LJJ agreed).
[251]   [1993] BCC 312 at 315; note *Re Grayan Building Services Ltd* [1995] BCC 554 at 574 per Hoffmann LJ (Henry and Neill LJJ agreed).
[252]   Comptroller and Auditor General, *The Insolvency Service Executive Agency: Company Director Disqualification – A Follow Up Report* The Stationery Office Ltd, London, 1999 at paras 1.15 and 1.6.

qualifications are required for appointment as a director,[253] by weeding out those who have proved to be glaringly unfit.'[254]

INSOLVENCY ACT 1986 (UK)

In many respects, the IA 1986 was a long time in coming. Whilst it is generally regarded as having its genesis in the Cork Report's recommendations,[255] which resulted from the review carried out by the Cork Committee during the late 1970s and the early 1980s, its pedigree can be traced back to 1926 and the Greene Report,[256] which was briefly considered above. Those reports, together with the Cohen Report[257] and the Jenkins Report[258] which were produced during the intervening years, are helpful to an appreciation for, and an understanding of, the current legislative framework.

The Insolvency Act emerged briefly in 1976. It was followed by a further Insolvency Act in 1985 ('IA 1985'), which implemented many of the recommendations found within the Cork Report.[259] This resulted in major reforms both to the law of individual bankruptcy and that relating to the winding-up of companies. The IA 1985 was in turn followed by the IA 1986 which consolidated the new, and the surviving earlier, legislation on these areas of the law. The result was to remove from the Companies Act 1985 (UK) all the provisions relating to winding-up and receiverships; areas of law pertaining to the dissolution of companies which can be traced back to the Joint Stock Companies Winding-up Act 1848 (UK).[260] This was followed by the CDD Act which consolidated all the remaining provisions empowering the courts to disqualify those undeserving of acting as directors, or being concerned in the management,[261] of British companies. These provisions had previously been split between the Insolvency Acts and the Companies Acts.[262]

As we have seen from the earlier part of this chapter, during the British companies legislative reforms of the mid-1980s, Companies Act 1985 (UK) s458 retained the criminal element of fraudulent trading, being that which formerly appeared in Companies Act 1948 (UK) s332. The civil sanction for those guilty of directorial misconduct involving misfeasance or breaches of fiduciary, legal or equitable duties was moved to IA 1986 ss212-214. This followed the Cork Report's recommendations which led to their enactment.[263] In keeping with those recommendations, fraudulent trading was extended to wrongful trading for those directors exhibiting a lesser degree

---

[253] Trebilcock M J, 'The Liability of Company Directors for Negligence' (1969) 32 MLR 499 at 502; cf. Company Law Amendment Committee, HMSO, London, Cmd 2657, 1926 at 53.

[254] Gower L C B, *Gower's Principles of Modern Company Law* (5th ed) Sweet & Maxwell Ltd, London, 1992 at 146.

[255] Report of the Review Committee on Insolvency Law and Practice, HMSO, London, Cmnd 8558, 1982.

[256] Company Law Amendment Committee, HMSO, London, Cmd 2657, 1926.

[257] Report of the Committee on Company Law Amendment, HMSO, London, Cmd 6659, 1945.

[258] Report of the Company Law Committee, HMSO, London, Cmnd 1749, 1962.

[259] Sealy L S, *Disqualification and Personal Liability of Directors* (4th ed) CCH Editions Ltd, Bicester, 1993 at para 103.

[260] Finch V, 'The Measures of Insolvency Law' (1997) 17 OJLS 227 at 228.

[261] Cf. Corporations Law s91A.

[262] Davies P L, *Gower's Principles of Modern Company Law* (6th ed) Sweet & Maxwell Ltd, London, 1997 at 51.

[263] *Re Farmizer (Products) Ltd* [1997] BCC 655 at 662 per Peter Gibson LJ (Potter and Butler-Sloss LJJ agreed).

of moral turpitude.[264] It is with these latter sections that we are here concerned for, as the learned authors of *Gower's Principles of Modern Company Law* note, 'they constitute what is probably the most extreme departure from the rule in *Salomon's* case yet achieved in the United Kingdom.'[265]

For the delinquent and fraudulent director whose egregious behaviour warrants prosecution, or whose dereliction has exposed his or her company and its creditors to the perils of insolvency, IA 1986 Part IV Chapter X must present as a minefield and, it is to be hoped, as a significant deterrent.[266] Part IV Chapter X captures malpractice before and during a company's liquidation and is directed at penalising directors *inter alios* both criminally and financially for their corporate misdeeds. At this point, we are concerned only with civil actions against directors brought by liquidators alleging causes of action which emerge in the course of the winding-up of a British company. In this respect, IA 1986 ss212-214 are apposite. All three are linked, as Peter Gibson LJ[267] in *Re Farmizer (Products) Ltd* observed, 'by the common thread that they enable directors and officers to be penalised for wrongdoing.'[268] Under these sections, the English courts are empowered to declare that an errant director is to restore the company's assets or make whatever contribution to the company's assets by way of compensation which the court thinks appropriate.[269] It is instructive to briefly consider the import of each section.

IA 1986 s212 permits the English courts to examine the conduct of a person concerned where it appears to the official receiver, the liquidator, or any creditor or contributory, that that person has misapplied or retained, or become accountable for, any money or other property of the company, or been guilty of any misfeasance or breach of any fiduciary or other duty in relation to the company.[270] Its pedigree extends back to Companies (Winding up) Act 1890 s10.[271] Section 212, in essence, as Hoffmann LJ explained in his judgment in *Re D'Jan of London Ltd*, 'is a summary procedure which used to be called a misfeasance summons but has been extended to include breaches of any duty including the duty of care.'[272] Its application by the English courts today, however, is largely uncontroversial.[273] Section 212 is not available to an

---

[264] Cf. *Australian Growth Resources Corporation Pty Ltd v van Reesema* (1988) 6 ACLC 529 at 539 per King CJ (Cox J agreed); note *Marchesi v Barnes* [1970] VR 434 at 438 per Gowans J; and *Re Living Images Ltd* [1996] BCC 112 at 116 per Laddie J; see Ford H A J and Austin R P, *Ford's Principles of Corporations Law* (6th ed) Butterworths Pty Ltd, Sydney, 1992 at 488-490.

[265] Davies P L, *Gower's Principles of Modern Company Law* (6th ed) Sweet & Maxwell Ltd, London, 1997 at 151.

[266] But as the Jenkins Report noted under its chapter on Enforcement of the Law, when looking at the position which prevailed in 1962, 'The value to the public of the Acts whose operation we have been asked to consider depends upon the extent to which they are effectively enforced.': Report of the Company Law Committee, HMSO, London, Cmnd 1749, 1962 at para 504.

[267] (Potter and Butler-Sloss LJJ agreed).

[268] [1997] BCC 655 at 660.

[269] *Re Farmizer (Products) Ltd* [1997] BCC 655 at 657 per Peter Gibson LJ (Potter and Butler-Sloss LJJ agreed).

[270] E.g., *Re Barton Manufacturing Co Ltd* [1999] 1 BCLC 740; cf. Corporations Law s598; note *Gamble v Hoffman* (1997) 15 ACLC 1314 at 1316 per Carr J; and *Re Property Force Consultancy Pty Ltd* [1997] 1 Qd R 300 at 304-316 per Derrington J.

[271] Cf. *In re Lands Allotment Company* [1894] 1 Ch 616.

[272] [1993] BCC 646 at 647.

[273] Schulte R, 'Corporate groups and the equitable subordination of claims on insolvency' (1997) 18 Co Law 2 at 9.

individual creditor to assert a personal right against a director,[274] nor does it enable the company to recover from a director a mere monetary claim owed to the company.[275] For present purposes, therefore, IA 1986 ss213-214 merit more attention and a brief discourse upon the more recent and interesting case-law advanced by the English courts in their interpretation, will repay analysis.

The provisions dealing with fraudulent trading presently found within IA 1986 s213 are generally the same as the relevant provisions formerly found within Companies Act 1948 (UK) s332; the residue of which is now carried forward into Companies Act 1985 (UK) s458, but only insofar as criminality associated with fraudulent trading is concerned. Decisions on the former, therefore, remain relevant to any deliberations by the English courts upon IA 1986 s213.[276] Unlike the criminal offence of fraudulent trading found within Companies Act 1985 (UK) s458, however, IA 1986 s213 only has application to civil proceedings and then only applies if the company concerned is in liquidation.[277] Companies Act 1985 (UK) s458 applies irrespective of whether or not the company concerned is, or has been, in the course of being wound up. In contrast with the former Companies Act 1948 (UK) s332,[278] applications for a declaration under IA 1986 s213 can be made only by the liquidator.[279]

How then does a liquidator establish that an errant director has been guilty of fraudulent trading under IA 1986 s213? To do so, involves the liquidator establishing that the company's business has been carried on, 'with intent to defraud creditors of the company or creditors of any other person, or for any fraudulent purpose'.[280] Implicit in that is the need, therefore, to demonstrate, albeit to the civil standard on the balance of probabilities,[281] that the director concerned had a fraudulent intent. Historically, this has proven to be no easy task as the following trilogy of cases makes clear. *In re William C Leitch Brothers Limited*[282] is a convenient starting point. There, the court was concerned with the words 'defraud' and 'fraudulent purpose' under the earlier, but corresponding, Companies Act 1929 (UK) s275(1). After observing that the true construction of s275 was a question of great difficulty, Maugham J went on to say that:

> In my opinion I must hold with regard to the meaning of the phrase carrying on business 'with intent to defraud creditors' that, if a company continues to carry on business and to incur debts at a time when there is to the knowledge of the directors no reasonable prospect of the creditors ever receiving payment of those debts, it is, in general, a proper inference that the company is carrying on business with intent to defraud.[283]

---

274   *Yukong Line Ltd of Korea v Rendsburg Investments Corp of Liberia (No. 2)* [1998] 4 All ER 82 at 99 per Toulson J.
275   *In re Etic Limited* [1928] Ch 861 at 873-876 per Maugham J.
276   *Re Farmizer (Products) Ltd* [1997] BCC 655 at 662 per Peter Gibson LJ (Potter and Butler-Sloss LJJ agreed).
277   But not necessarily 'insolvent' liquidation; cf. Insolvency Act 1986 (UK) s214.
278   Under which the application could also have been made by the official receiver, a creditor or a member.
279   *Re Oasis Merchandising Services Ltd* [1997] BCC 282 at 291 *per curiam*.
280   Insolvency Act 1986 (UK) s213(1); cf. Corporations Law s592(6).
281   Cf. Corporations Law s1332; and *Neat Holdings Pty Ltd v Karajan Holdings Pty Ltd* (1993) 67 ALJR 170 at 170-171 per Mason CJ, Brennan, Deane and Gaudron JJ.
282   [1932] 2 Ch 71.
283   *Ibid* at 77.

In re Patrick and Lyon Limited[284] is the second case in point and warrants attention. There, the court was also concerned with the words 'defraud' and 'fraudulent purpose' under Companies Act 1929 (UK) s275(1); a section which in Maugham J's judgment:

> [Is] a very remarkable section and one which is by no means easy to construe. ... I will express the opinion that the words 'defraud' and 'fraudulent purpose', where they appear in the section in question, are words which connote actual dishonesty involving, according to current notions of fair trading among commercial men, real moral blame.[285]

Leitch and *Patrick* were both cited in argument by the appellant in *R v Grantham*,[286] the last of our three cases for consideration. There, the Court of Appeal[287] was faced with an appeal against a conviction of fraudulent trading under Companies Act 1948 (UK) s332(3). In short, the argument was that the trial judge's direction to the jury in respect to s332 had misdirected them as to what it was they had to be satisfied upon before convicting the appellant. Within the trial judge's direction to the jury was this passage:

> [If] a man honestly believes when he obtains credit that although funds are not immediately available he will be able to pay them when the debt becomes due or within a short time thereafter, no doubt you would say that is not dishonest and there is no intent to defraud but if he obtains or helps to obtain credit or further credit when he knows there is no good reason for thinking funds will become available to pay the debt when it becomes due or shortly thereafter then, although it is entirely a matter for you this question of dishonesty, you might well think that is dishonest and there is an intent to defraud.[288]

The Court of Appeal in *Grantham* upheld the trial judge's direction to the jury. Lord Lane delivered the judgment of the Court of Appeal. In his Lordship's view, what the trial judge was saying to the jury in the court below was that insofar as the proper construction of the section was concerned, it was possible for them:

> [To] come to the conclusion that the appellant was acting dishonestly and fraudulently if he realised at the time when the debts were incurred that there was no reason for thinking that funds would become available to pay the debt when it became due or shortly thereafter. We do not think that the Judge was in error in this direction.[289]

Dishonesty is a difficult concept to grasp and to articulate in this context, and presents as a difficult evidentiary barrier to negotiate.[290] The Cork Committee acknowledged the difficulty of establishing dishonesty insofar as the criminal offence of fraudulent trading was concerned. Evidence provided to the Committee suggested a reluctance on the part of the English courts to entertain a claim of civil liability in the absence of dishonesty

---

[284]   [1933] Ch 786.
[285]   *Ibid* at 789-790.
[286]   (1984) 1 BCC 99,075.
[287]   (Lord Lane, Boreham and Stuart-Smith LJJ).
[288]   (1984) 1 BCC 99,075 at 99,078.
[289]   *Ibid.*
[290]   Schulte R, 'Corporate groups and the equitable subordination of claims on insolvency' (1997) 18 Co Law 2 at 9.

and the insistence upon a strict standard of proof.[291] Directors, irrespective of how recklessly or unreasonably they might have behaved, were escaping personal liability by persuading the courts of their honestly held belief that, 'there was light at the end of the tunnel'.[292] For this reason, civil liability was advocated by the Committee without: (i) proof of fraud or dishonesty; and (ii) requiring the criminal standard of proof.[293] It was against this background that the Cork Report recommended the substitution of an objective test for the subjective test which hitherto had prevailed,[294] and the introduction of a new concept of wrongful trading.[295] As the learned authors of *Gower's Principles of Modern Company Law* observe:

> It is this need to prove subjective moral blame that had led the Jenkins Committee in 1962 vainly to recommend the introduction of a remedy for 'reckless trading'[296] and the Cork Committee, 20 years later, successfully to promote it under the name of 'wrongful trading'.[297]

IA 1986 s214 is directed against wrongful trading and, 'measures a director's conduct against a minimum standard of commercial morality and competence.'[298] It was first introduced by IA 1985 s15.[299] What circumstances will constitute wrongful trading? Unlike IA 1986 s213, under s214 the court is empowered only if: (i) the company concerned has gone into insolvent liquidation;[300] (ii) at some time before the commencement of the winding-up of the company, the person concerned knew or ought to have concluded that there was no reasonable prospect that the company would avoid going into insolvent liquidation;[301] and (iii) that person was a director of the company at that time.

In such circumstances, a declaration can be made that that person is to make such contribution to the company's assets as the court thinks proper. But, where the court is satisfied that the director concerned then took every reasonable step to minimise the potential loss to the company's creditors as he or she ought to have taken, once they knew or ought to have concluded that there was no reasonable prospect that the company would avoid going into insolvent liquidation, no declaration can be made.[302] This is a demanding test, however, 'particularly as it does not contain any provision which limits the director's obligation merely to take reasonable steps to avoid loss to creditors.'[303]

---

[291] Cf. *Neat Holdings Pty Ltd v Karajan Holdings Pty Ltd* (1993) 67 ALJR 170 at 170-171 per Mason CJ, Brennan, Deane and Gaudron JJ.

[292] Report of the Review Committee on Insolvency Law and Practice, HMSO, London, Cmnd 8558, 1982 at paras 1776 and 1782.

[293] *Ibid* at para 1778.

[294] *Ibid* at para 1783.

[295] *Ibid* at para 1774 and chapter 44.

[296] Report of the Company Law Committee, HMSO, London, Cmnd 1749, 1962 at para 503(b).

[297] Davies P L, *Gower's Principles of Modern Company Law* (6th ed) Sweet & Maxwell Ltd, London, 1997 at 153.

[298] Schulte R, 'Enforcing wrongful trading as a standard of conduct for directors and a remedy for creditors: the special case of corporate insolvency' (1999) 20 Co Law 80 at 80.

[299] Effective 28 April 1986.

[300] *Re Hydrodan (Corby) Ltd* [1994] BCC 161 at 162 per Millett J.

[301] Insolvency Act 1986 (UK) s214(2); see *Re Oasis Merchandising Services Ltd* [1997] BCC 282 at 284 *per curiam*; and *Re Bath Glass Ltd* (1988) 4 BCC 130 at 133 per Peter Gibson J.

[302] Insolvency Act 1986 (UK) s214(3); cf. Corporations Law ss588H(5) and 588H(6), and 1317EA(4).

[303] Prentice D D, 'Creditor's Interests and Director's Duties' (1990) 10 OJLS 265 at 268.

In judging what facts the director concerned ought to have known or ascertained, what conclusions should have been drawn and what steps should have been taken, statutory guidance has been provided by the British Parliament. Under IA 1986 s214(4), a director's conduct is assessed against that of a reasonably diligent person with the general knowledge, skill and experience reasonably expected of someone carrying out the same functions having the general knowledge, skill and experience that that director has.[304] The standard, as Hazel Williamson QC[305] in *Re Brian D Pierson (Contractors) Ltd* explained, 'is thus an objective minimum, although it may be raised by the particular attributes of the director in question.'[306] That is to say, the errant director's conduct must be looked at objectively; albeit given his or her general knowledge, skill and experience.[307] Thus, notes Finch, 'the honest incompetent and unjustified optimist now has something to fear.'[308] Indeed, that was the case in *Re DKG Contractors Ltd,*[309] where John Weeks QC[310] found the directors' knowledge, skill and experience hopelessly inadequate for the task they undertook. Similarly, in *Re Produce Marketing Consortium Ltd*[311] the directors concerned were there found wanting. The judgment of Knox J in *Produce Marketing* merits attention as it was perhaps a harbinger of a more stringent attitude intended by the British Parliament to the requisite standard sought of directors of British companies in the context of insolvency. The following extract from his Lordship's judgment is pertinent:

> It is evident that Parliament intended to widen the scope of the legislation under which directors who trade on when the company is insolvent may ... be required to make a contribution to the assets of the company which, in practical terms, means its creditors. ... [The] test to be applied by the court has become one under which the director in question is to be judged by the standards of what can be expected of a person fulfilling his functions, and showing reasonable diligence in doing so.[312]

As the subjective test of the directors' duty to exercise care and diligence is more and more displaced by the English courts,[313] the lax behaviour hitherto tolerated of errant directors will gradually disappear.[314] As we have seen in earlier chapters of this book, and as mentioned above, the law in this area is developing. Illustrative of the development of the common law duty to exercise care and diligence in English company law in general, and in the present context of insolvency in particular, is the decision by Hoffmann LJ[315] in *D'Jan*.[316] Although *D'Jan* concerned an application by the liquidator pursuant to IA 1986 s212, his Lordship nonetheless accepted that the duty of care owed by a director at law is accurately stated in IA 1986 s214(4).

---

[304]   Insolvency Act 1986 (UK) s214(4); cf. Corporations Law s588G(2).
[305]   Sitting as a deputy High Court Judge.
[306]   [1999] BCC 26 at 49.
[307]   Ipp D A, 'The diligent director' (1997) 18 Co Law 162 at 166.
[308]   Finch V, 'Company Directors: Who Cares about Skill and Care?' (1992) 55 MLR 179 at 201.
[309]   [1990] BCC 903.
[310]   Sitting as a Chancery Judge.
[311]   (1989) 5 BCC 569.
[312]   *Ibid* at 594.
[313]   Editorial comment, 'Other people's money' (1996) 17 Co Law 98 at 98.
[314]   Gower L C B, *Gower's Principles of Modern Company Law* (5th ed) Sweet & Maxwell Ltd, London, 1992 at 589.
[315]   Sitting as a Chancery Judge.
[316]   [1993] BCC 646.

In finding the director concerned in *D'Jan* negligent, Hoffmann LJ considered that both objectively and subjectively the director did not show reasonable diligence and was, therefore, in breach of his duty to the company.[317] Although there were circumstances peculiar to the errant, but honest, director in *D'Jan* which permitted Hoffmann LJ to invoke Companies Act 1985 (UK) s727,[318] and thereby partly excuse some of the conduct complained of, but not all, it is now accepted that if the director concerned has failed the objective test, then such conduct cannot be excused by the court under s727 on the ground that he or she has acted honestly and reasonably.[319] His Lordship's reasons for exercising the discretion under s727 appear in the following extract from his judgment:

> I think that the economic realities of the case can be taken into account in exercising the discretion under sec. 727. His breach of duty in failing to read the form before signing was not gross. It was the kind of thing which could happen to any busy man, although, as I have said, this is not enough to excuse it. ... Mr D'Jan certainly acted honestly. For the purposes of sec. 727 I think he acted reasonably and I think he ought fairly to be excused for some, though not all, of the liability which he would otherwise have incurred.[320]

Applications under IA 1986 s214 can only be made by the liquidator within six years from the date on which the cause of action accrued;[321] namely, when the company went into insolvent liquidation.[322] Moneys recovered form part of the general assets of the company available to meet the claims of all creditors, and not merely those whose debts were contracted during the time when the trading was wrongful.[323] This is in keeping with traditional principles of insolvency law and enables a *pari passu* distribution of assets to be made in accordance with those principles and the statutory scheme of liquidation.[324] Vinelott J in *Re Purpoint Ltd* put the matter in this way:

> The purpose is to recoup the loss to the company so as to benefit the creditors as a whole. The court has no jurisdiction to direct payment to creditors or to direct that moneys paid to the company should be applied in payment of one class of creditors in preference to another. Moreover, creditors whose debts are incurred after the critical date in fact have no stronger claim than those whose debts were incurred

---

[317] *Ibid* at 648-649; see *Re Sherborne Associates Ltd* [1995] BCC 40.

[318] Cf. Corporations Law ss1317JA(2) and 1318.

[319] *Re Brian D Pierson (Contractors) Ltd* [1999] BCC 26 at 55 per Hazel Williamson QC (sitting as a deputy High Court Judge); and *Re Produce Marketing Consortium Ltd* (1989) 5 BCC 569; cf. Company Law Amendment Committee, HMSO, London, Cmd 2657, 1926 at para 47; and Law Commission, *Fiduciary Duties and Regulatory Rules* HMSO, London, Cm 3049, 1995 at para 12.18.

[320] [1993] BCC 646 at 649; cf. *Gamble v Hoffman* (1997) 15 ACLC 1314 at 1330 per Carr J.

[321] Limitation Act 1980 (UK) s 9(1); cf. Corporations Law s1317EC.

[322] *Re Farmizer (Products) Ltd* [1995] BCC 926 at 933-934 per Blackburne J; affirmed [1997] BCC 655 at 661-663 per Peter Gibson LJ (Potter and Butler-Sloss LJJ agreed).

[323] Davies P L, *Gower's Principles of Modern Company Law* (6th ed) Sweet & Maxwell Ltd, London, 1997 at 155; see *Re Oasis Merchandising Services Ltd* [1997] BCC 282 at 291 *per curiam*; note Insolvency Act 1986 (UK) s107.

[324] *Re Esal (Commodities) Ltd* [1997] 1 BCLC 705 at 715 per Peter Gibson LJ (Hirst and Ralph Gibson LJJ agreed); and *Re Oasis Merchandising Services Ltd* [1997] BCC 282 at 291 *per curiam*; note Insolvency Act 1986 (UK) s107; and Villiers C, 'Employees as creditors: a challenge for justice in insolvency law' (1999) 20 Co Law 222 at 228; cf. Schulte R, 'Corporate groups and the equitable subordination of claims on insolvency' (1997) 18 Co Law 2 at 2 and 11.

before that date. The former class also suffers to the extent that the assets of the company are depleted by wrongful trading.[325]

As mentioned in an earlier part of this chapter, the legislative framework contemplates that shadow directors and *de facto* directors both fall within the generic description of a 'director' under IA 1986 s214.[326] English company law would be a nonsense were it otherwise. Millett J in *Re Hydrodan (Corby) Ltd* made the point rather eloquently in his judgment where he said that:

> Liability cannot sensibly depend upon the validity of the defendant's appointment. Those who assume to act as directors and who thereby exercise the powers and discharge the functions of a director, whether validly appointed or not, must accept the responsibilities which are attached to the office.[327]

It should also be noted that IA 1986 s214 recognises that the person concerned may not be in a position to unilaterally put the company into liquidation. But if, as a reasonable director, he or she ought to have known that the company was heading towards insolvency, they must have done something to seek to prevent its continuing to trade in order to avoid the possibility of having to personally contribute to the payment of the company's debts.[328] Whilst this is not an analogue of the duty upon directors of Australian companies to prevent insolvent trading,[329] it is a positive step on the part of the British Parliament towards making directors of British companies in a parlous financial position, be more vigilant of their company's creditors' interests. By doing so, they also become more vigilant of their own.

PHOENIX COMPANIES

Before leaving this area of the law, mention should also be made of one last evil that is associated with delinquent directors: the so-called phoenix company.[330] The phoenix company is so called because from time to time it rises from the ashes of English and Australian company law left by companies either in, or on the brink of, insolvency.[331] The phoenix company has brought the law in this area into disrepute.[332] Its directors seek to walk away from their responsibilities to the company's creditors by transferring the remaining assets of the insolvent company to a newly formed company thereby

---

[325] [1991] BCC 121 at 128.

[326] Insolvency Act 1986 (UK) ss214(7) and 251; note Prentice D D, 'Creditor's Interests and Director's Duties' (1990) 10 OJLS 265 at 267-268.

[327] [1994] BCC 161 at 162; and *Re Richborough Furniture Ltd* [1996] BCC 155 at 169 per Timothy Lloyd QC (sitting as a deputy High Court Judge); cf. *Re Lo-Line Electric Motors Ltd* (1988) 4 BCC 415 at 422 per Browne-Wilkinson VC.

[328] *Secretary of State for Trade and Industry v Gash* [1997] 1 BCLC 341 at 349 per Chadwick J.

[329] Corporations Law s588G; see *Metropolitan Fire Systems Pty Ltd v Miller* (1997) 23 ACSR 699 at 701-703 per Einfeld J; and *Australian Securities Commission v Forem-Freeway Enterprises Pty Ltd* (1998-1999) 30 ACSR 339 at 340-341 per Madgwick J.

[330] See, e.g., *Re Bonus Breaks Ltd* [1991] BCC 546; *Penrose v Official Receiver* [1996] BCC 311; and *Re Lightning Electrical Contractors Ltd* [1996] BCC 950.

[331] Brennan M, 'The Phoenix Phenomenon' (1996) *Australian Accountant* 42 at 42-43.

[332] *Western Intelligence Ltd v KDO Label Printing Machines Ltd* [1998] BCC 472 at 473 per Jacob J.

enabling them to carry on business largely as before.[333] It was the repeated use by cynical directors of phoenix companies to shed corporate debts that raised public concern in this area.[334] From a corporate regulatory perspective, such companies have proven to be a thorn in the side of the DTI and also ASIC.[335] Given their prevalence, and persistence, over the years, it is hardly surprising that the Cork Committee, during its review in the late 1970s and the early 1980s, received much evidence to the effect that:

> [There] is a widespread dissatisfaction at the ease with which a person trading through the medium of one or more companies with limited liability can allow such a company to become insolvent, form a new company, and then carry on trading much as before, leaving behind him a trail of unpaid creditors, and often repeating the process several times. The dissatisfaction is greatest where the director of an insolvent company has set up business again, using a similar name for the new company, and trades with assets purchased at a discount from the liquidator of the old company.[336]

It was this widespread dissatisfaction with English company law, which permitted directors of British companies to abrogate their responsibilities to their companies' creditors,[337] which was instrumental in the Cork Committee formulating its recommendations in respect to *inter alia* fraudulent trading and wrongful trading. One specific measure recommended by the Cork Committee in order to combat phoenix companies in English company law,[338] is that now implemented by IA 1986 s216.[339] This provides a statutory ban upon directors of a British company which has gone into insolvent liquidation from being directly or indirectly concerned in a company of the same name as the insolvent company, or a name so similar as to suggest an association, for five years from the date upon which the original company went into liquidation. Directors who contravene s216 commit a criminal offence and are liable to imprisonment or a fine, or both.[340] Furthermore, by virtue of IA 1986 s217 such directors assume personal responsibility for all the relevant debts of the company concerned. This, in conjunction with IA ss213-214 and CDD Act ss6 and 10, ought to provide the DTI with an effective enforcement mechanism.[341]

In addition, by virtue of CDD Act s18(2), and the regulations made thereunder,[342] the Secretary of State shall continue to maintain the register of orders set up by him under Companies Act 1976 (UK) s29, and continued under Companies Act 1985 (UK)

---

[333] Department of Trade and Industry, *A Revised Framework for Insolvency Law* HMSO, London, Cmnd 9175, 1984 at para 54; and Hoffmann L H, 'The Fourth Annual Leonard Sainer Lecture' (1997) 18 Co Law 194 at 196.

[334] Finch V, 'The Measures of Insolvency Law' (1997) 17 OJLS 227 at 228.

[335] Hicks A, *Disqualification of Directors: No Hiding Place for the Unfit?* The Association of Chartered Certified Accountants, London, 1998 at 43-44.

[336] Report of the Review Committee on Insolvency Law and Practice, HMSO, London, Cmnd 8558, 1982 at para 1813.

[337] Cf. *Re Westmid Packing Services Ltd* [1998] 2 All ER 124 at 130 per Lord Woolf MR (Waller and Robert Walker LJJ agreed).

[338] Report of the Review Committee on Insolvency Law and Practice, HMSO, London, Cmnd 8558, 1982 at paras 1742 and 1774, and chapter 45.

[339] Formerly Insolvency Act 1976 (UK) s9.

[340] Insolvency Act 1986 (UK) s216(4).

[341] Cf. Milman D, 'Curbing the Phoenix Syndrome' [1997] JBL 224 at 225-226.

[342] Companies (Disqualification Orders) Regulations 1986 (SI 1986/2067).

s301.[343] The register is open to inspection upon the payment of such fee as may be specified, as publicity is crucial to its effectiveness.[344] It identifies cases in which: (i) a disqualification order is made; (ii) any action is taken by a court to vary or terminate such an order; and (iii) leave is granted by a court for a person subject to a disqualification order to do anything which the order would otherwise prohibit him or her from doing.[345]

These examples of statutory intervention by the British Parliament into English company law under the IA 1986, and the CDD Act which supplements and complements that, indirectly extend the directors' duty to exercise care and diligence in keeping with the, 'standards of probity and competence to which the law requires company directors to conform.'[346] Given the significant periods of disqualification which a court can order,[347] someone who has been derelict in their duties can be prevented from acting as a director or a manager of a British company for many years.[348] This may be in addition to the court making a declaration that the errant director concerned is to make a contribution to a company's assets.[349] Not only do such sanctions go some way towards protecting the British public,[350] they are also, 'more likely to encourage care and diligence than the possible liability for damages.'[351] Whilst other examples of statutory intervention can be found within British companies legislation,[352] their application is beyond the remit of this book.[353]

CIVIL PENALTY PROVISIONS

In contrast to English company law, the partial codification of directors' duties in Australian company law[354] has enabled the Australian Parliament to legislate for the provision of statutory compensation, not only in the context of insolvency, but in respect to the broader range of directors' duties generally.[355] As the earlier chapters of

---

[343] Hicks A, *Disqualification of Directors: No Hiding Place for the Unfit?* The Association of Chartered Certified Accountants, London, 1998 at 53-54; and Sealy L S, *Disqualification and Personal Liability of Directors* (4th ed) CCH Editions Ltd, Bicester, 1993 at para 207.

[344] Davies P L, *Gower's Principles of Modern Company Law* (6th ed) Sweet & Maxwell Ltd, London, 1997 at 690.

[345] Company Directors Disqualification Act 1986 (UK) s18(1).

[346] *Re Grayan Building Services Ltd* [1995] BCC 554 at 577 per Neill LJ.

[347] To a maximum of 15 years in some cases.

[348] Company Directors Disqualification Act 1986 (UK) s1(1).

[349] *Ibid* at s10(1).

[350] *Re Sevenoaks Stationers (Retail) Ltd* [1990] BCC 765 at 773 per Dillon LJ (Butler-Sloss and Staughton LJJ agreed); note *Re Grayan Building Services Ltd* [1995] BCC 554 at 577 per Henry LJ; *Re Richborough Furniture Ltd* [1996] BCC 155 at 166 per Timothy Lloyd QC (sitting as a deputy High Court Judge); *Re Continental Assurance Co of London plc* [1997] 1 BCLC 48 at 59 per Chadwick J; and *Re Blackspur Group plc* [1998] 1 BCLC 676 at 680 and 688 per Lord Woolf MR (Millett and Mummery LJJ agreed); cf. *Australian Securities Commission v Forem-Freeway Enterprises Pty Ltd* (1998-1999) 30 ACSR 339 at 349 per Madgwick J.

[351] Gower L C B, *Gower's Principles of Modern Company Law* (5th ed) Sweet & Maxwell Ltd, London, 1992 at 589.

[352] E.g., Companies Act 1985 (UK) ss310-347.

[353] See, e.g., Davies P L, *Gower's Principles of Modern Company Law* (6th ed) Sweet & Maxwell Ltd, London, 1997 at 623-640; and Walters A, 'Directors' duties and shareholder remedies' (1999) 20 Co Law 138 at 138-142.

[354] E.g., Corporations Law ss232 and 588G.

[355] *Ibid* at Parts 5.7B and 9.4B.

this book have highlighted, this was achieved as part of the Australian Government's clearly stated intention at the time to provide a sound and well-regulated environment for corporate activity.[356] One way in which the Australian Parliament has seen fit to keep abreast of public sentiment and business expectations in this regard, and combat some of the same sorts of criticisms which were directed to the Cork Committee during its review in the late 1970s and the early 1980s,[357] is by the introduction of civil penalty provisions under a new and radical regime found within Corporations Law Part 9.4B.[358]

Although essentially procedural in nature, it is considered that given the novelty of civil penalty provisions, mention ought be made of this remedy within the specific context of insolvency and in the light of the statutory duty upon directors of Australian companies to prevent insolvent trading.[359] But it should be remembered that civil penalty provisions have equal application across the whole gamut of directors' statutory duties, including those to act honestly on the one hand, and to exercise care and diligence on the other hand.[360] However, as Whincop has recently concluded, to the extent that civil penalty provisions create civil remedies, the statutory duties upon directors of Australian companies change little.[361] Nevertheless, civil penalty provisions within Australian company law do provide a good example of statutory intervention at work, and it is instructive to consider them in the light of the examples of statutory intervention examined above; being some of those which the British Parliament has introduced to date into English company law.[362]

Civil penalty provisions were also considered in chapter five of this book. It will be recalled from there that the Corporate Law Reform Act 1992 (Cth)[363] was enacted by the Australian Parliament, partly in response to the many recommendations for reform made by the Senate Standing Committee on Legal and Constitutional Affairs in its report on directors' duties ('Cooney Report').[364] Relevantly, the Senate Standing Committee recommended that wherever possible Australian company law should be decriminalised.[365] As a consequence, sanctions hitherto attracted by contraventions of directors' duties under the Corporations Law, have now been reformed.[366] It is suggested that the decriminalisation of directors' duties, as far as reasonably possible, will go some way towards overcoming the difficulties brought about by the intermixture

---

[356] Commonwealth, House of Representatives, Parliamentary Debates, 8 November 1990 at 3669.

[357] E.g., Report of the Review Committee on Insolvency Law and Practice, HMSO, London, Cmnd 8558, 1982 at paras 1742, 1759 and 1813.

[358] Added by Act No. 210 of 1992 and effective 1 February 1993.

[359] Corporations Law s588G; see *Metropolitan Fire Systems Pty Ltd v Miller* (1997) 23 ACSR 699 at 701-703 per Einfeld J; and *Australian Securities Commission v Forem-Freeway Enterprises Pty Ltd* (1998-1999) 30 ACSR 339 at 340-341 per Madgwick J.

[360] Corporations Law ss232(2) and 232(4); see Ford H A J, Austin R P and Ramsay I M, *Ford's Principles of Corporations Law* (9th ed) Reed International Books Australia Pty Ltd, Sydney, 1999 at paras 3.390, 8.360 and 9.288.

[361] Whincop M J, 'An Economic Analysis of the Criminalisation and Content of Directors' Duties' (1996) 24 ABLR 273 at 280.

[362] E.g., Insolvency Act 1986 (UK) ss212-214; and Company Directors Disqualification Act 1986 (UK) ss2, 4, 6, 8 and 10.

[363] Act No. 210 of 1992 and effective 1 February 1993 and 23 June 1993.

[364] Senate Standing Committee on Legal and Constitutional Affairs, *Social and Fiduciary Duties and Obligations of Company Directors* AGPS, Canberra, 1989.

[365] *Ibid* at 58; note House of Representatives Standing Committee on Legal and Constitutional Affairs, *Corporate Practices and the Rights of Shareholders* AGPS, Canberra, 1991 at 211-213; Baxt R, 'Can the Law Relating to Directors' Duties be Reformed?' (1990) 8 CSLJ 110 at 114-115; and Sealy L S, 'Reforming the Law on Directors' Duties' (1991) 12 Co Law 175 at 178.

[366] Bird H, 'The Problematic Nature of Civil Penalties in the Corporations Law' (1996) 14 CSLJ 405 at 409.

of criminal liability with civil liability within some provisions of the legislation which proscribes directorial misconduct.

This intermixture of criminal liability with civil liability can result in confusion insofar as the necessary burden of proof in civil proceedings is concerned. In English company law, for example, Companies Act 1948 (UK) s332 created not only a civil and a personal liability upon directors, but also a criminal offence. The constituent elements of the two were identical. The Cork Committee found that as a result, 'the Courts have consistently refused to entertain a claim to civil liability in the absence of dishonesty and, moreover, have insisted upon a strict standard of proof.'[367] This ultimately led to the enactment of Companies Act 1985 (UK) s458 which retained only the criminal element of fraudulent trading, being that which formerly appeared in Companies Act 1948 (UK) s332, and the enactment of IA 1986 s213 which only has application to civil proceedings taken in respect to fraudulent trading. Even so, in that context, and also for the purposes of CDD Act s6, the English courts have demonstrated a propensity to err on the conservative side. As Griffin notes:

> While the standard of proof remains formally moored to a civil standard, the satisfaction of that standard is more emphatic of a greater and more cogent degree of evidence than is normally required of the civil standard of proof.[368]

Corporations Law Part 9.4B implements the Senate Standing Committee's recommendations to the effect that: (i) criminal liability under the Corporations Law ought not apply in the absence of crimination; (ii) Corporations Law s232 be amended so that criminal liability only applies where conduct is genuinely criminal in nature;[369] and (iii) civil penalties be provided in the Corporations Law for breaches where no criminality is involved and that those suffering loss as a result of a breach be enabled to bring a claim for compensation.[370] By designating particular sections within the Corporations Law as civil penalty provisions, Part 9.4B draws those sections under its umbrella and provides civil and criminal consequences in the event of contravention, as appropriate.[371] These consequences are to be determined by separate proceedings, as the civil and criminal penalty regimes operate as alternatives.[372]

Should a director contravene a duty prescribed by either Corporations Law ss232(2) or 232(4), then he or she will be subject to Corporations Law Part 9.4B Division 2 which exposes that director to a pecuniary penalty specified by the court in an amount

---

[367] Report of the Review Committee on Insolvency Law and Practice, HMSO, London, Cmnd 8558, 1982 at paras 1759 and 1776.

[368] Griffin S, 'Standard of proof applicable to s6 of the Company Directors Disqualification Act 1986' (1997) 18 Co Law 24 at 25.

[369] Cf. *Proprietary Articles Trade Association v Attorney-General for Canada* [1931] AC 310 at 324 per Lord Atkin (Lords Blanesburgh, Merrivale, Russell and MacMillan agreed), 'Criminal Law connotes only the quality of such acts or omissions as are prohibited under appropriate penal provisions by authority of the State. The criminal quality of an act cannot be discerned by intuition; nor can it be discovered by reference to any standard but one: Is the act prohibited with penal consequences? Morality and criminality are far from co-extensive'.

[370] Senate Standing Committee on Legal and Constitutional Affairs, *Social and Fiduciary Duties and Obligations of Company Directors* AGPS, Canberra, 1989 at 189-191; note House of Representatives Standing Committee on Legal and Constitutional Affairs, *Corporate Practices and the Rights of Shareholders* AGPS, Canberra, 1991 at 211-213.

[371] Commonwealth, House of Representatives, Parliamentary Debates, 3 November 1992 at 2403; and Commonwealth, Senate, Parliamentary Debates, 12 November 1992 at 2853.

[372] Bird H, 'The Problematic Nature of Civil Penalties in the Corporations Law' (1996) 14 CSLJ 405 at 407.

not exceeding \$200,000.[373] *ASC v Donovan*[374] is apposite. There, one of the errant directors concerned received a civil penalty of \$40,000. In addition, by virtue of Corporations Law s1317EA(3)(a), the court may also make against the errant director, 'an order prohibiting the person, for such period as is specified in the order, from managing a corporation';[375] although no temporal range is stipulated. In *Donovan*, for instance, one of the errant directors concerned was prohibited from managing a corporation for ten years.

Like the disqualification provision found within CDD Act s6, for example, the thrust of a prohibition order within Corporations Law Part 9.4B is directed at the protection of the public and not punishment.[376] Section 1317EA(3)(a) is designed to prevent a corporate structure, 'being used by individuals in a manner which is contrary to proper commercial standards.'[377] This was recently reaffirmed by the Federal Court of Australia in *Australian Securities Commission v Forem-Freeway Enterprises Pty Ltd*.[378] There, the Federal Court was concerned with an errant director who had contravened a number of civil penalty provisions. The Federal Court prohibited him from managing a corporation for a period of 12 years. Madgwick J put the proposition in this way:

> I take it to be trite law that the purpose of the power in the court to prohibit an errant company officer from managing a corporation is protective of the public. This has fortunate and unfortunate consequences for the wrongdoer. He or she should, on the one hand, not be subject to any enlargement of the period of prohibition by reasons of or deriving from misplaced conceptions of punishment, such as 'general deterrence'. On the other hand, any hardship to the person concerned must play a lesser role in moderating a period of prohibition otherwise appropriate.[379]

By virtue of Corporations Law s1317EA(3)(b), the beneficiary of a civil penalty order is ordinarily the Commonwealth. Part 9.4B does permit under Division 5, however, an application by a company to the court for an order that the director concerned compensate the company in such amount as the order specifies.[380] Notwithstanding that compensation is sought by the company in such circumstances, Corporations Law s1317HE expressly preserves the company's right to seek non-statutory remedies from the director concerned. The importance of this will become evident in the next chapter of this book. Section 1317EA(3)(b) is punitive in character. Its underlying philosophy and rationale was explained by Cooper J in *ASC v Donovan* in the following manner:

[373] Corporations Law s1317EA(3)(b).
[374] (1998) 28 ACSR 583.
[375] Corporations Law ss230 and 599 also enable the court to prohibit a director from managing a company; cf. Company Directors Disqualification Act 1986 (UK) ss2, 4, 6, 8 and 10.
[376] Cf. *Re Lo-Line Electric Motors Ltd* (1988) 4 BCC 415 at 422 per Browne-Wilkinson VC; *Re Sevenoaks Stationers (Retail) Ltd* [1990] BCC 765 at 773 per Dillon LJ (Butler-Sloss and Staughton LJJ agreed); note *Re Grayan Building Services Ltd* [1995] BCC 554 at 577 per Henry LJ; *Re Richborough Furniture Ltd* [1996] BCC 155 at 166 per Timothy Lloyd QC (sitting as a deputy High Court Judge); *Re Continental Assurance Co of London plc* [1997] 1 BCLC 48 at 59 per Chadwick J; and *Re Blackspur Group plc* [1998] 1 BCLC 676 at 680 and 688 per Lord Woolf MR (Millett and Mummery LJJ agreed).
[377] *ASC v Donovan* (1998) 28 ACSR 583 at 602 per Cooper J.
[378] (1998-1999) 30 ACSR 339.
[379] *Ibid* at 349.
[380] Corporations Law s1317HA(1).

Its purpose in an appropriate case is to punish, but principally imposition of a pecuniary penalty is to act as a personal deterrent and a deterrent to the general public against a repetition of like conduct. The legislative deterrent effect is aimed at preventing a corporate structure being used by an individual in a manner which is contrary to proper commercial standards to the detriment of the company, its shareholders, creditors, investors and others dealing with it.[381]

Corporations Law s1317HA(2) permits a company to intervene in an application for a civil penalty order and, by virtue of sub-section (3), the company is entitled to be heard if the court is satisfied that the director concerned committed the contravention in relation to that company, but relevantly only on the question whether compensation should be ordered against that director in favour of the company because of the contravention. Similarly, Corporations Law s1317HD(1) facilitates an accounting in favour of the company for an amount equal to any profits made by an errant director because of an act or omission which contravenes a civil penalty provision; alternatively, in the event that the company has suffered loss or damage as a result of that act or omission, the director concerned must account to the company for an amount equal to the amount of that loss or damage.

For present purposes, it should be noted that Corporations Law ss232(6B) and 1317DA expressly provide that Corporations Law ss232(2), 232(4) and 588G are civil penalty provisions and, thus, are subject to the new regime.[382] Significantly, criminality associated with the breach of duties prescribed by ss232(2), 232(4) and 588G now only attaches where a director has contravened a civil penalty provision knowingly, intentionally or recklessly,[383] and either: (i) dishonestly and intending to gain, whether directly or indirectly, an advantage for that or any other person; or (ii) intending to deceive or defraud someone.[384] This carries into effect the Cooney Report's recommendation that criminal liability should only apply, 'where conduct is genuinely criminal in nature.'[385]

---

[381]   (1998) 28 ACSR 583 at 608.

[382]   *Metropolitan Fire Systems Pty Ltd v Miller* (1997) 23 ACSR 699 at 713 per Einfeld J.

[383]   Presumably in the *Derry v Peek* (1889) 14 App Cas 337 at 374 per Lord Herschell (Lords Halsbury LC and Watson agreed) sense; cf. *Regina v Mackinnon* [1959] 1 QB 150 at 153 per Salmon J; *The Queen v Phillips* [1971] 45 ALJR 467 at 478 per Windeyer J; *Manning v Cory* [1974] WAR 60 at 63 per Burt J; *Hyam v Director of Public Prosecutions* [1975] AC 55 at 74 per Lord Hailsham; *McL v Flavel* (1986) 4 ACLC 45 at 52-54 per Bollen J; *Brick and Pipe Industries Ltd v Occidental Life Nominees Pty Ltd* (1991-1992) 6 ACSR 464 at 478 *per curiam*; *Hatty v Pilkinton* (1992) 108 ALR 149 at 156-157 *per curiam*; and *Pollard v Commonwealth Director of Public Prosecutions* (1992) 8 ACSR 813 at 822-827 per Abadee J.

[384]   Corporations Law s1317FA(1); Corporations Law Schedule 3 provides a penalty for the breach of s1317FA(1) in the form of a fine not exceeding $200,000 and/or imprisonment for a term not exceeding five years; note *R v Martyn* [1954] SASR 161 at 165 per Napier CJ; *Hardie v Hanson* (1960-1961) 105 CLR 451 at 456-460 per Dixon CJ; *Welham v Director of Public Prosecutions* [1961] AC 103 at 124-129 per Lord Radcliffe (Lords Tucker, Keith and Morris agreed); *Marchesi v Barnes* [1970] VR 434 at 437-438 per Gowans J; *Scott v Metropolitan Police Commissioner* [1975] AC 819 at 839 per Viscount Dilhorne (Lords Reid, Diplock, Simon and Kilbrandon agreed); *R v Ghosh* [1982] 2 All ER 689 at 695-696 per Lord Lane CJ (Lloyd and Eastham JJ agreed); *Corporate Affairs Commission v Papoulias* (1990-1991) 20 NSWLR 503 at 506 per Allen J; *Feil v Commissioner of Corporate Affairs* (1991) 9 ACLC 811 at 816-818 per O'Bryan J; and *Chew v The Queen* (1991-1992) 173 CLR 626 at 633-634 per Mason CJ, Brennan, Gaudron and McHugh JJ, at 637 per Deane J and at 640 per Dawson J.

[385]   Senate Standing Committee on Legal and Constitutional Affairs, *Social and Fiduciary Duties and Obligations of Company Directors* AGPS, Canberra, 1989 at 190.

Thus, if the wisdom of the Senate Standing Committee is to be accepted,[386] then the removal of the criminal flavour from the statutory obligations of directors, by the introduction of the new civil penalty provisions regime under Corporations Law Part 9.4B, should add a fresh impetus to civil litigants seeking to avail themselves of statutory rights and remedies stemming from Australian companies legislation, where applicable. *Metropolitan Fire Systems Pty Ltd v Miller*[387] is a case in point. There, the Federal Court of Australia ordered the errant directors concerned to pay compensation by reason of their having caused their company to incur debts to Metropolitan Fire Systems Pty Ltd in breach of Corporations Law s588G.

The principal advantage of proceeding under the new Corporations Law Part 9.4B regime is that the proceedings are to be treated as civil proceedings and subject, therefore, to the rules of evidence and procedure applicable in hearing and determining civil matters,[388] and the civil standard of proof;[389] namely, the balance of probabilities.[390] It follows that the under-utilisation of Corporations Law ss232(2) and 232(4), which was earlier identified in chapter five of this book, may gradually be reversed.[391] By virtue of Corporations Law s1317EB(1), however, it will be ASIC which mainly brings these actions given its domain as Australia's corporate regulator.[392] As such, the challenge is now with ASIC, as Gething observes:

[To] use the regime it has at its disposal fully, effectively and creatively to ensure that directors comply with the civil penalty provisions in a way that maintains, facilitates and improves the performance of companies and the efficiency and development of the economy.[393]

Research conducted during 1998 by the Centre for Corporate Law and Securities Regulation, under the auspices of the University of Melbourne, however, suggests that ASIC has not fully taken up this challenge. The Centre found that ASIC had commenced only 14 civil penalty applications relating to ten case situations from the inception of civil penalty provisions on 1 February 1993.[394] Even so, it should be remembered that the sixth anniversary of the introduction into Australian company law of civil penalty provisions has only been reached, and the statutory import of Corpora-

---

[386] *Ibid* at 58.
[387] (1997) 23 ACSR 699.
[388] Corporations Law s1317ED(1).
[389] *Ibid* at s1332.
[390] Bird H, 'The Problematic Nature of Civil Penalties in the Corporations Law' (1996) 14 CSLJ 405 at 418; note *Neat Holdings Pty Ltd v Karajan Holdings Pty Ltd* (1993) 67 ALJR 170 at 170-171 per Mason CJ, Brennan, Deane and Gaudron JJ.
[391] *Airpeak Pty Ltd v Jetstream Aircraft Ltd* (1997) 15 ACLC 715 at 720-721 per Einfeld J; cf. *Mesenberg v Cord Industrial Recruiters Pty Ltd* (1996) 14 ACLC 519 at 526-527 per Young J; note Baxt R, 'Doubt on statutory derivative action' (1996) 12 Co Dir 4 at 5-6.
[392] *Metropolitan Fire Systems Pty Ltd v Miller* (1997) 23 ACSR 699 at 713 per Einfeld J; *Airpeak Pty Ltd v Jetstream Aircraft Ltd* (1997) 15 ACLC 715 at 720 per Einfeld J; cf. *Titlow v Intercapital Group (Australia) Pty Ltd* (1996) 20 ACSR 201 at 204 per Lehane J; note Corporations Law s1317HD(1); and Whincop M J, 'An Economic Analysis of the Criminalisation and Content of Directors' Duties' (1996) 24 ABLR 273 at 280.
[393] Gething M, 'Do We Really Need Criminal and Civil Penalties for Contraventions of Directors' Duties?' (1996) 24 ABLR 375 at 390.
[394] Bird H L, Gilligan G and Ramsay I M, *Regulating Directors' Duties – How Effective are the Civil Penalty Sanctions in the Australian Corporations Law?* The Centre for Corporate Law and Securities Regulation, The University of Melbourne, Parkville, 1999 at vii and 23.

tions Law Part 9.4B, and Corporations Law ss232 and 588G as a whole for that matter, remains in its infancy. Thus, its effectiveness is perhaps a little too early to judge. Needless to say, there is little case-law specifically on these new sections within Part 9.4B, although it is starting to emerge.[395] However, it is acknowledged that Part 9.4B has its genesis in, and is an analogue of, Trade Practices Act 1974 (Cth) Part VI. It is therefore considered likely that the Australian courts will look to, and draw upon, decisions which are affected by that legislation,[396] in the event that civil penalty provisions are availed of by ASIC more than presently seems to be the case.[397]

CONCLUSION

Nowhere is the balancing exercise which underpins the corporate regulation of directorial misconduct and decision-making more evident than in the context of insolvency. Within that context, the British and the Australian companies legislation which has been considered in this chapter is, 'designed to ensure that directors of companies act at an early stage when faced with the prospect of insolvency either to take remedial action or to initiate the appropriate insolvency procedure.'[398] This is an important feature of any well-regulated environment for corporate activity.[399]

The examples of statutory intervention on the part of the British and the Australian Parliaments which we have examined in this chapter will assist the corporate watchdogs in England and in Australia to carry out their responsibilities. The DTI, for instance, is now better equipped than at any other time to meet its fundamental objectives to, 'encourage, assist and ensure the proper regulation of British trade, industry and commerce, and to promote a climate conducive to growth and the national production of wealth.'[400] These laudable objectives are not too dissimilar to those of ASIC, its Australian counterpart.[401] Insofar as the DTI is concerned, or rather the Insolvency Service Executive Agency which has the day-to-day running of such matters and over which the DTI exercises executive responsibility,[402] it is the view of the learned authors of *Gower's Principles of Modern Company Law* that:

---

[395] *Australian Securities Commission v Major* (unreported, Federal Court of Australia, Queensland District Registry No. QG3011/96, Drummond J, 16 August 1996) and *Stargard Security Systems Pty Ltd v Goldie* (1994) 13 ACSR 805 were concerned with Corporations Law s588G and appear to be amongst the first decisions involving Corporations Law Part 9.4B; see also *ASC v Donovan* (1998) 28 ACSR 583; *Simar Transit Mixers Pty Ltd v Baryczka* (1998) 28 ACSR 238; *Australian Securities Commission v Spencer* (1997) 25 ACSR 143; *Metropolitan Fire Systems Pty Ltd v Miller* (1997) 23 ACSR 699; and *Airpeak Pty Ltd v Jetstream Aircraft Ltd* (1997) 15 ACLC 715; cf. *Mesenberg v Cord Industrial Recruiters Pty Ltd* (1996) 14 ACLC 519.

[396] E.g., *Trade Practices Commission v Prestige Motors Pty Ltd* (1994) 16 ATPR 42693; and *Trade Practices Commission v TNT Australia Pty Ltd* (1995) 17 ATPR 40161.

[397] Bird H L, Gilligan G and Ramsay I M, *Regulating Directors' Duties – How Effective are the Civil Penalty Sanctions in the Australian Corporations Law?* The Centre for Corporate Law and Securities Regulation, The University of Melbourne, Parkville, 1999 at vii and 23.

[398] Department of Trade and Industry, *A Revised Framework for Insolvency Law* HMSO, London, Cmnd 9175, 1984 at para 5.

[399] Commonwealth, House of Representatives, Parliamentary Debates, 8 November 1990 at 3669.

[400] Department of Trade and Industry, *A Revised Framework for Insolvency Law* HMSO, London, Cmnd 9175, 1984 at para 5.

[401] Australian Securities and Investments Commission Act 1989 (Cth) s1(2).

[402] Comptroller and Auditor General, *The Insolvency Service Executive Agency: Company Director Disqualification – A Follow Up Report* The Stationery Office Ltd, London, 1999 at para 1.5.

[Its] activities probably do far more to protect the interests of shareholders and creditors than the recent developments in the common law of directors' duties, whether by recognition of the interests of the creditors or by way of the development of an objective standard of care.[403]

As the British and Australian Parliaments statutorily intervene more and more into English and Australian company law, as it is suggested they will, each will constantly be faced with the need to enact laws to ensure compliance with certain minimum standards on the one hand, and the need to ensure that directors are not inhibited from carrying out their lawful day-to-day activities on the other hand.[404] It will then fall to the English judiciary and the Australian judiciary to enforce those laws by moving away from, 'the low standards of skill and diligence required of directors by the nineteenth-century judges.'[405] This is happening more and more in English and Australian company law as we confront the challenges of the 21st century. The experience of the past decade or so testifies to that. However, as we have seen from earlier chapters of this book, the circumstances in which directors ought be held accountable by the judiciary need to be carefully considered lest the scales tilt too far against the interests of commerce and snuff out the entrepreneurial flame.[406] This point is illustrated rather nicely by Scott J's judgment in *National Companies and Securities Commission v Hurley*, as the following extract makes clear:

> The management and direction of companies involves taking decisions and embarking upon actions which may promise much, on the one hand, but which are, at the same time, fraught with risk on the other. That is inherent in the life of industry and commerce. The legislature undoubtedly did not intend ... to dampen business enterprise and penalise legitimate but unsuccessful entrepreneurial activity.[407]

With the enactment of the IA 1986 and the CDD Act in English company law, and with the enactment of Corporations Law Parts 5.7B and 9.4B in Australian company law, within the context of insolvency, more stringent standards of care, skill and diligence have been imposed upon directors of British and Australian companies.[408] That ought inevitably lead to a further raising of directorial standards over time, not only in the

---

[403] Davies P L, *Gower's Principles of Modern Company Law* (6th ed) Sweet & Maxwell Ltd, London, 1997 at 690.

[404] Gething M, 'Do We Really Need Criminal and Civil Penalties for Contraventions of Directors' Duties?' (1996) 24 ABLR 375 at 389.

[405] Davies P L, *Gower's Principles of Modern Company Law* (6th ed) Sweet & Maxwell Ltd, London, 1997 at 656.

[406] Dwight F, 'Liability of Corporate Directors' (1907-1908) 17 YLJ 33 at 36, 'The canons of directorial responsibility are asserted bravely but almost invariably with a countervailing insistence upon preventing alarm to conscientious directors.'; note *Macquarie Bank Ltd v Fociri Pty Ltd* (1992) 10 ACLC 785 at 797 per Kirby P, 'There must be limits [to the imposition of greater liability] ... lest the brilliant idea which lay behind the separate legal personality of the corporation is undone to the disadvantage of the venturesome entrepreneurial spirit which is essential to driving a modern economy with its need for risk-taking.'

[407] (1995) 13 ACLC 1635 at 1642 per Scott J (Malcolm CJ and Anderson J agreed).

[408] Prentice D D, 'Directors, Creditors and Shareholders' in McKendrick E (ed), *Commercial Aspects of Trusts and Fiduciary Obligations* Clarendon Press, Oxford, 1992 at 80-81; note Herzberg A, 'Insolvent Trading' (1991) 9 CSLJ 285 at 294.

context of insolvency, but throughout English and Australian company law in general.[409] As a matter of practice opines Farrar:

> [We] should see directors bringing greater care and skill to their positions as they attempt to avoid the personal liability and disqualification provided by those Acts for directors who fail to reach an appropriate standard of conduct. The existing case-law must now be read in the light of these legislative developments.[410]

This chapter, and those preceding it, have sought to demonstrate that over time modern expectations of directors of British and Australian companies are gradually being realised. There is no doubt, in Malcolm's view, 'that the bar has been raised in accordance with changing expectations, both in the community and in the commercial world.'[411] It seems that at least in the context of insolvency, Menzies' oft quoted prophecy that, 'what is in general expected of directors will tend to become the measure of what is required of them',[412] has become self-fulfilling.

---

[409]   Davies P L, *Gower's Principles of Modern Company Law* (6th ed) Sweet & Maxwell Ltd, London, 1997 at 642-643.

[410]   Farrar J H, Furey N E, Hannigan B M and Wylie P, *Farrar's Company Law* (3rd ed) Butterworth & Co (Publishers) Ltd, London, 1991 at 397; see *Re Swift 736 Ltd* [1993] BCC 312 at 315 per Nicholls VC (Farquharson and Steyn LJJ agreed); *Re Grayan Building Services Ltd* [1995] BCC 554 at 577 per Henry LJ; *Re Living Images Ltd* [1996] BCC 112 at 115 per Laddie J; and *Re Richborough Furniture Ltd* [1996] 1 BCLC 507 at 520 per Timothy Lloyd QC (sitting as a deputy High Court Judge).

[411]   Malcolm D, 'Directors' Duties: The Governing Principles' in Ramsay I M (ed), *Corporate Governance and the Duties of Company Directors* The Centre for Corporate Law and Securities Regulation, University of Melbourne, Parkville, 1997 at 78.

[412]   Menzies D, 'Company Directors' (1959) 33 ALJ 156 at 164.

9

The Breach of Directors' Duties:
Are the Remedies Equitable?

INTRODUCTION

It is not intended that this chapter should provide an exhaustive analysis of the vast array of non-statutory, and statutory, remedies which are now available within English and Australian company law to redress breaches of directors' duties. The law of remedies is so broad a topic as to warrant a book in its own right. In the space available in this chapter, it is possible only to mention some of the more controversial and substantive aspects of, principally, equitable remedies given their revival in English and Australian company law.[1]

Throughout this book it has been argued that equity is alive and well.[2] Nowhere is this better demonstrated than in the modern application of equitable remedies;[3] refashioned by a judiciary more robust and interventionist than its predecessors, and applied in commercial and corporate circumstances considered more complex than at any earlier time.[4] Admittedly, within English and Australian company law, statutory remedies are playing an increasingly important role, but such remedies are largely procedural in nature and, thus, capable of somewhat less controversial application. In the previous chapter of this book we considered some of those statutory remedies which are today available to the English and Australian courts in order to curb directorial misconduct, and to make directors of British and Australian companies more accountable and responsible for their actions and inaction.

Whilst remedies lie at the sharp end of legal doctrine, the law of remedies is a much neglected subject in legal scholarship.[5] This is evident in practice where plaintiffs will

---

[1] *Royal Brunei Airlines Sdn Bhd v Tan* [1995] 2 AC 378 at 381-382 per Lord Nicholls (Lords Goff, Ackner and Steyn and Sir John May agreed); see McCormack G, 'Fiduciaries in a changing commercial climate' (1997) 18 Co Law 38; and Pascoe J, 'Equitable Remedies in Cases of Misapplied Company Funds: Recent Developments' (1996) 14 CSLJ 393.

[2] Editorial comment (1994) 15 Co Law 34 at 34.

[3] *Target Holdings Ltd v Redferns* [1995] 3 All ER 785 at 795 per Lord Browne-Wilkinson (Lords Keith, Ackner, Jauncey and Lloyd agreed); note *Warman International Ltd v Dwyer* (1994-1995) 182 CLR 544 at 559 *per curiam*, 'It is necessary to keep steadily in mind the cardinal principle of equity that the remedy must be fashioned to fit the nature of the case and the particular facts.'

[4] E.g., *Equiticorp Finance Ltd v Bank of New Zealand* (1993) 11 ACLC 952; *Bishopsgate Investment Management Ltd v Maxwell (No. 2)* [1994] 1 All ER 261; *Mallina Holdings Ltd v Biala Ltd* (1994) 15 ACSR 1; and *Daniels v Anderson* (1995) 13 ACLC 614; see Sealy L S, 'Directors' "Wider" Responsibilities – Problems Conceptual, Practical and Procedural' (1987) 13 MULR 164 at 169; and Sealy L S, '"Bona Fides" and "Proper Purposes" in Corporate Decisions' (1989) 15 MULR 265 at 265.

[5] Finn P D, *Essays on Damages* The Law Book Company Ltd, Sydney, 1992 at v.

often allege that directors have breached legal, equitable and/or statutory duties,[6] either because their lawyers misconceive or do not properly understand the precise nature of the duty, or duties, thought to have been owed in the circumstances,[7] or simply *ex abundanti cautela*. Alternative causes of action are pleaded,[8] and different remedies are sought.[9]

In practical terms it sometimes does not matter which of the plaintiff's claims is upheld. The very fact that a claim is upheld and the defendant stopped in his, her or its tracks and brought to account, satisfies the litigation and is often the all important *raison d'être*. On some occasions, the litigation serves to merely delay or intimidate.[10] But there are, of course, many occasions upon which it is imperative to recover company assets and, in these circumstances, claims need to be remedy specific. The wrongful disposal of company assets cases, the secret commissions or bribes cases, and the conflict of interest cases are apposite; and will be briefly considered in this chapter, as giving rise to either a constructive trust[11] or equitable compensation.[12] Additionally, within Australian company law, the range of remedies available has been further strengthened with the advent of Corporations Law Part 9.4B, and the introduction of civil penalty provisions, consequent upon the enactment of the Corporate Law Reform Act 1992 (Cth).[13] Civil penalty provisions were considered in the previous chapter of this book.

Within the law of remedies it is important to differentiate between the duties owed at law and those owed in equity as the remedies, consequent upon the particular breach, do differ.[14] This is so, as we shall see, notwithstanding that the superior courts in England and in Australia have administered law and equity concurrently for over 100

---

[6]   See, e.g., the line of authority in Australian company law which relevantly began with *Darvall v North Sydney Brick & Tile Co Ltd (No. 2)* (1989) 7 ACLC 659 through to the recent decision in *Daniels v Anderson* (1995) 13 ACLC 614.

[7]   *Australian Growth Resources Corporation Pty Ltd v van Reesema* (1988) 6 ACLC 529 at 535 per King CJ (Cox J agreed); *Girardet v Crease & Co* (1987) 11 BCLR (2d) 361 at 362 per Southin J; and *Wickstead v Browne* (1992-1993) 30 NSWLR 1 at 16 per Handley and Cripps JJA.

[8]   *Bishopsgate Investment Management Ltd v Maxwell (No. 2)* [1994] 1 All ER 261; *Kimberley Mineral Holdings Ltd v Triguboff* [1978] 1 NSWLR 364 at 366 per Needham J; and *Permanent Building Society v Wheeler* (1993-1994) 11 WAR 187; see Nolan R C, 'Maxwell's improper purposes' (1994) 15 Co Law 85 at 87; Mason K, 'Contract and Tort: Looking Across the Boundary from the Side of Contract' (1987) 61 ALJ 228 at 236; and Rickett C and Gardner T, 'Compensating for loss in equity: The evolution of a remedy' (1994) 24 VUWLR 19 at 29 and 48.

[9]   *Personal Representatives of Tang Man Sit v Capacious Investments Ltd* [1996] 1 AC 514 at 521 per Lord Nicholls.

[10]   *Financial Times*, 25 June 1999.

[11]   *Westdeutsche Landesbank Girozentrale v Islington London Borough Council* [1996] AC 669 at 714-716 per Lord Browne-Wilkinson (Lord Slynn agreed); see McCormack G, 'The remedial constructive trust and commercial transactions' (1996) 17 Co Law 3.

[12]   There is a long line of authority from, recently, *Attorney General for Hong Kong v Reid* [1994] 1 All ER 1, which extends back, at least, to *Keech v Sandford* (1726) Sel Cas t King 61, with rules and principles applicable to fiduciary duties in uncompromising terms often, but not always, resulting in what might well be thought to be positive hardship to the fiduciary concerned.

[13]   Added by Act No. 210 of 1992 and effective 1 February 1993.

[14]   Doyle J J, Commentary to Kearney, 'Accounting for a Fiduciary's Gains in Commercial Contexts' in Finn P D (ed), *Equity and Commercial Relationships* The Law Book Company Ltd, Sydney, 1987 at 212-214; and Davidson I E, 'The Equitable Remedy of Compensation' (1982) 13 Melb ULR 349 at 352 *et seq*; note *McKenzie v McDonald* [1927] VLR 134.

years.[15] Within these parameters, this chapter will also address the controversial question within English and Australian company law of causation *vis-à-vis* directorial breaches of fiduciary duties to act in good faith and for proper purposes and also, perhaps less controversially, breaches of legal and equitable duties to exercise care and diligence.

EQUITABLE v FIDUCIARY: A DISTINCTION?

The treatment by the textbooks on fiduciary law generally is superficial and lacking in areas of critical import. In the context of this book, where we are concerned with those cardinal duties of directors to act in good faith and for proper purposes on the one hand, and also to exercise care and diligence on the other hand, it is evident that little attention has been paid to the distinction which exists between equitable duties *per se* and the stricter fiduciary duties insisted upon by equity, and the doctrine of causation as it applies to fiduciaries. Consequently, the gloss applied to the law of remedies, within the context of directors' duties, belies the skein which lies beneath the surface of this complex, and at times baffling, area of company law.

These important and controversial issues are presently shrouded by the confusion which has permeated this area of the law;[16] largely, it would seem, through the imperfect understanding by many lawyers, judges and academics of the language of 19th century chancery and the inconsistent application of legal rules and equitable principles which grew out of that period in our legal history.[17] There has been a tendency amongst lawyers, judges and academics to treat the words 'fiduciary' and 'equitable' as synonymous and interchangeable; a tendency that adds to the confusion of an already complex and confused area of the law. *A fortiori* when speaking of directors' fiduciary duties.

Notwithstanding Sopinka J's caveat that, 'not all obligations existing between the parties to a well-recognised fiduciary relationship will be fiduciary in nature',[18] the very real differences which exist between these duties remains improperly understood and misconceived. All too often duties are characterised as fiduciary when, in truth, they are merely equitable or, perhaps, even legal. Modern authority, as Whincop has recently pointed out, 'is consistent with directors owing duties that are fiduciary, as well as non-fiduciary duties of care and diligence.'[19] A true fiduciary duty, for example, sits higher than a mere equitable duty, even though the equitable duty might be said to flow from the fiduciary relationship, and both fall for adjudication within the exclusive jurisdiction of courts of equity. Hence, it is not the case that all fiduciaries owe the same duties

---

[15] Consequent upon the Supreme Court of Judicature Acts, 1873 and 1875 (UK) from 1 November 1875; cf. *Peek v Gurney* (1873) LR 6 HL 377 at 393 per Lord Chelmsford; and *Nocton v Lord Ashburton* [1914] AC 932 at 957 per Viscount Haldane LC (Lord Atkinson agreed).

[16] *March v E&MH Stramare Pty Ltd* (1990-1991) 171 CLR 506 at 509 per Mason CJ (Toohey and Gaudron JJ agreed).

[17] Sealy L S, 'Directors' "Wider" Responsibilities – Problems Conceptual, Practical and Procedural' (1987) 13 MULR 164 at 164.

[18] *LAC Minerals Ltd v International Corona Resources Ltd* (1989) 61 DLR (4th) 14 at 61; see *Girardet v Crease & Company* (1987) 11 BCLR (2d) 361 at 362 per Southin J.

[19] Whincop M J, 'An Economic Analysis of the Criminalisation and Content of Directors' Duties' (1996) 24 ABLR 273 at 276.

in all circumstances.[20] The directors' duty to exercise care and diligence is, perhaps, the best example in the present context.[21]

This loose application of legal and equitable concepts and terminology does not merely offend against pedantry, but fosters confusion and misunderstanding which, in turn, can have significant consequences. This was graphically illustrated in *Girardet v Crease & Company*, where Southin J was critical of counsel for characterising an allegation of neglect against a solicitor as a breach of fiduciary duty, when in truth it was not, given that:

> [An] allegation of breach of fiduciary duty carries with it the stench of dishonesty – if not of deceit, then of constructive fraud.[22]

Thus, to fully appreciate the obligations and duties of directors, within the context of this book, it is of critical importance to understand the difference between the fiduciary duties to act in good faith and for proper purposes, and the equitable and legal duties to exercise care and diligence, which arise by virtue of the directors' office.

As was suggested in chapter one of this book, albeit there in a broader context, comparisons are sometimes drawn between directors and trustees.[23] In some of the older cases directors were referred to as trustees.[24] This can be traced back to a time when the English courts of chancery resorted to equitable principles said to be derived from the fiduciary relationship between directors, trustees and their companies. Thus, the authorities are replete with examples where courts of equity have regarded directors as trustees.[25] Consequently, whether through ignorance, misunderstanding or simply change in circumstance, the traditional application of the word fiduciary, as used by the judges in cases now centuries old, does not always accord with the way in which the word fiduciary is flung around now as if it applied to all breaches of duty by directors.[26] In this chapter, therefore, it is proposed to analyse the observations made by Ipp J,[27] in *Permanent Building Society v Wheeler*, which were briefly considered in chapter one of this book; namely:

---

[20] *Henderson v Merrett Syndicates Ltd* [1994] 3 All ER 506 at 543 per Lord Browne-Wilkinson.

[21] *Bristol and West Building Society v Mothew* [1996] 4 All ER 698 at 710-712 and 715 per Millett LJ (Otton LJ agreed); and *Permanent Building Society v Wheeler* (1993-1994) 11 WAR 187 at 237-238 per Ipp J (Malcolm CJ and Seaman J agreed).

[22] (1987) 11 BCLR (2d) 361 at 362; see *Barnes v Addy* (1874) 9 Ch App 244 at 251-252 per Lord Selborne LC; cf. *Consul Development Pty Ltd v D P C Estates Pty Ltd* (1974-1975) 132 CLR 373 at 396 per Gibbs J.

[23] Cf. *Mills v Mills* (1938) 60 CLR 150 at 185 per Dixon J; note Ford H A J, Austin R P and Ramsay I M, *Ford's Principles of Corporations Law* (9th ed) Reed International Books Australia Pty Ltd, Sydney, 1999 at para 8.050.

[24] *In re Forest of Dean Coal Mining Company* (1879) 10 Ch D 450 at 451 and 453 per Jessel MR; and *Hirsche v Sims* [1894] AC 654 at 667 per the Earl of Selborne; see Sealy L S, 'Fiduciary Relationships' [1962] CLJ 69; Finn P D, *Fiduciary Obligations* The Law Book Company Ltd, Sydney, 1977 at 89; Davies P L, *Gower's Principles of Modern Company Law* (6th ed) Sweet & Maxwell Ltd, London, 1997 at 598; and Ford H A J and Austin R P, *Ford's Principles of Corporations Law* (6th ed) Butterworths Pty Ltd, Sydney, 1992 at 487-488.

[25] *In re Caerphilly Colliery Company* (1877) 5 Ch D 336 at 342 per James LJ; and *In re Wincham Shipbuilding, Boiler, and Salt Company* (1878) 9 Ch D 322 at 328-329 *per curiam*.

[26] *Girardet v Crease & Company* (1987) 11 BCLR (2d) 361 at 362 per Southin J; note Sealy L S, 'Directors' "Wider" Responsibilities – Problems Conceptual, Practical and Procedural' (1987) 13 MULR 164 at 164, 'The language of nineteenth-century [*sic*] chancery is imperfectly understood by most lawyers and is inconsistently applied.'

[27] (Malcolm CJ and Seaman J agreed).

It is essential to bear in mind that the existence of a fiduciary relationship does not mean that every duty owed by a fiduciary to the beneficiary is a fiduciary duty. In particular, a trustee's duty to exercise reasonable care, though equitable, is not specifically a fiduciary duty ... Similarly ... a director's duty to exercise reasonable care, though equitable (as well as legal) is not a fiduciary obligation.[28]

As a consequence, the distinction between legal, equitable and fiduciary duties can well prove to be, as the balance of this chapter will demonstrate, of critical import in the light of the doctrine of causation, the related issues of foreseeability and remoteness traditionally associated with general law damages,[29] and the securing of a remedy considered appropriate in the circumstances.[30]

In particular, we shall analyse cases principally concerned with constructive trusts and equitable compensation. These are powerful remedies within equity's impressive array of remedies, developed over time, to regulate and circumscribe wrongful conduct on the part of defaulting fiduciaries and, thus, of particular relevance to errant directors.[31] Within this context it becomes, therefore, important to appreciate the fiduciary for what he or she really is. *A fortiori* in recent times as courts become more willing to allow equitable doctrine to infiltrate commercial law;[32] as the special relationship cases, and the partnership and joint venture cases, amply testify.[33]

But whether a person is designated a fiduciary through being a member of the recognised class of fiduciary,[34] or by reason of the particular relationship in which he or she finds themselves given such special circumstances as then exist, does not, of itself, elevate all responsibilities which they must undertake to a new level. Admittedly, much of what that person does, or ought to have done, will be clothed with the requirement that he or she meet the strict obligations which are associated with the fiduciary office; namely, utmost good faith, trust, confidence, honesty and integrity;[35]

---

[28] (1993-1994) 11 WAR 187 at 237-238; note Finn P D, *Fiduciary Obligations* The Law Book Company Ltd, Sydney, 1977 at 78, 'The varying usage is unimportant provided one always recognises that a person is *not* a "fiduciary" ... until a duty applies to him. When one does, he then becomes a "fiduciary" ... but for the purposes of that duty only.'; also Sealy L S, 'Some Principles of Fiduciary Obligation' [1963] CLJ 119 at 137-140; cf. *Eromanga Hydrocarbons NL v Australis Mining NL* (1988) 6 ACLC 906 at 913 per Malcolm CJ.

[29] *Re Dawson* [1966] 2 NSWR 211 at 215-216 per Street J; note Treitel G H, *The Law of Contract* (7th ed) Sweet & Maxwell Ltd, London, 1987 at 744 *et seq*; cf. Editorial comment, 'Target hit' (1995) 16 Co Law 258 at 258.

[30] For a discussion of the relevant equitable remedies see: *Hospital Products Ltd v United States Surgical Corporation* (1984-1985) 156 CLR 41 at 107-115 per Mason J; *Mallina Holdings Ltd v Biala Ltd* (1994) 15 ACSR 1 at 48-52 *per curiam*; and Meagher R P, Gummow W M C and Lehane J R F, *Equity Doctrines and Remedies* (3rd ed) Butterworths Pty Ltd, Sydney, 1992.

[31] Whincop M J, 'An Economic Analysis of the Criminalisation and Content of Directors' Duties' (1996) 24 ABLR 273 at 290.

[32] Cf. *Manchester Trust v Furness* [1895] 2 QB 539 at 545 per Lindley LJ; note Goodhart W and Jones G, 'The Infiltration of Equitable Doctrine into English Commercial Law' (1980) 43 MLR 489 at 489-490.

[33] E.g., *Allen v Hyatt* (1914) 30 TLR 444; *Coleman v Myers* [1977] 2 NZLR 225; *Glandon Pty Ltd v Strata Consolidated Pty Ltd* (1993) 11 ACSR 543; *Hospital Products Ltd v United States Surgical Corporation* (1984-1985) 156 CLR 41; *Fraser Edmiston Pty Ltd v AGT (QLD) Pty Ltd* [1988] 2 Qd R 1; *Chan v Zacharia* (1983-1984) 154 CLR 178; and *Mallina Holdings Ltd v Biala Ltd* (1994) 15 ACSR 1; see Rider B A K, 'Partnership Law and its Impact on "Domestic Companies"' [1979] CLJ 148; and McPherson B H, 'Joint Ventures' in Finn P D (ed), *Equity and Commercial Relationships* The Law Book Company Ltd, Sydney, 1987 at 19 *et seq*.

[34] Finn P D, *Fiduciary Obligations* The Law Book Company Ltd, Sydney, 1977 at 8 *et seq*.

[35] *Bristol and West Building Society v Mothew* [1996] 4 All ER 698 at 712 per Millett LJ (Otton LJ agreed).

but within that special duty category will be other non-fiduciary duties which that person is obliged to undertake. Duties which have no dependence upon the fiduciary office. In this respect, the following passage from Lord Browne-Wilkinson's speech to the House of Lords[36] in *Henderson v Merrett Syndicates Ltd* is instructive:

> The liability of a fiduciary for the negligent transaction of his duties is not a separate head of liability but the paradigm of the general duty to act with care imposed by law on those who take it upon themselves to act for or advise others. Although the historical development of the rules of law and equity have, in the past, caused different labels to be stuck on different manifestations of the duty, in truth the duty of care imposed on bailees, carriers, trustees, directors, agents and others is the same duty: it arises from the circumstances in which the defendants were acting, not from their status or description. It is the fact that they have all assumed responsibility for the property or affairs of others which renders them liable for the careless performance of what they have undertaken to do, not the description of the trade or position which they hold.[37]

Thus it is, for example, that solicitors who fall within the traditional class of fiduciary have a duty, 'in contract arising from an implied term (and also in tort) to conduct their clients' affairs with reasonable care and skill.'[38] Such a duty is not dependent on the fiduciary office and it would be imprudent to suggest otherwise. So too in the case of directors. It is neither necessary nor fair to expect each and every aspect of a director's working day to meet the exalted standards of a fiduciary. Hence there is no justification for subjecting someone to the rigorous scrutiny of equity, simply because that person just happens to be a fiduciary.[39] To do so, would be to ignore Lord Selborne LC's caveat in *Barnes v Addy* against undermining the sound doctrines of equity by making, 'unreasonable and inequitable application of them.'[40]

Within the fiduciary relationship which directors enjoy with their company, the activities of directors are prescribed by a compendium of legal rules, equitable principles and statutory enactment; many of which have nothing to do with fiduciary principles.[41] As La Forest J in *LAC Minerals Ltd v International Corona Resources Ltd* observed:

> [Not] every legal claim arising out of a relationship with fiduciary incidents will give rise to a claim for breach of fiduciary duty. ... It is only in relation to breaches of the specific obligations imposed because the relationship is one characterized as fiduciary that a claim for breach of fiduciary duty can be founded.[42]

---

[36] (Lords Keith, Goff, Browne-Wilkinson, Mustill and Nolan).
[37] [1994] 3 All ER 506 at 543.
[38] *Girardet v Crease & Company* (1987) 11 BCLR (2d) 361 at 362 per Southin J; see *Nocton v Lord Ashburton* [1914] AC 932 at 953-957 per Viscount Haldane LC (Lord Atkinson agreed).
[39] Cf. Law Commission, *Fiduciary Duties and Regulatory Rules* HMSO, London, Cm 3049, 1995 at paras 1.3 and 1.4.
[40] (1874) 9 Ch App 244 at 251; see *Chan v Zacharia* (1983-1984) 154 CLR 178 at 205 per Deane J; and *Boardman v Phipps* [1967] 2 AC 46 at 133 per Lord Upjohn.
[41] Meagher R P, Gummow W M C and Lehane J R F, *Equity Doctrines and Remedies* (3rd ed) Butterworths Pty Ltd, Sydney, 1992 at 131.
[42] (1989) 61 DLR (4th) 14 at 28.

Contrary to Lord Diplock's assertion in *United Scientific Holdings Ltd v Burnley Borough Council* that law and equity have surely mingled now,[43] the Judicature Acts did not fuse law and equity[44] as it is commonly suggested;[45] but rather provided for, 'the administration of the two systems of law by the one system of courts and by prescribing the paramountcy of equity'.[46] Undoubtedly, it is a fact that law and equity are convergent and, in all likelihood, will continue to converge so that ultimately the differences in origin between law and equity will become decreasingly important.[47] As matters presently stand, however, the law of remedies is predicated upon legal rules and equitable principles, and whilst there may be some confluence between the two,[48] in Ipp J's judgment in *Wheeler* there is:

> [A] fundamental distinction between breaches of fiduciary obligations which involve dishonesty and abuse of the trustee's advantages and the vulnerable position of beneficiaries, on the one hand, and, honest but careless dealings which breach mere equitable obligations, on the other.[49]

Fiduciary obligations are imposed so as to preclude the fiduciary from being influenced by personal considerations, or from actually misusing his or her position for personal advantage;[50] considerations which have no application whatsoever to, for example, a breach of the directors' duty to exercise care and diligence. Millett LJ in *Bristol and West Building Society v Mothew*, after referring to *Wheeler* and those passages from Ipp J's judgment extracted above, put the matter in this way:

> The nature of the obligation determines the nature of the breach. The various obligations of a fiduciary merely reflect different aspects of his core duties of loyalty and fidelity. Breach of fiduciary obligation, therefore, connotes disloyalty or infidelity. Mere incompetence is not enough. A servant who loyally does his incompetent best for his master is not unfaithful and is not guilty of a breach of fiduciary duty.[51]

---

43   [1978] AC 904 at 925; cf. *Maguire v Makaronis* (1996-1997) 188 CLR 449 at 489 per Kirby J; note Meagher R P, Gummow W M C and Lehane J R F, *Equity Doctrines and Remedies* (3rd ed) Butterworths Pty Ltd, Sydney, 1992 at 39 and 68.
44   Consequent upon the Supreme Court of Judicature Acts, 1873 and 1875 (UK) from 1 November 1875; cf. *Peek v Gurney* (1873) LR 6 HL 377 at 393 per Lord Chelmsford; and *Nocton v Lord Ashburton* [1914] AC 932 at 957 per Viscount Haldane LC (Lord Atkinson agreed); note Meagher R P, Gummow W M C and Lehane J R F, *Equity Doctrines and Remedies* (3rd ed) Butterworths Pty Ltd, Sydney, 1992 at 45, 'There was nothing in the Judicature Act which attempted to codify law and equity as one subject matter or which severed the roots of the conceptual distinctions between law and equity.'
45   Meagher R P, Gummow W M C and Lehane J R F, *Equity Doctrines and Remedies* (3rd ed) Butterworths Pty Ltd, Sydney, 1992 at 68; Stuckey-Clarke J, '"Damages" for Breaches of Purely Equitable Rights: The Breach of Confidence Example' in Finn P D (ed), *Essays on Damages* The Law Book Company Ltd, Sydney, 1992 at 74-76; and Davidson I E, 'The Equitable Remedy of Compensation' (1982) 13 Melb ULR 349 at 380; cf. *Coleman v Myers* [1977] 2 NZLR 225 at 359-360 per Cooke J.
46   Mason A, 'The Place of Equity and Equitable Remedies in the Contemporary Common Law World' (1994) 110 LQR 238 at 239.
47   *Ibid* at 258.
48   *United Scientific Holdings Ltd v Burnley Borough Council* [1978] AC 904 at 945 per Lord Simon.
49   (1993-1994) 11 WAR 187 at 247.
50   *Chan v Zacharia* (1983-1984) 154 CLR 178 at 198-199 per Deane J.
51   [1996] 4 All ER 698 at 712.

Because directors are fiduciaries their activities are inevitably supervised by courts of equity. Within the exercise of that jurisdiction, courts of equity are empowered to administer law and equity concurrently.[52] Within that administration, however, each discipline remains to be governed by its own rules and principles; although due recognition is paid to the maxim *aequitas sequitur legem*. Thus, the legal aspects of a fiduciary's duties will attract legal rules.[53] The fiduciary aspects of a fiduciary's duties will attract equitable principles.[54] Absent fiduciary incidents equitable doctrine will, in appropriate circumstances, still have application; for its jurisdiction is exercisable in the absence of adequate remedies at law, 'according to considerations of conscience, fairness, and hardship and other equitable features such as laches and acquiescence.'[55]

In these circumstances, although the particular remedy for breach of duty will depend upon the way the case has developed, 'equity and the law are set upon the same course.'[56] This is where, it is suggested, confusion has crept in. The distinction between equitable obligations *per se* and those stricter obligations which attach to fiduciary obligations, albeit still equitable, has all too infrequently been appreciated, or made.[57] One needs to distinguish between obligations enforced within the jurisdiction of courts of equity for reasons only that the miscreant is a fiduciary and, thus, falls within the equitable jurisdiction of the courts, and the defaulting fiduciary who is in breach of a fiduciary duty, in that he or she has demonstrated a lack of good faith, has been dishonest, has lacked integrity, has breached trust and/or confidence, or the like. In such cases, there is, 'ample justification on policy grounds for more stringent rules in the case of breaches of fiduciary obligations, but not where there has been honest but careless dealings.'[58]

CAUSATION, FORESEEABILITY AND REMOTENESS

The doctrine of causation is concerned with ascertaining or apportioning legal responsibility for a given occurrence;[59] which, as Lord Reid in *Stapley v Gypsum Mines Ld* explained, 'is a most difficult task.'[60] Causation often involves issues of intractable

---

[52] Cf. *Castlereagh Motels Ltd v Davies-Roe* (1966) 67 SR (NSW) 279 at 282-284 per Wallace P.

[53] *Attorney General v Blake* [1998] 1 All ER 833 at 846 per Lord Woolf MR (Millett and Mummery LJJ agreed).

[54] *Maguire v Makaronis* (1996-1997) 188 CLR 449 at 467 per Brennan CJ, Gaudron, McHugh and Gummow JJ.

[55] *Day v Mead* [1987] 2 NZLR 443 at 462 per Somers J; cf. *Warman International Ltd v Dwyer* (1994-1995) 182 CLR 544 at 559 *per curiam*; note Finn P D, 'Contract and the Fiduciary Principle' (1989) 12 UNSWLJ 76 at 76.

[56] *Day v Mead* [1987] 2 NZLR 443 at 458 per Somers J; see *Canson Enterprises Ltd v Boughton & Co* (1992) 85 DLR (4th) 129 at 152 per La Forest J; see Mason A, 'The Place of Equity and Equitable Remedies in the Contemporary Common Law World' (1994) 110 LQR 238 at 244.

[57] *Girardet v Crease & Company* (1987) 11 BCLR (2d) 361 at 362 per Southin J; note Davidson I E, 'The Equitable Remedy of Compensation' (1982) 13 Melb ULR 349 at 350.

[58] *Permanent Building Society v Wheeler* (1993-1994) 11 WAR 187 at 247 per Ipp J (Malcolm CJ and Seaman J agreed).

[59] *Stapley v Gypsum Mines Ld* [1953] AC 663 at 681 per Lord Reid; and *March v E & M H Stramare Pty Ltd* (1990-1991) 171 CLR 506 at 509 per Mason CJ (Toohey and Gaudron JJ agreed); see Rickett C and Gardner T, 'Compensating for loss in equity: The evolution of a remedy' (1994) 24 VUWLR 19 at 30 *et seq*; Ipp D A, 'Problems and Progress in Remoteness of Damage' in Finn P D (ed), *Essays on Damages* The Law Book Company Ltd, Sydney, 1992 at 14 *et seq*; and Treitel G H, *The Law of Contract* (7th ed) Sweet & Maxwell Ltd, London, 1987 at 753 *et seq*.

[60] [1953] AC 663 at 681.

complexity,[61] for it is not every breach of duty by a director that is compensable. Where the company has suffered no quantifiable loss, for instance, why should the breach be actionable?[62] There will be occasions where, for example, in the improper issue of shares and, indeed, in some of the conflict of interest cases, that directors will properly be enjoined from either engaging in, or proceeding with, such conduct.[63]

In this chapter, however, the interest lies with issues of quantum and that vexed question: is the establishment of a loss a prerequisite to the right of recovery? It is here that the distinction between legal, equitable and fiduciary duties manifests itself. In order to be actionable at law, there must be established a causal connection between the breach complained of and the loss said to flow from that breach; that is to say, did the breach of duty cause the loss sustained?[64] Or, by resorting to the but for test; *viz*, but for the breach, would the loss have occurred?[65]

It is then said that a defendant is not liable for loss which is too remote. In essence, the test of remoteness is whether the loss was within the reasonable contemplation of the parties;[66] or, as it is sometimes put, 'reasonably foreseeable as liable to result from the breach.'[67] Foreseeability is not a test of causation, but rather, 'it marks the limits beyond which a wrongdoer will not be held responsible for damage resulting from his wrongful act.'[68] Thus, once the defendant's actions have been held to be determinative of the loss suffered, the extent of that loss is then circumscribed by applying the test of reasonable foreseeability;[69] a test recently reaffirmed by the House of Lords in *Page v Smith*[70] and in *White v Chief Constable of the South Yorkshire Police*,[71] and by the High Court of Australia in *Bryan v Maloney*.[72]

Although causation, foreseeability and remoteness are quite different concepts,[73] nevertheless, some of the relevant considerations are the same.[74] In essence, their overall intent is to act as a control mechanism and delimit the remedial exposure to

---

[61] Stapleton J, 'Law, Causation and Common Sense' (1988) 8 OJLS 111 at 111.

[62] Cf. *Target Holdings Ltd v Redferns* [1995] 3 All ER 785 at 793 per Lord Browne-Wilkinson (Lords Keith, Ackner, Jauncey and Lloyd agreed).

[63] Corporations Law s1324.

[64] *Sherman v Nymboida Collieries Pty Ltd* (1963-1964) 109 CLR 580 at 590-591 per Windeyer J; *March v E & M H Stramare Pty Ltd* (1990-1991) 171 CLR 506 at 509 per Mason CJ (Toohey and Gaudron JJ agreed); and *Target Holdings Ltd v Redferns* [1995] 3 All ER 785 at 798 per Lord Browne-Wilkinson (Lords Keith, Ackner, Jauncey and Lloyd agreed).

[65] *Biala Pty Ltd v Mallina Holdings Ltd* (1993) 11 ACSR 785 at 852 and 854 per Ipp J; *Permanent Building Society v Wheeler* (1993-1994) 11 WAR 187 at 247 per Ipp J (Malcolm CJ and Seaman J agreed); *Bishopsgate Investment Management Ltd v Maxwell* [1993] BCC 120 at 136 per Chadwick J; and *Target Holdings Ltd v Redferns* [1995] 3 All ER 785 at 794 per Lord Browne-Wilkinson (Lords Keith, Ackner, Jauncey and Lloyd agreed).

[66] Treitel G H, *The Law of Contract* (7th ed) Sweet & Maxwell Ltd, London, 1987 at 744.

[67] *Victoria Laundry (Windsor) Ld v Newman Industries Ld* [1949] 2 KB 528 at 539 per Asquith LJ; cf. *Koufos v C Czarnikow Ltd* [1969] 1 AC 350.

[68] *Chapman v Hearse* (1961-1962) 106 CLR 112 at 122 *per curiam*.

[69] *Overseas Tankship (UK) Ltd v The Miller Steamship Co Pty* [1967] 1 AC 617 at 636 per Lord Reid.

[70] [1995] 2 All ER 736 at 753-754 per Lord Browne-Wilkinson and at 758-761 per Lord Lloyd (Lords Ackner and Browne-Wilkinson agreed).

[71] [1999] 1 All ER 1 at 39 per Lord Hoffmann (Lords Browne-Wilkinson and Steyn agreed).

[72] (1995) 128 ALR 163 at 165-166 and 171-172 per Mason CJ, Deane and Gaudron JJ; see *Burnie Port Authority v General Jones Pty Ltd* (1993-1994) 179 CLR 520 at 543 per Mason CJ, Deane, Dawson, Toohey and Gaudron JJ.

[73] Cf. *Smith New Court Securities Ltd v Scrimgeour Vickers (Asset Management) Ltd* [1996] 4 All ER 769 at 794 per Lord Steyn (Lords Browne-Wilkinson, Keith, Mustill and Slynn agreed).

[74] *Stinnes Interoil GmbH v A Halcoussis & Co (The 'Yanxilas' (No. 2))* [1984] 1 Lloyd's Rep 676 at 682 per Bingham J.

which a defendant might otherwise be put. Absent such control mechanisms, as Lord Lloyd in *Page* observed, 'a negligent defendant might find himself being made liable to all the world.'[75] Additionally, considerations of policy and value judgments, designed to limit legal responsibility for damage resulting from acts or omissions of the kind in question, are then addressed.[76] In the process, however, care must be taken to guard against the use of, 'subjective, unexpressed and undefined extra-legal values to determine legal liability.'[77] For, at the margins, public policy is a potent element in the matter.[78]

When examining the duty said to be owed by a particular fiduciary, it is important to keep in mind the source of that duty.[79] It will be recalled from chapter two of this book that the duty to exercise care and diligence, for example, can arise by virtue of: (i) fiduciary obligations; (ii) contract;[80] (iii) *Donoghue v Stevenson* principles;[81] or (iv) statute.[82] Insofar as contract is concerned, not only does its existence give rise to the duty, but its express and implied terms will confine and delimit the scope of the particular duty. The following passage from Lord Browne-Wilkinson's speech to the House of Lords in *Henderson v Merrett Syndicates Ltd* is apposite:

> [The] extent and nature of the fiduciary duties owed in any particular case fall to be determined by reference to any underlying contractual relationship between the parties. Thus, in the case of an agent employed under a contract, the scope of his fiduciary duties is determined by the terms of the underlying contract. Although an agent is, in the absence of contractual provision, in breach of his fiduciary duties if he acts for another who is in competition with his principal, if the contract under

---

[75] [1995] 2 All ER 736 at 759.

[76] *White v Chief Constable of the South Yorkshire Police* [1999] 1 All ER 1 at 32 per Lord Steyn; *March v E & M H Stramare Pty Ltd* (1990-1991) 171 CLR 506 at 535 per McHugh J; *Bryan v Maloney* (1995) 128 ALR 163 at 165-166, 169 and 172 per Mason CJ, Deane and Gaudron JJ; and *Murphy v Brentwood District Council* [1991] 1 AC 398 at 498 per Lord Jauncey; cf. *Glavanics v Brunninghausen* (1996) 19 ACSR 204 at 227-228 per Bryson J; see Ipp D A, 'Problems and Progress in Remoteness of Damage' in Finn P D (ed), *Essays on Damages* The Law Book Company Ltd, Sydney, 1992 at 14; and Hammond G, 'The Place of Damages in the Scheme of Remedies' in Finn P D (ed), *Essays on Damages* The Law Book Company Ltd, Sydney, 1992 at 193.

[77] *March v E & M H Stramare Pty Ltd* (1990-1991) 171 CLR 506 at 533 per McHugh J; cf. *Marc Rich & Co AG v Bishop Rock Marine Co Ltd* [1995] 3 All ER 307 at 332 per Lord Steyn (Lords Keith, Jauncey and Browne-Wilkinson agreed); see LLoyd-Bostock S, 'The Ordinary Man, and the Psychology of Attributing Causes and Responsibility' (1979) 42 MLR 143 at 167-168.

[78] Finn P D, 'Contract and the Fiduciary Principle' (1989) 12 UNSWLJ 76 at 93.

[79] *South Australia Asset Management Corporation v York Montague Ltd* [1997] AC 191 at 212 per Lord Hoffmann (Lords Goff, Jauncey, Slynn and Nicholls agreed).

[80] *Hospital Products Ltd v United States Surgical Corporation* (1984-1985) 156 CLR 41 at 97 per Mason J; *Lister v Romford Ice and Cold Storage Co Ltd* [1957] AC 555; *Day v Mead* [1987] 2 NZLR 443 at 452 per Cooke P; note Birds J R, 'A code of directors' duties?' (1974) 124 NLJ 1163 at 1165; Shepherd J C, 'Towards a Unified Concept of Fiduciary Relationships' (1981) 97 LQR 51 at 66; Corkery J F, *Directors' Powers and Duties* Longman Cheshire Pty Ltd, Melbourne, 1987 at 139; and Black A, 'Recent Developments in Directors' Duties' (1991) 7 ABR 121 at 123.

[81] [1932] AC 562; see *Castlereagh Motels Ltd v Davies-Roe* (1966) 67 SR (NSW) 279 at 283 per Wallace P and at 285 per Jacobs and Asprey JJA; and *Daniels v Anderson* (1995) 13 ACLC 614 at 663 per Clarke and Sheller JJA.

[82] Ford H A J and Austin R P, *Ford's Principles of Corporations Law* (6th ed) Butterworths Pty Ltd, Sydney, 1992 at 524.

which he is acting authorises him so to do, the normal fiduciary duties are modified accordingly.[83]

Two relatively recent decisions of the Privy Council shed light upon the necessary principles to apply in these circumstances to ensure that equity is not, 'prayed in aid to enlarge the scope of contractual duties.'[84] They are both worthy of brief study and, 'are to be welcomed for their refreshingly pragmatic approach.'[85] The first is *Kelly v Cooper*.[86] The facts were these. Two beachfront properties in Bermuda were purchased by Ross Perot.[87] The respondents were a firm of estate agents who marketed both properties. Kelly was the former owner of one of the properties. When he discovered that Perot had acquired both properties, Kelly took the view that his agents should have told him of Perot's interest in both properties as that was material information relating to the sale of his property. He refused to pay the agents' commission. The Privy Council[88] agreed that Perot's interest in buying both properties could have materially influenced the negotiations for the price at which Kelly's property was sold. In the result, however, the agents were entitled to their commission.[89]

Lord Browne-Wilkinson delivered the opinion of the Privy Council. His Lordship considered that it was not possible to say that all agents owe the same duties to their principals, but rather it was always necessary to have regard to the express or implied terms of the contract between them.[90] In finding no breach of duty, whether contractual or fiduciary, on the agents' part by not revealing Perot's interest in buying Kelly's property, the scope of the fiduciary duties owed by the agents to Kelly was defined by the terms of the contract of agency. That contract envisaged that the agents might have the conflict of interest ultimately complained of. Accordingly, in Lord Browne-Wilkinson's judgment:

> It cannot be sensibly suggested that an estate agent is contractually bound to disclose to any one of his principals information which is confidential to another of his principals. The position as to confidentiality is even clearer in the case of stockbrokers who cannot be contractually bound to disclose to their private clients inside information disclosed to the brokers in confidence by a company for which they also act. Accordingly in such cases there must be an implied term of the contract with such an agent that he is entitled to act for other principals selling competing properties and to keep confidential the information obtained from each of his principals. Similar considerations apply to the fiduciary duties of agents. The existence and scope of these duties depends upon the terms on which they are acting.[91]

83 [1994] 3 All ER 506 at 543-544.
84 *Clark Boyce v Mouat* [1994] 1 AC 428 at 437 per Lord Jauncey.
85 Jarvis K, 'Does the fiduciary bell toll?' (1996) 17 Co Law 51 at 53.
86 [1993] AC 205 (on appeal from the Court of Appeal of Bermuda).
87 The American businessman and sometime presidential candidate.
88 (Lords Keith, Ackner, Browne-Wilkinson, Mustill and Slynn).
89 See Law Commission, *Fiduciary Duties and Regulatory Rules* HMSO, London, Cm 3049, 1995 at paras 3.24-3.36; note Jarvis K, 'Law Commission report on fiduciary duties and regulatory rules' (1996) 17 Co Law 110 at 110-112.
90 [1993] AC 205 at 214.
91 *Ibid.*

The second of these two cases is *Clark Boyce v Mouat*.[92] There, the Privy Council[93] heard an appeal concerning Clark Boyce a firm of solicitors who carried out a conveyancing transaction on behalf of two clients, each with conflicting interests. At the material time Dorothy Mouat was a widow aged 72 years. She mortgaged her house to secure a loan for the benefit of her son Robert Mouat. He was guarantor and undertook primary liability for payment of the interest. It was agreed that Clark Boyce would act for Mouat and his mother subject to certain conditions. Ultimately, the loan fell into arrears and Mouat became bankrupt. When faced with repayment of the principal sum together with arrears of interest, Mrs Mouat brought proceedings against Clark Boyce alleging that they were in breach of contract, were negligent and had breached their fiduciary obligations to her by *inter alia* not refusing to act for her when they were acting for Mouat on the same transaction, and by failing to adequately advise her of the need for independent advice. In the result, it was determined that judgment should lie with Clark Boyce.[94] The opinion of the Privy Council was delivered by Lord Jauncey who reaffirmed that:

> There is no general rule of law to the effect that a solicitor should never act for both parties in a transaction where their interests may conflict. Rather is the position that he may act provided that he has obtained the informed consent of both to his acting. Informed consent means consent given in the knowledge that there is a conflict between the parties and that as a result the solicitor may be disabled from disclosing to each party the full knowledge which he possesses as to the transaction or may be disabled from giving advice to one party which conflicts with the interests of the other. If the parties are content to proceed upon this basis the solicitor may properly act.[95]

The trial judge in *Clark Boyce* was satisfied that: (i) Mrs Mouat was not concerned about the wisdom of the transaction; (ii) Mrs Mouat was intent upon ensuring that the transaction was given proper and full effect; (iii) the solicitors had done all that was reasonably required of them before accepting Mrs Mouat's instructions; and (iv) Mrs Mouat was fully aware of what she was doing and had rejected independent advice. The Privy Council considered Clark Boyce to be neither in breach of contract nor negligent in acting and continuing to act after Mrs Mouat had rejected the suggestion for independent advice. In doing so, Lord Jauncey found that:

> When a client in full command of his faculties and apparently aware of what he is doing seeks the assistance of a solicitor in carrying out a particular transaction, that solicitor is under no duty whether before or after accepting instructions to go beyond those instructions by proffering unsought advice on the wisdom of the transaction. To hold otherwise could impose intolerable burdens on solicitors.[96]

---

[92] [1994] 1 AC 428 (on appeal from the Court of Appeal of New Zealand).
[93] (Lords Goff, Jauncey, Lowry, Mustill and Slynn).
[94] See Law Commission, *Fiduciary Duties and Regulatory Rules* HMSO, London, Cm 3049, 1995 at paras 3.37-3.40; note Jarvis K, 'Law Commission report on fiduciary duties and regulatory rules' (1996) 17 Co Law 110 at 110-112.
[95] [1994] 1 AC 428 at 435.
[96] *Ibid* at 437.

Where *Clark Boyce* has particular appeal though is in the treatment by the Privy Council of the fiduciary duty of the solicitors in such circumstances. Lord Jauncey articulated that in this way:

> A fiduciary duty concerns disclosure of material facts in a situation where the fiduciary has either a personal interest in the matter to which the facts are material or acts for another party who has such an interest. It cannot be prayed in aid to enlarge the scope of contractual duties. Thus, there being no contractual duty on Mr. Boyce to advise Mrs. Mouat on the wisdom of entering into the transaction, she cannot claim that he nevertheless owed her a fiduciary duty to give that advice. Furthermore any duty of disclosure can only extend to the solicitor's knowledge of facts and not to his lack of knowledge thereof.[97]

In spite of the cautionary note struck by Fletcher Moulton LJ in *In re Coomber* of, 'the danger of trusting to verbal formulae',[98] this is an area of the law which continues to beguile and bedevil those who practise within it: largely, in Millett LJ's view, 'by unthinking resort to verbal formulae.'[99] Hence, there is here a particular need for vigilance to ensure that acts of omission and acts of commission by a fiduciary are only actionable where appropriate. This is of considerable importance to directors of British and Australian companies, and to their respective professional advisers. The recent developments in English and Australian company law concerning the doctrine of causation are informative and warrant particular attention in this respect.

CAUSATION: AN ENGLISH PERSPECTIVE

In English company law, there have been a number of recent decisions which have gone some way towards clearing the muddied waters into which the issue of causation had become submerged,[100] and in reaffirming equity's strict approach to the breach of fiduciary duties where appropriate.[101] Regrettably, some of the earlier decisions which re-ignited the academic and judicial interest in this challenging area of the law arose out of summary judgment applications only. These were disposed of at an early interlocutory stage of proceedings which, by virtue of the Court of Appeal's decision in *Balli Trading Ltd v Afalona Shipping Ltd*,[102] effectively precludes undue deliberation upon difficult questions of law.[103] Somewhat unusually, however, the second of the summary judgment applications which we consider in this chapter ended up being heard and decided by the House of Lords[104] in *Target Holdings Ltd v Redferns*.[105]

---

97 *Ibid.*
98 [1911] 1 Ch 723 at 728.
99 *Bristol and West Building Society v Mothew* [1996] 4 All ER 698 at 710.
100 E.g., *Bishopsgate Investment Management Ltd v Maxwell (No. 2)* [1994] 1 All ER 261; *Target Holdings Ltd v Redferns* [1995] 3 All ER 785; *Bristol and West Building Society v Mothew* [1996] 4 All ER 698; *Downs v Chappell* [1996] 3 All ER 344; and *Swindle v Harrison* [1997] 4 All ER 705.
101 *Nocton v Lord Ashburton* [1914] AC 932 at 963 per Lord Dunedin; see *Canson Enterprises Ltd v Boughton & Co* (1992) 85 DLR (4th) 129 at 161 per McLachlin J, 'Moreover the high duty assumed and the difficulty of detecting such breaches make it fair and practicable to adopt a measure of compensation calculated to ensure that fiduciaries are kept "up to their duty".'
102 [1992] TLR 406.
103 Nolan R C, 'Maxwell's improper purposes' (1994) 15 Co Law 85 at 87.
104 Editorial comment, 'Target hit' (1995) 16 Co Law 258 at 258.

The first decision to be considered emanates from *Bishopsgate Investment Management Ltd v Maxwell (No. 2)*,[106] a case which was considered in chapters two and four of this book. For present purposes, it should be recalled that Chadwick J, at first instance,[107] was faced with two principal issues. First, whether Maxwell was in breach of a tortious duty owed to Bishopsgate through an act of omission and also in breach of a fiduciary duty owed to Bishopsgate for an act of commission; namely, the improper transfer of shares to Robert Maxwell Group plc. Secondly, in the light of those matters, whether it was incumbent upon Bishopsgate to demonstrate a causal connection between the breaches complained of and the loss said to have been suffered as a result of Maxwell's omission and/or commission.

Thus, on the issue of causation, it necessarily fell to Chadwick J in *Bishopsgate* to distinguish between a cause of action grounded in the tort of negligence and equitable grounds for relief given the breach of a fiduciary duty. As to the former cause of action, it is incontestable that some causal connection must be proved.[108] Consequently, for an act of omission there must be established a causal nexus between the failure to act and the loss said thereby to have been caused.[109] In that respect, it is incumbent upon the plaintiff to prove that the default was *causa sine qua non* of the loss, rather than prove that it was *causa causans*.[110] Chadwick J was not prepared, however, for the reasons earlier alluded to, to investigate the requisite degree of proof in that regard upon an interlocutory application and, thus, quite properly gave leave to defend on the basis that there was a triable issue on causation.[111]

Nonetheless, Chadwick J did intimate that different considerations might apply regarding loss resulting from the breach of a fiduciary duty to that occasioned through neglect;[112] and it is with this aspect of causality *vis-à-vis* the breach of a fiduciary duty that *Bishopsgate* has particular appeal. It would seem from the judgment that Chadwick J was content to rely upon the but for test enunciated by Street J in *Re Dawson*,[113] as his Lordship considered that, 'it is necessary to show, at the least, that the loss would not have occurred if there had been no breach of the fiduciary duty.'[114] Chadwick J considered there to be a sufficient causal link between Maxwell's act of commission in wrongfully giving away company assets and the loss to the company thereby suffered. But there is a regrettable lack of analysis of the authorities within Chadwick J's judgment concerning the requirement of causation in the context of a breach of fiduciary duty.

---

cont.

[105] [1995] 3 All ER 785.

[106] [1994] 1 All ER 261.

[107] [1993] BCC 120.

[108] *Stapley v Gypsum Mines Ld* [1953] AC 663 at 681 per Lord Reid; and *March v E & M H Stramare Pty Ltd* (1990-1991) 171 CLR 506 at 509 per Mason CJ (Toohey and Gaudron JJ agreed); see Rickett C and Gardner T, 'Compensating for loss in equity: The evolution of a remedy' (1994) 24 VUWLR 19 at 30 *et seq*; Ipp D A, 'Problems and Progress in Remoteness of Damage' in Finn P D (ed), *Essays on Damages* The Law Book Company Ltd, Sydney, 1992 at 14 *et seq*; and Treitel G H, *The Law of Contract* (7th ed) Sweet & Maxwell Ltd, London, 1987 at 753 *et seq*.

[109] Cf. *Stovin v Wise* [1996] AC 923 at 944-945 per Lord Hoffmann (Lords Goff and Jauncey agreed).

[110] [1993] BCC 120 at 135-136 per Chadwick J; cf. *March v E & M H Stramare Pty Ltd* (1990-1991) 171 CLR 506.

[111] Nolan R C, 'Maxwell's improper purposes' (1994) 15 Co Law 85 at 87.

[112] [1993] BCC 120 at 135.

[113] [1966] 2 NSWLR 211 at 215.

[114] [1993] BCC 120 at 135.

In dismissing the appeal in *Bishopsgate*, Hoffmann LJ[115] also tackled the causality aspect by differentiating between Maxwell's acts of omission and commission. Insofar as Maxwell's alleged breach of duty constituted an omission, it was incumbent upon the plaintiff to prove that compliance would have prevented the damage. If, as Hoffmann LJ noted, 'it would have happened anyway, the plaintiff has failed to prove his case.'[116] But the more interesting aspect of the appeal concerns the giving away of company assets by Maxwell for no consideration. That was an act of commission and against which the company was entitled to expect the fullest protection available under fiduciary law. In such a case, Hoffmann LJ considered that:

> [The] cause of action is constituted not by failure to make inquiries but simply by the improper transfer of the shares to Robert Maxwell Group plc ... for a purpose outside the powers entrusted to the board.[117]

It was the improper transfer in *Bishopsgate* which caused the loss and, that of itself, established the necessary causal connection. Ralph Gibson LJ put the issue rather succinctly. In his Lordship's view, by signing the share transfers Maxwell misapplied the company's property for a purpose to which the company could not lawfully apply it; and, as such, 'the directors responsible must replace the property or make good the loss and it matters not that in so acting they acted honestly'.[118]

Disappointingly, however, from an academical and a practical perspective, there was a marked absence of relevant authority cited in *Bishopsgate* as to the application of the doctrine of causation in the context of a breach by directors of fiduciary duties; and, although admittedly this was beyond the scope of the appeal, the corresponding relationship, if any, between the requirement of causation in such circumstances when the directorial breach is merely equitable (as well as legal) rather than fiduciary in the sense described by Ipp J in *Permanent Building Society v Wheeler*.[119]

This approach to causality was reaffirmed nine months later by the Court of Appeal[120] in *Target Holdings Ltd v Redferns*[121] where the issue, once more, concerned the breach of a fiduciary duty; this time when a solicitor, acting contemporaneously for a mortgagor and a mortgagee, released mortgage moneys without authority before the execution of the mortgage documentation. The issue in *Target* was an analogue of that in *Bishopsgate* insofar as the breach was constituted by the wrongful payment of trust moneys by a defaulting fiduciary to a third party. The facts in *Target* exemplify that which the Full Federal Court of Australia in *Commonwealth Bank of Australia v*

---

[115] (Leggatt LJ agreed).

[116] [1994] 1 All ER 261 at 264.

[117] *Ibid* at 265; see *Target Holdings Ltd v Redferns* [1994] 2 All ER 337 at 353 per Peter Gibson LJ (Hirst LJ agreed).

[118] [1994] 1 All ER 261 at 269; see *Commonwealth Bank of Australia v Smith* (1991) 102 ALR 453 at 477 *per curiam.*

[119] (1993-1994) 11 WAR 187 at 237-238; note Finn P D, *Fiduciary Obligations* The Law Book Company Ltd, Sydney, 1977 at 78, 'The varying usage is unimportant provided one always recognises that a person is *not* a "fiduciary" ... until a duty applies to him. When one does, he then becomes a "fiduciary" ... but for the purposes of that duty only.'; also Sealy L S, 'Some Principles of Fiduciary Obligation' [1963] CLJ 119 at 137-140; cf. *Eromanga Hydrocarbons NL v Australis Mining NL* (1988) 6 ACLC 906 at 913 per Malcolm CJ.

[120] (Ralph Gibson, Hirst and Peter Gibson LJJ).

[121] [1994] 2 All ER 337.

Smith[122] so strongly decried; namely, the undesirable practice of one solicitor acting for both vendor and purchaser or, in the case of *Target*, mortgagor and mortgagee. The potential for conflict, in such circumstances, is ever present and there are countless decisions of the English and Australian courts which testify to the perils associated with such practices by a fiduciary. Some of the more controversial of these decisions are considered below.

The significance of the decision by the Court of Appeal in *Target* lies in its treatment of a fiduciary's duty to compensate for breach of trust, and to make immediate restitution for loss.[123] The principles associated therewith have direct application to the directors' fiduciary duty to act in good faith and for proper purposes. The judgment of the majority was delivered by Peter Gibson LJ[124] who considered that in circumstances where, 'the breach consists in the wrongful paying away of trust moneys so that there is an immediate loss, no inquiry is necessary: the causal connection is obvious.'[125] Consequently, the defaulting fiduciary is under an immediate obligation to restore those moneys to the trust fund, subject only to the trust giving credit for any moneys subsequently recovered, in keeping with general restitutionary principles.[126] In reaching this viewpoint, Peter Gibson LJ found support in, and quoted extensively from, Hoffmann LJ's judgment in *Bishopsgate*.

However, on appeal to the House of Lords,[127] the decision by the Court of Appeal in *Target* was reversed and the approach taken by Peter Gibson LJ to causation in such circumstances was departed from. Additionally, Hoffmann LJ's judgment in *Bishopsgate* was distinguished on its facts. In the view of the House of Lords in *Target*, on the present facts to be assumed as it was still at an interlocutory stage, it was demonstrated that no loss had in fact been incurred by reason of the breach of trust.[128] In spite of the fiduciary's breach, the mortgagee got exactly what it bargained for. The approach adopted in the Court of Appeal by Peter Gibson LJ was considered to be too harsh to the errant fiduciary in the circumstances.

Lord Browne-Wilkinson delivered the only reasoned speech of the House of Lords in *Target*; a judicious speech which contains an incisive commentary of the rules applicable to causation within the context of a fiduciary's breach of trust and the equitable obligation to either restore the trust *ante* the breach or to make good any loss suffered *post*, and by reason of, the breach in the form of equitable compensation.[129] In short, the moot point in *Target* was this: is a trustee liable to compensate his or her beneficiary not only for losses caused by the breach, but also for losses which the beneficiary would, in any event, have suffered even if there had been no such breach? Insofar as the breach of trust committed by Redferns was concerned, that left Target in exactly the same position as it would have been if there had been no such breach. The same amount of money was advanced. The same security was obtained. The same

---

[122] (1991) 102 ALR 453 at 478 *per curiam.*
[123] Cf. *Canson Enterprises Ltd v Boughton & Co* (1992) 85 DLR (4th) 129 at 157 per McLachlin J.
[124] (Hirst LJ agreed).
[125] [1994] 2 All ER 337 at 350; note Nolan R C, 'Targeting Trustees – Liability for Breach of Trust' [1994] CLJ 450 at 451.
[126] *Nocton v Lord Ashburton* [1914] AC 932 at 952 per Viscount Haldane LC (Lord Atkinson agreed).
[127] (Lords Keith, Ackner, Jauncey, Browne-Wilkinson and Lloyd).
[128] [1995] 3 All ER 785 at 799 per Lord Browne-Wilkinson (Lords Keith, Ackner, Jauncey and Lloyd agreed).
[129] Cf. *Maguire v Makaronis* (1996-1997) 188 CLR 449 at 469 per Brennan CJ, Gaudron, McHugh and Gummow JJ.

amount of money was received upon realisation of that security. In these circumstances, Lord Browne-Wilkinson was of the view that:

> In any ordinary use of words, the breach of trust by Redferns cannot be said to have caused the actual loss ultimately suffered by Target unless it can be shown that, but for the breach of trust, the transaction would not have gone through.[130]

Lord Browne-Wilkinson's speech is premised upon a thorough review of the authorities and provides an eloquent recapitulation of the legal rules and equitable principles which impact upon the doctrine of causation, as the following extract verifies:

> At common law there are two principles fundamental to the award of damages. First, that the defendant's wrongful act must cause the damage complained of. Second, that the plaintiff is to be put 'in the same position as he would have been in if he had not sustained the wrong for which he is now getting his compensation or reparation'[131] ... Although, as will appear, in many ways equity approaches liability for making good a breach of trust from a different starting point, in my judgment those two principles are applicable as much in equity as at common law. Under both systems liability is fault based: the defendant is only liable for the consequences of the legal wrong he has done to the plaintiff and to make good the damage caused by such wrong. He is not responsible for damage not caused by his wrong or to pay by way of compensation more than the loss suffered from such wrong. The detailed rules of equity as to causation and the quantification of loss differ, at least ostensibly, from those applicable at common law. But the principles underlying both systems are the same.[132]

The House of Lords in *Target* recognised that the common law rules of remoteness of damage and causation do not apply to breach of trust.[133] However, 'there does have to be some causal connection between the breach of trust and the loss to the trust estate for which compensation is recoverable, viz the fact that the loss would not have occurred but for the breach'.[134] This is consistent with the approach being taken in other Commonwealth jurisdictions.[135]

On this aspect of fiduciary law, and the interdependent requirement of causation, both *Bishopsgate* and *Target* elucidate and are eloquent of the equitable principles to be applied to infractions by defaulting directors who wrongfully dispose of company

---

[130] [1995] 3 All ER 785 at 791.

[131] *Livingstone v The Rawyards Coal Company* (1879-1880) 5 App Cas 25 at 39 per Lord Blackburn; note *Metcalfe v NZI Securities Australia Ltd* (unreported, Federal Court of Australia, New South Wales District Registry No. NG523/95, Sheppard, Burchett and Lindgren JJ, 26 March 1996) at 5.

[132] [1995] 3 All ER 785 at 792.

[133] Cf. Editorial comment, 'Target hit' (1995) 16 Co Law 258 at 258, 'Now using ideas like "remoteness of loss" in the context of equitable compensation may well raise the hackles of the traditional Chancery lawyer, who would assert that such hazy notions of the common law have no place in Equity. But is that really so?'

[134] [1995] 3 All ER 785 at 794 per Lord Browne-Wilkinson (Lords Keith, Ackner, Jauncey and Lloyd agreed).

[135] *Re Dawson* [1966] 2 NSWR 211 at 215 per Street J; *Permanent Building Society v Wheeler* (1993-1994) 11 WAR 187 at 247 per Ipp J (Malcolm CJ and Seaman J agreed); *Canson Enterprises Ltd v Boughton & Co* (1992) 85 DLR (4th) 129 at 163 per McLachlin J; cf. *Day v Mead* [1987] 2 NZLR 443 at 462 per Somers J, 'The assessment will reflect that which the justice of the case requires according to considerations of conscience, fairness, and hardship and other equitable features such as laches and acquiescence.'

assets. Although, as the learned editor of *The Company Lawyer* observes, the House of Lords in *Target* may not have adequately considered the justification for the strict approach which the Court of Appeal had earlier adopted in regard to the wrongful disposition of moneys by the defaulting solicitor in question.[136] Nonetheless, the approach taken by the Court of Appeal in *Bishopsgate*, and that taken by the House of Lords in *Target*, does emphasise the gravity with which the judiciary views any breach of a fiduciary duty. Infractions of fiduciary obligations are considered offensive to the revered equitable principles of trust, confidence, good faith, honesty and integrity. It is qualities such as these which courts of equity have, for so long, sought to promote.[137] Equity, as appears from the judgment of Hutley JA in *Walden Properties Ltd v Beaver Properties Pty Ltd*, 'has always been a jealous guardian of the rights of the person entitled to the benefit of the performance of fiduciary duties.'[138]

In English and Australian company law the principles of causation, foreseeability and remoteness of damage, as applied to breaches of duty at law and in equity, absent fiduciary incidents, do not apply to directorial breaches of fiduciary duties.[139] Moreover, as Mason notes, 'a fiduciary should not be held liable for loss that does not flow from a breach of fiduciary duty';[140] reaffirming in the process the view expressed by Davidson that, 'it is imperative to ascertain the loss resulting from breach of the relevant equitable duty'.[141] Thus, as Heydon quite properly points out in his case note on the Court of Appeal's decision in *Target*, in circumstances where there is no immediate loss and the causal connection not immediately obvious, the decision in *Bishopsgate* does not greatly assist in resolving the controversy concerning causation in a broader context.[142] The decision by the House of Lords in *Target*, however, is very much declaratory and elucidative of the doctrine of causation in this respect and the correct approach to be employed in its application.

In fiduciary law, the breach is often more contemptible than the loss thereby occasioned.[143] It is perhaps for this reason that equity has not always paid the same attention to issues of causation, foreseeability and remoteness of damage; issues regarded at common law as integral to any right of recovery, be it contractual or tortious.[144] This can be justified by reference to the preventive nature of the rules relating to fiduciaries and the historical approach by a court administering equity,[145] 'in

---

[136] Editorial comment, 'Target hit' (1995) 16 Co Law 258 at 258.
[137] Finn P D, *Fiduciary Obligations* The Law Book Company Ltd, Sydney, 1977 at 1; and Sealy L S, '"Bona Fides"' and "Proper Purposes" in Corporate Decisions' (1989) 15 MULR 265 at 265; see *LAC Minerals Ltd v International Corona Resources Ltd* (1989) 61 DLR (4th) 14 at 47 per La Forest J, 'The essence of the imposition of fiduciary obligations is its utility in the promotion and preservation of desired social behaviour and institutions.'
[138] [1973] 2 NSWLR 815 at 846.
[139] *Re Dawson* [1966] 2 NSWR 211 at 216 per Street J; and *Hill v Rose* [1990] VR 129 at 144 per Tadgell J.
[140] Mason A, 'The Place of Equity and Equitable Remedies in the Contemporary Common Law World' (1994) 110 LQR 238 at 244.
[141] Davidson I E, 'The Equitable Remedy of Compensation' (1982) 13 Melb ULR 349 at 354.
[142] See Heydon J D, 'Causal Relationships Between a Fiduciary's Default and the Principal's Loss' (1994) 110 LQR 328.
[143] *Maguire v Makaronis* (1996-1997) 188 CLR 449 at 465 per Brennan CJ, Gaudron, McHugh and Gummow JJ.
[144] *Swindle v Harrison* [1997] 4 All ER 705 at 715 per Evans LJ and at 733 per Mummery LJ; and *Downs v Chappell* [1996] 3 All ER 344 at 352 and 361 per Hobhouse LJ (Roch and Butler – Sloss LJJ agreed).
[145] Doyle J J, Commentary to Kearney, 'Accounting for a Fiduciary's Gains in Commercial Contexts' in Finn P D (ed), *Equity and Commercial Relationships* The Law Book Company Ltd, Sydney, 1987 at 213.

exercise of its jurisdiction "to keep persons in a fiduciary capacity up to their duty".'[146] Not surprisingly, therefore, equitable remedies have a different focus and emphasis than do common law remedies. Within Street J's seminal judgment in *Dawson*, his Honour was of the view that:

> [The] obligation to make restitution, which courts of equity have from very early times imposed on defaulting trustees and other fiduciaries is of a more absolute nature than the common law obligation to pay damages for tort or breach of contract.[147]

This viewpoint is consistent with that recently adopted by the Canadian Supreme Court[148] in *Canson Enterprises Ltd v Boughton & Co* where McLachlin J[149] pointed out that, 'equity is concerned, not only to compensate the plaintiff, but to enforce the trust which is at its heart.'[150] And, in this regard, Leeming's recent observations are also deserving of study:

> Ultimately, there is a fundamental difference in principle between damages and equitable compensation. The fact that a fiduciary has to subject his or her personal interest to that of his or her principal contrasts starkly with the common law's protection of individual freedom, qualified by a system of duties and obligations.[151]

It is instructive to consider the approach taken by the Canadian Supreme Court in *Canson*.[152] In issue was the extent of a solicitor's obligation for breach of fiduciary duty in failing to disclose that a third party was making a secret profit in the plaintiff's purchase of land, and whether or not the plaintiff could hold the solicitor liable for loss suffered due to the negligence of architects and engineers in subsequent construction on the land. Only part of the loss was recovered from the architects and the engineers. The plaintiff sought to recover the balance of the loss, the secret profit and consequential damages from the solicitor. The moot point was this: was the solicitor responsible only for losses directly flowing from his breach of duty, or was he also liable for loss caused by an intervening act unrelated to that breach; namely, the loss caused by subsidence of the building, the construction of which was known by the parties to be the purpose for acquiring the land? On the question of causality, McLachlin J[153] had this to say:

> While foreseeability of loss does not enter into the calculation of compensation for breach of fiduciary duty, liability is not unlimited. Just as restitution *in specie* is

---

[146] [1994] 2 All ER 337 at 353 per Peter Gibson LJ (Hirst LJ agreed); see *Nocton v Lord Ashburton* [1914] AC 932 at 963 per Lord Dunedin; and *Canson Enterprises Ltd v Boughton & Co* (1992) 85 DLR (4th) 129 at 160-161 per McLachlin J.

[147] [1966] 2 NSWR 211 at 216; see *Hill v Rose* [1990] VR 129 at 144 per Tadgell J.

[148] (Lamer CJC, Wilson, La Forest, L'Heureux-Dubé, Sopinka, Gonthier, Cory, McLachlin and Stevenson JJ).

[149] (Lamer CJC and L'Heureux-Dubé J agreed).

[150] (1992) 85 DLR (4th) 129 at 154.

[151] Leeming M, 'Causation and compensation for breach of fiduciary duty'(1996) 70 ALJ 537 at 540.

[152] (1992) 85 DLR (4th) 129 (on appeal from the British Columbia Court of Appeal).

[153] In a judgment deserving of study and which, 'contains an illuminating exposition of the rules applicable to equitable compensation for breach of trust': *Target Holdings Ltd v Redferns* [1995] 3 All ER 785 at 797 per Lord Browne-Wilkinson (Lords Keith, Ackner, Jauncey and Lloyd agreed).

limited to the property under the trustee's control, so equitable compensation must be limited to loss flowing from the trustee's acts in relation to the interest he undertook to protect.[154] ... The need for a link between the equitable breach and the loss for which compensation is awarded is fair and sound in policy ... The requirement that the loss must result from the breach of the relevant equitable duty does not negate the fact that 'causality' in the legal sense as limited by foreseeability at the time of breach does not apply in equity. ... Thus, while the loss must flow from the breach of fiduciary duty, it need not be reasonably foreseeable at the time of the breach ... A breach of fiduciary duty is a wrong in itself, regardless of whether a loss can be foreseen. Moreover the high duty assumed and the difficulty of detecting such breaches makes it fair and practical to adopt a measure of compensation calculated to ensure that fiduciaries are kept 'up to their duty'.[155]

In the result, the Canadian Supreme Court determined that the plaintiff's actual loss in *Canson*, as a consequence of the breach, was to be assessed with the full benefit of hindsight.[156] On a common sense view of causation,[157] the solicitor's breach of fiduciary duty could not be said to have caused the ultimate loss; notwithstanding that concepts of foreseeability and remoteness were not applicable in assessing equitable compensation.[158] A not dissimilar approach to that in *Canson* was taken by the New Zealand Court of Appeal[159] in *Day v Mead*, where Somers J ventured that equitable compensation, 'is not fettered by the requirements of foresight and remoteness which control awards of damages at law.'[160]

These decisions have recently enjoyed support in the English courts following a spate of litigation throughout the 1990s by finance providers as a consequence of the collapse of the property market in England and elsewhere. This litigation is designed to recover losses from professional advisers as the value of the securities taken has fallen.[161] Breach of contract, negligence and breach of fiduciary duty is often alleged. One such action against a solicitor which found its way to the Court of Appeal[162] following a successful summary judgment application was *Bristol and West Building Society v Mothew*.[163] This gave rise to important questions of principle in relation to a claim by a mortgagee seeking to recover from Mothew the solicitor who was acting for

---

[154] Cf. Davidson I E, 'The Equitable Remedy of Compensation' (1982) 13 Melb ULR 349 at 351.

[155] (1992) 85 DLR (4th) 129 at 160-161; see *Re Dawson* [1966] 2 NSWR 211 at 216 per Street J; note *Target Holdings Ltd v Redferns* [1995] 3 All ER 785 at 797-798 per Lord Browne-Wilkinson (Lords Keith, Ackner, Jauncey and Lloyd agreed).

[156] Cf. *Biala Pty Ltd v Mallina Holdings Ltd* (1993) 11 ACSR 785 at 852 per Ipp J, 'I am required by the rules of equity, in assessing compensation, to leave aside questions of causation (save that compensation will only be awarded for losses caused by the breach of fiduciary duties), foreseeability and remoteness, and to apply the full benefit of hindsight.'

[157] *March v E & M H Stramare Pty Ltd* (1990-1991) 171 CLR 506; and *Target Holdings Ltd v Redferns* [1995] 3 All ER 785.

[158] (1992) 85 DLR (4th) 129 at 163 per McLachlin J.

[159] (Cooke P, Somers, Casey and Hillyer JJ).

[160] [1987] 2 NZLR 443 at 461; see *Re Dawson* [1966] 2 NSWR 211 at 215-216 per Street J; *Coleman v Myers* [1977] 2 NZLR 225 at 359-362 per Cooke J; and *Witten-Hannah v Davis* [1995] 2 NZLR 141 at 149 per Richardson J (Casey J agreed); note Finn P D, *Fiduciary Obligations* The Law Book Company Ltd, Sydney, 1977 at 166-168.

[161] E.g., *South Australia Asset Management Corporation v York Montague Ltd* [1997] AC 191; and *National Home Loans Corp plc v Giffen Couch & Archer* [1997] 3 All ER 808.

[162] (Staughton, Millett and Otton LJJ).

[163] [1996] 4 All ER 698.

both mortgagors and mortgagee the loss arising from the mortgagors' subsequent default. *Bristol* provides an illustration of litigants resorting to equity and fiduciary law with a view to enlarging the fruits of their litigation by endeavouring to go outside the common law rules of causation and remoteness of damage which might otherwise limit, and perhaps even deny, recovery of their losses.[164]

The facts in *Bristol* were these. Mothew was required by Bristol and West Building Society ('Bristol') to submit a report on title and request for the advance cheque on a form which asked him to confirm that the title was good and marketable, and that to the best of his knowledge and belief the balance of the purchase moneys was being provided by the mortgagors personally without resort to further borrowing. Mothew provided such a report. In doing so, he negligently failed to disclose that the mortgagors were making arrangements for a second mortgage. When Bristol came to enforce its security following the mortgagors' default, it sought to recover the whole of its net loss on the transaction from Mothew. There was no allegation of bad faith on the part of Mothew. He admitted breach of contract and negligence, but denied breach of trust.

The leading judgment in the Court of Appeal was delivered by Millett LJ.[165] After a thorough review of the relevant authorities, his Lordship felt that the decision of the Court of Appeal[166] in *Downs v Chappell*[167] was binding upon him such that at law Bristol, 'will not have to prove that it would not have made the mortgage advance if it had known the true facts; but it will be required to establish what it has lost as a result of the existence of the second charge and the purchasers' indebtedness to the bank.'[168] On the summary judgment application that was not established. Thus, Bristol was only able to maintain the money judgment in the court below if it could invoke equitable principles. It is Millett LJ's treatment of those principles which has particular appeal.

In a refreshing judgment which drew heavily upon Commonwealth influence,[169] Millett LJ brought clarity to the expression 'fiduciary duty' in *Bristol* by emphasising the need to appreciate that there are duties peculiar to fiduciaries, the breach of which attracts legal consequences which differ from those consequent upon the breach of other duties given that, 'not every breach of duty by a fiduciary is a breach of fiduciary duty.'[170] Displaying his usual perspicuity, Millett LJ's review of the authorities led him to the view that it is inappropriate to elevate the obligation of a trustee or other fiduciary to use proper skill and care in the discharge of his duties to a fiduciary duty. As his Lordship explained, 'the fact that the source of the duty is to be found in equity rather than the common law does not make it a fiduciary duty.'[171] The following passage from Millett LJ's judgment is particularly helpful in this regard:

---

[164]   Cf. *Royal Brunei Airlines Sdn Bhd v Tan* [1995] 2 AC 378 at 381-382 per Lord Nicholls (Lords Goff, Ackner and Steyn and Sir John May agreed).

[165]   (Otton LJ agreed).

[166]   (Butler-Sloss, Roch and Hobhouse LJJ).

[167]   [1996] 3 All ER 344.

[168]   [1996] 4 All ER 698 at 707.

[169]   E.g., *Girardet v Crease & Company* (1987) 11 BCLR (2d) 361 at 362 per Southin J; *LAC Minerals Ltd v International Corona Resources Ltd* (1989) 61 DLR (4th) 14 at 28 per La Forest J; and *Permanent Building Society v Wheeler* (1993-1994) 11 WAR 187 at 237-238 per Ipp J (Malcolm CJ and Seaman J agreed).

[170]   [1996] 4 All ER 698 at 710; see *Attorney General v Blake* [1998] 1 All ER 833 at 843 per Lord Woolf MR (Millett and Mummery LJJ agreed).

[171]   [1996] 4 All ER 698 at 710.

Although the remedy which equity makes available for breach of the equitable duty of skill and care is equitable compensation rather than damages, this is merely the product of history and in this context is in my opinion a distinction without a difference. Equitable compensation for breach of the duty of skill and care resembles common law damages in that it is awarded by way of compensation to the plaintiff for his loss. There is no reason in principle why the common law rules of causation, remoteness of damage and measure of damages should not be applied by analogy in such a case.[172] It should not be confused with equitable compensation for breach of fiduciary duty, which may be awarded in lieu of rescission or specific restitution. This leaves those duties which are special to fiduciaries and which attract those remedies which are peculiar to the equitable jurisdiction and are primarily restitutionary or restorative rather than compensatory.[173]

In the result, Millett LJ found that whilst Mothew was in a potentially conflicting situation, that was not something of which Bristol could complain. The very reason why it chose Mothew to act for it was that he was acting for the mortgagors at the time. The potential conflict was, therefore, of Bristol's own making. Given that no allegation was made against Mothew that he acted in bad faith or that he deliberately withheld information because he wrongly believed that his duty to the mortgagors required him to do so, he was not guilty of a breach of fiduciary duty.[174] Mothew's inadvertent failure did not constitute want of fidelity. The fact that Mothew was acting for both parties did not contribute to his failure to fulfil his obligations to Bristol. Whilst that failure might constitute breach of contract and negligence, it did not constitute a breach of fiduciary duty on Mothew's part. The appeal was allowed and the money judgment set aside.

Swindle v Harrison[175] presents as another instance of a solicitor acting for both parties to a transaction being sued for the loss suffered upon an unsuccessful finance arrangement. There, a restaurant was purchased. Mary Harrison mortgaged her home to do so. Further moneys were to be borrowed against the restaurant premises. That did not happen and bridging finance could not be arranged in time. Moreover, one bank approached for finance communicated back to Swindle the solicitor that it was 'unhappy with the client'. That was not in turn communicated by Swindle to Harrison. Instead, Swindle himself offered to advance £75,000 for a two month period on reasonable terms.[176] The property and the business were then purchased. The business failed. Possession was taken of the house by which time its market value was considerably less than that due the financier.

In the action in *Swindle* for possession of the restaurant premises against Harrison, Swindle sought to recover the £75,000 loan. Harrison counterclaimed that she had lost the value of her equity in the home by reason of Swindle advancing those moneys and thereby enabling her to complete the restaurant purchase. At trial, Harrison alleged that Swindle should have advised her not to proceed and by not doing so was negligent. The trial judge rejected that allegation and found that even had Swindle given Harrison that advice she would have been undeterred and would have proceeded in any event. On appeal, that finding was not challenged.

---

[172] Cf. *Target Holdings Ltd v Redferns* [1995] 3 All ER 785 at 792 per Lord Browne-Wilkinson (Lords Keith, Ackner, Jauncey and Lloyd agreed).

[173] [1996] 4 All ER 698 at 711.

[174] *Ibid* at 714.

[175] [1997] 4 All ER 705.

[176] Cf. *Maguire v Makaronis* (1996-1997) 188 CLR 449.

In issue in *Swindle*, however, was whether in making the loan which enabled Harrison to proceed, Swindle was in breach of duty given that 'but for'[177] the loan, she would not have been able to complete the purchase. This somewhat audacious argument was rejected by the Court of Appeal.[178] On causation, the judgment of Evans LJ is instructive. In the absence of fraud, the test of causation was one of common sense and was essentially the common law approach. Here there was no allegation of fraud or of any breach of fiduciary duty which might be regarded as the equitable equivalent of fraud. Swindle's failure to disclose material facts to Harrison could not be said to have led to the making of the loan, 'even on a "but for" basis, precisely because disclosure of the true facts would not have affected her decision to accept it.'[179] In Evans LJ's judgment:

> Since she would have accepted the loan and completed the purchase, even if full disclosure had been made to her, she would have lost the value of the equity in her home in any event. She cannot recover damages or compensation for that loss, in my judgment, except on proof *either* that the plaintiffs acted fraudulently or in a manner equivalent to fraud *or* that she would not have completed the purchase if full disclosure had been made ie if the breach of duty had not occurred. She can do neither, and in my judgment her claim for damages must fail.[180]

Evans LJ referred to the appellate judgments in *Bristol* and *Target*.[181] His Lordship considered it to be well established that a general duty of skill and care is owed by a solicitor to his client, 'though its scope is always subject to the terms of his retainer in the particular case'.[182] Evans LJ went on to explain that:

> [What] I have called the stringent rule of causation or measure of damages does not apply as regards breaches of equitable duties unless the breach can properly be regarded as the equivalent of fraud. In other cases the plaintiff is entitled to be placed in the same position financially as he would have been in if the breach of duty had not occurred – not necessarily the same as he was in before it occurred.[183]

In this respect, the judgment of Mummery LJ in *Swindle* is illuminative and also particularly helpful to an appreciation for, and an understanding of, the pertinent issues touching upon the doctrine of causation as the following extract amply demonstrates:

> In considering the extent of liability for breach of fiduciary duty, it is not always necessary to consider all the matters which may be relevant in determining the extent of liability to pay damages for negligence. Foreseeability and remoteness of damage are, in general, irrelevant to restitutionary remedies for breach of trust or breach of

---

[177] *Smith New Court Securities Ltd v Scrimgeour Vickers (Asset Management) Ltd* [1996] 4 All ER 769 at 794-795 per Lord Steyn (Lords Browne-Wilkinson, Keith, Mustill and Slynn agreed); *March v E & M H Stramare Pty Ltd* (1990-1991) 171 CLR 506 at 515 per Mason CJ (Toohey and Gaudron JJ agreed); and *Fitzgerald v Penn* (1954-1955) 91 CLR 268 at 276-277 per Dixon CJ, Fullagar and Kitto JJ; see Weinrib E J, 'A Step in Factual Causation' (1975) 38 MLR 518 at 520-523 and 530.
[178] (Evans, Hobhouse and Mummery LJJ).
[179] [1997] 4 All ER 705 at 718.
[180] *Ibid*.
[181] [1995] 3 All ER 785.
[182] [1997] 4 All ER 705 at 716.
[183] *Ibid* at 717.

fiduciary duty. The liability is to make good the loss suffered by the beneficiary of the duty. It is, however, necessary to address the issue of causation. Although equitable compensation, whether awarded in lieu of rescission or specific restitution or whether simply awarded as monetary compensation, is not damages, it is still necessary for Mrs Harrison to show that the loss suffered has been caused by the relevant breach of fiduciary duty. Liability is not unlimited. There is no equitable by-pass of the need to establish causation.[184]

This is a complex area of English company law, and the doctrine of causation gives rise to important issues for the English courts. The spate of litigation witnessed during the 1990s has brought some of these issues sharply into focus. It is evident from our brief excursion above, into several of the more interesting and controversial cases which have recently come before the English courts, that a respectable body of jurisprudence upon the doctrine of causation is being formulated. As we have seen from some of the English authorities, the Australian experience is impacting upon, and coming to play an important role in the development of, English jurisprudence in this area. It is instructive, therefore, to examine the approach of the Australian courts to causation and witness how the Australian judiciary has approached some of the more intractable issues associated with that.

CAUSATION: AN AUSTRALIAN PERSPECTIVE

The leading Australian authority on the common law doctrine of causation is *March v E&MH Stramare Pty Ltd*,[185] where the High Court of Australia[186] examined the concepts of causation, foreseeability and remoteness within the context of a road accident and the usual allegations of negligence attendant on such. In the course of his reasons for decision, Mason CJ[187] considered that at common law the cause of a particular occurrence is, 'a question of fact which "must be determined by applying common sense to the facts of each particular case".'[188] For the purposes of the law of negligence, the question of causation arises in the words of Deane J:

> [In] the context of the attribution of fault or responsibility whether an identified negligent act or omission of the defendant was so connected with the plaintiff's loss or injury that, as a matter of ordinary common sense and experience, it should be regarded as a cause of it.[189]

In adopting this approach in *March*, the High Court of Australia was much influenced by the joint judgment of Dixon CJ, Fullagar and Kitto JJ in *Fitzgerald v Penn*, where their Honours observed that causation is ultimately a matter of common sense and, thus,

---

[184] *Ibid* at 733.
[185] (1990-1991) 171 CLR 506.
[186] (Mason CJ, Deane, Toohey, Gaudron and McHugh JJ).
[187] (Toohey and Gaudron JJ agreed).
[188] (1990-1991) 171 CLR 506 at 515; see *Stapley v Gypsum Mines Ld* [1953] AC 663 at 681 per Lord Reid; cf. Stapleton J, 'Law, Causation and Common Sense' (1988) 8 OJLS 111 at 124.
[189] (1990-1991) 171 CLR 506 at 522.

'is not susceptible of reduction to a satisfactory formula.'[190] Causation has an amorphous quality which, notwithstanding the many attempts over the years to define and describe,[191] continues to bedevil English and Australian jurists alike.

One test of causation, the but for test, has proved resilient and of general utility, but is neither exclusive nor definitive.[192] Although, when applied as a negative criterion of causation, the High Court of Australia in *March* considered it to have an important role to play.[193] In this regard, it is worth recalling Toohey J's remarks that the but for test is not and should not be a definitive test of causation since where negligence is in issue, causation is essentially a question of fact, 'into which considerations of policy and value judgments necessarily enter.'[194] In *Poseidon Ltd v Adelaide Petroleum NL*, the High Court of Australia[195] recently reaffirmed that the question of causation in civil actions is governed by the general standard of proof; namely, on the balance of probabilities.[196] The Court of Appeal in *Page v Smith (No 2)* recently did likewise.[197]

At common law, therefore, for the company to prove that a director's breach of duty caused loss to it, it must be established, upon a balance of probabilities, that a reasonable director in that director's position would have exercised reasonable care and diligence by acting in a way different to that which caused loss to the company. Nowhere is this approach better exemplified than in *Permanent Building Society v Wheeler* where, it will be recalled, the issue before the Western Australian Full Court[198] was whether one of the plaintiff building society's directors, by failing to express opposition to and vote against the adoption of certain resolutions, was in breach of a fiduciary duty by not exercising a reasonable degree of care and diligence in the exercise of his directorial powers and in the discharge of his duties.[199] The judgment of the Full Court was given by Ipp J, who reaffirmed the rule of equity that:

---

[190] (1954-1955) 91 CLR 268 at 277-278; note *Page v Smith (No 2)* [1996] 3 All ER 272 at 274-276 per Sir Thomas Bingham MR (Morritt and Auld LJJ agreed).

[191] *Haynes v Harwood* [1935] 1 KB 146 at 156 per Greer LJ; *Home Office v Dorset Yacht Co Ltd* [1970] AC 1004 at 1028-1030 per Lord Reid; and *Leyland Shipping Co v Norwich Union Fire Insurance Society Ltd* [1918] AC 350 at 370 per Lord Shaw.

[192] *Smith New Court Securities Ltd v Scrimgeour Vickers (Asset Management) Ltd* [1996] 4 All ER 769 at 794-795 per Lord Steyn (Lords Browne-Wilkinson, Keith, Mustill and Slynn agreed); see Weinrib E J, 'A Step in Factual Causation' (1975) 38 MLR 518 at 520-523 and 530.

[193] *March v E & M H Stramare Pty Ltd* (1990-1991) 171 CLR 506 at 515 per Mason CJ (Toohey and Gaudron JJ agreed); and *Fitzgerald v Penn* (1954-1955) 91 CLR 268 at 276-277 per Dixon CJ, Fullagar and Kitto JJ.

[194] (1990-1991) 171 CLR 506 at 524; see Weinrib E J, 'A Step in Factual Causation' (1975) 38 MLR 518 at 529 *et seq*; and Ipp D A, 'Problems and Progress in Remoteness of Damage' in Finn P D (ed), *Essays on Damages* The Law Book Company Ltd, Sydney, 1992 at 23.

[195] (Mason CJ, Brennan, Dawson, Toohey and Gaudron JJ).

[196] (1994) 68 ALJR 313 at 321 per Mason CJ, Dawson, Toohey and Gaudron JJ; note *Norwest Refrigeration Services Pty Ltd v Bain Dawes (WA) Pty Ltd* (1984-1985) 157 CLR 149 at 160 per Gibbs CJ, Mason, Wilson and Dawson JJ at 171-172 per Brennan J; and *Neat Holdings Pty Ltd v Karajan Holdings Pty Ltd* (1993) 67 ALJR 170 at 170 per Mason CJ, Brennan, Deane and Gaudron JJ.

[197] [1996] 3 All ER 272 at 274-276 per Sir Thomas Bingham MR (Morritt and Auld LJJ agreed).

[198] (Malcolm CJ, Seaman and Ipp JJ).

[199] (1993-1994) 11 WAR 187 at 235 per Ipp J (Malcolm CJ and Seaman J agreed).

[In] the management of the business of the trust, a trustee should exercise the same care and skill as an ordinary prudent man of business would exercise in conducting that business if it were his own.[200]

Ipp J considered that the relevant director in *Wheeler* owed the plaintiff building society a duty, both in law and in equity, to exercise reasonable care and skill, but that the equitable duty is not to be equated or termed a fiduciary duty.[201] After a thorough review of the authorities, Ipp J went on to conclude that:

The director's duty to exercise care and skill has nothing to do with any position of disadvantage or vulnerability on the part of the company.[202] It is not a duty that stems from the requirements of trust and confidence imposed on a fiduciary. In my opinion, that duty is not a fiduciary duty, although it is a duty actionable in the equitable jurisdiction of this court.[203]

Measured against the objective test enunciated by the Western Australian Full Court in *Australian Securities Commission v Gallagher*,[204] the relevant director in *Wheeler* was found to have breached his duty to exercise care and skill. That finding then led to the next enquiry: did the breach of duty cause loss to the plaintiff building society? In order to answer that question, resort must be had to the doctrine of causation and the attendant concepts of foreseeability and remoteness of damage, as earlier alluded to. In the circumstances, Ipp J considered that as regards matters of policy, 'the tortious duty not to be negligent, and the equitable obligation on the part of a trustee to exercise reasonable care and skill are, in content, the same.'[205]

Although Ipp J in *Wheeler* went to great lengths to differentiate between the breach of a fiduciary duty and that of an equitable duty, his Honour simply adopted *dicta* from Street J's judgment in *Re Dawson*,[206] and Tadgell J's judgment in *Hill v Rose*,[207] and considered that it was incumbent upon the plaintiff building society to demonstrate that but for the breach by the relevant director of his equitable duty to exercise reasonable care, the loss to the building society would not have occurred.[208] As the building society failed to establish this element of causality, so too, did its claim. Although the Western Australian Full Court applied the but for test in this instance, the result would have been no different, it is suggested, had the common sense test, advocated by the majority of the High Court of Australia in *March*,[209] been utilised. But, in Ipp J's view:

---

[200] *Ibid*; see *In re Whiteley* (1886) 33 Ch D 347 at 355 per Lindley LJ; and *Learoyd v Whiteley* (1887) 12 App Cas 727 at 733 per Lord Watson.
[201] (1993-1994) 11 WAR 187 at 239.
[202] Cf. *Hospital Products Ltd v United States Surgical Corporation* (1984) 156 CLR 41 at 102 per Mason J.
[203] (1993-1994) 11 WAR 187 at 239.
[204] (1993) 11 ACLC 286 at 294 per Pidgeon J (Franklyn and Walsh JJ agreed).
[205] (1993-1994) 11 WAR 187 at 247.
[206] [1966] 2 NSWLR 211 at 215.
[207] [1990] VR 129 at 144.
[208] Cf. *Target Holdings Ltd v Redferns* [1995] 3 All ER 785 at 794 per Lord Browne-Wilkinson (Lords Keith, Ackner, Jauncey and Lloyd agreed).
[209] (1990-1991) 171 CLR 506.

[A] court of equity, applying principles of fairness, should not require an honest but careless trustee to compensate a beneficiary for losses without proof that but for the breach of duty those losses would not have occurred.[210]

Within fiduciary law, the debate continues as to whether or not the breach of a fiduciary duty is subject to similar concepts; concepts notoriously vague and difficult to apply in practice, yet fundamental to the right to a remedy at law or in equity for a breach of duty absent fiduciary incidents.[211] The subtleties and nuances attendant on those concepts at law are, however, beyond the scope of this book; but were mentioned earlier in order to highlight the complexities which abound within the law of remedies generally.[212] To some extent, fiduciary law is not concerned with these contentious issues and, in this regard, the Australian case-law is shown to constitute a most distinguished contribution to equitable jurisprudence.

The leading Australian authority on the causation principles applicable to breaches of equitable obligations is the judgment of Street J in *Dawson*.[213] There, the New South Wales Supreme Court determined that an executor and trustee of a deceased estate, who had improperly paid away trust moneys, was under a duty to restore the estate in full notwithstanding that the effect of prevailing exchange rates at the time of restoration resulted in a much higher repayment figure. Street J's judgment recognised the obligation of a defaulting fiduciary as being essentially one of effecting a restitution to the company; such obligation being of, 'a personal character and its extent is not to be limited by common law principles governing remoteness of damage.'[214] Street J considered the trustee's actions to be a clear and deliberate breach for which the trustee was liable, 'to place the trust estate in the same position as it would have been in if no breach had been committed. Considerations of causation, foreseeability and remoteness do not readily enter into the matter.'[215] Street J went on to say in an oft quoted passage:

> The principles embodied in this approach do not appear to involve any inquiry as to whether the loss was caused by or flowed from the breach. Rather the inquiry in each instance would appear to be whether the loss would have happened if there had been no breach.[216]

---

[210] (1993-1994) 11 WAR 187 at 247; cf. *Biala Pty Ltd v Mallina Holdings Ltd* (1993) 11 ACSR 785 at 852 and 854 per Ipp J who applied the but for test in conjunction with, 'a common sense test of causation'; an approach consistent with that adopted by the House of Lords in *Target Holdings Ltd v Redferns* [1995] 3 All ER 785 at 797-798 per Lord Browne-Wilkinson (Lords Keith, Ackner, Jauncey and Lloyd agreed); see Ipp D A, 'Problems and Progress in Remoteness of Damage' in Finn P D (ed), *Essays on Damages* The Law Book Company Ltd, Sydney, 1992 at 23.

[211] *Permanent Building Society v Wheeler* (1993-1994) 11 WAR 187 at 247 per Ipp J (Malcolm CJ and Seaman J agreed); see Treitel G H, *The Law of Contract* (7th ed) Sweet & Maxwell Ltd, London, 1987 at 746.

[212] Ipp D A, 'Problems and Progress in Remoteness of Damage' in Finn P D (ed), *Essays on Damages* The Law Book Company Ltd, Sydney, 1992 at 14.

[213] [1966] 2 NSWR 211; cf. *Target Holdings Ltd v Redferns* [1995] 3 All ER 785 at 797 per Lord Browne-Wilkinson (Lords Keith, Ackner, Jauncey and Lloyd agreed).

[214] [1966] 2 NSWR 211 at 214-215.

[215] *Ibid* at 215; note *Biala Pty Ltd v Mallina Holdings Ltd* (1993) 11 ACSR 785 at 850-852 per Ipp J.

[216] [1966] 2 NSWR 211 at 215; see *Permanent Building Society v Wheeler* (1993-1994) 11 WAR 187 at 243-244 and 248 per Ipp J (Malcolm CJ and Seaman J agreed); and *Gemstone Corporation of Australia Ltd v Grasso* (1994) 12 ACLC 653 at 667 per Olsson J.

More recently in the Victorian Supreme Court in *Hill*,[217] Tadgell J explained that the aim of an equitable remedy is to restore the party, as nearly as possible, to the position in which he, she or it would have been in had there been no breach. In Tadgell J's judgment:

> The obligation imposed by courts of equity upon defaulting trustees and other fiduciaries is of a more absolute nature than the common law obligation to pay damages for tort or breach of contract. It follows that the obligation is not limited or influenced by common law principles governing remoteness of damage, foreseeability or causation. The question for consideration is not whether the loss was caused by or flowed from the breach. Rather ... 'the enquiry in each case [*sic*] would appear to be whether the loss would have happened if there had been no breach.'[218]

The Full Federal Court of Australia[219] in *Commonwealth Bank of Australia v Smith*,[220] considered the applicability of principles of causation, foreseeability and remoteness in the context of the breach by a local bank manager of a fiduciary duty owed to Smith, one of the bank's customers. The Full Court affirmed the trial judge's findings that the bank manager had assumed the mantle of financial adviser in circumstances where he must have known that the inexperienced Smith would rely on his advice and, thus, it was incumbent upon him, to eschew conflicting engagements, to make full and frank disclosure, and to encourage Smith to seek skilled independent advice.[221]

Smith had sought assistance from the bank manager in *Commonwealth Bank* in respect of purchasing the licensed leasehold of one of the several hotels in the vicinity of a small country town in South Australia. In addition to Smith being a customer of the bank, it transpired that the vendor of the business was also a customer of the bank, as a consequence of which the bank was in possession of sensitive information relevant to the business which ought to have been disclosed to Smith, but was not.[222]

In a joint judgment, Davies, Sheppard and Gummow JJ considered the bank manager in *Commonwealth Bank* to be under a duty to advise with due care and skill and that he had failed in this duty because the advice he gave about the appropriateness of the transaction was wrong given that he had no basis, let alone any reasonable basis, for making the statements which he did. Thus, in negligence, the cause of action was made out. As to the fiduciary relationship, their Honours reaffirmed that where a bank gives to a customer advice upon financial affairs, then in addition to any contractual rights the customer may have, 'the relationship between the parties may be such as to found either or both a common law duty of care and a fiduciary duty'.[223] As such, the question became, in Davies, Sheppard and Gummow JJ's joint judgment:

---

[217] [1990] VR 129.

[218] *Ibid* at 144; see *Re Dawson* [1966] 2 NSWR 211 at 215 per Street J; *Day v Mead* [1987] 2 NZLR 443 at 461 per Somers J; and *Permanent Building Society v Wheeler* (1993-1994) 11 WAR 187 at 244-245 per Ipp J (Malcolm CJ and Seaman J agreed).

[219] (Davies, Sheppard and Gummow JJ).

[220] (1991) 102 ALR 453.

[221] The causes of action upon which Smith relied were breach of Trade Practices Act 1974 (Cth) s52, negligent misstatement and breach of fiduciary duty.

[222] See *Bristol and West Building Society v Mothew* [1996] 4 All ER 698 at 713 per Millett LJ (Otton LJ agreed) who referred to this situation in these terms: 'The fact that he cannot fulfil his obligations to one principal without being in breach of his obligations to the other will not absolve him from liability. I shall call this "the actual conflict rule".'

[223] (1991) 102 ALR 453 at 475-476 *per curiam*.

[One] of (i) identifying the relevant incidents of that relationship and duties arising from it, and (ii) determining whether there had been a breach of duty leading to loss for which there was an obligation upon the bank to compensate[224] ... The crucial incident of the fiduciary relationship ... arose from the conflicting interests between the two sets of customers of the bank. ... In such a case, it is not to the point that the fiduciary himself may not stand to profit from the transaction he brings about between the parties. The prohibition is not against the making of a profit ... but of the avoidance of conflict of duties[225].[226]

The Full Federal Court of Australia in *Commonwealth Bank* accepted that the measure of damages was the same for the statutory breach and for negligence, and, from a practical perspective, the same for the breach of fiduciary duty. Their Honours approved Street J's judgment in *Dawson* to the effect that the bank was obliged to make restitution and in doing so was not necessarily limited by common law concepts of foreseeability and remoteness. As to the quantum of damages, the Full Court considered there to be no difference in result, 'whether one quantified the damages in tort or quantified compensation in equity.'[227]

In each of these cases there was an readily identifiable loss for which the court had no hesitation in compensating; given equity's strict attitude to the breach of a fiduciary duty.[228] Traditionally, where a fiduciary duty has been breached, equity did not look to the consequences in order to judge the reasonableness of the action. As McLachlin J in *Canson Enterprises Ltd v Boughton & Co* observed, the breach of a fiduciary duty, 'is a wrong in itself, regardless of whether a loss can be foreseen.'[229] Similar comments were made by Rowland J[230] in *Mallina Holdings Ltd v Biala Ltd*, where his Honour highlighted the universal acceptance of equity's strict approach which, once the breach is established, results in the application of remedies, 'not usually constrained by considerations of causation and foreseeability'.[231] The plaintiff, in Rowland J's judgment, 'need not suffer loss in order to succeed.'[232]

This attitude to the breach of a fiduciary duty is exemplified in *Gemstone Corporation of Australia Ltd v Grasso*,[233] where the South Australian Full Court[234] found Grasso, a director of Gemstone Corporation of Australia Ltd ('Gemstone'), to be in breach of his fiduciary duties to Gemstone by causing another company of which he

---

[224] Cf. *Gemstone Corporation of Australia Ltd v Grasso* (1994) 12 ACLC 653 at 663 per Olsson J.
[225] Cf. *Moody v Cox* [1917] 2 Ch 71 at 81-82 per Lord Cozens-Hardy MR; see *Nocton v Lord Ashburton* [1914] AC 932 at 957 per Viscount Haldane LC (Lord Atkinson agreed).
[226] (1991) 102 ALR 453 at 477 *per curiam*.
[227] *Ibid* at 480.
[228] *Nocton v Lord Ashburton* [1914] AC 932 at 963 per Lord Dunedin; see *Canson Enterprises Ltd v Boughton & Co* (1992) 85 DLR (4th) 129 at 161 per McLachlin J, 'Moreover the high duty assumed and the difficulty of detecting such breaches make it fair and practicable to adopt a measure of compensation calculated to ensure that fiduciaries are kept "up to their duty".'
[229] (1992) 85 DLR (4th) 129 at 161.
[230] (Pidgeon and Seaman JJ agreed).
[231] (1994) 15 ACSR 1 at 48.
[232] *Ibid* at 58; see *Furs Ltd v Tomkies* (1935-1936) 54 CLR 583 at 592 per Rich, Dixon and Evatt JJ; *Consul Development Pty Ltd v D P C Estates Pty Ltd* (1974-1975) 132 CLR 373 at 394-395 per Gibbs J; and *Green v Bestobell Industries Pty Ltd* [1982] WAR 1 at 4 per Burt CJ; note Austin R P, 'Fiduciary Accountability for Business Opportunities' in Finn P D (ed), *Equity and Commercial Relationships* The Law Book Company Ltd, Sydney, 1987 at 175 *et seq*.
[233] (1994) 12 ACLC 653.
[234] (Matheson, Prior and Olsson JJ).

was a director and shareholder to take up partly-paid shares in Gemstone when that other company never had any assets and, for that reason, could never answer any call on the Gemstone shares from its own resources.

In departing from the reasoning of the trial judge's finding that there could be no breach of a fiduciary obligation until a loss was caused, the South Australian Full Court in *Grasso* found that to be irrelevant in determining whether or not a director was in breach of fiduciary obligations to his or her company. In Matheson J's opinion, the court should not, in the case of non-disclosure by a director, be asked to determine what the company would have done had full disclosure been made as, 'such considerations are irrelevant.'[235] In Olsson J's view, the cause of action arises immediately the defaulting fiduciary enters into a relevant transaction in breach of his or her duty[236] and, thus, 'it is here that the exclusive jurisdiction in equity diverges from the common law approach – which directs its attention to a need for breach of duty and the concept of causation flowing from it.'[237]

It is trite fiduciary law that directors cannot be permitted to retain profits or benefits obtained by reason of their breach of a fiduciary duty.[238] Directors will be made to account for profits or benefits obtained in circumstances where there was a conflict, or possible conflict of interest and duty, or by reason of their having taken advantage of an opportunity, or of knowledge, derived by virtue of their directorships.[239]

In English company law, the House of Lords' decisions in *Aberdeen Railway Company v Blaikie Brothers*,[240] *Boardman v Phipps*,[241] and *Regal (Hastings) Ltd v Gulliver*,[242] amply testify to that, and are an analogue of the position in Australian company law. Thus, profits or benefits so obtained will be the subject of a constructive trust, with liability to account, as an equitable consequence.[243] Hence, in the words of Rich, Dixon and Evatt JJ in *Furs Ltd v Tomkies*, it is no answer to the application of the rule, 'that the profit is of a kind which the company could not itself have obtained, or that no loss is caused to the company by the gain of the director.'[244] These words were recently echoed by the High Court of Australia[245] in *Warman International Ltd v Dwyer*, where the High Court jointly pronounced that:

---

[235] (1994) 12 ACLC 653 at 656; see *Brickenden v London Loan & Savings Co* [1934] 3 DLR 465 at 469 per Lord Thankerton; *Gray v New Augarita Porcupine Mines Ltd* [1952] 3 DLR 1 at 15 per Lord Radcliffe; *Commonwealth Bank of Australia v Smith* (1991) 102 ALR 453 at 479 *per curiam*; and *Maguire v Makaronis* (1995) V Conv R 66314 at 66346 per Smith J.

[236] *Attorney General for Hong Kong v Reid* [1994] 1 All ER 1; see Nolan R C, 'The wages of sin: iniquity in equity following A-G for Hong Kong v Reid' (1994) 15 Co Law 3; and Watts P, 'Bribes and Constructive Trusts' (1994) 110 LQR 178.

[237] (1994) 12 ACLC 653 at 663; see *Brickenden v London Loan & Savings Co* [1934] 3 DLR 465 at 469 per Lord Thankerton.

[238] *Consul Development Pty Ltd v D P C Estates Pty Ltd* (1974-1975) 132 CLR 373 at 393 per Gibbs J; and *Queensland Mines Ltd v Hudson* (1978) 52 ALJR 399 at 401 per Lord Scarman.

[239] *Hospital Products Ltd v United States Surgical Corporation* (1984-1985) 156 CLR 41 at 107 per Mason J.

[240] (1854) 1 Macq 461.

[241] [1967] 2 AC 46.

[242] [1967] 2 AC 134.

[243] *Mallina Holdings Ltd v Biala Ltd* (1994) 15 ACSR 1.

[244] (1935-1936) 54 CLR 583 at 592; see *Hospital Products Ltd v United States Surgical Corporation* (1984-1985) 156 CLR 41 at 109 per Mason J.

[245] (Mason CJ, Brennan, Deane, Dawson and Gaudron JJ).

[It] is firmly established that the liability of a fiduciary to account for a profit or gain made in breach of fiduciary duty does not depend upon the person to whom that obligation is owed suffering a loss or injury; and it is ordinarily immaterial to the fiduciary's liability to account that the person to whom the fiduciary obligation is owed could not have earned the profit or gain.[246]

This view is incontestably correct, for underlying fiduciary obligations is the notion that inherent in the nature of the relationship itself, is a position of disadvantage or vulnerability on the part of one of the parties which causes that person to place reliance upon the other and requires the protection of equity acting upon the conscience of that other.[247] From that springs the requirement that directors shall not put themselves in a position where their interests and duties conflict or, if conflict is unavoidable, then they, 'shall resolve it in favour of duty and shall not, except by special arrangement, make a profit out of … [their] position.'[248]

Should either party to the relationship profit then such profit, or windfall,[249] ought stand to the company's account; the company being the more deserving of the two. To permit a defaulting fiduciary to retain a benefit improperly gained, even though the company can point to no corresponding loss, would seriously undermine fiduciary law and that which equity has striven to perpetuate.[250] This accords with the judgment of Gibbs J in *Consul Development Pty Ltd v DPC Estates Pty Ltd* that, 'the liability of the person in a fiduciary position does not depend on the fact that the person to whom the duty is owed has suffered injury or loss.'[251] Equity's supervision is premised upon the uncompromising principle articulated by Lord Herschell in *Bray v Ford*; namely, that:

It is an inflexible rule of a Court of Equity that a person in a fiduciary position … is not, unless otherwise expressly provided, entitled to make a profit; he is not allowed to put himself in a position where his interest and duty conflict. It does not appear to me that this rule is, as has been said, founded upon principles of morality. I regard it rather as based on the consideration that, human nature being what it is, there is danger, in such circumstances, of the person holding a fiduciary position being swayed by interest rather than by duty, and thus prejudicing those whom he was bound to protect.[252]

To this point then, within Australian company law, it clearly emerges that in the case of a breach of a fiduciary duty the courts are less concerned with concepts of causation,

---

[246] (1994-1995) 182 CLR 544 at 562 *per curiam*; see Nolan R, 'What to take into Account' [1996] CLJ 201.

[247] *Tate v Williamson* (1866) 2 Ch App 55 at 60-61 per Lord Chelmsford LC; and *Hospital Products Ltd v United States Surgical Corporation* (1984) 156 CLR 41 at 102 per Mason J.

[248] *Hospital Products Ltd v United States Surgical Corporation* (1984-1985) 156 CLR 41 at 142 per Dawson J (Wilson J agreed).

[249] *Reading v Attorney-General* [1951] AC 507.

[250] Finn P D, *Fiduciary Obligations* The Law Book Company Ltd, Sydney, 1977 at 1; and Sealy L S, '"Bona Fides" and "Proper Purposes" in Corporate Decisions' (1989) 15 MULR 265 at 265; see *LAC Minerals Ltd v International Corona Resources Ltd* (1989) 61 DLR (4th) 14 at 47 per La Forest J, 'The essence of the imposition of fiduciary obligations is its utility in the promotion and preservation of desired social behaviour and institutions.'

[251] (1974-1975) 132 CLR 373 at 394; see *Warman International Ltd v Dwyer* (1994-1995) 182 CLR 544 at 562 *per curiam*.

[252] [1896] AC 44 at 51; see *Boardman v Phipps* [1967] 2 AC 46 at 111 per Lord Hodson and at 123 per Lord Upjohn.

foreseeability and remoteness, than with condemning the breach itself. Within the disapprobation of the defaulting director which follows,[253] the courts invoke suitably flexible and elastic remedies,[254] for which equity is renowned, so as to achieve restitution through *inter alia* an award of equitable compensation or through the imputation of a constructive trust.[255] The recent decision of the High Court of Australia[256] in *Maguire v Makaronis*[257] is confirmatory of this approach and elucidative of its underlying philosophy. There, Mr and Mrs Makaronis executed a mortgage in favour of their solicitors in order to secure bridging finance for the purchase of a poultry farm. The solicitors did not either draw their clients' attention to the fact that they were to be the mortgagees or advise them to obtain independent legal advice. In the action brought to obtain possession of the mortgaged property following Mr and Mrs Makaronis' default on the loan, a declaration by way of counterclaim was sought that the mortgage was void.

The High Court of Australia in *Makaronis* considered the solicitors to be in breach of their fiduciary duties by entering into the mortgage absent their clients' informed consent to their interest in the transaction. The point in issue was whether or not those claiming equitable relief in such circumstances must affirmatively prove that their loss was caused by the breach.[258] In their joint judgment, Brennan CJ, Gaudron, McHugh and Gummow JJ distinguished the present situation from an action in tort to recover damages for a pecuniary loss caused, for example, by fraudulent misrepresentation on the basis that:

> Equity intervenes, particularly where the fiduciary is a solicitor, not so much to recoup a loss suffered by the plaintiff as to hold the fiduciary to, and vindicate, the high duty owed the plaintiff. Thus, whilst significant, inadequacy of the consideration or other improvidence of the transaction is not determinative.[259]

In *Makaronis* the majority in the High Court of Australia was of the view that issues of causation such as those which confront the recovery of damages in tort or contract, did not emerge in the present case. Their Honours considered that in the circumstances of this case, the solicitors' fiduciary duty forbade them to enter into the transaction with their clients absent fully informed consent and the equity for rescission was, therefore, immediately generated by breach of that fiduciary duty.[260] Whilst motivated by the

---

[253] Cf. *Maguire v Makaronis* (1995) V Conv R 66314 at 66329 per Nathan J, 'Equity invests in fiduciaries, especially solicitors, high degrees of trust and responsibility. If breach occurs some type of retribution follows.'

[254] Cf. *Nocton v Lord Ashburton* [1914] AC 932 at 952 per Viscount Haldane LC (Lord Atkinson agreed).

[255] *Barnes v Addy* (1874) 9 Ch D 244; *Nocton v Lord Ashburton* [1914] AC 932; *Boardman v Phipps* [1967] 2 AC 46; *Consul Development Pty Ltd v D P C Estates Pty Ltd* (1974-1975) 132 CLR 373; *Chan v Zacharia* (1983-1984) 154 CLR 178; *LAC Minerals Ltd v International Corona Resources Ltd* (1989) 61 DLR (4th) 14; *Hospital Products Ltd v United States Surgical Corporation* (1984-1985) 156 CLR 41; *Attorney General for Hong Kong v Reid* [1994] 1 All ER 1; *Bishopsgate Investment Management Ltd v Maxwell (No. 2)* [1994] 1 All ER 261; *Mallina Holdings Ltd v Biala Ltd* (1994) 15 ACSR 1; *Royal Brunei Airlines Sdn Bhd v Tan* [1995] 2 AC 378; and *Target Holdings Ltd v Redferns* [1995] 3 All ER 785.

[256] (Brennan CJ, Gaudron, McHugh, Gummow and Kirby JJ).

[257] (1996-1997) 188 CLR 449.

[258] *Ibid* at 478 per Kirby J.

[259] *Ibid* at 465 per Brennan CJ, Gaudron, McHugh and Gummow JJ.

[260] *Ibid* at 472.

policy of the law to hold fiduciaries to their duties, Brennan CJ, Gaudron, McHugh and Gummow JJ nonetheless jointly recognised that:

> Different considerations arise where the plaintiff seeks one or other of the further remedies referred to by the Lord Chancellor in *Nocton v Lord Ashburton*, namely an account of profits, as a personal rather than proprietary remedy, or, as another personal remedy, compensation for that which the plaintiff has lost 'by [the fiduciary] acting', to use the Lord Chancellor's phrase, in breach of duty. Likewise where what is sought is a proprietary remedy in the nature of a constructive trust. In these instances, there directly arises a need to specify criteria for a sufficient connection (or 'causation') between breach of duty and the profit derived, the loss sustained, or the asset held.[261]

The solicitors in *Makaronis* vainly urged the High Court of Australia to excuse them entirely for their breach of fiduciary duty on the basis that that had not caused any loss to their clients. In respect to this submission, Kirby J felt that a purely causative approach which relieved an errant fiduciary of liability unless it were shown that the breach of fiduciary duty caused such liability would have several disadvantages. In Kirby J's judgment:

> It would undermine the *Brickenden* rule which has the advantage of simplicity and the prophylactic consequence of discouraging fiduciary default.[262] Such default is inherent in the temptations to which people in the position of fiduciaries are commonly exposed. It is a rule which helps to fulfil the purposes of equity, which are somewhat different from those of the common law. These include, relevantly, ensuring the strict loyalty[263] and good faith to beneficiaries, the dutiful enforcement of obligations; the deterrence of breaches by fiduciaries of their powers, and, where such occurs, the ready restitution and reinstatement of the beneficiary to the fullest extent possible.[264]

This approach on the part of the High Court of Australia would seem to be somewhat more rigorous than that currently employed by the English judiciary;[265] due possibly to the very great number of defaulting directors and other fiduciaries before the Australian courts in recent years, and the inevitable reaction to that by the Australian judiciary. As we have seen from the earlier parts of this chapter, however, the English courts are

---

[261] *Ibid* at 468.
[262] Cf. Davies P L, *Gower's Principles of Modern Company Law* (6th ed) Sweet & Maxwell Ltd, London, 1997 at 655.
[263] Cf. *Attorney General v Blake* [1998] 1 All ER 833 at 841 per Lord Woolf MR (Millett and Mummery LJJ agreed), 'Equity does not demand a duty of undivided loyalty from a former employee to his former employer, and it does not impose a duty to maintain the confidentiality of information which has ceased to be confidential.'
[264] (1996-1997) 188 CLR 449 at 492.
[265] Finn P D, 'Fiduciary Law and the Modern Commercial World' in McKendrick E (ed), *Commercial Aspects of Trusts and Fiduciary Obligations* Clarendon Press, Oxford, 1992 at 40; note Aitken L, 'Developments in Equitable Compensation: Opportunity or Danger?' (1993) 67 ALJ 596 at 596; and Rickett C E F, 'Equitable Compensation: The Giant Stirs' (1996) 112 LQR 27 at 29.

coming to rely more and more upon Australian case-law within this context,[266] and also that from other Commonwealth jurisdictions.[267]

CONSTRUCTIVE TRUSTS AND EQUITABLE COMPENSATION

From the aggrieved party's perspective, the most critical aspect of company law is the achievement of an adequate remedy to best facilitate the restoration of that which is removed and compensation for that which is lost. It is axiomatic within English and Australian company law that it is for the plaintiff to choose his, her or its remedy; a choice governed by a number of varying factors, but made principally upon a cost-benefit analysis.[268] The characterisation of a defendant's wrongdoing as a breach of fiduciary duty is remedy led.[269] Inevitably, a plaintiff who establishes a breach of an equitable duty will have more flexibility and a broader range of remedies available than the plaintiff who must resort only to common law remedies.[270] As Doyle notes:

> [A] comparatively minor shift in the facts can move the parties from an area in which more restricted common law damages remedies are available to the area of the more ample equitable remedies.[271]

This highlights the significance of the special relationship cases, and the partnership and joint venture cases, where the facts can give rise to fiduciary obligations with consequent equitable remedies;[272] and further highlights the distinction made earlier in this chapter between the several duties which may exist within a fiduciary relationship, but which may not, necessarily, excite equitable relief. This was recently recognised by Lord Nicholls in *Royal Brunei Airlines Sdn Bhd v Tan* where his Lordship expressed the following opinion on behalf of the Privy Council:

> The proper role of equity in commercial transactions is a topical question. Increasingly plaintiffs have recourse to equity for an effective remedy when the person in default, typically a company, is insolvent. Plaintiffs seek to obtain relief from others

---

[266] E.g., *Re Dawson* [1966] 2 NSWR 211 at 215 per Street J; and *Permanent Building Society v Wheeler* (1993-1994) 11 WAR 187 at 237-238 per Ipp J (Malcolm CJ and Seaman J agreed).

[267] E.g., *Girardet v Crease & Company* (1987) 11 BCLR (2d) 361 at 362 per Southin J; and *LAC Minerals Ltd v International Corona Resources Ltd* (1989) 61 DLR (4th) 14 at 28 per La Forest J.

[268] Leeming M, 'Causation and compensation for breach of fiduciary duty' (1996) 70 ALJ 537 at 539.

[269] *Attorney General v Blake* [1998] 1 All ER 833 at 841 per Lord Woolf MR (Millett and Mummery LJJ agreed).

[270] Cf. *Canson Enterprises Ltd v Boughton & Co* (1992) 85 DLR (4th) 129 at 153 per La Forest J, 'It would be wholly inappropriate to interpret equitable doctrines so technically as to displace common law rules that achieve substantial justice in areas of common concern, thereby leading to harsh and inequitable results.'

[271] Doyle J J, Commentary to Kearney, 'Accounting for a Fiduciary's Gains in Commercial Contexts' in Finn P D (ed), *Equity and Commercial Relationships* The Law Book Company Ltd, Sydney, 1987 at 212.

[272] E.g., *Allen v Hyatt* (1914) 30 TLR 444; *Coleman v Myers* [1977] 2 NZLR 225; *Glandon Pty Ltd v Strata Consolidated Pty Ltd* (1993) 11 ACSR 543; *Hospital Products Ltd v United States Surgical Corporation* (1984-1985) 156 CLR 41; *Fraser Edmiston Pty Ltd v AGT (QLD) Pty Ltd* [1988] 2 Qd R 1; *Chan v Zacharia* (1983-1984) 154 CLR 178; and *Mallina Holdings Ltd v Biala Ltd* (1994) 15 ACSR 1; see Rider B A K, 'Partnership Law and its Impact on "Domestic Companies"' [1979] CLJ 148; and McPherson B H, 'Joint Ventures' in Finn P D (ed), *Equity and Commercial Relationships* The Law Book Company Ltd, Sydney, 1987 at 19 *et seq.*

who were involved in the transaction, such as directors of the company, or its bankers, or its legal or other advisers. They seek to fasten fiduciary obligations directly onto the company's officers or agents or advisers, or to have them held personally liable for assisting the company in breaches of trust or fiduciary obligations.[273]

Equity's remedies are flexible and elastic;[274] and, as we have seen, their application is strict so as to, 'keep persons in a fiduciary capacity up to their duty'.[275] The breach of a fiduciary duty attracts equitable remedies of a personal or proprietary nature considered appropriate to bring the defaulting fiduciary to account.[276] Notable among these remedies are constructive trusts and equitable compensation; both of which have received attention from English and Australian courts at the highest level.[277] It is a long established principle that should the improper exercise of directorial powers cause loss to the company, the directors concerned will be liable personally to compensate the company on the same basis that trustees are liable personally to restore trust property lost in breach of trust.[278]

As we have seen from the cases considered earlier in this chapter, directorial breaches of fiduciary duties often warrant restitutionary relief which involves the recovery of company assets, or its equivalent value; for the traditional obligation of a defaulting director is to effect restitution to the company.[279] But, because restitution *in specie* may not always be possible, equity awards compensation with the ideal of restoring to the estate that which was lost through the breach.[280] As a consequence, equitable compensation is essentially of a restitutionary nature and considerations of causation, foreseeability and remoteness do not readily enter into the matter.[281] In assessing equitable compensation, 'the court applies the full benefit of hindsight and ordinarily determines that compensation as at the date of the trial'.[282]

---

[273] [1995] 2 AC 378 at 381-382.

[274] *Nocton v Lord Ashburton* [1914] AC 932 at 952 per Viscount Haldane LC (Lord Atkinson agreed); see Sealy L S, 'Some Principles of Fiduciary Obligation' [1963] CLJ 119 at 137-140; and Shepherd J C, 'Towards a Unified Concept of Fiduciary Relationships' (1981) 97 LQR 51 at 77.

[275] *Nocton v Lord Ashburton* [1914] AC 932 at 963 per Lord Dunedin.

[276] Kearney J B, 'Accounting for a Fiduciary's Gains in Commercial Contexts' in Finn P D (ed), *Equity and Commercial Relationships* The Law Book Company Ltd, Sydney, 1987 at 187; note *Warman International Ltd v Dwyer* (1994-1995) 182 CLR 544 at 563 *per curiam*.

[277] *Barnes v Addy* (1874) 9 Ch D 244; *Nocton v Lord Ashburton* [1914] AC 932; *Boardman v Phipps* [1967] 2 AC 46; *Consul Development Pty Ltd v D P C Estates Pty Ltd* (1974-1975) 132 CLR 373; *Chan v Zacharia* (1983-1984) 154 CLR 178; *LAC Minerals Ltd v International Corona Resources Ltd* (1989) 61 DLR (4th) 14; *Hospital Products Ltd v United States Surgical Corporation* (1984-1985) 156 CLR 41; *Attorney General for Hong Kong v Reid* [1994] 1 All ER 1; *Bishopsgate Investment Management Ltd v Maxwell (No. 2)* [1994] 1 All ER 261; *Mallina Holdings Ltd v Biala Ltd* (1994) 15 ACSR 1; *Royal Brunei Airlines Sdn Bhd v Tan* [1995] 2 AC 378; and *Target Holdings Ltd v Redferns* [1995] 3 All ER 785.

[278] *In re Lands Allotment Company* [1894] 1 Ch 616 at 631 per Lindley LJ and at 638 per Kay LJ; cf. *Clough v Bond* (1838) 3 My & Cr 490 at 497 per Lord Cottenham LC.

[279] *Re Dawson* [1966] 2 NSWLR 211 at 214 per Street J; *Hill v Rose* [1990] VR 129 at 143-144 per Tadgell J; and *Day v Mead* [1987] 2 NZLR 443 at 451 per Cooke P; see Rickett C and Gardner T, 'Compensating for loss in equity: The evolution of a remedy' (1994) 24 VUWLR 19; and Davidson I E, 'The Equitable Remedy of Compensation' (1982) 13 Melb ULR 349 at 356.

[280] *Canson Enterprises Ltd v Boughton & Co* (1992) 85 DLR (4th) 129 at 157 per McLachlin J; see *Ex parte Adamson* (1878) 8 Ch D 807 at 819 per James and Baggallay LJJ; note Davidson I E, 'The Equitable Remedy of Compensation' (1982) 13 Melb ULR 349 at 351.

[281] Rider B A K, 'A Special Relationship on the Special Facts' (1978) 41 MLR 585 at 588-589.

[282] *Permanent Building Society v Wheeler* (1993-1994) 11 WAR 187 at 235 per Ipp J (Malcolm CJ and Seaman J agreed); note *Canson Enterprises Ltd v Boughton & Co* (1992) 85 DLR (4th) 129 at 162 per

In Lord Browne-Wilkinson's speech to the House of Lords in *Target Holdings Ltd v Redferns*, his Lordship encapsulated the relevant rules applicable to equitable compensation for breach of trust, as the following passage testifies:

> Equitable compensation for breach of trust is designed to achieve exactly what the word compensation suggests: to make good a loss in fact suffered by the beneficiaries and which, using hindsight and common sense, can be seen to have been caused by the breach.[283]

Consequently, equitable compensation can be more substantial than damages for breach of contract or tort. In Australian company law, it is widely accepted that courts have, 'an inherent power to award equitable compensation to relieve against loss occasioned by breach of fiduciary duty.'[284] So too in English company law, where English courts have proceeded upon this footing since, at least, the early 19th century.[285] The Court of Appeal's decision in *Bishopsgate Investment Management Ltd v Maxwell (No. 2)*, and the recent House of Lords' decision in *Target*, for example, amply testify to not only the enduring vitality of equitable compensation, but also to its increasing penetration into the law of remedies. These decisions suggest that equitable doctrine has an increasingly important role to play in today's complex commercial and corporate world. However, it is important to be vigilant to ensure that equitable doctrine only penetrates commercial transactions where appropriate.[286] Brennan CJ, Gaudron, McHugh and Gummow JJ in *Maguire v Makaronis* were alive to this as the following extract from their joint judgment verifies:

> From various decisions in recent years there appear attempts to throw a fiduciary mantle over commercial and personal relationships and dealings which might not have been thought previously to contain a fiduciary element. In some instances the forensic advantage sought to be gained has been ... less stringent time limitations. In others, the advantage sought has been the remedial constructive trust with the edge thereby conferred over unsecured creditors in an insolvent administration of the affairs of a defendant.[287]

cont.

McLachlin J; and *Target Holdings Ltd v Redferns* [1995] 3 All ER 785 at 797-798 per Lord Browne-Wilkinson (Lords Keith, Ackner, Jauncey and Lloyd agreed).

[283] [1995] 3 All ER 785 at 798.

[284] *Tavistock Holdings Pty Ltd v Saulsman* (1991) 9 ACLC 450 at 457 per Anderson J; see *McKenzie v McDonald* [1927] VLR 134; *Hill v Rose* [1990] VR 129; *Fraser Edmiston Pty Ltd v AGT (QLD) Pty Ltd* [1988] 2 Qd R 1; *Canson Enterprises Ltd v Boughton & Co* (1992) 85 DLR (4th) 129 at 143 per La Forest J; and *Nocton v Lord Ashburton* [1914] AC 932 at 952-953 per Viscount Haldane LC (Lord Atkinson agreed); note Davidson I E, 'The Equitable Remedy of Compensation' (1982) 13 Melb ULR 349 at 349; and Rickett C and Gardner T, 'Compensating for loss in equity: The evolution of a remedy' (1994) 24 VUWLR 19.

[285] Stuckey-Clarke J, '"Damages" for Breaches of Purely Equitable Rights: The Breach of Confidence Example' in Finn P D (ed), *Essays on Damages* The Law Book Company Ltd, Sydney, 1992 at 72.

[286] *In re Goldcorp Exchange Ltd* [1995] 1 AC 74 at 104 per Lord Mustill (Lords Templeman and Lloyd and Sir Thomas Eichelbaum agreed); note McCormack G, 'Fiduciaries in a changing commercial climate' (1997) 18 Co Law 38 at 39 and 41.

[287] (1996-1997) 188 CLR 449 at 463-464.

Equity has long recognised the efficacy of constructive trusts.[288] This potent equitable remedy has, however, been under-utilised in English and Australian company law through lack of attention to readily identifiable principles entitling relief in this form. In Australian company law it is said that equitable relief, by the imputation of a constructive trust, 'will only be granted if the principles of equity require that the owner of property should hold it to the use or benefit of another.'[289] In such circumstances, constructive trusts are imposed by equity without reference to the parties' intentions and, where appropriate, may be premised on the principle of unjust enrichment; which, as Dickson J[290] in *Pettkus v Becker* observed, 'lies at the heart of the constructive trust.'[291] Within his speech to the House of Lords[292] in *Westdeutsche Landesbank Girozentrale v Islington London Borough Council*, Lord Browne-Wilkinson spoke of constructive trusts in this way:

> Under an institutional constructive trust, the trust arises by operation of law as from the date of the circumstances which give rise to it: the function of the court is merely to declare that such trust has arisen in the past. The consequences that flow from such trust having arisen (including the possibly unfair consequences to third parties who in the interim have received the trust property) are also determined by rules of law, not under a discretion.[293]

From a restitutionary perspective, as the learned authors of *The Law of Restitution* pointed out in their third edition, 'a constructive trust should be imposed if it is just to grant a plaintiff the additional benefits which flow from the recognition of a right of property.'[294] In the case of a defaulting director, the imputation of a constructive trust will ensure that that director does not benefit from his or her wrongdoing which, from equity's perspective, is an important consideration,[295] and something which equitable compensation might not always achieve.[296]

In the 25 or so years since the decision in *Consul Development Pty Ltd v D P C Estates Pty Ltd*,[297] the High Court of Australia has, on occasion, considered the application of constructive trusts within the context of company law and also partnership law. The High Court of Australia in *Chan v Zacharia*, for example, when faced with a partnership dispute, considered the law to be firmly established that, 'a partner who, without the consent of his co-partner, obtains a renewal of a lease of the partnership premises in his own name, prima face holds the lease on a constructive trust for the partnership.'[298] The principles enunciated in *Chan* have direct application to

---

[288] *Barnes v Addy* (1874) 9 Ch App 244; and *Robinson v Abbott* (1894) 20 VLR 346.

[289] Mason A, 'The Place of Equity and Equitable Remedies in the Contemporary Common Law World' (1994) 110 LQR 238 at 250; see *Muschinski v Dodds* (1986) 60 ALJR 52 at 66 per Deane J.

[290] (Laskin CJC, Estey, McIntyre, Chouinard and Lamer JJ agreed).

[291] (1981) 117 DLR (3d) 257 at 273; see Austin R P, 'Fiduciary Accountability for Business Opportunities' in Finn P D (ed), *Equity and Commercial Relationships* The Law Book Company Ltd, Sydney, 1987 at 144.

[292] (Lords Goff, Browne-Wilkinson, Slynn, Woolf and Lloyd).

[293] [1996] AC 669 at 714.

[294] Goff R and Jones G, *The Law of Restitution* (3rd ed) Sweet & Maxwell Ltd, London, 1986 at 673.

[295] *Nocton v Lord Ashburton* [1914] AC 932 at 963 per Lord Dunedin.

[296] *Attorney General for Hong Kong v Reid* [1994] 1 All ER 1.

[297] (1974-1975) 132 CLR 373.

[298] (1983-1984) 154 CLR 178 at 181 per Gibbs CJ; see *Keech v Sandford* (1726) Sel Cas t King 61; and *Fraser Edmiston Pty Ltd v AGT (QLD) Pty Ltd* [1988] 2 Qd R 1.

company law. They were considered by the High Court of Australia in *Hospital Products Ltd v United States Surgical Corporation* to illustrate the accountability of fiduciaries, as constructive trustees, once it is established that they are liable to account for profits or benefits improperly obtained;[299] albeit, the majority decision in *Hospital Products* suggests a resistance to the imputation of constructive trusts within the context of commercial transactions.[300]

This resistance did not, however, manifest itself in *United Dominions Corporation Ltd v Brian Pty Ltd*, where the High Court of Australia considered the participants in a joint venture to be fiduciaries and, thus, the joint venture property was held upon trust.[301] Equally, when the High Court of Australia entertained *Muschinski v Dodds*, Deane J[302] accepted the predominately remedial character and availability of constructive trusts:

> [In] any case where some principle of the law of equity calls for the imposition upon the legal owner of property, regardless of actual or presumed agreement or intention, of the obligation to hold or apply the property for the benefit of another.[303]

Thus, constructive trusts award a right in property and can reflect, 'the right of the property holder to have changes in value accrue to his account rather than to the account of the wrongdoer.'[304] Consequently, as the Western Australian Full Court recently recognised in *Mallina Holdings Ltd v Biala Ltd*, constructive trusts are a most effective remedy where, 'there is a trust asset which can be followed and restitution *in specie* is given, together with all accrued benefits.'[305]

The decision by the Privy Council[306] in *Attorney General for Hong Kong v Reid*,[307] provides a dazzling example of the effect and import of constructive trusts within equity's impressive array of remedies for the breach of a fiduciary duty. The decision highlights the utility and appeal of constructive trusts and affords them a prominence within the law of remedies.[308] The decision also provides a salutary reminder to errant directors of equity's flexibility and tenacity in providing remedies capable of thwarting directorial misdeeds by, if necessary, tracing the proceeds of ill-gotten gains into a third party's hands, or into property.[309] Moreover, the following passage from Lord Browne-Wilkinson's speech to the House of Lords in *Westdeutsche* affirms the English courts' determination to recover ill-gotten gains, and the pre-eminent role which constructive trusts will come to enjoy in that respect:

[299] (1984-1985) 156 CLR 41 at 108 per Mason J.
[300] Austin R P, 'Constructive Trusts' in Finn P D (ed), *Essays in Equity* The Law Book Company Ltd, Sydney, 1985 at 196 *et seq*.
[301] (1984-1985) 157 CLR 1 at 11 per Mason, Brennan and Deane JJ (Dawson J agreed).
[302] (Mason J agreed).
[303] (1986) 60 ALJR 52 at 66; see *Mallina Holdings Ltd v Biala Ltd* (1994) 15 ACSR 1 at 57-58 *per curiam*.
[304] *LAC Minerals Ltd v International Corona Resources Ltd* (1989) 61 DLR (4th) 14 at 51 per La Forest J.
[305] (1994) 15 ACSR 1 at 58 *per curiam*.
[306] (Lords Templeman, Goff, Lowry and Lloyd and Sir Thomas Eichelbaum).
[307] [1994] 1 All ER 1 (on appeal from the Court of Appeal of New Zealand).
[308] Boyle A J, 'Attorney-General v Reid: the company law implications' (1995) 16 Co Law 131 at 133; cf. *Glavanics v Brunninghausen* (1996) 19 ACSR 204 at 225 per Bryson J.
[309] *Sinclair v Brougham* [1914] AC 398; cf. *El Ajou v Dollar Land Holdings plc* [1993] 3 All ER 717 and [1994] 2 All ER 685; and *El Ajou v Dollar Land Holdings plc (No. 2)* [1995] 2 All ER 213; note Nolan R, 'Arabian's rights' (1994) 15 Co Law 148; cf. Mountfort A G, 'Tracing: An Examination of the Applicability of Tracing Principles Today' (1996) 70 ALJ 54.

I agree that the stolen moneys are traceable in equity. But the proprietary interest which equity is enforcing in such circumstances arises under a constructive, not a resulting, trust. Although it is difficult to find clear authority for the proposition, when property is obtained by fraud equity imposes a constructive trust on the fraudulent recipient: the property is recoverable and traceable in equity.[310]

In *Reid* those ill-gotten gains constituted bribes which Reid, a public prosecutor in Hong Kong, took in return for obstructing the prosecution of certain criminals. Upon Reid's conviction, he was imprisoned and ordered to pay $HK12.4m being the value of assets derived from those bribes. Ultimately, the Attorney-General for Hong Kong registered caveats against the titles to certain land in New Zealand, owned by Reid and others, considered to have been bought with the bribe moneys. Disputation arose as to whether or not the Attorney-General had a caveatable interest in that land which, ultimately, led to this appeal. The New Zealand courts hearing *Reid* considered themselves bound by the English Court of Appeal's decision in *Lister & Co v Stubbs*,[311] a decision much criticised, but nonetheless intact for over 100 years;[312] and the effect of which was to deny any equitable or proprietary interest in the land.

The opinion of the Privy Council in *Reid* was delivered by Lord Templeman who had no hesitation in permitting the Attorney-General to trace the bribe moneys into the land, imputing a constructive trust in respect to that land, and declaring *Lister* to be no longer good law.[313] The significance of the decision, within the context of English and Australian company law, lies in the recognition of the immediacy with which equity acts upon a defaulting fiduciary. In Lord Templeman's view:

As soon as the bribe was received it should have been paid or transferred *instanter* to the person who suffered from the breach of duty. Equity considers as done that which ought to have been done.[314] As soon as the bribe was received, whether in cash or in kind, the false fiduciary held the bribe on a constructive trust for the person injured.[315]

---

310 [1996] AC 669 at 716.

311 (1890) 45 Ch D 1.

312 The New South Wales Court of Appeal in *D P C Estates Pty Ltd v Consul Development Pty Ltd* [1974] 1 NSWLR 443 considered *Lister & Co v Stubbs* (1890) 45 Ch D 1 to be anomalous and not to be extended beyond its own facts; see Goff R and Jones G, *The Law of Restitution* (3rd ed) Sweet & Maxwell Ltd, London, 1986 at 656 *et seq*; Meagher R P, Gummow W M C and Lehane J R F, *Equity Doctrines and Remedies* (3rd ed) Butterworths Pty Ltd, Sydney, 1992 at 156 *et seq*; and Nolan R C, 'The wages of sin: iniquity in equity following A-G for Hong Kong v Reid' (1994) 15 Co Law 3; cf. *Daly v Sydney Stock Exchange Ltd* (1986) 60 ALJR 371 at 374 per Gibbs CJ (Wilson and Dawson JJ agreed).

313 Thus, lending conclusive support to Lehane J R F, 'Fiduciaries in a Commercial Context' in Finn P D (ed), *Essays in Equity* The Law Book Company Ltd, Sydney, 1985 at 107 that the, '*Lister* ... heresy still remains finally to be eradicated.'; and, as foreshadowed by Kearney J B, 'Accounting for a Fiduciary's Gains in Commercial Contexts' in Finn P D (ed), *Equity and Commercial Relationships* The Law Book Company Ltd, Sydney, 1987 at 202.

314 Cf. *Muschinski v Dodds* (1986) 60 ALJR 52 at 65 per Deane J (Mason J agreed); see Gardner S, 'Two Maxims of Equity' [1995] CLJ 60 at 60-63.

315 [1994] 1 All ER 1 at 4-5; cf. *Zobory v Federal Commissioner of Taxation* (1995) 129 ALR 484 at 488 per Burchett J, 'But the equitable ownership of the moneys taken and invested by the applicant does not depend upon a court declaring the existence of a constructive trust.'

In reaching this landmark decision, the Privy Council in *Reid* was clearly influenced by the majority decision of the House of Lords in *Boardman v Phipps*,[316] where an honest fiduciary was there held to be a constructive trustee. It must follow, Lord Templeman reasoned, that:

> [A] fiduciary acting dishonestly and criminally who accepts a bribe and thereby causes loss and damage to his principal must also be a constructive trustee and must not be allowed by any means to make any profit from his wrongdoing.[317]

As the learned editor of *The Company Lawyer* recently opined, 'English judges have never been particularly enthusiastic about the prospect of those who have benefited by virtue of an unlawful act, whether amounting to a civil or a criminal wrong, retaining the fruits of their labours.'[318] Hence, the rules about bribes are prophylactic. They are designed to combat corruption and do not require proof that the principal's interests were in fact harmed.[319] *Attorney General v Blake*[320] is a case in point. It provides a useful insight into the ingenuity of the English judiciary in devising remedies considered appropriate to meet particular circumstances; remedies which adequately reflect the court's disapprobation of the distasteful practices sometimes before it.

In *Blake*, the Court of Appeal[321] heard argument as to whether or not a former member of the Secret Intelligence Services who became an agent for the Soviet Union, and betrayed his country by disclosing secret information of considerable value, should be enjoined from receiving any financial proceeds derived from the publication of his autobiography. It was argued that Blake was a fiduciary and that: (i) his duty to the Crown continued long after his service was terminated; and (ii) information gained during his employment was preserved even though it had ceased to be confidential.

The Court of Appeal in *Blake* considered the Crown's attempt to derive a fiduciary duty from a combination of two fiduciary relationships to be misconceived: both had come to an end.[322] The duty of loyalty which springs from the employer/employee relationship lasts only as long as the relationship which gives rise to it.[323] The duty of confidentiality which arises whenever information is imparted by one person to another in confidence, survives the termination of an employer/employee relationship, but it subsists only as long as the information remains confidential.[324] However, the particular appeal which *Blake* has lies in the Court of Appeal's treatment of the public law claims, and the public interest in denying a criminal his or her benefits derived from the crime perpetrated. Lord Woolf MR delivered the judgment of the Court of Appeal. In his Lordship's view:

---

[316] [1967] 2 AC 46.

[317] [1994] 1 All ER 1 at 11; see Ford H A J and Austin R P, *Ford's Principles of Corporations Law* (6th ed) Butterworths Pty Ltd, Sydney, 1992 at 516; and Oakley A J, 'The Bribed Fiduciary as Constructive Trustee' [1994] CLJ 31 at 32.

[318] Editorial comment, 'There and back again!' (1998) 19 Co Law 97 at 97.

[319] Davies P L, *Gower's Principles of Modern Company Law* (6th ed) Sweet & Maxwell Ltd, London, 1997 at 655.

[320] [1998] 1 All ER 833.

[321] (Lord Woolf MR, Millett and Mummery LJJ).

[322] Fung E T S, 'Spies, traitors and fiduciaries' (1998) 19 Co Law 219 at 219-220.

[323] [1998] 1 All ER 833 at 842 per Lord Woolf MR (Millett and Mummery LJJ agreed).

[324] *Ibid.*

An order restraining the defendant from receiving further benefits would not be open to any objection on the ground of retrospectivity or lack of proportionality: it only has prospective effect; it is a lesser penalty than a confiscation order under the legislation; it supports the criminal law in an area relating to the interests of national security; and it does not interfere with freedom of expression.[325]

The Court of Appeal considered *Blake* to be an exceptional case warranting the intervention by the Attorney-General through the institution of civil proceedings, 'in aid of the criminal law, to uphold the public policy of ensuring that a criminal does not retain profit directly derived from the commission of his crime.'[326] Blake was a notorious spy who had also dramatically escaped from prison. Notwithstanding that no remedy could be found in private law to deprive him of the fruits of his labours, given the public policy and the public interest considerations present, a remedy was found. As Lord Woolf MR explained:

[The] Attorney General has a legal right in public law to apply to the court for an injunction in a case of this kind. The money which will be subject to the injunction is money which is liable to confiscation, so that the injunction will serve the ordinary purpose of preserving assets subject to a claim pending adjudication. There is, of course, no prospect whatever that Mr Blake will ever return to this country and subject himself to the jurisdiction of the court, but in the circumstances of this case we consider that this is an argument for granting the injunction, not an objection for doing so.[327]

The recent decision of the Privy Council[328] in *Royal Brunei*[329] provides a further example of equity's ability to arrest egregious behaviour on the part of a fiduciary, and provide an appropriate remedy to not only recover assets in the hands of an undeserving third party, but also recover from a third party even though no trust property actually reached his, her or its hands. The essential facts in *Royal Brunei* were these. An insolvent travel agent company, of which Tan was the managing director and principal shareholder, owed money to Royal Brunei Airlines Sdn Bhd. The company had been appointed travel agent for the sale of passenger and cargo transportation. It was paid a sales commission. Moneys received by it on behalf of the airline were not paid into a separate bank account, but rather into the agent company's ordinary current account. It seems that moneys deposited were used for the agent company's ordinary business purposes, paying salaries, overheads and other expenses, and keeping down its overdraft.

Ultimately, the agent company in *Royal Brunei* became insolvent whereupon proceedings were commenced against Tan to recover moneys owed the airline. At first instance, the trial judge considered Tan liable as a constructive trustee. The Privy Council agreed.[330] The airline's claim was based upon the second limb of Lord Selborne

---

[325] *Ibid* at 849.
[326] *Ibid*.
[327] *Ibid* at 852.
[328] (Lords Goff, Ackner, Nicholls and Steyn and Sir John May).
[329] [1995] 2 AC 378 (on appeal from the Court of Appeal of Brunei Darussalam).
[330] Pascoe J, 'Equitable Remedies in Cases of Misapplied Company Funds: Recent Developments' (1996) 14 CSLJ 393 at 396.

LC's much quoted *dictum* from *Barnes v Addy*,[331] compendiously referred to as accessorial liability. In issue was whether or not the breach of trust, which is a prerequisite to accessorial liability, must itself be a dishonest and fraudulent breach of trust by the trustee. The opinion of the Privy Council was delivered by Lord Nicholls, who addressed the claim in this way:

> Liability as an accessory is not dependent upon receipt of trust property. It arises even though no trust property has reached the hands of the accessory. It is a form of secondary liability in the sense that it only arises where there has been a breach of trust. In the present case the plaintiff airline relies on the accessory limb. The particular point in issue arises from the expression 'a dishonest and fraudulent design on the part of the trustees.'[332]

The Privy Council in *Royal Brunei* considered dishonesty to be a necessary ingredient of accessorial liability. As we saw in the previous chapter of this book, the concept of dishonesty is difficult to grasp and to articulate.[333] In the context of accessorial liability, Lord Nicholls explained that, 'acting dishonestly, or with a lack of probity, which is synonymous, means simply not acting as an honest person would in the circumstances.'[334] That is measured objectively. His Lordship went on to explain that whilst honesty has a subjective connotation given that the type of conduct under scrutiny is assessed in the light of what a person actually knew at the time, as distinct from what a reasonable person would have known or appreciated, the standard of what constitutes honest conduct is not subjective.[335] For the most part, dishonesty is to be equated with conscious impropriety: carelessness is not dishonesty. Thus, it is advertent conduct, not inadvertent conduct, that the court must address in the context of accessorial liability. Lord Nicholls succinctly put the salient point in this way:

> A liability in equity to make good resulting loss attaches to a person who dishonestly procures or assists in a breach of trust or fiduciary obligation. It is not necessary that, in addition, the trustee or fiduciary was acting dishonestly, although this will usually be so where the third party who is assisting him is acting dishonestly.[336]

In the result, it was the opinion of the Privy Council in *Royal Brunei* that Tan did not meet the standard which would be observed by an honest person placed in his circumstances. Accordingly, Tan had no right to employ the money in the agent company's business. That was the breach of trust. The agent company's inability to pay the airline was the consequence of that breach of trust. The trial judge's order that Tan was liable as a constructive trustee to pay the amount in issue to the airline was restored by the Privy Council. This decision has important consequences for directors of British and Australian companies given that in their day-to-day stewardship opportunities will arise from which imprudent directors might become personally responsible for their company's debts through accessorial liability.

---

[331] (1874) 9 Ch App 244 at 251-252.
[332] [1995] 2 AC 378 at 382.
[333] Cf. *In re Patrick Lyon Limited* [1933] Ch 786 at 789-790 per Maugham J; and *R v Grantham* (1984) 1 BCC 99,075 at 99,078 per Lord Lane (Boreham and Stuart-Smith LJJ agreed).
[334] [1995] 2 AC 378 at 389.
[335] *Ibid.*
[336] *Ibid* at 392.

EPILOGUE

The decision by the Privy Council in *Attorney General for Hong Kong v Reid*,[337] and the courts' willingness to impute a constructive trust in appropriate circumstances which the various judgments in *Chan v Zacharia*,[338] *United Dominions Corporation Ltd v Brian Pty Ltd*,[339] *Royal Brunei Airlines Sdn Bhd v Tan*,[340] *Maguire v Makaronis*[341] and *Westdeutsche Landesbank Girozentrale v Islington London Borough Council*,[342] by way of example, clearly contemplate, have significant ramifications for the general body of unsecured creditors who might be adversely affected by the diminution in value of the estate which the imputation of a constructive trust will occasion. It was this consequence which largely influenced the Court of Appeal's reasoning in *Lister & Co v Stubbs*, and which there led to the finding that the relationship between the person receiving a bribe and his or her beneficiary was that of debtor and creditor, 'not that of trustee and *cestui que trust*.'[343] But, Lord Templeman[344] in *Reid* considered the decision in *Lister* to be inconsistent with equitable principles which deny to a fiduciary any benefit consequent upon a breach and which require a fiduciary to account immediately for the bribe. As to the concerns expressed by the Court of Appeal in *Lister* upon the impact of insolvency law, which the imputation of a constructive trust would cause, Lord Templeman considered that:

> If a trustee mistakenly invests monies which he ought to pay over to his cestui que trust and then becomes bankrupt, the moneys together with any profit which has accrued from the investment are withdrawn from the unsecured creditors as soon as the mistake is discovered. A fortiori, if a trustee commits a crime by accepting a bribe which he ought to pay over to his cestui que trust, the bribe and any profit made therefrom should be withdrawn from the unsecured creditors as soon as the crime is discovered.[345]

In his case note on *Reid*, Nolan makes the observation that the Privy Council did not there appear overly perturbed by the lack of, 'any thoroughgoing, certainly controversial and possibly disruptive, analytical reconsideration of the law of fiduciary duties viewed in a wider context, be that context the law of restitution or the law of insolvency.'[346] Thus *Lister*, as Nolan further observes, 'has apparently been laid to rest, but the arguments of policy as to when a person should or should not be adjudged to hold

---

[337] [1994] 1 All ER 1.

[338] (1983-1984) 154 CLR 178 at 181 per Gibbs CJ.

[339] (1984-1985) 157 CLR 1 at 11 per Mason, Brennan and Deane JJ (Dawson J agreed).

[340] [1995] 2 AC 378 at 381-382 per Lord Nicholls (Lords Goff, Ackner and Steyn and Sir John May agreed).

[341] (1996-1997) 188 CLR 449 at 463-464 per Brennan CJ, Gaudron, McHugh and Gummow JJ.

[342] [1996] AC 669 at 714-716 per Lord Browne-Wilkinson (Lord Slynn agreed).

[343] (1890) 45 Ch D 1 at 15 per Lindley LJ (Bowen LJ agreed); cf. *Daly v Sydney Stock Exchange Ltd* (1986) 60 ALJR 371; note Starke J G, 'The High Court and the Limits of the Doctrine of Constructive Trusts' (1987) 61 ALJ 241.

[344] (Lords Goff, Lowry and Lloyd and Sir Thomas Eichelbaum agreed).

[345] [1994] 1 All ER 1 at 9; cf. Allen T, 'Bribes and Constructive Trusts: A-G of Hong Kong v Reid' (1995) 58 MLR 87 at 90-91; and Jones A, 'Bribing the DPP: Should he Profit from Abusing his Position?' [1994] Conv 156 at 164-165.

[346] Nolan R C, 'The wages of sin: iniquity in equity following A-G for Hong Kong v Reid' (1994) 15 Co Law 3 at 9.

property on constructive trust will not go away so easily.'[347] *A fortiori* as equity further intrudes into the commercial world,[348] and as the substantive legal rules and equitable principles converge within the context of English and Australian company law, the impact of proprietary relief upon the general body of unsecured creditors may well undermine the traditional premise upon which insolvency law is based.[349]

Notwithstanding that the use of equitable remedies to redress directorial misconduct has long been central to English and Australian company law,[350] a by-product of the imposition of a constructive trust in circumstances where the trustee is insolvent is to disadvantage the general body of unsecured creditors. *A fortiori* where plaintiffs increasingly resort to equity seeking an effective remedy when the person in default, typically a company, is insolvent.[351] It is important, therefore, to consider the effect of the imputation of a constructive trust upon unsecured creditors for it is not difficult to conceive of situations where a constructive trust could seriously prejudice unsecured creditors' rights. This is why proprietary claims can be controversial and ought only be granted, 'when it is just to grant the plaintiff the additional benefit that flows from the recognition of a right of property.'[352] Lord Goff recognised the potential inequity of equitable proprietary remedies within the context of a commercial setting in *Westdeutsche*, as the following passage from his recent speech to the House of Lords attests:

> But why should the plaintiff bank be given the additional benefits which flow from a proprietary claim, for example the benefit of achieving priority in the event of the defendant's insolvency? After all, it has entered into a commercial transaction, and so taken the risk of the defendant's insolvency, just like the defendant's other creditors who have contracted with it, not to mention other creditors to whom the defendant may be liable to pay damages in tort.[353]

Whilst this complex and important issue is not the concern of this chapter, the point is worth noting as its implications are profound. However, the immediate effect of the decision in *Reid*,[354] and to a lesser extent the persuasive effect of *dicta* from *Chan*,[355] *United Dominions*,[356] *Royal Brunei*,[357] *Makaronis*[358] and *Westdeutsche*,[359] for example,

---

[347] *Ibid* at 10; see McCormack G, 'The remedial constructive trust and commercial transactions' (1996) 17 Co Law 3 at 7-9.

[348] Austin R P, 'Commerce and Equity – Fiduciary Duty and Constructive Trust' (1986) 6 OJLS 444 at 454-455.

[349] *Re Oasis Merchandising Services Ltd* [1997] BCC 282 at 291 *per curiam*; cf. Insolvency Act 1986 (UK) s107; note Villiers C, 'Employees as creditors: a challenge for justice in insolvency law' (1999) 20 Co Law 222 at 228; Schulte R, 'Corporate groups and the equitable subordination of claims on insolvency' (1997) 18 Co Law 2 at 2 and 11; Bean G M D, 'Debt subordination validated' (1994) 15 Co Law 52 at 52; Sealy L S, 'Directors' Duties – An Unnecessary Gloss' [1988] CLJ 175 at 177; and Report of the Review Committee on Insolvency Law and Practice, HMSO, London, Cmnd 8558, 1982 at para 1396.

[350] Pascoe J, 'Equitable Remedies in Cases of Misapplied Company Funds: Recent Developments' (1996) 14 CSLJ 393 at 393.

[351] *Royal Brunei Airlines Sdn Bhd v Tan* [1995] 2 AC 378 at 381 per Lord Nicholls (Lords Goff, Ackner and Steyn and Sir John May agreed).

[352] *LAC Minerals Ltd v International Corona Resources Ltd* (1989) 61 DLR (4th) 14 at 50 per La Forest J; see Goff R and Jones G, *The Law of Restitution* (3rd ed) Sweet & Maxwell Ltd, London, 1986 at 78.

[353] [1996] AC 669 at 684.

[354] [1994] 1 All ER 1.

[355] (1983-1984) 154 CLR 178 at 181 per Gibbs CJ.

[356] (1984-1985) 157 CLR 1 at 11 per Mason, Brennan and Deane JJ (Dawson J agreed).

[357] [1995] 2 AC 378 at 381-382 per Lord Nicholls (Lords Goff, Ackner and Steyn and Sir John May agreed).

will be to vanquish the inhibitory effects upon the development of constructive trusts within English and Australian company law for which the *Lister*[360] heresy must be partly to blame.[361] Thus, untrammelled by this spectre,[362] it is considered that constructive trusts will be better, and more frequently,[363] utilised by future English and Australian courts in a range of circumstances not hitherto considered appropriate.[364]

cont.
[358] (1996-1997) 188 CLR 449 at 463-464 per Brennan CJ, Gaudron, McHugh and Gummow JJ.
[359] [1996] AC 669 at 714-716 per Lord Browne-Wilkinson (Lord Slynn agreed).
[360] (1890) 45 Ch D 1.
[361] *Zobory v Federal Commissioner of Taxation* (1995) 129 ALR 484 at 487-488 per Burchett J.
[362] Cf. *Attorney General v Blake* [1996] 3 All ER 903 at 912 per Sir Richard Scott VC.
[363] Pascoe J, 'Equitable Remedies in Cases of Misapplied Company Funds: Recent Developments' (1996) 14 CSLJ 393 at 404.
[364] Rickett C E F, 'Equitable Compensation: The Giant Stirs' (1996) 112 LQR 27 at 29-30.

10

A New Millennium, A New Approach?

INTRODUCTION

English and Australian company law is such a dynamic area of law that it would be prosaic and presumptuous to attempt to draw conclusions in this chapter, and then seek to predict the direction in which the law relating to the duties upon directors of British and Australian companies will take as we move into the next millennium. It is, however, instructive to recapitulate upon some of those more interesting and striking aspects of company law which have been addressed throughout this book as they signify the way in which modern company law has developed over the past decade or so.

This chapter will not attempt to deal with each and every facet of company law addressed in previous chapters of this book, but rather select some only of the more salient and challenging features which we have considered. This epitome will provide a number of important foci for those intent upon identifying trends or areas in which traditional rules and principles have yielded in order to accommodate the requirements of today's complex and demanding commercial and corporate world. It will also signpost some of the more contentious and controversial aspects of company law which directors of the 21st century will need to confront in order to properly discharge the legal, equitable and statutory obligations and requirements of their office.[1]

DIRECTORS' DUTIES IN CONTEXT

While the duties of directors are many, the leading textbooks on English and Australian company law treat directors of British and Australian companies as being subject to two broad duties: (i) to act honestly, in good faith and for proper purposes; and (ii) to exercise care and diligence.[2] It is convenient to broadly categorise these duties in this way as the cases involving allegations of breach of the former duty raise very different

---

[1] Editorial comment, 'Directors – true or false?' (1997) 18 Co Law 129 at 129.
[2] Ford H A J, Austin R P and Ramsay I M, *Ford's Principles of Corporations Law* (9th ed) Reed International Books Australia Pty Ltd, Sydney, 1999 at paras 8.070 and 8.200-8.355; Davies P L, *Gower's Principles of Modern Company Law* (6th ed) Sweet & Maxwell Ltd, London, 1997 at 598-599; Ford H A J and Austin R P, *Ford's Principles of Corporations Law* (6th ed) Butterworths Pty Ltd, Sydney, 1992 at 430, 487 *et seq* and 524 *et seq*; Palmer F B, *Palmer's Company Law* (25th ed) Sweet & Maxwell Ltd, London, 1992 at paras 8.406 and 8.501 *et seq*; Farrar J H, Furey N E, Hannigan B M and Wylie P, *Farrar's Company Law* (3rd ed) Butterworth & Co (Publishers) Ltd, London, 1991 at 380; and Pennington R R, *Company Law* (6th ed) Butterworth & Co (Publishers) Ltd, London, 1990 at 583.

issues to those dealing with breach of the latter duty.[3] But it is important to be mindful that the image of company law projected by these textbooks as being all symmetry and design is, more often than not, not the case in practice.[4] Company law is often asymmetrical.

It is sometimes overlooked by academics and commentators alike that the obligations and rights consequent upon directors' duties do not always have, 'the same abstract uniformity that a legal text book may give them, but translate into practical gains and losses for the parties in the real world of people and property'.[5] Any attempt to categorise directors and to link duties to categories may over-simplify the reality that directors come in all shapes and sizes,[6] and that their duties range across a spectrum rather than fall into neatly defined categories.[7] It is against this backdrop that this book was written. Along the way we have encountered many complex, and at times intractable, issues. For some, that is the appeal of English and Australian company law.

But no matter how intriguing and intellectually stimulating English and Australian company law might be, its *raison d'être* must be the facilitation of enterprise.[8] However, in the pursuit of this, future developments in this challenging and complex field of the law are likely to be less orderly and more random than either the English and the Australian judiciary, or the British and Australian Parliaments would welcome. Practitioners of company law should not, however, despair over the vagaries which are associated with their particular discipline. Rather, they should be encouraged by the dynamic nature and ever changing face of this fascinating subject. By way of preface, Gower in his first edition wrote that:

Company Law, to those who specialise in it, is among the most fascinating of legal subjects. But its fascination is not always readily apparent to general practitioners or to the students of law, economics and accounting who try to master its intricacies. Indeed, they often regard it as technical and dull. This, perhaps, is because they find difficulty in viewing it in its historical and economic context and in grasping its underlying principles.[9]

Whilst English and Australian company law can indeed be technical, it is seldom dull. To fully appreciate its vitality and charm, however, it is imperative that company law

---

3   Sievers A S, 'Farewell to the Sleeping Director – The Modern Judicial and Legislative Approach to Directors' Duties of Care, Skill and Diligence' (1993) 21 ABLR 111 at 111.
4   Editorial comment (1994) 15 Co Law 34 at 34.
5   Sealy L S, 'The Enforcement of Partnership Agreements, Articles of Association and Shareholder Agreements' in Finn P D (ed) *Equity and Commercial Relationships* The Law Book Company Ltd, Sydney, 1987 at 99.
6   *In re City Equitable Fire Insurance Company Ltd* [1925] Ch 407 at 426-427 per Romer J; *Harris v S* (1976-1977) 2 ACLR 51 at 63-64 per Wells J; *Commonwealth Bank of Australia v Friedrich* (1991) 5 ACSR 115 at 125 per Tadgell J; *Standard Chartered Bank of Aust Ltd v Antico* (1995) 13 ACLC 1381 at 1436-1440 per Hodgson J; and *Australian Securities Commission v AS Nominees Ltd* (1995) 133 ALR 1 at 51-53 per Finn J; cf. *Dairy Containers Ltd v NZI Bank Ltd* [1995] 2 NZLR 30 at 90-91 per Thomas J; and *Re Richborough Furniture Ltd* [1996] 1 BCLC 507 at 524 per Timothy Lloyd QC; note Anderson C and Morrison D, 'Standard Chartered Bank of Australia Ltd v Antico: Towards a New Understanding of Insolvent Trading' (1996) 4 CCL 1 at 4-6; Baxt R, 'Shadow directors and Australian law' (1996) 70 ALJ 441 at 441-443; and Baxt R, commercial law note (1995) 69 ALJ 684 at 685-686.
7   Shepherd J C, *The Law of Fiduciaries* The Carswell Company Ltd, Toronto, 1981 at 347-348.
8   Editorial comment, 'Back to basics: company law reform' (1999) 20 Co Law 129 at 129.
9   Gower L C B, *Gower's Principles of Modern Company Law* (1st ed) Sweet & Maxwell Ltd, London, 1954.

be considered in context. At times this is overlooked by academics, practitioners and students alike. The learned editor of *The Company Lawyer* recently recognised this when he relevantly cautioned that:

> To appreciate its purpose and role, it [company law] needs to be cast against a background of history, economics and no doubt social policy. Company law, no matter how intriguing and intellectually stimulating is not and should never be an end in itself. Its raison d'être must be the facilitation of enterprise, although that is not to say that it is not right and proper that a good many other considerations need to be given attention en route.[10]

Modern English and Australian company law is multidimensional and multifaceted. Not only does it belie the perception portrayed by the leading textbooks of a well-ordered system of staid and static rules and regulations, universal in their application to companies of whatever size or form,[11] it is also undergoing a dynamic transformation: a new beginning.[12] During the past decade or so, English and Australian company law has become imbued with change. Within its remit, this book has endeavoured not only to highlight some of the more significant changes recently experienced in England and in Australia, but also to portray the implications of those changes. *A fortiori* within the intricate and exacting topic of directors' duties.

ARE DIRECTORS REPUTABLE?

The 1980s and the 1990s have involved directors of British and Australian companies in complex commercial dealings on a scale and magnitude not previously known in commercial and corporate life.[13] Whilst it is acknowledged that the greater number of such directors have responded diligently and with propriety to the inevitable challenges occasioned by these complexities, nonetheless, history will record those lesser lights who failed to meet levels of reasonable care and diligence and who either abandoned or flagrantly ignored the law's requirements of trust, confidence, good faith, honesty

---

[10] Editorial comment, 'Back to basics: company law reform' (1999) 20 Co Law 129 at 129.

[11] *In re City Equitable Fire Insurance Company Ltd* [1925] Ch 407 at 426-427 per Romer J; *Commonwealth Bank of Australia v Friedrich* (1991) 5 ACSR 115 at 125 per Tadgell J; and *Deputy Commissioner of Taxation v Austin* (1998) 16 ACLC 1555 at 1558-1560 per Madgwick J; note Shepherd J C, *The Law of Fiduciaries* The Carswell Company Ltd, Toronto, 1981 at 347-348.

[12] *Bishopsgate Investment Management Ltd v Maxwell (No. 2)* [1994] 1 All ER 261 at 264 per Hoffmann LJ (Leggatt LJ agreed) who recognised that the law, 'may be evolving in response to changes in public attitudes to corporate governance'; and *Re Grayan Building Services Ltd* [1995] BCC 554 at 577 per Henry LJ, 'The statutory corporate climate is stricter than it has ever been, and those enforcing it should reflect the fact that Parliament has seen the need for higher standards.'; note Committee on the Financial Aspects of Corporate Governance, *The Report on Compliance with the Code of Best Practice* Gee Publishing Ltd, London, 1995 at 8, 'Real progress in raising governance standards is being made and the task now is to maintain that momentum.'

[13] *Mirror Group Newspapers plc v Maxwell (No. 2)* [1998] 1 BCLC 638 at 641 per Ferris J; note the acquittal of George Walker (the former chairman and chief executive of Brent Walker) during October 1994 of a £19.3m fraud charge involving evidence so complex as to tax even the most erudite of jurors; and the acquittal of several businessmen during March 1995 of fraud-related charges, part-way through a trial scheduled to last six months, when the judge ruled that the evidence was too difficult for the jury to understand: *The Times*, 23 March 1995; cf. *The Times*, 20 July 1999 and 8 August 1999.

and integrity in favour of amorality, greed and selfishness. By doing so, they brought English and Australian company law into disrepute.[14]

The publicity associated with those larger than life corporate personalities mentioned at the outset of this book,[15] whose infamy during the late 1980s and the early 1990s has made them household names, does unfortunately tend to distort, and detract from, the widely held view that the greater number of directors of British and Australian companies do act with diligence and propriety befitting their positions of trust and responsibility. This is a view which has by and large persisted in England since 1926 when the committee chaired by Wilfrid Greene KC noted that:

> The evidence satisfies us that the great majority of limited companies both public and private are honestly and conscientiously managed. Cases in which fraud or lesser forms of dishonesty or improper dealing occur are comparatively few, and the public interest which such cases naturally arouse tends to divert attention from the vast number of honestly conducted concerns and to create an exaggerated idea of the evils connected with limited companies and their activities.[16]

As we move into the next millennium, therefore, the corporate spotlight will remain upon directors of British and Australian companies and the enormous power and influence which they wield over corporate assets and also creditors, employees, shareholders and others.[17] As we saw in chapter one of this book, this can have serious ramifications for local, national and international communities. The modern corporate sector in England and in Australia has a profound effect on everyday life. It is crucial to the creation of national wealth.[18] Accordingly, where a company is fraudulently, or even negligently, operated the potential for economic and social harm is tremendous. Bad and incompetent management places shareholders, creditors, employees, suppliers and consumers at risk.[19] Hence the ability, honesty, industry, ethical and moral outlook of directors affects many aspects of community life.[20] That directors need to be careful, skilful and diligent, and also honest and reputable is, therefore, of vital concern to the community at large.[21]

A WIDER CORPORATE CONSTITUENCY

Throughout this book we have witnessed a tendency to depart at times from the traditional repository of directors' duties in favour of a wider corporate constituency

---

[14] E.g., *Bishopsgate Investment Management Ltd v Maxwell (No. 2)* [1994] 1 All ER 261; *Commonwealth Bank of Australia v Friedrich* (1991) 5 ACSR 115; *Linter Group Ltd v Goldberg* (1992) 10 ACLC 739; *Equiticorp Finance Ltd v Bank of New Zealand* (1993) 11 ACLC 952; and *State of South Australia v Clark* (1996) 19 ACSR 606; note *The Times*, 29 April 1999.

[15] Robert Maxwell in England and Alan Bond in Australia.

[16] Company Law Amendment Committee, HMSO, London, Cmd 2657, 1926 at para 7.

[17] *The Sunday Times*, 25 April 1999; cf. *The Australian*, 23 April 1997; note Department of Trade and Industry, *Modern Company Law: For a Competitive Economy* (a consultative document) HMSO, London, 1998 at para 3.7; and Department of Trade and Industry, *Modern Company Law: The Strategic Framework* HMSO, London, 1999 at para 5.1.14.

[18] Senate Standing Committee on Legal and Constitutional Affairs, *Social and Fiduciary Duties and Obligations of Company Directors* AGPS, Canberra, 1989 at 7.

[19] Rider B A K, 'Amiable Lunatics and the Rule in Foss v Harbottle' [1978] CLJ 270 at 286-287.

[20] *The Australian Financial Review*, 2 January 1996.

[21] Company Law Amendment Committee, HMSO, London, Cmd 2657, 1926 at paras 8-9.

than that of the company's shareholders.[22] This is a development which English and Australian case-law and statute, particularly with respect to creditors, has recently entertained.[23] As a consequence, conventional English and Australian company theory is being gradually displaced in favour of a wider corporate constituency which contemplates the recognition of disparate interests,[24] long considered anathema to corporate membership.[25] As Sealy observes:

> [We] may now be moving into a new era in company law, in which directors will be required to take into account interests over and above those represented by the shareholders.[26]

The traditional acceptance that the duties upon directors of British and Australian companies are confined to their companies has, therefore, come under pressure. As we saw in chapters one and six of this book, more and more interest groups, historically considered unqualified for admission to corporate membership, now compete for recognition in modern English and Australian company law.[27] The list of those considered to be on the periphery includes employees, customers, suppliers, consumers, contractors, competitors, creditors, local and national interests, exports, welfare and the environment.[28] These interest groups have traditionally been considered extraneous to company law.[29]

We have considered the ongoing debate as to whether or not directors of British and Australian companies these days owe duties to, for example, the company's shareholders and its creditors direct or, indeed, to an even wider corporate constituency, or

---

[22] Wedderburn K W, 'Trust, Corporation and the Worker' (1985) 23 OHLJ 203 at 223-232; and Stapledon G P, *Institutional Shareholders and Corporate Governance* Clarendon Press, Oxford, 1996 at 8.

[23] Prentice D D, 'Directors, Creditors and Shareholders' in McKendrick E (ed), *Commercial Aspects of Trusts and Fiduciary Obligations* Clarendon Press, Oxford, 1992 at 76.

[24] *Financial Times*, 8 July 1999: 'The issue is between the supporters of the traditional view of the corporation as an agent for the shareholders and the fashionable alternative of a stakeholder corporation taking into account wider interests.'; and *Financial Times*, 21 July 1999.

[25] Sealy L S, 'Directors' "Wider" Responsibilities – Problems Conceptual, Practical and Procedural' (1987) 13 MULR 164 at 173-174.

[26] Sealy L S, 'The Enforcement of Partnership Agreements, Articles of Association and Shareholder Agreements' in Finn P D (ed) *Equity and Commercial Relationships* The Law Book Company Ltd, Sydney, 1987 at 109.

[27] Heydon J D, 'Directors' Duties and the Company's Interests' in Finn P D (ed), *Equity and Commercial Relationships* The Law Book Company Ltd, Sydney, 1987 at 134; and Renard I A, Commentary to Heydon, 'Directors' Duties and the Company's Interests' in Finn P D (ed), *Equity and Commercial Relationships* The Law Book Company Ltd, Sydney, 1987 at 137; note *Financial Times*, 8 July 1999; and *The Times*, 21 July 1999.

[28] Ford H A J and Austin R P, *Ford's Principles of Corporations Law* (6th ed) Butterworths Pty Ltd, Sydney, 1992 at 466-470; Senate Standing Committee on Legal and Constitutional Affairs, *Social and Fiduciary Duties and Obligations of Company Directors* AGPS, Canberra, 1989 at 11; Sealy L S, 'Directors' "Wider" Responsibilities – Problems Conceptual, Practical and Procedural' (1987) 13 MULR 164 at 170; and Sealy L S, 'Reforming the Law on Directors' Duties' (1991) 12 Co Law 175 at 178.

[29] Wedderburn K W, 'Trust, Corporation and the Worker' (1985) 23 OHLJ 203 at 223-230; Sealy L S, 'Directors' "Wider" Responsibilities – Problems Conceptual, Practical and Procedural' (1987) 13 MULR 164; Sealy L S, 'The Enforcement of Partnership Agreements, Articles of Association and Shareholder Agreements' in Finn P D (ed) *Equity and Commercial Relationships* The Law Book Company Ltd, Sydney, 1987 at 109-110; Prentice D D, 'Directors, Creditors and Shareholders' in McKendrick E (ed), *Commercial Aspects of Trusts and Fiduciary Obligations* Clarendon Press, Oxford, 1992 at 73 *et seq*; note Panel on Take-overs and Mergers, *The City Code on Take-overs and Mergers* London, 1993 at General Principle 9; Companies Act 1985 (UK) ss309 and 719; Insolvency Act 1986 (UK) s187; *Financial Times*, 8 July 1999; and *The Times*, 21 July 1999.

whether their interests must simply be taken into account.[30] There are some circumstances where a fiduciary relationship may exist, for example, between a director purchasing a shareholder's shares and that shareholder.[31] Conceptually, directors' duties in these circumstances raise quite different issues. But as Sealy stresses:

> [The] issue is not whether any of these 'wider' interests merits recognition and protection, but whether this can be satisfactorily achieved within the framework of company law as we know it, through the conceptual and remedial vehicle of directors' duties.[32]

Within the remit of this book, we have examined the developing argument that the conventional treatment of English and Australian company law should be departed from so as to impart upon directors of British and Australian companies an obligation to recognise, and to take into account, the company's creditors' interests as part of their day-to-day management obligations and responsibilities.[33] It is clear that support is mounting for the definition of a duty upon directors, 'to act bona fide in the interests of the company as encompassing creditor interests in some circumstances.'[34]

Within the context of insolvency there now exists an obligation upon directors of British and Australian companies to have regard for their insolvent company's creditors' interests: statutorily and non-statutorily. Within Australian company law we have considered the novel regime introduced by Corporations Law Part 5.7B.[35] This statutorily obliges directors to prevent insolvent trading by their Australian companies and provides statutory remedies in default thereof.[36] This is a radical departure from traditional company law tenets. Within English company law the enactment of the Company Directors Disqualification Act 1986 (UK) ('CDD Act') and the Insolvency Act 1986 (UK) ('IA 1986') has not only permitted the disqualification of directors from holding office and also the payment of compensation to their companies for their directorial misconduct, but has generally raised the, 'standards of probity and competence to which the law requires company directors to conform.'[37] This statutory intervention represents, as Prentice observes, 'one of the most important developments in company law this century.'[38] It was examined in detail in chapter eight of this book.

30 Stapledon G P, *Institutional Shareholders and Corporate Governance* Clarendon Press, Oxford, 1996 at 8; cf. *The Australian Financial Review*, 2 January 1996.
31 *Allen v Hyatt* (1914) 30 TLR 444 at 445 per Viscount Haldane LC; *Coleman v Myers* [1977] 2 NZLR 225 at 323 *et seq* per Woodhouse J, at 328 *et seq* per Cooke J and at 370 *et seq* per Casey J; *Glandon Pty Ltd v Strata Consolidated Pty Ltd* (1993) 11 ACSR 543 at 547 per Mahoney JA; and *Glavanics v Brunninghausen* (1996) 19 ACSR 204 at 215-219 and 222-224 per Bryson J; see Barrett R I, 'Directors' Duties to Creditors' (1977) 40 MLR 226 at 226-227.
32 Sealy L S, 'Directors' "Wider" Responsibilities – Problems Conceptual, Practical and Procedural' (1987) 13 MULR 164 at 173.
33 Cf. *Financial Times*, 8 July 1999; and *The Times*, 21 July 1999.
34 Farrar J H, Furey N E, Hannigan B M and Wylie P, *Farrar's Company Law* (3rd ed) Butterworth & Co (Publishers) Ltd, London, 1991 at 386.
35 Added by Act No. 210 of 1992 and effective 23 June 1993.
36 Powers L, 'Can the Court Excuse Insolvent Trading?' (1996) 7 JBFLP 160 at 160; Mannolini J J, 'Creditors' Interests in the Corporate Contract: A Case for the Reform of our Insolvent Trading Provisions' (1996) 6 AJCL 14 at 26-30; Grawehr P, 'A Comparison Between Australian and European Insolvent Trading Laws' (1996) 14 CSLJ 16; and Noble T, 'When Does a Company Incur a Debt Under the Insolvent Trading Provisions of the Corporations Law?' (1994) 12 CSLJ 297 at 297-298 and 308-309.
37 *Re Grayan Building Services Ltd* [1995] BCC 554 at 577 per Neill LJ.
38 Prentice D D, 'Creditor's Interests and Director's Duties' (1990) 10 OJLS 265 at 277.

OBJECTIVITY v SUBJECTIVITY: A CHANGE IN FOCUS

Few would argue that today the objective test is to be preferred over the subjective test when subjecting the duty upon directors of British and Australian companies to exercise care and diligence to scrutiny. Even so, it is not possible to eliminate subjectivity. There will be a residual subjective element present as it applies to skill and the knowledge and experience that a particular director brings to bear.[39] As we have seen from the earlier chapters of this book, the subjective test enjoyed pre-eminence during the 19th century,[40] and for much of the 20th century as well.[41] However, if the Australian experience can be relied upon, it is suggested that its demise in English company law is imminent.[42] The following passage from Tadgell J's judgment in *Commonwealth Bank of Australia v Friedrich*[43] explains why. There, his Honour noted that as the complexity of commerce has gradually intensified:

> [The] community has of necessity come to expect more than formerly from directors whose task it is to govern the affairs of companies ... In response, the parliaments and the courts have found it necessary in legislation and litigation to refer to the demands made on directors in more exacting terms than formerly; and the standard of capability required of them has correspondingly increased.[44]

Notwithstanding that the standard of care and diligence ought to be viewed objectively,[45] this area of the law continues to be pre-eminently an area where the legal result is highly sensitive to the particular facts,[46] and each case is to be determined upon its own merits.[47] As Finch explains, directors, 'do not form a homogeneous category and necessary skills vary according to differences in the sizes and purposes of companies, complexities of management structures, reliance on expert advisers and roles of the

---

[39] Ipp D A, 'The diligent director' (1997) 18 Co Law 162 at 163; note Ford H A J, Austin R P and Ramsay I M, *Ford's Principles of Corporations Law* (9th ed) Reed International Books Australia Pty Ltd, Sydney, 1999 at para 8.330; see *State of South Australia v Clark* (1996) 19 ACSR 606 at 628 per Perry J; cf. Insolvency Act 1986 (UK) s214(4).

[40] E.g., *Turquand v Marshall* (1869) 4 Ch App 376 at 386 per Lord Hatherley LC; *In re Denham & Co* (1884) 25 Ch D 752 at 766 per Chitty J; and *In re Cardiff Savings Bank* [1892] 2 Ch 100 at 108-109 per Stirling J.

[41] E.g., *In re Brazilian Rubber Plantations and Estates Ltd* [1911] 1 Ch 425 at 427 per Neville J; *Transvaal Lands Company v New Belgium (Transvaal) Land and Development Company* [1914] 2 Ch 488 at 500 per Swinfen Eady LJ; and *Pavlides v Jensen* [1956] Ch 565 at 570 per Danckwerts J.

[42] Cf. *Bishopsgate Investment Management Ltd v Maxwell (No. 2)* [1994] 1 All ER 261 at 264 per Hoffmann LJ (Leggatt LJ agreed); note Senate Standing Committee on Legal and Constitutional Affairs, *Social and Fiduciary Duties and Obligations of Company Directors* AGPS, Canberra, 1989 at 29.

[43] (1991) 5 ACSR 115.

[44] *Ibid* at 126.

[45] E.g., *Norman v Theodore Goddard* [1992] BCC 14 at 15 per Hoffmann J; *Re D'Jan of London Ltd* [1993] BCC 646 at 648-649 per Hoffmann LJ; V*risakis v Australian Securities Commission* (1992-1993) 9 WAR 395 at 451 per Ipp J (Malcolm CJ agreed); *Daniels v Anderson* (1995) 13 ACLC 614 at 662 per Clarke and Sheller JJA; *Androvin v Figliomeni* (1996) 14 ACLC 1461 at 1470 per Owen J (Kennedy and Franklyn JJ agreed); and *Re Barings plc* [1998] BCC 583 at 586 per Sir Richard Scott VC.

[46] *Re Manlon Trading Ltd* [1995] 4 All ER 14 at 17 per Peter Gibson LJ.

[47] *Re Barings plc (No 5)* [1999] 1 BCLC 433 at 484 per Jonathan Parker J; note Malcolm D, 'Directors' Duties: The Governing Principles' in Ramsay I M (ed), *Corporate Governance and the Duties of Company Directors* The Centre for Corporate Law and Securities Regulation, University of Melbourne, Parkville, 1997 at 60 and 78.

particular directors'.[48] Hence, it is not surprising that there is no catholicon available to the English and Australian courts, applicable to each and every case, to enable the courts to assess whether or not the director concerned has fallen below the standard expected of them. The presence of a residual subjective element ensures that. Given that directors need have no special qualifications at all for office,[49] this is an area where subjectivity is bound to encroach upon objectivity irrespective of the undesirability of its doing so.[50]

Even though the law surrounding directors' duties is today in a state of flux, in the light of such decisions as *Norman v Theodore Goddard*,[51] *Vrisakis v Australian Securities Commission*,[52] *Re D'Jan of London Ltd*,[53] *Daniels v Anderson*,[54] and *Androvin v Figliomeni*,[55] where objective tests were applied, it is clear that subjectivity is rapidly losing ground to objectivity as the applicable test. Sir Richard Scott VC's judgment in *Re Barings plc* marks a further advance towards the development of an objective standard of care and diligence in English company law.[56] So too does Jonathan Parker J's judgment in *Re Barings plc (No 5)*.[57] This is to be welcomed. By way of comparison, in Australian company law the test of the reasonable person is now enshrined in statute law.[58] Within the context of insolvency, for instance, the duties upon directors of Australian companies operate, 'in the objective rather than the subjective sphere. The question is whether beliefs or expectations are "reasonable" in an objective sense.'[59]

The law regarding the duty upon directors of British and Australian companies to exercise care and diligence continues to evolve in response to changes in public attitudes to corporate governance.[60] This is a welcome change to, 'the low standards of skill and diligence required of directors by the nineteenth-century judges.'[61] It is to be encouraged. As directors of British companies take up the challenges of the 21st

---

[48] Finch V, 'Company Directors: Who Cares about Skill and Care?' (1992) 55 MLR 179 at 203; cf. *Deputy Commissioner of Taxation v Austin* (1998) 16 ACLC 1555 at 1558-1560 per Madgwick J.
[49] Trebilcock M J, 'The Liability of Company Directors for Negligence' (1969) 32 MLR 499 at 502.
[50] Cf. Insolvency Act 1986 (UK) s214(4); note Law Commission, *Company Directors: Regulating Conflicts of Interests and Formulating a Statement of Duties* HMSO, London, Cm 4436, 1999 at paras 5.19-5.20 and 5.38.
[51] [1992] BCC 14.
[52] (1992-1993) 9 WAR 395.
[53] [1993] BCC 646.
[54] (1995) 13 ACLC 614.
[55] (1996) 14 ACLC 1461.
[56] [1998] BCC 583 at 586.
[57] [1999] 1 BCLC 433.
[58] E.g., Corporations Law s232(4); note *State of South Australia v Clark* (1996) 19 ACSR 606 at 628 per Perry J, 'The predominantly objective requirement now imposed by the law finds expression in s232(4) of the Corporations Law'.
[59] *Androvin v Figliomeni* (1996) 14 ACLC 1461 at 1470 per Owen J (Kennedy and Franklyn JJ agreed).
[60] Stapledon G P, *Institutional Shareholders and Corporate Governance* Clarendon Press, Oxford, 1996 at 8; Whincop M J, 'An Economic Analysis of the Criminalisation and Content of Directors' Duties' (1996) 24 ABLR 273 at 277 and 291; Prentice D D and Holland P R J, *Contemporary Issues in Corporate Governance* Oxford University Press, Oxford, 1993; and Farrar J H, 'Corporate Governance, Business Judgement and the Professionalism of Directors' (1993) 6 CBLJ 1 at 2; note Committee on the Financial Aspects of Corporate Governance, *The Report of the Committee on the Financial Aspects of Corporate Governance* Gee and Co Ltd, London, 1992; and Committee on Corporate Governance, *Final Report* Gee Publishing Ltd, London, 1998; cf. The American Law Institute, *Principles of Corporate Governance: Analysis and Recommendations* St Paul, 1994.
[61] Davies P L, *Gower's Principles of Modern Company Law* (6th ed) Sweet & Maxwell Ltd, London, 1997 at 656.

century, it is considered that the English courts will more and more resort to the objective test as being the standard applicable to their determination of whether a particular director's conduct has met the requisite standard of care and diligence, or whether such conduct ought attract their disapprobation. It is evident that the traditional approach to the duty upon directors to exercise care and diligence is being gradually departed from.[62] As the subjective test of the directors' duty to exercise care and diligence is more and more displaced by the English courts,[63] the lax behaviour hitherto tolerated of errant directors will gradually disappear.[64]

Within Australia company law, on the other hand, there has been a dramatic upsurge in activity attending the duty to exercise care and diligence during the past decade or so. What traditionally was seen as a somewhat lacklustre duty, and a particularly ineffective part of the courts' weaponry in controlling errant directors' conduct, has been revitalised. This duty now assumes a prominence which has placed it to the forefront of the Australian courts' remedial arsenal.[65]

Insofar as the cardinal duty upon directors of British and Australian companies to act honestly, in good faith and for proper purposes is concerned, we have also witnessed a change in focus. The earliest cases, as Sealy notes, were mostly about property; whereas, more recently, the cases are more concerned with the exercise by directors of their powers.[66] As a consequence, the English and the Australian judiciary's techniques in combating improper directorial conduct and decision-making have shifted in emphasis from a determination of whether or not such conduct was *bona fide* in the company's interests, to a determination of whether or not such conduct was for proper purposes.[67] In the former case, subjective criteria held sway. In the latter case, objective criteria assumes paramountcy.[68]

The duty upon directors of British and Australian companies to exercise powers for proper purposes has come to be regarded as separate from the duty to exercise powers *bona fide* in the interests of the company,[69] and is presently enjoying attention from

---

[62] *Norman v Theodore Goddard* [1992] BCC 14 at 15 per Hoffmann J; *Re D'Jan of London Ltd* [1993] BCC 646 at 648-649 per Hoffmann LJ; and *Re Barings plc* [1998] BCC 583 at 586 per Sir Richard Scott VC.

[63] Editorial comment, 'Other people's money' (1996) 17 Co Law 98 at 98.

[64] Gower L C B, *Gower's Principles of Modern Company Law* (5th ed) Sweet & Maxwell Ltd, London, 1992 at 589.

[65] V*risakis v Australian Securities Commission* (1992-1993) 9 WAR 395 at 451 per Ipp J (Malcolm CJ agreed); *Daniels v Anderson* (1995) 13 ACLC 614 at 662 per Clarke and Sheller JJA; and *Androvin v Figliomeni* (1996) 14 ACLC 1461 at 1470 per Owen J (Kennedy and Franklyn JJ agreed).

[66] Sealy L S, 'Directors' "Wider" Responsibilities – Problems Conceptual, Practical and Procedural' (1987) 13 MULR 164 at 168.

[67] *Gambotto v WCP Ltd* (1995) 13 ACLC 342; *Kokotovich Constructions Pty Ltd v Wallington* (1995) 13 ACLC 1113; *Bishopsgate Investment Management Ltd v Maxwell (No. 2)* [1994] 1 All ER 261; and *Re BSB Holdings Ltd (No. 2)* [1996] 1 BCLC 155.

[68] *Androvin v Figliomeni* (1996) 14 ACLC 1461 at 1470 per Owen J (Kennedy and Franklyn JJ agreed); *Daniels v Anderson* (1995) 13 ACLC 614 at 662 per Clarke and Sheller JJA; *Lyford v Commonwealth Bank of Australia* (1995) 13 ACLC 900 at 914 per R D Nicholson J; *Carter v Drake* (1992-1993) 9 WAR 82 at 94 per Malcolm CJ; and V*risakis v Australian Securities Commission* (1992-1993) 9 WAR 395 at 451 per Ipp J (Malcolm CJ agreed).

[69] Wedderburn K W, 'Shareholders' Control of Directors' Powers: A Judicial Innovation?' (1967) 30 MLR 77 at 79; Parsons R W, 'The Director's Duty of Good Faith' (1967) 5 MULR 395 at 419; and Birds J R, 'Proper Purposes as a Head of Directors' Duties' (1974) 37 MLR 580; cf. Slutsky B V, case note (1974) 37 MLR 457 at 460; Burridge S J, 'Wrongful Rights Issues' (1981) 44 MLR 40 at 50; and Sealy L S, 'Company – Directors' Unconstitutional Acts' [1992] CLJ 229.

English and Australian courts of the highest authority.[70] The proper purposes test or, as it is also referred to, the collateral purposes test,[71] allows the acts of directors to be reviewed by the courts upon a more objective basis than that which has been traditionally applied in relation to *bona fides*.[72] Notwithstanding that directors may have acted honestly in what they believe to be in the company's interests, they may nevertheless be liable to the company if they have exercised their powers for a purpose different from that for which the powers were conferred upon them.[73] Strict adherence to the *bona fides* doctrine can permit of too much subjectivity in the directors' decision-making process.

The attractiveness of the proper purposes doctrine in English and Australian company law is that it introduces an objective element which permits English and Australian courts with a more interventionist disposition to monitor more closely directors' decision-making.[74] It is significant that the proper purposes doctrine has application where the directors' good faith is not challenged.[75] Thus, subjective honesty on the part of directors is no longer, of itself, sufficient to justify a decision or a course of conduct improperly taken.[76]

DELEGATION

It is clear from the recent cases in English and Australian company law that traditional rules and principles are being refashioned and applied in circumstances which evidence a somewhat revivified English and Australian judiciary.[77] In today's complex commercial and corporate world, delegation is playing a critical role in sound business practice and proper corporate governance.[78] As the day-to-day business of management

---

[70] *Gambotto v WCP Ltd* (1995) 13 ACLC 342; and *Bishopsgate Investment Management Ltd v Maxwell (No. 2)* [1994] 1 All ER 261.

[71] *Darvall v North Sydney Brick & Tile Co Ltd (No. 2)* (1989) 7 ACLC 659 at 676 per Kirby P; *Equiticorp Finance Ltd v Bank of New Zealand* (1993) 11 ACLC 952 at 1018 per Clarke and Cripps JJA; *Permanent Building Society v Wheeler* (1993-1994) 11 WAR 187 at 193, 218, 226 and 234 per Ipp J (Malcolm CJ and Seaman J agreed); and *Re BSB Holdings Ltd (No. 2)* [1996] 1 BCLC 155 at 243 per Arden J.

[72] *Greenhalgh v Arderne Cinemas Ld* [1951] Ch 286 at 291 *per curiam*; and *Richard Brady Franks Ltd v Price* (1937) 58 CLR 112 at 135-136 per Latham CJ and at 216-217 per Isaacs J; note Birds J R, 'Making Directors do their Duties' (1980) 1 Co Law 67 at 70.

[73] *Fraser v Whalley* (1864) 2 H & M 10; *Punt v Symons & Co Ltd* [1903] 2 Ch 506; *Piercy v S Mills & Company Ltd* [1920] 1 Ch 77; *Ngurli Ltd v McCann* (1954) 90 CLR 425; *Hogg v Cramphorn Ltd* [1967] Ch 254; and *Howard Smith Ltd v Ampol Petroleum Ltd* [1974] AC 821.

[74] Sealy L S, '"Bona Fides" and "Proper Purposes" in Corporate Decisions' (1989) 15 MULR 265 at 266; and Sealy L S, 'Company – Directors' Unconstitutional Acts' [1992] CLJ 229.

[75] *Hogg v Cramphorn Ltd* [1967] Ch 254; see Wedderburn K W, 'Shareholders' Control of Directors' Powers: A Judicial Innovation?' (1967) 30 MLR 77.

[76] *Permanent Building Society v Wheeler* (1993-1994) 11 WAR 187 at 218 per Ipp J (Malcolm CJ and Seaman J agreed); and *Bishopsgate Investment Management Ltd v Maxwell (No. 2)* [1994] 1 All ER 261 at 268-269 per Ralph Gibson LJ.

[77] E.g., *Norman v Theodore Goddard* [1992] BCC 14 at 15 per Hoffmann J; *Vrisakis v Australian Securities Commission* (1992-1993) 9 WAR 395 at 451 per Ipp J (Malcolm CJ agreed); *Daniels v Anderson* (1995) 13 ACLC 614 at 662 per Clarke and Sheller JJA; *Androvin v Figliomeni* (1996) 14 ACLC 1461 at 1470 per Owen J (Kennedy and Franklyn JJ agreed); and *Re Barings plc* [1998] BCC 583 at 586 per Sir Richard Scott VC.

[78] See Prentice D D and Holland P R J, *Contemporary Issues in Corporate Governance* Oxford University Press, Oxford, 1993; Committee on the Financial Aspects of Corporate Governance, *The Report of the Committee on the Financial Aspects of Corporate Governance* Gee and Co Ltd, London, 1992; Farrar J H, 'Corporate Governance, Business Judgement and the Professionalism of Directors' (1993) 6 CBLJ

intensifies, the delegation of tasks by directors of British and Australian companies is becoming increasingly important. As we have seen, absent reasonable grounds for suspicion, a director is justified in trusting his or her co-directors and the other officers of the company to perform honestly those duties which may properly be delegated or left to them.[79] However, duties must not be entrusted to an obviously inappropriate or unqualified person.[80] This is an interesting area of the law which is still developing. Hence the particular circumstances in each case are clearly relevant.[81]

The Australian approach to delegation is exemplified by Rogers CJ's decision in *AWA Ltd v Daniels*;[82] an approach recently amplified on appeal by the joint judgment of Clarke and Sheller JJA in the New South Wales Court of Appeal in *Daniels v Anderson*.[83] This approach is not dissimilar to that recently preferred in England. In *Norman v Theodore Goddard*,[84] for example, Hoffmann J mentioned two principles relevant to the extent of the duty of care owed by a director of a British company. His Lordship put the second of these in this way:

> [As] *Romer* J said in *Re City Equitable Fire Insurance Co Ltd* [1925] Ch 407 at p. 429, 'Business cannot be carried on upon principles of distrust' and 'Men in responsible positions must be trusted … until there is reason to distrust them'.[85]

It would be inappropriate and unreasonable to expect directors of British and Australian companies to act as insurers. The frenetic pace at which business operates today in England and in Australia could simply not be sustained were directors obliged as a matter of course to check up on co-directors each and every step of the way, irrespective of the particular circumstances involved. Nor could business operate if, in default thereof, directors were to be made personally liable.[86] However, there are limits. In this respect, the recent decision of the Court of Appeal[87] in *Re Westmid Packing Services Ltd*[88] is pertinent. Lord Woolf MR delivered the judgment of the Court of Appeal. In doing so, his Lordship relevantly accepted as correct the following propositions:

---

cont.

1; Whincop M J, 'An Economic Analysis of the Criminalisation and Content of Directors' Duties' (1996) 24 ABLR 273; and Stapledon G P, *Institutional Shareholders and Corporate Governance* Clarendon Press, Oxford, 1996.

[79] *In re Brazilian Rubber Plantations and Estates Ltd* [1911] 1 Ch 425 at 438 per Neville J; note *Re Barings plc (No 5)* [1999] 1 BCLC 433 at 487 per Jonathan Parker J; and *Daniels v Anderson* (1995) 13 ACLC 614 at 663-666 per Clarke and Sheller JJA; see Davies P L, *Gower's Principles of Modern Company Law* (6th ed) Sweet & Maxwell Ltd, London, 1997 at 643-644.

[80] It will be recalled that one of the grounds on which the directors in *In re City Equitable Fire Insurance Company Ltd* [1925] Ch 407 were held to have breached their duties, was that they had allowed the managing director to usurp functions not delegated to him and had permitted the company's stockbrokers to retain large sums without security in a manner more appropriate to bankers than to brokers.

[81] *Dovey v Cory* [1901] AC 477 at 488 per Lord Macnaghten; note Law Commission, *Company Directors: Regulating Conflicts of Interests and Formulating a Statement of Duties* HMSO, London, Cm 4436, 1999 at para 5.36.

[82] (1992) 10 ACLC 933 at 1015.

[83] (1995) 13 ACLC 614 at 663-666.

[84] [1992] BCC 14.

[85] *Ibid* at 16.

[86] *Dovey v Cory* [1901] AC 477 at 485-486 per the Earl of Halsbury LC.

[87] (Lord Woolf MR, Waller and Robert Walker LJJ).

[88] [1998] 2 All ER 124.

[The] collegiate or collective responsibility of the board of directors of a company is of fundamental importance to corporate governance under English company law. That collegiate or collective responsibility must however be based on individual responsibility. Each individual director owes duties to the company to inform himself about its affairs and to join with his co-directors in supervising and controlling them. A proper degree of delegation and division of responsibility is of course permissible, and often necessary, but not total abrogation of responsibility.[89]

Delegation is but one important function which directors of British and Australian companies regularly perform in the course of the day-to-day management of their companies.[90] It is inextricably interwoven with their duty to exercise care and diligence. Irrespective of what a particular director's status might be, directors are duty bound to keep themselves regularly informed of their company's affairs.[91] It is incumbent upon directors to participate in the supervision and monitoring of their fellow directors and those to whom they delegate functions.[92] In this respect, Jonathan Parker J's recent judgment in *Re Barings plc (No 5)*[93] greatly contributes to the development in English company law of the duty upon directors of British companies to exercise care and diligence, and elucidates some of the issues which pertain to delegation. His Lordship considered that the following general propositions could be derived from the authorities:

(i) Directors have, both collectively and individually, a continuing duty to acquire and maintain a sufficient knowledge and understanding of the company's business to enable them properly to discharge their duties as directors. (ii) Whilst directors are entitled ... to delegate particular functions to those below them in the management chain, and to trust their competence and integrity to a reasonable extent, the exercise of the power of delegation does not absolve a director from the duty to supervise the discharge of the delegated functions. (iii) No rule of universal application can be formulated as to the duty referred to in (ii) above. The extent of the duty, and the question whether it has been discharged, must depend on the facts of each particular case, including the director's role in the management of the company.[94]

Barings (No 5) is an important case. Jonathan Parker J's judgment provides impetus for the further expansion of the common law duty upon directors of British companies to exercise care and diligence by requiring them to take: (i) positive action to inform themselves about their company's affairs; and (ii) responsibility for the reasonable supervision and control of those to whom they delegate specific tasks and functions. As his Lordship explained, directors must appreciate that having delegated a particular function, they remain responsible and accountable for such delegated functions and will retain a residual duty of supervision and control.[95] This was the approach of the New

---

[89] *Ibid* at 130; note *Re Landhurst Leasing plc* [1999] 1 BCLC 286 at 346 per Hart J.

[90] Ford H A J, Austin R P and Ramsay I M, *Ford's Principles of Corporations Law* (9th ed) Reed International Books Australia Pty Ltd, Sydney, 1999 at para 8.330.

[91] *Re Westmid Packing Services Ltd* [1998] 2 All ER 124 at 130 per Lord Woolf MR (Waller and Robert Walker LJJ agreed).

[92] *Daniels v Anderson* (1995) 13 ACLC 614 at 663-666 per Clarke and Sheller JJA.

[93] [1999] 1 BCLC 433.

[94] *Ibid* at 489.

[95] *Ibid* at 487.

South Wales Court of Appeal in *Daniels*;[96] an approach which is gradually coming to enjoy wider support in English company law as well.[97]

STATUTORY INTERVENTION: BRINGING DIRECTORS TO ACCOUNT

Within English and Australian company law a number of attempts have been made by the British and Australian Parliaments over the past 15 years or so in order to make directors of British and Australian companies more responsible and accountable. This book has examined at length the more significant statutory provisions and legislative initiatives directed towards achieving this. Chapters seven and eight of this book, for instance, analysed in detail the development of the statutory machinery in English company law within the CDD Act for disqualifying errant directors from acting as directors, or being in any way concerned in the management, of British companies by reason of their unfitness to do so: either generally,[98] or given that they have engaged in either fraudulent trading[99] or wrongful trading[100] within the context of insolvency. We also analysed the legislative framework within IA 1986 ss212-214 which the British Parliament has provided.[101] This permits the liquidator to apply to the court for an order that the errant directors concerned are to restore the company's assets or make whatever contribution to the company's assets by way of compensation which the court thinks appropriate.[102] Whereas these sections of the IA 1986 are aimed at enlarging the company's assets for the benefit of the creditors along the lines of traditional insolvency law principles,[103] the CDD Act has a different emphasis, and seeks to remove egregious directors from office.[104]

By its enactment of Corporations Law s588G,[105] the Australian Parliament has undoubtedly introduced a novel concept into Australian company law within the traditional framework of directors' duties.[106] The implementation of a statutory duty upon directors to prevent insolvent trading by their Australian companies, in conjunction with those statutory, and non-statutory, duties explored in the previous chapters of

---

[96] (1995) 13 ACLC 614 at 663-666 per Clarke and Sheller JJA.

[97] Davies P L, *Gower's Principles of Modern Company Law* (6th ed) Sweet & Maxwell Ltd, London, 1997 at 643-644.

[98] Company Directors Disqualification Act 1986 (UK) ss6 and 8.

[99] *Ibid* at ss4, 6, 8 and 10; and Companies Act 1985 (UK) s458; see Insolvency Act 1986 (UK) s213.

[100] Company Directors Disqualification Act 1986 (UK) ss6, 8 and 10; see Insolvency Act 1986 (UK) s214.

[101] Cf. Company Directors Disqualification Act 1986 (UK) ss4, 6, 8 and 10.

[102] *Re Farmizer (Products) Ltd* [1997] BCC 655 at 657 per Peter Gibson LJ (Potter and Butler-Sloss LJJ agreed).

[103] *Re Esal (Commodities) Ltd* [1997] 1 BCLC 705 at 715 per Peter Gibson LJ (Hirst and Ralph Gibson LJJ agreed); and *Re Oasis Merchandising Services Ltd* [1997] BCC 282 at 291 *per curiam*; note Insolvency Act 1986 (UK) s107; and Villiers C, 'Employees as creditors: a challenge for justice in insolvency law' (1999) 20 Co Law 222 at 228; cf. Schulte R, 'Corporate groups and the equitable subordination of claims on insolvency' (1997) 18 Co Law 2 at 2 and 11.

[104] See Sealy L S, *Disqualification and Personal Liability of Directors* (4th ed) CCH Editions Ltd, Bicester, 1993; note Farrar J H, Furey N E, Hannigan B M and Wylie P, *Farrar's Company Law* (3rd ed) Butterworth & Co (Publishers) Ltd, London, 1991 at 397; cf. *Re Swift 736 Ltd* [1993] BCC 312 at 315 per Nicholls VC (Farquharson and Steyn LJJ agreed); *Re Grayan Building Services Ltd* [1995] BCC 554 at 577 per Henry LJ; and *Re Living Images Ltd* [1996] BCC 112 at 115 per Laddie J.

[105] Added by Act No. 210 of 1992 and effective 23 June 1993.

[106] Noble T, 'When Does a Company Incur a Debt Under the Insolvent Trading Provisions of the Corporations Law?' (1994) 12 CSLJ 297 at 297.

this book, provide the Australian judiciary with a flexible and powerful array of remedies in order to combat directorial misconduct and decision-making. In contrast, in English company law there is no corresponding duty upon directors of British companies to prevent insolvent trading. As Chadwick J in *Secretary of State for Trade and Industry v Gash* observed:

> The companies legislation does not impose on directors a statutory duty to ensure that their company does not trade while insolvent; nor does that legislation impose an obligation to ensure that the company does not trade at a loss.[107]

In spite of this, the introduction into English company law of the CDD Act and the IA 1986, and the frequency with which the English courts are today approached for declaratory relief in respect to these Acts,[108] has endowed the English judiciary with effective measures designed to, 'protect the public, and in particular potential creditors of companies, from losing money through companies becoming insolvent when the directors of those companies are people unfit to be concerned in the management of a company.'[109] As mentioned earlier in this chapter, this significant statutory intervention represents, 'one of the most important developments in company law this century.'[110] Thus, notwithstanding the absence from the British statute books of a statutory duty upon directors to prevent insolvent trading by their British companies, revived and refashioned traditional legal rules and equitable principles,[111] coupled with the limited but effective measures provided for under the CDD Act and the IA 1986,[112] do provide the English judiciary with an array of remedies comparable to those which their Australian counterparts have become accustomed to deploying.

It is suggested that the British and Australian Parliaments will seek to legislate more and more in the area of directors' duties.[113] Such legislation will be directed towards raising the overall standards of directorial conduct and decision-making on the part of directors of British and Australian companies in keeping with the community's, and the commercial world's, changing expectations.[114] This will naturally have profound implications for the directors of the next century. *A fortiori* as the common law relating to the directors' duty to exercise care and diligence continues to evolve, and the objective standard of care and diligence further develops at the expense of subjectiv-

---

[107] [1997] 1 BCLC 341 at 348.

[108] Comptroller and Auditor General, *The Insolvency Service Executive Agency: Company Director Disqualification – A Follow Up Report* The Stationery Office Ltd, London, 1999 at paras 1.6 and 1.15.

[109] *Re Sevenoaks Stationers (Retail) Ltd* [1990] BCC 765 at 773 per Dillon LJ (Butler-Sloss and Staughton LJJ agreed); note *Re Grayan Building Services Ltd* [1995] BCC 554 at 577 per Henry LJ; *Re Richborough Furniture Ltd* [1996] BCC 155 at 166 per Timothy Lloyd QC; *Re Continental Assurance Co of London plc* [1997] 1 BCLC 48 at 59 per Chadwick J; and *Re Blackspur Group plc* [1998] 1 BCLC 676 at 680 and 688 per Lord Woolf MR (Millett and Mummery LJJ agreed).

[110] Prentice D D, 'Creditor's Interests and Director's Duties' (1990) 10 OJLS 265 at 277.

[111] Cf. Malcolm D, 'Directors' Duties: The Governing Principles' in Ramsay I M (ed), *Corporate Governance and the Duties of Company Directors* The Centre for Corporate Law and Securities Regulation, University of Melbourne, Parkville, 1997 at 60 and 80.

[112] *Re Blackspur Group plc* [1998] 1 BCLC 676 at 681 per Lord Woolf MR (Millett and Mummery LJJ agreed).

[113] E.g., Corporate Law Economic Reform Program Bill 1998 (Cth).

[114] Cf. Malcolm D, 'Directors' Duties: The Governing Principles' in Ramsay I M (ed), *Corporate Governance and the Duties of Company Directors* The Centre for Corporate Law and Securities Regulation, University of Melbourne, Parkville, 1997 at 78.

ity.[115] It will be with some trepidation, therefore, that directors will take up the challenges which the 21st century will hold for them.

Whether or not legislation further intervenes into English company law and insolvency law, it is considered that the English courts will more and more resort to the objective test as being the standard applicable to their determination of whether a particular director's conduct ought attract their disapprobation, and result in that director's disqualification on the basis that he or she is unfit to be concerned in the management of a British company.[116] This is entirely consistent with the British parliamentary intent behind the enactment of the CDD Act.[117] Nicholls VC[118] recognised this in *Re Swift 736 Ltd* as the following extract from the Vice-Chancellor's judgment makes clear:

> Limited liability is a valuable tool in the promotion of trade and business, but it must not be misused. Those who make use of limited liability must do so with a proper sense of responsibility. The director disqualification procedure is an important sanction introduced by Parliament to raise standards in this regard. Those who take advantage of limited liability must conduct their companies with due regard to the ordinary standards of commercial morality. They must also be punctilious in observing the safeguards laid down by Parliament for the benefit of others who have dealings with their companies.[119]

Within the context of insolvency, the English courts have developed a substantial body of jurisprudence in respect to the appropriate standard of care and diligence expected of directors of British companies. This is of recent origin. It is a function of the increasing number of proceedings being instituted by the Secretary of State for Trade and Industry ('Secretary of State') and the liquidator for relief considered appropriate under the CDD Act and the IA 1986 respectively.[120] It should be remembered, however, that the CDD Act is directed towards the abuse of limited liability, 'and the obligations of a businessman to his creditors rather than general questions of corporate government.'[121] As Lord Hoffmann recently pointed out:

> The Company Directors Disqualification Act is concerned with an altogether different problem. The directors against whom applications for disqualification are made are for the most part sole traders, beneficial owners of the whole issued share capital

---

[115] E.g., *Norman v Theodore Goddard* [1992] BCC 14 at 15 per Hoffmann J; *Vrisakis v Australian Securities Commission* (1992-1993) 9 WAR 395 at 451 per Ipp J (Malcolm CJ agreed); *Daniels v Anderson* (1995) 13 ACLC 614 at 662 per Clarke and Sheller JJA; *Androvin v Figliomeni* (1996) 14 ACLC 1461 at 1470 per Owen J (Kennedy and Franklyn JJ agreed); and *Re Barings plc* [1998] BCC 583 at 586 per Sir Richard Scott VC.

[116] Company Directors Disqualification Act 1986 (UK) s6(1).

[117] See, e.g., Walters A and Davis-White M, *Directors' Disqualification: Law & Practice* Sweet & Maxwell Ltd, London, 1999 at chapter 2; note *Re Grayan Building Services Ltd* [1995] BCC 554 at 577 per Henry LJ.

[118] (Farquharson and Steyn LJJ agreed).

[119] [1993] BCC 312 at 315; note *Re Grayan Building Services Ltd* [1995] BCC 554 at 574 per Hoffmann LJ (Henry and Neill LJJ agreed).

[120] E.g., Comptroller and Auditor General, *The Insolvency Service Executive Agency: Company Director Disqualification – A Follow Up Report* The Stationery Office Ltd, London, 1999 at paras 1.6 and 1.15.

[121] Hoffmann L H, 'The Fourth Annual Leonard Sainer Lecture' (1997) 18 Co Law 194 at 197; cf. *Secretary of State for Trade and Industry v Tjolle* [1998] BCC 282 at 290 and 300-301 per Jacob J.

of a company using the corporate structure simply for the advantages of limited liability.[122]

Notwithstanding the growing body of case-law, the lack of a yardstick, universal in its application to a director's obligations in all circumstances, and against which the standard of care and diligence required of the ubiquitous director can be measured, makes it very difficult to formulate meaningful guidelines to be followed by the English and Australian courts in order to delimit unacceptable behaviour.[123] As Lord Hoffmann pointed out when he gave the Leonard Sainer Lecture in London on 26 November 1996, 'where the law does not require any kind of qualification for becoming a director, it is not easy to fix an *ex post facto* standard of competence for disqualification.'[124] As such, each case must inevitably be determined upon its own merits;[125] an approach entirely consistent with authority.[126]

There is some uniformity, however, to the approaches now being taken by the English courts to the requisite standard required of directors of British companies. This is provided by IA 1986 s214(4),[127] and is consistent with that recently applied in respect to disqualification orders made by the courts pursuant to CDD Act s6. The recent judgments of Sir Richard Scott VC in *Re Barings plc*[128] and Jonathan Parker J in *Re Barings plc (No 5)*[129] are apposite. More and more applications are being brought under the CDD Act each year by the Secretary of State to have errant directors disqualified.[130] This, in conjunction with those applications brought by the liquidator pursuant to the IA 1986, ought lead to a better consistency in approach and a raising of directorial standards over time.[131] As a matter of practice opines Farrar:

> [We] should see directors bringing greater care and skill to their positions as they attempt to avoid the personal liability and disqualification provided by those Acts for directors who fail to reach an appropriate standard of conduct. The existing case-law must now be read in the light of these legislative developments.[132]

The impact which statutory intervention has had upon the duties of directors of British and Australian companies over the past 15 years or so has been profound. The statutory machinery which the British and Australian Parliaments have provided has enabled the

---

[122] Hoffmann L H, 'The Fourth Annual Leonard Sainer Lecture' (1997) 18 Co Law 194 at 196.
[123] Ipp D A, 'The diligent director' (1997) 18 Co Law 162 at 165.
[124] Hoffmann L H, 'The Fourth Annual Leonard Sainer Lecture' (1997) 18 Co Law 194 at 197.
[125] Malcolm D, 'Directors' Duties: The Governing Principles' in Ramsay I M (ed), *Corporate Governance and the Duties of Company Directors* The Centre for Corporate Law and Securities Regulation, University of Melbourne, Parkville, 1997 at 60 and 78.
[126] *Re Manlon Trading Ltd* [1995] 4 All ER 14 at 17 per Peter Gibson LJ.
[127] *Re Brian D Pierson (Contractors) Ltd* [1999] BCC 26 at 49 per Hazel Williamson QC (sitting as a deputy High Court Judge); and *Re D'Jan of London Ltd* [1993] BCC 646 at 648-649 per Hoffmann LJ.
[128] [1998] BCC 583 at 586.
[129] [1999] 1 BCLC 433.
[130] Comptroller and Auditor General, *The Insolvency Service Executive Agency: Company Director Disqualification – A Follow Up Report* The Stationery Office Ltd, London, 1999 at paras 1.6 and 1.15.
[131] Davies P L, *Gower's Principles of Modern Company Law* (6th ed) Sweet & Maxwell Ltd, London, 1997 at 642-643.
[132] Farrar J H, Furey N E, Hannigan B M and Wylie P, *Farrar's Company Law* (3rd ed) Butterworth & Co (Publishers) Ltd, London, 1991 at 397; see *Re Swift 736 Ltd* [1993] BCC 312 at 315 per Nicholls VC (Farquharson and Steyn LJJ agreed); *Re Grayan Building Services Ltd* [1995] BCC 554 at 577 per Henry LJ; *Re Living Images Ltd* [1996] BCC 112 at 115 per Laddie J; and *Re Richborough Furniture Ltd* [1996] 1 BCLC 507 at 520 per Timothy Lloyd QC.

English and Australian courts to redress instances of egregious behaviour on the part of directors for their misconduct and decision-making. By doing so, the courts have been able to generally raise the, 'standards of probity and competence to which the law requires company directors to conform.'[133] Directors of British and Australian companies must tread cautiously, therefore, as they take up the challenges of the 21st century.

RECENT LEGISLATIVE INITIATIVES: MODERNISING COMPANY LAW

It is apparent from the previous chapters of this book that significant change has occurred in Australian company law, more so than in English company law, over the past decade or so: especially within the area of directors' duties. Fresh legislative initiatives on the part of the Australian Parliament,[134] for instance, complement and supplement the recent developments in this area of the law by the Australian judiciary.[135] These initiatives encourage judges of a robust and interventionist disposition to exact even higher standards from directors of Australian companies, as company law responds to the times.[136]

The recent Corporate Law Economic Reform Program,[137] which has been partially implemented by the Australian Parliament, is an example of the determination which the Australian Government has for progressing a modernised and revitalised Australian company law into the 21st century. It is suggested that such initiatives and developments on the part of the Australian Parliament, and the Australian judiciary, will further assuage the business community's demands for raised levels of directorial responsibility and greater accountability. Moreover, these initiatives and developments accord with today's ideals of corporate governance.[138] Insofar as the duty to exercise care and diligence is concerned, for example, Perry J in *State of South Australia v Clark* has lately acknowledged that:

---

[133] *Re Grayan Building Services Ltd* [1995] BCC 554 at 577 per Neill LJ.

[134] E.g., Corporations Legislation Amendment Act 1991 (Cth); Corporate Law Reform Act 1992 (Cth); Corporate Law Reform Act 1994 (Cth); First Corporate Law Simplification Act 1995 (Cth); Company Law Review Act 1998 (Cth); Managed Investments Act 1998 (Cth); and Financial Sector Reform (Amendments and Transitional Provisions) Act 1998 (Cth). Moreover, further initiatives are to be re-introduced into the Australian Parliament with the Corporate Law Economic Reform Program Bill 1998 (Cth) expected to be enacted in the first half of 2000.

[135] *Morley v Statewide Tobacco Services Ltd* (1992) 8 ACSR 305; *Commonwealth Bank of Australia v Friedrich* (1991) 5 ACSR 115; and *AWA Ltd v Daniels* (1992) 10 ACLC 933; note Explanatory memorandum, *Corporate Law Reform Bill 1992* CCH Australia Ltd, Sydney, 1992 at 25.

[136] *Daniels v Anderson* (1995) 13 ACLC 614 at 663-666 per Clarke and Sheller JJA; note Fidock R, 'Landmark call for Judgement Rule' (1996) 12 Co Dir 47 at 47; and Baxt R, commercial law note (1995) 69 ALJ 571 at 575.

[137] Ford H A J, Austin R P and Ramsay I M, *Ford's Principles of Corporations Law* (9th ed) Reed International Books Australia Pty Ltd, Sydney, 1999 at para 3.030.

[138] See Prentice D D and Holland P R J, *Contemporary Issues in Corporate Governance* Oxford University Press, Oxford, 1993; Committee on the Financial Aspects of Corporate Governance, *The Report of the Committee on the Financial Aspects of Corporate Governance* Gee and Co Ltd, London, 1992; Farrar J H, 'Corporate Governance, Business Judgement and the Professionalism of Directors' (1993) 6 CBLJ 1; Whincop M J, 'An Economic Analysis of the Criminalisation and Content of Directors' Duties' (1996) 24 ABLR 273; and Stapledon G P, *Institutional Shareholders and Corporate Governance* Clarendon Press, Oxford, 1996.

Recent appellate decisions in Australia have gone a long way towards clarifying and re-expressing the duty of care owed by directors of a company vis á vis the company in terms more closely reflecting contemporary attitudes.[139]

English company law on the other hand has proven to be somewhat more reticent and impervious to change;[140] seemingly rooted in a bygone era,[141] hamstrung by outmoded conservative policies, and steadfast in its refusal to respond to the times.[142] It should be noted, however, that on 4 March 1998 the President of the Board of Trade announced the launch of a fundamental review of the framework of core English company law. This is to be welcomed. The consultation paper published at that time by the Department of Trade and Industry ('DTI') outlines the nature of the problems which the review is designed to address and its objectives, and relevantly provides that:

> The object of the review will be to bring forward proposals for a modern law for the modern world. The Government is determined that the nation should have an up-to-date framework which promotes the competitiveness of UK companies and so contributes to national competitiveness and increased prosperity.[143]

In February 1999, the DTI released its consultation document entitled *Modern Company Law: The Strategic Framework*. This document identifies as an issue of general importance to the review those interests which English company law should serve and the means by which it should do so.[144] In addition, the Law Commission published in September 1999 its eagerly awaited report entitled *Company Directors: Regulating Conflicts of Interests and Formulating a Statement of Duties*. This report revives the push for the partial codification of the duty upon directors of British companies to exercise care and diligence.[145] The Law Commission considers that the case for partial codification is a powerful one,[146] and advocates the enactment of a twofold objective/subjective test as the standard by which the duty upon directors of British companies to exercise care and diligence should be adjudged.[147]

Hence changes in English company law are mooted. Moves are afoot. But, quite properly, these things take time. The aim of the Company Law Review Steering Group, for instance, is to enable the DTI to publish a detailed White Paper in or about March

---

[139] (1996) 19 ACSR 606 at 627.

[140] Finn P D, 'Fiduciary Law and the Modern Commercial World' in McKendrick E (ed), *Commercial Aspects of Trusts and Fiduciary Obligations* Clarendon Press, Oxford, 1992 at 40; and Sealy L S, 'Fiduciary Obligations, Forty Years On' (1995) 9 JCL 37 at 52-53.

[141] Department of Trade and Industry, *Modern Company Law: For a Competitive Economy* (a consultative document) HMSO, London, 1998 at para 1.1.

[142] Cf. *Bishopsgate Investment Management Ltd v Maxwell (No. 2)* [1994] 1 All ER 261 at 264 per Hoffmann LJ (Leggatt LJ agreed) who recognised that the law, 'may be evolving in response to changes in public attitudes to corporate governance'; and *Re Grayan Building Services Ltd* [1995] BCC 554 at 577 per Henry LJ, 'The statutory corporate climate is stricter than it has ever been, and those enforcing it should reflect the fact that Parliament has seen the need for higher standards.'

[143] Department of Trade and Industry, *Modern Company Law: For a Competitive Economy* (a consultative document) HMSO, London, 1998 at para 1.2.

[144] Department of Trade and Industry, *Modern Company Law: The Strategic Framework* HMSO, London, 1999 at chapter 5.1.

[145] Law Commission, *Company Directors: Regulating Conflicts of Interests and Formulating a Statement of Duties* HMSO, London, Cm 4436, 1999 at paras 4.48, 5.19-5.20 and 5.38.

[146] *Ibid* at para 4.31.

[147] *Ibid* at paras 5.19-5.20 and 5.38.

2001.[148] Given the breadth of the DTI's review, even this looks to be a tight timetable.[149] Furthermore, in the event that the recent views of the Law Commission advocating partial codification are embraced, and ultimately enacted, by the British Parliament, it will be some time before English company law benefits from that.

PARTIAL CODIFICATION

By way of preface, Ford wrote in his first edition that, 'Company law is founded on enacted law but the legislation is not a self-sufficient code.'[150] This is as true today as when it was first written over 25 years ago: in English and Australian company law. Insofar as it deals with the duties upon directors of Australian companies, the Corporations Law is a partially codified reflection of current judicial trends; the culmination of English and Australian judicial development of those legal rules and equitable principles considered appropriate to control and regulate directorial conduct and decision-making.[151]

In spite of its daunting size,[152] the Corporations Law has achieved a reasonable and workable balance in reconciling fundamental concepts, legal rules, equitable principles and policies within the clearly stated legislative intent behind its enactment.[153] This has been achieved largely through the adoption of broad general principles which leave the law flexible and permit the courts considerable latitude in which to manoeuvre,[154] rather than by resorting to a body of rigid rules.[155] Conceptually, this is important as many of these principles are based on current mores, philosophy, economic and social conditions; and, thus, are subject to change. Australian company law encourages this as the partial codification of directors' duties is such that the general law is expressly preserved.[156]

In contrast to the statutory duty upon directors of Australian companies to exercise care and diligence in Australian company law,[157] there is no corresponding statutory provision in English company law in either the Companies Act 1985 (UK) or the Companies Act 1989 (UK); notwithstanding an earlier attempt in the Companies Bill 1978 (UK) to codify directors' duties.[158] However, it should be noted that the Law

---

[148] Department of Trade and Industry, *Modern Company Law: For a Competitive Economy* (a consultative document) HMSO, London, 1998 at paras 1.5 and 8.2-8.3.

[149] Law Commission, *Company Directors: Regulating Conflicts of Interests and Formulating a Statement of Duties* HMSO, London, Cm 4436, 1999 at para 1.7.

[150] Ford H A J, *Principles of Company Law* (1st ed) Butterworths Pty Ltd, Sydney, 1974.

[151] Cf. *State of South Australia v Clark* (1996) 19 ACSR 606 at 627 per Perry J.

[152] Ipp D A, 'The diligent director' (1997) 18 Co Law 162 at 162.

[153] Commonwealth, House of Representatives, Parliamentary Debates, 26 February 1992 at 192, 'In developing the new Corporations and Securities Legislation the aim was to balance the conflicting interests of efficient business, shareholders and creditors, civil liberties and effective law enforcement, so as to achieve a workable result.'

[154] Cf. Lloyd D, 'Codifying English Law' (1949) 2 CLP 155 at 165.

[155] *Canson Enterprises Ltd v Boughton & Co* (1992) 85 DLR (4th) 129 at 136 per La Forest J.

[156] Corporations Law s232(11); note *The Governor and Company of the Bank of England v Vagliano Brothers* [1891] AC 107 at 144-145 per Lord Herschell.

[157] Corporations Law s232(4).

[158] Department of Trade, *The Conduct of Company Directors* Cmnd 7037, 1977 at paras 2-4; note Rider B A K, 'The Conduct of Company Directors' (1978) 128 NLJ 27 at 27-28; Birds J R, 'Making Directors do their Duties' (1980) 1 Co Law 67 at 68; and Gower L C B, *Gower's Principles of Modern Company Law* (5th ed) Sweet & Maxwell Ltd, London, 1992 at 551.

Commission's recently published report entitled *Company Directors: Regulating Conflicts of Interests and Formulating a Statement of Duties*, has as one of its central recommendations that the duty upon directors of British companies to exercise care and diligence should be partially codified.[159] The Law Commission considers the case for partial codification to be a powerful one. The advantage of partial codification of directors' duties, in the Law Commission's view, is that it achieves a balance between certainty and flexibility. It is argued that this would make English company law more coherent and improve the international dimension.[160] Whilst there might be some scepticism over aspects of the report, the Law Commission's overall objectives are laudable.

The Australian approach to partial codification of the duties upon directors of Australian companies, however, should allay any concerns which English lawyers, judges and academics might have at the prospect of English company law going the same way, in the event that the Law Commission's recent recommendations in this respect are accepted, and ultimately enacted, by the British Parliament. Moreover, as the Law Commission went to some lengths in its report to stress:

> It will, however, be clear from the Act that the intention of our *partial codification* is to state the principal duties and not to alter them in any respect. As with any Act of Parliament, the courts should give effect to the meaning of the words used by Parliament. In the event of any ambiguity in the statutory statement, the courts could have regard to the general law that the statute was intended to codify.[161]

Whilst concern is expressed, from time to time, regarding the necessity for commerce to be able to operate within a legal system which is certain, and therefore predictable, and within which decisions may be made with confidence,[162] it is not possible nor, indeed, desirable to constrict equitable doctrine in such a way.[163] Because fiduciary law so dominates this area of English and Australian company law, there is a certain impossibility about codifying directors' duties.[164] There are so many matters to be taken into account that codification *per se* could not deal with them all. The Law Commission is of the view that full codification of the duties upon directors of British companies would be undesirable given that the law governing directors' duties is dynamic and continues to develop.[165] The Law Commission's reasons for this viewpoint were amplified in this manner:

---

[159] Law Commission, *Company Directors: Regulating Conflicts of Interests and Formulating a Statement of Duties* HMSO, London, Cm 4436, 1999 at paras 4.48, 5.19-5.20 and 5.38.

[160] *Ibid* at para 4.31.

[161] *Ibid* at para 4.36.

[162] *Maredelanto Compania Naviera SA v Bergbau-Handel GmbH (The Mihalis Angelos)* [1971] 1 QB 164 at 205 per Megaw LJ.

[163] Kennedy G A, 'Equity in a Commercial Context' in Finn P D (ed), *Equity and Commercial Relationships* The Law Book Company Ltd, Sydney, 1987 at 17.

[164] Beatson J, 'The Relationship Between Regulations Governing the Financial Services Industry and Fiduciary Duties under the General Law' in McKendrick E (ed), *Commercial Aspects of Trusts and Fiduciary Obligations* Clarendon Press, Oxford, 1992 at 56; and Law Commission, *Fiduciary Duties and Regulatory Rules* HMSO, London, Cm 3049, 1995 at paras 12.2 and 17.2; cf. *The Australian Financial Review*, 6 November 1995.

[165] Law Commission, *Company Directors: Regulating Conflicts of Interests and Formulating a Statement of Duties* HMSO, London, Cm 4436, 1999 at para 4.27.

We expect that the law will need to continue to evolve incrementally as circumstances require. The commercial context is constantly changing. It is important that the law retains the capacity to develop. For this reason we think that a *full codification* of directors' duties would not be desirable. To set out in statute duties that were still developing might restrict their ability to adapt to changing circumstances.[166]

Even though legislation in English and Australian company law is omnipresent and imposes multifarious duties upon directors of British and Australian companies over a wide range of issues,[167] it is considered virtually impossible for parliament to do other than provide guidance for the courts concerning the standards demanded of directors in the light of the business community's expectations.[168] The British and Australian Parliaments cannot legislate for, nor statutorily impose, corporate integrity.[169] The recent trend within Australian company law to partial codification of directors' duties recognises this.[170] Irrespective of whether or not the recent views of the Law Commission advocating the partial codification of the duty upon directors of British companies to exercise care and diligence are ultimately embraced by the British Parliament,[171] legal rules and equitable principles will continue to prove a driving force in setting, enforcing and remedying the conduct and decision-making of directors of British companies well into the next millennium. The same will be true for directors of Australian companies.[172]

THE PRE-EMINENCE OF EQUITY

English and Australian company law has long paid homage to, 'age-old principles of honesty, equity and disclosure'.[173] As a consequence, the courts of equity have always jealously guarded the fiduciary obligations owed by directors of British and Australian companies. By doing so, the courts have sought to adapt those obligations to reflect

---

[166] *Ibid* at paras 4.27-4.28.
[167] Harper J B and Browne A A, 'The Duties and Liabilities of a Director in 1973' (1973) 47 ALJ 447 at 454.
[168] During the second reading of the Corporations Legislation Amendment Bill 1991 (Cth), the Attorney-General proclaimed the need for the timely and effective enforcement of companies and securities laws to, 'clearly establish the standards of behaviour that the community is entitled to expect of its corporate directors': Commonwealth, House of Representatives, Parliamentary Debates, 29 May 1991 at 4213; cf. *The Australian Financial Review*, 6 November 1995.
[169] Cf. *Re Swift 736 Ltd* [1993] BCC 312 at 315 per Nicholls VC (Farquharson and Steyn LJJ agreed); *Re Grayan Building Services Ltd* [1995] BCC 554 at 577 per Henry LJ; and *Re Living Images Ltd* [1996] BCC 112 at 115 per Laddie J; note Farrar J H, Furey N E, Hannigan B M and Wylie P, *Farrar's Company Law* (3rd ed) Butterworth & Co (Publishers) Ltd, London, 1991 at 397; and *The Australian Financial Review*, 2 January 1996.
[170] Corporations Law s232(11); note *The Governor and Company of the Bank of England v Vagliano Brothers* [1891] AC 107 at 144-145 per Lord Herschell; and Senate Standing Committee on Legal and Constitutional Affairs, *Social and Fiduciary Duties and Obligations of Company Directors* AGPS, Canberra, 1989 at 37-38.
[171] Law Commission, *Company Directors: Regulating Conflicts of Interests and Formulating a Statement of Duties* HMSO, London, Cm 4436, 1999 at paras 4.48, 5.19-5.20 and 5.38.
[172] Cf. *Australian Securities Commission v AS Nominees Ltd* (1995) 133 ALR 1 at 6 per Finn J, 'I would note in passing that here the emphasis in legal principle will be on the law of trusts and of fiduciary obligation more so than on company law.'
[173] *Coleman v Myers* [1977] 2 NZLR 225 at 358 per Cooke J.

changes in public opinion which, after all, ultimately makes the law.[174] Equitable doctrine has come to assume a high profile within commercial and company law,[175] notwithstanding the increasing importance of British and Australian companies legislation.[176] Furthermore, it is considered that equitable doctrine will continue to play an increasingly important role in the development and refinement of company law well into the next millennium. *A fortiori* as equity continues to infiltrate commercial and corporate life,[177] and as the English and Australian courts come more and more to realise the benefits and utility of equitable doctrine in controlling, regulating and remedying directorial misconduct and decision-making.

It is important to recognise, however, that given English company law's long and distinguished pedigree, the legal rules and equitable principles which evolved from the unincorporated association or joint stock company,[178] and which developed within the context of trusts law will, at times, require to be refashioned in order to fit, and be properly applied to, the intricacies of modern commercial and corporate life. For, as the learned authors of *Snell's Principles of Equity* note, 'the prevailing judicial climate seems to favour the refinement of existing rules rather than the creation of new doctrines.'[179] However, it should be borne in mind that the rationale and philosophy underlying these traditional rules and principles may not necessarily reflect today's complex commercial and corporate requirements.[180]

Notwithstanding the statutory duty in Australian company law upon directors of Australian companies to act honestly, this area of the law remains dominated by equitable principles;[181] principles which vitally affect the directors' obligations to their Australian companies. It is evident that independently of statute, 'the law has pitched the standard of honesty very high for directors, and this has been done simply enough by regarding a director as a person who occupies a fiduciary position.'[182] Equity, as Christie notes, 'retains a primary role in ensuring that directors comply with the highest standards of conduct towards their companies.'[183] In the recent decision handed down by the Western Australian Full Court[184] in *Fitzsimmons v R*, Owen J echoed these remarks as the following extract from his Honour's judgment attests:

---

[174] Dodd E M Jr, 'For Whom are Corporate Managers Trustees?' (1931-1932) 45 Harv LR 1145 at 1160.

[175] Kennedy G A, 'Equity in a Commercial Context' in Finn P D (ed), *Equity and Commercial Relationships* The Law Book Company Ltd, Sydney, 1987 at 1; note *Australian Securities Commission v AS Nominees Ltd* (1995) 133 ALR 1 at 6 per Finn J, 'I would note in passing that here the emphasis in legal principle will be on the law of trusts and of fiduciary obligation more so than on company law.'

[176] *AWA Ltd v Daniels* (1992) 10 ACLC 933 at 1012 per Rogers CJ.

[177] Cf. *Manchester Trust v Furness* [1895] 2 QB 539 at 545 per Lindley LJ; note Goodhart W and Jones G, 'The Infiltration of Equitable Doctrine into English Commercial Law' (1980) 43 MLR 489 at 489-490.

[178] Gower L C B, 'Some Contrasts Between British and American Corporation Law' (1955-1956) 69 Harv LR 1369 at 1371-1372; note *Daniels v Anderson* (1995) 13 ACLC 614 at 656 per Clarke and Sheller JJA.

[179] Baker P V and Langan P St J, *Snell's Principles of Equity* (28th ed) Sweet & Maxwell Ltd, London, 1982 at 11.

[180] Cf. Gibson P, 'Introduction' in McKendrick E (ed), *Commercial Aspects of Trusts and Fiduciary Obligations* Clarendon Press, Oxford, 1992 at 1.

[181] Although, actionable fraud or deceit would give rise to a claim in damages at law: *Lagunas Nitrate Company v Lagunas Syndicate* [1899] 2 Ch 392 at 434-435 per Lindley MR; and *Castlereagh Motels Ltd v Davies-Roe* (1966) 67 SR (NSW) 279 at 283-284 per Wallace P and at 285 per Jacobs and Asprey JJA.

[182] Menzies D, 'Company Directors' (1959) 33 ALJ 156 at 157.

[183] Christie M, 'The Director's Fiduciary Duty not to Compete' (1992) 55 MLR 506 at 519.

[184] (Murray, Owen and Parker JJ).

It is a fundamental principle governing corporate governance that the relationship between a director and the company is a fiduciary one. The law imposes strict fiduciary and statutory obligations on a director so as to ensure high standards of loyalty in the performance of the duties of office.[185]

Throughout this book it has been argued that equity is alive and well.[186] Nowhere is this better demonstrated than in the modern application of equitable remedies,[187] refashioned by a judiciary more robust and interventionist than its predecessors, and applied in commercial and corporate circumstances considered more complex than at any earlier time.[188] Admittedly, within English and Australian company law, statutory remedies are playing an increasingly important role, but such remedies are largely procedural in nature and, thus, capable of somewhat less controversial application. In chapter eight of this book we considered some of those statutory remedies which are today available to the English and Australian courts in order to curb directorial misconduct, and to make directors of British and Australian companies more accountable and responsible for their actions and inaction. But as Finn J recently pointed out in *Australian Securities Commission v AS Nominees Ltd*, albeit there in the context of an application for a winding up order, 'the emphasis in legal principle will be on the law of trusts and of fiduciary obligation more so than on company law.'[189] Given the increasing infiltration by equity into modern commercial and corporate life,[190] when coupled with such pronouncements on the part of the English and Australian judiciary,[191] there can be little doubt that equity will retain its pre-eminence in English and Australian company law well into the next millennium.

EQUITABLE v FIDUCIARY: THERE IS A DIFFERENCE

To fully appreciate the obligations and duties upon directors of British and Australian companies within the context of this book, it is of critical importance to understand the difference between the fiduciary duties to act in good faith and for proper purposes, and the equitable and legal duties to exercise care and diligence, which arise by virtue of the

---

[185] (1997) 23 ACSR 355 at 357.

[186] Editorial comment (1994) 15 Co Law 34 at 34.

[187] *Target Holdings Ltd v Redferns* [1995] 3 All ER 785 at 795 per Lord Browne-Wilkinson (Lords Keith, Ackner, Jauncey and Lloyd agreed); note *Warman International Ltd v Dwyer* (1994-1995) 182 CLR 544 at 559 *per curiam*, 'It is necessary to keep steadily in mind the cardinal principle of equity that the remedy must be fashioned to fit the nature of the case and the particular facts.'

[188] E.g., *Equiticorp Finance Ltd v Bank of New Zealand* (1993) 11 ACLC 952; *Bishopsgate Investment Management Ltd v Maxwell (No. 2)* [1994] 1 All ER 261; *Mallina Holdings Ltd v Biala Ltd* (1994) 15 ACSR 1; and *Daniels v Anderson* (1995) 13 ACLC 614; see Sealy L S, 'Directors' "Wider" Responsibilities – Problems Conceptual, Practical and Procedural' (1987) 13 MULR 164 at 169; and Sealy L S, '"Bona Fides" and "Proper Purposes" in Corporate Decisions' (1989) 15 MULR 265 at 265.

[189] (1995) 133 ALR 1 at 6.

[190] *Royal Brunei Airlines Sdn Bhd v Tan* [1995] 2 AC 378 at 381-382 per Lord Nicholls (Lords Goff, Ackner and Steyn and Sir John May agreed); and *Bristol and West Building Society v Mothew* [1996] 4 All ER 698 at 701 per Millett LJ (Otton LJ agreed).

[191] *Chan v Zacharia* (1983-1984) 154 CLR 178 at 181 per Gibbs CJ; *United Dominions Corporation Ltd v Brian Pty Ltd* (1984-1985) 157 CLR 1 at 11 per Mason, Brennan and Deane JJ (Dawson J agreed); *Maguire v Makaronis* (1996-1997) 188 CLR 449 at 463-464 per Brennan CJ, Gaudron, McHugh and Gummow JJ; and *Westdeutsche Landesbank Girozentrale v Islington London Borough Council* [1996] AC 669 at 714-716 per Lord Browne-Wilkinson (Lord Slynn agreed).

directors' office. This difference is often neglected as the treatment by the textbooks on fiduciary law generally is superficial and lacking in areas of critical import. It is evident that little attention has been paid to the distinction which exists between equitable duties *per se* and the stricter fiduciary duties insisted upon by equity. In this respect, the following observations by Ipp J[192] in *Permanent Building Society v Wheeler* are pertinent:

> It is essential to bear in mind that the existence of a fiduciary relationship does not mean that every duty owed by a fiduciary to the beneficiary is a fiduciary duty. In particular, a trustee's duty to exercise reasonable care, though equitable, is not specifically a fiduciary duty ... Similarly ... a director's duty to exercise reasonable care, though equitable (as well as legal) is not a fiduciary obligation.[193]

In a refreshing judgment, which referred to Ipp J's remarks in *Wheeler* and which drew heavily upon other Commonwealth influence,[194] Millett LJ[195] also brought further clarity to the expression 'fiduciary duty' in *Bristol and West Building Society v Mothew*.[196] There, his Lordship emphasised the need to appreciate that there are duties peculiar to fiduciaries, the breach of which attracts legal consequences which differ from those consequent upon the breach of other duties given that, 'not every breach of duty by a fiduciary is a breach of fiduciary duty.'[197] Displaying his usual perspicuity, Millett LJ's review of the authorities led him to the view that it is inappropriate to elevate the obligation of a trustee or other fiduciary to use proper skill and care in the discharge of his duties to a fiduciary duty. As his Lordship explained, 'the fact that the source of the duty is to be found in equity rather than the common law does not make it a fiduciary duty.'[198]

As a consequence, the distinction between legal, equitable and fiduciary duties can well prove to be critical in the light of the doctrine of causation, the related issues of foreseeability and remoteness traditionally associated with general law damages,[199] and the securing of a remedy considered appropriate in the circumstances.[200]

---

[192] (Malcolm CJ and Seaman J agreed).

[193] (1993-1994) 11 WAR 187 at 237-238; note Finn P D, *Fiduciary Obligations* The Law Book Company Ltd, Sydney, 1977 at 78, 'The varying usage is unimportant provided one always recognises that a person is *not* a "fiduciary" ... until a duty applies to him. When one does, he then becomes a "fiduciary" ... but for the purposes of that duty only.'; also Sealy L S, 'Some Principles of Fiduciary Obligation' [1963] CLJ 119 at 137-140; cf. *Eromanga Hydrocarbons NL v Australis Mining NL* (1988) 6 ACLC 906 at 913 per Malcolm CJ.

[194] E.g., *Girardet v Crease & Company* (1987) 11 BCLR (2d) 361 at 362 per Southin J; and *LAC Minerals Ltd v International Corona Resources Ltd* (1989) 61 DLR (4th) 14 at 28 per La Forest J.

[195] (Otton LJ agreed).

[196] [1996] 4 All ER 698.

[197] *Ibid* at 710; see *Attorney General v Blake* [1998] 1 All ER 833 at 843 per Lord Woolf MR (Millett and Mummery LJJ agreed).

[198] *Ibid*.

[199] *Re Dawson* [1966] 2 NSWR 211 at 215-216 per Street J; note Treitel G H, *The Law of Contract* (7th ed) Sweet & Maxwell Ltd, London, 1987 at 744 *et seq*; cf. Editorial comment, 'Target hit' (1995) 16 Co Law 258 at 258.

[200] For a discussion of the relevant equitable remedies see: *Hospital Products Ltd v United States Surgical Corporation* (1984-1985) 156 CLR 41 at 107-115 per Mason J; *Mallina Holdings Ltd v Biala Ltd* (1994) 15 ACSR 1 at 48-52 *per curiam*; and Meagher R P, Gummow W M C and Lehane J R F, *Equity Doctrines and Remedies* (3rd ed) Butterworths Pty Ltd, Sydney, 1992.

CAUSATION, FORESEEABILITY AND REMOTENESS

We have seen that in English and Australian company law infractions of fiduciary obligations are considered offensive to the revered equitable principles of trust, confidence, good faith, honesty and integrity. It is qualities such as these which courts of equity have, for so long, sought to promote.[201] As La Forest J in *LAC Minerals Ltd v International Corona Resources Ltd* observed, 'The essence of the imposition of fiduciary obligations is its utility in the promotion and preservation of desired social behaviour and institutions.'[202] Equity, as appears from the judgment of Hutley JA in *Walden Properties Ltd v Beaver Properties Pty Ltd*, 'has always been a jealous guardian of the rights of the person entitled to the benefit of the performance of fiduciary duties.'[203]

As we saw in the previous chapter of this book, in fiduciary law the breach is often more contemptible than the loss thereby occasioned.[204] Hence principles of causation, foreseeability and remoteness of damage, as applied to breaches of duty at law and in equity absent fiduciary incidents, do not apply to directorial breaches of fiduciary duties.[205] Although a fiduciary, as Mason notes, 'should not be held liable for loss that does not flow from a breach of fiduciary duty'.[206] This reaffirms Davidson's view that, 'it is imperative to ascertain the loss resulting from breach of the relevant equitable duty'.[207]

Equity has not always paid the same attention to issues of causation, foreseeability and remoteness of damage which the common law regards as integral to any right of recovery, be it contractual or tortious.[208] This can be justified by reference to the preventive nature of the rules relating to fiduciaries and the historical approach by a court administering equity,[209] 'in exercise of its jurisdiction "to keep persons in a fiduciary capacity up to their duty".'[210] Not surprisingly, therefore, equitable remedies have a different focus and emphasis than do common law remedies. This viewpoint is consistent with that recently adopted in other Commonwealth jurisdictions. In *Canson Enterprises Ltd v Boughton & Co*, for instance, McLachlin J[211] pointed out that, 'equity is concerned, not only to compensate the plaintiff, but to enforce the trust which is at its heart.'[212]

---

[201] Finn P D, *Fiduciary Obligations* The Law Book Company Ltd, Sydney, 1977 at 1; and Sealy L S, '"Bona Fides"' and "Proper Purposes" in Corporate Decisions' (1989) 15 MULR 265 at 265.

[202] (1989) 61 DLR (4th) 14 at 47.

[203] [1973] 2 NSWLR 815 at 846.

[204] *Maguire v Makaronis* (1996-1997) 188 CLR 449 at 465 per Brennan CJ, Gaudron, McHugh and Gummow JJ.

[205] *Re Dawson* [1966] 2 NSWR 211 at 216 per Street J; and *Hill v Rose* [1990] VR 129 at 144 per Tadgell J.

[206] Mason A, 'The Place of Equity and Equitable Remedies in the Contemporary Common Law World' (1994) 110 LQR 238 at 244.

[207] Davidson I E, 'The Equitable Remedy of Compensation' (1982) 13 Melb ULR 349 at 354.

[208] *Swindle v Harrison* [1997] 4 All ER 705 at 715 per Evans LJ and at 733 per Mummery LJ; and *Downs v Chappell* [1996] 3 All ER 344 at 352 and 361 per Hobhouse LJ (Roch and Butler – Sloss LJJ agreed).

[209] Doyle J J, Commentary to Kearney, 'Accounting for a Fiduciary's Gains in Commercial Contexts' in Finn P D (ed), *Equity and Commercial Relationships* The Law Book Company Ltd, Sydney, 1987 at 213.

[210] *Target Holdings Ltd v Redferns* [1994] 2 All ER 337 at 353 per Peter Gibson LJ (Hirst LJ agreed); see *Nocton v Lord Ashburton* [1914] AC 932 at 963 per Lord Dunedin; and *Canson Enterprises Ltd v Boughton & Co* (1992) 85 DLR (4th) 129 at 160-161 per McLachlin J.

[211] (Lamer CJC and L'Heureux-Dubé J agreed).

[212] (1992) 85 DLR (4th) 129 at 154.

This is a complex area of English and Australian company law, and the doctrine of causation gives rise to important issues for the English and Australian courts. The spate of litigation witnessed during the 1990s has brought some of these issues sharply into focus. It is evident from our brief excursion in the previous chapter of this book into several of the more interesting and controversial cases which have recently come before the courts, that a respectable body of jurisprudence upon the doctrine of causation is being formulated. The Australian case-law is shown to constitute a most distinguished contribution to equitable jurisprudence in this regard. This is impacting upon, and coming to play an important role in, the development of English jurisprudence in this exacting area of the law.

Within Australian company law, it clearly emerges that in the case of a breach of a fiduciary duty the courts are less concerned with concepts of causation, foreseeability and remoteness, than with condemning the breach itself. Within the disapprobation of the defaulting director which follows,[213] the courts invoke suitably flexible and elastic remedies,[214] for which equity is renowned, so as to achieve restitution through *inter alia* an award of equitable compensation or through the imputation of a constructive trust.[215] The recent decision of the High Court of Australia[216] in *Maguire v Makaronis*[217] is a testament to this approach. In respect to a vain submission from the solicitors concerned that they should be excused entirely for their breach of fiduciary duty, on the basis that that had not caused any loss to their clients, Kirby J felt that a purely causative approach which relieved an errant fiduciary of liability unless it were shown that the breach of fiduciary duty caused such liability would have several disadvantages. In Kirby J's judgment:

It would undermine the *Brickenden* rule which has the advantage of simplicity and the prophylactic consequence of discouraging fiduciary default.[218] Such default is inherent in the temptations to which people in the position of fiduciaries are commonly exposed. It is a rule which helps to fulfil the purposes of equity, which are somewhat different from those of the common law. These include, relevantly, ensuring the strict loyalty[219] and good faith to beneficiaries, the dutiful enforcement of obligations; the deterrence of breaches by fiduciaries of their powers, and, where

---

[213] Cf. *Maguire v Makaronis* (1995) V Conv R 66314 at 66329 per Nathan J, 'Equity invests in fiduciaries, especially solicitors, high degrees of trust and responsibility. If breach occurs some type of retribution follows.'

[214] Cf. *Nocton v Lord Ashburton* [1914] AC 932 at 952 per Viscount Haldane LC (Lord Atkinson agreed).

[215] *Barnes v Addy* (1874) 9 Ch D 244; *Nocton v Lord Ashburton* [1914] AC 932; *Boardman v Phipps* [1967] 2 AC 46; *Consul Development Pty Ltd v D P C Estates Pty Ltd* (1974-1975) 132 CLR 373; *Chan v Zacharia* (1983-1984) 154 CLR 178; *LAC Minerals Ltd v International Corona Resources Ltd* (1989) 61 DLR (4th) 14; *Hospital Products Ltd v United States Surgical Corporation* (1984-1985) 156 CLR 41; *Attorney General for Hong Kong v Reid* [1994] 1 All ER 1; *Bishopsgate Investment Management Ltd v Maxwell (No. 2)* [1994] 1 All ER 261; *Mallina Holdings Ltd v Biala Ltd* (1994) 15 ACSR 1; *Royal Brunei Airlines Sdn Bhd v Tan* [1995] 2 AC 378; and *Target Holdings Ltd v Redferns* [1995] 3 All ER 785.

[216] (Brennan CJ, Gaudron, McHugh, Gummow and Kirby JJ).

[217] (1996-1997) 188 CLR 449.

[218] Cf. Davies P L, *Gower's Principles of Modern Company Law* (6th ed) Sweet & Maxwell Ltd, London, 1997 at 655.

[219] Cf. *Attorney General v Blake* [1998] 1 All ER 833 at 841 per Lord Woolf MR (Millett and Mummery LJJ agreed), 'Equity does not demand a duty of undivided loyalty from a former employee to his former employer, and it does not impose a duty to maintain the confidentiality of information which has ceased to be confidential.'

such occurs, the ready restitution and reinstatement of the beneficiary to the fullest extent possible.[220]

This approach on the part of the High Court of Australia seems to be a little more rigorous than that of the English judiciary at present.[221] Nonetheless, the English courts are coming to rely more and more upon Australian case-law within this context,[222] and also that from other Commonwealth jurisdictions.[223] By doing so, the English courts are displaying new levels of determination and also a measure of ingenuity in devising remedies considered appropriate to meet particular circumstances;[224] remedies which adequately reflect the court's disapprobation of the distasteful practices sometimes perpetrated by venal directors, and other fiduciaries before it.[225]

EQUITABLE REMEDIES

From the aggrieved party's perspective, the most critical aspect of company law is the achievement of an adequate remedy to best facilitate the restoration of that which is removed and compensation for that which is lost. It is axiomatic within English and Australian company law that it is for the plaintiff to choose his, her or its remedy. A plaintiff who establishes a breach of an equitable duty will have more flexibility and a broader range of remedies available than the plaintiff who must resort only to common law remedies.[226] Equity's remedies are diverse and continuing.[227] As such, the characterisation of a defendant's wrongdoing as a breach of fiduciary duty is remedy led.[228] As Doyle notes:

> [A] comparatively minor shift in the facts can move the parties from an area in which more restricted common law damages remedies are available to the area of the more ample equitable remedies.[229]

---

[220] (1996-1997) 188 CLR 449 at 492.

[221] Finn P D, 'Fiduciary Law and the Modern Commercial World' in McKendrick E (ed), *Commercial Aspects of Trusts and Fiduciary Obligations* Clarendon Press, Oxford, 1992 at 40; note Aitken L, 'Developments in Equitable Compensation: Opportunity or Danger?' (1993) 67 ALJ 596 at 596; and Rickett C E F, 'Equitable Compensation: The Giant Stirs' (1996) 112 LQR 27 at 29.

[222] E.g., *Re Dawson* [1966] 2 NSWR 211 at 215 per Street J; and *Permanent Building Society v Wheeler* (1993-1994) 11 WAR 187 at 237-238 per Ipp J (Malcolm CJ and Seaman J agreed).

[223] E.g., *Girardet v Crease & Company* (1987) 11 BCLR (2d) 361 at 362 per Southin J; and *LAC Minerals Ltd v International Corona Resources Ltd* (1989) 61 DLR (4th) 14 at 28 per La Forest J.

[224] *Westdeutsche Landesbank Girozentrale v Islington London Borough Council* [1996] AC 669 at 716 per Lord Browne-Wilkinson (Lord Slynn agreed).

[225] E.g., *Attorney General v Blake* [1998] 1 All ER 833; and *Royal Brunei Airlines Sdn Bhd v Tan* [1995] 2 AC 378.

[226] Cf. *Canson Enterprises Ltd v Boughton & Co* (1992) 85 DLR (4th) 129 at 153 per La Forest J, 'It would be wholly inappropriate to interpret equitable doctrines so technically as to displace common law rules that achieve substantial justice in areas of common concern, thereby leading to harsh and inequitable results.'

[227] *Gemstone Corporation of Australia Ltd v Grasso* (1994) 12 ACLC 653 at 658 per Prior J; see *Day v Mead* [1987] 2 NZLR 443 at 451 per Cooke P.

[228] *Attorney General v Blake* [1998] 1 All ER 833 at 841 per Lord Woolf MR (Millett and Mummery LJJ agreed).

[229] Doyle J J, Commentary to Kearney, 'Accounting for a Fiduciary's Gains in Commercial Contexts' in Finn P D (ed), *Equity and Commercial Relationships* The Law Book Company Ltd, Sydney, 1987 at 212.

This highlights the significance of the special relationship cases, and the partnership and joint venture cases, where the facts can give rise to fiduciary obligations with consequent equitable remedies;[230] and further highlights the distinction made earlier in this chapter between the several duties which may exist within a fiduciary relationship, but which may not, necessarily, excite equitable relief.[231] The propriety of bringing actions based upon allegations that fiduciary obligations have not been met, and the frequency with which such actions are now being brought, was recently addressed by Lord Nicholls in *Royal Brunei Airlines Sdn Bhd v Tan* where his Lordship expressed the following opinion on behalf of the Privy Council:

> The proper role of equity in commercial transactions is a topical question. Increasingly plaintiffs have recourse to equity for an effective remedy when the person in default, typically a company, is insolvent. Plaintiffs seek to obtain relief from others who were involved in the transaction, such as directors of the company, or its bankers, or its legal or other advisers. They seek to fasten fiduciary obligations directly onto the company's officers or agents or advisers, or to have them held personally liable for assisting the company in breaches of trust or fiduciary obligations.[232]

Equity's remedies are flexible and elastic.[233] As we have seen their application is strict so as to, 'keep persons in a fiduciary capacity up to their duty'.[234] It is a long established principle that should the improper exercise of directorial powers cause loss to the company, the directors concerned will be liable personally to compensate the company on the same basis that trustees are liable personally to restore trust property lost in breach of trust.[235] The breach of a fiduciary duty attracts equitable remedies of a personal or proprietary nature considered appropriate to bring the defaulting fiduciary to account.[236] Notable among these remedies are constructive trusts and equitable compensation. These have both received attention from English and Australian courts at the highest level.[237]

[230] E.g., *Allen v Hyatt* (1914) 30 TLR 444; *Coleman v Myers* [1977] 2 NZLR 225; *Glandon Pty Ltd v Strata Consolidated Pty Ltd* (1993) 11 ACSR 543; *Hospital Products Ltd v United States Surgical Corporation* (1984-1985) 156 CLR 41; *Fraser Edmiston Pty Ltd v AGT (QLD) Pty Ltd* [1988] 2 Qd R 1; *Chan v Zacharia* (1983-1984) 154 CLR 178; and *Mallina Holdings Ltd v Biala Ltd* (1994) 15 ACSR 1; see Rider B A K, 'Partnership Law and its Impact on "Domestic Companies"' [1979] CLJ 148; and McPherson B H, 'Joint Ventures' in Finn P D (ed), *Equity and Commercial Relationships* The Law Book Company Ltd, Sydney, 1987 at 19 *et seq*.

[231] *Permanent Building Society v Wheeler* (1993-1994) 11 WAR 187 at 237-238 per Ipp J (Malcolm CJ and Seaman J agreed); and *Bristol and West Building Society v Mothew* [1996] 4 All ER 698 at 710 per Millett LJ (Otton LJ agreed).

[232] [1995] 2 AC 378 at 381-382.

[233] *Nocton v Lord Ashburton* [1914] AC 932 at 952 per Viscount Haldane LC (Lord Atkinson agreed); see Sealy L S, 'Some Principles of Fiduciary Obligation' [1963] CLJ 119 at 137-140; and Shepherd J C, 'Towards a Unified Concept of Fiduciary Relationships' (1981) 97 LQR 51 at 77.

[234] *Nocton v Lord Ashburton* [1914] AC 932 at 963 per Lord Dunedin.

[235] *In re Lands Allotment Company* [1894] 1 Ch 616 at 631 per Lindley LJ and at 638 per Kay LJ; cf. *Clough v Bond* (1838) 3 My & Cr 490 at 497 per Lord Cottenham LC.

[236] Kearney J B, 'Accounting for a Fiduciary's Gains in Commercial Contexts' in Finn P D (ed), *Equity and Commercial Relationships* The Law Book Company Ltd, Sydney, 1987 at 187; note *Warman International Ltd v Dwyer* (1994-1995) 182 CLR 544 at 563 *per curiam*.

[237] *Barnes v Addy* (1874) 9 Ch D 244; *Nocton v Lord Ashburton* [1914] AC 932; *Boardman v Phipps* [1967] 2 AC 46; *Consul Development Pty Ltd v D P C Estates Pty Ltd* (1974-1975) 132 CLR 373; *Chan v Zacharia* (1983-1984) 154 CLR 178; *LAC Minerals Ltd v International Corona Resources Ltd* (1989) 61 DLR (4th) 14; *Hospital Products Ltd v United States Surgical Corporation* (1984-1985) 156 CLR

The decision by the Privy Council[238] in *Attorney General for Hong Kong v Reid*,[239] provides a dazzling example of the effect and import of constructive trusts within equity's impressive array of remedies for the breach of a fiduciary duty. The decision highlights the utility and appeal of constructive trusts and affords them a prominence within the law of remedies.[240] The decision also provides a salutary reminder to errant directors of equity's flexibility and tenacity in providing remedies capable of thwarting directorial misdeeds by, if necessary, tracing the proceeds of ill-gotten gains into a third party's hands, or into property.[241] Moreover, the following passage from Lord Browne-Wilkinson's speech to the House of Lords in *Westdeutsche Landesbank Girozentrale v Islington London Borough Council* reaffirms that the English courts are determined to recover ill-gotten gains wherever reasonably possible, and the pre-eminent role which constructive trusts will come to enjoy in that respect:

> I agree that the stolen moneys are traceable in equity. But the proprietary interest which equity is enforcing in such circumstances arises under a constructive, not a resulting, trust. Although it is difficult to find clear authority for the proposition, when property is obtained by fraud equity imposes a constructive trust on the fraudulent recipient: the property is recoverable and traceable in equity.[242]

As the learned editor of *The Company Lawyer* recently opined, 'English judges have never been particularly enthusiastic about the prospect of those who have benefited by virtue of an unlawful act, whether amounting to a civil or a criminal wrong, retaining the fruits of their labours.'[243] The recent decision of the Privy Council[244] in *Royal Brunei*[245] is a case in point. It provides a useful insight into equity's ability to not only arrest egregious behaviour on the part of a fiduciary, and provide an appropriate remedy to recover assets in the hands of an undeserving third party, but also to recover from a third party even though no trust property actually reached his, her or its hands.

The decision by the Privy Council in *Reid*,[246] and the willingness of the English and Australian courts to impute a constructive trust in appropriate circumstances which the various judgments in *Chan v Zacharia*,[247] *United Dominions Corporation Ltd v Brian Pty Ltd*,[248] *Royal Brunei*,[249] *Maguire v Makaronis*[250] and *Westdeutsche*,[251] by way of

cont.

41; *Attorney General for Hong Kong v Reid* [1994] 1 All ER 1; *Bishopsgate Investment Management Ltd v Maxwell (No. 2)* [1994] 1 All ER 261; *Mallina Holdings Ltd v Biala Ltd* (1994) 15 ACSR 1; *Royal Brunei Airlines Sdn Bhd v Tan* [1995] 2 AC 378; and *Target Holdings Ltd v Redferns* [1995] 3 All ER 785.

[238] (Lords Templeman, Goff, Lowry and Lloyd and Sir Thomas Eichelbaum).
[239] [1994] 1 All ER 1 (on appeal from the Court of Appeal of New Zealand).
[240] Boyle A J, 'Attorney-General v Reid: the company law implications' (1995) 16 Co Law 131 at 133; cf. *Glavanics v Brunninghausen* (1996) 19 ACSR 204 at 225 per Bryson J.
[241] *Sinclair v Brougham* [1914] AC 398; cf. *El Ajou v Dollar Land Holdings plc* [1993] 3 All ER 717 and [1994] 2 All ER 685; and *El Ajou v Dollar Land Holdings plc (No. 2)* [1995] 2 All ER 213; note Nolan R, 'Arabian's rights' (1994) 15 Co Law 148; cf. Mountfort A G, 'Tracing: An Examination of the Applicability of Tracing Principles Today' (1996) 70 ALJ 54.
[242] [1996] AC 669 at 716.
[243] Editorial comment, 'There and back again!' (1998) 19 Co Law 97 at 97.
[244] (Lords Goff, Ackner, Nicholls and Steyn and Sir John May).
[245] [1995] 2 AC 378 (on appeal from the Court of Appeal of Brunei Darussalam).
[246] [1994] 1 All ER 1.
[247] (1983-1984) 154 CLR 178 at 181 per Gibbs CJ.
[248] (1984-1985) 157 CLR 1 at 11 per Mason, Brennan and Deane JJ (Dawson J agreed).

example, clearly contemplate, have significant ramifications for English and Australian company law. Such an approach is demonstrative of a determination that constructive trusts will be better, and more frequently,[252] utilised by future English and Australian courts in a range of circumstances not hitherto considered appropriate.[253] This serves to remind us of equity's vitality and penetration into areas not normally reached by the common law.

A MORE INTERVENTIONIST APPROACH BY THE COURTS?

As we have seen throughout this book, the Australian judges have become far more interventionist than their predecessors.[254] As a consequence, in the last decade or so, corporate Australia has witnessed a dramatic tightening up of directorial responsibility and increased accountability, and the way in which directors of Australian companies are now required to go about their business.[255] The English judges on the other hand seem to have been a little more reticent in this respect. Although the recent cases do suggest a redefinition of traditional values in the context of a modern commercial and corporate setting. This strongly favours increased levels of responsibilities and greater accountability on the part of directors of British companies.[256] In the light of this, the following concerns recently identified by the learned editor of *The Company Lawyer* are increasingly likely to be met:

> That high standards of directors should be enforced by the law we accept as funda-
> mental. If an individual accepts that office and if there is then a failure in those
> standards, the office of director should not be available to that individual. Accord-
> ingly, it is important to ensure that those who become directors understand that they
> contribute to major decisions, are obliged to take an overview and are obliged to
> receive and have regard to information to enable them to take decisions.[257]

---

cont.

[249] [1995] 2 AC 378 at 381-382 per Lord Nicholls (Lords Goff, Ackner and Steyn and Sir John May agreed).

[250] (1996-1997) 188 CLR 449 at 463-464 per Brennan CJ, Gaudron, McHugh and Gummow JJ.

[251] [1996] AC 669 at 714-716 per Lord Browne-Wilkinson (Lord Slynn agreed).

[252] Pascoe J, 'Equitable Remedies in Cases of Misapplied Company Funds: Recent Developments' (1996) 14 CSLJ 393 at 404.

[253] Rickett C E F, 'Equitable Compensation: The Giant Stirs' (1996) 112 LQR 27 at 29-30.

[254] *Kokotovich Constructions Pty Ltd v Wallington* (1995) 13 ACLC 1113 at 1125 per Kirby ACJ (Priestley and Handley JJA agreed), '[Whilst] Courts should hesitate before interfering with management decisions which have been reached bona fide … this principle is of no application where, as in this case, the management decision was not *bona fide* arrived at. Indeed, it would be absurd to suggest that a court should forsake its responsibility to uphold the law in such a situation. If a director breaches his or her fiduciary duty in exercising a power for an improper purpose, not only is it desirable that the courts should intervene. They have a duty to do so.'

[255] In a line of authority which relevantly began with *Darvall v North Sydney Brick & Tile Co Ltd (No. 2)* (1989) 7 ACLC 659 through to the recent decision in *Daniels v Anderson* (1995) 13 ACLC 614.

[256] *Bishopsgate Investment Management Ltd v Maxwell (No. 2)* [1994] 1 All ER 261 at 264 per Hoffmann LJ (Leggatt LJ agreed) who recognised that the law, 'may be evolving in response to changes in public attitudes to corporate governance'; and *Re Grayan Building Services Ltd* [1995] BCC 554 at 577 per Henry LJ, 'The statutory corporate climate is stricter than it has ever been, and those enforcing it should reflect the fact that Parliament has seen the need for higher standards.'

[257] Editorial comment, 'Directors – true or false?' (1997) 18 Co Law 129 at 129.

In such circumstances, and for such reasons, challenges are now being made to the English and the Australian judiciary's traditional approach of non-intervention with the internal management of companies.[258] It is considered that today's judges should be more alert for ulterior purposes of private advantage than were their predecessors. They should be prepared to intervene and interdict by reference to the real purposes which primarily motivate directors' actions. Statements by directors of British and Australian companies about their subjective intention, whilst relevant, are no longer conclusive of their *bona fides* or of the purposes for which they acted as they did.[259] It is suggested that the days when directors could shield themselves from scrutiny by asserting that they acted honestly and with good intention are gone.[260] Today's Australian courts, probably more so than their English counterparts, are more inclined to vigilance and to subject such purposes to analysis to see whether or not they should be accepted.[261] Kirby P in *Darvall v North Sydney Brick & Tile Co Ltd (No. 2)* put the proposition in this way:

> Directors of corporations cannot immure themselves from a scrutiny of their purposes by asserting that they acted honestly and with good intention for this or that legitimate purpose. The purpose may be scrutinised by a court to see if this assertion should be accepted. The directors cannot, by donning blinkers, ignore the plain facts disclosed to them and then assert that they acted bona fide in the best interests of the company. A more rigorous standard of conduct is required by the law.[262]

With the pre-eminence of the proper purposes doctrine, and its current resurgence in popularity with the English and Australian courts,[263] it is considered likely that the judiciary will become more vigilant and more involved in reviewing directors' decision-making in order to determine whether in fact decisions which directors assert on oath, as having been made *bona fide* in the interests of the company as a whole, accord with a strict application of the proper purposes doctrine.[264] Mere assertion of subjective honesty will no longer be considered enough to hold the day.[265]

---

[258] *Carlen v Drury* (1812) 1 V & B 154 at 158 per Lord Eldon; *Burland v Earle* [1902] AC 83 at 93 per Lord Davey; *Shuttleworth v Cox Brothers and Company (Maidenhead) Ltd* [1927] 2 KB 9 at 23 per Scrutton LJ; *Howard Smith Ltd v Ampol Petroleum Ltd* [1974] AC 821 at 832 per Lord Wilberforce; and *Harlowe's Nominees Pty Ltd v Woodside (Lakes Entrance) Oil Company NL* (1969-1970) 121 CLR 483 at 493 *per curiam;* note Sealy L S, 'The Director as Trustee' [1967] CLJ 83 at 100-101; and Editorial comment, 'Directors – true or false?' (1997) 18 Co Law 129 at 129.

[259] *Permanent Building Society v Wheeler* (1993-1994) 11 WAR 187 at 218 per Ipp J (Malcolm CJ and Seaman J agreed); and *Bishopsgate Investment Management Ltd v Maxwell (No. 2)* [1994] 1 All ER 261 at 268-269 per Ralph Gibson LJ.

[260] *Darvall v North Sydney Brick & Tile Co Ltd (No. 2)* (1989) 7 ACLC 659 at 679 per Kirby P.

[261] *Advance Bank Australia Ltd v FAI Insurances Ltd* (1987) 5 ACLC 725 at 742-743 per Kirby P (Glass JA agreed); and *Kokotovich Constructions Pty Ltd v Wallington* (1995) 13 ACLC 1113 at 1123-1125 per Kirby ACJ (Priestley and Handley JJA agreed).

[262] (1989) 7 ACLC 659 at 679.

[263] *Gambotto v WCP Ltd* (1995) 13 ACLC 342; *Kokotovich Constructions Pty Ltd v Wallington* (1995) 13 ACLC 1113; *Bishopsgate Investment Management Ltd v Maxwell (No. 2)* [1994] 1 All ER 261; and *Re BSB Holdings Ltd (No. 2)* [1996] 1 BCLC 155.

[264] *Kokotovich Constructions Pty Ltd v Wallington* (1995) 13 ACLC 1113 at 1125 per Kirby ACJ (Priestley and Handley JJA agreed).

[265] *Permanent Building Society v Wheeler* (1993-1994) 11 WAR 187 at 218 per Ipp J (Malcolm CJ and Seaman J agreed); and *Bishopsgate Investment Management Ltd v Maxwell (No. 2)* [1994] 1 All ER 261 at 268-269 per Ralph Gibson LJ.

Although the cases are replete with caveats reminding judges not to second guess business decisions,[266] when faced with allegations that those business decisions are improper, more and more are today's judges obliged to test those decisions against objective criteria.[267] It is inevitable that that will require the directors of British and Australian companies whose decisions are under attack to give evidence of their subjective intentions in that regard. That in turn obliges judges to step upon dangerous ground for proper purposes focuses upon the decision itself and, 'calls for a more interventionist line, reviewing the business judgments of business men.'[268] The decision in *Kokotovich Constructions Pty Ltd v Wallington* is apposite as the following extract from the judgment of Kirby ACJ[269] amply attests:

> [Whilst] Courts should hesitate before interfering with management decisions which have been reached bona fide ... this principle is of no application where, as in this case, the management decision was not *bona fide* arrived at. Indeed, it would be absurd to suggest that a court should forsake its responsibility to uphold the law in such a situation. If a director breaches his or her fiduciary duty in exercising a power for an improper purpose, not only is it desirable that the courts should intervene. They have a duty to do so.[270]

But as Ipp J[271] in *Permanent Building Society v Wheeler* reminded us, the issue is, 'not whether a management decision was good or bad; it is whether the directors acted in breach of their fiduciary duties.'[272] That involves an inquiry into, and a determination of, whether but for the improper purpose the directors would have performed the act impugned.[273] It is suggested that tomorrow's English and Australian courts will be increasingly prepared to conduct such an inquiry.

COMMERCIAL PRAGMATISM

Rogers CJ observed in *AWA Ltd v Daniels* that modern companies legislation has, 'evolved in response to the demands of changing company structures and commercial practices.'[274] The legal rules and equitable principles which breathe life into British and

---

[266] *Equiticorp Finance Ltd v Bank of New Zealand* (1993) 11 ACLC 952 at 977 per Kirby P; note *The Times*, 21 July 1999.

[267] *Androvin v Figliomeni* (1996) 14 ACLC 1461 at 1470 per Owen J (Kennedy and Franklyn JJ agreed); *Daniels v Anderson* (1995) 13 ACLC 614 at 662 per Clarke and Sheller JJA; *Lyford v Commonwealth Bank of Australia* (1995) 13 ACLC 900 at 914 per R D Nicholson J; *Carter v Drake* (1992-1993) 9 WAR 82 at 94 per Malcolm CJ; and V*risakis v Australian Securities Commission* (1992-1993) 9 WAR 395 at 451 per Ipp J (Malcolm CJ agreed).

[268] Sealy L S, 'Company – Directors' Unconstitutional Acts' [1992] CLJ 229 at 229.

[269] (Priestley and Handley JJA agreed).

[270] (1995) 13 ACLC 1113 at 1125.

[271] (Malcolm CJ and Seaman J agreed).

[272] (1993-1994) 11 WAR 187 at 218; see *Japan Abrasive Materials Pty Ltd v Australian Fused Materials Pty Ltd* (1998) 16 ACLC 1172 at 1180 per Templeman J; cf. *Carter v Drake* (1992-1993) 9 WAR 82 at 94-95 per Malcolm CJ; *Mills v Mills* (1938) 60 CLR 150 at 185 per Dixon J; and *Howard Smith Ltd v Ampol Petroleum Ltd* [1974] AC 821 at 838 per Lord Wilberforce.

[273] *Darvall v North Sydney Brick & Tile Co Ltd (No. 2)* (1989) 7 ACLC 659 at 676 per Kirby P; and *Kokotovich Constructions Pty Ltd v Wallington* (1995) 13 ACLC 1113 at 1124 per Kirby ACJ (Priestley and Handley JJA agreed).

[274] (1992) 10 ACLC 933 at 1013.

Australian companies legislation must do likewise.[275] In the application of refashioned legal rules and equitable principles to today's complex commercial and corporate disputes, the English and the Australian judiciary would be well-advised to adopt a common sense approach to the question of remedies and company law in general. Such an approach is in keeping with that enunciated by the House of Lords in *Target Holdings Ltd v Redferns*,[276] and by the High Court of Australia in *March v E & M H Stramare Pty Ltd*,[277] and that applied by the Western Australian Full Court in *Mallina Holdings Ltd v Biala Ltd*.[278] By doing so, a measure of commercial pragmatism will be brought to bear upon the resolution of today's complex commercial and corporate disputes[279] in a way which accords with modern ideals of corporate governance,[280] and which promotes confidence in English and Australian company law by the application of accessible, fair, reasonable and workable remedies.

Commercial pragmatism, or the 'commercial reality principle' as Malcolm labels it,[281] is more and more proving a decisive factor in the resolution of complex commercial and corporate disputes which so dominate today's Australian corporate sector.[282] The approach favoured by the New South Wales Court of Appeal[283] in *Equiticorp Finance Ltd v Bank of New Zealand*[284] is fitting.[285] However, whilst there are benefits which flow from a pragmatic approach, one needs to ensure that there is no debasement to the integrity of English and Australian company law, and that companies operate according to the law.[286] Kirby P sought to preserve that ideal in *Equiticorp* and was quick to point out that:

---

[275] Menzies D, 'Company Directors' (1959) 33 ALJ 156 at 165.

[276] [1995] 3 All ER 785 at 798 per Lord Browne-Wilkinson (Lords Keith, Ackner, Jauncey and Lloyd agreed).

[277] (1990-1991) 171 CLR 506.

[278] (1994) 15 ACSR 1.

[279] *Equiticorp Finance Ltd v Bank of New Zealand* (1993) 11 ACLC 952 at 1019 per Clarke and Cripps JJA; *Glandon Pty Ltd v Strata Consolidated Pty Ltd* (1993) 11 ACSR 543 at 547-548 per Mahoney JA; *Bishopsgate Investment Management Ltd v Maxwell (No. 2)* [1994] 1 All ER 261; *Mallina Holdings Ltd v Biala Ltd* (1994) 15 ACSR 1; and *Daniels v Anderson* (1995) 13 ACLC 614; see Sealy L S, 'Directors' "Wider" Responsibilities – Problems Conceptual, Practical and Procedural' (1987) 13 MULR 164 at 169; and Sealy L S, '"Bona Fides" and "Proper Purposes" in Corporate Decisions' (1989) 15 MULR 265 at 265.

[280] See Committee on the Financial Aspects of Corporate Governance, *The Report of the Committee on the Financial Aspects of Corporate Governance* Gee and Co Ltd, London, 1992; cf. The American Law Institute, *Principles of Corporate Governance: Analysis and Recommendations* St Paul, 1994; Stapledon G P, *Institutional Shareholders and Corporate Governance* Clarendon Press, Oxford, 1996 at 8; Farrar J H, 'Corporate Governance, Business Judgement and the Professionalism of Directors' (1993) 6 CBLJ 1 at 2; and Whincop M J, 'An Economic Analysis of the Criminalisation and Content of Directors' Duties' (1996) 24 ABLR 273 at 277 and 291.

[281] Malcolm D, 'Directors' Duties: The Governing Principles' in Ramsay I M (ed), *Corporate Governance and the Duties of Company Directors* The Centre for Corporate Law and Securities Regulation, University of Melbourne, Parkville, 1997 at 60.

[282] *Gray Eisdell Timms Pty Ltd v Combined Auctions Pty Ltd* (1995) 13 ACLC 965 at 974 per Young J; cf. Muir G, 'Contract and Equity: Striking a Balance' (1985) 10 Adel LR 153 at 183, 'But pragmatism must not always triumph over principle'.

[283] (Kirby P, Clarke and Cripps JJA).

[284] (1993) 11 ACLC 952; see Baxt R, 'Duties to a Corporate Group – One Step Forward or Two Steps Backwards?' (1994) 22 ABLR 138.

[285] (1993) 11 ACLC 952 at 1019 per Clarke and Cripps JJA.

[286] *Gray Eisdell Timms Pty Ltd v Combined Auctions Pty Ltd* (1995) 13 ACLC 965 at 974 per Young J; cf. Muir G, 'Contract and Equity: Striking a Balance' (1985) 10 Adel LR 153 at 183, 'But pragmatism must not always triumph over principle'.

The law has not yet come to the point of ignoring the requirements of due formality. Such requirements are protective of shareholders, creditors, employees and the community. The suggested imperative of 'realism' and the *Realpolitik* of corporate control does not authorize courts to ride roughshod over the due observance of company law.[287]

In the continued quest for higher standards this approach will become the norm, rather than the exception, as English and Australian judges take a more commercial and pragmatic approach to the duties owed by directors of British and Australian companies,[288] in keeping with the business community's aspirations.[289] This trend is evident from, for example, the way in which the English and the Australian judiciary are reassessing the proper purposes doctrine. We saw that in chapters four and five of this book. By doing so, the English and the Australian judiciary are tending to favour the promotion of commercial certainty, tempered with a degree of commercial pragmatism,[290] in the light of the business community's expectations,[291] in order to resolve today's complex commercial and corporate disputes.[292] It can be argued, therefore, that the old values and traditions are no longer enough, and that a fresh approach is required to the complex and challenging topic of directors' duties in modern company law. This is being gradually embraced by the English and Australian courts, and also by the British and Australian Parliaments, and will have profound implications for directors of British and Australian companies of the 21st century.

EPILOGUE

Whilst there are many loose threads throughout this book, no apology is offered for not better drawing them together. To draw all these loose threads together would be a task of *Sisyphean* proportion. A task made all the more difficult in modern English and Australian company law by the impossibility of formulating a rule of universal application to the duties upon directors of British and Australian companies, given that different conduct on the part of directors will be required in order to meet different situations.[293] The rigours of today's commercial and corporate world place exacting

---

[287] (1993) 11 ACLC 952 at 979; cf. *Brady v Brady* (1987) 3 BCC 535 at 552-553 per Nourse LJ, 'But there is a higher principle at stake, which is that the formalities of company law must be rigorously upheld.'

[288] Malcolm D, 'Directors' Duties: The Governing Principles' in Ramsay I M (ed), *Corporate Governance and the Duties of Company Directors* The Centre for Corporate Law and Securities Regulation, University of Melbourne, Parkville, 1997 at 60, 78 and 80.

[289] Baxt R, 'The Role and Responsibilities of Nominee Directors in a Contested Takeover' a paper presented at the Corporate Law Workshop, conducted by the Business Law Section of the Law Council of Australia, Melbourne, October 1993 at 66.

[290] *Gray Eisdell Timms Pty Ltd v Combined Auctions Pty Ltd* (1995) 13 ACLC 965 at 974 per Young J; cf. Muir G, 'Contract and Equity: Striking a Balance' (1985) 10 Adel LR 153 at 183, 'But pragmatism must not always triumph over principle'.

[291] *Equiticorp Finance Ltd v Bank of New Zealand* (1993) 11 ACLC 952 at 1019 per Clarke and Cripps JJA.

[292] E.g., *Equiticorp Finance Ltd v Bank of New Zealand* (1993) 11 ACLC 952; *Bishopsgate Investment Management Ltd v Maxwell (No. 2)* [1994] 1 All ER 261; *Mallina Holdings Ltd v Biala Ltd* (1994) 15 ACSR 1; and *Daniels v Anderson* (1995) 13 ACLC 614; see Sealy L S, 'Directors' "Wider" Responsibilities – Problems Conceptual, Practical and Procedural' (1987) 13 MULR 164 at 169; and Sealy L S, '"Bona Fides" and "Proper Purposes" in Corporate Decisions' (1989) 15 MULR 265 at 265.

[293] *Gould v The Mount Oxide Mines Ltd* (1916-1917) 22 CLR 490 at 531 per Isaacs and Rich JJ; see *Vrisakis v Australian Securities Commission* (1992-1993) 9 WAR 395 at 404 per Malcolm CJ.

demands upon British and Australian companies and those who manage them.[294] It is inevitable that the proper performance of directors' duties will be dictated by a host of circumstances;[295] circumstances impossible, and inappropriate, to catalogue given the need for directors to be able to adjust to their company's peculiarities, needs and requirements.[296]

This book has sought to demonstrate that over time the public's, and the business community's, expectations of directors of British and Australian companies are being gradually realised. There is no doubt, in Malcolm's view, 'that the bar has been raised in accordance with changing expectations, both in the community and in the commercial world.'[297] It seems that Menzies' oft quoted prophecy that, 'what is in general expected of directors will tend to become the measure of what is required of them',[298] has become self-fulfilling. *A fortiori* within the context of insolvency, but increasingly outside that context as well.[299] In reference to this observation by Menzies, Tadgell J in *Commonwealth Bank of Australia v Friedrich* noted that this has been borne out over the years and that as the complexity of commerce has gradually intensified:

> [The] community has of necessity come to expect more than formerly from directors whose task it is to govern the affairs of companies ... In response, the parliaments and the courts have found it necessary in legislation and litigation to refer to the demands made on directors in more exacting terms than formerly; and the standard of capability required of them has correspondingly increased.[300]

This book has also sought to highlight some of the judicial and legislative steps which have been recently taken by the English and Australian courts, and by the British and Australian Parliaments, to actually raise levels of responsibility and accountability of directors of British and Australian companies more in keeping with contemporary public sentiment and the business community's aspirations.[301] These judicial and legislative steps are designed to restore corporate integrity to the benefit of those millions of men and women in England and in Australia whose lives are affected by,

---

[294] *Deputy Commissioner of Taxation v Austin* (1998) 16 ACLC 1555 at 1559 per Madgwick J; cf. *Canadian Aero Service Ltd v O'Malley* (1974) 40 DLR (3d) 371 at 381 per Laskin J.

[295] *Commonwealth Bank of Australia v Friedrich* (1991) 5 ACSR 115 at 125 per Tadgell J; and *Howard Smith Ltd v Ampol Petroleum Ltd* [1974] AC 821 at 835 per Lord Wilberforce.

[296] *Statewide Tobacco Services Ltd v Morley* (1990) 2 ACSR 405 at 431 per Ormiston J.

[297] Malcolm D, 'Directors' Duties: The Governing Principles' in Ramsay I M (ed), *Corporate Governance and the Duties of Company Directors* The Centre for Corporate Law and Securities Regulation, University of Melbourne, Parkville, 1997 at 78.

[298] Menzies D, 'Company Directors' (1959) 33 ALJ 156 at 164.

[299] E.g., *Norman v Theodore Goddard* [1992] BCC 14 at 15 per Hoffmann J; V*risakis v Australian Securities Commission* (1992-1993) 9 WAR 395 at 451 per Ipp J (Malcolm CJ agreed); *Daniels v Anderson* (1995) 13 ACLC 614 at 662 per Clarke and Sheller JJA; *Androvin v Figliomeni* (1996) 14 ACLC 1461 at 1470 per Owen J (Kennedy and Franklyn JJ agreed); and *Re Barings plc* [1998] BCC 583 at 586 per Sir Richard Scott VC.

[300] (1991) 5 ACSR 115 at 126.

[301] See Prentice D D and Holland P R J, *Contemporary Issues in Corporate Governance* Oxford University Press, Oxford, 1993; Committee on the Financial Aspects of Corporate Governance, *The Report of the Committee on the Financial Aspects of Corporate Governance* Gee and Co Ltd, London, 1992; Farrar J H, 'Corporate Governance, Business Judgement and the Professionalism of Directors' (1993) 6 CBLJ 1; Whincop M J, 'An Economic Analysis of the Criminalisation and Content of Directors' Duties' (1996) 24 ABLR 273; and Stapledon G P, *Institutional Shareholders and Corporate Governance* Clarendon Press, Oxford, 1996.

and are dependent upon, a set of rules and principles facilitative of a duly regulated and properly enforced system of company law.[302]

English and Australian company law provides a compendium of legal, equitable and statutory duties and remedies capable of enforcing and remedying directors' conduct and decision-making. Within the context of this book, it is considered that Australian company law in particular, with its morass of legal rules, equitable principles and statutory enactment, all operating within the legislative framework of the Corporations Law, goes a considerable distance towards achieving a duly regulated and properly enforced system of company law. English company law, on the other hand, is lagging some way behind. There is a gap. However, if the recent initiatives and recommendations of the Law Commission are embraced by the British Parliament,[303] and if the DTI's fundamental review of core company law is conducted thoroughly and extensively and within its timetable,[304] and permits of fresh ideas and thinking beyond the traditional model, then there is no reason why the first decade of the 21st century ought not see English company law prosper and close that gap. But in order to do so, it is incumbent upon the English courts and the British Parliament to accept that classical theories that were once unchallengable, 'must yield to the facts of modern life.'[305]

---

[302] *The Sunday Times*, 25 April 1999; cf. *The Australian*, 23 April 1997; note Department of Trade and Industry, *Modern Company Law: The Strategic Framework* HMSO, London, 1999 at para 5.1.14; Department of Trade and Industry, *Modern Company Law: For a Competitive Economy* (a consultative document) HMSO, London, 1998 at i and at para 3.7; HM Treasury, *Financial Services and Markets Bill: A Consultation Document, Part One* HMSO, London, 1998 at foreword; Committee on the Financial Aspects of Corporate Governance, *The Report of the Committee on the Financial Aspects of Corporate Governance* Gee and Co Ltd, London, 1992 at para 1.1; and Senate Standing Committee on Legal and Constitutional Affairs, *Social and Fiduciary Duties and Obligations of Company Directors* AGPS, Canberra, 1989 at 7.

[303] Law Commission, *Company Directors: Regulating Conflicts of Interests and Formulating a Statement of Duties* HMSO, London, Cm 4436, 1999 at paras 4.48, 5.19-5.20 and 5.38.

[304] Department of Trade and Industry, *Modern Company Law: For a Competitive Economy* (a consultative document) HMSO, London, 1998; and Department of Trade and Industry, *Modern Company Law: The Strategic Framework* HMSO, London, 1999.

[305] *Teck Corporation Ltd v Millar* (1972) 33 DLR (3d) 288 at 314 per Berger J.

Select Bibliography

Aitken L, 'Developments in Equitable Compensation: Opportunity or Danger?' (1993) 67 ALJ 596

Alcock A, 'Insider dealing – how did we get here?' (1994) 15 Co Law 67

Alcock A, 'The draft Financial Services and Markets Bill' (1998) 19 Co Law 258

Allen R E, *The Concise Oxford Dictionary of Current English* (8th ed) BCA, London, 1990

Allen T, 'Bribes and Constructive Trusts: A-G of Hong Kong v Reid' (1995) 58 MLR 87

Andenas M and Savla S, 'Serious fraud and s34 of the Criminal Justice and Public Order Act 1994' (1998) 19 Co Law 66

Andenas M, 'The future of EC company law harmonisation' (1994) 15 Co Law 121

Anderson C and Morrison D, 'Standard Chartered Bank of Australia Ltd v Antico: Towards a New Understanding of Insolvent Trading' (1996) 4 CCL 1

Ansell S, 'Directors' and Officers' Liability Insurance – Recent Reforms and Developments in Australia and New Zealand' (1995) 23 ABLR 164

Arden M, 'Foreword' (1999) 20 Co Law 161

Arden M, 'Time for an English Commercial Code?' [1997] CLJ 516

Arora A, 'When Directors are Personally Liable' (1981) 2 Co Law 201

Attorney-General (Cth), *Proceedings on Behalf of a Company (Statutory Derivative Action) Draft Provisions and Commentary* Canberra, 1995

Austin R P, 'Commerce and Equity – Fiduciary Duty and Constructive Trust' (1986) 6 OJLS 444

Austin R P, 'Constructive Trusts' in Finn P D (ed), *Essays in Equity* The Law Book Company Ltd, Sydney, 1985

Austin R P, 'Fiduciary Accountability for Business Opportunities' in Finn P D (ed), *Equity and Commercial Relationships* The Law Book Company Ltd, Sydney, 1987

Austin R P, case note (1996) ACS 279

Australian Law Reform Commission, Report No. 27, *Standing in Public Interest Litigation* AGPS, Canberra, 1985

Australian Law Reform Commission, Report No. 45, *General Insolvency Inquiry* AGPS, Canberra, 1988

Australian Law Reform Commission, Report No. 68, *Compliance with the Trade Practices Act 1974* AGPS, Canberra, 1994

Australian Law Reform Commission, Report No. 78, *Beyond the door-keeper: Standing to sue for public remedies* AGPS, Canberra, 1996

Australian Stock Exchange, *Exposure Draft: Proposed Listing Rule Amendments* Australian Stock Exchange Ltd, Sydney, 1994

Australian Stock Exchange, *Listing Rules Simplification* ASX Exposure Draft, Australian Stock Exchange Ltd, Sydney, April 1995

Australian Stock Exchange, *Listing Rules Simplification* ASX Exposure Draft, Australian Stock Exchange Ltd, Sydney, June 1995

Australian Stock Exchange, *Official Listing Rules* Australian Stock Exchange Ltd, Sydney, 1987

Axworthy C S, 'Corporate Directors – Who Needs Them?' (1988) 51 MLR 273

Bagge J, 'The future for enforcement under the new Financial Services Authority' (1998) 19 Co Law 194

Baker P V and Langan P St J, *Snell's Principles of Equity* (28th ed) Sweet & Maxwell Ltd, London, 1982

Barnard J W, 'The Hampel Committee Report: a transatlantic critique' (1998) 19 Co Law 110

Barrett R I, 'Directors' Duties to Creditors' (1977) 40 MLR 226

Barrett R I, 'Directors' Fiduciary Duties' (1985) 59 ALJ 46

Barrett R I, case note (1982) 56 ALJ 189

Barrett R I, case note (1982) 56 ALJ 600

Barry P, *The Rise and Fall of Alan Bond* Transworld Publishers (Australia) Pty Ltd, Sydney, 1990

Baxt R, 'Can nominating companies be vicariously liable for the negligence of their nominee directors?' (1995) 69 ALJ 684

Baxt R, 'Can the Law Relating to Directors' Duties be Reformed?' (1990) 8 CSLJ 110

Baxt R, 'CLERP – Two Steps Backward and One Step Forward' (1998) 26 ABLR 376

Baxt R, 'CLERP a breakthrough for directors' (1998) Co Dir 27

Baxt R, 'Company Law Reform by No Half Measures! – The CLERP Program Really "Takes Off"' (1998) 26 ABLR 217

Baxt R, 'Conflict of Interest: Byrnes v The Queen' (1996) 14 CSLJ 54

Baxt R, 'Directors Cannot Escape Liability by Doing Nothing' (1990) ABLR 405

Baxt R, 'Doubt on statutory derivative action' (1996) 12 Co Dir 4

Baxt R, 'Duties of directors with respect to creditors' (1989) 63 ALJ 846

Baxt R, 'Duties to a Corporate Group – One Step Forward or Two Steps Backwards?' (1994) 22 ABLR 138

Baxt R, 'Judges in their Own Cause: The Ratification of Directors' Breaches of Duty' (1978) 5 MULR 16

Baxt R, 'Misuse of corporate position by company directors' (1995) 69 ALJ 940

Baxt R, 'Reforming the law relating to company directors' (1990) 64 ALJ 345

Baxt R, 'Second Guessing Directors' Decisions on Takeovers – A Mixed Message from the New South Wales Court of Appeal' (1990) 8 CSLJ 26

Baxt R, 'Shadow directors and Australian law' (1996) 70 ALJ 441

Baxt R, 'Sleeping Directors Get a Second Chance' (1992) 20 ABLR 78

Baxt R, 'The Duties of Directors of Public Companies – The Realities of Commercial Life, The Contradictions of the Law, And the Need for Reform' (1976) BLR 289

Baxt R, 'The Role and Behaviour of Company Directors – Phase 2' (1990) 18 ABLR 53

Baxt R, 'The Role and Responsibilities of Nominee Directors in a Contested Takeover' a paper presented at the Corporate Law Workshop, conducted by the Business Law Section of the Law Council of Australia, Melbourne, 1993

Baxt R, 'What Price an Informed Securities Market?' (1994) 22 ABLR 58

Baxt R, 'Will Section 574 of the Companies Code Please Stand Up! (And will Section 1323 of the Corporations Act Follow Suit)' (1989) 7 CSLJ 388

Baxt R, *Afterman & Baxt's Cases and Materials on Corporations and Associations* (5th ed) Butterworths Pty Ltd, Sydney, 1988

Baxt R, case note (1970) 44 ALJ 37

Baxt R, case note (1974) 48 ALJ 319

Baxt R, case note (1986) 60 ALJ 102

Baxt R, case note (1987) 5 CSLJ 247

Baxt R, case note (1988) 62 ALJ 643

Baxt R, case note (1989) 7 CSLJ 344

Baxt R, case note (1991) 65 ALJ 352

Baxt R, case note (1993) 67 ALJ 694

Baxt R, commercial law note (1994) 68 ALJ 758

Baxt R, commercial law note (1995) 69 ALJ 571

Baxt R, company law note (1994) 12 CSLJ 178

Bean G M D, 'Debt subordination validated' (1994) 15 Co Law 52

Beatson J, 'The Relationship Between Regulations Governing the Financial Services Industry and Fiduciary Duties under the General Law' in McKendrick E (ed), *Commercial Aspects of Trusts and Fiduciary Obligations* Clarendon Press, Oxford, 1992

Beck S M, 'An Analysis of Foss v Harbottle' in Ziegel J S (ed), *Studies in Canadian Company Law* Butterworth & Co (Canada) Ltd, Toronto, 1967

Beirne N and Herring A, 'Financial services regulation and the Internet in the UK' (1998) 19 Co Law 264

Belcher A, 'Compliance with the Cadbury Code and the reporting of corporate governance' (1996) 17 Co Law 11

Bennetts K J, 'Expectations of Financial Support – Grounds for Avoidance of Directors' Liability Under Section 592, Corporations Law' (1991) 9 CSLJ 268

Berle A A Jr, 'Corporate Decision-Making and Social Control' (1968-1969) 24 Bus Law 149

Berle A A Jr, 'Corporate Powers as Powers in Trust' (1930-1931) 44 Harv LR 1049

Berle A A Jr, 'For Whom Corporate Managers are Trustees: a Note' (1931-1932) 45 Harv LR 1365

Bhattacharyya G, 'Re Hydrodan (Corby) Ltd – shadow directors and wrongful trading' (1994) 15 Co Law 151

Bird H L, Gilligan G and Ramsay I M, *Regulating Directors' Duties – How Effective Are The Civil Penalty Sanctions In The Australian Corporations Law?* The Centre For Corporate Law and Securities Regulation, The University of Melbourne, Parkville, 1999

Bird H, 'The Problematic Nature of Civil Penalties in the Corporations Law' (1996) 14 CSLJ 405

Birds J R, 'A code of directors' duties?' (1974) 124 NLJ 1163

Birds J R, 'Making Directors do their Duties' (1980) 1 Co Law 67

Birds J R, 'Proper Purposes as a Head of Directors' Duties' (1974) 37 MLR 580

Birds J R, 'The demise of ultra vires?' (1986) 7 Co Law 203

Birds J R, 'The Permissible Scope of Articles Excluding the Duties of Company Directors' (1976) 39 MLR 394

Bishop W and Prentice D D, 'Some Legal and Economic Aspects of Fiduciary Remuneration' (1983) 46 MLR 289

Black A, 'Recent Developments in Directors' Duties: A Postscript' (1991) 8 ABR 10

Black A, 'Recent Developments in Directors' Duties' (1991) 7 ABR 121

Blanchard J, 'Honesty in Corporations' (1996) 14 CSLJ 4

Boros E J, *Minority Shareholders' Remedies* Clarendon Press, Oxford, 1995

Bosworth-Davies R, 'Powers granted to the SIB under FSA 1986, s59' (1994) 15 Co Law 119

Boyle A J and Sykes R, *Gore-Browne on Companies* (44th ed) Jordan Publishing Ltd, Bristol, 1995

Boyle A J, 'Attorney-General v Reid: the company law implications' (1995) 16 Co Law 131

Boyle A J, 'Indemnifying the Minority Shareholder' [1976] JBL 18

Boyle A J, 'Minority Shareholders' Suits for Breach of Directors' Duties' (1980) 1 Co Law 3

Boyle A J, 'The Derivative Action in Company Law' [1969] JBL 120

Boyle A J, 'The Judicial Review of the Special Litigation Committee: The Implications for the English Derivative Action after Smith v Croft' (1990) 11 Co Law 3

Boyle A J, 'The Minority Shareholder in the Nineteenth Century: A Study in Anglo-American Legal History' (1965) 28 MLR 317

Boyle A J, 'The new derivative action' (1997) 18 Co Law 256

Boyle A J, 'The Prudential, the Court of Appeal and Foss v Harbottle' (1981) 2 Co Law 264

Bradley C, 'Corporate Control: Markets and Rules' (1990) 53 MLR 170

Brennan M, 'The Phoenix Phenomenon' (1996) *Australian Accountant* 42

Brown S R and Grogan P R, *Company Directors* (3rd ed) The Law Book Company Ltd, Sydney, 1974

Burke J, *Osborn's Concise Law Dictionary* (6th ed) Sweet & Maxwell Ltd, London, 1976

Burridge S J, 'Wrongful Rights Issues' (1981) 44 MLR 40

Callaway F H, Commentary to Sealy, 'The Enforcement of Partnership Agreements, Articles of Association and Shareholder Agreements' in Finn P D (ed), *Equity and Commercial Relationships* The Law Book Company Ltd, Sydney, 1987

Carroll R, 'Third Party Liability for Corporate Activity: Recent Developments' (1996) 26 UWALR 332

Cassidy J, 'An Evaluation of Section 232(4) of the Corporations Law and the Directors' Duty of Due Care, Skill and Diligence' (1995) 23 ABLR 184

Chernov A, 'The Role of Corporate Governance Practices in the Development of Legal Principles Relating to Directors' in Ramsay I M (ed), *Corporate Governance and the Duties of Company Directors* The Centre for Corporate Law and Securities Regulation, University of Melbourne, Parkville, 1997

Chow K C K, 'Proper Purpose Doctrine and the Companies Bill' (1979) 129 NLJ 123 and 135

Christie M, 'The Director's Fiduciary Duty not to Compete' (1992) 55 MLR 506

Comerford A and Law L, 'Directors' Duty of Care and the Extent of "Reasonable" Reliance and Delegation' (1998) 16 CSLJ 103

Committee on Corporate Governance, *Final Report* Gee Publishing Ltd, London, 1998

Committee on Corporate Governance, *The Combined Code* Gee Publishing Ltd, London, 1998

Committee on the Financial Aspects of Corporate Governance, *The Code of Best Practice* Gee and Co Ltd, London, 1992

Committee on the Financial Aspects of Corporate Governance, *The Report of the Committee on the Financial Aspects of Corporate Governance* Gee and Co Ltd, London, 1992

Committee on the Financial Aspects of Corporate Governance, *The Report on Compliance with the Code of Best Practice* Gee Publishing Ltd, London, 1995

Commonwealth, House of Representatives, Parliamentary Debates, 13.4.89 – 8.6.94 inclusive

Commonwealth, Senate, Parliamentary Debates, 14.10.88 – 12.11.92 inclusive

Companies and Securities Advisory Committee, *Report on a Statutory Derivative Action* Canberra, 1993

Companies and Securities Law Review Committee, Report No. 12, *Enforcement of the Duties of Directors and Officers of a Company by Means of a Statutory Derivative Action* Canberra, 1990

Companies and Securities Law Review Committee, Report No. 9, *Director's Statutory Duty to Disclose Interest (Companies Act s228) and Loans to Directors (Companies Act s230)* Melbourne, 1989

Company Law Advisory Committee to the Standing Committee of Attorneys-General, *Second Interim Report* CGPO, Canberra, 1969

Company Law Amendment Committee, HMSO, London, Cmd 2657, 1926

Comptroller and Auditor General, *The Insolvency Service Executive Agency: Company Director Disqualification – A Follow Up Report* The Stationery Office Ltd, London, 1999

Conway H M and Manuell R J, 'Duties of Company Directors and Ratification by General Meetings' (1977-1979) 8 Syd LR 493

Cooke R, 'The Place of Equity and Equitable Doctrines in the Contemporary Common Law World: A New Zealand Perspective' in Waters D W M (ed), *Equity, Fiduciaries and Trusts 1993* Thomson Canada Ltd, Toronto, 1993

Corkery J F, *Directors' Powers and Duties* Longman Cheshire Pty Ltd, Melbourne, 1987

Corporations Law Simplification Task Force, *Officers and related party transactions: Proposal for simplification* Canberra, 1995

Cranston R, 'Directors' Duties – Indemnity and Ratification' a paper presented at the Sydney Law Review Conference, conducted by the University of Sydney, Faculty of Law, Bowral, 1987

Currie C, 'Civil enforcement as a regulatory device: the use of the civil law as a means of enforcing securities law violations' (1996) 17 Co Law 139

Dabner J, 'Directors' Duties – The Schizoid Company' (1988) 6 CSLJ 105

Davidson I E, 'The Equitable Remedy of Compensation' (1982) 13 Melb ULR 349

Davies J D, 'Equitable Compensation: "Causation, Foreseeability and Remoteness"' in Waters D W M (ed), *Equity, Fiduciaries and Trusts 1993* Thomson Canada Ltd, Toronto, 1993

Davies P L, 'Directors' Fiduciary Duties and Individual Shareholders' in McKendrick E (ed), *Commercial Aspects of Trusts and Fiduciary Obligations* Clarendon Press, Oxford, 1992

Davies P L, case note [1980] JBL 415

Davies P L, *Gower's Principles of Modern Company Law* (6th ed) Sweet & Maxwell Ltd, London, 1997

Dawson F, 'Acting in the Best Interests of the Company – For Whom are Directors "Trustees"?' (1984) 11 NZULR 68

DeMott D A, 'Shareholder Litigation in Australia and the United States: Common Problems, Uncommon Solutions' (1987) 11 Syd LR 259

Department of Trade and Industry, *A Revised Framework for Insolvency Law* HMSO, London, Cmnd 9175, 1984

Department of Trade and Industry, *Accounting Simplifications* (a consultative document) HMSO, London, 1995

Department of Trade and Industry, *Company Law Review: Proposals for Reform of Sections 151-158 of the Companies Act 1985* (a consultative document) HMSO, London, 1993

Department of Trade and Industry, *Company Law Review: Proposals for Reform of Part XII of the Companies Act 1985* (a consultative document) HMSO, London, 1994

Department of Trade and Industry, *Company Law Review: The Law Applicable to Private Companies* (a consultative document) HMSO, London, 1994

Department of Trade and Industry, *Directors' Remuneration* (a consultative document) HMSO, London, 1999

Department of Trade and Industry, *Financial Services in the United Kingdom: A new framework for investor protection* HMSO, London, Cmnd 9432, 1985

Department of Trade and Industry, *Model Articles of Association for Partnership Companies (Table G)* (a consultative document) HMSO, London, 1995

Department of Trade and Industry, *Modern Company Law: For a Competitive Economy* (a consultative document) HMSO, London, 1998

Department of Trade and Industry, *Modern Company Law: The Strategic Framework* HMSO, London, 1999

Department of Trade and Industry, *Proposals for Reform of Part VI of the Companies Act 1985* (a consultative document) HMSO, London, 1995

Department of Trade and Industry, *Resolutions of Private Companies* (a consultative document) HMSO, London, 1995

Department of Trade and Industry, *Simpler Procedures for Summary Financial Statements* (a consultative document) HMSO, London, 1995

Department of Trade, *The Conduct of Company Directors* Cmnd 7037, 1977

Digby Q, 'Eliminating Minority Shareholdings' (1992) 10 CSLJ 105

Digby Q, 'Flexibility in the Administration of the Takeovers Code' (1991) 9 CSLJ 343

Dignam A, 'A principled approach to self-regulation? The report of the Hampel Committee on Corporate Governance' (1998) 19 Co Law 140

Dine J, 'The governance of governance' (1994) 15 Co Law 73

Dixon O, 'Concerning Judicial Method' (1955-1956) 29 ALJ 468

Dodd E M Jr, 'For Whom are Corporate Managers Trustees?' (1931-1932) 45 Harv LR 1145

Dodd E M Jr, 'Is Effective Enforcement of the Fiduciary Duties of Corporate Managers Practicable?' (1934-1935) 2 UCLR 194

Dodds J, 'New Developments in Directors' Duties – The Victorian Stance on Financial Competence' (1991) 17 MULR 132

Doyle J J, Commentary to Kearney, 'Accounting for a Fiduciary's Gains in Commercial Contexts' in Finn P D (ed), *Equity and Commercial Relationships* The Law Book Company Ltd, Sydney, 1987

Dwight F, 'Liability of Corporate Directors' (1907-1908) 17 YLJ 33

Easterbrook F H and Fischel D R, 'Close Corporations and Agency Costs' (1985-1986) 38 SLR 271

Editorial comment (1964-1965) 38 ALJ 251

Editorial comment (1994) 15 Co Law 34

Editorial comment (1996) 14 CSLJ 3

Editorial comment, '"Guinness" and human rights – the common law "remembered"' (1997) 18 Co Law 33

Editorial comment, 'Back to basics: company law reform' (1999) 20 Co Law 129

Editorial comment, 'Civilising the criminal law' (1998) 19 Co Law 161

Editorial comment, 'Day of the civil sanction?' (1996) 17 Co Law 257

Editorial comment, 'Director disqualification: upping the ante?' (1999) 20 Co Law 97

Editorial comment, 'Directors – true or false?' (1997) 18 Co Law 129

Editorial comment, 'Financial Services and Markets Bill: individuals beware' (1998) 19 Co Law 225

Editorial comment, 'Fraud and the civil law: further development' (1997) 18 Co Law 1

Editorial comment, 'Getting tough with the market' (1998) 19 Co Law 289

Editorial comment, 'How many regulators?' (1996) 17 Co Law 34

Editorial comment, 'Is Company Law Still in a Muddle?' (1991) 12 Co Law 42

Editorial comment, 'Only mad cows and Englishmen' (1997) 18 Co Law 65

Editorial comment, 'Other people's money' (1996) 17 Co Law 98

Editorial comment, 'Personal liability for directors' (1998) 19 Co Law 129

Editorial comment, 'Practical academia?' (1996) 17 Co Law 161

Editorial comment, 'Reforming directors' duties' (1999) 20 Co Law 1

Editorial comment, 'Target hit' (1995) 16 Co Law 258

Editorial comment, 'The new company law' (1999) 20 Co Law 257

Editorial comment, 'There and back again!' (1998) 19 Co Law 97

Editorial comment, 'To live in interesting times' (1997) 18 Co Law 193

Editorial comment, 'Unsung heroes?' (1996) 17 Co Law 130

Editorial comment, 'When will we ever learn?' (1996) 17 Co Law 66

Ehrlich E, *Nil Desperandum: A Dictionary of Latin Tags and Useful Phrases* (1992 ed) BCA, London, 1992

Explanatory memorandum, *Corporate Law Economic Reform Program Bill 1998* CCH Australia Ltd, Sydney, 1999

Explanatory memorandum, *Corporate Law Reform Bill 1992* CCH Australia Ltd, Sydney, 1992

Farrar J H and Russell M, 'The Impact of Institutional Investment on Company Law' (1984) 5 Co Law 107

Farrar J H, 'Abuse of Power by Directors' [1974] CLJ 221

Farrar J H, 'Corporate Governance, Business Judgement and the Professionalism of Directors' (1993) 6 CBLJ 1

Farrar J H, 'The Obligation of a Company's Directors to its Creditors Before Liquidation' [1985] JBL 413

Farrar J H, 'The Responsibility of Directors and Shareholders for a Company's Debts' (1989) 4 Canta LR 12

Farrar J H, 'The Role and Responsibilities of Nominee Directors in a Contested Takeover' a paper presented at the Corporate Law Workshop, conducted by the Business Law Section of the Law Council of Australia, Melbourne, 1993

Farrar J H, Furey N E, Hannigan B M and Wylie P, *Farrar's Company Law* (3rd ed) Butterworth & Co (Publishers) Ltd, London, 1991

Ferran E, 'The Reform of the Law on Corporate Capacity and Directors' and Officers' Authority' (1992) 13 Co Law 124 and 177

Fidock R, 'Landmark call for Judgement Rule' (1996) 12 Co Dir 47

Finch V, 'Company Directors: Who Cares about Skill and Care?' (1992) 55 MLR 179

Finch V, 'Directors' duties towards creditors' (1989) 10 Co Law 23

Finch V, 'The Measures of Insolvency Law' (1997) 17 OJLS 227

Finn P D, 'Contract and the Fiduciary Principle' (1989) 12 UNSWLJ 76

Finn P D, 'Controlling the Exercise of Power' (1996) 7 PLR 86

Finn P D, 'Fiduciary Law and the Modern Commercial World' in McKendrick E (ed), *Commercial Aspects of Trusts and Fiduciary Obligations* Clarendon Press, Oxford, 1992

Finn P D, 'The Fiduciary Principle' in Youdan T G (ed), *Equity, Fiduciaries and Trusts* The Law Book Company Ltd, Toronto, 1989

Finn P D, 'The Liability of Third Parties for Knowing Receipt or Assistance' in Waters D W M (ed), *Equity, Fiduciaries and Trusts 1993* Thomson Canada Ltd, Toronto, 1993

Finn P D, *Equity and Commercial Relationships* The Law Book Company Ltd, Sydney, 1987

Finn P D, *Essays in Equity* The Law Book Company Ltd, Sydney, 1985

Finn P D, *Essays on Damages* The Law Book Company Ltd, Sydney, 1992

Finn P D, *Fiduciary Obligations* The Law Book Company Ltd, Sydney, 1977

Ford H A J and Austin R P, *Ford's Principles of Corporations Law* (6th ed) Butterworths Pty Ltd, Sydney, 1992

Ford H A J, Austin R P and Ramsay I M, *Ford's Principles of Corporations Law* (7th ed) Reed International Books Australia Pty Ltd, Sydney, 1995

Ford H A J, Austin R P and Ramsay I M, *Ford's Principles of Corporations Law* (9th ed) Reed International Books Australia Pty Ltd, Sydney, 1999

Ford H A J, *Principles of Company Law* (1st ed) Butterworths Pty Ltd, Sydney, 1974

Ford H A J, *Principles of Company Law* (3rd ed) Butterworths Pty Ltd, Sydney, 1982

Ford H A J, *Principles of Company Law* (4th ed) Butterworths Pty Ltd, Sydney, 1986

Ford H A J, *Principles of Company Law* (5th ed) Butterworths Pty Ltd, Sydney, 1990

Fraser H, 'Directors' interests in contracts: fair and foul dealing' (1994) 15 Co Law 46

Frommel S N, 'The right to silence and the powers of the Serious Fraud Office' (1994) 15 Co Law 227

Fung E T S, 'Spies, traitors and fiduciaries' (1998) 19 Co Law 219

Gardner S, 'Two Maxims of Equity' [1995] CLJ 60

Gething M, 'Do We Really Need Criminal and Civil Penalties for Contraventions of Directors' Duties?' (1996) 24 ABLR 375

Gibson P, 'Introduction' in McKendrick E (ed), *Commercial Aspects of Trusts and Fiduciary Obligations* Clarendon Press, Oxford, 1992

Goff R and Jones G, *The Law of Restitution* (3rd ed) Sweet & Maxwell Ltd, London, 1986

Goff R and Jones G, *The Law of Restitution* (4th ed) Sweet & Maxwell Ltd, London, 1993

Goldberg A H, 'Who'd be a Company Director' a paper presented at the Second Business Lawyers' Conference, conducted by the Business Law Section of the Law Council of Australia, Melbourne, 1989

Goodhart W and Jones G, 'The Infiltration of Equitable Doctrine into English Commercial Law' (1980) 43 MLR 489

Gower L C B, 'A Comment' (1967) 30 MLR 259

Gower L C B, 'Some Contrasts Between British and American Corporation Law' (1955-1956) 69 Harv LR 1369

Gower L C B, *Gower's Principles of Modern Company Law* (1st ed) Sweet & Maxwell Ltd, London, 1954

Gower L C B, *Gower's Principles of Modern Company Law* (5th ed) Sweet & Maxwell Ltd, London, 1992

Gower L C B, *Review of Investor Protection Report: Part I* HMSO, London, Cmnd 9125, 1984

Grantham R, 'Directors' Duties and Insolvent Companies' (1991) 54 MLR 576

Grantham R, 'The Doctrinal Basis of the Rights of Company Shareholders' (1998) CLJ 554

Grantham R, 'The Judicial Extension of Directors' Duties to Creditors' [1991] JBL 1

Grawehr P, 'A Comparison Between Australian and European Insolvent Trading Laws' (1996) 14 CSLJ 16

Gray J, 'Dishonesty plus breach of fiduciary duties can add up to fraud' (1995) 16 Co Law 315

Gray T, *Ode on a Distant Prospect of Eton College* (1747) The Concise Oxford Dictionary of Quotations (3rd ed), Oxford University Press, Oxford, 1993

Greenwood C, 'The Tin Council Litigation in the House of Lords' [1990] CLJ 8

Gregory R, 'What is the Rule in Foss v Harbottle?' (1982) 45 MLR 584

Griffin S, 'Standard of proof applicable to s6 of the Company Directors Disqualification Act 1986' (1997) 18 Co Law 24

Hahlo H R, 'Codifying the Common Law: Protracted Gestation' (1975) 38 MLR 23

Hahlo H R, 'Here Lies the Common Law: Rest in Peace' (1967) 30 MLR 241

Hammond G, 'The Place of Damages in the Scheme of Remedies' in Finn P D (ed), *Essays on Damages* The Law Book Company Ltd, Sydney, 1992

Hannigan B M, 'The Reform of the Ultra Vires Rule' [1987] JBL 173

Harper J B and Browne A A, 'The Duties and Liabilities of a Director in 1973' (1973) 47 ALJ 447

Harwood R, 'The SIB's exercise of its enforcement powers' (1995) 16 Co Law 271

Hawke N, 'Creditors' Interests in Solvent and Insolvent Companies' [1989] JBL 54

Hein L W, 'The British Business Company: Its Origins and Its Control' (1963) 15 UTLJ 134

Herzberg A, 'Insolvent Trading' (1991) 9 CSLJ 285

Heydon J D, 'Causal Relationships Between a Fiduciary's Default and the Principal's Loss' (1994) 110 LQR 328

Heydon J D, 'Directors' Duties and the Company's Interests' in Finn P D (ed), *Equity and Commercial Relationships* The Law Book Company Ltd, Sydney, 1987

Hicks A, 'Directors' Liability for Management Errors' (1994) 110 LQR 390

Hicks A, *Disqualification of Directors: No Hiding Place for the Unfit?* The Association of Chartered Certified Accountants, London, 1998

Hill J, 'Protecting Minority Shareholders and Reasonable Expectations' (1992) 10 CSLJ 86

Hill J, case note (1986) 60 ALJ 525

Hilmer F G, *Strictly Boardroom: Improving Governance to Enhance Company Performance* The Business Library, Melbourne, 1993

HM Treasury, *Financial Services and Markets Bill: A Consultation Document, Part One* HMSO, London, 1998

HM Treasury, *Financial Services and Markets Bill: A Consultation Document, Part Two* HMSO, London, 1998

HM Treasury, *Financial Services and Markets Bill: A Consultation Document, Part Three* HMSO, London, 1998

Hoey A, 'Disqualifying delinquent directors' (1997) 18 Co Law 130

Hoffmann L H, 'The Fourth Annual Leonard Sainer Lecture' (1997) 18 Co Law 194

Hopkins J, case note [1990] CLJ 220

Hopt K J, 'Directors' Duties to Shareholders, Employees, and Other Creditors: A View from the Continent' in McKendrick E (ed), *Commercial Aspects of Trusts and Fiduciary Obligations* Clarendon Press, Oxford, 1992

House of Representatives Standing Committee on Legal and Constitutional Affairs, *Corporate Practices and the Rights of Shareholders* AGPS, Canberra, 1991

Howard C, 'Current Takeover Law' (1985) 15 Melb ULR 31

Hurst T R, 'Self Regulation versus Legal Regulation' (1984) 5 Co Law 161

Institute of Chartered Accountants in England & Wales, *Internal Control* (a consultative document) Institute of Chartered Accountants in England & Wales, London, 1999

Institute of Chartered Accountants in England & Wales, *Internal Control: Guidance for Directors on the Combined Code* Institute of Chartered Accountants in England & Wales, London, 1999

Instone R, 'Powers and Objects' (1978) 128 NLJ 948

Instone R, 'Unfairly Prejudiced Directors' (1986) 136 NLJ 973

Ipp D A, 'Problems and Progress in Remoteness of Damage' in Finn P D (ed), *Essays on Damages* The Law Book Company Ltd, Sydney, 1992

Ipp D A, 'Problems with "control" in fraud-on-the-minority actions' (1997) 18 Co Law 88

Ipp D A, 'The diligent director' (1997) 18 Co Law 162

Jarvis K, 'Does the fiduciary bell toll?' (1996) 17 Co Law 51

Jarvis K, 'Law Commission report on fiduciary duties and regulatory rules' (1996) 17 Co Law 110

Joffe V, 'Majority Rule Undermined?' (1977) 40 MLR 71

Jones A, 'Bribing the DPP: Should he Profit from Abusing his Position?' [1994] Conv 156

Jones G, 'Unjust Enrichment and the Fiduciary's Duty of Loyalty' (1968) 84 LQR 472

Kahn-Freund O, 'Some Reflections on Company Law Reform' (1944) 7 MLR 54

Kearney J B, 'Accounting for a Fiduciary's Gains in Commercial Contexts' in Finn P D (ed), *Equity and Commercial Relationships* The Law Book Company Ltd, Sydney, 1987

Keeton G W, 'The Director as Trustee' (1952) 5 CLP 11

Kennedy G A, 'Equity in a Commercial Context' in Finn P D (ed), *Equity and Commercial Relationships* The Law Book Company Ltd, Sydney, 1987

Kennett G R, case note (1989) 63 ALJ 502

Kent W and Vary L, 'Compulsory Acquisition of Shares' (1991) 9 CSLJ 261

Kidd C J F, 'Stare Decisis in Intermediate Appellate Courts Practice in the English Court of Appeal, the Australian State Full Courts, and the New Zealand Court of Appeal' (1978) 52 ALJ 274

Kirby M, 'Corporate Governance, Corporate Law and Global Forces' in Ramsay I M (ed), *Corporate Governance and the Duties of Company Directors* The Centre for Corporate Law and Securities Regulation, University of Melbourne, Parkville, 1997

Kluver J, 'Derivative Actions and the Rule in Foss v Harbottle: Do We Need a Statutory Remedy?' (1993) 11 CSLJ 7

Law Commission, *Company Directors: Regulating Conflicts of Interests and Formulating a Statement of Duties* HMSO, London, Cm 4436, 1999

Law Commission, Consultation Paper No. 124 (Summary), *Fiduciary Duties and Regulatory Rules* HMSO, London, 1992

Law Commission, Consultation Paper No. 142, *Shareholder Remedies* HMSO, London, 1996

Law Commission, Consultation Paper No. 153, *Company Directors: Regulating Conflicts of Interests and Formulating a Statement of Duties* HMSO, London, 1998

Law Commission, *Fiduciary Duties and Regulatory Rules* HMSO, London, Cm 3049, 1995

Law Commission, *Shareholder Remedies* The Stationery Office Ltd, London, Cm 3769, 1997

Leeming M, 'Causation and compensation for breach of fiduciary duty' (1996) 70 ALJ 537

Lehane J R F, 'Fiduciaries in a Commercial Context' in Finn P D (ed), *Essays in Equity* The Law Book Company Ltd, Sydney, 1985

Lindgren K E, 'The Fiduciary Nature of a Company Board's Power to Issue Shares' (1971-1972) 10 UWALR 364

Lindgren K E, case note (1973) 11 UWALR 68

Lloyd D, 'Codifying English Law' (1949) 2 CLP 155

LLoyd-Bostock S, 'The Ordinary Man, and the Psychology of Attributing Causes and Responsibility' (1979) 42 MLR 143

Lodge M, 'Barnes v Addy: The Requirements of Knowledge' (1995) 23 ABLR 25

London Stock Exchange Ltd, *Consultative document on the dissemination of price sensitive information* The International Stock Exchange of the United Kingdom and Republic of Ireland Ltd, London, 1993

London Stock Exchange Ltd, *Guidance on the dissemination of price sensitive information* The International Stock Exchange of the United Kingdom and Republic of Ireland Ltd, London, 1994

London Stock Exchange Ltd, *The Listing Rules* The International Stock Exchange of the United Kingdom and Republic of Ireland Ltd, London, 1999

Long J, 'Policing the markets – SIB's role' (1994) 15 Co Law 83

Loss L, 'The Fiduciary Concept as Applied to Trading by Corporate "Insiders" in the United States' (1970) 33 MLR 34

Lowry J, 'Reconstructing shareholder actions: a response to the Law Commission's consultation paper' (1997) 18 Co Law 247

Macfarlan R B S, 'Directors' Duties after the National Safety Council Case Directors' Duty of Care' (1992) 9 ABR 269

Mackenzie A L, 'The Employee and the Company Director' (1982) 132 NLJ 688

Malcolm D, 'Directors' Duties: The Governing Principles' in Ramsay I M (ed), *Corporate Governance and the Duties of Company Directors* The Centre for Corporate Law and Securities Regulation, University of Melbourne, Parkville, 1997

Mannolini J J, 'Creditors' Interests in the Corporate Contract: A Case for the Reform of our Insolvent Trading Provisions' (1996) 6 AJCL 14

Mason A, 'The Place of Equity and Equitable Doctrines in the Contemporary Common Law World: An Australian Perspective' in Waters D W M (ed), *Equity, Fiduciaries and Trusts 1993* Thomson Canada Ltd, Toronto, 1993

Mason A, 'The Place of Equity and Equitable Remedies in the Contemporary Common Law World' (1994) 110 LQR 238

Mason K, 'Contract and Tort: Looking Across the Boundary from the Side of Contract' (1987) 61 ALJ 228

Maughan C W and Copp S F, 'The Law Commission and economic methodology: values, efficiency and directors' duties' (1999) 20 Co Law 109

McCormack G, 'Fiduciaries in a changing commercial climate' (1997) 18 Co Law 38

McCormack G, 'The remedial constructive trust and commercial transactions' (1996) 17 Co Law 3

McDermott P M, 'Jurisdiction of the Court of Chancery to Award Damages' (1992) 109 LQR 652

McDonough D D, *Annotated Mergers and Acquisitions Law of Australia* (3rd ed) The Law Book Company Ltd, Sydney, 1993

McKendrick E, *Commercial Aspects of Trusts and Fiduciary Obligations* Clarendon Press, Oxford, 1992

McLachlin B M, 'The Place of Equity and Equitable Doctrines in the Contemporary Common Law World: A Canadian Perspective' in Waters D W M (ed), *Equity, Fiduciaries and Trusts 1993* Thomson Canada Ltd, Toronto, 1993

McPherson B H, 'Joint Ventures' in Finn P D (ed), *Equity and Commercial Relationships* The Law Book Company Ltd, Sydney, 1987

Meagher R P, Gummow W M C and Lehane J R F, *Equity Doctrines and Remedies* (3rd ed) Butterworths Pty Ltd, Sydney, 1992

Menzies D, 'Company Directors' (1959) 33 ALJ 156

Mescher B, 'Personal Liability of Company Directors for Company Debts' (1996) 70 ALJ 837

Millett P J, 'Tracing the Proceeds of Fraud' (1991) 107 LQR 71

Milman D, 'Curbing the Phoenix Syndrome' [1997] JBL 224

Mitchell V, 'Company law reviews in Australia and the United Kingdom' (1999) 20 Co Law 98

Mitchell V, 'The Concept of "Honesty" Under Section 232(2) of the Corporations Law' (1994) 12 CSLJ 231

Mitchell V, 'The High Court and Minority Shareholders' (1995) 7 Bond LR 58

Moran L J, 'Missing links and missed opportunities' (1997) 18 Co Law 264

Mountfort A G, 'Tracing: An Examination of the Applicability of Tracing Principles Today' (1996) 70 ALJ 54

Muir G, 'Contract and Equity: Striking a Balance' (1985) 10 Adel LR 153

Mullender R, 'Negligent misstatement and the personal liability of company directors' (1997) 18 Co Law 153

Mullender R, 'Negligent misstatement, company directors and the House of Lords' (1999) 20 Co Law 121

Nakajima C, 'Putting the pieces together – insider liability' (1994) 15 Co Law 88

Nakajima C, 'Signing without reading' (1994) 15 Co Law 123

Nakajima C, *Conflicts of Interest and Duty* Kluwer Law International Ltd, London, 1999

New Zealand Law Commission, Report No. 9, *Company Law Reform and Restatement* Wellington, 1989

Noble T, 'When Does a Company Incur a Debt Under the Insolvent Trading Provisions of the Corporations Law?' (1994) 12 CSLJ 297

Nolan R C, 'Maxwell's improper purposes' (1994) 15 Co Law 85

Nolan R C, 'Targeting Trustees – Liability for Breach of Trust' [1994] CLJ 450

Nolan R C, 'The wages of sin: iniquity in equity following A-G for Hong Kong v Reid' (1994) 15 Co Law 3

Nolan R, 'Arabian's rights' (1994) 15 Co Law 148

Nolan R, 'Care and skill in Australia – Daniels v Anderson' (1996) 17 Co Law 89

Nolan R, 'Disclosure of directors' interests' (1995) 16 Co Law 216

Nolan R, 'What to take into Account' [1996] CLJ 201

Nottle R, 'Disclosure: The New Listing Rule on Corporate Governance Practices' (1996) ACS 281

O'Donovan J, 'The Impact of the Corporate Law Reform Act 1992 on Directors' Duties' a paper circulated at University of Western Australia Law School, 1993

O'Donovan J, *The Law of Company Liquidation* (3rd ed) The Law Book Company Ltd, Sydney, 1987

Oakley A J, 'The Bribed Fiduciary as Constructive Trustee' [1994] CLJ 31

Ong K T W, 'Disqualification of directors: a faulty regime?' (1998) 19 Co Law 7

Organisation for Economic Co-operation and Development, *OECD Principles of Corporate Governance* OECD Publications, Paris, 1999

Osler, Hoskin & Harcourt, *Directors' Duties* Toronto, 1993

Owen-Conway S, 'The Equitable Jurisdiction of the Inferior Courts in Western Australia' (1979-1982) 14 UWALR 150

Palmer F B, *Palmer's Company Law* (25th ed) Sweet & Maxwell Ltd, London, 1992

Panel on Take-overs and Mergers, *The City Code on Take-overs and Mergers* London, 1993

Parliamentary Joint Committee on Corporations and Securities, *Report on the Corporate Law Economic Reform Program Bill 1998* AGPS, Canberra, 1999

Parsons R W, 'The Director's Duty of Good Faith' (1967) 5 MULR 395

Partridge R J C, 'Ratification and the Release of Directors from Personal Liability' [1987] CLJ 122

Pascoe J, 'Equitable Remedies in Cases of Misapplied Company Funds: Recent Developments' (1996) 14 CSLJ 393

Pascoe J, 'Review of Australia's corporate regulator' (1996) 17 Co Law 91

Passmore C, 'Directors' Duties: Australian Style' (1997) 18 Co Law 158

Payne J, 'Bigger and Better Guns for Minority Shareholders?' [1998] CLJ 36

Pennington R R, 'Reform of the Ultra Vires Rule' (1987) 8 Co Law 103

Pennington R R, *Company Law* (6th ed) Butterworth & Co (Publishers) Ltd, London, 1990

Pickering M A, 'Shareholders' Voting Rights and Company Control' (1965) 81 LQR 248

Polack K, 'Companies Act 1985 – "The Interests of the Company"' [1988] CLJ 24

Polack K, 'Companies Act 1985 – Scope of Section 153' [1988] CLJ 359

Poole J, 'Abolition of the Ultra Vires Doctrine and Agency Problems' (1991) 12 Co Law 43

Posner R A, 'The Rights of Creditors of Affiliated Corporations' (1975-1976) 43 UCLR 499

Powers L, 'Can the Court Excuse Insolvent Trading?' (1996) 7 JBFLP 160

Prentice D D and Holland P R J, *Contemporary Issues in Corporate Governance* Oxford University Press, Oxford, 1993

Prentice D D, 'Creditor's Interests and Director's Duties' (1990) 10 OJLS 265

Prentice D D, 'Directors, Creditors and Shareholders' in McKendrick E (ed), *Commercial Aspects of Trusts and Fiduciary Obligations* Clarendon Press, Oxford, 1992

Prentice D D, 'Expulsion of Members from a Company' (1970) 33 MLR 700

Prentice D D, 'Restraints on the Exercise of Majority Shareholder Power' (1976) 92 LQR 502

Prindl A R and Prodhan B, *Ethical Conflicts in Finance* Blackwell Publishers, Oxford, 1994

Promotion of Non-Executive Directors, *A Practical Guide for Non-Executive Directors* PRO NED Ltd, London, 1987

Rajak H, *A Sourcebook of Company Law* Jordan & Sons Ltd, Bristol, 1989

Ramsay I M, 'Enforcement of Corporate Rights and Duties by Shareholders and the Australian Securities Commission: Evidence and Analysis' (1995) 23 ABLR 174

Ramsay I M, *Corporate Governance and the Duties of Company Directors* The Centre for Corporate Law and Securities Regulation, University of Melbourne, Parkville, 1997

Ramsay I M, *Gambotto v WCP Ltd: Its Implications for Corporate Regulation* The Centre for Corporate Law and Securities Regulation, University of Melbourne, Parkville, 1996

Redmond P, 'Safe Harbours or Sleepy Hollows: Does Australia Need a Statutory Business Judgment Rule?' in Ramsay I M (ed), *Corporate Governance and the Duties of Company Directors* The Centre for Corporate Law and Securities Regulation, University of Melbourne, Parkville, 1997

Redmond P, 'The Reform of Directors' Duties' (1991) 15 UNSWLJ 86

Redmond P, *Companies and Securities Law Commentary and Materials* (2nd ed) The Law Book Company Ltd, Sydney, 1992

Reinhardt G, 'The Availability of Tracing to the Insolvency Administrator – Is the Remedy Adequate?' (1996) 4 ILJ 74

Renard I A, Commentary to Heydon, 'Directors' Duties and the Company's Interests' in Finn P D (ed), *Equity and Commercial Relationships* The Law Book Company Ltd, Sydney, 1987

Report of the Committee on Company Law Amendment, HMSO, London, Cmd 6659, 1945

Report of the Company Law Committee, HMSO, London, Cmnd 1749, 1962

Report of the Review Committee on Insolvency Law and Practice, HMSO, London, Cmnd 8558, 1982

Rickett C and Gardner T, 'Compensating for loss in equity: The evolution of a remedy' (1994) 24 VUWLR 19

Rickett C E F, 'Equitable Compensation: The Giant Stirs' (1996) 112 LQR 27

Rider B A K and Ashe M, *The Fiduciary the Insider and the Conflict* Brehon Sweet & Maxwell, Dublin, 1995

Rider B A K, 'A Special Relationship on the Special Facts' (1978) 41 MLR 585

Rider B A K, 'A Tarnished Knight and Another DoT Volte-Face' (1981) 2 Co Law 194

Rider B A K, 'Amiable Lunatics and the Rule in Foss v Harbottle' [1978] CLJ 270

Rider B A K, 'Changes in Company Law – Directors' Duties' (1978) 128 NLJ 1116

Rider B A K, 'Changes in Company Law – Directors' Private Transactions' (1978) 128 NLJ 1138

Rider B A K, 'Partnership Law and its Impact on "Domestic Companies"' [1979] CLJ 148

Rider B A K, 'Percival v Wright – Per Incuriam' (1977) 40 MLR 471

Rider B A K, 'The Conduct of Company Directors' (1978) 128 NLJ 27

Rider B A K, 'The Fiduciary and the Frying Pan' [1978] Conv 114

Rider B A K, Abrams C and Ashe M, *Guide to Financial Services Regulation* (3rd ed) CCH Editions Ltd, Bicester, 1997

Rider B A K, Abrams C and Ferran E, *Guide to the Financial Services Act 1986* (2nd ed) CCH Editions Ltd, Bicester, 1989

Riley C A, 'Directors' duties and the interests of creditors' (1989) 10 Co Law 87

Riley C A, 'The Final Report of the Hampel Committee on corporate governance' (1998) 19 Co Law 179

Riley C A, 'The Law Commission's questionable approach to the duty of care and skill' (1999) 20 Co Law 196

Riley C A, 'The values behind the Law Commission's consultation paper' (1997) 18 Co Law 260

Riley C A, book review (1994) 57 MLR 992

Ritson L, 'The "Proper Purposes" Duty of Directors and Defensive Measures against Company Takeovers' (1982-1985) 10 Syd LR 627

Rixon F G, 'Competing Interests and Conflicting Principles: An Examination of the Power of Alteration of Articles of Association' (1986) 49 MLR 446

Robert-Tissot S P, 'A fresh insight into the corporate criminal mind: Meridian Global Funds Management Asia Ltd v The Securities Commission' (1996) 17 Co Law 99

Rumble G A, 'The Commonwealth/State Co-Operative Basis for the Australian Wheat Board and the National Companies and Securities Commission: Some Constitutional Issues' (1980) 7 Adel LR 348

Ryan C L, *Company Directors Liabilities, Rights and Duties* (3rd ed) CCH Editions Ltd, Bicester, 1990

Sarker R, 'Maxwell: fraud trial of the century' (1996) 17 Co Law 116

Sarker R, 'New lease of life for the SFO' (1995) 16 Co Law 213

Sarker R, 'Reform of the financial regulatory system' (1998) 19 Co Law 11

Sarker R, 'The Serious Fraud Office – quo vadis?' (1995) 16 Co Law 56

Savla S, 'SFO, powers under the Criminal Justice Act 1987, s2 and the Police and Criminal Evidence Act 1984' (1996) 17 Co Law 19

Schmitthoff C M, 'The Origin of the Joint-Stock Company' (1939-1940) 3 UTLJ 74

Schmitthoff C M, 'The Wholly Owned and the Controlled Subsidiary' [1978] JBL 218

Schulte R, 'Corporate groups and the equitable subordination of claims on insolvency' (1997) 18 Co Law 2

Schulte R, 'Enforcing wrongful trading as a standard of conduct for directors and a remedy for creditors: the special case of corporate insolvency' (1999) 20 Co Law 80

Sealy L S and Milman D, *Annotated Guide to the 1986 Insolvency Legislation* (3rd ed) CCH Editions Ltd, Bicester, 1991

Sealy L S, '"Bona Fides" and "Proper Purposes" in Corporate Decisions' (1989) 15 MULR 265

Sealy L S, 'A Company Law for Tomorrow's World' (1981) 2 Co Law 195

Sealy L S, 'A Setback for the Minority Shareholder' [1982] CLJ 247

Sealy L S, 'Company – Directors' "Duties" and Exempting Articles' [1987] CLJ 217

Sealy L S, 'Company – Directors' Unconstitutional Acts' [1992] CLJ 229

Sealy L S, 'Company Directors' Powers – Proper Motive but Improper Purpose' [1967] CLJ 33

Sealy L S, 'Company Law – Protection of Minority Shareholders' [1976] CLJ 235

Sealy L S, 'Directors' "Wider" Responsibilities – Problems Conceptual, Practical and Procedural' (1987) 13 MULR 164

Sealy L S, 'Directors' Duties – An Unnecessary Gloss' [1988] CLJ 175

Sealy L S, 'Fiduciary Obligations, Forty Years On' (1995) 9 JCL 37

Sealy L S, 'Fiduciary Relationships' [1962] CLJ 69

Sealy L S, 'Foss v Harbottle – A Marathon Where Nobody Wins' [1981] CLJ 29

Sealy L S, 'Reforming the Law on Directors' Duties' (1991) 12 Co Law 175

Sealy L S, 'Some Principles of Fiduciary Obligation' [1963] CLJ 119

Sealy L S, 'The "Disclosure" Philosophy and Company Law Reform' (1981) 2 Co Law 51

Sealy L S, 'The bell tolls for ultra vires' (1986) 7 Co Law 90

Sealy L S, 'The Director as Trustee' [1967] CLJ 83

Sealy L S, 'The Enforcement of Partnership Agreements, Articles of Association and Shareholder Agreements' in Finn P D (ed) *Equity and Commercial Relationships* The Law Book Company Ltd, Sydney, 1987

Sealy L S, 'Undue Influence and Inequality of Bargaining Power' [1975] CLJ 21

Sealy L S, *Cases and Materials in Company Law* Cambridge University Press, Cambridge, 1971

Sealy L S, *Disqualification and Personal Liability of Directors* (4th ed) CCH Editions Ltd, Bicester, 1993

Sealy L, 'No relief for the minority shareholder' (1995) 16 Co Law 178

Senate Legal and Constitutional References Committee, *The Investigatory Powers of the Australian Securities Commission* AGPS, Canberra, 1995

Senate Standing Committee on Legal and Constitutional Affairs, *Social and Fiduciary Duties and Obligations of Company Directors* AGPS, Canberra, 1989

Shapira G, 'Liability of corporate agents: Williams v Natural Life Ltd in the House of Lords' (1999) 20 Co Law 130

Sheikh S, 'Curbing top pay bonanza' (1995) 16 Co Law 117

Shepherd J C, 'Towards a Unified Concept of Fiduciary Relationships' (1981) 97 LQR 51

Shepherd J C, *The Law of Fiduciaries* The Carswell Company Ltd, Toronto, 1981

Sheridan L A and Keeton G W, *The Law of Trusts* (11th ed) Barry Rose Publishers Ltd, Chichester, 1983

Sievers A S, 'Farewell to the Sleeping Director – The Modern Judicial and Legislative Approach to Directors' Duties of Care, Skill and Diligence' (1993) 21 ABLR 111

Sievers A S, 'The National Safety Council Case' (1991) 9 CSLJ 338

Slutsky B V, case note (1974) 37 MLR 457

Spender P, 'Compulsory Acquisition of Minority Shareholdings' (1993) 11 CSLJ 83

Stamp M, 'Reform of the Ultra Vires Rule: A Consultative Document' (1986) 136 NLJ 962 and 971

Stapledon G P, 'Disincentives to Activism by Institutional Investors in Listed Australian Companies' (1996) 18 Syd LR 152

Stapledon G P, 'Exercise of Voting Rights by Institutional Shareholders in the UK' (1995) 3 Corp Gov: Inter Rev 144

Stapledon G P, 'The CLERP Proposal in Relation to Section 232(4): The Duty of Care and Diligence' (1998) 16 CSLJ 144

Stapledon G P, 'The Structure of Share Ownership and Control: The Potential for Institutional Investor Activism' (1995) 18 UNSWLJ 250

Stapledon G P, *Institutional Shareholders and Corporate Governance* Clarendon Press, Oxford, 1996

Stapleton J, 'Duty of Care: Peripheral Parties and Alternative Opportunities for Deterrence' (1995) 111 LQR 301

Stapleton J, 'Law, Causation and Common Sense' (1988) 8 OJLS 111

Starke J G, 'Liability of Individuals Connected with Company' (1991) 65 ALJ 300

Starke J G, 'The High Court and the Limits of the Doctrine of Constructive Trusts' (1987) 61 ALJ 241

Steel T, 'Defensive Tactics in Company Takeovers' (1986) 4 CSLJ 30

Stratton I, 'Non-executive directors: are they superfluous?' (1996) 17 Co Law 162

Stuckey-Clarke J, '"Damages" for Breaches of Purely Equitable Rights: The Breach of Confidence Example' in Finn P D (ed), *Essays on Damages* The Law Book Company Ltd, Sydney, 1992

Study Group on Directors' Remuneration, *Directors' Remuneration* Gee Publishing Ltd, London, 1995

Sugarman D, 'Is company law founded on contract or public regulation? The Law Commission's paper on company directors' (1999) 20 Co Law 162

Sugarman D, 'Reconceptualising company law: reflections on the Law Commission's consultation paper on shareholder remedies: Part 2' (1997) 18 Co Law 274

Sugarman D, 'Reconceptualising company law: reflections on the Law Commission's consultation paper on shareholder remedies: Part 1' (1997) 18 Co Law 226

Sykes T, *The Bold Riders* Allen & Unwin Pty Ltd, St Leonards, 1994

Teele R, 'A Fifth Exception to the Rule in Foss v Harbottle?' (1995) 13 CSLJ 329

Teele R, 'Collapse of the State Bank of South Australia: Implications for Directors' (1996) 14 CSLJ 56

Teele R, 'The Necessary Reformulation of the Classic Fiduciary Duty to Avoid a Conflict of Interest or Duties' (1994) 22 ABLR 99

The American Law Institute, *Principles of Corporate Governance: Analysis and Recommendations* St Paul, 1994

The Companies and Securities Advisory Committee, *Report on Reform of the Law Governing Corporate Financial Transactions* AGPS, Canberra, 1991

The Companies and Securities Law Review Committee, *Report on Indemnification, Relief and Insurance in Relation to Company Directors and Officers* AGPS, Canberra, 1990

The Toronto Stock Exchange Committee on Corporate Governance in Canada, *Where Were the Directors?* Toronto, 1994

Tomasic R and Bottomley S, *Directing the Top 500 – Corporate governance and accountability in Australian companies* Allen & Unwin Pty Ltd, St Leonards, 1993

Trebilcock M J, 'The Liability of Company Directors for Negligence' (1969) 32 MLR 499

Treitel G H, *The Law of Contract* (7th ed) Sweet & Maxwell Ltd, London, 1987

Trethowan I, 'Directors' Personal Liability for Insolvent Trading: At Last, a Degree of Consensus' (1993) 11 CSLJ 102

Tunc A, 'The Judge and the Businessman' (1986) 102 LQR 549

Veasey E N, 'The Defining Tension in Corporate Governance in America' in Ramsay I M (ed), *Corporate Governance and the Duties of Company Directors* The Centre for Corporate Law and Securities Regulation, University of Melbourne, Parkville, 1997

Villiers C, 'Employees as creditors: a challenge for justice in insolvency law' (1999) 20 Co Law 222

Virgo G, 'Stealing from the Small Family Business' [1991] CLJ 464

Wallace G and Young J McI, *Australian Company Law and Practice* The Law Book Company Ltd, Sydney, 1965

Walsh J K, 'The Exercise of Powers in the Interests of a Company' (1967-1968) 8 UWALR 176

Walters A and Davis-White M, *Directors' Disqualification: Law & Practice* Sweet & Maxwell Ltd, London, 1999

Walters A, 'Directors' duties and shareholder remedies' (1999) 20 Co Law 138

Walters A, 'Enforcing Wrongful Trading' in Rider B A K (ed), *The Corporate Dimension* Jordans, London, 1998

Walters A, 'Williams v Natural Life Health Foods Ltd' (1996) 17 Co Law 247

Watts P, 'Bribes and Constructive Trusts' (1994) 110 LQR 178

Wedderburn K W, 'Control of Corporate Litigation' (1976) 39 MLR 327

Wedderburn K W, 'Derivative Actions and Foss v Harbottle' (1981) 44 MLR 202

Wedderburn K W, 'Multinationals and the Antiquities of Company Law' (1984) 47 MLR 87

Wedderburn K W, 'Shareholders' Control of Directors' Powers: A Judicial Innovation?' (1967) 30 MLR 77

Wedderburn K W, 'Shareholders' Rights and The Rule in Foss v Harbottle' [1957] CLJ 194

Wedderburn K W, 'Shareholders' Rights and the Rule in Foss v Harbottle' [1958] CLJ 93

Wedderburn K W, 'The Social Responsibility of Companies' (1985) 15 Melb ULR 4

Wedderburn K W, 'Trust, Corporation and the Worker' (1985) 23 OHLJ 203

Wedderburn K W, 'Ultra Vires in Modern Company Law' (1983) 46 MLR 204

Wedderburn K W, 'Ultra Vires or Directors' Bona Fides?' (1967) 30 MLR 566

Weiner J L, 'The Berle-Dodd Dialogue on the Concept of the Corporation' (1964) 64 Colum LR 1458

Weinrib E J, 'A Step in Factual Causation' (1975) 38 MLR 518

Weir T, 'Statutory Auditor not Liable to Purchaser of Shares' [1990] CLJ 212

Whincop M J, 'A Theoretical and Policy Critique of the Modern Reformulation of Directors' Duties of Care' (1996) 6 AJCL 72

Whincop M J, 'An Economic Analysis of the Criminalisation and Content of Directors' Duties' (1996) 24 ABLR 273

Whincop M J, 'Developments in Directors' Statutory Duties of Honesty and Propriety' (1996) 14 CSLJ 157

Whincop M J, 'Directors' Statutory Duties of Honesty and Propriety' in Ramsay I M (ed), *Corporate Governance and the Duties of Company Directors* The Centre for Corporate Law and Securities Regulation, University of Melbourne, Parkville, 1997

Whincop M J, 'Of Fault and Default: Contractarianism as a Theory of Anglo-Australian Corporate Law' (1997) 21 MULR 187

Whincup M, '"Inequitable Incorporation" – the Abuse of a Privilege' (1981) 2 Co Law 158

Whitford K, 'The Year That Was: An Overview of Corporate Law 1995' (1996) 6 AJCL 1

Wilberforce R O, 'Law and Economics' [1966] JBL 301

Yeung K, 'Disentangling the Tangled Skein: The Ratification of Directors' Actions' (1992) 66 ALJ 343

Youdan T G, *Equity, Fiduciaries and Trusts* The Law Book Company Ltd, Toronto, 1989

Ziegel J S, *Studies in Canadian Company Law* Butterworth & Co (Canada) Ltd, Toronto, 1967

Index

1. Arthur R. Pinto and Gustavo Visentini (eds), *The Legal Basis of Corporate Governance in Publicly Held Corporations: A Comparative Approach* (1998)
(ISBN 90-411-9663-3)

2. Betty M. Ho, *Public Companies and their Equity Securities: Principles of Regulation Under Hong Kong Law* (1998)
(ISBN 90-411-9648-X)

3. Chizu Nakajima, *Conflicts of Interest and Duty: A Comparative Analysis in Anglo-Japanese Law* (1999)
(ISBN 90-411-9698-6)

4. Stefan N. Frommel and Barry A.K. Rider (eds), *Conflicting Legal Cultures in Commercial Arbitration: Old Issues and New Trends* (1999)
(ISBN 90-411-1227-8)

5. T. Baums and E. Wymeersch, *Shareholder Voting Rights and Practices in Europe and the United States* (1999)
(ISBN 90-411-9750-8)

6. George P. Gilligan, *Regulating the Financial Services Sector* (1999)
(ISBN 90-411-9757-5)

7. Bruce S. Butcher, *Directors' Duties: A New Millennium, A New Approach?* (2000)
(ISBN 90-411-9788-5)

KLUWER LAW INTERNATIONAL – THE HAGUE, LONDON, BOSTON